WESTERN POLITICAL THOUGHT

*An Historical Introduction from the Origins
to Rousseau*

by

JOHN BOWLE

Lecturer in Modern History, Wadham College, Oxford

JONATHAN CAPE
THIRTY BEDFORD SQUARE
LONDON

FIRST PUBLISHED 1947

PRINTED IN GREAT BRITAIN IN THE CITY OF OXFORD
AT THE ALDEN PRESS
BOUND BY A. W. BAIN & CO. LTD., LONDON

CONTENTS

CONTENTS

BOOK TWO

THE POLITICAL THOUGHT OF THE MIDDLE AGES

CONTENTS

BOOK THREE

THE POLITICAL THOUGHT OF THE RENAISSANCE AND THE AGE OF RATIONALISM

7

CONTENTS

PREFACE

THE purpose of this book is to describe the main evolution of Western political thought in its historical context, and to analyse the texts of the most important writers. Existing works deal admirably with theory, but not with the social background which conditions thought. To fill this gap the present volume was designed.

The task has been one of selection and compression, and the author has preferred a full account of representative thinkers rather than a superficial account of many, though writers have been included whose influence has not been immediate but whose thought had a great future, and quotations made from documents which illustrate the outlook of a given age. Thus, in the seventeenth century, the works of Grotius, Hobbes, and Locke are naturally given priority, but an account of the political ideas of Spinoza has also been included, and the mentality of the Dark Ages has been illustrated by citations from Cassiodorus and Gregory of Tours. Throughout, it has been the author's aim to present the outstanding ideas of the great masters of political science, to relate them to one another, to the circumstances and intellectual climate of their time and to the continuity of historical evolution. This juxtaposition is intended to help the reader make his own judgement; the aim of the work has been an impartial presentation, though the author has indicated his own views, particularly in the concluding chapter.

The survey is, of course, in no sense a work of research, but rather an introduction to a very great subject; a degree of over-simplification has been unavoidable, and in concentrating on essentials the study of minor influences has had to be sacrificed. It was planned, in the first place, as an introduction to the study of political theory, and forms no substitute for a first-hand knowledge of the works described or the books treating them in greater detail, of which a bibliography is given at the end of this volume. It is primarily intended to help those beginning the subject to get their bearings, and set about the study of the texts and fuller interpretations with clearer minds, though it may be also that specialists in other fields will have use for an account of a subject which, after all, trenches on many aspects of life, for the political philosophers, as well as the poets, are the unacknowledged legislators of mankind.

9

PREFACE

In recent years the growing interest in political theory outside academic circles has led the author to believe there is a growing body of readers, especially in this country, the British Commonwealth and in America, who might like such a work. More particularly, he believes that those engaged in politics and administration may find interest in an account of the historical development of the dominant tendencies of Western political thought. Many philosophers have interpreted history in the light of political theory; it may be there is room for a more historical interpretation, with special reference to the contribution of English writers. And never has a widespread understanding of the tradition of civilized political thought been more urgent than it is to-day.

It has been necessary, owing to the scope of the subject, to design the work in two volumes, and it seemed suitable to end the first at the Industrial Revolution, that great landmark which changed the scale of history and heralded the advent of modern mass society. It is intended to complete the survey in a second volume dealing with the nineteenth and twentieth centuries.

The author has received encouragement and advice from many quarters. His principal debt is to Lord Lindsay, Master of Balliol, who read the manuscript in the original draft and made many suggestions which saved it from errors and omissions, and whose understanding and wide vision have been a real inspiration. The author's thanks are also due to Dr. C. M. Bowra, Warden of Wadham, for his advice on the chapters dealing with Antiquity; to Sir Charles Grant Robertson and Mr. Lionel Curtis; to Professor d'Entrèves; to Professor R. M. Dawkins and Professor Stuart Piggott; to Major B. E. Urquhart of the U.N.O. secretariat, who helped plan the original scheme; to Mr. J. S. P. Bradford, of the Pitt Rivers Museum; and to Professor J. Simmons. Finally he would like to thank Mrs. Neville-Smith, who typed a difficult manuscript with patience and judgement, and Miss C. V. Wedgwood for her help in discussing the arrangement of the book.

JOHN BOWLE

Wadham College
Oxford
April 1947

TO
E.B.B.

in gratitude and affection

BOOK ONE

THE POLITICAL THOUGHT OF ANTIQUITY

CHAPTER I

THE PRIMITIVE BACKGROUND

§ I

'SINCE men aim at the good,' says Aristotle, 'the State, which is the highest form of community, aims at the highest good.' And again, '. . . the good lawgiver should inquire how states may participate in the good life'. With trenchant clarity the greatest master of political thought recalls the values without which power is meaningless and defines the purpose of civilized society.

Of the nature of the good life many opinions have been held; but all the great thinkers are agreed that the State ought to further, directly or indirectly, their various interpretations of it. The purpose of this volume is to examine representative definitions, given down the ages, of the aim of society in the light of different conceptions of the good life; to describe the historical setting in which these definitions were made; and to attempt some assessment of the wisdom of the old writers in the light of modern knowledge. But before embarking upon a survey of the main tendencies of Western political thought it will be well to take account of a novel aspect of our own outlook and of the light thrown on political problems by this new knowledge.

During the last century and a half, the perspective of thought has been radically altered by a new apprehension of the antiquity of man. Political theory now appears a late, relatively artificial phenomenon, comparable to the conscious as opposed to the subconscious mind. Though fine-spun, and biologically speaking, recent ideas have profoundly influenced the course of events, the study of archaeology, prehistory and anthropology depicts a background which conditions all theoretical speculation. Modern research, as well as political experience, sees human society heavily controlled by forces atavistic, instinctive, to logical analysis often blind, yet for that reason perhaps the more in harmony with the mysterious tides of life.

During long millennia which dwarf written record, the sparse forebears of mankind displayed an animal solidarity. If we may illuminate prehistory by comparison with modern primitives, there was apparently little individuality or family sense, and the earliest social pattern was matriarchal and totemistic. These hunters and scavengers were not organized, as is often supposed, through a misleading comparison with the higher apes, in small family units dominated by a savage and polygamous Old Man. The earliest men, collaterals and ancestors of modern man, lived not in isolated families but in bands and hordes. When, in the Upper Palaeolithic, Homo Sapiens became the dominant human type, his societies were socially solid and mentally co-conscious; they had to be to survive. The basis of the earliest communities is primarily the pack.

In view of this evidence, the ancient assumption that civilization derives from a social compact, reflecting the deliberate choice of rational individuals, has long disappeared, and history is seen as a branch of a relatively new science of biology, concerned with a creature which owes much of its success to an intense sociability. Yet this solidarity is instinctively directed to the survival of the group, and aims, on its primitive level, at a measure of the good life. The sense of community and purpose, stressed by so many political thinkers, reflects, therefore, a long biological pedigree, and later conceptions of natural law and world order are in part rationalizations of a desire for a primitive solidarity later individualism has broken down. The sense of common purpose implied in Aristotle's dictum thus goes back to the earliest beginnings; the inherited instincts of humanity are against an unbridled individualism, and the majority of political thinkers have greatly overestimated the rationality of mankind. Political theory, then, must reckon with an intensely strong social instinct, older than family loyalty or individual enterprise, a solidarity upon which the leader, the thinker, the inventor, has to build — the patient material which later suffers the tyranny and devastation of fighting men out of control within the society and of barbarians who attack it from without. In view of this background, it seems also apparent that the conflict between the individual and authority is unusual in primitive conditions, since the basis of society is instinctive and men not yet much individualized.

Although, indeed, the resulting conservatism may have discouraged enterprise, early communities, within their limitations, were probably psychologically better adjusted than many later societies. This solidarity, this urge to 'swing together', is as old as humanity itself; it would seem that any social system must cater for

leadership in civilized communities will be bound up with religion, the heir of magic, and with science, the heir of both. This hypothesis is, in fact, borne out by the evidence of recorded history, which reinforces the conclusion that in a healthy society, with a sound relationship between rulers and ruled, the mass of the people and their leaders are permeated with a common pattern of ideas, the masses reflecting, in some degree, the aims of the leaders of thought and action. It would seem indeed impossible to maintain effective and dynamic government unless it retains popular prestige and consequent support; if the relation fails, the leaders are left in a blind alley and the rest leaderless. This hypothesis would seem strengthened by later evidence from the history of the River Valley civilizations of the Middle East, of the City State in its successful phases, of mediaeval Europe of the twelfth and thirteenth centuries, and by many examples in modern times. In all these stages of development the full force of the community is brought to bear on a vigorous expansion of social life, while talented individuals are given scope within the framework, backed by the support of the rest. The result may be recognized in brilliant artistic achievement; Greek, mediaeval, Renaissance and eighteenth-century art all reach their finest phases as the expression of a healthy society that believes in itself. When, on the other hand, as in the later Roman empire and during the waning Middle Ages, the community sense is broken, the binding force of common ideas loosed, there is loss of confidence, irrelevance of purpose and a sense of lowered vitality. A period of frustration sets in; each man is for himself and the driving force is lost or turns self-destructive. There is a miasma of real decadence, only lifted when a new idea wins through, compatible alike with contemporary knowledge and popular needs. The outlook of the *élite* then ceases to be negative and they swing back into their proper place, in line with the drive of the whole society.

Obviously the same pattern of ideas cannot be valid for all societies, since metaphysics and ethics must fit expanding knowledge; but all magic, religion and science in their varying forms have a social function as the binding link between rulers and ruled, and a society with an effective but inferior religion, such as militant nationalism, may well oust a more civilized one, in which the healthy relationship is broken, should that civilization fail to develop a dynamic mythos of its own. The moral for contemporary society would seem plain.

it and guide it into right channels. The attempt of an anal
minded minority to impose a plan which ignores irrational
is bound to fail. Graeco-Roman Stoic rationalism was swep
by Christianity; again, the rationalism of the eighteenth cent
overwhelmed by national and romantic enthusiasm, while
own time the compromises of liberal thought have gone down
mass movements of the Left and Right. Societies, then, like
duals, cannot live by reason alone; yet such a conclusion d
render organized common sense powerless, but gives it new w
for it follows that the wise ruler must take account of the d
of the whole man, and reason admit its own limitations, m
dispassionate assessment of the medium in which it has to
Such, then, would appear the first conclusion to be draw
the study of prehistory, supplemented by the evidence of
anthropology. The basic material achievements of our speci
in part the result of an intense and irrational sociability,
enabled mankind to survive the rigours of the palaeolithic
to combine to build the agricultural and, later, the urban
tions of civilized life.

§ II

The second conclusion, bound up with the first, points
need of common beliefs for the healthy functioning of
Through long millennia, stability and monotony were t
dominant note. For civilization to emerge, stability was not
it had to be combined with initiative. This initiative, the rec
tion of individual enterprise with communal conservatism
about through primitive magic, the centre of the earlies
pattern which can be detected in simple agricultural comn
of prehistoric times or the present.

The medicine man was the first person of enterprise. The
original, was crushed down in an immemorial conservatism
the field of magic and, later, religion there appeared the fi
carious development of artistic, poetic and musical abilit
magician-priest was permitted to be odd; out of the conserv
the dark past he might emerge if he could pay his way.

Assuming, then, that the life of societies, like that of indi
ought to display a healthy continuity, a steady elaborati
strengthening of an original theme, it may be expected that

B   17

The second conclusion which follows from the study of primitive communities is thus the importance of the social function of magic and religion, for early societies are inspired by common beliefs, and progress came about through common ideas. Whatever the nature of these beliefs, they appear to perform an essential social function without which no society can long survive. In degenerate forms they may poison a whole culture; in a healthy form, compatible with contemporary knowledge, they will inspire its greatest achievements, as in Sumer or Egypt, where a theocracy may impose a highly satisfactory cultural pattern. It would seem that the attempt of eighteenth- and nineteenth-century rationalism to do without such motives and create a society of calculating rational individuals was doomed to failure.

In view, then, of the importance of these beliefs, which for good or ill have played so great a part in human history, it will be well to glance in particular at the nature of primitive magic and religion, and compare the motives they reflect with the inspiration of modern societies.

§ III

The earliest beliefs of mankind would appear to have centred on interests common to the whole group, on food, fertility, and magic intended to secure command over environment.

If we base our conclusions on the evidence from the study of palaeolithic and neolithic communities, supplemented by the evidence of modern anthropology, it would seem that ritual and art are bound up with food and hunting. For example, palaeolithic man probably scratched his brilliant drawings on cave interiors to secure his kill, and the same preoccupation naturally appears in most primitive societies. Food supply comes first; here is a salutary lesson for political theorists. In the elaboration of later theory, men have too often lost sight of this plain necessity. If modern societies with their technical skill set about creating plenty with the whole-hearted drive of the primitive group in pursuit of its prey or the early Egyptians invoking the Nile flood, modern economic problems would be nearer solution. Further, squabbling over the kill is bad business; there is no evidence that our ancestors habitually tried to tear one another to pieces in sharing it out. The full drive of the community, under the pressure of environment, was brought to bear on the struggle for

existence; the back of the effort unbroken by individualistic monopoly or other-worldly obsessions. It looks as though here, too, a
healthy social pattern implies the drive of combined enterprise
inspired by common beliefs.

The second preoccupation, shading into the first, was the fertility
cult, natural from the earliest times and still prevalent in primitive
societies. It was reinforced after the neolithic revolution, which saw
the cultivation of crops and the domestication of animals. As is well
known, the emergence of the corn king, at first a fertility mascot, is
an early step in the evolution of kingship. The king is the embodied
luck of the tribe, bound up with the productivity of the land and the
control of the elements, rather than the war leader or the administrator. Modern constitutional monarchy, which focuses the continuity and the tradition of the state, standing aside from executive
preoccupations and responsibilities, is a reversion to this original and
healthy leadership; hence in part its survival, where royal despotism
has failed.

The fertility cult is one of immense power, focusing the community
in a way far more beneficial than that other form of solidarity, war.
War alone is an equally intoxicating stimulant, but increasingly
suicidal and with a much shorter pedigree as a human institution.
It appears there is little evidence for its wide prevalence in the
earliest societies; generally there was too much room and too little
to plunder. The fertility ritual, on the other hand, goes back to the
remotest times; and to peg communal emotion on anything so
sensible as food and fertility is obviously wiser than to concentrate
on dreams of military domination.

The third element, pervading the first two in the primitive mind,
is magic, the attempt to control environment. This may be 'imita-
tive' or 'contagious', and gives rise to the positive method of sorcery
and the negative method of taboo. Now savage, crazy, and erroneous
as the magician's hypothesis may be, and concerned often with pro-
pitiating spirits and ancestors as much as with the control of environment, it is perverted science. As the great anthropologist Frazer
observes, it is a 'theory of thought'. 'In magic', he says, 'man depends on his own strength to meet the difficulties and dangers that
beset him on every side.'[1] He believes in a certain established, if
fantastic, order of nature, which helps him, even if for the wrong
reason, to feel more at home in the world. A confidence, however

[1] FRAZER, *The Golden Bough*. Abridged edition, p. 712. Macmillan (1925).

misplaced, in his witch doctors to control natural forces, is better than uneasy bewilderment.

When magic fails, he falls back on a negative attitude to his surroundings which he regards as the sport of uncontrollable anthropomorphic beings. But with the rise of science, the old positive attitude towards environment is resumed, this time on a contrasting basis of fact.[1] The attempt to master nature begins again, on a very different scale and with very different results. Science may be said in some sense to be magic that works, and the prestige of modern science has its precedents. The attempt to control environment, the basis of civilization, has therefore its parallel, if perverse and unsuccessful, in primitive societies.

Initiative in the earliest communities, then, centres on interests common and intelligible to all; on food supply, fertility and magical practices, often, indeed, bound up with the cult and propitiation of the ancestral dead, but primarily concerned to control environment. It would appear likely, moreover, that a healthy civilization ought to reflect this pattern in a higher form. Such a society would aim at a basic standard of welfare which all would work together to attain, at a solid material progress, at control over environment, and the consequent possibility of elaborating the moral, intellectual and aesthetic values which constitute the good life.

As to the basis of that good life, there would now appear no mystery. Modern society is the heir to an accumulated intellectual, moral and artistic inheritance, which, independently of any metaphysical justification, provides a realized basis for values emergent in the life process at the highest power apprehendable by the human mind, values which are the most vivid expression of material evolution and as much bound up with it and dependent on it as the flower with its roots.

How comes it, then, that history, for all its overriding record of advance, shows so frequent a falling off in this constructive effort? It may well be that the key to the problem, to the manifold perversions of political thought and practice, comes from that aspect of society which differs most radically from the primitive pattern.

[1] 'Thus the keener minds . . . come to reject the religious theory of nature as inadequate and to revert in a measure to the older standpoint of magic, by postulating explicitly what in magic had been only implicitly assumed, to wit, an inflexible regularity in the order of natural events, which if carefully observed enables us to foresee the future and act accordingly. In short, religion regarded as an explanation of nature is replaced by science.' FRAZER, ibidem.

The dynamic phase of social development comes with the emergence of self-conscious individuals out of the stable group. It implies
a new promise and a new risk; new possibilities of enterprise and
power, a transformation of outlook. Individuality means a wider
awareness, a new grip on the world; it means, also, loneliness and
guilt. The fruit of the tree of knowledge brings a new and sometimes
destructive point of view. In taking the hard step out of the close
routine of the group life, the individual may be sundered from his
roots and turn anti-social. Along with the promise of the constructive, benevolent leadership which made civilization, the conflict
between individual and community developed as well. This change
is reflected in the religious field; men may, indeed, attain a new
sense of duty and honour, but they may become obsessed with the
cult of a personal salvation, or thwarted in their desire for individualistic power, break out into violence or subside into a cynical
pessimism.

Fully developed initiative, along with its obvious benefits, tends
therefore towards a conflict between individual and society, following
a widening gap between the outlook of the majority and the freer and
more intellectualized outlook of highly developed individuals at the
top. There are greater possibilities both for good and evil than are
apparent in the stable routine of primitive communities. To restore
this early solidarity, imperilled by excessive individualism, it would
appear desirable to retain the stability of the earlier phase, while
retaining the initiative and intellectual freedom of later individualism; to translate primitive solidarity and fundamental good sense
into large-scale policy and organization, and to restore the sundered
relationship between the leaders and the mass in pursuit of practical
and biologically reputable objectives, which alone can form a
foundation for higher values.

Anthropological studies depict early societies as healthy when
striving towards such objectives; a secure food supply, a numerous
population, a culture permeated by common beliefs through which
comes leadership, the whole on its primitive level rooted in a way
of life to which man is naturally adapted. Obvious as these objectives
appear, they are imperfectly attained by modern governments, in
spite of a technical skill out of all proportion to that displayed by
early societies. A second world war and an atomic revolution may,

indeed, force us to a new realism both in international and economic affairs, with perhaps more hopeful prospects for the future; but it is clear we have something yet to learn from our ancestors, who made a better success of a more unpromising situation.

These would appear to be some of the lessons to be learnt from the contemplation of the primitive background to articulate political thought. This background is a habit of animal custom adapted to environment, enabling the primitive group to survive, shot through with gleams of initiative centring on magic and, later, on religious rites. The basic preoccupation with food and fertility is strictly limited, the environment meagre and squalid; yet the primitive community sets a standard of good sense without which subsequent higher values would never have been realized. It is close to the stream of animal life from which all civilizations derive; it can be ignored only at our peril.

§ V

Such, then, would seem some outstanding conclusions of prehistory and anthropology of which we must take account when examining the answers given to the question of the purpose of society. For all their limitations, prehistory and anthropology form a heartening and constructive foundation for historical studies. The deepest instincts of mankind have given rise to a sense of common purpose, reinforced by beliefs which are an expression of man's nature. These beliefs have welded early societies into constructive effort, reinforced individual enterprise and gone far to keep it under control. After their fashion, these societies have aimed instinctively at a basic prosperity which could form the foundation of more elaborate values. Here is no conflict between Church and State, that disastrous result of salvationist individualism and ascetic hatred of life; no cult of violence, of destruction for its own sake arising from greed, guilt and egotism; rather there is constructive purpose, plodding, limited, with its nose to the ground, but concerned with a slow mastery of environment to ensure a limited version of the good life.

A further lesson to be drawn from prehistoric and anthropological studies is the variety and flexibility of human institutions. Though any healthy society may be expected to display the solidarity and harmony already noted, an inexhaustible variety of social pattern has been realized in widely contrasting situations in space and time.

Although, then, certain societies have realized higher values than others, there would appear to be no one ideal pattern valid for all circumstances. This relativity of outlook distinguishes modern political thought from the more dogmatic idealism of the past. Further, society is conceived of as in process of continuous evolution, while the great majority of political thinkers have hitherto regarded it as static or caught in a pattern of cyclic recurrence. It follows that the modern view of society is more interesting; in a sense more optimistic. There is no last word to be said about history or political science, and although the statesman or political thinker can profit by the experience of the past, he is no longer crushed by the weight of precedent and precept.

This comparative optimism is reinforced by a new time sense. While regarding recorded history as a very short episode in the evolution of mankind, modern knowledge sees this relatively short time-span as a prelude to a vast future. It would seem likely that civilized society, if it can control the power science has thrust upon it, is only at the beginning of a very long road, with the whole recorded past only a prelude to a wider evolution of power and consciousness. Judging from the intellectual and material progress achieved, in spite of setbacks, in the last six thousand years — and upon such data we may fairly base our conclusions — the promise, though not the certainty, of similar and greater achievement must appear a reasonable expectation. In spite of the numerous examples of the decline of high civilizations, the considered judgement of cautious authorities on prehistoric and anthropological studies is encouraging. During the last decades, following certain Continental movements of thought, a false impression has been put about of the 'decadence' of civilization. On the contrary, the evidence goes to show its intense vitality and, in particular, the unbroken constructive drive of the Western tradition and its inheritors. Judged by the basic standard of biological success, man has fantastically outdistanced his competitors. In an animal world increasingly specialized and so apparently falling off in the evolutionary struggle, he has maintained the adaptability for further advance; while, by intellectual and aesthetic standards, human history shows a steady enrichment and growing diversity of experience. Though the great minds of Antiquity, the Middle Ages, the Renaissance, and the seventeenth and eighteenth centuries displayed a comparable individual power to the thinkers of modern times, they had not behind them the accumulated knowledge and professional skill of which we now dispose. The fundamental endowment of mankind, the preservation and transmission of experience through speech and writing, has built up an expanding inheritance of incomparably greater scope.

It may be said, therefore, that the conclusions which follow from the realization of the antiquity of man, from the evidence of prehistoric and anthropological studies and from the contemplation of the sweep of history in the light of modern knowledge, reinforce the Aristotelian concept of the state as a community with a constructive common purpose. Modern investigation, moreover, displays a wonderful diversity of social pattern, and sets the period of recorded history in its place, not only as a culmination of a prehistoric past, but as a possible prelude to a future full of promise. Prehistoric studies, further, affirm the fact of progress, intellectual and material, and scout the pessimism which, following recent metaphysical fashions, has tended to infect the historical outlook. If we base our conclusions not on abstract generalities, but, following the English tradition, on the results of scientific field-work and applied common sense, we are justified in a cautious optimism, in a belief in the reality of human progress towards the good life. Alien as may appear the millennia of animal evolution which precede the emergence of mankind, and paralysing the discrepancy between the brief period of civilized life and the ages which preceded it, the basis of solid achievement is there. With this background in mind, we will turn to examine the political ideas which inspired the early societies of the great river valleys of the Middle East, civilizations from which the material culture of western Europe derives.

CHAPTER II

THE TEMPLE STATE AND SACRED
CITY: MIDDLE EASTERN EMPIRE

§ 1

THE foundation of cities and formulation of law, the creation of a bureaucratic tradition and of the routine of organized society, occurred not in Europe but in Mesopotamia and Egypt. Modern conditions obscure the fundamental unity of civilization, and the 'racial' and 'national' divisions of our time can best be discounted by an understanding of the unity of European cultural origins.

European culture derives from the river valleys of the Near East; here, in a favourable but initially exacting environment, the first steps were made. The neolithic peasant cultures of the North formed the basis on which Near Eastern ideas could work, but they did not originate the great inventions. As a stone thrown into a pond sends concentric ripples widening and fading to the distant edge, so the technique and ideas of the river valleys expanded into the North. Over the Greek islands, up the Danube valley, along the coasts of the Great Sea, the early traders and colonizers pushed out and carried the rudiments of civilization with them; the common origins of European culture must be sought along the great rivers.

The conditions which brought about the rise of the river valley civilizations are imperfectly known; apparently with the slow recession of the European ice-cap, a climatic change took place in what is now the desert belt, Sahara-Arabia-Sind. What had been grassland, good for animals and men, began to dry up, leaving only the great river valleys fertile and habitable. After the worst desiccation was over a moister phase encouraged the first steps in cultivation to be taken about the sixth millennium.

The movement into the valleys did not take place until after the initial neolithic revolution;[1] the use of cereal crops and the domesti-

---

[1] See *Man Makes Himself*, by V. GORDON CHILDE, Watts (1936), for an introduction to the study of the origins of civilization and an excellent short account of the neolithic and urban 'revolutions' – an ungainly term for these gradual processes, but one which brings home their importance. Prof. J. B. S. Haldane has well said that, looked at from the purely practical point of view, there have been two major events in human history: the neolithic and the industrial revolutions. To-day we may add a third.

cation of animals are the advances which distinguish the new stone age cultures from those of palaeolithic and mesolithic times. The neolithic way of life had evolved its routine before the valley settlements were made; man was equipped to tackle the riverine jungles into which he penetrated. A primitive agriculture, supplemented by hunting over a wide area, need not mean permanent settlement; but, once in the river valleys, man settled down; the river flood, by renewing the fertility of the land, made casual migration unnecessary. Having moved into these restricted areas, Near Eastern man was confronted with unprecedented conditions, which demanded a different adaptation and provided a new stimulus; the answer to this challenge, in a favourable climate, was the rise of civilization.

Meanwhile, in the North, the recession of the ice had given mesolithic Europe a new environment. With the spread of an Atlantic climate, the forest crept northward and imposed a new way of life; the mesolithic peoples adapted the palaeolithic hunting culture, designed for cold, to more temperate conditions; they settled along the sea and lake shores. At the same time there was a gradual infiltration northwards by neolithic settlers equipped with the rudiments of farming method. In Thessaly and on the Danube peasant cultures appear by 3500 B.C., and there is evidence of neolithic influence from North Africa in Spain. These areas of stability and self-sufficiency settled and widened; the neolithic colonists interbred with the remnants of older stock and by the third millennium the population of Europe had greatly increased. Here was a foundation on which the cultural influences of the Near East were to react; vital enough, in time, to give its own interpretation to the Eastern influence. Parallel with this development, the river valley settlements had gradually evolved an urban way of life, the practical basis of civilization, already old by the time the European peasant communities had stabilized.

The cultures of Mesopotamia and Egypt are fundamentally similar, though there are important differences of climate and institutions. Both are based on great rivers, both are urbanized, built up and controlled by priesthoods and priest-kings and supported by the labour of a docile and numerous peasantry; both are static, and for all their massive stability, lack the initiative and variety of Europe.

To turn first to Mesopotamia. The environment presented more formidable difficulties than Egypt, and its subjugation demanded intensive communal enterprise. This effort is the root of the whole Mesopotamian achievement; the foundations of the city are religious, controlled by priests, centring on the cult of the god to whom the city belonged. The urban habit of life was based on certain great inventions and discoveries — the wheel, the ship, writing, and the measurement of time. The Sumerians created this civilization and the means of defending it.

Their origins are not yet fully clear, but it is thought they came originally from the western mountains of Iran, bordering on Mesopotamia, and imposed themselves on a native aboriginal population. Their racial type is distinctive; they were a broad-headed solid people of business-like appearance. Behind them was a Central Asian neolithic culture, and even the pre-Sumerian swamp-dwelling populations of the southern Euphrates had achieved an elementary but settled way of life,[1] in face of considerable difficulties.

The country has been well described as follows, 'The great southern lake (north of Basra), known as the Khor Hammar, between the sea and the river mouths, is girt with flat land fringed with high reed beds; little islands rise sporadically out of the water, barely lifting their heads above the high tide, and when they do they support the reed huts and families of a few marsh dwellers of a low type . . . The shore line is marked by low level banks of dull sepia, fringed with reeds, withered to dark brown in winter save where some plantation of palm trees here and there along a canal marks civilization. In prehistoric times there had been great settlements to the south and west of these lakes . . . Here on the Euphrates flats they had made their dwellings, laid the foundations of many cities.' The extremes of temperature found in this area are notable; in the summer the average is 110°, rising to a maximum of 126°; in winter the thermometer often reaches freezing point.[2]

The clearing of these swamps and thickets was an undertaking which implied a strong social discipline; the construction of canals and the control of floods demanded systematic measurement and thought. Once the initial settlement had been made, the fertility of

[1] See *Cambridge Ancient History*, vol. I, pp. 494-503.   [2] *C.A.H.*, vol. I, p. 360.

the land, the abundance of game and fish, the extensive cultivation of the date palm — the staple of this civilization — made for an increase in wealth and population. The resulting pride in solid material achievement is apparent from the earliest Sumerian records, and their rulers identify themselves with the community of their subjects. The word 'patesi', the title of their princes, signifies literally the 'tenant farmer' of the civic god.

Now the conception of the city as a sacred and communal enterprise implies the beginning of purposive social thought. The object of the community is so much taken for granted that early civilizations did not, so far as we know, speculate about it; but, different as was to be the ethos of the polis, the idea of the temple state is at the back of the Cretan and Mycenaean palace and the Greek city, with its clear formulation of aim. It is an institution which spreads over the Levant and the Near East, intimately bound up with the Minoan and Greek religion, the foundation of later and more sophisticated speculation. It persists, with certain modifications, as the cultural unit of the Graeco-Roman world, the basis of the civilization of antiquity.

Such an achievement, made in the face of formidable difficulties, is the result of intelligent co-operative enterprise, a monument of good sense and adaptation. These facts reinforce modern anthropological conclusions already described.

Sumerian civilization appears to have combined a primitive solidarity with inventive genius; at the same time, the tomb at Ur, with its guards and women voluntarily massacred in a great pit, should leave no illusions about Sumerian religion.

'In the death pit', writes Sir Leonard Woolley, 'lay 74 bodies. Against the north-west wall were five men servants carrying knives or axes and a sixth lay a little in front of the platform edge. The remaining sixty-eight were women, their bodies arranged for the most part in neat rows; . . . nearly all were richly adorned with gold and silver ornaments. Twenty-eight wore the conventional headdress of gold hair-ribbons, wreathes of gold leaves, big lunate earrings, dog-collars of gold and lapis triangles . . . By each body was a little cup of copper or of limestone, and each one had one or more cockle shells containing green paint.'[1]

Whether this immolation should be regarded as a touching example of faith or as a landmark in the bloodstained annals of

[1] WOOLLEY, 'Excavations at Ur', *Journal of the Society of Antiquaries* (October 1929).

superstition, we must leave the reader to decide. It is notable that then, as often subsequently, the women bore the brunt of it. The sacrifice marks, at any rate, a milestone in the history of human solidarity.

Already, then, in the fourth millennium before Christ, under the baking Near Eastern sun, there rose the great temples and the great ziggurats, the whole beehive priestly accumulation of habit and business which laid the foundations of civilized life, of the immemorial Mesopotamian routine. To this day, the clumsy peasant irrigation, the buckets swung upwards on their creaking hoists, the docile laden asses trotting through the flat land, are in direct unmodified descent from antiquity.

This social structure was, of course, highly artificial. If the irrigation were to fail, drought would destroy the harvest and famine sweep away a population out of all proportion to the area which carried it. The city remained the unit throughout, controlling its own irrigation area; and the successive conquerors of the land, native or external, could not at first impose a centralized despotism, only a general supremacy over a number of cities. The two most notable Sumerian rulers are Sargon of Akkad (*c.* 2870) and Dungi (*c.* 2456); both of them left Codes of Law, but the most famous code was made by the Semite Hammurabi of Babylon (2123-2081), whose power was on a greater scale, but the basis of whose state was Sumerian.

The Prologue of this document shows a highly responsible conception of kingship; the code itself throws much light on Mesopotamian civilization, and the Epilogue, which concludes with a stupendous curse lasting for three pages, attempts to ensure the perpetual observance of the laws.[1]

As a prelude to their detailed provisions, 'Hammurabi, the High Prince', declares his purpose 'to uphold justice in the land, to banish the proud and the oppressor, that the great shall not despoil the weak . . . to rise like the sun over the Black Headed Race'. 'Ham-

---

[1] I have used throughout the translation of the code contained in *Babylonian and Assyrian Laws and Contracts*, C. W. H. JOHNS (Library of Ancient Inscriptions, Edinburgh, 1904). On the difficulties of translation the editor remarks: 'When an ancient king called himself a "rabid buffalo", it doubtless gave him satisfaction, but it would be very rude for us to do so. On the other hand, it is very tiresome for an English reader to read a sentence 300 lines in length before coming to the principal verb. Such a sentence is here broken up into short clauses . . . This is done, not because the translator is entirely ignorant of grammar, but in pity for the reader.' Appendix I, p. 389 (for the Code, see pp. 44-67).

murabi', he says, 'The Good Shepherd, am I, the Completer of Plenty.'

There follows an account of the restoration of cities, of temples rebuilt and re-endowed, of the defeat of the Elamites. 'As a God, King of the City, knowing and far seeing, I looked to the plantations of Dilbat and constructed its granaries for Ib the God, . . . as Overlord I gave fresh life to Erech, furnishing abundance of water to its people; I completed the tower of Eanna . . . As a Leader and King of the City I made the settlements on the Euphrates to be populous . . . As the Shepherd of my People, in the midst of Agade of the wide squares, I settled the rules and set straight the Tigris. High of purpose, great King, a very sun of Babylon, I caused light to arise upon Sumer and Akkad.'

It is a fine conception of government, stated in the dawn of history, constructive and protective, not predatory.

The Laws, in 282 short clauses, cover a wide range, designed not merely for the punishment of crime but for the regulation of a complex society. They begin with provisions dealing with spells, false witness, theft, lost property and runaway slaves; they punish officials for neglect or evasion of duty, and declare the responsibility of the temple and the treasury for their ransom. Provisions dealing with rents and debts encourage enterprise in cultivation;[1] obligations to maintain the irrigation system are fixed. 'If a man has let out the waters and they flood the young plants in his neighbour's field', he is liable to be fined.[2] Penalties are also provided for anyone who steals a 'watering machine'. If sheep get into a field and eat off the grass crop without its owner's consent, compensation must be paid. The relations between merchants and their agents are defined; the responsibility of bankers for deposits, and of the owners of granaries for stored corn, are enforced; if the corn rots, they must pay damages. Penalties for assault and for matrimonial irregularities follow; drowning is the usual punishment, particularly for women. But there are not the savage punishments of later militaristic Near Eastern tyrannies, though it seems hard that the keeper of a beer shop should be drowned for charging too much, or for harbouring 'seditious slanderers'.[3] Penalties for assault vary with the status of the persons concerned; if a patrician has knocked out the tooth of an equal, his tooth shall be knocked out;[4] but if he has knocked out the tooth of a plebeian, he shall pay one-third of a mina of silver. Brutal

[1] Clauses 40-8.   [2] Clause 56.   [3] Clauses 108-9.   [4] Clause 200.

31

assault on a man of higher rank is punished with sixty blows of an ox-hide scourge.[1] Surgeons were paid or punished according to results. 'If a surgeon has operated with a bronze lancet or has removed a cataract . . . he shall take 10 shekels of silver'; if he has caused the patient's death, 'his hands shall be cut off'.[2] The same penalty applies to anyone who excises a slave's brand-mark.

There follow detailed regulations for the hire of boats and for traffic on the river, for the hire and treatment of oxen and responsibility for them. 'If a man has hired an ox and has broken its horn, cut off its tail or torn its muzzle, he shall pay one quarter of its value.[3] On the other hand, if a man has hired an ox and 'God has struck it', the hirer shall make an affidavit and go free; and if a bull runs wild and gores a man, the owner is not responsible, though, if the animal is known to be wild, he is expected to blunt its horns and shut it up. The wages of field-labourers and herdsmen are fixed; stone-cutters, tailors, potters and builders are to be given a fair price, but the builder is to be put to death if the house he has put up falls down and kills the owner. Ordeal is usual (again the river is convenient), particularly for allegations of unchastity in a wife.

It will be seen that the conception of justice behind the Code was, for the time, constructive, not unreasonable; its provisions, though drastic, are in advance of those of the Franks and Burgundians nearly three millennia after it. The state is in truth regarded as a real commonwealth, though it has its social inequalities and is based on slavery: there is evidently a capable bureaucracy well in its stride.

In conclusion, the opening of the Epilogue runs: 'The judgements of righteousness which Hammurabi, the powerful King, settled and caused the land to receive, a sure polity and a gracious rule. I am Hammurabi, the superb King . . . The flesh of the land I made to rejoice. I extended the dwellings of the people in security.' The boast of this founder of civilization, four thousand years ago, seems justified.

This early utterance of law is already thoroughly Oriental in expression. The aims of government are security and plenty, the religion behind them practical and in the main wise; at the same time, the ornate utterance and self-glorification of Oriental despotism are already recognizable.

After Hammurabi, Mesopotamia was conquered by successive

---

[1] Clause 202. [2] Clauses 215 and 218. [3] Clause 248.

invaders, but the Sumerian basis of this culture remained. New rulers might proclaim themselves the successors of Marduk and impose a more brutal conception of conquest, but the same foundations persist.

The political ideas behind this society, it will be apparent, are largely inarticulate assumptions; in so far as they are rationalized, they centre on the cult of the god-king, who is the representative of the community and the mediator with its god. In Mesopotamia everything centres on the dwelling of the patesi; the palace is known as 'The House of the Man'; just as in Egypt the term 'Pharaoh' means 'He of the Great House'. Round this sacred focus the scribes and priests cluster and swarm; it is an organic, healthy and static civilization.

§ I I I

Turning to the parallel Egyptian development, we find it dependent on the Nile, with a rather similar economic organization, though more centralized. The Egyptian valley was easier to defend, bordered on both sides by sheer desert and not seriously threatened from the South. The danger came from sea raids in the Delta and from Semitic attacks over the Sinai peninsula. The military development of Egypt, though formidable, was therefore comparatively late. There was less independence of individual cities; they were swamped in a large scale domination. The Nile flood remained the dominant fact of the environment; it was the business of the Pharaoh and the priests to deal with it, to ensure its regular appearance and provide for the conservation of the water; as in Mesopotamia, measurement and calculation were among the most important functions of the ruling class.

The pre-dynastic Egyptians were a long-headed, lightly built people of mixed Hamitic and Mediterranean origin; superimposed on them was another race of Armenoid affinities who probably came from Syria and originally out of Middle Asia. They were physically and mentally superior to the aborigines; they adapted and developed the pre-dynastic culture. Egypt was united, and the first dynasty founded by Menes, King of Upper Egypt, about 3400 B.C.; the pyramid age and the full splendour of the Old Kingdom date from the fourth dynasty, c. 2900-2750. By this time the bureaucratic organization of the Egyptian state is already in being. Centring on

c   33

the Pharaoh, who is absolute in the land,[1] the scale and wealth of Egypt surpasses anything in Mesopotamia. The whole structure rests on the patient labour of the fellaheen: 'So far as the life of the common people is concerned, Egypt is the most unchanging country in the world; it has changed even less than China. The life of the fellah of the XIIth or even of the IVth dynasty is much the same as to-day.'[2] Political changes might alter the ruling dynasty, or place increased power in the hands either of the Pharaoh or of the local feudatories, but the whole structure of society was an absolutism more or less effectively centralized.

'The king was housed in a brick and mud palace with a double gate, typifying the double kingdom, made gay with painted stripes and panelling and with streamers flying from great cedar poles that stood before it brought from Lebanon by sea. It was no doubt surrounded by the smaller but similar palaces of the nobles, much as the palace of the Japanese Mikado . . . stood at Kyoto, surrounded by the palaces of his court nobles or Kuge.'[3]

There is nothing in Egyptian history to suggest that any conception of self-government or personal freedom ever penetrated the peasantry, who suffered and accepted heavy taxation, forced labour and military conscription as part of the nature of things. The power of the Pharaoh, and, under him, of his officials, was absolute, sanctioned by the whole weight of the religions which permeated and obsessed Egyptian life. There is indeed, behind the splendour of Egyptian art and the massiveness of Egyptian monuments, a fundamental pessimism and lack of originality; it was an almost indestructible civilization, but it lacked resilience. The obsession with death which makes this culture so extraordinary and its monuments so impressive, overshadowed and paralysed thought. Their conception of an after-life was material; where the mediaeval Christian prayed for the souls of the departed, the Egyptian is concerned to see that they are fed.[4] Their morality was pedestrian and comparable to that of the Chinese. 'A good name' and social approval, the usual worldly wisdom, tinged with the fatalism of the East, was as far as they

---

[1] The beginnings of his authority were, of course, primarily religious – he was a totem figure, subject to religious controls, e.g. the evidence of the 'sed' ceremony, which possibly derived from a fertility sacrifice at the expense of an aboriginal Pharaoh.

[2] *C.A.H.*, vol. I, chap. viii, p. 317.

[3] *C.A.H.*, vol. I, chap. vii, p. 280.

[4] A usual form of prayer was 'Thousands of bread and beer for the owner of this tomb'; in the most elaborate tombs they even provided lavatories for the dead. *Vide* QUIBELL, *Excavations at Sakkara*, 1912-14, plate 31.

reached. Magic rather than good works safeguards the passage of the dead to the next world; the formula is painted on the coffin-lid. The traditional and vaunted wisdom of the Egyptians did not include philosophical or political speculation.

The early Egyptians saw questions of government in personal terms, as the East has always seen them. The admonitions and parables which have come down, generally in fragmentary form, go back as far as the Old Kingdom; they are wisdom-books, rather similar on a smaller scale to those of the Old Testament.

The Admonitions of Ptahopt (c. 2600 B.C.) date from the pyramid age. Ptahopt, who was a retired official, gives advice to his son — pedestrian, sensible and worldly.[1] He exhorts him to 'do right' that his days may be long in the land . . . 'Thou shalt attain my years of life; they are not a few that I have spent on the earth; I have attained 110 years of life, while the King gave me rewards above those of the ancestors, because I did righteousness unto the King even to the grave.' He is mainly concerned with the wise conduct of personal relationship with one's family, with the bureaucracy and with 'great men'.

It is well, for example, when dining with a superior, not to look at his plate, but at one's own; not to stare at him; to laugh when he laughs; to be circumspect of speech. 'Let thy mind be deep and thy speech scanty . . .'; if he is a self-made man, appear unaware of it. All worldly success is precarious and it is wise to conciliate one's colleagues. Most important of all is the proper conduct of family life: 'If thou art a successful man, establish thy household; be not avaricious towards thine own kin; impoverished is he that over-reaches his brethren, greed . . . sunders fathers and mothers, husbands and wives; there is no tomb for the avaricious.'

Ptahopt can be easy-going as well. It is right to be cheerful, to take enjoyment as it comes; no prosperity is enjoyable if a man is 'harassed'. It is right also to be amiable and urbane in public life; the administrator should be gracious to the client. He should be allowed to pour out what is in his mind first, and 'heard kindly'.

The wise man is recognized by his knowledge: 'His heart is the balance for his tongue; his lips are correct in speaking, his eye in seeing . . . Established is the man who does righteousness, who walketh according to the way.'

[1] There is an admirable account of this side of Egyptian thought in BREASTED, *Dawn of Conscience*, Scribners (New York 1934), to which I am indebted for many of the quotations which follow.

Character, responsibility, the circumspect amenities of a stable life; these are the notes struck in this document of the twenty-seventh century before Christ. It contains the usual wisdom of the East, later to be expressed with fuller sophistication in the book of Ecclesiasticus, its disillusionment in the book of Job.

With the decline of the Old Kingdom the theme of the 'vanity' of 'wisdom', merging into a platitudinous staleness running into lamentation, begins to appear. Amiability and good sense give place to complaint and denunciation. The Pharaoh Amenhemet (*fl.* 2000-1970 B.C.), after a successful attempt to rally the decline of the feudal age, advises his son cynically 'That thou mayest increase good, harden thyself against all subordinates. The people regard him who terrorizes them; fill not thy heart with a brother; know not a friend, nor make to thyself intimates. For a man has no people in the Day of Evil.'[1]

The bitterness of these observations was justified by the Pharaoh's own experience, the occasion of the composition of his work being, on internal evidence, his own escape from assassination. 'It was after the evening meal,' he writes. 'Night had come, lying upon my couch I relaxed. Behold weapons were flourished . . . I awoke to fight, utterly alone.'[2]

But the most vivid expression of disillusionment is the 'Admonition of Ipuwer'.[3] The document is an exhortation by the scribe Ipuwer to the king, contrasting the evils of the time with the good days of the past, and it presents a picture of severe social dislocation.

'There is war in the land,' he writes, '. . . the river is blood. There is pestilence in the land . . . The Desert is throughout the land; the Nomes are laid waste, a foreign tribe has come into Egypt . . . The Corn of Egypt is common property; the crocodiles are glutted; men go to them of their own accord. The builders of the Pyramids are become farm labourers; the poor complain — "How terrible it is. What am I to do?" Cattle moan because of the state of the land.' Worst of all, the dead are not even buried, but flung in the river.

---

[1] BREASTED, op. cit., p. 206.
[2] BREASTED, *Ancient Records of Egypt*, vol. I, pp. 228-31.
[3] *The Admonitions of an Egyptian Sage*, from the *Hieratic Papyrus in Leiden*, Leipzig, 1909, edited and illustrated by A. G. GARDINER. There is an introduction explaining the kind of research which has gone to the translation and interpretation of this fragmentary and obscure papyrus. The hieroglyphic text is reproduced at the end and is of great interest. 'The document', says Professor Gardiner, 'is incoherently arranged', and, following Gardiner, I have, quoting from his translation, given an artificial impression of arrangement.

'The Nile overflows not, no-one ploughs for it.' Ipuwer exhorts the king to appease the Gods, to observe his office meticulously. 'Remember to chew Naton . . . to prepare the white bread. Remember to erect flagstaffs, and to renovate the offering loaves; remember to *observe regulations and to adjust dates*. Remember to slaughter oxen and to offer geese upon the fire.'

To point his denunciation of the king, he contrasts the good things of prosperity with present catastrophes. 'It is good when the net is drawn in, when the birds are made fast, when the hands of men build pyramids, when the ponds are dug, and the roads are passable; when the magnates of the districts stand and look on at the rejoicing in their houses, the need of every man is satisfied with a couch in the shade; it is good when fine linen is spread out on the day of the New Year.' The last paragraph gives a clear picture of Egyptian everyday life and values, not unattractive.[1]

Their ideas of justice are illustrated by the anonymous tale of the 'Eloquent Peasant' which dates from the feudal age, the gist of which is as follows.

The asses of a Faiyum peasant are stolen by a bailiff employed by the King's Grand Steward, Rensi. The peasant gets access to Rensi as he is about to embark on his state barge, and the great man brings the case before his subordinate officials. One and all advise that it be dismissed, but the peasant is allowed to plead his own case. This he does with such eloquence that Rensi is amused, telling the king he has discovered 'one of these peasants who is beautiful of speech'. He leads the peasant on, suspending judgement, and he has the speech written down. The suppliant makes nine appeals, all recorded and shown to the king, who is pleased and orders justice to be done.

The peasant's 'eloquence' runs the gamut of Oriental flattery, humour, beseeching and reproach. 'It is the breath of thy nostrils to do justice — , Thou art great and therefore responsible; thou art at one with the balances; if they are deflected, thou art deflected . . . Thy tongue is the plummet of the balances, thy breath is the weight, thy two lips are the beam.' The steward, he says, ought to be 'the rudder of the whole land': the practical similes are notable. Exasperated, the peasant turns to denunciation. 'Thou art set for a dam for

---

[1] As one would expect, there is slender evidence for any 'Messianic' ideas in Ipuwer's Admonitions. The hypothesis is based on a very obscure and corrupt passage, and Gardiner concludes that 'there is too much uncertainty in the matter for it to be made the basis of far-reaching conclusions as to the influence of Egyptian on Hebrew literature'. Op. cit., Introduction, p. 15.

the poor man to save him from drowning, but behold thou art the flood that sweeps him away . . . Thou hast not given me requital, according to the good word which came out of the mouth of Re himself, "Speak the truth; do the truth".[1]

Here is apparent a conception of justice not as arbitrary, but as following rules; it is bound up, as the comparisons constantly show, with the idea of measurement, order, and correct routine.

All the Egyptian documents quoted, though some are cynical or pessimistic, show much the same sensible conception of government as is apparent in Hammurabi's Code; they express an outlook only possible in a highly organized state. These Oriental societies, stable, wise within their limitations and conservative, carried on through all the vicissitudes of the centuries. They laid the foundations of civilized life.

§ IV

With the transformation of government into large-scale military empires in the second millennium, the conception of Near Eastern kingship expands and deteriorates; a series of competing empires clashed and succeeded each other — the Hyksos in Egypt, the Babylonians in Mesopotamia, the Hittites in Asia Minor, and, worst of all, the Assyrians.

These great military empires developed through various causes. There had always been predatory nomads and mountaineers watching with avid eyes the fat settlements of the valleys. Successively they broke in, successively they were absorbed — there was 'corn in Egypt'. Again, the increasing demands of civilization encouraged rulers to send their caravans after the timber and metals which the river lands did not provide; trade led to military commitments, finally to imperialist expansion.

Next, within the society, the central government might weaken; as it became more militarized, a warrior aristocracy grow up. Further, the Pharaoh or the Priest-King, not content with his placid routine, irked perhaps by theocratic domination, might break out as a war leader, refuse to play the priestly game and surround himself with a fighting nobility which in time became feudalized. These in turn, when the king was weak or young, would set up for themselves; there would be a phase of military disorder. Thus the warrior

[1] BREASTED, op. cit., pp. 180-7.

king and the warrior aristocracy emerged; they brought a fiercer note into the civilization of the East.

The co-operative enterprise of early civilizations was followed by a phase of military conflict on a great scale and the fruits of good sense and stability squandered. With the risk of large-scale warfare, government and social organization harden; henceforward the successful ruler must depend less on religious and magical prestige, more on material force.

The most formidable and best administered of the great Semitic empires was the Assyrian, built up after the collapse of the Hittite power in Asia Minor, reaching its fullest extent in the eighth and seventh centuries of the first millennium B.C. Their hideous art, depicting figures half animal and half human, and bombastic triumphal inscriptions, are well known. Their religion was repulsive and their morals shocking; they were obsessed with devil-worship and preoccupied with omens; their cruelty was remarkable even by the standards of the contemporary Near East. It was indeed this cruelty which enabled them to impose an almost Roman order, and indirectly to preserve much of the Babylonian inheritance. But their empire was a ferocious and sombre tyranny.

The Assyrian king was absolute, though in practice influenced by fear of the priesthood; Assyrian laws were efficient, comprehensive, and of the utmost savagery — Hammurabi's Code would have been too mild for them. They split ears and noses, castrated offenders, and flogged them to death; the variety of vices for which their penalties provide indicates a society of peculiar brutality.[1]

Although it had evolved the most highly specialized military technique of any of the peoples of the ancient world, the Assyrian domination was broken and the Assyrian state wiped out by the Medes and Babylonians in 612 B.C. Professor Toynbee says of them: 'By Asshurbanipal's time (regnabat 669-625 B.C.), on the eve of the great catastrophe, two centuries of steady progress in the art of war had produced an Assyrian army which was well prepared for every task, as it was scientifically divided into a number of specialized arms. There were the chariotry and the demi-cataphract horse archers; the heavy foot archers, armoured from helmet to boots, and the light foot archers who risked their lives in head-bands, loin-cloths and sandals; the hoplites, armed like the heavy foot archers, except that

---

[1] See SCHIEL, *Recueil des Lois Assyriennes* (Paris 1921). A remarkable catalogue of crime.

they carried spear and shield instead of bow and quiver; and the peltasts, likewise carrying spear and shield, but wearing in lieu of a cuirass a pectoral secured by crossed shoulder straps. There was probably also a corps of engineers, for there was certainly a siege train — not, indeed, of catapults, but of battering rams and rolling towers — and, when these engines had done their work and the walls of the enemy fortress had been breached, the Assyrian directors of military operations knew how to cover the storming parties with volleys of arrows from massed batteries of archers . . . The Assyrians were firm believers in the sovereign value of the offensive.'[1] This 'war machine' within a century and a half had sacked Damascus, Samaria, Babylon, Sidon, Memphis, Thebes, and Susa. 'The loss and misery which Assyria inflicted on her neighbours is beyond calculation.'[2]

Such was the sequel to the patient building up of civilization by earlier Near Eastern communities; and the situation can be paralleled, on a lesser scale, by the imperialist activities of Egypt and Babylon. It is the measure of the cultural vitality of the Temple State that its civilization was not destroyed by the monstrous conflicts of the military empires it later sustained.

§ v

Looking back, then, over the main lines of the political and social development of Mesopotamia and Egypt, we may recapitulate as follows. First, the dawn of civilization came in the Near East. Here massive societies grew up which no amount of violence could wholly break; they had a stubborn vitality and a wealth without any precedent. But they were materialistic and conservative, and they did not evolve speculative thought. 'Writing and numeration, astronomy and mathematics, were all invented in the East to be pinned to the service of a static civilization, dominated by the temple and the court, and it was the hard mould of urban culture that kept that civilization static . . . The "changeless East" invented civilization only to stagnate it.'[3] But the initial steps had been taken, the foundations secured. Here, in spite of a later superimposed militarism, is the cardinal fact. Later, as the scale and wealth of these societies develop, and warrior dynasties successively impose their

[1] TOYNBEE, *A Study of History*, vol. IV, pp. 468-84.
[2] TOYNBEE, ib.
[3] CHRISTOPHER HAWKES, *The Prehistoric Foundations of Europe*, Methuen (1940), pp. 382-3.

rule, the resources of civilization are increasingly devoted to military ends. The king becomes not merely the beneficent law-giver, whose interest is bound up with the city and the city's god, and who defends it against aggression from without, but the predatory despot of unbridled ambition and terrible power, who massacres whole populations and razes cities to the ground, who impales and flays his captives and transfers peoples like cattle from one part of a great empire to another. The conception of rule behind this later hyper-trophied development is unconstructive and degenerate. The ruling race, Hittite or Assyrian, employing new weapons, chariots and iron, imposes itself, a conquering military minority, on a mass of subject peoples. The ruler proclaims his identity with the local gods, but he has little constructive to contribute. The ordinary process of Oriental conquest runs its course; the rulers collect a steady tribute, spent on luxury and war; living thus, they do little to develop the resources of the communities which sustain them. Finally they are smashed by other and more ferocious invaders who impose the same cycle again.

The price of large-scale rule had been large-scale war, but, in spite of all this, effective government had been established on an increas-ingly great scale; and the blood-stained Hittite and Assyrian empires were succeeded by the Persian, which was far more intelligent, and created an imperial structure, from which Alexander and the Romans directly inherited a tradition of empire never envisaged by the Greek world. Thus the Near East gave Europe not only the foundations of material culture but the tradition of imperial rule, which, for all its cruel pedigree, provided through its Hellenistic and Roman inter-pretations the framework of Graeco-Roman society. But the rise of the Near Eastern empires is an aspect of secondary importance for our immediate purpose, which is to trace the spread of the river valley civilization to Europe and, in particular, the Greek reinterpre-tation of the culture of the temple state, transmitted through the Minoan-Mycenean civilization of the bronze-age Aegean.

CHAPTER III

THE GREEK CITY STATE: PLATO

§ 1

The cultures of the Levant and Mediterranean, and of the Graeco-Roman world from which modern civilization derives, were organized in terms of the City State: the Greek version of the Sacred City, combined with the Near Eastern idea of divine kingship and empire, was the foundation of the world of antiquity.

For the development of political thought the emergence of the Greek City State is of cardinal importance. The heavy routine of Near Eastern empire, the bureaucracy of Egypt and Mesopotamia, the feckless irresponsibility of the iron-age tyrants of the Old Testament, give place to something new. The free play of speculative intelligence, the brilliant formulation of the vocabulary of thought in a language expressive of the subtlest shades of meaning, the purposive coherence of Greek ideals — all these things mark the greatest step forward that political speculation has ever made.

The foundations had been laid in the river valleys; the fundamental inventions, without which the Greek city would have been impossible — writing, the wheel, the ship, the calendar — these had been achieved, but it is not until Greek intelligence has raised the essential problems of thought that political theory in the full sense can be said to begin. For all their practical inventive genius, the priest-ridden societies of Mesopotamia and Egypt never displayed the intellectual initiative of the Greeks; the docile Near Eastern peoples had taken the world as they found it; the Greek intellect probes to the foundations of life.

The historical background of the Greek city has only fairly recently been made known. The discoveries of Schliemann at Mycenae and of Sir Arthur Evans in Crete have proved that behind the brilliance of fifth-century Greece there lies a phase of heroic barbarism depicted in the Homeric poems; that, behind the period in which the Greek newcomers from the steppe were raiding and wrecking the civilization of the Levant, there lies a whole history of high cultural achievement centring on Crete.

The Minoan empire, based on sea power and secure over centuries, produced an art of the first quality, a sophisticated way of life, and a script at present indecipherable but evidently advanced; its civilization derived both from Egypt[1] and from Asia Minor.

Further, there is now evidence that Sumerian influence had penetrated north over the Caucasus and affected the steppe peoples of South Russia; the kurgans in which the Caucasian copper-age chieftains were buried are the counterparts of the great Sumerian tombs. We find, therefore, a warrior steppe people directly linked with the oriental beginnings of civilization. The Mycenaean invaders who came originally, in all probability, out of South Russia into Greece, had already a distinctive culture of their own which blended with the Minoan influence and contributed a more virile strain to the peoples of the Levant. By the middle of the seventh century B.C. a distinctive European culture has been evolved.

The Minoan-Mycenaean influence conditions the whole development of classical Greece. Recent research has confirmed how widespread and persistent were the social and religious ideas of this lost world in antiquity. The Dorian invasions swamped the Mycenaean cities, but there was no break in continuity. The high Greek civilization was the result of barbarian vigour from the north, crossed with the southern culture of the Levant, which it smashed but never killed. The most brilliant phase of Greek art and thought may perhaps be compared with the twelfth-century Renaissance in northern France. It is a similar phenomenon; vigorous barbarians, tamed by an ancient civilization, create an intellectual and artistic renaissance which combines strength and integrity of vision with technical skill from an older tradition. But it is dangerous to push this comparison too far; the Levantine culture must have been materially a small affair compared with the far-flung might of Graeco-Roman and Byzantine civilization from which the twelfth-century Renaissance derived.

The geographical setting of Greece naturally conduced to variety and vitality. The invigorating clear air, the cool but sunny winters, the small-scale and intricate configuration of the peninsulas and islands, combined to foster intelligence and enterprise. 'With accum-

[1] 'The intimate connection of Minoan Crete with the Nile valley, which goes back to predynastic times, has been demonstrated by a long series of discoveries extending from the southern plain of Mesara to the site of Knossos, so that any criticism of the reaction of Egyptian elements on the early Cretan religion stands self-condemned.' SIR ARTHUR EVANS, *The Earlier Religions of Greece in the Light of Cretan Discoveries* (1931).

ulated energy from the steppe, but with less power of or need for work in the more southern latitudes, these early invaders would combine energy with leisure, which is the basis of all art . . . The seasonal work implied seasonal idleness, heroic games, perennial war'[1] — hence the brilliance and hence the weakness of Hellenic civilization.

The beginnings of Greek speculation can be traced to the seaboard of Asia Minor; the ports and islands of this beautiful coast provided an environment at once stimulating and comparatively easy. The outlook of the Ionian thinkers was profoundly original; it was scientific. They regarded man as one with other phenomena, to be studied objectively; they are thus sharply differentiated from their Mesopotamian and Egyptian forerunners. This lucid objectivity, which strikes down to fundamentals, is unequalled until scientific method emerges again in the sixteenth century.

Homer, an Ionian Greek, shows this objectivity of judgement, and his widespread influence, coming when it did, profoundly affected Greek thought. 'The ordinary Greek', wrote a modern scholar, killed in the last war, 'was subject to the superstitions of an immature people as much as any other, but the appearance of such a giant as Homer in an age when the Greeks could hardly be said to be civilized was a portent which had incomparable results to Greek thought as a whole; and by stating simple human problems of life and death and suffering and happiness in their simplest forms he drew Greek thought aside from the darker things which might have engulfed it. Homer acted as a purge for all that was barbaric and retrogressive in a barely established society. In this way Homer was a forerunner of the Ionian method of thought.'[2] The achievements of Heraclitus and Hippocrates are well known; Archelaus of Miletus is thought to have influenced Socrates, and it is likely that the Socratic method had its origin in Ionian Greece.

By the fifth century B.C. the Greek world was already swarming with itinerant sophists to whom Socrates has given a bad name, but

[1] LYDE, *Continent of Europe*, Macmillan (1930), p. 158. Professor Lyde believes the actinic rays of the Levantine sun were in the long run harmful; that this overstimulus combined with progressive desiccation between 400 B.C. and A.D. 600 and endemic malaria to account for the 'racial suicide' of the Greeks. Yet Greece was the intellectual life of Rome and Byzantium long after her political collapse. For the decay of their fighting qualities, however, this explanation is interesting; the draining off of Greek manpower into Asia in the Hellenistic age obviously further contributed to the decline.

[2] STANLEY CASSON, *The Discovery of Man*, p. 42. Hamish Hamilton (1939).

who played an important part in spreading the habit of speculative thought. They were concerned not with practical science but with problems of conduct. Such problems do not require specialized technical knowledge, and the discussion of them would be attractive to the quick-witted audience from which the philosophers got their living. These early sophists are the successors of the itinerant poets and soothsayers of Homeric times and form the link between the beginnings and subsequent Greek thought. The restless and intricate minds of Ionian Greece turned away from practical speculation to those problems of ethics and politics with which this study is primarily concerned.

The outstanding quality of Greek speculation was a clear analysis of terms, a striking to the root of a problem; in the later phases this distinction is often swamped in pettiness and elaboration, but the inspiration lived on. The virility and directness of the early Greek spirit is already apparent in the archaic statues in which the savage elements have not yet been softened out. The sculpture of the period shows the calibre of these people at their best. There is a formidable solidarity and serenity of poise together with a hard intelligence which dwarfs most subsequent achievement.

The force and gravity of antique public sculpture persists into full Roman times; and, if coarsened in the later period, gives us the measure of the scale and force of antiquity at its full tide, the echoes of its prestige persisting in the legends of the successor peoples who camped amid its ruins. And, as the inspiration of the Roman sculpture was Greek, so also was the idiom of the Roman political thought.

The Socratic attitude began by demolishing the conventional certainties of behaviour by a ruthless analysis; the next stage was to build up a set of ethical rules on an intellectually satisfactory basis. Questioning the nature of right conduct, Socrates concludes that it is something clear cut, which can in the last resort be defined and therefore taught. Hence the didactic nature of Greek thought; far from theorizing *in vacuo*, that curse of much Western European and most Eastern practice, the Greek thinkers tried to find out what the good life was, and to act upon it. Hence the good sense and coherence of Aristotle's definition of the end of the State — that the aim of the State is the good life. Socrates and Plato are concerned to frame rules for making the good life possible in societies. Such an approach is apt to be over-intellectual, and an impression of stark artificiality sometimes crops up in the *Republic* and even, in a less

45

degree, in the *Politics*. The Greek ethics and political theory are often geometrically rigid and take little account of the subconscious motives which largely determine conduct.

Further, it is well to remember that the earlier Greek political theory, for all its originality and nobility of thought, to a large extent takes the institution of slavery for granted; it was the price paid for the existence of a leisured class in such an economic and geographical setting. The Ionian thinkers, in particular, living under Persian influence along the Asiatic coast and in the islands, would have been accustomed to it; and the Spartans, whose example was widely admired, were a small and hated minority ruling over a Helot population.

§ II

The political thought of the polis is expressed with the greatest clarity and imaginative beauty by Plato, and Plato derives his inspiration from Socrates (469-399 B.C.). Of this extraordinary man comparatively little is directly known, though Plato's account of him has made him famous; he perished through his own will to die for his principles and because his revolutionary method of analysis was felt to be anti-social by his contemporaries. His immediate political sympathies, so far as he had any, were probably with the landowning oligarchy who opposed the trading urbanized Athens which had grown up in the fifth century, but there is no reason to suppose that the government of the day was anxious to kill him. In advanced old age he deliberately chose death rather than exile, and displayed contempt for the court which tried him, suggesting that he deserved 'free quarters at the Prytaneum' as a reward for his good influence. His personality and outlook are best described in Plato's *Apology*, which gives an account of his defence at his trial; in the *Phaedo*, which describes his last hours and death, and in the famous *Symposium*.

The philosophical position of Socrates cannot be here examined, but the attitude of mind for which he stands must be understood, for from it derives the political outlook expressed not only by Plato, but indirectly by the Stoics and Epicureans.

Socrates' great achievement was to set the highest value on personality and reason; he held that the supreme interest of man is the bettering of his own soul, the expansion and discipline of mind and character; and he communicated this passion for improvement to

46

his disciples. One of them said of him, 'This Marsyas' (an allusion to Socrates' odd appearance) 'makes me think life is not worth living so long as I am what I am.' Socrates, a disturbing influence, put moral and intellectual values into the forefront of life; the business of a man is to lead the good life in the light of rational knowledge. The self-mastery and virility of thought and conduct behind this attitude is in the best European tradition; it puts intellectual honesty and personal independence before any political or theological loyalties, and Socrates himself affirmed these values for all time in the dignity and serenity of his death. The force of his personality and the fame of his ending make him the first hero and martyr of European thought.

Socrates himself held that he was inspired by his 'daimon' to make men realize their ignorance, and to compel them to face facts. Such an attitude was no more popular in Athens than it would be in most cities to-day; but Athenian delight in speculation for its own sake, the novelty which such an approach had for them, may be compared with the similar speculative enterprise shown in Renaissance Italy, in Elizabethan England, and among the Russian intellectuals of the nineteenth century.

But there is no feverish romantic note in the Greek thought, in the Greek balanced rationality, expressed also in the restraint and excellence of their lyric poetry.[1] Economy, understatement, a poignant focusing of an exact situation, all these qualities are apparent, reinforced with a powerful analytical judgement and fine ironical humour, in the mind of Socrates depicted in the *Symposium* and the *Apology*.

In the light of these firm values the function of government is clear; it is to ensure the good life. The city should produce men of the highest intellectual and spiritual integrity, develop their personalities and talents, and ensure that each man should have the scope or limitations for which his qualities fit him. Ethical and rational standards are to determine political practice.

The natural result of this outlook is the aristocratic and intellectualized view of the City State, which finds its fullest expression in the writings of Plato. Since the political crises of our own time are forcing us to consider some radical solution to our own larger-scale problems as an alternative to destruction, this first trenchant attempt

[1] See C. M. BOWRA, *Greek Lyric Poetry*, a brilliant exposition of this aspect of Greek genius. Also the *Oxford Book of Greek Verse*, in translation, Oxford University Press.

to moralize and rationalize politics has a particular interest to the twentieth century.

Plato's[1] political thought falls into three phases: first, the *Republic* (*c.* 378 B.C.) represents the thought of his early maturity and surpasses his later work in literary and aesthetic quality; the second phase is represented by the short dialogue, the *Statesman* (*c.* 365); and the third by the *Laws*, which was the work of his old age, written between 360 and 348, and which is far more rigid and authoritarian. All are the product of a profound disillusionment with actual political life. 'I at last perceived', he writes in the famous Seventh Epistle, 'that the constitution of existing states is bad, and their institutions all but past remedy without the combination of radical measures and fortunate circumstances; and I was driven to affirm that . . . the human race will never see the end of trouble until genuine philosophers should come to hold political power, or those who hold political power should by some divine appointment become philosophers.' The disastrous Peloponnesian War and the execution of Socrates had disgusted Plato with political affairs, though he thought it his duty to take part in politics and did so at Syracuse with little success.

On that occasion he thus defined his attitude to the prospect of political power: 'Now, if ever, is the moment for the realization of all our hopes of a personal union between philosophy and political power in a state of large calibre. These, with many others in the same strain, were the arguments with which Dion sought to prevail upon me . . . So I long debated and hesitated whether I should go . . . till in the end I inclined to his opinion that, if ever a philosopher was to set himself to realize his ideas about legislation and government, this was just the occasion for making the experiment . . . These were the considerations which led me to take the bolder course and set out from home, not at all in the spirit with which some people have credited me, but under a most powerful moral compulsion not to lose my self-respect, as I was in danger of losing it if I were to be

[1] Born 427 at Athens of aristocratic family; as a youth came under the influence of Socrates, who was forty years his senior. Left Athens in 399 after Socrates' death, and wrote the first series of dialogues as a memorial to him. Travelled in the Levant and probably Egypt. First visited Syracuse 387. In 387 returned to Athens and founded the Academy, so called from the 'Grove of Academus' near the Kephissus. The Academy was designed to be a school of political science; the *Republic* a programme on which such science should proceed. In 367 he paid his second visit to Syracuse, to instruct Dionysus the Younger, Tyrant of that city. The mission ended in failure and Plato returned to Athens. He died in 346 B.C.

convicted in my own judgement of being simply nothing but a mere voice — a fellow who never took action, not even a hand's turn if he could help it.'[1]

The *Republic* is primarily a philosophical discussion, a profound inquiry into the nature of the good life; the ideal city is brought in almost incidentally to the ethical theme. It is impossible in a short space to give a full account of the book, one of the outstanding achievements of the human mind. It is available in many good translations,[2] and the reader unfamiliar with it is advised to study the full text.

The *Republic* shows disillusionment, not only with democratic Athens, but with political human nature; Plato believes there is a right science of human government, 'a kingly science', which includes the whole art of living. The social coherence of the City State, inherited from its beginnings, is taken for granted and sophisticated into a balanced social order in which each man does 'the things appropriate to him at the right time'. It is the same with Aristotle; the 'conflict' between individual and community is not yet admitted; politics are a means to the end of the individual good life. Both Plato and Aristotle assume that the full development of personality coincides with the common good; when they envisage the development of the self-conscious individual who asks, 'What shall I do to be saved?', who breaks out from the community into a destructive independence, they invoke the remedy of education.

This healthy outlook brings the political thought of the πολις, alien though its setting may be, into line with modern evidence which shows the individual linked with the group in a way more fundamental than political theory from the Hellenistic period to the late eighteenth century would generally admit.

Now Plato was convinced that the 'kingly science' was something which could be known; he is no romantic dreamer, but determined to construct a right science of politics of geometrical precision. The authority which he gives his 'guardians', and which he would assign his philosopher king if he could find him, is given because they are experts; they stand in relation to the rest of the citizens as the physi-

---

[1] Plato, Letter No. 7; quoted by TOYNBEE in *A Study of History*, vol. VI, pp. 257-8.
[2] I have quoted throughout from the translation made by the present Master of Balliol (Dent, 1926, revised edition). See also the admirable Introduction, which works out the consequences of Plato's philosophical thought and gives a clear guide to the intricacies of the book.

cian to a patient; they know, and have a right to power. Hence the disconcerting ruthlessness of Plato's thought.

The resulting view of the State is profoundly undemocratic. Most men have to be told what is good for them, as they have not the sense to conduct their affairs themselves. Such an outlook, natural enough in any age, is in practice apt to demoralize both rulers and ruled; the 'human cattle' the watchdogs guard, soon stop being worth guarding, and power corrupts the guardians themselves. This fact, of course, Plato must have known and, as will be seen from the *Statesman* and the *Laws*, his later thought admits it, at least by implication.

Now it follows that since there is a kingly science of government it should be put into action. The *Republic* implies, in fact, a 'revolt of the competent', though Plato was well aware of the practical impotence of philosophers in politics. 'A very small band', he writes, 'is left of those who worthily associate with philosophy . . . Those who have become members of it and can taste the blessedness of this prize can all discern the madness of the many and the almost universal rottenness of all political action. The philosopher . . . is like a man in a den of wild beasts'[1] (VI, 496). There is, further, in Plato a strain of puritanical dislike of ordinary human motives, alien to the spontaneity of Greek poetry and art, a strict introspection and self-discipline. The Semitic conflict between body and soul, between matter and spirit, is foreshadowed in many of the dialogues. Hence the extreme rigour of the Platonic political scheme, which, severe enough in the *Republic*, in the *Laws* reaches an inhuman intensity. Only a small minority, he argues, have any insight into government, and Plato compares the philosophic ruler to an artist: 'A city will never know happiness unless its draughtsmen are artists who have a pattern of the divine.' They must paint on a 'clean canvas': 'They will look at natural justice and beauty and temperance and all the other virtues and produce a human copy after their likeness, so combining and mixing from various institutions the colour and likeness of true manhood' (VI, 501). The philosopher king, by his insight, possesses knowledge; the multitude, on the other hand, judges only by opinion, and the only way to guide them in the right path is in terms of opinions suitable to their minds, since they cannot come at the truth at all. This principle opens up strange possibilities; the

---

[1] It is notable how many of the writers to whom Greek civilization owes its fame, express similar sentiments about the society in which they lived.

Catholic Church and modern authoritarian states have been known to act on it.

The kind of state at which the philosopher aims strives for a harmonious balance or principle of justice, not at all in the modern sense of the enforcement of public law, but in the sense of creating a pattern which fits the intellectual, physical, and psychological needs of different kinds of men, each kind contributing according to his ability. Now this clearly set out purpose, that the supreme end of the State is the moral perfection of its citizens, overrides many of the normal impulses of life; if human nature conflicts with it, so much the worse, says Plato, for human nature. Aristotle, with greater good sense, attempts to adapt the State to human needs as they are; and Plato indeed aims to do so, though without much success, in the *Laws*.

But the *Republic*, the prototype of all Utopias, must be studied within its own convention. The ideal state is divided into three kinds of men: a small class of rulers; a larger class of civilians, merchants and craftsmen; and a third class of slaves, who are presumably taken for granted, though not directly mentioned, and who sustain the whole structure. The ruling minority are in turn divided into the guardians and the ἐπίκουροι, who enforce their decisions. They are selected according to ability, and their elaborate education continues up to the age of 35. Women who show the necessary talent are admitted to this class — an extraordinary idea in such a context of time and place. These rulers are to renounce all the usual human interests of family ambition and affection and private property, since such interests are incompatible with the best life and the perfect state. It is notable, though, that this prohibition does not extend to the ordinary civilians, who are, naturally, allowed within limits to carry on business and to maintain families. For the rulers, however, there is nothing for it but to do away with such things. It is a desperate remedy. For the guardians marriage is abolished, not only because family ambition breaks the unity of the state, but because human breeding ought to be planned and not casual.[1] Plato holds, with some justice, that no one would tolerate such breeding of animals; it is ridiculous, he maintains, not to apply biological knowledge to a supremely important problem. It must be confessed that this short cut has been made more convincing

[1] There is here, of course, no question of lax morality. On the contrary, Plato's design is the result of intellectual austerity. Similarly, property is abolished for the guardians, not because Plato was a communist in the modern sense, but because it interferes with the good life of a select minority.

in our own day by an increased knowledge of the mechanism of heredity. Further, Plato maintains, women of outstanding ability should not waste their energy in child-bearing and domestic interests.

The object of the education which is to be the backbone of Plato's state is very fully defined. It is indeed with education as much as with politics that Plato is concerned. His object is to impart a balanced insight into essentials and an all-round harmony of body and mind. The whole being must be disciplined by will; Plato distrusts the subconscious mind, and aims at subjugating and sublimating it. The man who is 'ridden by the baser desires' is the slave of the worst kind of tyranny: 'This terrible, fierce and lawless class of desires exists in every man, even in those who have the appearances of being decent people' (IX, 572). The attractive and beautiful temptations are the most insidious and lead gradually to the moral suicide of the 'greedy soul'. 'The just man will fix his eyes on the constitution within him and watch that nothing therein is shaken by excess or poverty' (IX, 591). The man who is at war with himself is helpless before the chances of life; the 'reasonable man, if he meets with misfortunes . . . will bear it much more easily than other people' (X, 601). He will, in a fine phrase, 'conceal an intimate sorrow'. Poets, in so far as they encourage emotional abandonment and 'impulses which should be withered', are immoral. 'Be quite sure that only such specimens of poetry as are hymns to the gods or praises of good men will be received into the city.' 'So much is at stake — much more than people think — in a man becoming good or bad; and therefore he must not be seduced by honour or money or any office, or even by poverty, to neglect justice and virtue.' Everything is subordinate to this hard moral purpose, this exacting ideal.

Thus the *Republic* is primarily a moral treatise of deep insight, the political Utopia subordinate to the main theme. Whether one admires or dislikes Plato's ideal, the subordination of politics to an ethical purpose, which Plato, like Aristotle, takes for granted, is clearly of the utmost value. Here, at the beginning of political thought, the cardinal principles are set out. First, that the development of the individual is only possible in the medium of the community; second, that political aims should never violate morality; and third, that the statesman's activity should be directed towards a clear aim. That these ideals should have been stated in the idiom and within the limitations of the πολις does not make them the less permanently valid or incapable of adaptation and enlargement into a wider setting. A deepened psychological knowledge and a more powerful economic and social organization might well reinforce them. But always the limitations of the human medium must be remembered; a purposive adaptation defeats its own ends if it works against the tide of human nature; if it arrogates to itself a monopoly of moral judgement and cramps or distorts the humanity it aims to improve, depriving men of the moral freedom which makes virtue worth attainment.

Such, then, are some outstanding aspects of Plato's *Republic*. The scope of the book is so great and its philosophic import so profound, influential, and well known, that this account of it has been deliberately confined to a small compass; a first-hand knowledge of the text, as of Aristotle's *Politics*, is one of the first essentials to the study of political theory.

The *Statesman* and the *Laws*, on the other hand, are less familiar; often, indeed, neglected, and it is well to give some description of them.

In the *Statesman*[1] Plato admits that the best must be made of existing institutions, though there is a 'scientific' form of government which is the only right one, as there is a right medical science or a right science of navigation, and the ideal state would be ruled by a philosopher king who would follow the rules of this science. Since in practice such a ruler cannot be found, he proceeds to analyse different kinds of actual governments on the lines followed later by Aristotle, and to define the function of the ruler within these limits. The problem is still envisaged as purely ethical and the conclusions reached artistically attractive, though practically unconvincing.

The dialogue begins, after preliminaries which are heavy going, with the statement that the kingly man or statesman exercises the 'art of herding human beings' (p. 43); he studies the science of 'tending men in common'. Plato then proceeds to a curious account of the origins of evil. In the Golden Age, when the earth was directed by God, there came a time when the Creator, as it were, let go of the machine, which turned backwards and reversed the processes of life. 'So long as the world was under the guidance of the pilot, it produced little evil and great good, but in becoming separated from him it grew forgetful . . . and disorder prevailed more and more; whereupon

---

[1] The *Statesman* or *Politicus* is cast in the form of a discussion between Socrates, a stranger from Elis, and a subsidiary and contributing audience. The important part of the dialogue is contained in the second half. References are to the Loeb edition, Heinemann (1925).

the Creator took charge again.' During the period of confusion men were 'in great straits'; they were thrown on their own resources, and the craft of ruling grew up under these conditions. After various digressions, Plato comes down to defining the nature of regal government. Just as a physician has science behind him, so too must the ruler. Among forms of government, one is pre-eminently right, and is the only real government, in which 'the rulers are found truly possessed of science' (pp. 132-3).

All other forms of government must be considered as imitated from this. But lawgivers must legislate for particular cases and times. How, then, can they lay down rigid rules? And is the statesman justified in forcing his subjects to be good even against their inherited traditions which, though sound, may be improved upon? (p. 143). However unskilful physicians or sea-captains may be, the ordinary layman cannot give advice on their art. It follows that, even if existing laws are bad, if they are arbitrarily altered by people who are not experts, they will be made worse. 'No multitude is capable of acquiring any kind of art, and if there is a kingly art neither the collective body of the wealthy nor the whole people could ever acquire the science of statesmanship.' The true form of government is by a single ruler who rules with science, but since 'no king is produced in our states who is, like the ruler of the bees in their hives, pre-eminently fitted to govern', it follows that we must 'follow in the track' of the perfect government by making written laws. 'It is our duty to see which of these not right forms of government is the least difficult to live with.'

He proceeds to discuss the three forms of government: monarchy, the rule of the few, and the rule of the many. These he subdivides into four forms: royalty, tyranny, aristocracy, oligarchy; 'but to the rule of the many we give but a single name, "democracy" '. 'The principle of lawfulness and lawlessness bisects them.' Monarchy keeping the laws is the best; aristocracy, intermediate; but democracy is 'unable to do anything great, either good or bad'. If the law is broken, democracy is the least bad, for it is incapable of going to extremes.

Plato then discusses the arts by which the statesman rules; by persuasion and speech, by command, by legal judgements; but the art which co-ordinates all these is statecraft. It is compared to the art of weaving (p. 175), and should be directed to the achievement of a 'balanced mean'. There are two kinds of men, the courageous and the docile; the kingly art assigns to each his position. 'This, then, let us declare, is the end of the statesman's activity; the direct interweaving of the characters of restrained and courageous men, when the kingly science has drawn them together by friendship . . . into a common life . . . and, omitting nothing which ought to belong to a happy state, rules and watches over them.'

Thus the *Statesman* is remarkable for the clear statement that there is an absolute and correct method of government, as there is a correct geometry, and for the insistence that the ruler is a kind of artist, who in practice must accept the limitations of his material.

In the *Laws*[1] Plato works out the thought already defined in the *Statesman*. Since it is impossible to find a philosopher king, the second best but only practicable alternative is to reinforce intensive education by rigid customs and conventions. He never fully develops a concept of a universal Natural Law; such an idea would have taken him outside the polis, the social context of his thought. The rule of Law, for Plato, remains the rule of custom and convention; it is thought of as 'a golden leading string', and men as puppets. It is an inferior substitute for the ideal outlined in the *Republic*. The thought is dominated throughout by the idea of harmony; the community, in Plato's view, should reflect certain absolute values of beauty and concord it is the highest duty of man to realize. 'The pattern of political life should be organic, the movement of society something of the nature of a complex and well-ordered rhythm, analogous to a dance. Yet for all their fine background, the *Laws* imply a static and rigid organization.

The central theme is that balance and self-control, reinforced by rules which are the result of experienced wisdom, will create a good state likely to further the moral development of its citizens. As in the *Statesman*, the middle way is admired; it is achieved by education and good laws, which dominate every aspect of life and which tend to destroy moral responsibility.

The discussion opens, after very few preliminaries, with an account of the Spartan state organized for war. War as an end in itself is not enough; education for the good life is more important, and actually produces better soldiers. 'Education is the way to produce good men,

[1] The setting is in Crete. Clinias the Cretan, in company with an Athenian and a Spartan – all represented as elderly men – are walking from Knossos to the Cave of Dicte, the birthplace of Zeus. It appears that the Cretan has been given permission to refound Knossos, long deserted; hence arises a detailed discussion as to the best way of planning a city. The translation quoted is by Prof. A. E. TAYLOR, Dent (1934).

and, once produced, such men will live nobly and vanquish their enemies in the field into the bargain.'

All aspects of education are subordinated to the training of character. The pleasures of wine and music, for example, are regarded as a means of inculcating self-control.

It is in this light that Plato reviews the history of political institutions. After treating of the old myth of a peaceful state of nature of which the present is a degenerate sequel, he complains that under modern conditions good rulers are difficult to find. 'Cambyses the Elder', he says, 'would brook no equal, and began by making away with his own brother. Then, what with strong drink and want of education, he went out of his mind and lost his throne. . . The Persians have never had a real "Great King" who has been more than nominally such, and the cause of this in my own theory is not accidental; it is the evil life commonly led by the sons of autocrats and rich men.'[1]

Absolutism is indeed an unsatisfactory form of government. Extreme democracy, on the other hand, is equally bad; in Persia there is too much despotism, in Athens too much democracy. The remedy is a proper balance between liberty and authority; wise laws, obeyed by good men, because they have the law in their own hearts.

Pursuing his idea of harmony, Plato insists that the best state should have a mixed constitution reflecting a balance of forces, since stability results from the tension of opposites.

As for the situation of the city, it must be fertile, with access to the sea, but export trade must not swamp its balance, for greatness consists not in wealth and empire but in the minds of the citizens, in frugality and self-sufficiency, in a middling, ordered way of life. To perfect this harmonious pattern, the citizens are limited to five thousand and forty, with their property strictly limited, and 'our society must have neither gold nor silver'.[2] Further, anti-social elements must be eradicated; a farmer, says Plato, would never hesitate to cull his herd. There are to be thirty-seven curators of laws, all elderly men, and a council of three hundred and sixty. There is to be a smooth succession of magistrates, of city commissioners, of priests and priestesses, of authorities for music and physical training, and a minister for education, the most important of all the magistrates. Plato also advocates very detailed marriage regulations[3] and his advice on the treatment of slaves is unlikely to make their masters

[1] *Laws*, bk. III, 695-6.   [2] Bk. V, 744.   [3] Bk. VI, 775.

popular. There must, he says, be no spoiling of them: 'Our language to servants should commonly be that of a simple command, and there should be no familiar jesting with servants of either sex.' He thinks it shocking, for example, that householders should be called in the morning by their servants: the head of the household should be up and about first. Public officials should cut down their sleep and often work at night, thus being a source of fear to evil-doers, of awe and reverence to the good.

Turning again to the key problem of education — 'Now we have our boys and girls born' — Plato insists on their strict supervision. 'The privacy of home life screens . . . many little incidents not in keeping with the legislators' advice.'[1] After the age of three, therefore, all children should be 'collected at the local sanctuary'. Further, their games should be standardized: 'Change is always highly perilous, and innovators are always changing the children's character behind your back.' Here Plato's assumption of the wickedness of the natural man is apparent; he refers to the normal desires for food, drink, and sexual satisfaction as 'unwholesome'; they must be checked, he insists, by 'fear, laws and true discourse'.

The young, of course, put up a good fight, as he admits. 'Now of all wild young things a boy is the most difficult to handle . . . He is the craftiest, most mischievous, most unruly of brutes, so the creatures must be held in check.' They must, indeed, never be let out of sight of their attendants.

In the interest of harmony freedom of expression must also be curtailed. Selected citizens may compose panegyrics and censures on one another, but authors must be respectable; they must have 'done something noble', besides merely being able to write well; they will then be licensed by the minister of education. As for athletics, Plato regards them as most important, but feels 'uneasy apprehensions about how to manage such a society . . . where the young of both sexes are in the pink of condition'. 'Severe laws and moral disapproval' can, of course, do much; it is remarkable, he thinks, what public opinion can do when indulgence is attended with a sense of shame.

His criminal code is ruthless. Sacrilege is punishable by death, the offender being 'buried in silence beyond the borders'. Suicides are to be 'buried ignominiously in nameless spots'; treason, theft, and subversion of the laws are all heavily dealt with, and reverence must

[1] Bk. VII, 788.

be shown to the old.[1] As for religion, the young must be taught that 'He who provides for the world had disposed all things for its perfection, even to the minutest particulars', and made to understand that 'the world is not made for them but they for it'.[2] Impiety is heavily punished; informers are to report to the magistrates, and officials failing to take action are to be prosecuted. If the culprit preaches 'atheism merely out of folly', he is to be imprisoned for five years, his only visitors being the members of the Nocturnal Council, who shall 'admonish' him. If after this he still remains incorrigible, he is to be put to death, by this time probably a happy release. The really dangerous atheists, on the other hand, 'full of subtlety and guile, of the kind that furnishes all sorts of impostors and, on occasion, dictators, demagogues and generals — they deserve more than one death or even two': they must be blotted out, incarcerated for life in the common prison. Plato thus anticipates the procedure of the Inquisition and the Gestapo and makes the first reasoned defence of religious persecution. Before his time, it had generally been taken for granted.

In conclusion, Plato tackles the problem which lies in wait for all authoritarian states — how to ensure the loyalty and vigilance of the officials on whom it depends. The keystone to the whole structure is to be the Nocturnal Council; it is to hold regular sessions every morning from daybreak until after sunrise. It shall contain priests of the first grade, the ten senior acting curators of the laws, the elected minister of education and any retired holders of that office. Each member shall associate with himself a person of thirty or forty years, as he deems best, the younger men to serve as 'scouts in every branch of affairs'. This body, he emphasizes, 'is to be the sheet anchor of the State, the safeguard of all our hopes'.[3] If we can once create this admirable Council, then we must deliver the State into its keeping . . . The dream on which we touched a while ago in our talk will have found fulfilment in working fact, when we have seen our men scrupulously elected, duly educated, settled at the end of the process in the State's central fortress and established there as guardians, whose like we have never seen for perfection as protectors.' Such are the hard conclusions of Plato's old age; they point to the dangers of the idealist approach in politics.

Though the *Republic*, and not the *Laws*, must be taken as representative of Plato's finest political thought, and the earlier work was to

[1] Bk. IX, 879.　　　　[2] Bk. X, 903.　　　　[3] Bk. XII, 961.

be far more important, the *Laws* display the cruelty of the aesthete, latent in all imposed patterns of perfection. This disappointing sequel results, it may be thought, from the nature of Plato's ideas; though he aims at a balanced moderation, he desires it with such passion as to make his thought unstable and ruthless.

Yet the *Republic*, the *Statesman*, and the *Laws* together form the first great landmark in Western political thought. The fine and astringent quality of Plato's mind, the cutting down to essentials, the power of classification, the profound moral sense, which sees the purpose of the community in terms of the good life — all display the virile Hellenic qualities which reflect the environment already described. Here, in the setting of the eastern Mediterranean, in a world derivative both from the steppe and the Minoan civilization of which Hellas was the heir, is the first full impact on political speculation of an ordered, a European mind; the first and original attempt to design a plan whereby political science, reflecting the geometrical perfection of an abstract idea, may build and control an ordered society.

CHAPTER IV

THE GREEK CITY STATE: ARISTOTLE

§ I

THE classification of minds naturally Platonic and naturally Aristotelian is ancient and exact, but Aristotle studied in the Academy for
twenty years and was deeply influenced by Platonic thought. Both
Plato and Aristotle, indeed, aim at the same thing, the creation of a
body of knowledge on which a statesman can proceed; but while
Plato taught that knowledge reflects a pattern of abstract ideas,
Aristotle, by a stubborn investigation of facts, built up hypotheses
based on empirical observation.

It has been already remarked that Greek thought was the result
of the impact of a conquering, originally steppe people out of the
North on the culture of the Levantine world; it was tinged therefore
by an aristocratic outlook. Plato, in particular, reflects this outlook;
after an age of conquest had come an age of assimilation, of leisured
cultivation of aesthetic and moral perceptions. Such a point of view,
serene, dignified and touched with a spacious sense of proportion
and self-discipline, is none the less static and conservative. A cult of
balanced intellect and emotion, an unhurried contemplation of the
excellencies of the soul, is the fine flower of the way of life of the class
to which Plato belongs. In Plato's writings, for all their powerful
argument and close reasoning, the moral and aesthetic elements
predominate, and facts are interpreted in the light of abstract
ideas.

Aristotle, on the other hand, is primarily a scientific thinker, the
embodiment of massive and impersonal analysis. He follows the
facts with complete objectivity. The Middle Ages called him '*The
Philosopher*' and his influence on scholastic knowledge was long
overwhelming. Aristotle's definitions recur again and again as the
starting point of political theory; of all books on the subject, the
Politics, in the view of the present writer, is the most influential and
the most profound. It is the book which must be mastered before all
others.

Aristotle, besides being a shrewd judge of character and situations, is the greatest of early scientists.[1] The *Politics* are only a small part of his writings, and scientific interests overshadow his ethical and political thought. Aristotle's immensely powerful, classifying, assimilative mind breaks away from the clear-cut geometrical pattern of the *Republic* and the *Laws*; the *Politics* is a difficult and confused book, a quarry of arguments and profound definitions, the thought behind them becoming apparent as the argument proceeds. The philosophical premises are similar to Plato's, but Aristotle does not argue about them; where Plato is set on constructing a planned state in the light of assumed principles and will often brush aside practical objections, Aristotle is constantly testing his hypothesis by the facts. There is a sense, in reading the *Politics*, of being in touch with a mind of immense power, with enormous reserves; but Aristotle in this work has little consideration for the reader, following out his own thought for his own satisfaction without much regard for his audience. Sometimes there seems a staggering callousness and lack of imagination; at others a penetrating insight; and there is ironical humour and biting understatement. The book is the work of a master intellect, not over-touched with pity, drawing on great erudition.

The Good at which Aristotle aims is severely practical. In spite of the difficult and often confused arrangement of his argument, the main conclusions are clear, the definitions valid; subsequent political thought has worked largely in terms of them. It is probable Aristotle is the greatest master of political science — the very casualness of his exposition makes it the more impressive.

It is impossible to do justice to the *Politics*[2] in a short space; but in the succeeding pages some attempt will be made to give an impression of the book's more outstanding features and of the general drift of its thought.

It is now generally supposed that the *Politics* in its present form is composed of lecture notes not extant until four hundred years after Aristotle's death. The first book, which was probably written later than the rest, is a general introduction to the whole work.

---

[1] Born 384 B.C. at Stagira in the Thracian peninsula, son of a physician. From 367 to 347 studied under Plato at Athens. After Plato's death he left Athens and settled at Atarneus, at the court of Hermias. In 343 he became tutor to Alexander of Macedon. 355 returned to Athens and formed the Peripatetic School; during this period he wrote most of his books. In 323 he thought it best for his own safety to leave Athens 'so as not to give the Athenians a second chance of sinning against philosophy'. He died in Euboea, 322. His extant works were not well known in antiquity outside a small circle; the study of them was revived by Andronicus of Rhodes in the time of Cicero.

[2] See JOWETT's translation here quoted, edited H. C. W. Davis, O.U.P. (1923).

Books II and III, VII and VIII, possibly the earliest, deal with the ideal state and its foundations. Finally, inserted between books III and VII, the IVth, Vth and VIth books are an analysis of actual states and political events.

The composition of the *Politics* extended over about fifteen years, and from being originally a mainly ethical treatise it became a more detailed and scientific appreciation of the political facts.

The first book, the general introduction, opens with an inquiry into the nature of the State, 'Since', says Aristotle, 'men aim at the good, the State, which is the highest form of community, aims at the highest good.' He proceeds to trace the biological and economic origins of the πολις, making his famous and profound definition that man is a 'political animal'. By the gift of speech and sense of moral values, man is distinguished from the other animals. The solitary man 'is either a beast or a god'; it follows that human institutions can be scientifically classified and the behaviour of men studied objectively; it should thus be possible to deduce the laws which govern a given society. The State and individuals composing it form an organic whole, for the State is as natural to man as the family or the clan; it is as natural as water to a fish, the medium without which human faculties can never come to their full compass. 'For man,' says Aristotle, 'when perfected, is the best of animals; but when separated from law and justice he is the worst of all, since armed injustice is the most dangerous; and he is equipped at birth with the arms of intelligence and wit, moral qualities which he may use for the worst ends.'[1]

'The principle of order', he continues, 'in political society is justice, the bond of men in states'; and by justice Aristotle implies a far-reaching principle of harmonious balance. He assumes throughout the dependence of the individual on the community; he would have given short shrift either to 'the noble savage', the 'honnête homme' or the 'economic man'.

Breaking away from the wider problems he has raised, he then examines the structure of the household, the question of property and the nature and office of a slave, whom he defines as one 'by nature not his own, but another's, a human being but also a possession' (I, 5). He goes so far as to compare slaves with tame animals, a view in sharp contradiction to subsequent Stoic and Christian values; the Good aimed at by Aristotle is something only valid for a

[1] I, 2.

minority. This conclusion is certainly disconcerting, but in taking slavery for granted he was following an intelligible course, considering the facts of his environment and the comparatively flimsy economic basis of the Greek cities — indeed of Mediterranean civilization generally in that age.

The philosopher next turns to property and money-making, legitimate and otherwise (I, 8). 'There are many different kinds of men, as there are of animals; in the lives of men, too, there is a great difference. The laziest are shepherds, who lead an idle life and get their substance without trouble from tame animals which they follow, cultivating a sort of living farm . . . Others support themselves by hunting, which is of different kinds; some, for example, are pirates . . .' Others practise more subtle arts of acquisition, both 'necessary' money-making and 'unnecessary'. Aristotle objects to usury as 'unnatural', and regards all transactions which demand the use of coined money with suspicion; this argument, which reinforced the Christian distrust of riches and money-making, had a deep effect upon mediaeval economic thought.

Finally, returning to the subject of households and their management, he raises the question of the relations between husbands, wives, and children, and touches on the importance of education.

Such are the main topics of the first book; it will be apparent that it is disjointed though profound. The vital principles enunciated in it are as follows: the setting of man and the State in a biological frame, the statement that man is a political animal, and the formulation of the aim of the State, which is the 'highest good'.

Book II, which begins Aristotle's discussion of the ideal State, is mainly concerned with a criticism of Plato's *Republic*. The two challenging Platonic ideas of community of property and of women are discussed and refuted. In the well-ordered State, are the citizens to have all things, nothing, or some things in common? 'The State', says Aristotle, 'is made up of different kinds of men, not only so many men. The principle of reciprocity is the salvation of States.' Here he points the way to the mediaeval doctrine that the State is made up of a balance of co-operating interests, an organic whole. This idea of 'reciprocity' has often dominated European political theory; it runs particularly strongly through English political thought and finds eloquent expression in Burke.

Aristotle then makes the curious point that community of wives and children seems better suited to husbandmen than to 'guardians', and remarks, rightly, 'There are many difficulties in community of women'. In a state having women and children in common, affection would be 'watery' and morale low. Next the disadvantages of communal property are pointed out (II, 5). Laws advocating it, he says, have 'a specious appearance of benevolence . . . Men readily listen to it and are easily induced to believe that in some wonderful manner everybody will become everybody else's friend . . .' 'These evils, however,' he concludes brutally, 'are due to a very different cause, the wickedness of human nature.'

Further, the guardians in Plato's ideal state, he maintains, would probably quarrel: 'And if the guardians are not happy, who are?' Surely not the artisans or the common people? Of Plato's *Laws*, he remarks, 'In the *Laws* there is hardly anything but laws' — a pretty shrewd criticism. Socrates' city would, in any case, be too big; 5000 families would require a territory the size of Babylonia (II, 6). Property limitation should be related to the number of children; if there are too many of them, the property law will be defied, and men of ruined fortunes are subversive. This leads him to the subject of crime.

'Want is not the sole incentive to crime . . . The greatest crimes are caused by excess, not by necessity.' This is certainly true of revolutions and popular revolts, as of wars of expansion or conquest. The best solution of the problem of property, he concludes, is to train the nobler natures not to desire more and to prevent the lower from getting more; that is to say, they must be kept down, but not ill treated.

Proceeding to discuss the proposals of Hippodamus of Miletus, 'who invented the art of planning cities', he deals with judicial questions and law courts. There follows a discussion of the merits and demerits of the Spartan polity and whether kings are an advantage or disadvantage to the State. The Spartans, he says, refuse to pay their taxes, so that the city is poor and the citizens greedy, then he turns to deal with Crete and Carthage, the chapter ending with an account of various well-known law-givers. 'Draco has left laws, but there is no peculiarity in them worth mentioning except the severity of the punishments . . . Andronymus of Rhegium gave laws to the Chalcidians of Thrace; some of them relate to homicide and to heiresses, but there is nothing remarkable in them.'

Such in bare outline are the main subjects discussed in the second book; it is concerned with a series of particular problems and examples, and contains only incidentally statements of general theory.

The third book contains political definitions as important as the first. Aristotle again defines the State and citizenship. A state 'is a body of citizens sufficing for the purposes of life' (III, 1). 'Like the sailor', the citizen is a member of a community. 'Now sailors have different functions, for one is a rower, another a pilot, another a lookout man. All have a common object, namely safety in navigation.' It follows, since men are so intimately bound up with states, if a state is bad, the man who is a good citizen in it must be a bad man. Further, there must be variety within the State, 'for the State may be compared to a living being, composed of dissimilar elements', and therefore, 'the virtue of all citizens cannot possibly be the same any more than the excellence of the leader of a chorus is the same as that of the performer who stands by his side'.

Aristotle then proceeds to a definition of the three kinds of state similar to that made by Plato and constantly employed in subsequent political thought. They are royalty, aristocracy, and constitutional government. Of these the perversions are tyranny, oligarchy, and democracy. The merits and demerits of these forms of government and the claims of different elements in the State to rule are exhaustively discussed. Surprisingly, he remarks that for men of preeminent virtue there is no law; they are themselves a law. 'Anyone would be ridiculous who attempted to make laws for them; they would probably retort what, in the fable of Antisthenes, the lion said to the hare, "Where are your claws?", when, in the council of the beasts, the latter began haranguing and claiming equality for all. And for this reason democratic states have instituted ostracism.' After raising this fundamental problem, Aristotle embarks on a discussion of monarchy and whether it is more advantageous to be ruled by the best men or the best laws. He decides that the best law is preferable, for it is passionless. 'He who bids the law rule may be deemed to bid God and reason alone rule, but he who bids men rule adds the element of the beast; for desire is a wild beast, and passion perverts the minds of rulers, even if they are the best of men.' This principle is obviously of great importance and points the way to a wider conception of law.

Then follows the later, more concrete analysis of particular constitutions and states, which forms the middle section of the *Politics*, inserted between the more general discussions contained in the chapters which make up the beginning and ending of the work.

The fourth book, in common with the fifth and sixth, abandons the discussion of general principles after the first few pages, and proceeds to a detailed and most interesting study of institutions. 'Political writers, though they often have excellent ideas, are often unpractical (IV, 1) . . . We are concerned with what forms of government are most tolerable in different conditions, and the causes of the ruin and preservation of states.'

There are bound to be different forms of government; states differ just as animals do, according to their combinations of differences. 'For animals cannot be the same which have different kinds of mouths and ears . . . In like manner, forms of government, as I have repeatedly said, are composed of different elements' (IV, 4). Aristotle then describes the various kinds of democracies and the nature of demagogues; next come aristocracies and 'polities', or constitutional governments, which are a fusion between democracy and aristocracy. After an examination of tyranny, he decides that the worst form is that of the arbitrary power of an individual 'who is responsible to no one and governs all alike with a view to his own advantage and not of his subjects and, therefore, against their will. No free man, if he can escape from it, can endure such a government' (IV, 10). Returning to the best kind of constitution, it should, he considers, show a preponderance of the middle-class interest, 'for those who are of the middle condition pass through life safely and are most amenable to reason'. Friendship will be most likely amongst equals, and large states are more stable than small ones because they contain a larger middling element. But, Aristotle remarks fatalistically: 'It has now become a habit among citizens of states not even to care about equality; all men are seeking for dominion, or, if conquered, to submit.' There follows a discussion of the duties of assemblies, magistrates, and law courts; of how such institutions actually work and how it is best to distribute offices.

The fifth book is concerned with the causes of revolutions and how they can be avoided. 'Inferiors revolt in order that they may be equal, and equals that they may be superior' (V, 2). Revolutions spring from a disproportionate increase in any one part of the State; they are often occasioned by trifles; some are gradual and imperceptible, others sudden. The best way to avoid them is to preserve a friendly atmosphere and 'never wrong the ambitious in a matter of honour or the common people in a matter of money'. Office must not be monopolized by a few families; the ruler should also invent terrors and keep distant dangers near so as to maintain loyalty, and 'give moderate honour for a long time, rather than great honour for a short time. For men are easily spoilt; not everyone can bear prosperity' (V, 8). Above all, every state should be so administered and so regulated by law that its magistrates cannot possibly make money; but the best guarantee of stability is education, adapted to the form of government of the State.

He describes how tyrannies are often overthrown. 'There are two chief motives which induce men to attack tyrannies — hatred and contempt.' The time-honoured methods of the tyrant are noted; he must 'lop off' those who are too high, take any means to prevent people from knowing one another well, and prohibit intelligent discussion. He sows quarrels among his subjects and impoverishes them for the support of his guards; the people, if kept hard at work, are prevented from conspiring. Aristotle has no illusions about tyrants; they are fond of bad men and dislike anyone of independence; but women and slaves support them, for under them they 'have a good time'. The better kind of tyrant must be austere and wide awake, for a 'drunken or drowsy tyrant' is despised and attacked. He should appear to do everything for the public good and be particularly earnest in the service of the gods, though his religion must not be thought foolish and he must be the hero of the multitude. 'Let his disposition be virtuous, or at least half virtuous, and if he must be wicked, let him be half wicked only.' The whole picture is a masterly performance, outclassing Machiavelli on his own ground, and valid in any age. The book ends with a criticism of Plato's views on the causes of revolutions.

The sixth book deals with the organization of democracies and oligarchies. In a democracy a man can live as he likes; officials are chosen 'by all out of all', and paid. The best kind of democracy is agricultural, for few farmers want the nuisance of office. Next comes 'pastoral' democracy; the citizens are the best trained of any for war — robust in body and 'able to camp out'. Mob democracy is the worst and finds many supporters since 'most persons would rather live in a disorderly than in a sober manner' (VI, 4). Demagogues maintain their power by bribing the electorate, and the poor are always receiving and always wanting more and more, for 'such help is like water poured into a leaky cask'. Turning to oligarchy, he finds it is most usual in country adapted for cavalry (VI, 7); only rich men can afford to keep horses. There follows a discussion of the right distribution of offices and the need for auditors to scrutinize public accounts. Priests are included among state officials and regarded as simply a branch of the State; there is, of course, no question of any distinction between spiritual and lay power.

With the sixth book ends the section of the *Politics* concerned with detailed observations on the actual working of states; it is thought to have been written and inserted later than both the second and third, the seventh and the eighth books.

The seventh book breaks away from detailed observations to return to more general topics. The best life, both for individuals and states, is the life of virtue, having external goods enough for the performance of good actions. 'True happiness is more often found with those who are most highly cultivated in mind and character and have only a moderate share of external goods, than among those who possess external goods to a useless extent but are deficient in higher qualities' (VII, 1). The subordination of politics to ethical purpose is here apparent, as elsewhere in the *Politics*. Having defined his objective, Aristotle builds up a picture of the kind of city likely to realize it and of the education on which it must be founded.

The seventh book is one of the wisest achievements of the Greek mind. He dismisses the widely held view that power is good in itself, although it is on this assumption that most politics are conducted. 'Although in most cities, laws may be said generally to be in a chaotic state, still if they aim at anything they aim at the maintenance of power' (VII, 2). 'Warlike pursuits, though generally to be deemed honourable, are not the supreme end of all things, but only a means, and the good law-giver should inquire how states may participate in the good life.'

The size of the city must be moderate, for experience shows that very large cities cannot be very well governed; the State, like a ship, must be the right size. It must be self-sufficing, and in size and extent such 'as may enable the inhabitants to live temperately and liberally in the enjoyment of leisure' (VII, 4). It should be well situated near the sea, but not on it, and have a climate which will produce people like the Hellenes, high spirited and intelligent. There follows an anatomy of the various parts of the State, which co-operate together, and the famous definition that 'a state is not a mere aggregate of persons, but a union of them sufficing for the purposes of life' (VII, 4).

As to common meals, there is general agreement that the well-ordered city should have them. The best arrangement of property is as follows: 'The land must be divided into two parts, one public and the other private . . . half the public land being appropriated to the service of the gods, the other used to defray the cost of the common meal'; the private land should, of course, be fairly distributed. Returning to the city's situation, he concludes that cities which lie towards the east wind are the healthiest; there should be an abundance of springs and fountains, and the water should be pure: 'this latter point is by no means a secondary consideration' (VII, 2). Strong walls are a necessity, more especially since 'catapults and siege engines have been brought to such perfection'; there should be two agorai or piazzas, one for citizens and one for traders.

At this point, Aristotle, remarking that these are details and dependent in any case on fortune, returns to the discussion of what makes for true happiness, which can only be secured by proper education. Animals are creatures of habit, but man alone has reason; education should foster reason that it may control appetite. This statement raises the whole question of education and the rearing of children (VII, 16). Marriage should take place at the age when the parents are most likely to have fine children. Aristotle considers this age to be eighteen for women and thirty-seven for men, and that marriage should take place in the winter at the season of the north wind. The best parents will not be those who are over-athletic: 'The temperament of an athlete is not suited to the life of a citizen, or to health, or to the procreation of children, any more than an invalid or exhausted constitution', but one which is a mean between them. As to the problem of over-population, he remarks: 'Let there be a law that no deformed child shall live, but where there are too many and the state of feeling is averse to the exposure of offspring, let abortion be provoked before sense and life have begun.' Having settled that question, he turns to adultery: 'Let it be held disgraceful if during the time of bearing children anything of the sort occurs. Let the guilty persons be punished by a loss of their privileges in proportion to the offence.'

Directions follow for the education of the children. 'The food which has most milk is best suited for human beings', but the less wine the better, and 'from their natural warmth' he says, rather unsympathetically, 'children may easily be trained to bear cold'. Children must also be kept from all bad company and indecency of speech and must not go to the theatre until they are of an age 'to sit at the public table and drink strong wine' (VII, 17). They must be allowed exercise and amusement, so long as it is not vulgar; and Plato is wrong 'in attempting to check the loud crying and screaming of children, for these contribute towards their growth and in a manner exercise their bodies'. This scientific observation points the contrast between the two men; the one over-riding scientific truth in the interest of aesthetics and moral theory, and often inflicting suffering without a qualm; the other studying the facts, observing that the best kind of children are those who are not badgered and over-disciplined, and drawing a wise conclusion.

The short eighth book, after a further inquiry into the principles of education, is mainly concerned with the function of music. It is a most curious and interesting chapter. There are three things which are notable. First, the aristocratic quality of the ideal of education set out; secondly, the insight shown into educational method; and thirdly, the odd view of music expressed. Nowhere in the book does the Greek mind seem more alien than in this last aspect.

In the discussion of education, it is repeatedly emphasized that children should be uncontaminated by any vulgar influence. 'Any occupation, art or science which makes the . . . free man less fit for the exercise or practice of virtue is vulgar. Wherefore we call those arts vulgar which tend to deform the body, and likewise all paid employments, for they absorb and degrade the mind. There are also some liberal arts quite proper for a free man to acquire, but only to a certain degree, and if he attend to them too closely, the same evil effects will follow' (VIII, 2).

Things must be done for their own sakes, not to benefit others. Leisure is thought of the utmost importance; the good man must clearly be an amateur and never a technician. True, children have to be taught some useful things, 'but to be always seeking after the useful does not become exalted souls'. There is here apparent a touch of romanticism, an idealizing of an aristocratic way of life.

Aristotle is well aware, with his unerring psychological insight, that in education habit must come before reason. Therefore physical training is most important, though children must not be brutalized (VIII, 4); that is the Spartan mistake. As a matter of fact, among barbarians and among animals courage is rarely found associated with ferocity: 'No wolf or other wild animal will face a really noble danger. Such dangers are for the brave man' (VIII, 4). What is noble, not what is brutal, should have the first place.

Aristotle then turns to the question of music in education. He obviously appreciates music, but thinks it may well be demoralizing and seems afraid that the specialism of first-class skill may distort the personality. Music must play a great part in education and character is deeply affected by it; children should be allowed to perform themselves, in part because it gives them something to do. 'The rattle of Archytas, which people give to their children in order to amuse them and prevent them from breaking anything in the house, is a capital invention, for the young cannot be quiet; musical education is a rattle or toy for children of larger growth' (VIII, 6). They are to learn for themselves, 'but to stop short of the arts which are practised at professional contests'. The important question whether the child has musical talent, Aristotle does not raise. 'Let the young pursue their studies until they are able to feel delight in noble melodies and rhythms, not merely in that common part of music in which every slave or child, and even some animals, find pleasure.' The flute is disqualified because it requires too great skill: 'besides, the flute is not an instrument which has a good moral effect; it is too exciting.' He goes on worrying at the moral defects of this instrument; Athene invented the thing only to throw it away 'because it made the face ugly', and it contributes nothing to the mind.

Music, like poetry, affords 'purgation' to the feelings. He even concedes that the vulgar may be allowed to hear the kind of music they like, and 'professional musicians may be allowed to practise this sort of music before an audience of a lower type'. But for purposes of education, modes and melodies should be employed which are 'ethical', such as the Dorian — 'It is evident that our youth should be taught the Dorian music'.

The chapter ends with the profound observation that education should be based on three principles: 'the mean, the possible, the becoming, these three.'

The 'mean' implies a just balance of faculties, mental and physical, the whole disciplined by a habit of calm and self-control. Education should inculcate long views and a grasp of essentials, an integrity based on a just pride, a wide range of interests balanced by a grasp of the facts.

The 'possible' means, perhaps, two things: first, that no man can achieve what is beyond humanity to win — there should be no reaching for the stars; secondly, that a man's education and ambition should fit his ability.

Finally the 'becoming' is the result of the achievement of the 'mean' and the 'possible'. The development of a man's full faculties in the way appropriate to his talent and surroundings, which gives him style and assurance, is the true mark of a right adaptation in the human and the animal world.

Such in brief outline are the outstanding ideas in Aristotle's *Politics*. The analysis is profound, the purpose noble, and the setting foreign. All the essential problems are raised, and the truth stated that man is, and must be, a political animal; that the community and the individual are bound up together.

Plato and Aristotle were near enough to the primitive beginnings to take the organic quality of the State for granted, while their thought displays the highest moral insight. Aristotle, assuming that the end of the πολις is the good life, has said the last word about the State within the limitations of a slave-owning world. With the break-up of the closed world of the πολις and diffusion of self-consciousness, conflict developed further between the individual and the community. Further, salvationist and other-worldly religions took the moral heart out of the City State. Yet the attempt to solve the problem by calling in a law of nature imposed from without and not emergent from the community can never be satisfactory, and the modern world is probably coming back to an Aristotelian view in a different setting. Modern science directed by Aristotelian ethical values, reinforced by a *caritas* which Aristotle does not conspicuously display, and by modern psychological knowledge, might further extend the possibilities of the good life.

Here, then, at the beginnings of political speculation stands a master whose genius has been vindicated by the course of subsequent thought. Where Plato attempts to impose a pattern of events, Aristotle, with an equally strong ethical purpose, wrestles with the facts and deduces his principles from them. Aristotle combines a scientist's respect for the facts with the shrewd judgement of a man of the world; further, he has a clear vision of the moral purpose of society, which is to secure the good life, to produce individuals at once in harmony with the State and fulfilling themselves through it, and yet realizing in themselves those aristocratic moral, physical, and intellectual values to which men, alone of animals, are able to attain.

Both Plato and Aristotle thus created the vocabulary of subsequent political speculation. Both wrote against a background of political failure. The cause of the political collapse of the Greek cities is an historical problem of great interest; the following reasons may in part be assigned for it.

The speculations of Plato and Aristotle do not offer any satisfactory solutions of the problems of inter-state rivalry and war; they took them for granted, and these problems ultimately wrecked the independence and prosperity of Greece. The Greek spirit was strong enough to stave off the oriental land power of Persia, to the benefit of subsequent European civilization, though actually the Ionian Greeks under Persian domination were allowed wide intellectual freedom. But the Greeks failed to resolve their own dissensions, and, as the European nation states of our own time threaten to do, fought themselves to a standstill and forfeited their political freedom to superior power. But the collapse was only political. The subsequent empire of Alexander Hellenized the Near East, and ultimately Greek intellectual life, focusing on Alexandria, gained in some respects by the greater scale and system the Hellenistic world gave it.

For the whole way of thought of the Levant, and afterwards of Rome, was Greek, and the Christian Greeks of Byzantium preserved through the darkest times a standard of civilization unparalleled in the West; it is well, therefore, not to talk too much about Greek political failure. But, as has been emphasized, the institution of slavery differentiates the Greek society sharply from our own; their attitude to women was more oriental than is generally admitted, while the custom of enslaving captive citizens taken in war must have debased and demoralized the old conception of citizenship. But the most important cause of political decadence was probably similar to that which operated under parallel conditions in Renaissance Italy — that the Greeks, like the Renaissance Italians, were too clever to make their institutions work. Their incessant discussion and analysis, degenerating, often, into an intellectual fidgeting for its own sake, characteristic of the Greek mind off the rails in subsequent Byzantine theological disputes, together with the competition of brilliant unscrupulous personalities in a society on a rather small-scale geographical and economic basis, made, at its best, for pioneer speculation and the greatest advances in thought, but at its average, and at its worst, was incompatible with any permanent political stability. The common sense of the casually co-operative Franks or Anglo-Saxons in the North laid the foundations of solider institutions, while the far-flung lucidity of Roman genius organized Greek ideas into the stable if rigid framework of the Empire.

It may well be that city states, while culturally they are the most valuable social units — and the Greek, Italian, French, Flemish, and German cities have produced between them most of the greatest art and music — are not, in the long run, capable of building large-scale enduring political structures. The great empires, in their turn, while comparatively barren in their cultural and artistic achievement, create organizations of far greater scale, providing, within their framework, the medium within which art and thought can be expanded, elaborated, and appreciated, though in turn they become debased and vulgarized, and the process has to start over again. Certainly the Greek cities, though they civilized their masters, depressingly failed to solve problems of which, like ourselves, they must have been poignantly aware.

These limitations, then, made the Greek polis in the short view a failure; the City State broke up from within through internal disruption and economic insufficiency, and from without through inter-state war. The assumption that the City State was psychologically, morally, and intellectually satisfying, which runs through the *Republic* and the *Politics*, therefore fell to the ground, as did the other assumption that 'barbarians' were incapable of adequate government, in face of the facts of Macedonian and Roman power.

At the same time, this immediate political failure counts for little beside the importance of the Greek contribution to political thought, the statement of political and social problems as problems, questions to be discussed intelligently and objectively, in terms of the good life. The moral sensibility and intellectual brilliance of the Greek mind is joined, in its finer phases, to a proud self-respect which comes down from Homeric times, the result of a combination of warrior and Levantine qualities, at once hard and subtle. It has something in common with the good sense of the heroic age of the North, though with a much wider and richer range of awareness. This Greek ideal was behind the major achievements of antiquity and the source of their continuing vitality; it has much in common with the scientific-humane outlook, emerging, on a wider stage, in our own day. The very grammar and vocabulary of political thought are Greek; it was indeed through Greek initiative that the habit of political speculation originated at all, and Europe, having assimilated the material and static culture of the Near East, set the mind ranging over fields of political speculation the Near East had never known.

CHAPTER V

ALEXANDER AND THE HELLENISTIC
WORLD: STOICS AND EPICUREANS

§ 1

THE swamping of the cities of old Greece by the military power of
Macedon, and the subjugation by Alexander of the Near East, had
its effects on political thought. The break-up of the limited loyalties
of the City State gradually cast men out into an impersonal world
of large-scale government and universalized religions; it also created,
for good and ill, a new conception of world power. The spread of
ideas of universal monarchy and universal law, deriving out of
Oriental king-worship and Greek philosophy, is also most important.

The Hellenistic kingship was absolute, founded on conquest in an
Eastern setting. After Alexander's death the dynasties created by
his generals adapted themselves with varying success to the areas
they had conquered; the Ptolemies in Egypt in particular taking
over the semi-divine Egyptian monarchy. The deliberate cult of the
ruler as a god, intelligible and natural in an Oriental setting, and
deriving from the oldest traditions of the East, made a focus of
loyalty for the strange mixture of peoples and languages over which
the power of these rulers extended. From the Hellenistic world,
Rome, when she had expanded into empire, adapted the idea as a
sanction for her military empire, but the Greeks of the earlier period
would not have liked it; it went ill with the other traditions of Rome,
and it marks the heavy price paid for an extended, vulgarized power.
The cult of the semi-divine ruler was profoundly alien to the traditions and, indeed, to the biting intelligence of earlier Greece.

The idea of world rule, though bound up with the trappings of
Oriental despotism, is something of new and outstanding importance
in European thought; it is the inspiration behind the realized
achievements of Augustus, behind the Papacy and the Holy Roman
Empire of the Middle Ages.

How far can the credit for it be given to Alexander? He was a
man of action and of brilliant intellect; Aristotle had been his tutor,
and probably circumstances combined with the bent of his mind to

produce a new conception of kingship, 'harmonizing the State as God does the Universe'. How far the cult of Hercules and of Ammon, based on a universalized sun-worship, influenced his political ideas, it is difficult to determine.[1]

One thing is certain; his career revolutionized men's political ideas. In Europe and the East the impression his exploits made, the legends to which his career gave rise, and the cultural influence he exercised through his Hellenizing policy and foundation of cities, all combined to create an imperial prestige which resounded to the confines of the known world.

A modern authority writes: 'Alexander transformed what had been a gentle infiltration into a flood. His spectacular overthrow of the Persian Empire enhanced the prestige of Hellenism, and made the Greeks the ruling race of the East. It is tolerably clear that Alexander moved steadily away from the standpoint of the average contemporary Greek and his master Aristotle, that the barbarian was by nature inferior to the Greek; towards the end of his reign two lofty ideas seem to have dominated his mind. He felt himself to be the apostle of Hellenism; it was his mission to carry Greek culture over the barbarian world. The instrument which he chiefly used to promote this policy was the celebration of musical and gymnastic games, and, of course, intermarriage. He deliberately founded cities where he could just as well have founded trading stations or garrison towns.'[2]

Thus Alexander fused Greek traditions with the organization and ideas of Eastern empire. And the Persian state was in many aspects politically advanced; the threat made by this great power to Greece in the fifth century and Greek accounts of it, have given a false impression of the barbarism of the Persian government.[3] For all the dynastic entanglements of the Archeminids, the Persian Empire was organized on a scale undreamt of in Hellas. The Peloponnesian war and its sequel had demonstrated the political bankruptcy of Greece. Philip and Alexander dealt with that, and when the phalanx had smashed its way across Asia with a consoli-

---

[1] For an interesting discussion of the whole problem, see W. W. TARN, 'Alexander and the Unity of Mankind' (*Proceedings of the British Academy*, vol. XIX, p. 135), and the same author's chapter on Alexander in the *C.A.H.*, vol. VI.

[2] A. H. M. JONES, *The Greek City*, O.U.P. (1940).

[3] Witness Herodotus' picture of Xerxes, who is portrayed as quite irresponsible and without any of the merits which the Persian kings in fact displayed. Flogging of the Hellespont with iron chains and impaling captives alive were good enough for him, Herodotus implies, and it all makes a capital story.

dated sea power behind it, the Macedonian conqueror found himself in a world which demanded a new outlook altogether.

So the extension of Greek culture into Asia was repaid by a new conception of great-scale rule. The Persian organization was there; Alexander had only to tighten it and reform its finance to take over the whole structure of Persian government in Asia and Egypt. The foundation of Alexandria, one of the greatest of cities, shows his economic and social vision. With the conquest of Susa and Persepolis, he was master of treasure and authority unknown to any previous European — the successor of the great king. He took over the whole accumulated tradition of Near Eastern empire, of the ancient, stable civilizations of Babylon and Egypt. For the subject races he became the successor of Marduk and Ammon; for the Persians, if not a god, a ruler as absolute as Darius or Xerxes.

Of the extraordinary sequel, the Indian expedition, there is not space here to tell; of Porus' wounded elephants trumpeting and trampling their way out of the battle of the Jhelum; of the vision of an eastern ocean which led the conqueror on till the army mutinied and ended the advance; of the famous reconciliation of Greeks and Persians at Opis, where Alexander drank to the harmony of both races; of the end, at thirty-two, from fever, on the verge of a great expedition to Arabia. It is in many ways the strangest tale in history; its political implications were to extend far into space and time. Through Alexander the tradition of world empire became acclimatized in Europe, later to be realized and reinterpreted by Rome.

§ 11

As Alexander's conquests dwarfed the old Greek ideas of the limited City State, Greek thinkers elaborated an outlook more individualized and more universal. The old ideal of citizenship was limited in two ways; first, it was confined to a minority; secondly, it failed to take account of any political unity beyond the πολις.

Thus, besides the introduction of new ideas of kingship and empire, the Hellenistic age saw the development of the universalized philosophies of Epicureanism and Stoicism, of religious and social organizations going beyond the polis and often incompatible with its full vitality: they supplied a new sanction for conduct in a universal Natural Law and Natural Reason, common to all men and transcending local political loyalties.

78

The idea that an individual can be self-sufficient and have no business with the 'world' is profoundly alien to earlier Greek thought. It is more akin to the political abnegations of the East; it destroys the assumption, so attractive in the writings of Plato and Aristotle, that the moral interests of the State and the individual naturally coincide. This new distinction between private and public life immediately raises problems familiar in later political speculation. It was later reinforced by the rise of universalized religions aiming at personal salvation, and represents a serious break with the organic, healthy traditions the polis inherited from its primitive origins. Further, the mystery religions which had long permeated the Levant, with their underground organizations and orgiastic practices, tended to undermine earlier, more virile, loyalties of civic patriotism and ideals of balanced personal development, though they provided a psychological compensation for the over-intellectualized ethics of the Greeks.

But these new ideas still assumed a static world order, in sharp contrast with the Christian outlook or with modern ideas of progress. Neither the outlook of the polis nor of the new philosophies saw the cosmic process or society as driving towards any purpose or leading towards any perfection. Society is thought of as a degenerate expression of a better world in the past, or else as an aspect of a cyclic recurrence of events which may go on indefinitely. There is indeed a certain static pessimism behind the deeper thought of antiquity, if also an absence of crusading animosity and a wide tolerance of religious views, if not subversive of social order. In part, no doubt, this attitude was due to relative lack of control over natural forces, and to the rhetorical and literary bias of their education.

Further, Semite asceticism had not yet made men afraid. They sought and found satisfaction in present experience, instead of projecting their zest for living into the future, in this world or the next. The coarse Roman interpretation of the Hellenistic way of life led, as will be seen, to its reaction in the fourth and fifth centuries; but a study of Hellenistic art and literature shows the widespread prevalence of a cultivated, serene, and disciplined way of life. These men knew how to make the most of the good things of the world, and, without rising to any height of religious or philosophical virtue, achieved a good life for many of those born to prosperity. The ordinary amenities of Mediterranean life—the gardens, the olive groves, the vintage and the sea — all were long accepted and enjoyed by generations of civilized men before the social order began to crumble, and the priests of a new religion appeared among the ruins, with their new hope and their unworldly eyes. Further, the Hellenistic age set much store on the cultivation of friendship and the affections of family life. And indeed they were well at home in the world. All this must be set against the results of political failure, which, though deadly in the long run, were not the dominating and immediate preoccupation which misapplied science has made them in our own day.

The Hellenistic philosophies, then, were not merely a compensating movement for the political inadequacy of the old ideal of the polis; they were often the inspiration of a widespread tradition of living, within its limitations, humanistic and benevolent, which contributed a great deal to inspire the habits of order and good sense, later imposed by the practical genius of Rome. The civilization of antiquity was a tremendous achievement, both in space and time; and though it grew old and went under, it long framed a way of living which must be regarded with respect.

As might be imagined, the *élite* of this civilization display a wide mental range and political grasp. The Hellenistic thinkers have become citizens of the world. They retain the Greek conviction, inherited from Ionian beginnings and shared with Plato and Aristotle, that there is a correct pattern of conduct which can be known; but with greater sophistication and altered political conditions, they have moved away from the strong community sense of the City State into a wider world. Though they retain the scientific detachment of early Greek thought, they have broken out beyond the primitive solidarity and limitation of the originally tribal city. In the attempt to find a permanent world of values apart from the limited community of the polis, they formulated what was later to become, translated into political terms, the concept of an all-pervading Natural Law, based on the reason and instinct of man, in harmony with the Logos, the spirit of the universe.

This extremely influential idea, destined to persist through the centuries in varying interpretations, appears again and again, in both Christian and rationalistic guise, to be explained away and yet constantly return in a new shape. It largely determines political thought from Cicero to the eighteenth century.

The conviction of an order behind the natural world goes back to the earliest Greek writers. The Greek philosophers saw in nature a fundamental principle of harmony, of proportion. This originally geometrical and practical concept was applied just as much to political theory as to physics or music. It was reinforced by the Greek idea of Fate, whereby gods and men were punished if they overstepped the bounds. Behind the flux of circumstance there remain the eternal rules, of which the physical world, in all its diversity, is the changing expression. To transfer this originally practical idea of measure and harmony to philosophy and politics was natural; it is apparent, though, in terms of the City State, in Aristotle's conception of Law, in Plato's science of government, but the Hellenistic period saw its development in a wider field.

Here are the beginnings of an outlook which appears constantly in political theory; the view which maintains that the cosmic process is moral and part of a divine plan; that when men follow their 'natural reason' they are acting in harmony with their own interests and their highest good; that the writ of human values runs in the universe, the writ of a benevolent cosmic order in human society. Conversely, of that other view which maintains that the natural processes are blind, indifferent or even evil; that human society achieves its own values only in its private garden, cultivated in spite of nature; that laws are only conventions, that man is the 'rebel of nature' and 'the stars blindly run'.

There is also a third view, which regards values as emergent; which holds that in man and his societies the cosmic process becomes conscious of itself, and makes its 'natural law' as it goes along. Which would maintain that, since human consciousness is the highest form of awareness men can apprehend, it is through an expansion of consciousness only, so far as can be known, the cosmic process realizes itself in time. It follows that a society which best promotes the awareness of individuals is the best; that the social pattern which promotes this end is the right one, ensures a greater scope for living and therefore reflects an emergent 'Natural Law': the 'Law of Nature' is in fact immanent and not either transcendent or subhuman. But this third view was not to be formulated for many centuries.

With the political failure of the polis, then, the early setting of man as a political animal was breaking up. Government had to find its sanction in a wider and vaguer concept of Natural Reason, common to all men, expressed as a universal principle applicable everywhere. The basis of an optimistic view of politics became, therefore, more tenuous, for men were attempting something even more difficult than to find the ideal pattern of a City State and aiming to expand its benefits outside a small privileged class. In this comprehensive form, the idea of Natural Law evolved; in the course of this study the various interpretations given to it will be traced.

The Hellenistic age thus formulated philosophies which attempted to find a new moral sanction for politics outside the community of the polis, and of these philosophies the Stoic and the Epicurean are the most famous. The Stoic thought was the more constructive, and provided an interpretation of politics which greatly influenced the Romans, who transposed Stoic ideals of Natural Reason and Law into the practical medium of their legal system.

But not all the Hellenistic thinkers took the austere Stoic view; others formulated a different answer; and, before turning to the Stoic outlook, it will be well to take account of the Epicurean.

Both Stoics and Epicureans share a Socratic hardness of mind and clarity of thought, expressed in their disillusionment and emphasis on will and self-control. Epicurus (341-270 B.C.),[1] who founded his school in Athens in 306, thinks it impossible to find a moral pattern behind society and rejects the idea of a benevolent Natural Law altogether. Like Hume in the eighteenth century, he regards social values as relative; the universe, independent of divine government, evolves the processes of life automatically, and the rules of human conduct have no sanction beyond utility. Men, if they act according to natural instinct, are selfish and predatory, and the only reason for keeping the rules is that it pays in the long run to do so. Consequently standards of conduct vary in time and space, and what is right conduct in one context is wrong in another. The wise man, therefore, regards these differences with toleration and rejects the ideas of a moral order of nature or Natural Law altogether. It follows, then, since the game is like that, it is best not to play; to keep out of politics and set about preserving one's own comfort as far as possible under adverse circumstances. A wary individualism is the only answer to a cosmic order so insultingly evil.

By the standards of the Temple State or the polis, this outlook is

[1] Epicurus, a native of Samos. Bought a garden outside Athens, where he taught his principle of 'unobtrusive living'. He extolled the virtues of 'wisdom, temperance, courage and friendship'. 'Pleasure', he wrote, 'is not a succession of banquets and revels, nor enjoyment of boys and women, nor of fish or whatever may load an expensive table . . . but a sober calculation that examines the grounds for every choice.' (*Epistle to Menoeclos*.)

highly sophisticated and profoundly anti-social. It reflects a new widespread self-consciousness, rare in earlier, more primitive communities. Here, in an increasingly complicated society, is the individual — contemplative, baffled by circumstance, putting up his defences against a world in which he feels increasingly separate. 'Live unobtrusively' was the sum of this negative attitude, which could easily become parasitic on an over-ripe society. There was no need to fear the gods; if they existed, they did not interfere with human life: 'Above all, leave God out', they said.

The terrors of an after-life are also eliminated: 'Death, the king of terrors, is no concern of ours, since when we exist death is not present; when death is come, then we are not.'

The Epicureans were not, of course, the sensualists they have been painted; the aim of life was happiness, detachment. This could never be so long as men were ridden by passions, and a sensible moderation and self-control alone could achieve serenity. Further, a kindly attitude to others ought to be cultivated, since all are victims of the same fate; and the wise man will do his best to undermine the grosser superstitions which distort men's lives.

Such an attitude would result in political quietism unlikely to convert or control barbarians or frighten men of action into decent behaviour. It also weakened the traditional loyalty to the city's gods; it may be regarded as politically negative, except in so far as it encouraged a humanitarian attitude to all men.[1]

The Stoic philosophy is more constructive; it greatly influenced the Romans, and later statements of Christianity were affected by it. The Stoic school at Athens was founded in 301 B.C. by Zeno,[2] whose Phoenician-Semitic origin is probably reflected in the austerity of his doctrine. In common with the Epicureans, the Stoics preached

[1] Its most famous expression is Roman, Lucretius, *De Rerum Natura*.

[2] Zeno (342-270 B.C.), a Cypriote merchant, who settled in Athens. According to Diogenes Laertius, whose account must be treated with reservations (Bk. VII, vol. II, Loeb edition, q.v.), 'He had a wry neck, was lean, tall and swarthy . . . They say he was fond of eating green figs and of basking in the sun . . . He was of a frowning countenance; he was very niggardly too, clinging to meanness unworthy of a Greek. It is said that he had more than a thousand talents when he came to Greece and that he lent this money on maritime ventures. He disliked, they say, to be brought too near to people, so that he would take the end seat of a couch, thus saving himself at any rate from one half of such inconvenience.' He was shipwrecked on a voyage from Phoenicia to Piraeus with a cargo of 'purple' at the age of thirty. He settled in Athens and devoted himself to philosophy, becoming the pupil of Crates. Zeno used to discourse pacing up and down the painted colonnade 'which is called the Colonnade of Pisianax . . . hither, then, people came thenceforth to hear Zeno and this is why they were known as the men of the Stoa or Stoics (colonnade: Latin – porticus – loggia or porch).

detachment, but aimed also at an ideal of selfless duty. They set much store by will and the planned practice of virtue. Life was a burden and a pilgrimage, in which to play a noble part was its own reward. There was no heavenly city at the end; the world process went its way of cyclic recurrence with profound indifference to the fates of men.

The wise man, therefore, seeks to become invulnerable by a deliberate cultivation of 'apathy', insensitiveness, and a self-discipline, which, though the world crash about him, would render him impervious to disaster. The early Greek rationalists had evolved the idea of pattern and order. The Stoics went further and identified the Logos with the world soul. They emphasized the brotherhood of man, since all participated in a common reason. This permanent world of values dwarfs the ordinary affairs of life, which are only significant as they contribute to or interfere with it. The philosopher exists fully only on this plane; though he ought to play his part nobly on the stage of the world. He accepts certain obligations of conduct, the convention of his station and his duties. To do what is becoming is the obligation of the good man; it is a proud and admirable creed, and not an easy one. Suicide becomes legitimate when circumstances make the good life impossible and the only seemly thing to do is to put an end to oneself. Instead of making a pathetic individual protest against fate, it is best to conform with the drift of things. Here man finds fulfilment in harmony with the will of a process indifferent to him. The ideal is a fine one, the more so as it holds out no hope of reward. The dignity of character achieved and admired by the leaders of Graeco-Roman civilization owed more to it than to any other philosophy; it directly affected politics, for the sense of duty, of playing one's part in the transient show, sustained the high morale of many Roman administrators and elevated the spirit of Roman Law. Stoicism influenced men in positions of great power in the ancient world, and contributed to the efficiency of government.

Yet, in Professor Toynbee's view, this Stoic philosophy was 'handicapped by a fatal lack of zest'. This negative melancholy temper is manifest in the *Meditations* of Marcus Aurelius, the historic philosopher king who dutifully carried on his shoulders the burden of governing the whole *Orbis Romanus*. 'Human life! Its duration is momentary . . . its physical organism perishable, its consciousness a vortex, its destiny dark, its repute uncertain; in fact the material element is a rolling stream . . . life a war and a sojourning in a far country, fame oblivion. What can see us through? One thing and one thing only — Philosophy; and that means keeping the spirit within us unspoiled and undishonoured . . . and taking what comes contentedly, as all part of the process to which we owe our own being.'[1]

Thus the two famous philosophies, transcending the City State, unite in apprehending a universal life-process and in attempting to meet the needs of individual loneliness. Both discern a pattern behind life and institutions, though it is indifferent to human values. The Stoics go farther and maintain that Natural Law or Providence governs a world in which, through all the preponderance of evil, it is the duty of good men to uphold the nobler values which are their own reward. Here, then, is the contribution which Stoicism made both to Roman Law and to Christianity. A moral law of nature comprehending all men can become the sanction behind large-scale government; translated into Roman legal terms, following the definitions of Cicero, it was transmitted to the Middle Ages and beyond.

§ I I I

Another aspect of the Hellenistic world is the persistence and popularity of the primitive mystery religions. Like the Hellenistic philosophies, these sacramental cults were the business not of the polis but of the individual, and take no account of political responsibilities. They tap the dimmest subconscious springs of conduct and are yet concerned with personal salvation. A psychologically satisfactory pattern of ritual, independent of the state religion, these mysteries are consistently attacked by Plato. They fall under two main headings: the Eleusinian and the Orphic. The latter produced a complicated theological literature.

The Eleusinian mysteries centred on an agricultural ritual; the Orphic on a complicated and revolting mythology. The ideal of renewal, following subconscious release of energy provoked through secret ritual, is common to all these rites. By sacramental communion the desiccation and loneliness of the individual is appeased. Going back to the primitive beginnings of ritual, to the witch doctor, who, in animal guise in the palaeolithic cave, performed the ritual drama

---

[1] *Marcus Aurelius Antoninus, to Himself*, bk. II, quoted by TOYNBEE, *A Study of History*, vol. III, p. 253.

before the representation of to-morrow's kill, the guardians of the mystery enact a symbolical death and resurrection which brings fulfilment and release. This rebirth into a new life, this 'grace', is attained by 'communion' in the ritual passion play. The sufferings and triumph of the god somehow embody the experience of the worshippers.

The Eleusinian mysteries took place in spring and autumn; they centred on the resurrection of Persephone and the new corn. Just as seed sown in the earth lives again,[1] so the soul of the initiate is guarded in its passage through the underworld into reincarnation; by the 'grace' of witnessing the rites, 'salvation' will be assured. There is no ethical code, no creed; the thing is largely magical. The Eleusinian mysteries were conducted by the sacred families who monopolized them from the earliest beginnings of Greek history to the fifth century A.D.

The Orphic cult was more complicated, better organized, and more widespread. Like Mithraism and Christianity, it was a universal religion. The theology which sustained it was roughly as follows. Out of primeval night, Time fashioned Earth and Heaven; from their union, Eros, the life spirit, generated the gods. Then Zeus, by his daughter Persephone Kore, begat Zagreus, the horned infant, and endowed him with power over the earth; but he was cut to pieces and eaten by the Titans, whom Zeus in anger slew. From drinking the heart's blood of Zagreus, the Earth-Mother Semele rebore him as Dionysus, and from the remnants of the Titans Zeus made men.

The origin of man is thus steeped in sin; yet through the crime of the Titans he is linked with God, for they had eaten the Son of Heaven. The central rite of the Orphic mystery was the symbolic consumption of the flesh of Dionysus. So the participants re-enacted the primal sin, yet shared the virtue of the risen God and attained redemption out of a world dead in wickedness. The Orphic mystery differed from the Eleusinian in its emphatic sense of guilt. Both these rituals have in common the assuagement of individual fear and guilt; the one by grace offers immortality, the other, by sacrament, salvation. Their persistence during the first four centuries of the Christian era is significant.

In these cults religious emotion is divorced from the State. The

---

[1] Being ignorant of the chemistry of germination, the Hellenistic thinkers, both pagan and Christian, thought of the sown corn as actually dead, e.g. St. Paul, 'Foolish man, what you sow never comes to life unless it dies'. 1 Cor. xii, 37. The analogy with 'resurrection' is thus reinforced, though in point of fact the corn does not 'die' at all.

priests are no longer the responsible officials of a traditional ritual, bound up, as in Egypt and Mesopotamia or the primitive city, with the pride and achievement of the ruling, politically conscious, minority. They stand for values above or below the political community, the beginnings of a Church within the State.

§ IV

In addition to the new vision of great-scale rule, the new philosophies and mystery religions, there is another memorable aspect of the Hellenistic period, its cultural achievement. The foundation of the library at Alexandria was a landmark in the consolidation and professionalizing of knowledge.[1] The reception and elaboration of Greek ideas in this Egyptian setting has, indeed, been compared to the assimilation of Renaissance ideas in the sixteenth century by the North. The actual scale of organized learning and encyclopaedic arrangement in the Hellenistic universities goes far beyond the world of Socrates and Plato. 'The Alexandrian school diffused a splendour over the civilized world which lasted longer than that shed by any University afterwards, whether of Paris, Bologna or Padua. Long after the creative power of Greek genius was exhausted, encyclopaedic knowledge and Greek sophistry were to be found in the library and museum of Alexandria . . . In this foundation of the first Lagidae, Ptolemy Philadelphus and Euergetes, all the methods of the philosophies, as well as of the exact sciences, were fostered for centuries.'[2]

The main achievements of Alexandrian scholarship were in the sphere of medicine, astronomy, and mathematics. The names of Galen, Claudius Ptolemy, and Euclid are famous; all date from the Hellenistic period. In philosophy Plotinus, in history Plutarch and Dio Cassius, are well known, and the poetry and literature of the age, though its quality may not have been high, and the bulk of it has now perished, was widespread in volume and technically proficient. Further, this increased level of technical skill made possible the bureaucratic efficiency of Roman times.

Moreover, during the long phase of its prosperity, the social structure of the Hellenistic world was materially splendid. The cities were, it is true, deprived of initiative in major policy and singularly

[1] See TARN, *The Hellenistic World*, London (1927).
[2] GREGOROVIUS, *Hadrian*, bk. II, chap. vii.

cut off from the country districts around them, but the civic oligarchy into whose hands the control of affairs increasingly devolved were lavish, though often undiscriminating, patrons of the arts, of literature and of building, competing with one another in the splendour of their setting. The same pattern is familiar all over the world of antiquity. The public buildings, the amphitheatre, the elaborate baths and libraries, the gymnasia, the last the centre of an athletic and intellectual culture in the tradition of the polis, the mainspring of this society, and largely confined to the richer classes. Many famous cities lived on the prestige of their universities, and they employed a great number of professors of rhetoric and philosophy. The prestige of Greek ideas made the Orientals anxious to follow the fashion and imitate their conquerors. The practice of athletics[1] was reinforced by improved sanitation; town planning and public medical services and communications were relatively efficient.

Thus was realized and sustained an ordered and powerful society; its tradition persisted through the period of decline. Politically, then, the widespread cult of the Divine Ruler and the concept of Universal Empire, briefly realized by Alexander in the Near East and the Levant, was afterwards taken over and developed by Rome. The Eastern tradition of semi-divine kingship was acclimatized to Europe, and a wider conception of royalty in part derived from it, through Byzantium and the Holy Roman Empire and the kings by Divine Right of the sixteenth and seventeenth centuries.

Further, the Hellenistic philosophies stress the value of individual personality, and its independence of circumstance. The idea of a universalized Law of Nature that knows neither bond nor free, of the brotherhood of man, transcending class distinction, is already widely extant before the coming of Christianity, and invoked by Roman thought as a sanction for government.

Again, the mystery religions, with their sacramental cults, ritual, and salvationism, became increasingly pervasive. Finally, the steady elaboration of a civilized social life, of learning and education, the maintenance of a vigorous intellectual tradition and a degree of professionalized knowledge, formed the medium in which the culture of the Augustan world expanded, and the doctrines of Christianity were formulated, and which was strong enough to outlive, if in a changed and limited form, the decline of the civilization of antiquity.

[1] Even the Jews bought the privilege of having a gymnasium from the astute Antiochus Epiphanes, with disastrous repercussions among their own nationalists.

CHAPTER VI

ROME: THE RULE OF LAW

§ I

THE heir to the conquests of Alexander was Rome, the business-like, uncouth city out in the West. The debt which civilization owes to Rome is incalculable, but the Roman mind was not speculative; it was practical, military, legalistic. The genius of this people was to create the political and military framework of universal empire, to realize the imperial idea foreshadowed by Alexander.

The scale of their achievement is staggering even by modern standards. The empire at its greatest stretched from Mesopotamia to Scotland; the disciplined tramp of the heavy-armed legionaries imposed the habit of peace in the remotest confines of Brittany and Spain, the Balkans and Roumania, in Palestine and Egypt and the boundaries of Iran. The structure of the Byzantine and Western mediaeval world was created by the Romans, the framework of political and ecclesiastical order.

To understand this people one must be aware of the limitations of their early beginnings. The tradition was that of a tenacious farming stock. The Etruscan element in Rome, too, was not a gentle one; the Etruscans, who came from Asia Minor, had a hard-bitten inheritance, and their influence persisted in the more primitive aspects of Roman religion.

The Roman contribution to political thought is primarily in the development of an all-embracing Public Law, and the designing of great-scale institutions which kept the peace over a wider area of space and time than has ever been achieved in Europe, before or since. It will be well, therefore, to concentrate on the nature of their Law and the structure of the empire. Three outstanding men will be the focus of our study: Cicero, as the exponent of Roman political and legal theory; Augustus, the architect of the empire; and Justinian, the Byzantine emperor of the sixth century, who codified Roman Law when the shadows had drawn in round the declining empire in the West.

Great as was the Roman achievement, it was founded throughout on military force; it is the first example in Europe of organized power on a great scale. Successive wars of aggression, won by superior discipline and the systematic routine of fortifying camps, building roads and ensuring supply services in an age when such a technique was generally unknown, steadily enlarged the confines of the Roman Peace. Roman success was due not only to the excellence of their discipline but to the weakness of their opponents. In the North, the Iron Age Belgae, their most formidable enemies, relied on the chariot charge, terrible to primitive people. But these early armoured troops were easily thrown into confusion if the Roman formation held, and behind the Roman front line was a supply organization which the barbarians could not hope to imitate. At the same time, for all the efficiency of their organization, the Romans had their primitive side. The whole conduct of a campaign might turn on the interpretation of the auguries or on the phase of the moon.

In its military aspect, indeed, the power of Rome was an ugly thing, founded on a brutal militarism and a harsh discipline; this side of the imperial power must be set against the theoretical idealism of the Hellenized Stoic lawyers. Moreover, the Romans accepted slavery as completely as the Greeks; even the Christian Justinian takes it as a matter of course, and their treatment of criminals and captives is outstanding in its savagery even by the standards of antiquity — witness the mass crucifixion of the Spartacist slaves, or the fate of the Jewish prisoners after the sack of the temple by Titus, set to fight to the death in the arena.

But along with this brutality, without which no large-scale government in that age could have existed, there went an efficiency and solid integrity which was new. Roman dignity and seriousness reflected a conviction of superior mission, an ideal of impartial justice, and Rome tolerated native institutions, so long as they did not interfere with government, a mark of unusual political sagacity and one of the reasons for the empire's success.

It was over internal politics that Rome failed; the old institutions and the republican tradition could not stand up to the burden of world power, and the influx of slaves and treasure from war. Demoralized by success and its economic sequel, the Roman stock lost grip, and Cicero (106-43 B.C.) wrote against a background of political failure which only dictatorship could remedy. Julius Caesar perished not because the dictatorship at which he aimed was incompatible with the interests of Rome — on the contrary, it was to be its salvation — but because with his personality and record he could never disguise the reality Augustus was able to conceal.[1]

Cicero is the most important Roman transmitter of Greek political thought.[2] The terms coined by him are used constantly by subsequent writers and his grasp of politics strengthened Greek ideas. The massive realities of large-scale government were never far absent from the Roman mind; Cicero translated Stoic philosophical ideas into Latin legal terms employed by subsequent Roman and ecclesiastical lawyers. To discuss the function of government in terms of legal rights is un-Greek; the Roman influence, for good and ill, legalized the vocabulary of political thought.

While the flexible Roman law was able to absorb Greek ideas, Roman common sense prevented the ossification and complexity of the Egyptian and Hebrew codes. Law became compatible with a progressive society, no longer the 'Law of the Medes and Persians which altereth not'. Above all, Rome took from the Hellenistic world the idea of Natural Law, *Ius Naturale*, which was thus brought down to earth and linked up with the *Ius Gentium*, the 'Law of the peoples'. *Ius Naturale* became something more practical, and the *Ius Gentium* more general. All these ideas were crystallized by the legists, who distinguished three kinds of Law: *Ius Civile*, *Ius Gentium* and *Ius Naturale*, the term *Ius* implying custom based on what is right.

The Roman outlook thus became more humane, less narrow, less conservatively religious, at once practical and informed with a comprehensive ideal of justice. The *Ius Gentium*, with its immediate flexibility and freedom from archaic custom — the early Romans would have considered the foreigners for whom it was designed outside the pale of their own formal and sacred code — proved in the long run the principal medium whereby the idea of universal law was brought to bear on politics, the Hellenistic idea of Natural Law defined and put to practical purpose as the sanction for government.

The *Republic*[3] of Cicero, though long lost, contains the fullest state-

[1] See FERRERO's *Julius Caesar* for a masterly account of the Italy of Caesar's time. R. SYME, *The Roman Revolution*, O.U.P. (1939), thinks that, for all his genius, Caesar did not see a way out: *'exitum non reperiebat'*.
[2] Polybius, who lived as a hostage in Rome during the Punic War, and who chronicled the struggle in his great history, in which he sets himself to account for the Roman rise to the domination of the ancient world, was a political philosopher of considerable note. See his sixth book, which contains reflections on politics anticipating Machiavelli. But his outlook is Hellenistic and he wrote in Greek.
[3] The *Republic* was written between 54 and 52 B.C. in the form of a dialogue assumed to have taken place in 129 B.C. in the garden of Scipio Africanus the Younger. It is divided into three 'days' of conversation. On the first day books I and II raise the

ment of the Roman ideal of government and world-embracing law representative of Roman upper middle-class tradition. We are here in direct contact with a reinterpretation of Stoic and Platonic ideals. The Greek thought is by no means simply accepted; it is given a new and more concrete interpretation and some aspects of it are rejected.

The ideal sketched in the *Republic* is not a city laid up in heaven — that would have been most unsatisfying to a Roman — but an attempt is made to deduce the nature of the best commonwealth by a survey of Roman history; the principle of justice or harmony in a commonwealth is plainly stated, and the role of the statesman glorified. The book begins with a preface praising the *métier* of the statesmen and arguing against the Epicurean view that the good man ought to hold aloof from politics. Cato is cited as an example of one who sacrificed private life for public duty. This calling is the highest of all, since where the philosopher merely exhorts, the statesman can compel. His aim is plain: 'to make human life nobler and richer by our thought and effort' (I, 2). 'There is no activity in which man comes nearer to godhead than to found new cities or to preserve those already founded' (I, 7). Cicero proceeds to an account of a house party on the country estate of Scipio Africanus the Younger, who lived about seventy years before his own time.

It is an appropriate setting for the discussion — these affable, stately men of affairs, conscious of the power behind the state they serve, proud of the public achievement of Rome, rather plethoric and heavy, but able, powerful, and serious. The contrast with the setting of the Platonic dialogues is striking. There is none of the artistic sense, the playfulness and banter of the Socratic method; these Romans discuss wisely and plainly, as among sensible men, what is 'useful for the State'. 'Let us ask Scipio what form of government he considers best (I, 20) . . . He is conversant with Penaetius and Polybius.' Scipio answers he is not satisfied with the works on this subject, 'which the greatest and wisest of the Greeks have left; nor, on the other hand, am I bold enough to rate my own opinion

---

question of the nature of the commonwealth, and by tracing out the history of Rome, attempt to find the ideal state and to sketch the ideal statesman. On the second day, book III discusses the foundations of justice and defines it. Book IV is fragmentary and concerned with education. The third day includes books V and VI; V is almost entirely lost; VI contains Scipio's 'Dream'. Much of the text, of which the fragments were discovered in the early nineteenth century, was familiar to mediaeval thinkers, in part through the use made of it by Lactantius.

upon this highly . . . but listen to me as a Roman, trained by experience and maxims learned at home rather than from books.' He goes straight to a business-like definition of the State: ' *"Est igitur"*, *inquit Africanus*, *"Res publica, res populi"*.' (I, 25); a people is not merely 'a mob of men come together anyhow', but an association *'iuris consensu et utilitatis communione sociatus'*.[1]

The dialogue then proceeds to discuss various forms of government. The Greek classifications are awkwardly imposed on the Roman experience but they are permeated with a Roman good sense.

Citizens should be equal before the Law: 'If we cannot equate citizens' wealth, and equality of innate abilities is impossible, the legal rights at least of citizens of the same commonwealth should be equal': *'Quid est enim civitas nisi iuris societas?"*[2] Ranging over the various methods of government — in the Greek convention monarchy, oligarchy, democracy — Scipio decides that a combination of all three is the best. 'The ruling power of the State is like a ball, snatched from kings by tyrants, from tyrants by aristocracies or the people' and from them again by an oligarchy or another tyrant. He concludes that there is no form of government so good as the Roman, and proposes to show his audience why.

The second book is therefore devoted to a survey of Roman history, followed by a portrait of what a statesman ought to be. He proceeds to study the history of an actual state, rather than follow Plato in inventing an ideal one. The Roman commonwealth is based on the genius not of one founder but of many men working together; it grew up gradually as an expression of their combined abilities. Rome grew great by its own efforts, *'concilio et disciplina'*.[3] Scipio, then, scouts the legend that King Numa Pompilius was a pupil of Pythagoras and imbued with Greek ideas. A long survey of Roman history leads to the idea of a state which combines different elements harmoniously. 'What musicians call harmony in a song is concord in the State'; this 'harmony' is equated by Scipio with the term 'justice'; in his sense it means the harmonious social expression of the moral instincts of man; it is a misleading term to anyone who thinks of justice as simply the fair enforcement of Law. This 'justice' is further explained in Book III; Philus, for whom is cast the role of

[1] 'United by acceptance of Law and by common enjoyment of its practical advantages.'
[2] I, 32. 'For what is the State but a fellowship in Law?'
[3] 'By deliberation and training.'

advocatus diaboli, questions its reality, quoting the famous dialogue between Alexander and the pirate. '*Nam cum quaeretur ex eo quo scelere impulsus mare haberet infestum uno myoperone*, "*Eodem*", inquit, "*Quo tu orbem terrae*".'[1] Government, he maintains, is nothing but piracy on a large scale; the Roman eye for the main chance cannot pretend it is not better to be wicked, successful and respected, than to be a good man in misery. What is true for private life is true in public affairs: 'There is no state so stupid that it would not prefer to rule unjustly rather than be enslaved and in the right' (III, 18).

The answer is an assertion and definition of Natural Law as a sanction for government. '*Est quidem vera lex, recta ratio naturae congruens*' — 'There is in fact a true law, right reason, in accordance with nature; it applies to all men, is unalterable and eternal . . . There will not be one law in Rome, another in Athens, one now, another later on, but one law for all people at all times; one master and ruler over us all, the inventor, promulgator and enforcing judge' (III, 22). This view of Law, the backbone of the best Roman imperialism, was destined to dominate and haunt the mind of Europe till our own day. The lapidary Roman phrases (it is significant how many words of English are needed to translate them) clinch the thought and stamp it into the mind. Through the jurists and the Fathers it came down, Christianized, through mediaeval times and beyond.

The fourth book is fragmentary, interesting for the light it throws on Roman views of Greek education. 'Our people have never wished to have any system of education for the freeborn youth which is either definitely fixed by law or officially established and uniform in all cases, though the Greeks expended much vain labour to find it.' The Romans felt uncomfortable at the antics of the Greek training: '*Iuventutis vero exercitatio quam absurda in gymnasiis!*' They go about naked and are no better than they should be and their military training is amateurish — '*Quam levis epheborum illa militia!*' (IV, 4). And as for Plato's views about property, they are shocking.

The fifth book, also fragmentary, returns to the main theme, and defines the purpose of the State. 'Just as the aim of the pilot is a successful voyage, of the physician, health, of the general, victory, so the aim of the *moderator reipublicae . . . beata civium vita proposita est*.' The *beata civium vita* is deadly practical, '*ut opibus firma, copiis locuples,*

---

[1] 'For when he was asked what was the evil motive that drove him to terrorize the seas with a single privateer, he answered, "The same that drives you to terrorize the whole earth".'

gloria ampla, virtute honesta sit.[1] There is no nonsense about spiritual unrest or fulfilment here — all is material, efficient, sane. No wonder, in the short view, they succeeded.

The sixth book contains the curious and weird passage known as the *Somnium Scipionis*. The ghost of Africanus the Elder appears to Scipio Aemilianus, who is visiting the aged Masinissa in Africa. After prophesying the dreamer's future and showing him the kingdoms of the earth and their limitations, the insignificance even of the Roman empire and the vanity of human life, the ghost declares that fame itself is ultimately a dead thing, for the greatest reputation is blotted out by the forgetfulness of posterity, and whatever a man's celebrity, the generations which have come before him cannot have known his fame. After an account of the cosmic order, of one sphere circling another, of the earth immobile in the centre of the lowest, and of the music of the spheres,[2] the spirit explains that only a love of right and duty can set a man on the 'road to the skies', to the place in the Milky Way where the shades of the great dead have their being. 'Spirit' alone, which is 'spontaneous motion', can survive death, and the souls of the ignoble haunt the mundane sphere. The reward of the great statesman is the immortality of the stellar heaven.

This ideal of Universal Law, of just administration and its reward, is further worked out in the first book of the *Laws*.[3] Cicero declares that Law is a natural force, the mind and reason of the intelligent man (I, 6). *Recta ratio* is common to God and man. 'This provident, sagacious, many-sided, acute, remembering animal which we call man, shares with the gods a *virtus* which is nothing else but its own nature carried out to its fullest expression' (I, 8). Man is thus born for justice (I, 10). *Lex* is '*Recta ratio in iubendo et vetando*'; the expression of right reason in action. It is an absolute value, based on the nature of things, originating in the natural inclination of men to help each

---

[1] The 'happy life for the citizens' is to be 'stable with wealth, rich with resources, spacious with glory, honourable with virtue'.

[2] The uppermost sphere, which revolves more rapidly, gives out a high shrill note; the lowest revolving sphere, that of the moon, has the deepest tone.

[3] The *Laws*, written later than the *Republic* (*c.* 47 B.C.), takes the form of a discussion between Cicero, his brother Quintus, and some others at Cicero's estate at Arpinum by the River Liris. It is likely that there were originally six books. The first book gives a philosophical definition of Natural Law on the lines of the *Republic*. The second book carries on this thought and then gives a deliberately archaic specimen code of religious laws suitable for any state, which are fully analysed in turn. The third book does the same for Constitutional Law. The outlook and scope of both these codes is very limited after the statement of Cicero's principles in the first chapter. The manuscript which has come down dates from the ninth century.

other, compared by Cicero to the impulse to friendship. The good man instinctively 'loves his friend as himself', so the *virtus*, of which justice is the expression, is instinctive. It follows there is an absolute standard of right immanent in nature, otherwise it could not exist, says the practical Roman; and it is independent of utility. Were it based merely on decrees and edicts, 'the decrees of fools could change the laws of nature, and good would become bad'. We know what is right in the same way as a farmer can instinctively recognize the *virtus* of a good horse (I, 16), and 'the law which a Roman *interrex* proposed, that a Dictator might put to death with impunity anyone he wished without a trial', flies in the face of justice which exists in its own right. The book ends with a passage in which the mind of the just man is glorified. He is *civis totius mundi*, citizen of the whole world; he must bear his part in public affairs, 'rule the peoples, stabilize the Laws, castigate wrong, uphold the good, praise famous men' — the Roman programme of duty and order.

Fine as these definitions are, there is reason to believe that the material mind of Rome, which felt uncomfortable at the Greek brilliance, had not the spiritual power and creativeness to sustain this high purpose. The second and third books are an anti-climax. In the second book Cicero composes a specimen table of religious laws in deliberately archaic form, which he claims are 'in agreement with nature'. Actually they are very limited, very pagan and old-fashioned. There is little here beyond the old City State doctrine of correct routine, of decency and right behaviour, of a purely social religion. 'They shall approach the gods in purity', celebrate with their slaves when the day's work is done; the priests shall perform their offices, the vestal virgins tend their fire. 'Prodigies and portents shall be referred to the Etruscans if the Senate so decrees.' The sooth-sayers are to consult the omens, the rites of ancestral piety are to be observed, '*sacra privata perpetuo memento, in urbibus delubra habento . . . lucos in agris habento et larum sedes, sacra solemnia obeunto*' — they shall perform the established rites. We are not here beyond the decent pieties of the City State, the solid archaic rules. These rules, says Cicero, are certainly in agreement with nature: 'This completes, I believe, my consideration of the whole subject of religion.'

Again, in the third book, the functions of the magistrate are set out. He is a 'speaking law': 'there is nothing so completely in accordance with the principles of justice and the demands of nature as government'. There follows a similar deliberately archaic code.

'Commands shall be just, there shall be right of appeal from a magistrate's decision, but in war no appeal against the commander.' The structure of aediles, praetors, censors and their functions is fully worked out, and how the senatorial order shall be an example for the rest, and how a man may not hold the same office twice, save after an interval of ten years. All is detailed, sensible, pedestrian, static, and bears little on the political situation of Cicero's day. He is looking back to an aristocratic republic which has already failed.

This lack of originality and spiritual power may in part explain the ultimate Roman failure; it looks as if the Greek ideas, though superbly expressed, had not, perhaps, got through as far as at first seems apparent, though they were given a precise and resounding definition which carried them over into the Middle Ages and beyond.

But if Cicero, for all his powerful definitions of the nature of Law, looked back to a limited ideal, there emerged out of the republican failure the great bureaucratic and military structure of imperial rule which was to go a long way to realize the conception of universal justice and order which at his best Cicero could grasp. It was to be under the Principate that this achievement was brought about; under it Graeco-Roman society, of which Europe is still the heir, stabilized and continued on a scale and for a duration which makes it the dominant fact of Western history.

§ 11

The architect of the empire was Augustus, an enigmatic figure whose personality has been variously described.[1] He and his administrators created the first structure of imperial government in Europe. The habit of order which the Roman rule imposed, and the

---

[1] Caius Octavius (*imperabat* 27 B.C.-A.D. 14), great-nephew of Julius Caesar. He came of equestrian family, his grandfather being a provincial banker. ('*Ipse Augustus nihil amplius quam equestri familia ortum se scribit*'; Suetonius.) His father married the daughter of Caesar's sister, Julia, and was made Governor of Macedonia. Octavius passed by adoption into the Julian house, changing his name to C. Julius Caesar Octavianus; when Princeps he was styled Imperator Caesar Divi Filius Augustus. Alternative views of his character are expressed by modern writers. Buchan, whose work is one of popularization, regards Augustus as a great gentleman, but Syme sees him as the ruthless party leader of a successful syndicate. Both agree that the condition of Italy was so bad that dictatorship was the only solution. Syme, in particular, gives a vivid picture of the irresponsible plutocrats of the last days of the republic, 'secluded like indolent monsters in their fashionable villas'. He quotes Crassus' remark that 'no man was really rich who could not keep his own army'. Such a situation required the implacable and unerring realism Augustus certainly displayed, and it is probable that the second picture is the more accurate. BUCHAN, *Augustus*, Hodder & Stoughton (1937). SYME, op. cit. See also *C.A.H.*

stability of the empire over centuries, created a respect for institutions never wholly lost, which influenced all subsequent political thought; it will be well, therefore, to look at the outline of its organization and at its limitations.

The Constitutional Principate was based on the authority of the Imperator, delegated to him, in theory, by the senate and people of Rome, and reinforced by the cult of the ruler as a god. The imperial bureaucracy, which had its beginnings under Augustus and reached its greatest efficiency under Hadrian and the Antonines, was something new in Western Europe and derived its model from the Persian and Hellenistic monarchies; it was the backbone of the empire. Drawn at first from freedmen in the personal service of the household of Augustus, it was later gradually reinforced by an aristocracy of officials, recruited increasingly from the civic classes. This cosmopolitan bureaucracy carried on for centuries, through all the vicissitudes of changing emperors and economic and military conflict; it survived in an unbroken continuity in Byzantium; its tradition never died, the Catholic Church, and, in part, the Holy Roman Empire, had their roots in it.

The Princeps controlled a well-paid long-service army, small for its enormous task, the total force probably between 300,000 and 450,000 men; it held the frontiers and garrisoned the provinces. The taxation which supported the bureaucracy and the army was comparatively light in the earlier empire; later, economic collapse at the centre imposed the crushing burden that was one of the major causes of the decline. Financial affairs were dealt with by a special bureau of the imperial household in a systematic manner hitherto practised only in the East, notably in Egypt; the organization of the provinces, with which the republic had shown itself unfit to deal, was adequately tackled; governors, pro-consuls, and legates were better chosen and kept in close touch with the central authority; imperial procurators supervised their financial policy.

The Roman administration formed a framework of order superimposed on a society organized in terms of City States, and by the extension of the Roman citizenship, which reached its widest extent at the end of the second century (there were between four and five million citizens) went some way, though not far enough, to create a loyalty beyond local patriotism. It aimed at the maintenance of order and routine: in spite of the political corruption which haunted it at the centre, it long succeeded in that aim.

The weakness of this constitution was its dependence on the Princeps; the principate was not hereditary, but actually Augustus selected his successor. Unhappily the Julio-Claudian house threw up personalities which could hardly have been more unsuitable. If the Princeps was a neurotic, as were Nero and Caligula, there was no way out but a palace revolution. Further, the praetorian soldiers, the imperial bodyguard, played a sinister part in Roman high politics, and in the later empire the central authority became increasingly militarized. Moreover, the imperial conception of government was static, and lack of economic understanding, combined with an over-legalistic outlook, led to mishandling of the economic situation.

The causes of the final decline were economic, political, and psychological. Militarism, economic failure, the ruin of the best qualities of the Roman State through the competition of foreign elements of the basest origin; the brutal disregard of aesthetic and moral standards by the plutocracy of the empire, encouraged the view that all government can be is a necessary evil for keeping society together. An undercurrent of disgust with 'the world' is already apparent in the writings of Seneca, who represents the Romanized version of Stoicism in decline.

It is not surprising that Seneca, who attempted to educate Nero and ultimately committed suicide, should display a pessimistic view of life. His outlook shows the dualist escapism of Roman society, already apparent in the first century; a fine but not a warmhearted humanitarianism. Government already comes to be regarded as a remedy for wickedness, a far cry from the healthy co-operation of younger societies; all sorts of evils are condoned, for the world is like that. And, indeed, even by the time of Nero, a brutal self-indulgence and unbridled sensuality were threatening the austere traditions of earlier Rome; finally, after the golden age of Hadrian and the Antonines in the second century, standards became militarized and debased. The blood and sweat of later pagan antiquity, the disregard for human life, the public gloating over games and crucifixions, the roaring vulgarity of the later empire, are all too apparent from the denunciations of the Christian Fathers, and the mosaic pictures of popular gladiators and their patrons tell their own tale;[1] while as early as the first century the cultivated Petronius gives a bad enough account of Roman society in the *Satyricon*, a work

[1] See M. H. SWINDLER, *Ancient Painting*, plates 441, 520, 521, 640 (Yale, 1929).

99

written with a modern insight, and there is no reason to suppose that Martial's epigrams or the satires of Juvenal are unrepresentative of their age.

The Stoic distaste for this kind of atmosphere represents an important facet of Roman life, for all the practical and legal achievements of the empire. It paved the way for the Christian assumption, expressed by St. Augustine, that the secular state is rooted in iniquity, or at best only justifies itself by performing the duties of the police for the benefit of the righteous: the blunders and excesses of the later empire unduly discredited the possibilities of the secular state.

There is not here occasion to follow the phases of prosperity, decline and reorganization which succeeded one another in the decadence of the empire. It should be borne in mind as one of the causes of the decline that the empire was in no way analogous to a modern great state. A bureaucracy and an army, inspired by their own *esprit de corps*, held together a civilization of City States, all owing loyalty to the semi-divine emperor. There was civic duty and bureaucratic efficiency, but not patriotism; passive gratitude for the benefits of the empire, but they had no word for membership of a nation in the modern sense. Further, the cities became politically demoralized, since major decisions of war and justice were taken out of their hands. Civic patriotism gradually died; as the machine ran down, the economic position deteriorated, and the central government applied a compulsion constantly evaded. In the end there was a huge unwieldy bureaucracy, a cumbrous machine, which lumbered on out of its own inertia, and a 'dreary individualism' which 'despaired of the republic'.[1] With the upper middle class crushed, there remained the great landowners on their self-sufficing estates, the soldiers, the peasantry, and the urban mob. There is evidence that the culture of the cities was not shared by either town or country proletariat, who often spoke a different language from the curiales. From the beginning, too, the Roman government had taken the side of the rich; the whole weight of moral and speculative ideas was conservative, and neither the cities nor the imperial bureaucracy understood the rudiments of economic science.

As we have seen, in the *Meditations* of Marcus Aurelius, in whose reign the ideals of civic upper classes were best realized, there is a close revelation of the mind of a ruler carrying out his duty in a highly civilized world, from which the spiritual tide is running out.

[1] See A. H. M. JONES, op. cit., pp. 303-4.

Throughout, the imperial structure carried on, the routine of ordinary life was apparently secure, but society was becoming increasingly pessimistic, static and centralized; the divine aspect of the emperor, initiated by Augustus in a formal and political manner, was to be translated by the time of Constantine into a theocratic authority which combined the prestige of the pagan empire with the new sanction of Christianity.

The marvel is that the structure held, though subjected to an intolerable political and financial strain. That it did hold so long is of the utmost importance for Western culture, for the habit of mind was created which assumed the existence of a European order, sustaining a peaceful and mighty civilization which awed the barbarians and of which the tradition has never died.

§ III

The survival of the political thought of antiquity was largely due to the carapace of Law which protected it. Roman Law, defined by the great jurists, systematized, condensed, and preserved by Justinian's officials in the sixth century, was carried over into medi-aeval times through Byzantine influence as well as through Patristic and Western thought.

Justinian[1] (A.D. 527-565) inherited the autocratic and theocratic tradition of the later empire. 'This Macedonian peasant, seated on the throne of the Caesars, was the successor and heir of the Roman Emperors. Few princes realized the imperial dignity to a more marked degree than this *parvenu*, or have done more to maintain the ancient traditions . . . Justinian was less a Byzantine than the last of the Roman Emperors.'[2]

The immense work of reorganization undertaken by him included what was to be, in the long view, his most important contribution to European development, the revision and consolidation of the dis-

---

[1] Born at Taurisium near Uskub, the nephew of Justin, commander of the palace guard, who ousted the Emperor Anastasius by a *coup d'état* in 518. Succeeded to the empire in 527; in 523 married Theodora, daughter of the bear-keeper of the Hippodrome, a woman of outstanding beauty and ability who exercised equal power with her husband. When, on the occasion of the Nika riots in 532, Justinian was on the verge of flight from the capital, it was Theodora who remarked, 'The purple is a good winding sheet', and held her ground. After her death, in 548, Justinian became increasingly obsessed with theological controversy and unable to cope with the military and economic problems which threatened the empire. He died, in 565, after a reign of great achievement against heavy odds.

[2] *Vide* C. DIEHL, *C.M.H.*, vol. II, p. 3.

persed and voluminous records of Roman Law. In 528 he appointed a commission, under his minister Trebonian, to set about this task, already in part attempted by the Theodosian Code.[1] In 529 Justinian's lawyers produced the *Codex*, in which two thousand rolls of roughly three million lines were reduced to one book a twentieth of this size, the *Digest* or *Pandects* (533), a text-book of condensed legal literature, amended and brought up to date, and the *Institutes*, a manual for students in the law schools. Through the Byzantine pomposity of the preamble of the last, its purpose is clear: 'In the name of the Lord Jesus Christ, the Emperor Caesar Flavius Justinian, conqueror of the Alemanni, the Goths, the Franks, the Germani, the Alani, the Vandals, the Africans, pious, prosperous, renowned, victorious and august, greeting to the youth desirous of studying the Law. The Imperial Majesty should be armed with laws as well as glorified with arms, that there may be good government in times both of war and of peace, and the Ruler of Rome may not only be victorious over his enemies, but show himself as scrupulously regardful of justice . . . With deepest application and forethought and by the blessing of God, we have attained both these objects. We called together the distinguished man Trebonian and the illustrious Theophilus and Dorotheus, Professors of Law, and specially commissioned them to compose, by our authority and advice, a book of Institutes of the ancient jurists. Receive then these laws with your best powers and with the eagerness of study, and show yourself so learned as to be encouraged to hope . . . that you may have ability to govern such portion of the State as may be entrusted to you. Given at Constantinople by the Emperor, Father of his Country.'

These three books together preserved in a compendious and accessible form a great deal of what was best in Roman Law and formed a basis for subsequent development.

The condensation had been made just at the right time. Though the very memory of Justinian's Code died out in the West during the Dark Ages, it continued to be accepted in the Byzantine world, and the basis of ecclesiastical Law was Roman. The prestige of Roman Law, the generations of superior force behind it, were carried on by Byzantium into the Dark Ages, and the revived study of Roman Law profoundly affected the outlook and idiom of political thinkers and

---

[1] For an exhaustive account of the sources with which Justinian's lawyers had to contend, *vide* J. B. BURY, *C.M.H.*, vol. II, chap. 3. See also H. D. HAZELTINE, 'Roman and Canon Law in the Middle Ages', *C.M.H.*, vol. V, chap. xxi.

administrators when civilization again took the initiative in the West in the eleventh and twelfth centuries. It was to be the inspiration of a legal renaissance in Lombardy, Bologna, and Provence.[1] Justinian's lawyers, indeed, only reproduced and defined; their conception of Natural Law is confused; yet they transmitted the vocabulary and principles of Roman Law to the Middle Ages and into modern times. Though the task of enforcing an all-embracing Law was beyond the strength of governments during the Dark Ages, and Roman Law survived mainly as a personal attribute, in the same way that Visogoths and Lombards carried their own Law with them, when at length effective central government re-emerged, the practical qualities and comprehensiveness of the Roman system gave it the decisive advantage over other codes, and provided a basis of study when Law ceased to be regarded as a branch of theology and became again the object of research in universities.

Looking back, then, over the long and splendid course of Roman history, it will be apparent that the empire realized and sustained over centuries a degree of civilization new to Europe, that it created the framework which held together the City State civilization of antiquity and allowed the ideas of Hellenism and Christianity to permeate the known world, leaving a tradition of European order inherited by the Catholic Church and revived in the Renaissance tradition of thought and education. It combined a conception of great-scale rule, first brought into Europe by Alexander, with a genius for military and civil organization far surpassing the Eastern bureaucratic structure on which it was modelled, and it made in a language of terse and memorable splendour a definition of Greek political ideas in a form which could be understood and remembered in the West, together with a tradition of flexible law and administrative ability new in the history of mankind.

---

[1] *Vide* VINOGRADOFF, *Roman Law in Mediaeval Europe*, edited F. de Zulueta (Oxford, 1929), for a brilliant account of the problem of the survival of Roman Law.

CHAPTER VII

CHRISTIANITY AND THE JEWISH
TRADITION

§ 1

THE world of antiquity, in the tide of its changing development, had submerged the small organic community of the City State and created a great structure of imperial power and Law which welded in a common culture two-thirds of Europe and the Near East; it had produced universalized philosophies, of which Stoicism is the most distinguished, and a literature of the highest order; it had fulfilled the promise of earlier cultures and set the stage for later European history. But the Greeks and Romans were, by modern civilized standards, callous, sensual, and ultimately pessimistic; from the Middle Ages till the nineteenth century most European thinkers have had an outlook more compassionate and more optimistic than that of representative Graeco-Roman thought.

This contrast was due to the influence of Christianity, which, together with the Hellenistic thought of antiquity, has given Western political thought a characteristic outlook. Christianity brought into the world a new pity and a new hope, if it brought also a new fear; a new promise of salvation and a new sense of sin. The 'good news' of the Gospels, once heard, flooded life with a pervading light; men's minds could not be the same after it. The effect of this change was radical, and expressed itself directly and indirectly in subsequent European thought. First in the Patristic and Catholic statement and re-statement of Christian social ideals, beginning with the Fathers and St. Augustine, and developing its full range in the great structure of thought built up in the thirteenth century by St. Thomas Aquinas, who attempted to state, in philosophical terms, the place of human society in a Divine plan, and to define political problems in terms of it. The speculation of mediaeval thinkers never departed from the Christian idiom, and it is not till Machiavelli and the Renaissance that a purely secular tradition reasserts itself, while the counter-reformation restates the Catholic theory of politics to fit the conditions of the sixteenth century.

In the second place, Christian influence is expressed directly through Protestant thought and indirectly through the tradition of humanitarianism common to nearly all European and American speculation, up till the end of the nineteenth century. Thus the most militant English and American agnostics of the last century were Christian in their ethical outlook, and reformist humanitarianism owes more than it cares to acknowledge to the tradition whose theological assumptions it cannot accept. It remained for the totalitarian movements of the twentieth century to make a frontal attack on both the Christian and humanitarian positions; the political thought of Europe until very recent times has been, consciously and unconsciously, predominantly in terms of the Christian outlook.

There are two aspects of early Christianity: the Gospel itself, which transcends the limitation of its immediate setting, and the Hellenistic-Jewish tradition in terms of which Pauline Christianity is expressed. The first, most revolutionary and original aspect is apparent in the 'glad tidings' of pity and love which run through both the Gospels and the Epistles of St. Paul. The realization of the values of the Sermon on the Mount implied a social revolution, both of the Roman Empire and of subsequent societies, at a cost practical men have always shuddered to contemplate. It has never yet been made on a large scale, but the effect of the teaching on the political theory has been indefinite, indirect, and profound. Respect for personality and the treatment of individuals as ends, not as means, were greatly reinforced by it, and no later vision has ever superseded this central aspect of the Christian revelation; it remains, as it has always remained, the ultimate challenge.

A reading of the Sermon on the Mount and the Parables must bring home to anyone the sublimity of the teaching of Jesus, whether or not he be regarded as the Incarnate God. The impression given in the Gospels is of a personality of overwhelming power, beyond the grasp of the men who recorded it. Their very limitations make the story the more convincing. There is the imprint of a formidable magnetism. The personality depicted is strenuous and fierce as well as profoundly compassionate; the narrative sweeps forward to its climax, the record of a shattering career, packed into a short lifetime, for the Founder of Christianity died at thirty.

This revolutionary morality, preached by an itinerant prophet in the sun-bitten East, has an Eastern disregard for compromise, an Eastern intensity of spiritual power. The original Gospel 'takes no thought for the morrow'; it declares that 'he that loseth his life shall find it'. 'An astounding reality that crashed into the shadowy life of every day and brought with it the sound of many waters, with the blaze of sun and rainbow, with the voice of creation and the rapture of new love . . . "Behold, I make all things new".'[1] Plainly, we are here in touch with a level of consciousness beyond that of ordinary humanity.

The Greek thought had aimed at a balanced σωφροσύνη of body and mind, a harmonious moral rightness. The Greek 'good life' was an aristocratic, aesthetic ideal; Aristotle takes it for granted that there are 'natural slaves', though Stoic teaching is less exclusive. The 'good life' is also highly intellectualized; virtue is a kind of knowledge. The Gospel, on the other hand, implies a complete awareness of the whole man, its 'charity' the bounty of a happy adjustment to life, not the reasoned humanitarianism of the 'good man'. Further, the idea of human equality expressed in the Gospels reinforces with a new and intense emotional drive the pagan Stoic ideals of Natural Law and self-sufficiency, and irradiates them in the new light of the living fatherhood of God. Where the pagan virtues had tended to be negative and pessimistic, the Christian outlook, as expressed in the Gospels and many passages of St. Paul, is one of dynamic vigour and joy.[2] The conviction that the Kingdom of Heaven is within you — something at once immediately present, yet beyond time — that the individual is sustained by an all-pervading Providence, whether it be explained in terms of a subconscious release of energy or of transcendental revelation, is the fact with which history has had to deal.

The political aspect of this religion was naturally revolutionary; to 'render unto Caesar the things that are Caesar's, and unto God the things that are God's' does not sound, on the face of it, a socially subversive attitude; it is in making the distinction at all that the political sting of the remark lies.

Platonic and Aristotelian political theory assumed that the City State ought to and could give scope for the realization of the full range of values of the 'good life'. To separate the religious and social spheres is to strike at the roots of this position, and to strike far more

---

[1] GERALD HEARD, The Social Substance of Religion, p. 207. Allen & Unwin (1931).
[2] Of all the artistic representations of this spirit, none surpasses the central figure over the west door at Chartres. The sculptor in the spring of the twelfth-century northern French Renaissance has exactly caught the eager alertness, the lightning ability of the Jesus of the Gospels, a very different personality from the Divine Pantokrator of Byzantine art, though not from the beardless Hellenistic Christ.

positively than the Hellenistic philosophies and mystery religions had done. Again, the Stoic self-sufficient individual could conform to the emperor-worship of his day; the values for which he stood were not militant and expansive, but aimed rather at self-preservation and a saving of dignity. For the Christian, on the other hand, if the claims of 'the world' encroached upon those of God, there could only be one loyalty. In spite of a theoretical respect for existing rulers as ordained by Providence, or even 'sent to try us', there could be only one answer to the demand to worship Caesar. Hence in part the distrust and hatred the early Christians aroused in the minds of otherwise comparatively humane men. Hence also the persecutions, which, looked at in this light, are intelligible. Since, for the Christian, the perfect pattern of behaviour had been revealed for all time in the person of the Incarnate God, all life must be viewed in relation to it. Nothing is significant except in terms of this faith that could 'remove mountains', of which the dynamic quality has constantly emerged through the stifling structure of organized religion; for the conflict with the 'world' has worked out within the Church as often as outside it.[1]

The teaching of Jesus thus links up with and transcends the Hellenistic philosophies. It takes ultimate values out of the political arena altogether and sets them in a timeless eternity; it pulls the individual out of the organic community of the City or Temple State and sets him in relation to a world order beyond them. It undermines the whole structure of the more primitive, less individualized community and the psychological solidarity which had kept earlier societies strong and stable, if insensitive. Further, and notably in the writings of St. Paul, the distinction is asserted between the elect and the 'secular' authority. The original unity of the social structure is broken, and the religious sense, which was the binding force of the Temple State and the Sacred City, is canalized into a community which can only come to terms with government either by simply passing it by politely, or else by converting and subordinating it to a Christian purpose.

Government, indeed, was regarded by the early Christians as a transitory thing: they lived in the expectation of an imminent Apocalypse. St. Paul believed that 'the present order of things is

[1] This conflict is nowhere better illustrated than in DOSTOIEVSKI's *Brothers Karamazov*. The Christ returns on the eve of an *auto da fé* in Seville. The Grand Inquisitor recognizes Him – and condemns Him to the flames. See *The Brothers Karamazov*, translated C. GARNETT. Heinemann (1912), pp. 259-77.

passing away', and refers to the brethren 'whose lot has been cast in the closing hours of the world'.[1] This conviction shelves the problem of the Christian attitude to authority, but, as the expectation died and the power and scale of Christian organization grew, this solution was not enough. In Augustine's *De Civitate Dei*,[2] the most comprehensive statement of Christian political thought of the fifth century, the same secular power, though not yet subordinated to a theocracy (it remained for the mediaeval papacy and the Calvinists to make that claim), is regarded as fulfilling its mission only in co-operating with the Church to promote the Christian life and its power as justified only if it does so.

Moreover a ruthless disregard of the practical, of the politically expedient, is apparent in the Gospels.

It is likely that the environment of the disciples made this natural; Professor Whitehead writes: 'The Galilean peasantry, having regard to their climate and simplicity of life, were neither rich nor poor; they were unusually intellectual for a peasantry, by reason of their habits of study of historical records; they were protected from disturbance from within and from without by the guardian structure of the Roman empire . . . Their own society was of the simplest . . . they were ignorant even of the services that the empire was rendering them. The alternation of Procurators was like that of the seasons, some were better and some were worse; but all alike, seasons and Procurators of Judaea, issued from an inscrutable order of things. The tone of life of this peasantry provided an ideal environment in which concepts of ideal relations between rational beings could be formulated — concepts devoid of ferocity, concepts kindly and shrewd . . . a gracious mode of life, combined with a fortunate ignorance, endowed mankind with its most precious instrument of progress, the impracticable ethics of Christianity.'[3]

This attitude made understanding between primitive Christianity and the secular state impossible if the spirit of the original message was preserved. As the apocalyptic element weakened, political accommodation became easier, but the early Christian ethic was incompatible with the local loyalties of the City State or with the power politics, and indeed with the organization, of Rome.

[1] 1 Cor. x, 12.
[2] *Vide infra*, Bk. I, chap. viii.
[3] A. N. WHITEHEAD, *Adventures of Ideas*, Cambridge (1933), pp. 19-20.

Such, then, is the nature and political implication of the original teaching, the first and most important aspect of Christianity. It is with St. Paul that the second aspect, the specifically Jewish influence, for good and ill, becomes forcefully articulate. Where the Gospel is concerned with a way of living, in the light of a mystical experience of eternal life, with an expansion of consciousness, St. Paul, though apprehending the Gospel teaching and inspired by it, runs true to the type of Semitic religious genius, both prophetic and priestly.

In a famous passage from the *Seven Pillars of Wisdom*, T. E. Lawrence has well described this uncompromising Semitic outlook: 'Semites had no half tones in their register of vision. They were a people of primary colours, or rather of black and white, who saw the world always in contrast . . . their thoughts were at ease only in extremes. They inhabited superlatives by choice . . . their convictions were by instinct, their activities intuitional. Their largest manufacture was of creeds; almost they were monopolists of revealed religions. Three of these efforts had endured among them, two of the three had also borne export (in modified form) to non-Semitic peoples. Christianity, translated into the diverse spirits of Greek and Latin and Teutonic tongues, had conquered Europe and America. Islam, in various transformations, was subjecting Africa and part of Asia. These were Semitic successes. Their failures they kept to themselves. The fringes of the desert were strewn with broken faiths. *The common base of all the Semitic creeds*, winners or losers, *was the ever-present idea of world worthlessness* . . . The Semite hovered between lust and self-denial. They were incorrigibly children of the idea, feckless and colour blind, *to whom body and spirit were for ever and inevitably opposed.*'[1]

This sense of 'world worthlessness', of conflict between body and spirit, is at the root of the Pauline interpretation of Christianity; it was later to be emphasized and elaborated by St. Augustine. Further, the Platonic contrast between the ideal and actual, which runs through Hellenistic thought, reinforced the native dualism of St. Paul's outlook. St. Paul, indeed, broke away from the Jewish Law, believing the way out could not come by that means. But his point of view remains typically Jewish in his blinding vision of God's

---

[1] T. E. LAWRENCE, *Seven Pillars of Wisdom*, Cape (1937), pp. 40-2. The italics are the present writer's.

omnipotence, of the abject condition of man, the overwhelming sense of sin, the passion for 'salvation'.[1]

In face of this annihilating 'fear of the Lord', there is only one answer. Not 'works', the observance of the Law, but redemption by faith. St. Paul found the salvation he had sought from the Jewish Law in Christ, by whose sacrifice the elect are saved. He emphasizes the sacramental element in Christianity, which is paralleled, on a lower plane, in the theology of the Hellenistic mystery cults, with their communion and salvation by vicarious sacrifice.[2] Further, in addition to the Jewish sense of world worthlessness and sin, the idea of a chosen people had come to dominate the Jewish mind since the Captivity. This idea is specifically transferred from the Jews to the Christians by St. Paul, together with the conception of divine purpose and ultimate judgement which runs through the prophetic books of the Old Testament.

St. Paul apprehended the essential 'charity' of the Gospels; but he was also a convert, bred and disciplined in the Law, at once a religious genius and an organizer in the Rabbinic tradition. It will be well to deal with these two aspects of his mind separately.

In the great Epistles, Romans and Corinthians, where the first aspect is apparent, he works out the thought which was to dominate the Christian Church, applying the idea of a chosen people of the elect to all Christians, Gentile as well as Jew. Salvation, as we have seen, is by faith, not by the Law. The Gospel 'is God's Saving Power for everyone who has faith, for the Jew first and for the Greek as well. As it is written, "by faith shall the righteous live".'[3] There are, St. Paul insists, two kinds of men. God at the Judgement will render 'to everyone according to what he has done, eternal life to those who, by patiently doing good, aim at glory, heaven and immortality, but anger and wrath to those who are wilful . . . anguish and calamity . . . for the Jew first and for the Greek as well, but glory, honour and peace to everyone who does good, for the Jew first and for the Greek as well. There is no partiality about God.'[4] All have sinned, he

---

[1] It should be remembered that the salvationist element in Christianity is very primitive and cannot be attributed solely to St. Paul. It is probable that he was only one of many missionaries, the record of whose activities has been lost. See Dr. A. M. HUNTER, *Paul and his Predecessors*, Nicholson & Watson (1940).

[2] *Vide supra*, Bk. I, chap. v.

[3] Romans i, 16-17. I have throughout used Moffat's translation of the New Testament, sacrificing the beauty of the language of the Authorized Version for clarity of meaning.

[4] Romans ii, 6-11.

reiterates, but '*we are justified by faith* . . . Let us enjoy the peace we have with God *through* our Lord Jesus Christ. Through him we have got access to this grace, when we have our standing and triumph in the hope of God's glory . . . Not only so, but we triumph even in our troubles . . . But God proves his love for us by this; Christ died for us when we were still sinners. Much more, then, now that we are justified by his blood, shall we be saved by him from wrath'.[1]

The obsession of 'world worthlessness', of sin, of the conflict of body and spirit, is constantly reiterated. 'I do not act as I desire to act; on the contrary, I do what I detest; miserable wretch that I am, who shall rescue me from this body of death? God will; thanks be to Him through Jesus Christ our Lord.'[2] The interests of the flesh, he insists, mean death; the interests of the spirit, life and peace. Having stated this fundamental conflict, St. Paul goes on to distinguish between those who are 'called' and the rest of the world. 'For he decreed of old that those whom he predestined should share the likeness of his Son, that he might be the first-born of a great brotherhood.'[3] This is the compensation for the persecution, the obscurity, the bitterness the faithful minority must face; the words proclaim a fighting creed. 'If God is for us, who shall be against us? Who is to condemn the elect of God? . . . Who can ever part us from Christ's love? Can anguish or calamity, or persecution, or famine, or nakedness, or danger, or the sword?'[4]

The later success of Christianity obscures the conditions of its early beginnings; the early Christians were bitterly despised; they were even thought drunk or mad. After the Pentecostal visitation it was said, 'These men are brimful of new wine'.[5] The high priests were 'astonished to discover how outspoken Peter and John were, and to discover that they were uncultured persons and mere outsiders'.[6] On their side the Christians were uncompromising: 'You killed the Pioneer of Life . . . The God of our Fathers raised Jesus whom you had murdered by hanging him on a gibbet . . . As with your fathers, so with you! Which of the prophets did your fathers fail to persecute?'[7] Paul himself bewildered the Roman authorities; Felix and Festus were interested, but nonplussed. 'The questions at issue referred to their own religion and to a certain Jesus who had died; Paul said he was alive.'[8] Festus told Paul, 'Much learning hath made thee mad'. The high priests, astutely, took the line with the Romans

---

[1] Romans, v, 1-11.   [2] ib., vii, 15, 24.   [3] ib., viii, 29.   [4] ib., viii, 32, 35.
[5] Acts ii, 13.   [6] ib., iv, 13.   [7] ib., iii, 14; v, 30; vii, 52.   [8] ib., xxv, 19.

that Paul's influence was subversive of order. 'The fact is that we have found this man a perfect pest.'[1] Scorn, incomprehension, ridicule, torture — Pauline Christianity had to face it all. Naturally they hated the world; they cut themselves passionately apart.

For Israel itself had failed: 'By this lapse salvation has passed to the Gentiles . . . I tell you this, you Gentiles, that I lay great stress on my office, in the hope somehow of making my fellow Jews jealous and managing thus to save some of them.'[2] St. Paul proceeds to the famous simile of the wild olive: 'You have been grafted on, *like a shoot of wild olive*, to share the rich growth of the olive's stem . . . Remember in your pride that the stem supports you, not you the stem . . . It is only a partial insensibility which has come over Israel.'[3]

This outlook was reinforced by an attack on pre-Christian values:

'It is written,
I will destroy the wisdom of the sages,
I will confound the insight of the wise.
Sage, scribe, critic of this world, where are they all?'[4]

The world, says St. Paul, as Job had said before him, is given over to evil; it is only by a conviction of the blinding omnipotence of God, and by Faith in Christ, that sanity and hope can be retained. 'No one understands the thoughts of God.'[5] The point of view is typical of the East.

In face of this tremendous fact, the elect must separate themselves from the wicked and maintain a morality different from the world's. 'I maul and master my body, lest, after preaching to other people, I am disqualified myself.'[6] The community of Christians combine in the consciousness of salvation, sustained by the operation of the Holy Spirit. 'Now you are Christ's Body, and severally members of it . . . Yet I will go on to show you a still higher path',[7] and there follows the superb passage in praise of Charity, a triumphant definition of Faith, of which the Resurrection is the proof. 'If there is no such thing as a Resurrection from the dead . . . and if Christ did not rise, then our preaching has gone for nothing, and your faith has gone for nothing too . . . Ah, if in this life we have nothing but a mere hope in Christ, we are of all men to be pitied most. But it is not so! Christ did rise from the dead and he is the first to be reaped of those who sleep in death.

---

[1] Acts, xxiv, 5.   [2] Romans xi, 13-14.   [3] ib., xi, 17-18, 25.
[4] 1 Corinthians i, 19-20.   [5] ib., ii, 11.   [6] ib., ix, 27.   [7] ib., xii, 27, 31.

> For since by man came death,
> By man came also the resurrection of the dead.
> For as in Adam all die,
> Even so in Christ shall all be made alive.'[1]

For the elect, such an outlook makes other values insignificant. Sustained by this conviction, the blessed minority, by its 'spiritual glow', can 'overcome evil with good'. Meanwhile, respect should be paid to constituted government; the existing authorities have been constituted by God; the magistrate is God's servant. 'Pay them all their respective dues; tribute to this one, taxes to another, respect to this man, honour to that.'[2] The attitude has much in common with Stoicism, though the Christian had a joyful secret where the Stoic had a sad one.

Political questions and all life are also viewed in the light of the imminent Second Coming. Christians should sit loosely to the ties of the present life. 'Let those who mix in the world live as if they were not engrossed in it, for the present phase of things is passing away.'[3] This side of the Pauline teaching reflects the Gospel in its attitude to political problems. In so far as it takes account of them, men's politics are to be changed by a change of heart. No one inspired by the morality of the Sermon on the Mount and the mystical experience behind it, or by the 'Charity' of the Epistles, could be anything but critical of the worldly compromises and deceptions by which government is carried on. And no one, having St. Paul's burning sense of election and apocalyptic conviction, can be deeply concerned with secular affairs. So long as the Christians, following the Gospel, showed the 'world' by example they possessed a secret it did not know, so long the challenge remained unanswerable. But Pauline Christianity, following its Jewish side—the second, Rabbinic, organizing aspect of St. Paul — might easily seek to subdue the world with its own weapons and establish a theocratic and imposed power. With the success of the movement and the waning of apocalyptic hope, theocratic ideas inevitably crept in. The transition from the original tiny group to an organized movement on a great scale is already apparent in the mind of St. Paul, who, besides being a mystic, is an able organizer, well capable of wielding power. Thus St. Paul countenances two attitudes to government: one brushes it aside as a

---

[1] I Cor. xv, 13-22 (20-2 from Authorized Version).   [2] Romans xiii, 1-4, 7.
[3] I Corinthians vii, 31.

passing phenomenon of this world; the other sanctions the God-given power of priest and magistrate. And though St. Paul wrote the Epistles in the heat of immediate business, he was legislating for generations unborn. His precepts were to echo and re-echo down the European centuries.

Thus Christianity developed its twofold attack: on the one hand the dynamic 'charity' of the Founder—a source of perennial power; on the other, and closely bound up with it, the Pauline outlook, scriptural and Rabbinic, with a pattern of purpose and redemption, a passionate sense of sin and ultimate judgement, and a trend, as the apocalyptic hope faded, towards conservatism and theocracy.

This salvationist emphasis on redemption was the way of thought predominant both in the Jewish and in much of the Hellenistic world. St. Paul was a Jew, though a Hellenized Jew, and the demonology which colours the epistles derives from the later Rabbinic tradition. 'The first impression produced by a perusal of his letters is clear and strong, namely, that it is the Jewish element which predominates and that very greatly; that the Hellenistic element, so far as it is present at all, is not central but superficial. Those who come to his letters with a fair acquaintance with the Old Testament have no sense of passing from one intellectual atmosphere to another. The idiom of his thought is Hebrew.'[1] Far from his citizenship of Tarsus diluting this Hebraism, it probably increased it. 'An Hebrew of the Hebrews', he was passionately monotheistic, convinced of the blinding omnipotence of God, of the abject state of men. His mind centres on 'salvation'—what all the competing religions offered.

The evidence does not support the widely accepted theory that St. Paul gave Christianity its sacramental character, nor was he so much influenced by Hellenistic mystery cults as virtually to have created a new religion to that found in the Gospels. But St. Paul's references to 'the prince of this world' and to 'principalities and powers' are concerned with the belief in evil spirits and devils, assimilated to Jewish thought during the Babylonian exile, and with the astrological influences which were thought to affect human life. It was from 'bondage' to these 'Powers' that Christ was said to have delivered men. Through the act of dying, Christ 'divested himself of the flesh' and so escaped from the medium whereby they could get at him. Further for St. Paul it was axiomatic that all men are

---

[1] C. ANDERSON SCOTT. *Christianity According to St. Paul,* Cambridge University Press (1927), p. 3. See also EDWYN BEVAN, *The Hellenistic Age.*

'under sin' through the transgression of Adam, who, as founder and head of the human race, by that transgression entailed sin and death on his descendants; it was from the dominion of sin and death that Christ redeemed His followers.

So St. Paul focuses two traditions: the Caritic tradition of the Gospel, and Judaism, touched with Hellenistic influence. Such a synthesis was the natural medium for the spread of the original teaching, which includes and transcends it. St. Paul, indeed, translates the Gospel into the idiom of his time. Perhaps, without such a translation, inspired by the Founder's teaching of pity and love, the original Gospel might never have come through. St. Paul's was an appropriate mind to interpret the teaching to his contemporaries, his way of thought intelligible both to Gentile and Jew.

Within this interpretation, with all its profound political repercussions, carried outside the Jewish pale to the Gentile world, three revolutionary principles emerge. First a dynamic Charity; second the conviction of brotherhood and salvation in Christ; third Hebraic dualism. To be sure of the loving Fatherhood of God, to feel the certainty of salvation, to have all things in common, to return evil with good, the outlook was to alter the atmosphere and purpose of government, save the classical tradition from the bankruptcy to which the governing classes of antiquity were to bring it, and, having tamed the barbarian invaders, to inspire much of what was best in the civilization of mediaeval Europe.

But, along with this 'salt of the earth', this redeeming Charity, which appears again and again in the history of religion, in the great missionaries and mystics, went also a rigid, ferocious, and Judaized cosmology. As the apocalyptic hope faded, the third element in the Pauline scheme was emphasized; the Jewish Old Testament tradition, with its terror of Hell and the Judgement, its sense of 'world worthlessness', increasingly dominated Christian ideas.

The first of these three elements have already been examined; it will be well to glance briefly at the nature of the last, the specifically Jewish outlook, prophetic and priestly, spiritual and political, for this influence was destined deeply to affect European political thought. Christianity came to Europe in terms of the Jewish sacred books; and the history of this Eastern people was to be far more familiar, for many generations, to the majority of Europeans than the history of their own forebears, the Old Testament as much as the

New, colouring their individual and political outlook. It is necessary, therefore, to examine the spiritual and secular teaching of pre-Christian Jewish writings.

§ III

It will at once be found that the prophets and the book of Job anticipate in varying degrees the teaching of the Gospel itself. The teaching of Jesus, in particular, is indeed the culmination and transfiguration of Old Testament prophecy. The priestly tradition, on the other hand, is limited, ascetic, and exclusive; it was not for nothing that the Jews rejected and crucified the Founder of Christianity and 'stoned the prophets which were before' Him. The uncompromising moral sense and monotheism of the prophets had lifted the Jewish mind out of the ordinary run of fertility cult and image worship, and the religious genius of Isaiah anticipates the power of the Pauline Epistles. But the prophetic outlook was both fierce and denunciatory; they were in constant conflict with the secular authority, anticipating the Patristic and mediaeval clash between spiritual and lay power. Moreover, the price of Jewish moral sense and monotheism had been the loss of the solid unity of the Temple State, an ascetic denunciation of ordinary 'religion', the binding force of the traditional Near Eastern and Levantine community. 'Bring no more oblations,' writes Isaiah, 'Incense is an abomination unto me; the new moons and Sabbaths, the calling of assemblies I cannot away with. It is iniquity, even the solemn meeting.'[1]

The new phase of self-conscious asceticism is in full conflict with the older, less individualized, community religion, and all is dwarfed by an overriding sense that the community is lost in sin, that its misfortunes are the judgement of God, a God who may yet have mercy if the people repent: 'Though your sins be as scarlet, they shall be as wool.'[2]

On the moral plane, the success of the astute and worldly was a constant outrage to the moral sense of the prophets; this new conscience breaks through the natural conservatism of an Oriental society. 'Wherefore', asks Jeremiah, 'doth the way of the wicked

[1] See Isaiah. i, 13.   [2] ib., i, 18.

prosper? Wherefore are they happy that deal very treacherously?'[1] The balance must and shall be redressed. This pattern of thought is constantly apparent in the minds of Jewish writers, and finds its nineteenth-century expression in Marx, who invokes a similar inevitable justice, while repudiating the theological sanction. 'He, shall come', writes Hosea, 'as an eagle against the House of the Lord because they have transgressed my covenant and trespassed against my Lord . . . for they have sown the wind and they shall reap the whirlwind.'[2]

The ordinary injustices of life and the ordinary compensations are intolerable to Isaiah; only a revolution in the whole conduct of the world is enough. 'And there shall come forth a rod out of the stem of Jesse, and a branch shall grow out of his roots, and the Spirit of the Lord shall rest upon him, the spirit of wisdom and understanding, the spirit of counsel and might, the spirit of knowledge and the fear of the Lord . . . the wolf also shall dwell with the lamb, and the leopard shall lie down with the kid, and the calf and the young lion and the fatling together and a little child shall lead them.'[3]

Here is a challenge to the problem of evil, anticipating the Gospel.

Further, running through the prophetic books, is the conviction of redemption. It is thoroughly Pauline, a vision of a new heaven and a new earth, and of the punishment, too, of the rich and worldly. 'For thus saith the Lord God; Behold I, even I, will both search my sheep and seek them out . . . I will deliver them out of all places where they have been scattered in the cloudy and dark day . . . I will seek out that which was lost and bring again that which was driven away . . . but I will destroy the fat and strong, I will feed them with judgement.'[4]

The revenge of the Lord is merciless, for the wicked are past redemption. 'Can the Ethiopian change his skin or the leopard his spots? Then may ye also do good who are accustomed to evil. Therefore I will scatter them as the stubble that passeth away by the wind of the wilderness.'[5]

There are here two ideas springing from the Semitic conviction of world worthlessness. On the one hand, the demand for righteousness, for a moral standard beyond 'worldly' values, for a God to whom justice is a burning concern, developing in Isaiah into a

---

[1] Jeremiah xii, 1. [2] Hosea viii, 1-7. [3] Isaiah xi, 1-6.
[4] Ezekiel xxxiv, 11-12, 16. [5] Jeremiah xiii, 23-4.

vision of a transfigured world. On the other hand, there is a real hatred for the normal run of life, the desire for savage and pitiless revenge. Both these aspects of Jewish religion passed over into Patristic and mediaeval Christianity.

Finally, overriding all, is the Eastern sense of the utter omnipotence of Fate and God, monotheistic, world wide. The book of Job is the most remarkable expression of this outlook; it combines the traditional wisdom of the East, as expressed in Proverbs and Ecclesiasticus, with a deeper religious insight. The Oriental acceptance of Fate, with its dignity and limitation, develops into an assertion that human categories of thought are incapable of apprehending the ways of God. To some degree the book anticipates the outlook of Spinoza, another Jew of genius. Job, confronted with material disaster, bows to God's inscrutable will. 'The Lord', he says, 'hath given and the Lord hath taken away; blessed be the name of the Lord . . . What? shall we receive good at the hand of God, and shall we not receive evil?'[1] For His ways are inscrutable, often apparently unjust. 'He destroyeth the perfect and the wicked . . . He will laugh at the trial of the innocent . . . He is not a man as I am that I should answer Him . . . Thine hands have made me, yet thou dost destroy me . . . Who can understand the thoughts of God?'[2]

It is impossible to contend with a force beyond human control and human values; Job asks only for death, though he still maintains his personal integrity, convinced that his own conduct has never deserved the evils that have fallen upon him. But Job's humiliation is still incomplete; the pride which still sustained him is blasted by a final assertion of Divine omnipotence. 'Then the Lord answered Job out of the whirlwind, and said, "Who is this that darkeneth counsel by words without knowledge? . . . Where wast thou when I laid the foundations of the earth? . . . Gavest thou the goodly wings unto the peacocks? . . . Canst thou draw out leviathan with an hook?" '[3]

Finally, like St. Paul, Job makes the final, inevitable, submission: 'I am vile . . . things are too wonderful for me . . . I repent in dust and ashes.'[4]

The Oriental abjection of man before omnipotent power is nowhere better expressed, though the book ends with the rehabilitation of Job into prosperity. The outlook is typically Pauline, but without

---

[1] Job i, 21; ii, 10.
[2] ib., ix, 22-3, 32; x, 8.
[3] ib., xxxviii, 2, 4; xxxix, 13; xli, 1.
[4] ib., xlii, 3, 6.

the New Testament Caritas. There is a strenuous insight into the realities of life, into the mystery and power beyond the universe. A people that could produce such a book in that age was indeed a portent to be reckoned with.

Such, then, is the prophetic contribution to the Jewish tradition. Turning now to the priestly and Rabbinic side of Judaism, we shall find that its influence, and particularly its political influence, was often pernicious.

The sense of the omnipotence of an all-pervading God, apparent in the prophetic books, had developed out of a savage and limited conception of the Yahweh of the earlier Old Testament, and the Jewish priesthood never got beyond the tribal outlook. They were obsessed with a material vindication of Israel; incapable of viewing political problems objectively, but only in the light of impending judgement and retributive vengeance, of the exact fulfilment of covenanted promises. A fanatical nationalism had been increased by the precariousness and poverty of their geographical position and the political catastrophes which were its consequence; it is significant that the period during and after the captivity saw the definition of their outlook.

Carried off to Babylon in 586 B.C., the Jewish priesthood had been allowed by the Persian Cyrus to re-establish itself after 538. This post-exilic regime was still dependent on the Persians; it was a fierce and narrow theocracy with little political sense. 'None of the grave and serious obligations of a commonwealth standing on its own basis hampered the priests of the Temple of Jerusalem in setting up the Kingdom of Jahweh on earth.'[1] They were more intolerant, more priest-ridden, and more backward than the Jewish communities of the rest of the Near East. This regime formed the centre of a cult of the Mosaic Law which held together the great extra-Palestinian communities with unbreakable tenacity. The Pentateuch was compiled during the Persian age, from the sixth century B.C. The Creation story, borrowed in part from Babylonian sources, is indeed world-embracing, but after the Flood and the appearance of the Patriarchs, the vision of God becomes exclusive. The Jews are depicted as a priestly people, the Chosen of God, destined to rule over a subservient Gentile world. It is exactly the compensatory pattern of ideas which might be expected.[2] The conception of an

[1] MOMMSEN, *Roman Provinces*, vol. II, chap. xi, p. 161.
[2] The Books of Nehemiah and Ezra are particularly illuminating for this period.

elect people, and of theocracy as a right form of government, was deeply to influence Christian thought, while the uncompromising Jewish claims brought disaster upon themselves. An odium, too, which the early Christians inherited and which encouraged their hatred of the 'world'.

The importance and wealth of the scattered Jews of the Near East made the fanaticism of Jerusalem intolerable to Rome. They swarmed in Alexandria, in Mesopotamia, and Asia Minor; government could not ignore this influence, extending from Palestine over the vastly greater population of the Diaspora, and the period of the Gospels and early Christianity coincided with a gradual climax of the enmity between Jerusalem and the empire. A wave of anti-Semitism was sweeping over the East; with the sack of the Temple by Titus in A.D. 70 the temporal power of the Jewish theocracy was blotted out.

The effect on the early Christians, still largely an Hebraic sect, was twofold. On the one hand, many were infected with an abiding hatred of secular power. The Book of Revelation expresses this loathing of Rome. 'The Apocalypse furnishes us with clear evidence that as a matter of fact the Jewish hatred of the Roman government was at one time and in some circles common among Christian men . . . It is at least obvious that we have in it an expression of the most intense hatred of the Roman oppressor.'[1] On the other hand, the collapse of the power of orthodox Jewry allowed the Christians more easily to break free. The earthly Jerusalem had been destroyed; the ideal could be the better projected into heaven. Meanwhile the Jewish remnant, withdrawn into itself, created the tradition which was to sustain their race through the centuries of persecution before them. For, besides the older priestly tradition, they had developed the formidable and detailed elaboration of the Law, the cult of the sacred books. A new tradition grew up, centring on the formalism Jesus attacked and St. Paul found inadequate for salvation. The Law runs parallel in the Old Testament with the spiritual intuitions of the Prophets.

So the third element in Christianity, the Jewish influence, prophetic and priestly, brought a new outlook into Western political thought; directly, through the mind of St. Paul; indirectly, through Christian study of the Jewish Old Testament. The Oriental intensity

[1] CARLYLE, *History of Mediaeval Political Theory in the West*, Blackwood (1893), vol. I, p. 93.

of vision; the scorn and incapacity for balanced living; the passion for justice; the elaborate, repetitive poetry, full of fire, but heavy with the emphasis of an ingrained materialism, all profoundly coloured the outlook of mediaeval and modern Europe.

So the effect of Christian teaching was to be threefold. First, through the challenge of a new way of life, of a new expansion of consciousness, expressed in the Gospels; second, through Pauline Salvationism; third, through the old Jewish outlook, with its intense moral purpose, its tendency to exclusiveness and theocracy, transferred to the community of the elect. Politically this influence led to a profound change; the spiritual centre of gravity was removed out of the traditional civic setting and away from the formal religion of the empire. There grew up a state within a state, an underground organization, which, like the Mithraic cult, filled the spiritual emptiness left by the inadequacy of the traditional 'pietas' for any but an aristocratic minority. Further, a new element of purpose is brought into political thought by Christianity. The outlook of antiquity was static, and society was not conceived of as driving towards a goal, life being regarded as its own justification. In contrast, the Christian outlook, as expressed in the Gospels, is restless and dynamic; it regards men as capable of moral progress. All things are possible; men's hearts can be changed, their awareness expanded into an apprehension of eternal life. The faith in a future and better life, that 'we see now in a glass darkly, but then face to face', was revolutionary. Subsequent belief in progress and free will, vital and original elements in Western civilization, derive directly from the implications of Christ's teaching. The impulse to 'give men their heads', to 'believe in' them, since personality is not intrinsically evil, derives in part from Greek thought and in part from the 'Charity' of the Gospel; it is fundamental to later political theory.

At the same time, the Jewish side of Christianity also broke up the static outlook of pagan antiquity, though it substituted a narrower and more rigid world view, devoid of the progressive qualities of the Caritic teaching. Pauline Christianity took over from Jewish thought the conviction that God was working His purpose out in Time. The Jewish mind, with its fatalistic worship of power, had long forecast the future as a divine plan working out to its inevitable end, the redemption of Israel. And indeed a materialistic determinism runs through Jewish thought. It makes a formidable fighting creed, justifying the pent-up hatred of the exiled, the outcast, and the poor; obstinate in adversity, ruthless in success. Hostility and persecution could be met with the Charity of the original teaching, but the Jewish elements in the Pauline interpretation could lend themselves to a more obviously militant answer in the traditional terms — to a retrogressive direct attack by the elect of the world. Such an outlook is constantly apparent in the writings of the Fathers, and it provoked, as much as it answered, the persecutions. As will be seen, the attitude of Tertullian to the culture of antiquity was to be bitterly hostile, and the triumph of Christianity must have seemed a deplorable and improbable contingency to most contemporary opinion.

The tolerance and the curiosity of the Graeco-Roman ruling classes prevented this originally obscure movement being crushed in its beginnings. The sophistication which enabled Pilate to ask 'What is truth?' was impossible to the Jewish bystanders; among the Gentiles alone could Christianity gain a wide hearing. And indeed this tolerance and humanitarianism of the Hellenistic world was not incompatible with the Charity of the Gospels, though perhaps a less spectacular thing compared with it; nor was the Greek ideal of a balanced development of the facets of personality, or the Roman ideal of a stolid duty, common sense, fairness, and self-disciplined honour, unworthy of comparison.

But 'to love thy neighbour as thyself', without distinction of class or creed, was a strange precept in the slave-owning, militarist, oligarchic world of antiquity; it was a new and softening influence in human affairs. Where the best thought of the Graeco-Roman philosophers was austere and negative, this mass movement, which must have appeared disconcerting and hysterical, possessed immense force. The breakdown of the social order in the later empire was its opportunity, and in three centuries it had so permeated the mind of antiquity that the atmosphere and purpose of government was changed; Western civilization was given a new outlook, more enterprising and more humane, more intense, and more intolerant.

And the movement grew and engulfed all kinds of men, so that the original Caritas was diluted by the influence of executive types, burdened with the cares of office, and by eager partisans, ready to persecute. These men gloried in the Old Testament vision of life as a dramatic working out of the fierce judgement of an omnipotent

God, and in the division of mankind into the elect, saved by the Divine Sacrifice, and the reprobate world. But, along with this new intolerance and transcending it, the teaching of Jesus of Nazareth, with its message of love and hope, its bounty of spiritual power, its conviction of new life, was to sweep over Europe and the world.

CHAPTER VIII

THE TRIUMPH OF CHRISTIANITY: ST. AUGUSTINE

§ I

THE triumph of Christianity was brought about not only by the power of the Christian Gospel but by the social situation which developed in the late empire. The limitations of Graeco-Roman society have already been suggested; the second and third centuries saw attempts at reconstruction, but the fundamental defects remained. Political and economic collapse was reflected in deteriorating morale, and men turned the more eagerly to the religions which had long been creeping into the empire out of the East.

Mithraism and Christianity were the most widespread cults, the latter sustained by an increasingly self-sufficient economic organization and by an appeal transcending class barriers. The fourth century saw the Church's temporal triumph and the full definition of doctrine, the result of a cumulative and uncompromising drive. With the economic decline, the discontented masses were ripe to stampede into new religious movements; it was fortunate for the future that the dominant movement was Christian.

The breakdown of the civilization of antiquity, the biggest cultural disaster the world has so far seen, led to a predominance of emotional motives and a degradation of intellectual standards. The loss of grip among the educated minority and the transference of power to military adventurers, often of barbarian origin, is reflected in a coarseness of artistic production and an atmosphere of mass emotion; already, by the time of Constantine, credulity and fear are the note of this decadent world.

In such a setting the Christian Church alone had the vitality and the organization to take over a bankrupt society; with Constantine, Christianity becomes an established religion of the empire. Naturally the interpretation put upon it by contemporaries was after their own lights; apart from the intellectual contribution of the Fathers, Christian standards shared, though to a less degree, the degradation of the age. The vulgar apprehension of the original Gospel was elementary by the fourth century.

The emperor had always been Pontifex Maximus, the focus of the imperial cult; with the conversion he merely assumed a fresh spiritual power. But the kind of religion with which the empire had been bound up was profoundly social, rooted in pagan observance of appropriate ritual, linked closely to 'worldly' interests by traditional rites. With the establishment of Christianity, the imperial government was committed to an Eastern religion with its values set outside the present life and with an attitude to government which was ultimately hostile. After the first phase of gratitude and dependence, the bishops claimed a spiritual jurisdiction of their own, and St. Augustine, by the fifth century, stated a theory of society which was bound to work out in the long run to the disparagement of government and pave the way for the theocratic claims of the mediaeval Church. Thus triumphant official Christianity in its patristic interpretation worked out to its conclusion the diminution of the power of what came to be regarded as the 'secular arm'.

The motives which led to the establishment of Christianity are perhaps best understood by a glance at the political circumstances of the day. The rally under Diocletian had been temporary; Constantine,[1] the most capable of the competing successors, emerged and attempted a new solution. The background out of which he fought his way was unpromising, with similarities with the worst aspects of our own century. The resulting state of mind of his apologists and panegyrists is both partial and superstitious. The *Vita Constantini* of Eusebius and the writings of Lactantius, both contemporaries, make curious reading; the former is already mediaeval in its outlook. Eusebius, in addition to his *Ecclesiastical History*, wrote a detailed account of Constantine's life; Lactantius, among other voluminous writings, gives a shocking survey of the dynastic mêlée from which Constantine emerged.

The politics of the time are obscure, and rendered bewildering by the similar names of rival and coincident emperors. Diocletian and his co-emperor, Maximian the Herulian, were succeeded by Galerius Maximian, who married Diocletian's daughter. He reigned in conjunction with Constantius Chlorus, Constantine's father. As a youth,

---

[1] Constantine (A.D. 288-337). Born at Nish, Yugoslavia. Son of the Emperor Constantius Chlorus. In 306 proclaimed co-emperor at York. 312, marched on Rome. Granted toleration of Christians by the Edict of Milan; convoked the Council of Nicaea, 325. Founded Constantinople, 326.

Constantine was held hostage by Diocletian, but on the latter's abdication remained in the power of Galerius Maximian, who, according to Lactantius, was a peculiarly ferocious character.[1] On his father's death, Constantine was proclaimed co-emperor with Galerius at York (A.D. 306); in the resulting dynastic struggle, which involved a campaign against Maxentius, he saw the famous vision which led him partially to adopt Christianity.

Eusebius recounts the episode as follows: 'An astonishing sign sent by God appeared to the Emperor, one which if it had been described by anyone else would have hardly been believed by the audience . . . He said that, at midday, he saw, with his own eyes, the sign of the cross appearing in the sky above the sun, with the inscription *"Hac Vince"*. At the sight he and all the soldiers who saw the miracle were completely astounded — *vehementer obstupefacti*. And again, that night, Christ appeared to Constantine with that sign which had appeared in the sky and advised him to use a military *signum* similar to that which he had seen. This advice Constantine followed.'[2] The connection with the sun is significant; it looks as though Constantine was attempting to reconcile the sun cult with Christianity; a wise political move.

Moreover, the sequel was victory. Maxentius, who had built a bridge of boats over the Tiber, was trampled to death by his retreating soldiers. Though Constantine, after the battle, gave thanks to Jupiter as well, he subsequently had his standard, the numinous '*Labarum*', guarded by picked troops, borne before his armies.

'It was like this,' says Eusebius, 'to a long spear encased in gold was fixed a sail-yard (antenna); at the top of the spear was a crown

[1] 'He exceeded in wickedness the worst princes that ever were. There was a barbarous brutality in his temper, together with a cruelty not known to those who were of Roman extraction. *And no wonder . . . for his mother was born beyond the Danube.*' Constantine did well to escape from him, for his amusements were unpleasant. 'What', writes Lactantius, 'shall I say of his diversions? He had some Bears . . . the biggest and fiercest that could be found (that were by consequence the liker unto himself) and when he intended to divert himself he ordered one of them to be brought out and a man to be thrown to him to be ate up by morsels. At the spectacle he used to burst out most indecently with laughter.' He is alleged to have roasted Christians over slow fires, keeping them alive as long as possible by throwing cold water in their faces. He found an expedient for dealing with the unemployed; they were rounded up, taken out to sea and drowned. As Lactantius describes it, his end was hideous. See Burnet's translation: *A Relation of the Deaths of the Primitive Persecutors, Englished by Gilbert Burnet, D.D., in which he hath made a large preface concerning persecution*, Amsterdam, 1687.

[2] EUSEBII PAMPHILI, *De Vita Beatissima Imperatoris Constantini* (MIGNE, *Patrologia latina*, vol. VIII, bk. I, chap. xxviii). The language of Eusebius is already of a crudity and clumsiness shocking to those trained in classical Latin.

set with jewels and gold, and on this was a sacred sign, that is to say, the two initial letters of the name Christ, the letter C in the middle. These letters the Emperor, from that time onwards, carried on his helmet. From the bar which crossed the spear obliquely there hung a kind of purple sail, ornamented with precious stones strung together . . . and the length of the sail equalled its breadth.'[1]

Constantine, further, took about with him a mysterious tabernacle. 'There was a tabernacle outside the camp, where he poured forth his prayers to God. Then, *velut diviniore actu impulsus*, he would bound out of it (*prosiliere solebat*) and give the order to march . . . and the soldiers would at once charge the enemy, cutting to pieces everyone they met, without distinction of age.'[2]

The sense of the immediate situation is clear enough. The age was far gone in pessimism and spiritually bankrupt; a rigid, social structure and a crushing taxation draining the life out of the cities. Diocletian had made Mithraism the religion of the empire; Julian the Apostate, getting a family revenge on the memory of Constantine,[3] was later to endeavour to create a new synthetic religion of his own; the rulers of the tormented empire, lungeing this way and that in the gathering twilight which was to deepen into the dark ages, tried one expedient after the other. Constantine, it would seem, a man of his age, with the weight of this crumbling world on his shoulders, dependent on illiterate legionaries drawn from all parts of the empire and outside it, himself brought up in the atmosphere of the camp, exploited and later believed the new popular religion. So the *Labarum*, surrounded by the picked troops, was trundled into battle, and vindicated by a series of crushing victories. Finally, at the end of the successful reign, came the lavish building of the church at Jerusalem, and the consecration of the first cathedral at Constantinople — later to be rebuilt on a greater scale by Justinian — where the empire was to make a fresh start.

These events brought about a revolution, unbelievable a century before; Constantine, far from persecuting the formerly despised sect,

---

[1] Op. cit., bk. II, chap. xxviii.

[2] He was also alive to the arts of propaganda. He had a picture hung outside the palace 'for all to see, in which the sign of the cross was placed at the top and, below, the enemy, the foe of mankind, in the form of a dragon . . . The emperor wished the dragon to be represented as pierced through the middle of the belly with spears and cast into the foaming depths of the sea, and this the picture displayed, in various colours.' (Bk. II, chap. iii).

[3] For Julian's views of his uncle, *vide* 'The Works of Julian the Apostate', Loeb edition and translation.

is now preoccupied to bring the Christian bishops to agreement, and sets himself to compose their doctrinal feuds. There is an interesting picture of him at the Council at Nicaea. The bishops — and there were 318 of them — became involved in controversy. 'Some began to make allegations against others . . . and when this had gone on for some time on both sides . . . the Emperor, listening to it all patiently, attended to the controversies most carefully, and, supporting what each party said in turn, gradually reconciled the bitterest opponents. And when he had addressed them all calmly, using the Greek language, of which he was not ignorant, he was exceedingly pleased and joyful.'[1]

Naturally, the Emperor wanted a safe solution. 'I am convinced', he wrote towards the end of his life, 'that the *greatest safety and prosperity* will be enjoyed everywhere, when God through the true and righteous and *from their agreement concerning His Divinity*, shall deign to draw all men unto himself.'[2]

It is a far cry from the days of Augustus and Hadrian. Caesar, *religiosissimus Augustus*, wrestles with the complications of patristic theology, because, if Christianity is to be the religion of the empire, it must be defined and its definitions command respect. And, indeed, an alliance with the Church, the best organized and the most self-sufficient of the competing religions within the empire, toughened by persecution and attracting the best intellect of the day, was the obvious move. Constantine[3] had won to his side the greatest social force of his time. The Council of Nicaea marks the triumph of organized Christianity, but at a price. It may be thought the leaders of the Church, as from an exceeding high mountain, saw the kingdoms of this world and thought the prospect worth the risk. They were, in fact, hardly in a position to choose; the impression from the documents of the time is almost slavish gratitude to any ruler who will stop the persecution and impose peace; their tone is one of adulation and of triumph.

'Those who have set themselves in opposition to God are now laid

---

[1] EUSEBIUS, op. cit.

[2] Letter to the Persian King, Shapur, quoted by N. H. BAYNES, 'Constantine and the Christian Church', *Proceedings of the British Association*, vol. XV, q.v., for a full discussion of the problem.

[3] 'Canny to the end, aware of the cruel necessities which from time to time confront the politician, he had delayed the ceremony of baptism till the last hour . . . He died as a neophyte, clad in the white robe of innocence, the one human being who enjoyed the distinction of being deified as a pagan god, while at the same time he was venerated as a Christian saint.' C. N. COCHRANE, *Christianity and Classical Culture*, O.U.P. (1940), p. 212.

in the dust. Where are now the glorious and renowned names of Jovius and Heraclius? God has blotted them out and razed them out of the world.'[1]

Naturally, then, the bishops did not yet claim spiritual authority over Caesar; but the alliance marks a revolution. In the words of the *Cambridge Ancient History*: 'Constantine, sitting among the Christian bishops at the Council of Nicaea, in his own person marks the beginning of Europe's Middle Age.' A new outlook had captured the seats of power of the ancient world and set the stage for fresh developments of thought.

But Constantine among the bishops retains the religious authority of the pagan emperors, exercising it in a new field. His Byzantine successors retained this authority unimpaired, and the conflict between Church and State did not develop in the Eastern empire. Sustained by a bureaucracy and a splendour in the direct tradition of antiquity, the Basileus retained in his own person the sacred character for which his imitators in the West were constrained to win the sanction of the Papacy.

The loss of contact with the East and the breakdown of secular rule was the papal opportunity; it was the Bishop of Rome, not the Byzantine Patriarch, who was to develop the theocratic outlook implicit in the teaching of the Christian Fathers, already defined by the fourth century. Where the old culture had broken down, there the full implication of the Patristic attitude was to be realized.

§ 11

The nature of this attitude will now be our concern. The Patristic mind was the medium through which the political thought of antiquity was largely transmitted to the Middle Ages; it dominated the theological outlook of Europe up to the seventeenth century, and since politics were to be discussed in terms of theology from St. Augustine to Machiavelli and beyond, it is well to examine Patristic thought with care.

The political ideas of the Fathers change with the growing responsibilities of the Church. They develop from Tertullian, through St. Ambrose, to the full statement of political theory in St. Augustine's *City of God*, a book of cardinal importance which must be examined in some detail.

---

[1] LACTANTIUS, op. cit.

How hostile to secular government the early Fathers could be is apparent in the writings of Tertullian,[1] who lived during the period of the fiercest persecutions. Tertullian is the earliest of the Fathers, and his writings deeply influenced both Cyprian and St. Augustine; he is, in a sense, the creator of Patristic literature and his affinities are with the fiercest of the Old Testament Prophets. It is significant that, like St. Augustine, he came from North Africa.

Tertullian's outlook is thoroughly anti-social; he expresses bitter hatred of the world, and repudiates all contact with pagan culture. The sooner a man is out of the world, the better; there can be no health in it. *'Quid Athenae Hierosolymis?'*[2] he asks — 'We have no need of curiosity since Jesus Christ.' The Christian should 'mourn when the heathen rejoice, and rejoice when they weep', a strange inversion of the Gospel teaching. He asserts what was later to become the Protestant position, insisting that the laity are on the same spiritual footing as the priesthood, and attacks ecclesiastical as well as secular authority. He is a religious genius of sombre outlook and brilliant eloquence, unable to reconcile his interpretation of the Gospel with the compromises and organization of the growing Church. He spent his life in controversy and died an old man, unreconciled to the opponents whom his eloquence had castigated in a flood of sermons, treatises, and letters.

An outlook suited to a persecuted minority is unsuited to the holders of executive office, and it was natural that the uncompromising attitude of Tertullian should give way, in the fourth century, to the more responsible utterances of St. Ambrose,[3] already a pillar of society. While Tertullian emphasized the unworldly and, indeed, vindictive attitude of the early Fathers to society, St. Ambrose's writings imply a shouldered responsibility, while St. Augustine later formulates and sums up the outlook of the triumphant Church, com-

---

[1] Tertullian (*c.* A.D. 155-222), born at Carthage of well-to-do parents, and highly educated both in Latin and Greek literature. He studied Law in Rome, and won reputation as a lawyer. Converted to Christianity, *c.* 193. Travelled in Greece and the Levant and returned to Carthage (197), where he produced the first volume of his writings, in controversy with the Gnostics, the Jews, and the Orthodox clergy.

For an account of his historical setting, see GLOVER, *Conflict of Religions in the Early Roman Empire* (1909).

[2] 'What has the child of Jerusalem to do with Athens?'

[3] St. Ambrose (*c.* 340-97). Born at Trier, where his father was Governor. Prefect of Liguria. His attempt to mediate between the contending parties, Orthodox and Arian, over the vacant bishopric of Milan led to his appointment to the bishopric himself. He played a decisive part in the high politics of his age. For a full account of him, see DR. HOMES DUDDEN's *Life and Times of St. Ambrose*, O.U.P., 2 vols.

promising between the extreme position expressed by Tertullian and the excutive preoccupations of the great bishop.

St. Ambrose was a formidable figure, with a sophisticated tradition behind him. The Church, in his view, is to be a corporate body, appointing its own bishops, exhorting and judging the world, upholding an unworldly morality, with a right and duty of interference in secular affairs when religious principles are involved. In the disputation with Symmachus before the Emperor Valentinian II, he repudiates the pagan plea for toleration since the Christian revelation has finally superseded all other doctrines. He advocates warfare against Arian heretics, and claims an authority for the priesthood over the laity which Tertullian never sanctions. Highly educated in Hellenistic learning, he translates the old Roman executive tradition of ordered government into Christian terms; in that sense he is a forerunner of Gregory the Great and the thirteenth-century Papacy.

§ III

Where St. Ambrose points the way towards the development of the huge organization of the mediaeval Church, St. Augustine,[1] with his contrasting African background, formulates the political theory behind it; his work is the most complete and influential expression of the Patristic outlook. St. Augustine's *De Civitate Dei* may be taken as the summing up of a development which had taken place over three centuries. The extent to which the Jewish Scriptures, the third element in Christianity, had coloured and, indeed, submerged the

---

[1] St. Augustine (354-430). Son of Patricius, a pagan landowner of Thagaste in Algeria, and Monica, his Christian wife. His father's outlook appears to have conflicted with his mother's. 'If we may generalize from the scanty data preserved for us, women and family ambition would seem to have been his father's chief preoccupations . . . It was Augustine's tragic destiny to combine in a small and sickly body the souls of both his parents and a fastidious intellect which served both souls in turn . . . In him the two souls appear as nature and grace.' (PROFESSOR E. R. DODDS, in *Hibbert Journal*, April 1928. Professor Dodds regards this conflict as the psychological explanation of St. Augustine's outlook.) In 370 he went to the University of Carthage and joined the Manichaeans. He became a schoolmaster at Thagaste; in 377 a teacher of rhetoric at Carthage, and in 384 Professor of Rhetoric at Milan. In 387 he was converted to Christianity. Returning to Africa in 388, he became, seven years later, Bishop of Hippo (the modern Bona in Algeria). By 400 he had written the *Confessions*, a document of importance for the understanding of his other works. From 413 to 426, in the midst of a crowd of administrative duties, he wrote the *De Civitate Dei*. He died in 430, with the Vandals outside the walls of his city. The translation of the *De Civitate Dei* here quoted was made by John Healey in the early seventeenth century. It renders the majestic Latin better than a modern version, but St. Augustine's full eloquence can only be appreciated in the original. References to the Latin text are here made from Dombart's edition, Teubner, 1927.

Gospel teaching, will be apparent from this book. The *Confessions* and the *De Civitate Dei* form only a part of St. Augustine's writings; an enormous correspondence has survived, and over five hundred sermons. He was primarily a religious genius; and it is impossible here to investigate his theological position. Where Tertullian had brushed aside the intellectual justification of Christianity, and indeed gloried in doing so, St. Augustine is a highly trained metaphysician, well skilled to use the dialectic of his day. It is indeed even claimed that his spiritual experience supersedes the best classical thought. The classical outlook, it is argued, was over-intellectualized; the Greek and Roman philosophers were attempting to live by reason alone and never tapped the spiritual energy of the whole man.[1] It is maintained that in the doctrine of the Trinity St. Augustine found the final symbol of the complete harmony of the whole man: 'That is, that knows, that wills.' By surrender to a power beyond the self, personality regains its full integrity, and a harmony of intelligence, will, and energy is secured; 'Sapientia' is substituted for 'Scientia'; wisdom for analytical knowledge.

In the history of political thought, St. Augustine was to be enormously influential. His *Confessions* and the *Retractationes* — a survey of his intellectual development, written in the year of his death — are landmarks in psychological history. There is none of the dignified reserve of the classical philosophers; St. Augustine was fascinated with himself; before his tempestuous vitality self-consciousness disappears. For this lack of reticence he has been called modern. His writings are indeed the record of an ultra-sensitive mind dealing with the demands of an exacting life, and of a powerful intellect which finally found peace by an act of faith.

The *De Civitate Dei* was a *livre de circonstance*. The immediate cause of its composition is stated by Augustine as follows: 'Rome having been stormed and sacked by the Goths, under Alaric their King, the pagans made an attempt to attribute the calamity to the Christian religion . . . It was this which kindled my zeal for the name of God and prompted me to undertake the defence of the City of God against its assailants.' The book is long and diffuse; it is divided into twenty-

[1] There is an extensive and able treatment of the whole problem in COCHRANE, op. cit., chap. ii. It is argued that the 'Scientia' of the classical world was barren, and the author refers to 'the errors of scientific understanding in its effort to become an instrument of control'. But to equate the rhetorical and literary 'scientia' of antiquity, so ignorant of technology and statistics, with the full range of modern scientific understanding and the integrity of modern scientific method is surely an arbitrary proceeding, in spite of the range and excellence of the author's argument.

two chapters, of which the last twelve include a statement of St. Augustine's view of society. 'Of these twelve books,' he says, 'the first four contain an account of the origin of these two cities, the City of God and the City of this world; the second four treat the history of the Pagans; the third and last four their deserved destinies.'

The conception of the two societies is, of course, biblical; Jerusalem, the Holy City, is contrasted with Babylon; but modern research has tended to show that Augustine partially derived his theme from Ticonius the Donatist who, in his work on the *Apocalypse*, had interpreted the Book of Revelations on similar lines.[1]

The *De Civitate Dei* goes very deep; it raises the whole question of the function of the State in terms of St. Augustine's view of the problem of evil. Its assumptions are profoundly pessimistic, and gravely affected mediaeval and subsequent thought.

'What river of eloquence', he writes, 'could ever suffice to set forth the wretchedness of this life?' The world is divided into two societies, of God and of the devil; the two overlap, and the only basis for a righteous social order would be for the first to permeate and absorb the second. Society is nothing but the individuals who make it up ('What is Rome but the Romans?'); if all followed Christ, the conflict would be annulled. But, as St. Augustine is well aware, they do not all follow Christ. The best that can be hoped of civil society is for it to be a 'secular arm' which enforces the Church's will. Starting from the Ciceronian definition that justice (*aequitas*) ought to 'give every man his due', St. Augustine asserts that man, through sin, denies his due to God. Unregenerate society is therefore incapable of *aequitas*; government is concerned only with the outward man; only an inward change of heart can alter society.

The natural man, if he follows his instinct, sets too much store on life as experienced in the limited range of consciousness he enjoys. Hence a greedy egotism, an inflammation of selfishness, whereby man becomes the slave of his own lust, whether for power and acclamation, or for the more obvious appetites. The conflict of competing egotisms turns the world into a present hell. From this blind alley of addiction, there is only one escape; the transcendence of self in Christ, and the obstacle to the transcendence of self is spiritual pride, the pride of life.

---

[1] *Vide* N. H. BAYNES, *The Political Ideas of St. Augustine's 'De Civitate Dei'*, Historical Association Pamphlet, No. 104 (1936).

St. Augustine, like Hegel or Marx, saw the world process as a vast drama unfolding itself in Time. His conception of human fate is Miltonic, and the plot determined by an unusually complicated way of experience. He was a man well endowed to appreciate the variety and colour of life. In contrast to the cold determinism of Calvin, his outlook is vigorous and comprehensive, if to-day hectic and strange.[1] The *De Civitate Dei* is a large, discursive work with none of the remorseless lucidity of Calvin's *Institutes*. St. Augustine's own nature contained contradictory elements; these he projects with force and eloquence on to the cosmic process. There are thus two aspects of his thought which may be distinguished; the one intelligible to our own age, and the other only to be understood by an investigation of the fifth century. On the one hand, his outlook on life and the psychological motives revealed in it; on the other, the theological idiom in which that outlook is expressed.

The author of the *De Civitate Dei* was a highly strung intellectual of violent passions and wide range of mind. It may be he was taught by experience that there are in the world a creative minority of the sensitive, the intelligent and the good, but that the world is largely dominated by coarser types, who trample on the values recognized by the few. Seldom have they trampled more effectively than in the early fifth century. This reading of the social facts was reinforced by the conflict in Augustine's own personality between an evidently African sensuality and a strong sense of sin, illustrated by the spiritual struggles recorded in the *Confessions*. Life is thought of as a contest in which the *turbidus calor* of the natural man is suppressed by self-discipline which aims at the reward of salvation.

The tremendous phrases of the Latin original do full justice to the conflict in Augustine's mind. He dwells with reiterated emphasis on the wickedness of his childhood;[2] on the ardours of his adoles-

---

[1] Augustine can refer to 'the brightness of the light of the sun, moon and stars, the shades of the woods, the colours and smells of flowers . . . the many forms of beasts and fishes, and the strange alterations in the colour of the sea' (XXII). He is well aware, too, of the precariousness of existence: 'What fears, what calamities, are heaped on the heart of men . . . So are we afflicted . . . with cold, storms, deluges, lightnings, falls of houses, fury of beasts, stinging of scorpions, biting of mad dogs (a strange accident wherein a beast most sociable and familiar with man shall sometimes become more to be feared than a lion or dragon). What miseries do navigators now endure! What man can walk anywhere free of sudden accidents? One coming home from the Court (being sound enough on his feet), fell down, broke his leg, and died of it.' These utterances are not those of a cloistered intellectual who thinks only in abstractions.

[2] *In stante innocentia puerilis? non est, Domine, non est.* – 'Is this childish innocence? O Lord, it is not.'

cence;[1] on his *variis et umbrosis amoribus* — 'various and shady loves'. He kept a mistress, *sed unam tamen* — but only one. *'Veni Carthaginem'*, he says, *'et circumstrepebat undique sartago flagitiosorum amorum'* — 'To Carthage then I came, and a cauldron of unholy loves sang all about my ears.'

His conversion was accompanied by acute psychological crisis; it occurred in the garden of his lodging at Milan. 'There was a little garden at our lodging, which we had the use of . . . *illuc me abstulerat tumultus pectoris'* — 'thither I had been drawn by the tumult of my breast'. His agony of mind was intolerable; he felt that ordinary converts were stealing a march upon him. *'Surgent indocti et caelum rapiunt . . . et nos, cum doctrinis nostris sine corde'.*[2] He flung himself weeping under a fig tree. Suddenly, over the wall, he heard the voice of a child, crying incessantly: *'Tolle, lege; tolle, lege.'* — 'Take and read.' He thought at first the words were a sort of game or nursery rhyme, but could not place them; then the conviction came over him they were a divine command. He took up the Epistles of St. Paul, opened them at random and read: 'Not in rioting and drunkenness, not in chambering and wantonness, not in strife and envying . . .'[3] He experienced immediate and complete conversion It is a record of spiritual torment, culminating in hard-won peace.

Three motives, then — disgust at the brutality of the world, an intense preoccupation with sin, and a passionate hunger for redemption — colour the thought of the *De Civitate Dei*. The whole is expressed, in the idiom of its time and enriched with great imaginative range, eloquence, and vitality. The cosmic drama is expressed in terms of the Jewish sacred books; it is through St. Augustine, next to St. Paul, that the Semitic outlook determines European thought, for he consistently emphasizes the second, the Hebraic, strain in Christianity.

He begins with the fall of Adam: 'All mankind was in the first man.' (*Omnes enim fuimus in illo uno qui per feminam lapsus est in peccatum* — 'For we all were in that one man who through woman fell into sin.')[4] With the Fall, humanity became sullied with passion.[5] The

---

[1] *Exhalabantur nebulae de limosa concupiscentia carnis et scatebra pubertatis . . . atque offuscabant cor meum* (II, 2).

[2] 'The unlearned rise and take heaven by storm, and we — with all our learning but without a heart — we wallow in the flesh.'

[3] Romans xiii, 13.　　　　[4] XIII, 14.

[5] *Nam postea quam praecepti facta transgressio est, confestim, gratia deserente divina, de corporum suorum nuditate confusi sunt. Unde etiam foliis ficulneis pudenda texerunt; quae prius eadem membra erant sed pudenda non erant. Senserunt ergo novum motum inobedientis carnis suae . . . Tunc ergo coepit caro concupiscere adversus spiritum, cum qua*

race could no longer be propagated by a passionless act of will. Man's nature was debased with the admission of 'concupiscential disobedience in the members against the will, and thereby was bound to death by necessity'.[1] 'Justly is man ashamed of this lust.' In books XIV and XV St. Augustine comes back again and again to a morbid analysis of natural impulse. He regrets that God should have allowed the satisfaction of instinct to be enjoyable.[2] 'All these evils are belonging to man and arise out of the root of that error and perverse affection which every son of Adam brings into the world with him.'[3] In Adam all fell; man, but for redeeming grace, is irretrievably damned.

Given this inherited wickedness, 'God's purpose is to restore men by Grace by means of a man, born of the condemned seed of mankind, and by gathering so many into Grace, *we should supply the places of the fallen angels and so preserve, or perhaps augment, the number of the heavenly inhabitants*'.[4] There are, in consequence, 'two sorts of men; those that live according to the flesh and according to the spirit, either in kind. All would have been cast long ago into the second death that has no end, had not the undue grace of God acquitted some from it.'[5]

Such in brief outline is the sequence of St. Augustine's thought. Naturally his conceptions of heaven and hell are in accordance with this doctrine and with the imagination of his time.[6] Of the material reality of hell he is not in doubt, and quotes the authority of Jesus for it. ' "Better for them to go halt into life than having two feet to be cast into Hell" . . . Oh, in whom would not this thunder from the

---

[1] XIII, 3.   [2] XIV, 26.   [3] XXII, 22.   [4] XXII, 1.   [5] XIV, 1.
[6] XIII, 18. ('Against the Platonists that oppose the elevation of the body up to heaven by arguments of elementary ponderosity.') He debates by what contrivance God can transport the righteous up to heaven, and his idea of an after-life leads him to face various problems which interested his contemporaries. He discusses the view that men becomes Lares if they have behaved well, Lemurs if they have behaved badly, and dismisses it (IX, 11). He inquires whether infants rise again in the stature they died in: 'The sudden and strange power of God', he concludes, 'will give them their full stature.' Cut hair and nails will not return to deform the body; scattered limbs will be reassembled, 'but all spiritualized'.

---

controversia nati sumus, trahentes originem mortis (XIII, 13). – 'For after the command had been disobeyed, straightway, upon the departure of divine grace, they were ashamed at the nakedness of their bodies. Whence also they covered their shameful parts with fig leaves, those parts that had been the same before but had not been shameful. They were conscious, therefore, of a new impulse of their rebellious flesh. So then did the flesh begin to lust against the spirit; *and with this conflict were we born, bringing with it the source of death*.'

mouth of God strike chill terror?'[1] He questions whether the human body can endure perpetual burning and speculates why the devils do not themselves burn. They have, he says: 'Bodies of condensed air, and that this air is passible and may suffer burning the heating of baths proves . . . But that Hell, that lake of fire and brimstone, shall be real, and the fire corporeal, burning both men and devils, the one in flesh, the other in air . . . Christ hath spoken it.'[2]

The world to St. Augustine, is thus divided into a minority of the Elect, destined to fill the gaps left in heaven by the evil angels, and the reprobate, the majority, who organize themselves apart from God. Hence the division between the citizens of the *Civitas Dei* and the citizens of the *Civitas Terrena*. The goal in which social wickedness is overcome and spiritual unrest appeased is the Pax Aeterna, the Visio Dei. The chief end of man is 'to glorify God and enjoy Him for ever'; the aim of society, 'peace of all things in a well-disposed order'.[3]

The world process into which St. Augustine projects this drama of sin and redemption he compares with 'the grand melody of some ineffably rare master of song'.[4] Human life is a preparation for a heavenly goal, and history the education of the human race. Man, long embedded in the static philosophies of the ancient world, becomes the pilgrim of eternity. This dramatic conception dominated men's minds throughout the Middle Ages.

Thus the sense of world worthlessness, the conviction of the wickedness of man, and the vision of life as dominated by a divine purpose or judgement, of an *élite* minority who will be rewarded in an afterlife, gained ground and emphasis, often at the expense of Caritic Christianity, of the way of life which, if rightly followed, will result in the immediate apprehension of eternal life.

If Augustine's outlook be accepted, it follows that the reality behind the social order is a divine plan, expressed in a world-wide process that dwarfs the ordinary interests of civilized life. The Hellenistic way of living becomes insignificant or meaningless before the searing vision of this North African genius. Gone are the amenities and affections ordinary good men cherish. For pagans they are flattened out before this theological sirocco; for Christians transcended and sublimated in the divine purpose. It follows, therefore, that the political outlook is profoundly altered. The Stoic sense of high ethical mission and natural order, already apparent in Cicero

[1] XXI, 9.   [2] XXI, 10.   [3] XIX, 13.   [4] Letter to Marcellinus.

and the *Meditations* of Marcus Aurelius, is swept into this world-embracing vision: government becomes moral only if it furthers the purpose of God. Without God the bloodstained politics of secular empire are but the expression of the 'large-scale brigandage' (*magna latrocinia*) of unsanctified power. The Hellenistic ideal of harmony, including all men, gives place to a division between the elect and the unrighteous; the hell of secular society unredeemed by Christianity is not even capable of improvement. Indeed, to try to improve it 'without God' is futile and impious. Society organized 'apart from God' is beyond redemption; it is what humanity with its fallen nature deserves, *meritum peccatorum*. Only in the light of the Christian revelation can the secular power be sanctified and aspire to be instead *remedium peccatorum*.

St. Augustine insists, therefore, that the State must be closely bound up with the Christian Church, and can never be divorced from it without losing its *raison d'être* in the moral order, though the exact relation between the two he does not define. There is not yet in the *De Civitate Dei* any specific subordination of the civil power to a theocracy, though St. Augustine's attitude points the way to it and the dualism at the root of his thought was the foundation of the temporal claims of the mediaeval Papacy. He has too fine a religious sense (in spite of the demonology and credulity in which it is involved) to commit himself thus far. Yet the intrinsic evil of the reprobate world, in which the secular ruler is by his very nature enmeshed, makes his function spiritually inferior to that of the Church. The Christian ruler needs the Church for guidance in the spiritual life: the bishops need the help of the secular law to deal with secular affairs; in theory they ought to work together in harmony, but the moment they cease to do so the spiritual authority will be invoked. St. Augustine has stated the fundamental axiom that the secular state was spiritually dead unless it made a close alliance with the Church, and human life itself only intelligible and significant in the light of the doctrine of the Fall and the Redemption.

In assessing the thought of this religious genius, it is well to distinguish between the general position, arguable in any age, that human society, if unredeemed by higher spiritual values, is an actively evil thing, most men being naturally wicked when judged by the higher standards evolved by the few, and the theological outlook of St. Augustine. A reading of the full text of *De Civitate Dei* will indicate how large a part a sense of the intrinsic wickedness of human instincts played in the author's mind; we have here an example of the ascetic reaction to the ordinary routine of pagan observances made dynamic by a positive theology. The conflicts in Augustine's personality, resulting from an overmastering sense of sin; from his desire for atonement and peace; from his apprehension of the evil of the world and of the contrast between the creative minority, the spiritual and intellectual aristocracy among men, with the brute force and stupidity of the lower types, all had found their expression.

§ I V

By the fifth century, then, with the final collapse of the Western empire, both the government and the political thought of antiquity had been transformed. The Church, now established as the official religion of the empire, had undertaken vast social responsibilities, built up a complex hierarchy, and formulated an elaborate creed and ritual. In addition to the administrative achievement, destined to survive the dark centuries of barbarism, the influence of the Christian scriptures and the writings of the Fathers, which together formed an overwhelming body of literature, profoundly altered the intellectual background of Europe. Henceforward the surviving tradition of civilization was to be interpreted in theological terms, and learning to be concerned primarily with biblical and Patristic subjects. Until the fourteenth century the classical tradition that came through was successfully subordinated to this new interpretation. Political thought became something very different from that of Hellas or of Rome, concerned with the precedents of biblical history and quoting the authority of the inspired books. And this submission to authority was reinforced by the prestige of the organized Church.

This reintroduction of a dominant religious *motif* into political thought is nothing new; the cities of Mesopotamia and Egypt were built mainly on theocratic enterprise; the polis centred on the city's gods. But the religion of St. Augustine is different from the routine worship of the Temple State and the Sacred City; it is utterly different from the rites which held together and satisfied primitive agricultural societies; the direct line of descent is out of the prophetic utterances of the Old Testament, that burning moral vision of 'world worthlessness' which had broken the 'pillars' of the fertility cult and slain the prophets of Baal. In St. Augustine, indeed, religion takes the centre of the stage, but it is a dynamic religion, reinforced by a sense of guilt and built round a dogmatic structure precisely and frighteningly defined; it had indeed come to bring not peace but a sword. During the Patristic age, the fierce and elaborate accentuation of the denunciatory, ascetic, aspect of Christianity tends to swamp the Caritic tradition, which was the fundamental core of the faith, and which St. Augustine, for all his strange cosmology, understands. With the need to convert the barbarians, and the expansion of missionary effort in the North, with the subsidence of the cloud of metaphysical argument which fogged the mind of Roman antiquity, the simpler and in the long run more powerful Caritas of the Gospels came again into its own.

Although the victory of the Patristic outlook makes a profound break with the past — and naturally the political ideals of the polis and the negative self-sufficiency of Stoic and Epicurean philosophies had little place in St. Augustine's highly emotional outlook — the political responsibilities and intellectual sophistication of the leaders of the Church made the abandonment of classical culture less complete than might be expected. In particular, in the political sphere, the influence of Cicero on Christian thinkers, as upon so many of the writers of antiquity, is constantly apparent, and the idea of Natural Law, so important in the Roman contribution to political thought, was swept up into the patristic world-view. The Ciceronic universal providence behind Right Reason and Just Law could be adapted easily into the Augustinian scheme. Natural Law could be invoked as the sanction behind both secular and ecclesiastical authority; Christianized, it was constantly so evoked in mediaeval speculation. As will be later apparent, St. Thomas Aquinas largely bases his political thought on this idea.

At the same time, the Patristic view of the intrinsic wickedness of man, and the insistence that only in terms of the Christian revelation of the redemption and the after-life, can human values have significance at all, gave Graeco-Roman ideas a content which was altogether new. An almost Manichaean dualism, a conflict between light and darkness, reinforced with an Hebraic and ancient sense of guilt and atonement, drives home the sharp antithesis between 'matter' and 'spirit'. A view not supported by modern knowledge, which tends to regard personality as an event in space-time, a body-mind, or 'chord', including the whole gamut of consciousness and subconsciousness, from the most bestial instinct to the most ethereal intuitions. Indeed, the tenuous basis of 'matter', revealed by modern physics, and the new conception of time, would seem incompatible with Augustinian dualism.

Besides displaying this overriding dualism, the Patristic outlook is conditioned by the certain prospect of immortality, with the short span of life insignificant compared with the vistas of heaven and hell; important only as a time of probation, with its values in terms of the rewards and punishments of a tremendous sequel. To see life thus, 'under the stare of eternity', changes the whole balance of thought. The Greeks put their values into the present. Constantly Greek poetry reiterates the beauty of the fleeting moment; the pride of achievement; the pain and pleasure of love; and laments the precariousness of human happiness, the brief span of youth, the losses of war, the penalties of old age. Yet the Greek would rather be a slave among the living than a king among the dead; the after-life, in so far as they gave a thought to it, was regarded as a grey and tenuous thing. Virgil expresses the same feeling about the dead in the sixth book of the *Aeneid*; they achieve a brief return to full consciousness only by drinking blood.

Set against this the overwhelming idea of the Second Coming and the Last Judgement, later expressed in innumerable windows and frescoes, and in the sculpture of the great cathedrals; the idea which dominated men's minds and tamed the barbarians; the imminent apocalyptic vision. Where the Greek statues, their eyes heavy with thought, express the brooding but clear-sighted dignity of a disciplined humanism, mediaeval artists were to represent the joy of ecstasiated rapture and the degradation of remorseful sin.

It was indeed an extraordinary change. The political and social situation of the fourth century had made the success of an emotional religion inevitable. The interests of Constantine made the alliance between Caesar and the well-organized and powerful Christian community natural, and the tide of intellectual development ran the same way. The climate of classical thought was changed from a static, intellectualized morality by the dynamic theological outlook of the Fathers as well as by the Caritas of the Gospel itself.

Thus Patristic Christianity captured the thought and society of antiquity. The early Christians had been simple men; but with Augustine the position is elaborately defined. The movement had spread and succeeded among the town proletariat and the socially obscure — *latebrosa et lucifugax natio*. With success, sophistication, and responsibility, an elaborate framework of thought and organization emerged, the latter largely modelled on the civic structure and bureaucracy of the empire; while the independent economic basis of the Christian State within the State was secured. Faced, then, with the gathering storm of the succeeding centuries, when all else was foundering, the Christian Church stood out, the gaunt bulwark on which the tides of barbarism were to break, and which was to shelter the rudimentary culture that survived. As the lights went out, one by one, over the Mediterranean world, there remained the guttering beacon of the new faith.

BOOK TWO

THE POLITICAL THOUGHT OF THE MIDDLE AGES

CHAPTER I

THE DARK AGES

§ I

THE causes of the gradual collapse of the Roman Empire, intellectual and spiritual, political and economic, have been extensively analysed; [1] one thing is agreed — there was a slow decline into barbarism. A degradation of intellectual standards, a general coarsening and technical incompetence, overtook thought, art, and architecture; elementary memories of civilized practice survived, illiteracy became general; and only by stressing the most superstitious and thaumaturgic aspects of its doctrine, by desperate expedients of assimilation of pagan cults and by shady political manœuvres, the Church managed to preserve the rudiments of the past.

The decline was mainly due to the failure of the ruling classes of antiquity to civilize the mass of slaves and subject peoples on whom their generally callous way of life depended; to their incapacity to tackle economic problems, either in the sphere of finance or organization, so that there sources of the empire were squandered at the centre, Italy was ruined and the currency went to pieces; to the decimation of the old Roman stock through civil war and political proscription, and to the increasing importation of barbarians to guard the frontier. Given this fundamental weakness, it is easy to see that the strategic threat on the Danube, together with internecine feuds between the emperors, could have only one conclusion, once the outer barbarians were on the move, though their numbers were comparatively small. It is remarkable that Byzantium, the Eastern heir of Rome, so long preserved itself, and by adaptation of limited resources faced out over centuries the threat of a peculiarly mischievous and formidable collection of enemies, right up to the final debacle in 1453.

In the West the continuity of any kind of cultural standards was extremely tenuous; the intellectuals defended themselves under the sanction of religion, and in a barbarian society, the flame of intelligence was kept flickering but alive.

The period is at once the decadent sequel to antiquity and the

---

[1] *Vide*, in particular, ROSTOVSTEFF, *Social and Economic History of the Roman Empire*, O.U.P. (1926).

beginning of mediaeval development. It produced no political theory in the full sense of the term; merely crude and distorted statements of general principles, derived from Roman thought, transmitted by the curious monastic communities which formed islands of literacy amid the surrounding barbarism. The fifth and sixth centuries, which saw the invasions in Britain and the most extensive folk migrations in Gaul, Italy, and Spain, naturally brought political ideas to an elementary level; and memories of patristic thought are revealed in the crudest form by their barbarized interpreters. Yet since this age is so important and so formative, it will be well to glance at the outlook of some of its representative minds, in the absence of works of systematic political theory.

The kind of thought which survived will appear startlingly childish. It was timid and clumsy, flat and dull; weighed down with a sense of inferiority; highly self-conscious — a quality which infected most subsequent mediaeval thought — and concealing its poverty with a *babu* elaboration of words. It is indeed a sinister warning of a civilization's decline: there is a loss of natural gaiety and drive, an obsession with the past, a sense of the futility and inferiority of secular society, an adulation — alternating with strident denunciation — of incalculable barbarian patrons.

St. Augustine's view that secular power, unless sanctified, is a 'brigandage', was indeed borne out by the conditions of the day. Any centres of culture that remained were clerical or under clerical influence, sustained by the spiritual force of Christianity and the awe which it provoked. Thus, when political thought again became articulate, order was generally identified with the spiritual power and the *sacerdotium* often preferred to the *regnum*. It is a refugee mentality which emerges from the barbarian centuries, and its atmosphere is in part due to the monastic medium through which it was transmitted.

Monkish institutions, alien to classical civilization, first appear in Egypt and derive from pre-Christian origins. They were new to Europe, and there is evidence that the idea arrived in Egypt as early as the Persian conquest, when there are indications of the presence of Buddhist missionaries there: the tonsure and the rosary would further point to such an influence. The social and economic breakdown which isolated the great estates in the West made for conditions under which these communities could become acclimatized. The monastic achievement was indeed remarkable; manuscripts were preserved and copied; chronicles made; a degree of education kept alive; a routine preserved; but the limitations of monastic writing should not be forgotten. Monasticism was a desperate expedient, and by the sixth century what political ideas remained came down through a monastic medium. The resulting impoverishment of thought, in its mosaic of stock quotations — the lack of originality, the rigid conservatism — still conditions Thomism six centuries later; not till the Renaissance, with the revival of humanist ideals, did the spirit of Antiquity begin to be understood.

In the first place, then, the intellectual bottleneck of the Dark Ages too often narrowed the rich variety of classical thought into a theological nightmare, in which the old ideas are subservient to a dualism in the worst Patristic tradition. In the second place an elementary rationalism is at a premium: argument proceeds in a geometrical manner, crude but clear. They clung to this way of thought, and the sheer process of reasoning, always subordinate to theological beliefs, took on a magical flavour. In the third place, the disorder of the time, which put the Church on the defensive, provoked, against barbarian excesses, a constant assertion of the validity of Law and of the trusteeship of power. This last, the most valuable of the political legacies of the Middle Ages, runs, as will be seen, like a thread through mediaeval thought. That it did so, preserving and strengthening the best thought of Antiquity, is due to the influence of Christian beliefs, which were strong enough to master barbarian idolatry of persons and of power.

On these bare foundations the later edifice of scholastic political theory was to be built. In spite of the elementary level of the Dark Ages, distorted memories of Hellenistic ideals, of universal Natural Law, of Roman justice that rendered every man his due, survived in terms of the Augustinian outlook and the Christian doctrine of Redemption and brotherhood. In the circumstances of that age it was a great achievement.

§ II

For by the sixth century the situation had shockingly deteriorated. This decadence will be apparent from the outlook of Cassiodorus; while, a generation later, the most important transmitter of mediaeval political ideas, Isidore of Seville, shows a staggering crudity of mind.

The writings of Cassiodorus illustrate the difficulties of the time and the persistence of the Roman administrative tradition. Most of his letters were written while he was minister to Theodoric; the *Institutes* were composed in his old age in the monastery which he had founded and to which he had retired. Isidore of Seville, wrote in the early seventh century, during the period of the Visigothic domination of Spain. He composed an encyclopaedia which tried to tabulate and preserve the whole range of contemporary knowledge; he is perhaps the most influential of all the transmitters of classical knowledge and his etymological writings handed down political ideas of great importance, particularly for Thomist thought.

To turn first to Cassiodorus.[1] In the *Institutes* we have a document which aims at giving a condensed account of the knowledge of the time; in the letters he wrote on behalf of the illiterate Gothic king, a first-hand record of the mentality and politics of the sixth century; both show interesting limitations.

The former are divided into two parts; the first gives an outline, *divinarum litterarum*, supplemented by topics relevant to the conduct of monastic life. The second, strictly subordinated to the first, is an outline of secular knowledge; it is contained in seventy-two pages of the Oxford text. The following extracts from the Introduction to the second book will indicate its quality. Cassiodorus, enumerating the contents, gives these reasons for grouping them under seven headings: 'A number which, repeated continuously through succeeding weeks, stretches illimitably to the whole world's end.' The proof, he says, of this arresting thought is given by the use of the number in Holy Scripture to enumerate 'anything which is continuous or endless'. There follows a passage on numbers in general. 'Now the creation of God has evidently been made with number, since He Himself says in the Gospel, "Even the hairs of your head are numbered". Similarly, the creation has been planned with measurement . . . as

---

[1] Cassiodorus Senator, Flavius Magnus Aurelius; born at Squillace, in Calabria, *c.* 480, of Roman official family; Consul at Rome, 514. He became the principal minister of the Gothic king, Theodoric, not an easy position, and survived the dynastic feuds which were the sequel to the king's death in 526, when the queen regent, Amalasnuetha, was murdered in her bath by Theoduhad. He continued to make the best of the Gothic rulers until 540, when, after the collapse of the Gothic kingdom before the Byzantine armies under Belisarius, he retired to his estate between Aspromonte and the sea. He converted the place into a monastery and set to work deliberately to preserve what knowledge, classical as well as Christian, he could. He also wrote a commentary on the Psalms and compiled a Church history. He died in 575. See *Letters of Cassiodorus*, translated and edited HODGKIN, Frowde (1886); and R. A. B. MYNORS, *Cassiodori Institutiones*, Oxford (1937).

He Himself bears witness: "Which of you by taking thought can add one cubit to his stature?" ' The devil, on the other hand, has no concern with order: 'Hence it is obvious that the evil works of the devil are limited neither by weight, measurement nor number.' It was through this sort of medium that mediaeval knowledge emerged, and it still deeply affected the sophisticated scholasticism of the thirteenth century.

The letters depict clearly the society of the day. On the one hand, Cassiodorus lives in a world still thinking in terms of the complicated bureaucratic structure of the late empire. There are the *nobilissimi*, the *illustres*, the *spectabiles*, the *clarissimi*; the hierarchy of official classes who still sustained the crumbling structure Cassiodorus spent his life shoring up. On the other hand, the barbarians; the Gothic kings, Theodoric, Athelaric, Witigis, whom he served and in whose names most of the letters are written. Finally, on the edge of civilization, there appear and disappear the real barbarians, the Frankish, Burgundian, and German rulers, who have to be propitiated and dealt with after their kind.

Cassiodorus is constantly concerned with the reparation of walls and aqueducts: 'We are anxious', he writes, 'to keep the walls of Rome in good repair . . . See that this is done. The persons to whom money was entrusted for the rebuilding of the walls of Rome have been embezzling it.'[1] The aqueducts are the object of special care: 'We desire you at once to root up the shrubs growing in the Signine channel, which interfere with the purity of the water supply in the aqueduct of Ravenna; vegetation is the peaceable overturner of buildings.'[2]

He had endless difficulties to contend with. 'We regret to learn from your report that the brazen elephants placed in the Via Sacra are falling to pieces. This is to be regretted, that whereas the animals live in the flesh for more than a thousand years, their brazen effigies should be so soon crumbling away. It is most desirable that we should preserve the image of these creatures.'[3]

[1] Bk. II, letter 34.
[2] Bk. V, letter 38.
[3] Cassiodorus cannot resist a long disquisition on the natural history of the elephant, in which the following points deserve quotation: 'The living elephant, when it is prostrate on the ground, as it often is when helping man to fell trees, cannot get up again unaided. This is because it has no joints to its feet, and accordingly you see numbers of them lying about as if dead until men come to help them up again . . . The elephant always walks cautiously, mindful of the hunter's pit which was the beginning of their captivity. At its master's bidding it exhales its breath, which is said to be

Public post-horses, moreover, are being loaded with private documents. 'This must cease; what can the poor quadruped do when pressed by a too great burden? It succumbs.'[1]

He is constantly concerned with problems of defence and with the training of the militia. 'War needs rehearsal and preparation. Therefore let your illustrious Sublimity provide the inhabitants of Salona with arms. The necessity for drill and practice is shown by the combats of young bullocks and the playhuntings of young puppies', he adds, irrelevantly.[2]

The barbarians have to be tactfully dealt with. 'The Lord of the Burgundians, Gundebad, has earnestly requested that we should send him a clock which is regulated by water, and one, also, which is marked by the embracing illumination of the immense sun . . . It would be a great gain to us that the Burgundians should daily look on something sent by us which will appear to them to be little short of miraculous. Exert yourself, therefore, O Boethius, to get this thing put in hand . . . What a wonderful art is mechanics!'

Boethius,[3] as a person of culture, is also asked to find a harper for Clovis. 'The King of the Franks has asked us to send him a harper. We felt that in you lay our best chance of complying with this request, because you, being such a lover of music yourself, will be able to introduce us to the right man.' There follows elaborate reflections about the nature of music, and the letter ends 'Be sure to get us that *Citharoedus*, who will go forth like another Orpheus to charm the beast-like hearts of the barbarians'.[4]

Clovis was the most dangerous of them: 'If Clovis succeeds in his unprovoked aggression, none of his neighbours will be safe; he is prepared to shake the kingdoms of all of us; he ought to desist from his attacks and seek redress from the law of nations.'

[1] Bk. V, letter 5.   [2] Bk. I, letter 40.

[3] The influence of Boethius (482-525) on the mediaeval outlook was destined to be considerable. The *De Consolatione Philosophiae* is, however, an echo of pre-Christian antiquity, rather than typical of the new concern with salvation which actuates all the most representative writings of the age. As is well known, he was a poet of some merit. His translation of Aristotle's *Organon*, a treatise on formal logic, was his most lasting contribution to mediaeval knowledge. His intention of translating the whole of Plato and Aristotle into Latin was frustrated by his execution by the Ostrogoth Theodoric.

[4] Bk. II, letter 40.

a remedy for the human headache. There is a sort of kingly dignity in its appearance and it seems to despise scurrilous jests.' This ancient belief was still widely prevalent in the seventeenth century; see Sir Thomas Browne, *Enquiry into Vulgar and Common Errors*, bk. III, chap. i.

The barbarians within the borders were also a problem, and the mercenary troops a nuisance. They were apt to get out of hand, particularly on festive occasions. Writing on behalf of Theodoric to the Goths of Samnium, he says: 'Come into our royal presence on the eighth day before the Ides of June, there solemnly to receive our royal largesse; but let there be no excesses by the way, no plundering of the harvest of the cultivators nor trampling down of their meadows. *Civilitas* must be kept intact.'[1] To the officer in charge at Avignon: 'We charge you to see that no violence happens at Avignon; let the Romans feel that our troops are come for their defence and not for their annoyance.' The Gepid mercenaries are encouraged to accept payment in money rather than live off the country, to them a more natural proceeding.

It is evident from Cassiodorus' letters, apart from their disarming pedantry, that the Gothic government is doing its best under atrocious difficulties; they admire the Roman tradition and are anxious to live up to it. The mixture of moralizing and high flown writing with business is curious; but even in these times a plodding sense of responsibility persists.

The writings of Isidore of Seville cover a wider theoretical field, of direct importance to political theory. They contain political ideas of greater influence than Isidore ever grasped; definitions of Natural Law and kingship, of the tradition of Roman government, taken and distorted from classical writers, in the interest of a grotesque etymology.

The contribution of Isidore to the survival of ideas about Law are contained in the fifth book of his *Encyclopaedia*; about government, in the ninth book (sections 3-4); and about war in the eighteenth (1-12). They form only a small part of this large and extraordinary collection, ranging over all the field of knowledge. Starting with an outline of grammar, rhetoric, mathematics, and astronomy (chapters 1-3), Isidore proceeds to an alarming account of the medical science of his day. The sixth and seventh chapters are theological, and the eighth deals with the organization of the Church. Next there follows a survey of biological and anatomical knowledge, section 11 on portents and 12 on animals being particularly odd. There follow accounts of metals, agriculture, forestry, sport, and war; in the last chapter are included detailed accounts of chariot racing and gladiatorial games. After a passage about ships, he proceeds to an

[1] Bk. V, letter 26.

anatomy of clothes and finishes with an account of meals and cooking, beds and vehicles — *instrumentis hortorum et equorum*. The whole is contained in two thick volumes of the Oxford text.[1]

In book IX Isidore gives an account of the languages and races of men, for which he works out a fantastic Old Testament pedigree. He regards the races of northern Europe as savages. The Germans are so called *quod sint inmania corpora, inmanesque nationes saevissimis duratae frigoribus*[2]— 'They are fierce and unconquered, living by hunting and plunder; the depth of their barbarity is apparent in the hideousness of their speech.' The Saxons are outstanding pirates; the Franks particularly fierce; and the Gauls ('Galli', so called from the Greek 'gala', milk, owing to the whiteness of their skins) show 'a sharp wit, as one would expect from their climate'; the Brittones are so called *eo quod bruti sint* — 'Because they are stupid'.

He proceeds (IX, 3) to an etymological definition which was to have a most important bearing on the subsequent theory of kingship, and which could be interpreted as setting the king under the Law: *Regnum a regibus dictum, reges a regendo*.[3] 'The king holds his title by doing right; there is an ancient proverb': *Rex eris si recte facias; si non facias, non eris* — 'You will be king if you do right; if you do not do right, you will not be king.' This point of view crudely foreshadows mediaeval ideas of kingship and is echoed by Bracton in the thirteenth century; it could have a very different interpretation from the ideas of absolutism then current in the Eastern empire.

He also transmits the idea of Natural Law. All laws are either divine or human; divine laws are derived from nature, human laws from custom; divine law is called *fas*, human law *jus*. 'Law is either natural or civil or *jus gentium*; natural law is common to all peoples and is maintained everywhere by natural instinct rather than by definite statutes . . . civil law is that which every State ordains for itself in matters human and divine. *Jus gentium* concerns the occupation of territory, buildings and fortifications, war, the position of prisoners of war and of slaves, exiles, peace treaties, armistices and the inviolable sanctity of envoys . . . *jus militare* contains the

---

[1] *Isidori Hispalensis Episcopi Etymologiae*, edited W. M. LINDSAY, Oxford (1911). Isidore (c. 560-636). Born at Seville and entered a monastery. Succeeded his brother as Archbishop of Seville, 599. The *Etymologiae* were his last work, written between 622 and 633. He also wrote a commentary on the Old Testament, concerned with allegories; a defence of the Christian Faith against the Jews; a history of the Goths, and a *Chronicon de sex aetatibus*, a comprehensive history from the Creation to A.D. 615.
[2] 'Because of their huge bodies, and vast tribes hardened in savage cold.'
[3] 'Kingship is called from Kings, Kings from ruling.'

formalities of declaring war, the conclusion of treaties, the process
of attacking and engaging the enemy at a given signal, and also
that of retreat' (V). Thus Isidore preserves and hands on the extremely important concept of natural law (*instinctu naturae, non con-
stitutione aliqua*). 'A law should be honourable, just and practicable;
it shall be in accordance with nature and the custom of the country;
it shall suit both place and time; it shall be necessary, useful and
clear, and not containing any obscure expression to deceive people.
It shall be drawn up not for private advantage to anyone, but for
the common good of the citizens.'

His chapters on war (book XVIII) start with tracing its origin.
'The first person to make war was Ninus, King of the Assyrians.
Not content with his own dominions and breaking the peace of
human society, he began to devastate other men's territory, and to
subjugate or massacre free peoples, and he brought all Asia into a
new servitude. From this time the world learned to batten on mutual
bloodshed by alternate slaughter.' Isidore maintains that there are
four kinds of war: 'Just, unjust, civil and, worse than civil (*plus
quam civile*), war between relatives.' Following Cicero, he distinguishes between just and unjust wars; he separates war from sedition
or revolution; *Bellum igitur est totum, pugna unius diei, proelium pars
pugnae est* — 'Therefore war is total, battle lasts for a day and a fight
is part of a battle'.

Most of Isidore's ideas can be traced to a debased acquaintance
with Cicero, Lucan, and Virgil, mixed with extensive biblical knowledge. His prime concern is with etymologies, not with subjects, and
he displays remarkable ingenuity in inventing false derivations. For
example, GLADIUS is so called *quod* GULAM *dividit, id est cervicem secat;*[1]
INSULAE *dictae quod* IN SALO *sint, id est in mari;*[2] ROTA *dicta quod quasi*
RUAT*; est enim machina de qua e flumine aqua extrahitur;*[3] LAPIS *dictus quod*
LAEDAT PEDEM;[4] VOMER *dictus quod* VI HUMUM *eruat, seu ab* EVOMENDO
terram.[5] *Vetus Testamentum ideo dicitur quia veniens Novo cessavit* — 'The
Old Testament was so called because, with the arrival of the New,
it ceased.'[6]

Isidore's thought is indeed elementary, if ingenious. But under the

---

[1] XVIII, vi. 'Because it cuts the throat, that is to say cuts off the head.'
[2] XIV, vi. 'Islands are so called because they are in the salt, that is, in the sea.'
[3] XX, xv. 'A pump is so called because it goes round like a wheel; for it is a machine
by means of which water is extracted from the river.'
[4] XVI, iii. 'A stone is so called because it hurts the foot.'
[5] XX, xiv. 'A plough is so called because it heaves up the soil by force, and because
it vomits up the earth.'   [6] VI, i.

conditions of the day it is remarkable that the *Etymologiae* could have been written at all.

The background against which he wrote must be reckoned with. Illiteracy and brutality were the rule over most of Europe, among the people at large, and at most of the petty courts of the barbarian kings. The record of the Gothic, Anglo-Saxon, and Frankish princely houses is a shocking one, and these people were among the first to be Christianized. Certainly there is another side to the picture; a naive sudden conversion running into childlike excesses of piety; an access of temper with the ancestral gods, leading to fitful attempts to get a better deal out of the new religion; an intelligent ruler entering into reasoned debate with the missionaries; but these instances are the exception, and are over-emphasized by the monastic chroniclers. It is well to realize the kind of thing with which the Church had to deal. The following example could be paralleled, if not surpassed, in other chronicles of the times. It is worth remembering this dominant side of life in understanding the thought of the age.

A contemporary account of the Frankish court of the late sixth century, the period of Isidore's youth, comes down in the Chronicle of Gregory of Tours,[1] who writes a Latin worthy of the subject to which he devoted himself. Painfully aware of his own rusticity, he apostrophizes himself in the preface of his work: *O rustice et idiota, quid nomen tuum inter scriptores indi aestimas? Putasne ut bos piger palaestrae ludum exerceat? . . . Non tibi latet quod sim inops litteris.*[2] His editor remarks succinctly that 'a study of the manuscript is enough to prove his sincerity'.

His account of the Merovingian Queen Fredegunde's attempt to get rid of her daughter is worth quoting in the original. The queen employed the time-honoured stratagem of inviting the princess, who was called Rignunth, to choose what she would from a chest containing jewellery belonging to her dead father. The eager girl plunged head and shoulders into the treasure box, whereupon her mother tried to suffocate her with the lid. *Apprehenso mater opertorio archae, super cervicem eius illisit — quod cum in fortitudine premerit, atque*

---

[1] Georgius Florentius, Bishop of Tours. Took the name of Gregory on entering the Church. He came of a well-to-do Gallo-Roman family. Bishop of Tours, 573. Died, 585, ten years after Cassiodorus. Wrote the *History of the Franks*, 575-85, translated and edited DALTON, O.U.P., 2 vols.

[2] 'Oh rustic and silly man, why do you imagine that your name can be set among the writers? Do you think that a fat ox can do circus tricks? It cannot be concealed from you that I am weak at letters.'

gulam ejus axis inferior ita attereret, ut etiam oculi ad crepandum parati essent.[1]
Fortunately, one of her maids gave the alarm and the queen was
prevented from completing her design.

The behaviour of Queen Fredegunde outside her family was even
more outrageous; she specialized in poisoning and murder, and
used to provide her assassins with drugs to keep their courage up
before embarking on their operations. The early Merovingian
aristocracy were as savage as their rulers, and expressed themselves
by elementary and cruel jokes, of which many examples can be
found in the chronicles.

Under conditions of this sort it is remarkable that anything survived. One barbarous characteristic made for some continuity of
tradition; a reverence for a misunderstood memory of the past. The
conservatism of barbarian peoples preserved, parrot-like, the rudiments of civilization. If they regarded the Romans as 'giants' or
'demons', the barbarians had an immense respect for the memory of
Rome. They deliberately imitated Roman institutions, Roman
dress and Roman art; and the ghastly results they achieved were
better than deliberate destruction. There is no parallel, even in the
boisterous activities of the Vandals, with the systematic rooting out
of civilized life undertaken by the Huns under Attila, or later, by the
Mongols in Mesopotamia. Further, the barbarian invasions revital-
ized Europe. The later empire had arrived at an *impasse*; the
crushing taxation; the veritable caste system, the general decay of
initiative, all indicated a society ossified and cumbrously out of gear.
There could be no new beginning without a phase of disintegration;
without the Dark Ages there could have been no twelfth-century
Renaissance.

§ I I I

We have now glanced at the minds of an executive statesman of
the sixth century; of a Spanish bishop of the seventh; and at the kind
of behaviour found at the barbarian courts. Between them they
explain why the period was not in a condition for speculative
political thought. But out of this welter of barbarism, with the
monks holding on desperately to their debased knowledge, there

---

[1] 'Her mother seized the lid of the chest and crashed it on to her neck, intending
that the violent force and the pressure of the lower edge on her throat should cause
her very eyes to start out of her head.' (XI. 34.)

emerged one institution which had never lost its continuity; the Papacy. It was the remaining focus of civilized initiative, the last positive element in the classical tradition. From this centre the revival of culture radiated in the sixth century; round it the forces of the future were destined to rally, and out of it the missionary effort, whereby civilization made its counter attack, was to come.

Throughout much of Europe the episcopal and parish organization remained. Once the Papacy had secured its position in Rome, there were elements beyond the Alps ready to answer a wider leadership; and the desperate situation which had developed even in Italy by the end of the sixth century was retrieved by the re-establishment of the papal power under Gregory the Great.[1] The victories of Justinian's generals in the first part of the century had not prevented the decay of the Byzantine power by the end of it; the Lombard invaders and the trail of warfare over Italy had dislocated economic life and spread misery and pestilence over the peninsula. Forced down to a bare fight for survival, the Church produced a statesman who not only consolidated the Roman base, but struck outward with a missionary drive to the north, which was to bring in good returns in the dark years to follow.

Gregory displayed a fierce ascetic energy. His writings show that he cared for nothing besides the work of conversion and consolidation. His *Pastoral Rule* shows him a wise administrator, and his letters to St. Augustine of Canterbury, quoted in Bede's *Ecclesiastical*

---

[1] Gregory the Great. Born *c.* 540, of Christian Roman family of good position. 573, Prefect of the city; converted his palace into a Benedictine monastery and became a monk. From 579 to 585 Gregory lived in Constantinople as representative of the Pope, where he is said to have converted the patriarch Eutychius to a belief in the material reality of eternal punishment. In 590 he became Pope. He died in 604. There is no evidence that he originated the Gregorian method of chanting or wrote the hymns attributed to him. He is best known in England for the legend of the Anglian 'slaves'. It runs as follows. Struck by their fair-haired and innocent appearance, when exposed for sale by a Jew in the bewildering inferno of the slave market, he is said to have inquired their country of origin. According to Bede, he followed up his well-known comment 'Non Angli sed Angeli', by asserting that the inhabitants of Deira should be saved 'De ira Dei' and as their king was Aelle they should sing 'Alleluia'. He is said to have set out himself to convert the English, but a locust settled on the book he was reading on the third day of his journey. He concluded it meant 'locus sta' (i.e. 'stay where you are'), and abandoned the project. The evidence of the whole story is, according to DR. HOLMES-DUDDEN, very weak (*Gregory the Great*, Longmans (1905), p. 191, note). THE VENERABLE W. H. HUTTON, on the other hand, in the *C.M.H.*, vol. II, p. 237, thinks it authentic: 'There is no reason', he says, 'to doubt the familiar story.' The legend is an English tradition, and first appears in the life of St. Gall, which says: 'Est narratio Romam venisse quidam ex nostra natione forma et crinibus candidati albis, crispes juvenes et decores.' 'There is a story that certain of our nation came to Rome, of fair hair and complexion — fresh and elegant young men.' Bede is the first to call them slaves and to mention the Jew.

History, show his shrewdness in dealing with barbarians. Augustine writes him a series of questions, all of which he answers undaunted in a practical and decisive way. For example, 'after mature deliberation on the affairs of the English', he decides that 'the temples of that nation ought not to be destroyed, but let the idols which are in them be destroyed . . . for the temples are well built and it is requisite that they be converted from the worship of devils to the worship of the true God . . . that they may the more familiarly resort to the places to which they have been accustomed'. They are still to be allowed their ritual cattle-killing (he refers to the autumnal slaughter in the 'Blood Month' — November), but 'to the praise of God'. It is impossible, he says, to efface everything at once from their obdurate minds, and he is ready to work through the medium of the old customs.

He co-ordinated and directed the economic policy of the Papacy. By sheer force of personality he overawed the Lombards, who threatened Rome; he is a figure of similar calibre to Hildebrand and Innocent III. His statement of the papal position is uncompromising; outside the Church there can be no salvation. 'The Holy Universal Church proclaims that God cannot be worshipped save within herself and asserts that all who are without her pale shall never be saved.' The Church is apostolic, and Rome its head. 'To all who know the Gospels, it is plain that to St. Peter, the Prince of the Apostles, Our Lord committed the care of the whole Church.' Though he is *servus servorum Dei*, on the Bishop of Rome devolved the succession: 'I know of no Bishop who is not subject to the Holy See.' His attitude to the secular power is still ambiguous, and he makes no theocratic claim, merely asserting the priority of conscience.[1]

Gregory shows also the credulity and pessimism of his age. In spite of his immense activity, he cares nothing for life. 'Our Lord desires to find us ready, and shows us the misery of a worn out world in order to divert our love from it . . . Be alert and watchful; those who love God should shout with joy at the end of the world . . . The world grows old and hoary and through a sea of troubles hastens to approaching death.'

It says much for the executive flair and sense of civic order of the Roman stock that Gregory's will was not paralysed by this outlook.

---

[1] *Quod Imperator fecerit, si canonicum est, sequimur. Si vero canonicum non est, in quantum sine peccato nostro, portamus.* — 'What the Emperor does, if it be canonical we follow. If it be uncanonical, we put up with it in so far as we may without sin.' Ep. 11, quoted HOLMES-DUDDEN, *Gregory the Great*, Longmans (1905), p. 414.

On the contrary, he consistently displayed formidable energy. Thus, at a critical moment in the history of the Church, an organizer of the first calibre emerged in Italy; he turned a difficult corner, while the missionary effort which coincides with his pontificate, linking up with the Celtic revival of the sixth century, bore fruit of surprising quality in the North.

For out on the fringe of civilization, in the north-west, Christendom was to find unexpected allies. First in the independent Celtic Church, later among the Anglo-Saxons, who, converted by both Roman and Celtic missionaries, were to exercise a powerful cultural effect on the Continent.[1] These influences combined with the drive from Rome, with all its formidable organization behind it, to imbue the barbarian converts with a new sense of the purpose of government. The limited and often bloody-minded outlook of tribalism gave place to a sense of trusteeship and of participation in a universal society.

The survival of Celtic Christianity from Roman times in Ireland, Wales, Cornwall and other parts of the West Country provided a source of new power. St. Patrick's ministry in Ireland during the fifth century had its sequel in the sixth, with the settlement of St. Columba on Iona, and the spread of missionary influence over Western Scotland. In a world of soft air and brown water, with the tang of peat smoke on the wind, where the rain drifted across landscapes of heather and sea, there had grown up a form of Christianity reflecting a different background from the harder Mediterranean environment. A new spirituality was realized in strange hermit colonies in their beehive huts, looking out, solitary, on the Atlantic.

Manuscript illumination — later to contribute to the art of the great sculptors of the twelfth century — drew new vitality from Celtic artists, and Celtic influence was, indeed, already spreading over the Continent by the time of Gregory the Great. St. Columbanus in the late sixth century was carrying it to Gaul and Germany, and it had penetrated to Northumbria. It was here, among the Anglo-Saxons of northern England, that Celtic and Roman influences combined, the latter related to St. Augustine's mission to Kent. Here there grew up a remarkable culture. The Southern influence arrived first with Paulinus; the Celtic influence later with St. Aidan. In consequence there was a blend of Celtic and Roman tradition which inspired the Northumbrian culture in particular. Here the

---

[1] See LEVISON, *England and the Continent in the Eighth Century*, O.U.P. (1946).

Anglo-Saxon scholars carried on the tradition of learning through a dark time, and by their influence on the Carlovingian court contributed a good deal towards the re-establishment of civilized standards among the Franks.

The Venerable Bede[1] is the best known representative of this English development. He displays a new cultural initiative. His *Ecclesiastical History* and his letters are of particular interest, and he helped to reinforce the traditional tribal obligations of the barbarian rulers with a constructive and touching piety.

Bede realized the degradation of his age. Following Isidore, he imagined he was living in the last of the six phases of human history, which were divided as follows: the Creation, the Flood, Abraham, David, the Babylonian captivity, and the Incarnation. The entire process was to take 3952 years, so that there were not many more years to run. As a geographer, also, he took a depressing view of his situation, since he imagined that England lay on the uttermost edge of the world. His interest in chronology is determined by a desire to find out the correct date of Easter. But, through the fog of the early eighth century, his character is attractive and full of good sense; he was evidently a teacher of genius and his influence extended indirectly to the Carloving renaissance. His pupil Egbert founded the school at York which produced Alcuin, who, in turn, is thought to have attempted, though without success, to teach Charlemagne to write.

The monasteries in which Bede spent his life, Monkswearmouth and Jarrow, were founded by Benedict Biscop, a young Northumbrian nobleman, who had decided to forsake the world. The society in which Bede lived, though elementary and insecure, was a healthy one; the missionaries who had converted these uncorrupted barbarians were picked men, and the barbarians themselves uncontaminated by the decadence of the old civilization. His letters throw an interesting light on the conditions of his time, on Anglo-Saxon attempts to avoid military service by the foundation of bogus monasteries, and on the prestige of a man of God in a barbarous world. There is something attractive in the thought of Bede's

---

[1] The Venerable Bede (672-735). Born and brought up in monastic territory on the Tyneside. Entered the monastery at the age of seven and spent his life there. He exercised a formative influence over the culture of his day, and was one of the greatest minds of his age. He died translating the Gospel of St. John and Isidore of Seville (*de libris Isidori episcopi excerptiones quasdam*), and indeed to translate Isidore into Anglo-Saxon may well have taxed anybody's powers.

English scholars, in their thatched Northumbrian huts, in the depths of the eighth century, laboriously transcribing the magic words of salvation through the cold and the pale sunlight of northern winters. 'I do not', he said, 'want my boys to read a lie' — *nolo ut pueri mei mendacium legant.*

Bede's thought is often elementary, but he conserves knowledge and asserts the humane values; he records the increasing control of the Church over the lay rulers, and has the vitality to start writing work of his own. He greatly contributed to the cultural tradition of Northumbria, afterwards revived in Wessex.[1]

Thus the native clergy, Celtic and Anglo-Saxon, began a cultural leadership which gave them increasing social influence. The missionary drive from Rome was bearing fruit in the North; the Anglo-Saxon culture penetrating into France and Germany encouraged similar development on the Continent.

So in the North the Christian tradition took root. We are no longer down to a slavish imitation of the past, but find a new initiative, backed by barbarian vitality. The Christian missionaries embodied the best aspects of Christianity, of the original Gospel — that alone could have impressed the barbarians. The miasma of Byzantine theological controversy could not live in the North.

It is indeed remarkable how kindly the Anglo-Saxons took to

---

[1] Bede already shows the perennial English interest in the cuckoo. In his poem about the bird, Spring personified exclaims,

> Opto rursus veniat cuculus, carissima ales,
> Omnibus iste solet fieri gratissimus hospes,
> In tectis modulans rutilo bona carmina rostro.

To this Winter replies,

> Non veniat cuculus, nigris sed dormiat antris
> . . . *Omnia disturbat.*

The dialogue continues for eleven stanzas, until it is closed by the intervention of 'Palaemon', the shepherd,

> Desine plura, Hiems, rerum tu prodigus, atrox,
> Et veniat cuculus pastorum dulcis amicus . . .
> Salve, dulce decus, cuculus, per saecula, salve.

The sense of this poem may be roughly rendered as follows:
Spring: I hope the cuckoo comes again, best beloved of guests, singing his goodly songs on the roof-tops with orange tawny bill.
Winter: We don't want the cuckoo. Let it sleep in black caves. It disturbs everything.
Shepherd: Give over, winter, you wasteful, cruel creature, and let the cuckoo come, the shepherds' sweet friend. Welcome, cuckoo, our charming ornament, welcome down the years.

Cuculus, sive Veris et Hiemis conflictus, Bedae Venerabilis Poemata II, *The Works of Bede*, vol. I, edited by DR. GILES (1843).

Christianity, considering their record in the fifth century, when they
had the reputation of particular savagery. Already by the eighth
century the Northumbrian Cynewulf is giving his native interpretation of the new religion in the *Dream of the Rood*, a poem
which even in translation has already the authentic beat of later
English accented verse. The following vision of the Crucifixion
is fine poetry:[1]

> Then the young hero,
> Who was God Almighty,
> Firm and unflinching
> Stripped himself.
> He mounted on the high cross,
> Brave in sight of many,
> When he was minded
> To redeem mankind.

The Anglo-Saxon vision of heaven is homely, with its stress on the
reunion of friends. 'There shall be song of angels, the delight of the
blessed; there shall be the face of the Lord brighter than the sun
for the happy ones; there shall be the love of friends; life without
death . . . rest without strife for those who did right, peace henceforth without dissension between friends happy in heaven.' We are
a long way from the metallic splendours of the Hebrew apocalypse.

Thus the classical inheritance, transmitted from antiquity in
Christian terms, was reinterpreted in the North. The barbarian
peoples are beginning to assimilate the southern culture, reduced to
the elementary terms they can compass by the ordeal of the Dark
Ages, and with it the concept of the trusteeship of power.

Out of the despairing resignation of the fifth century, through the
anxious labours of Cassiodorus and the credulities of Isidore, through
the administrative genius of Gregory and the missionary drive from
Rome, there has emerged in the North an outlook crude, resilient,
and healthy. The petty barbarian kingdoms are touched to a new
sense of European community; coaxed into a new way of life, a new
political morality. The assimilation of this Caritic aspect of Christianity was to produce a new concept of government, to be expressed
in the labours of Charlemagne and Alfred; it contrasts with the grim
materialism of the old barbarian outlook, for all its high qualities, so
pessimistic.

[1] See GORDON, *Anglo-Saxon Poetry*, Everyman edition, p. 262.

L

By the eighth century, then, out of the North-west, came a fresh wind to shred away the sullen clouds that had long brooded over the Continent. Irish and Anglo-Saxon missionaries began to play their part in clearing the wreckage the decline of the empire had left behind, while in the South the Papacy consolidated its power for its bid for European supremacy. The tide of civilization, reinforced with the new vitality of the converted barbarians, by the ninth century sets fully towards its mediaeval goal.

CHAPTER II

THE RISE OF MEDIAEVAL CIVILIZA-TION: THE BARBARIAN CONTRIBUTION

§ I

THERE were to be two dominant influences in mediaeval political thought: on the one hand, the Christianized tradition of antiquity, coming down through monastic and missionary influence, centred on the Papacy, bringing with it memories of Universal Law, great-scale administration, and a common civilization; on the other, the barbarian contribution of a degree of self-government and the elements of representative institutions. The survival of the first influence has been traced in the last chapter; we will now turn to the second.

The native barbarian institutions, working on a small scale and embedded in a slow-moving agricultural framework, gradually began an original and far-reaching progress unknown to the ancient world.

The barbarian peoples were capable of self-government and rudimentary co-operation, while tribal kingship, tamed and organized by the Church, was to develop into an effective, though not a despotic, method of government. This kind of rule later made for the emergence of semi-autonomous, self-governing bodies, the mediaeval guilds and corporations, which possessed a vitality the bureaucratic structure had long drained out of the cities of the South. The beginnings of self-government and a capacity for give and take begin to be apparent in very early times among these self-sufficient, level-headed peoples of the North.

The barbarian contribution falls naturally under three heads: Anglo-Saxon, Frankish, and Scandinavian.

The first developed a habit of local government and responsibility; the second an attempt at European order in the huge empire of Charlemagne, which marks the emergence of western Europe out of the Dark Ages and a new political initiative in the North-west; and the third, the Scandinavian contribution, a new legal and maritime enterprise. All three overlapped and heightened one another; combined, they altered the outlook of European political thought.

An examination of early Anglo-Saxon laws, of the organization of Charlemagne's household and of Scandinavian customs, will illustrate these respective barbarian contributions. But first it will be well to look at the new society which grew out of the ruins of Antiquity. Through the collapse of monetary relationships and the social paralysis of the later empire, civic administration had gradually lost touch with the country districts. Towns decayed or became walled fortresses; trade dwindled to a precarious traffic in the smaller luxuries; the peasants huddled for protection round the nucleus of the great estates, increasingly militarized, either for protection against slinking war bands or because the Romanized landowners had been butchered and replaced by barbarians, who gradually adopted a sub-Roman way of life, a debased version of the culture they had helped to destroy. This society was provincial, purely agricultural, and thoroughly inefficient, but it carried on. Other centres of order were the urban bishoprics, often coincident with the *civitates* of the older regime, and the parishes, formed as the country districts were gradually Christianized.

The barbarian institutions emerged from this background; they generally centred on a Christianized tribal kingship. Reinforced by religious sanctions and enriched by a few generations of comparative security, the barbarian kingdoms became more formidable; Alfred and Pepin were able to establish their power on a scale impossible for their ancestors in the fifth and sixth centuries. Further, they could count on organic and indestructible peasant institutions, growing up as the invaders settled into the soil and interbred with the original stock, as the Teutonic barbarians stabilized by absorption into the native village communities.

Among the Teutonic and Scandinavian peoples tribal decisions had generally been taken in the assembly of free men. Although they possessed slaves and treated anyone not a fighting man with contempt, their early kings remained war leaders whose position was justified partly by descent and more by personality; there could be no question of despotism and still less of bureaucracy in such a society. But the consciousness, mainly fictitious, of common descent, made for a patriarchial feeling, which emerges particularly after the adoption of Christianity in the outlook of Charlemagne and of Alfred, who still styles himself *Rex Saxonum*. In England this solidarity with the reigning family survived, territorialized, linking up with the institutions of shire and hundred moot into a common authority to form an organic basis for government, once society had been pulled together by Norman efficiency.

It was round the early tribal kingship, as it settled into the newly won lands, that the rudiments of ordered society began to form. Gradually the rulers extended their authority by enforcing an increasingly comprehensive law, which ceased to be merely personal and tribal. Under primitive conditions the individual looks not to government for his protection, but to his own kindred and clan. He may look first to his paternal or maternal relations; the common assumption is the same; the only method of securing justice is through blood feud, or at best through agreed fines. The substitution of payment in money or in kind for blood feud marks an important advance; the next stage comes when the king takes over the responsibility of enforcing the fine. He thus implies a new idea, that not only had the crime wronged the individual and the kindred against which it had been committed, but that the act of violence had done something new, and broken the 'King's peace' also. Thus the transition is made from the rule of tribal, personal law to a social order differently organized from that of the South; and this transition involves a territorial conception of law and society which absorbs and supersedes the primitive tribal and clan loyalties.

The transition from the first stage to the second is illustrated from many tables of barbarian law: the development of Anglo-Saxon law provides a convenient illustration. The following examples are taken from the earliest known legal document in the English language, the laws of Aethelbert, who was converted by Augustine. They date from about the year 610; they are mainly detailed penalties for physical assault, but here is the beginning of the idea of the Public Peace.[1] The laws are almost exclusively concerned with fines for violence, rape, and theft; they are drawn up under ninety short headings; apart from the first, they show little Christian influence, harking back to heathen custom. The first is concerned, naturally under the circumstances, with the protection of Church property, thus putting it into the existing social system. 'Breach of the peace shall be compensated doubly when it affects the Church or a meeting place.' Apart from this precaution, extra fines are imposed for violence in the king's presence. 'If a King's liege is molested in the King's house, double compensation and fifty shillings

[1] ATTENBOROUGH, *The Laws of the Earliest English Kings*, Cambridge University Press (1922).

to the King.' 'If the King is feasting in anyone's house and any sort of offence is committed there, twofold compensation shall be paid.' The laws proceed to a tariff of penalties for murder and for the unauthorized loan of weapons. Provision is also made that *wergild* shall be paid up in time. 'If one man slays another, he shall pay twenty shillings before the grave is closed and the whole within forty days.' Payment for murder is thus arranged by instalments; there follow graded penalties for assault and damage to property. Damage to ears, eyes, teeth, noses, etc., is carefully assessed. 'If one man strikes another on the nose with his fist, three shillings.' (*Gif man operne mid fihste in naso slaeð*,[1] *III scill*) (57). For seizing a man by the hair, the fine is fifty *sceattas* (33). Finger-nails are a shilling apiece, toe-nails ten *sceattas*. If a freeman abducts the wife of another, he shall pay him her *wergild*, procure him a new wife (*other wif*), and deliver her at the husband's home (*aet ham*). Fifty shillings is paid for criminal assault on a widow of the best class, twenty for assault on one of the second class, twelve on one of the third, while assault on a fourth-class widow is assessed at six shillings.

Such are the earliest known utterances of English Law, comparable in some respects to the laws of Hammurabi already examined. They throw an unhappy light on the behaviour of our ancestors, but such a tariff is a landmark in social progress.

The laws of Ine of Wessex, which date from about eighty years later, are less exclusively devoted to the more obvious crimes, and more influenced by Christianity. Grouped under seventy-six headings and enforced by the king, they begin with provisions connected with the Church. Early baptism of infants is most important; if the child dies unbaptized, the guardian forfeits his entire property. Slaves must not work on Sundays. Church dues must be paid at Martinmas. The right of sanctuary is asserted. 'If anyone fights in a monastery, 120 s. fine; in an Alderman's house, 60 s. compensation to the owner and 60 s. fine.' This high penalty is enforced 'even if the fight takes place in the open'. But if two men quarrel over their cups, and one 'endures it patiently', he need not pay. There are many clauses dealing with theft. 'He who captures a thief shall have ten shillings; the thief shall be given up to the king and his kinsmen swear to have no vendetta against the captor' — an important provision; a man need not incur blood feud through doing a public service.

The agricultural life of Anglo-Saxon England can be sensed from

[1] In Anglo-Saxon the signs þ and ð signify 'th'.

these laws. The provisions are exact. 'If rent for pasturage of pigs be paid in kind, every third pig shall be taken when the bacon is three fingers thick, every fourth when it is two fingers thick, every fifth when it is a thumb thick.' 'A ewe with her lamb (*mid hire giung sceape*) is worth a shilling until a fortnight after Easter.' A sheep shall retain its fleece until after midsummer (*Sceap sceal gongan mid his fliese oð midne sumor*) (69). A cow's horn is worth twopence, an ox's tail a shilling and a cow's tail fivepence (*Cuuhorn bith twegea paeninga, oxan taegl bið scill weorð, cus bið fifa*). 'If ceorls have a common meadow to fence . . . and some have fenced their portion and others not, so that the cattle get in and eat up the grass, those responsible for the gap shall compensate the others' (42). Careless setting fire to woodlands is severely punished: 'He shall pay sixty shillings, because fire is a thief (*fyr bið theof*).'

Owners ought to make the best of their land. 'He who has a holding of twenty hides shall show twelve hides of land under cultivation when he means to leave' — a very large area, so large that the provision may be mainly deterrent. There are further penalties for breaking into the premises of the king or a bishop, and the custom of clearing oneself by an oath is widely employed.

It will be seen that by Ine's day there is already some sense of general responsibility and accepted authority. The Anglo-Saxons had made the first transition into territorialized law. How, on the other hand, it was possible to remain in the primitive stage is shown by the complications in which the Welsh, lacking Anglo-Saxon common sense, involved themselves right up to the thirteenth century, when the old responsibility of the kindred was still being zealously calculated.

It was a natural but gradual development. Migrations and new conditions had disintegrated the original tribal arrangements. The overlapping of different kinds of law was incompatible with any ordered government; it was difficult either to keep up the old system or to create a new one. One expedient was to form 'guilds' and artificial 'brotherhoods' going beyond the kindred, a widespread Anglo-Saxon practice; but the only permanent solution was for a central authority to impose law which applied equally to all in a given territory, with and through the co-operation of the military aristocracy, which is increasingly rooted to the soil. Hence the provision 'Every man must have a lord'. 'With regard to lordless men from whom no legal satisfaction can be obtained, we have declared that their relatives shall be commanded to settle them in a fixed residence where they shall be amenable to Public Law.'[1] These rudimentary governments tried to pin men down into the social organization of the manor, of the local courts, of the land. Thus social distinction comes not only through birth but through property; the tribal and clan society, which widely persists in Ireland and Scotland, is superseded by an order which serves better both the interest of the king's government, which can impose its very sketchy authority only through the good will of the *thegnage* and of the magnates with whom its interests are bound up.

So the primitive loyalties of clan, sept, and kindred are replaced by a combined effort to keep a degree of order, to assist rather than hinder the royal government in its struggle for a rudimentary peace, since, in the long run, order pays those who have a 'stake in the country'. Here is the beginning of a common-sense conception of government, with a healthy respect for property; it foreshadows an outlook later to assert itself with particular strength in England and in North America.

§ 11

While this practical and gradual development was at work in England, there occurred on the Continent a more ambitious Frankish initiative; nothing less than the revival in the West of a Christianized barbarian version of the Empire itself.

The Frankish empire of Charlemagne is the greatest political achievement of its age, and marks a reorientation of European culture. Based on northern France, Belgium, and the Rhineland, there had emerged by the ninth century a political institution which, though it drew its title from the past, was largely a new creation. The concept of the Holy Roman Empire, for all its vagueness, marks the revival of the idea of European order in the West and the defini-tion of a structure of royal government which was to be the model for subsequent European kingship. Further, with the Carloving dynasty, the political centre of gravity of western Europe shifted to the North; initiative and institutions became Franco-Teutonic. The squalid barbarism of the Merovingian court was giving place to a vigorous, constructive, if over-ambitious phase. The Merovingian Frankish dynasty was still a continuation of the decadent Roman

---

[1] ATTENBOROUGH, *Laws of Aethelstan*, op. cit.

tradition; it looked to the Mediterranean for its cultural contacts and foreign policy. The Carloving dynasty, on the other hand, for all Charlemagne's alliance with the Papacy, was a North-western power; it looked away from the Mediterranean, no longer the high-way of commerce and centre of civilization it had been throughout antiquity, but now a barrier. Arab corsairs had paralysed seaborne trade; they had established themselves in Provence; they harried the coasts of Southern France and overran Sicily; the whole North African coast and most of Spain was lost to Christendom; western Europe from the eighth century till the First Crusade was on the defensive.

The economic results of the Mohammedan aggression were disastrous; the coinage became debased and the trade with the Levant through Venice interrupted. It was a most serious situation, and the Papacy was right to come to terms with the Transalpine military power which formed what was left of European defence. For the Arab expansion contributed to the de-Romanizing of the North, though the personal qualities of the Merovingian rulers in the seventh century, true to their tradition in the sixth, had already accentuated the cultural and political decline.[1]

With the enfeeblement of the monarchy and the weakening of economic and political links with the South, the Germanic element in the Frankish kingdom came to the fore, while the influence of the native aristocracy increased. Pepin, who was illiterate, stands culturally for an anti-Romanizing and barbarian movement. When finally, in 751, the papal decision in Pepin's favour 'relegated the poor Merovingian king to a monastery and no one troubled further about him', the Teutonic influence had prevailed. 'The home of Western Christendom was displaced towards the North; it was represented by the line Rome-Metz-York; Rome, the mistress, lay no longer at the centre but at the periphery; the unitary culture of the Mediterranean centre was shattered.'[2] So it came about that the Roman empire became Germanized, and ultimately, under

---

[1] 'When Chilperic ascended the throne in 715, it was 25 years since any Frankish king had lived to reach his majority. The explanation may be found in the debauchery of these princes. Most of them were doubtless degenerates. Clovis II died insane. . . None of these kings had any influence whatever; they were the puppets of the Mayors of the Palace, against whom they did not even attempt to react. Not one of them attempted to have his Mayor of the Palace assassinated, as the Roman emperor had formerly done at Ravenna; on the contrary, *it was they who were assassinated*. They lived under the tutelage of their mothers or sometimes of their aunts.' PIRENNE, *Mohammed and Charlemagne*, Allen & Unwin, p. 191.

[2] SCHUBERT, *History of the Early Middle Ages*, quoted by Pirenne.

Barbarossa, 'romantic', a thing the original empire certainly never was. Latin disappeared as a colloquial medium; it became a learned tongue, which the Anglo-Saxon missionaries mainly responsible for the Carloving renaissance and for Christian missionary efforts in the interior of Germany, regarded as a foreign and sacred speech.

Charlemagne's household was the centre of government for the whole empire; its officers his executive ministers. Thus the frame was set, afterwards taken for granted in subsequent European government, which differs a good deal from the official structure of antiquity or of Byzantium. The constable (*comes stabuli*), originally in charge of the horses; the chamberlain, originally in charge of the treasure and clothes; the seneschal, in charge of the meals; all expanded into the great offices of state at the courts of mediaeval and subsequent times. The chancellor, originally responsible for the royal documents, and the king's council, or immediate entourage, develop into something more precise and permanent. Further, the feudal count, in charge of a district, and the feudal seigneur, responsible to the king for his vassals, are both in part of Frankish origin. The model of much mediaeval political organization was created at the court of Charlemagne.

Though it owed a good deal to sub-Roman influences as well, a revived conception of great-scale government dates from this period. The Carlovings, in contrast to their Merovingian predecessors, no longer trundled to the tribal 'Mayfield' in a ceremonial ox wagon, or wore their hair long because it was a sacrilege to cut it, or were raised at their accession on a shield, amid the uncouth acclamations of the assembled warriors; they proclaimed themselves kings 'by the grace of God', with the full ceremony of coronation, anointing, throne and sceptre, ever since traditional in the West.

Charlemagne himself is a figure of the greatest interest. Convinced of the sacredness of his mission, he aimed, like Alfred, at educating his nobility. The advance he began depended on his own personality; politically without adequate foundations, in the short run it proved premature, but the tradition of a divinely sanctioned ruler, combining the attributes of a Frankish warrior with those of a Justinian, persisted in the West, and was later to dominate the secular aspect of mediaeval political theory.

Of Charlemagne personally more is known than might be expected; the reality is different from the figure of legend. In the *Vita Karoli Magni*, Einhardt, his chaplain, wrote a first-hand account of his personality and household. The extent of Charlemagne's dominions is best shown in the list of the metropolitan cities of the empire contained in his will. They are as follows: Rome, Ravenna, Milan, Fiuli, Gratz, Köln, Mainz, Salzburg, Trier, Sens, Bésançon, Lyons, Rouen, Rheims, Arles, Vienne, Moutier in the Tarantaise, Embrun, Bordeaux, Tours, and Bourges. The centre of this huge accumulation was the palace and cathedral at Aachen, where the insignia of empire were preserved.

Einhardt writes: 'It was on account of the warm baths that he built his palace at Aachen . . . he not only invited his sons to bathe with him, but also his chief men and friends . . . so that at times one hundred men or more would be bathing together.' He was very skilful in swimming, 'no man being able to outstrip him'. Of his personal habits and appearance, Einhardt gives a detailed account. He was a big man, 'nearly seven feet tall . . . the top of his head was round, his eyes large and animated, his nose somewhat too long, his hair white and his face bright and pleasant . . . although his neck was too thick and his belly too prominent, still his good proportions concealed these defects'. He was so voluble in speech that 'he seemed like a schoolmaster' (*didasculus appareret*); his appetite was large, though he was temperate with wine, and he liked best 'roast meat which the hunters brought on a spit and of which he partook more largely than any other food. While he was dining he listened to music or reading . . . he derived much pleasure from the works of St. Augustine, especially from his book called *Civitas Dei*.'[1]

Charlemagne had fourteen children by four successive wives and five concubines. 'He was so careful in bringing up his sons and daughters that he never dined without them, and they always accompanied him on his journeys. His daughters were very fair and he loved them passionately.' He would never consent, says Einhardt, to give them in marriage, but kept them all at home, with unfortunate results.

In addition to the main household at Aachen, there was also a palace at Ingelheim near Mainz, and one at Nymvegen in Holland. This vast but premature attempt at European domination used the Rhineland not as a frontier but as a base; had it proved practicable, the age-old conflict between the French and Germans might have been resolved. The effort failed, and Europe fell back into the

---

[1] EINHARDT, *Life of Karolus the Great*, translated and edited Glaister, Bell (1877), pp. 74-6.

disastrous division, since come to be thought natural, which has long handicapped Western civilization. But the prestige of the Carloving experiment remained enormous,[1] and the tradition of the Holy Roman Empire persisted effectively in European politics right up to the time of Charles V. Further, Charlemagne extended his rule over Saxony and the Upper Danube, initiating the German drive in the East. Coming when it did, his empire marks another turning point out of the Dark Ages into the constructive phase of early mediaeval development.

§ III

Such, then, was the Frankish contribution. We will now turn to the Scandinavian. According to legend, towards the end of his life, Charlemagne, riding along the shore, saw the first Viking war-boats and wept — and indeed they were to be the scourge of Europe for the next two centuries.

The Viking heathen were even more formidable than their Teutonic forerunners, they displayed more initiative and intellectual power; they were efficient and constructive. This virile strain probably contributed more to European civilization than any of the other barbarians.

The organization displayed in the Viking expeditions is remarkable; they could co-operate on a large scale. 'Fleets comprising hundreds of ships were gathered together without any appointed leader; seven, nine, fifteen, or even a greater number of "kings" are named as chieftains of the Scandinavians . . . "We are all equal", are the words placed by a Norman legend in the mouths of the Vikings as a reply to a Frankish messenger who inquired for their leader. Yet all these individual wills subordinated themselves to a common decision; obedient to their self-given laws, the Vikings sailed to victory over the great kings of the West and their unruly vassals.'[2]

[1] Charlemagne's great reputation brought him an embassy from Haroun al Raschid, the Caliph of Bagdad, who sent him, among other *ingentia dona*, an elephant called Abulabaz. It arrived at Pisa, in the charge of a Jew, in 801. A 'fleet' was prepared to bring it into Gaul, and it was brought a year later to Aachen. The animal survived until 810, when it succumbed when accompanying its master on an expedition into Denmark. Neither this elephant, nor the various other ones which made their appearance on and off through the Middle Ages, induced mediaeval artists to modify the extraordinary convention in which they depicted these animals, or shook the faith of zoologists in the fantastic ideas about their behaviour, which they inherited from the Dark Ages, *vide supra*, p. 149n.

[2] AXEL OLRICK, *Viking Civilization*, Allen & Unwin (1930) p. 98.

They were more than a match for the cumbrous levies of their opponents. *The Anglo-Saxon Chronicle*, which refers to the invaders in a bewildered way as 'the Army', tells how they consistently out-manœuvred the slow-moving *Fyrd*. 'When the King's men should have gone out to meet them as they went up, then went they home; and when they (the Danes) were in the East, then were the King's men detained in the West, and when they were in the South, then was the Army in the North.' The perfidy and mobility of the Danes shocked and deceived their opponents — 'And this year the Army stole into Wareham, a fort of the West Saxons. The King afterwards made peace with them, and they gave him as hostages those that were worthiest in the Army and swore with oaths on the Holy Bracelet . . . that they would readily go out of his kingdom. Then, under colour of this, their cavalry stole by night into Exeter.'

Their discipline, too, was remarkable for that age. The following Viking code throws light on the organization of a war-boat and shows the standard expected and enforced.

'(1) This was the beginning of their Law; that there should no man enter that was older than sixty, and none younger than eighteen winters. (2) Never should kinship be taken account of, when men wish to enter that were not of their league. (3) No man should run before a man of like power or like weapons. (4) Every man should avenge the other as he would his brother. (5) None there should speak a word of fear or dread, however perilous things might be. (6) All that they took in warfare should be brought to the *stang* or *pole*, little or big, that was of any value, and if a man had not done this he must be driven out. (7) None there shall kindle discussion or waken quarrel. (8) And if tidings come, no man should be so rash as to tell it to anyone, but all tidings to the captain. (9) No man should bring a woman into the fort. (10) None should be abroad three nights together.'[1] Another code provides that 'no man shall have a sword longer than an ell, so close were they to go; no man shall bind a wound till the same hour next day'.[1]

In addition to their piratical enterprise, the Scandinavians early showed their capacity for legal organization and routine. For example, from very early times there is provision for the observation of the peace and the ending of feuds, often through oaths and the co-operation of neighbours. There is a rudimentary attempt at self-

---

[1] VIGFUSSON and YORK POWELL, *Origines Icelandicae*, Oxford (1905), vol. I, bk. II, p. 324.

government, in the absence of effective central authority. 'All knew
how it standeth concerning the feud between N. and N.; but now
their friends have come between them and are wishing to see them
at one. There was feud between N. and N., but now they are at
peace.' This was a formula of the oath:

> Ye two shall share knife
> And carven steak
> (*Deila knif oc koet stycce*)
> As friends and not as foes.

The pact was ratified: 'As the meter meted, and the teller told, and
the doomsman doomed, and the givers gave, and the receivers
received and carried away, with full fee and paid ounce, handselled
(presented) to them that ought to have it.' After the taking of the
oath, the following formula was used: 'Now are N. and N. at accord
whenever they meet, on land, on water, on ship or snowskate, on
sea, on horseback, to share oar and bilgescoop, bench and bulwark
if need be.' If they broke the truce: 'It was the old heathen custom
in our land that if a man was outlawed for breach of truce, the
twelve men named for his peace ought to take the right of out his
money.' 'But there is a law in Norway and over the Danish tongue
that if a man observe not his peace or truce, that the man be outlawed throughout Norway, and he shall never come back to the land
again.' It would have been hard to enforce this law, but the oath-
breaker is liable to be 'hunted as far as men hunt wolves . . . He shall
be outcast from Church and Christian men, from every world save
hell woe.'

The moot or 'Thing' played an important part in Scandinavian
life. 'No man shall bring either weapons or drink to the law court,
and if it be taken thither it shall be taken away; half the weapon
and half the outlawry fine and half to the men of the moot. But the
mootmen shall have all the drink . . . Let men sit at the moot with
quiet and seemly behaviour and let no man go away till the moot is
closed.' These regulations date from Christian times, but there are
similar provisions in the earlier customs.

A full expression of the Scandinavian polity was achieved in
Iceland, where, remote from southern influence, the descendants of
some of the toughest elements on the mainland developed a characteristic and original social order. We have a full description of the
organization of the Icelandic Great Moot or Althing. 'A law court

shall also be held every summer at the All Moot and it shall sit ever in the place where it hath long been; and there shall be three raised places, so broad that there be room on each of them for four twelves of men. There are twelve men of each quarter that have seats in the law court, and the law Speaker also . . . Men shall take to them a law Speaker, and settle upon whom it shall be. It is also well if all men are agreed on this man, but if any law court man withstand him whom most men wish for, then shall lots be cast to see in what quarter the law speaking is to go.'[1]

The good sense and clear grasp of detail shown throughout these laws is strikingly apparent. At the same time, the heathen Vikings had a wicked side to them. The fighting aristocracy are portrayed in their literature as beautiful, brave, and capable of fine feeling, in contrast to the treacherous, ugly slaves. The worst crime is kin-killing, which can only be expurgated by religious rites and lifelong exile. The next is treason, for which men are torn to death by wild bulls and hunted by dogs;[2] adultery in a wife is punished by trampling by horses, or the archaic penalty of cutting off the nose. Wager of battle is a usual method of settling quarrels, with an elaborate code of challenge, acceptance, conditions, and penalties. It was held usually on an island in a sort of prize ring; the combatants fought with sword and shield by alternate strokes, the senior having the first blow and neither being expected to give ground. They buried their illustrious dead in great barrows; they gambled at dice; they admired riddles; they played chess and staged competitions in 'tongue-play', in which the women also took part, scolding for a stake. They camouflaged their tents black and used fighting dogs in battle, and they had a habit of bone-throwing after dinner, as St. Elphege learnt to his cost, for he was martyred by this means.

They were a cruel people; the sagas are full of stored-up revenges, in which the women play as ruthless a part as the men. They practised human sacrifice in the blood-stained groves of Upsala, far into historic times; they hacked 'blood eagles' on the backs of priests and drove nails into their brains; they flayed their victims alive, burnt whole families in their beds, and pitched their bivouacs, by choice, among the piled-up dead of northern battlefields. But they respected cunning — Odin was a god of runes as well as war —

---

[1] *Origines Icelandicae*, pp. 345-7.
[2] See *The Danish History of Saxo Grammaticus; fl. c.* 1200, edited YORK POWELL, Folk Law Society (1894).

and they had a shrewd eye for trade. Their merchants combined for plunder and profit, uniting in self-protective convoys for the better prosecution of their business. Viking settlements in the Irish coast towns captured or developed the Irish trade, while the native peasantry was relegated to the interior. In the east their cities of Kiev and Novgorod monopolized the traffic in wax and honey, furs and slaves on the Dnieper, the Dneister, and the Don. The great water-roads of Russia, the centre of the emerging Kiev-Russian state, were first exploited and secured by the organizing ability of the Swedish grand princes of Kiev, while the foundations of early Russian Law are Scandinavian.[1]

The self-sufficient qualities bred in the bone of these men, who wrested a living from the northern seas and planted their windswept homesteads in Iceland and the Hebrides, in the dales and moors of Northern England and the Isle of Man, in Ireland and Normandy, in Sicily and the Levant, whose fleets terrorized the Mediterranean, and who entered as Verangians the service of Byzantium, expressed themselves in tough institutions and hard traditions which kept their descendants vigorous and enterprising for generations, even under demoralizing conditions of success. Their literature displays admirable characteristics, in spite of its harshness and pessimism. The Icelandic sagas, written down in the twelfth century but originating in earlier times, give the best impression of their mentality. From a welter of personal animosities and blood feud emerges a dour common sense, respect for legal contracts and points of law. Cut off from the normal civilization of the Middle Ages, the Icelandic settlements, made deliberately by men who would not bear the authority of the Norwegian kings, present the essence of the Viking qualities.[2] There is a Homeric admiration for character and a dominance of practical motives. The great man of the sagas is independent, self-reliant, bound by the same 'community of prosaic interests' as his dependants; he 'sails his own ship'.[3]

[1] Sir Bernard Pares, *History of Russia*, Cape (1937), pp. 20 and ff.
[2] See *The Saga of Njal*, Everyman edition; and *Egil's Saga*.
[3] See W. P. Ker, *Epic and Romance*, Macmillan (1897), for the best account of the Scandinavian and Teutonic literature of this age. The ethical standards of these people, at their best, are, he says, 'equally marked out from the . . . cheapness of popular morality on the one hand and the ostentation of oriental or chivalrous society on the other'. He compares the interest in character, so remarkable in the sagas, with that found in the writings of Crabbe and Hardy in their more peaceful worlds. It was an intense and limited society. 'They had nothing much else to think of than other people's affairs.' The result is an acute and modern self-consciousness, plainly set out, for there is nothing romantic about them.

Thus both the laws and the sagas depict a primitive and brutal society, but one redeemed by common sense. 'The most singular thing in the heroic age of Iceland is that the heroes knew what they were about . . . They possessed a self-consciousness, a hard and positive clearness of understanding, such as is found nowhere else in the Middle Ages and very rarely in any polity.'[1] The Njal Saga portrays a strong sense of order conflicting with the tradition of primitive blood feud. The routine of 'riding to the Thing' persists through all the complications of the plot. The characters stand out in a hard light; how a man faces adversity is coolly judged; there is a summing up and balancing of evidence expected and admired by these people and much is required of a man.[2] This individualism, good sense, and self-reliance were the finest of the barbarian qualities.

§ I V

Such, then, were the respective Anglo-Saxon, Frankish, and Scandinavian contributions to the new Europe; all, in spite of their original barbarity, unite in seeing facts as they are, in a level-headed grasp of essentials. The political sense these qualities imply shows great promise; it was to be one of the foundations of subsequent democratic self-government. Christianized and influenced by Roman Law, Anglo-Saxon, Frankish, and Scandinavian reliability was to prove an invaluable element in the European, and subsequently the American, tradition. The defined and more rigid institutions of the South break down; the balance is redressed by the instinct for responsibility and the adaptable institutions of the North.

A sense of fair play, a capacity to look at political problems without excitement, to work together in the public interest, was shown by the Anglo-Saxons, who otherwise could never have made their curious institutions work; while the Scandinavians, and in particular the Latinized Vikings of Normandy, politically the most successful of them all, show a clear-cut realism and a sense of legal order alien to the Celtic peoples and lost to north-western Europe since Roman times. The spirit of the barbarian peoples was thus destined, in alliance with Roman Christianity, to make a distinctive and original

[1] KER, op. cit., p. 68.
[2] In Anglo-Saxon poetry there is the same exacting standard. The famous *Song of Maldon*, written as late as the tenth century, expresses the old barbarian ethic of resistance to hopeless odds and defiance of ruin, 'Thought the harder, heart the keener, mood the more, as our might lessens'.

contribution to European political thought. This development runs parallel to the transmission of the knowledge and tradition of Mediterranean antiquity traced in the last chapter.

So the Western world passed through the worst period of cultural decline, when barbarism and decadence joined hands, and re-emerged in the ninth century with the barbarian influence swamping and invigorating the remnant of the old order. Anglo-Saxon, Scandinavian, and Frankish political sense, military force and vision, and the drive of the Latin Papacy, create new shapes out of the chaos of the Dark Ages. Europe re-emerges with new institutions and a new outlook, and the stage is set for the development of mediaeval society. Feudalism, kingship, the empire, the Papacy, all are there; it will be the purpose of the following chapters to examine their interaction and their effect on political thought.

CHAPTER III

FEUDALISM AND KINGSHIP

§ 1

THE most articulate aspect of mediaeval political thought centres on the theory of Christendom and the conflict between ecclesiastical and lay power which arose from it, but following on from our account of the barbarian contribution, it will be well first to deal with the secular aspect of mediaeval political theory; with the development of feudal ideas, with mediaeval kingship and its theoretical subordination to Law. The feudal idea of contract, together with the concept of the ruler as the leader of the folk, whose function is to declare and enforce the common custom but not to make it, was to combine in the long run with the Roman tradition of Law which came down from antiquity, in the main through the Law Schools of Italy.

The theoretical subordination of kingly power, the focus of a new large-scale political integration, to a wider law, is illustrated both by feudal documents on the one hand and, on the other, by the best known political expression of the twelfth-century Renaissance, the non-feudal *Policraticus* of John of Salisbury, which directly influenced Bracton in the thirteenth century.

First, then, we must glance at the origins of feudal custom and at the king's relation to it; next, take account of the ideas of contract to which that custom gave rise; and finally, examine the non-feudal doctrine of kingship as a public power, set out in the *Policraticus*, a document of singular interest.

European society in the Middle Ages had grown up out of the ruins of antiquity, the barbarian interpretation of the Christianized tradition of Rome. As the Roman Empire had been cosmopolitan and world-embracing, so mediaeval Christendom, its heir, remained cosmopolitan. The unity of European culture was expressed by the Church, the universities, and the fighting aristocracy, later elaborated in the great European orders of chivalry. The political ideas behind this society are in theory clear and comprehensive; in the *universitas* of Christendom there can be no sovereign 'state', though the emperor may claim some shadowy authority. The mediaeval 'realm' was a nucleus of ordered government within the great order of Christendom; in relation to the 'estates' within such a realm the king at once represented the whole *communitas regni*, and held the balance between the various interests which made it up.

Mediaeval kingship was therefore, ideally, held in trust. The king is under God and Natural Law; the law was not 'in the king's breast'. If he said it was, he was *Tyrannus*, not *Princeps* — the ancient distinction is already made by Isidore. Within the great family of Christendom, the secular ruler held his proper place. Further, both feudal law and tribal custom put the king under the Law. The barbarian tradition of responsible and limited monarchy could link up with the Roman and Canonist tradition of universal law. It was only when mediaeval civilization broke down that the naked power of the sovereign ruler began to emerge. It was a desperate expedient; by strict mediaeval standards, a phenomenon of decadence.

The Middle Ages saw the building up of a great Christian community, united by a common religion, participating in a common culture. The monuments of this civilization cover the length and breadth of Europe: the cathedrals and the solid parish churches; the gaunt ruins of the strongholds of the feudal baronage; the tradition, still so much alive, of the European universities. This civilization came to its maturity and its decline. With growing sophistication, the simple motives of its creation began to flag; while its attitude to scientific knowledge, comparable to that prevalent in the traditional East, made for grave technical incompetence. The waning of the faith which had inspired the early Middle Ages; the loss of prestige by the Church; economic expansion; all these things ended in the disruption of the fifteenth century. But the traditional political theory remained. For all its difficult conventions, there is a line of direct descent between the highly systematic mediaeval theory of the rule of Law, the subjection of power to moral ends, and the assertion of limited monarchy and later of popular sovereignty. Moreover, the barbarian habit of participation in government — in particular Anglo-Saxon and Scandinavian good sense and judgement, respect for Law and instinct for legal procedure — were crystallized in mediaeval thought and institutions. They persisted through the phase of absolutism which was the price paid for the organization of power on a national scale. Mediaeval political thought asserted two great traditions: the unity of European civilization and the limitation of power through subjection to Law.

The first focus of power in the barbarian state was the monarchy. It has been shown, already, how by the time of Charlemagne the rulers had been tamed and won over by the Christian Church. Already closely identified with the bishops and higher clergy, the national kingship, with success, increasingly depends on a clerical bureaucracy, steeped in the southern tradition, and upon professional lawyers who are building up their own code of constitutional practice. By the twelfth century a systematic work of mediaeval political theory has been written; the *Policraticus* of John of Salisbury. This work sets out the place of kingship in society, and insists that the king is subject to the rule of law. Before examining it, we must trace the developments that made its appearance possible.

§ 11

Generally speaking, in France, England, and Christian Spain, a degree of centralized government exists by the late twelfth century; and it was indeed in Spain that representative institutions seemed most promising. In Germany and Italy, tribal and provincial elements and the European preoccupations of the emperor on the one hand, civic independence and papal power on the other, prevented the consolidation of a central authority.

It was to be in England that the mediaeval realm reached its most lasting influence; and here systematic political thought appears in the later twelfth century. It was here, moreover, that government was most effectively sustained by revived legal and bureaucratic routine. Since, moreover, it was to be in England that the secular mediaeval political inheritance was best preserved and had the greatest future, inspiring as it did the whole world-wide Anglo-Saxon tradition, it will be well to study English developments closely, as most representative of their time. The English realm was geographically suited to centralization, as were Norman Sicily and the small kingdoms of northern Spain. In geographically less coherent areas, the great provincial duchies of France and the empire, the Communes of the Low Countries and north Italy, defied the periodical visitations of the rulers of the Germanies and France.

The foreground of it all was feudalism; the background, the toiling peasantry, who had been spreading over Europe since neolithic times. National monarchy grew in part out of feudal monarchy, and this feudal inheritance, together with the tradition of Christian

piety and French ideas of chivalry and romance, makes the mediaeval king different from the kings of antiquity. The feudal king, as
he develops gradually into a national king, brings his feudal appara-
tus with him, tending in time to work it into the tradition of centralized government and law revived from antiquity.

He contributes something new to the theory of government, and
feudal institutions, modified and adapted, are turned to new uses
by new occasions. The feudal method of government implied, when
adapted to a degree of central authority, a corporative idea of the
realm. Feudal arrangements implied a bargain between overlord
and vassal, and this idea was liable to be transferred to the relation
between the different estates in a kingdom. Moreover, the feudal
outlook implied, in theory, an attempt by all parties to keep their
bargain in accordance with custom, the obligation of both lord and
vassal to find out and admit the rulings of feudal law. A man had
the right to be tried by his peers, and the king the obligation to consult his vassals. This obligation linked up with the tribal and
traditional function of the barbarian kings, to find out what the
tribal law is in consultation with the wise men or the oldest men,
and to interpret, not to make, existing custom. Thus in this aspect
royal power is not arbitrary, but implies consultation with both
feudal and traditional elements in the realm. Here, it would seem,
are the beginnings of the important idea of the kingdom as a balance
of interests, in part expressed through a parliament.

It is probable that the origins of feudalism go back into Roman
times, as well as deriving from barbarian custom. The magnates of
the late empire surrounded themselves with their *clientes* and *bucel-
larii*, private military gangs, which they equipped and rewarded
themselves. The custom of commendation, accompanied by hand-
shaking, goes back as far as the second century,[1] and the barbarian
following also derives from very early times. The Frankish *Pueri*, the
Lombard *Gesindi*, the Anglo-Saxon *Thegns*, and, in Germany, what
Tacitus calls the *Comitatus* — all these barbarian institutions link up
with Roman custom. Both have two principles in common: first,
the personal relation of patron and client, leader and follower, and
second the obligation of the patron to provide equipment and the
means of livelihood. Translate this, as it was bound to be translated,

---

[1] *Vide* DOPSCH, *Economic and Social Foundations of European Civilization*, chap. ix,
for a full discussion of this problem. Dopsch goes so far as to say that modern research
points to some degree of feudalization of public authority in the later Roman period.

into land tenure, and the basis of feudalism is secured. The use of heavy cavalry by the barbarians also goes back very far; the mediaeval knight has an unbroken pedigree to antiquity, though in the Middle Ages his equipment becomes more elaborate and more difficult to come by. The constant civil wars of the Merovingian period and dynastic rivalries during the break-up of Charlemagne's empire had further increased the power of the fighting aristocracy; by the end of the tenth century feudal arrangements were the most practicable method of government.

The feudal expedient (system is a misleading word) thus resulted from the breakdown of large-scale government and paid standing armies, from the social dislocation of the declining empire, from the strength of the tie of personal loyalty among barbarian peoples, and from the supremacy of the mounted knight on a trained war horse.

The numbers of the feudal host were very small,[1] but their training was highly specialized and their equipment expensive. In the early Middle Ages the knights had it all their own way.[2] Sweating under the thick leather beneath chain and ring mail, armed with a lance and a clumsy sword, swung up and brought down in a great cutting arc (see the way it is carried in contemporary seals, well back to strike), and protected on the left side by a huge kite-shaped shield, they had better control of their horses than the Roman cavalry since the use of the stirrup had been learned from the Huns in the fifth century. Only the Byzantine Kataphracts, who carried a bow as well as even fuller equipment for close fighting, could stand up to them.

The castle was the other determining fact of the feudal age. It developed out of a crude structure of wood, placed on a mound and protected from fire by undressed hides. The square stone keep of Norman times was the main key to the military situation. The

---

[1] William the Conqueror's expedition is thought to have amounted to not more than 5000 men. 'It seems that the most plausible number we can assume for William's army is somewhere round 5000 men. Somewhere about 2000 of them were probably fully equipped knights with trained horses, of whom about 1200 sailed from Normandy and about 800 from other districts, while the remaining 3000 men would be made up of contingents of footmen and archers and the crews that manned the ships. In that age, however, 5000 men were an almost fabulously large force to collect and keep embodied for any length of time.' *Cambridge Mediaeval History*, vol. V, p. 498. See also the Bayeux Tapestry for the number of retainers necessary to 'service' the knights. Reproduction by E. MACLAGAN, King Penguin books, 1945.

[2] There was only one answer to the feudal horseman, before the effective use of gunpowder, and that was the Welsh longbow, with a rate of fire with which the crossbow could not compete and a striking power derived from the extreme thickness of the yew stave, as the French discovered in the Hundred Years War.

masonry was extremely tough, and prolonged mediaeval warfare generally resolved itself into sieges; the castles could be starved out, but seldom taken by direct assault.

Both the feudal horseman and the castle were very expensive, particularly the former. Apart from the scarcity of weapons and armour, he needed, besides his war-horse, three or four horses for transport, and at least five men to keep the whole unit in proper condition. The central government being weak, and scarcity of coin making payment in kind compulsory, the fighting men had to live off the land. From the earliest times they were granted estates in return for service, and these *fiefs*, in feudal society, have become hereditary. There is no need here to go into the elaboration of feudal tenure; economically it was based on the self-sufficient manor, and develops fully only in open country where such arrangements are possible.[1] In Wales and Scotland, Switzerland and the Pyrenees, feudal society never came to its typical evolution, while the urbanized nobility of the Italian cities were different from their social equals in the North.

The feudal relationship was intimate and the clash of unbridled personalities determined its working; hence the frequent impression of anarchy. All centred on the relationship of lord and vassal; the Assizes of Jerusalem[2] (*c.* 1180) give a clear definition of the vassals' obligation and their right of 'diffidation' or legalized rebellion.

'. . . *L'ome deit au seignor reverence en totes choses, fermement et enterinement . . . et l'ome deit plus au seignor par le fei qui il li est tenus, que le seignor a l'ome.*' If a man finds his lord in danger of death or in prison, he must '*remonter le et geter le de cel perill*'; he should, if necessary, give him his own horse '*ou sa beste sur que il chevauche, c'il la requiert, et aider le, à son pooir, à son cors sauver.*' The barbarous French brings home the essentials of the situation.

In return, the lord undertakes to protect and further the honour and interest of the vassal, but if there be conflict between overlord and vassals, they have no right to resist him by force; '*Ne contre vostre cors*', they say, '*nos ne porteremes armes*', unless, of course, they have formally renounced their service after stating their case to their peers in the feudal court; they then have a full 'right' of rebellion. This respect for the letter of the Law is typical; feudal law is theoretically

---

[1] *Vide* VINOGRADOFF, *C.M.H.*, vol. VI, Feudalism.

[2] BEUGNOT, *Paris* (1841). They form a very full treatise on feudal ideas, since they are a synthesis of European feudal custom made deliberately for the new crusading state. Quoted CARLYLE, op. cit., vol. III, p. 27.

exact, but the rules could not be regularly enforced. Indeed the arrogance and truculence of the feudatories is apparent from any contemporary chronicle; they lacked common sense, too, being generally insolvent and often reduced to living by plunder, apart from the natural pleasure they took in hunting, brawling, and combat. When there was not a private or public war to take part in, they deliberately organized mass tournaments in which men were killed for the fun of the thing. The elaborate and generally harmless 'tourneys' of the later Middle Ages were very different from the barbarous large-scale combats (*conflictus gallicus*) of the twelfth century, and the bestial qualities of the early mediaeval aristocracy should not be obscured by the apparent splendours of later chivalry.

There is, then, little speculation among feudal theorists, though we find in Beaumanoir a glimpse of theoretical grasp and rudimentary ideas about the origins of kingship. Men, he says, were originally '*franc et d'une miesme franchise, car chascuns set que nous descendimes tuit d'un pere et d'une mere. Mais quant li pueples commenca a croistre et guerres furent commencié*' . . . those who '*avoient talent de vivre en pes*', knowing they could never get it if they were all '*assez grands sires*', elected a king.[1]

As has been pointed out, the relation between vassal and lord was personal and depended on both sides keeping certain unwritten rules. The feudal king himself, 'first among equals', was obliged in theory to give protection as much as his vassals to render service. This confusion between private personal obligations and public service, though it made for disorder, brought home some sense of responsibility in the only way intelligible to these men.

Apart from this defined relation between lord and vassal, feudal society also secured to those within its pale the right to trial by their social equals. It assumed a rudimentary co-operation among the same class. Even the king could in theory be brought to book if he broke his feudal contracts, though there was no effective machinery for enforcing a penalty.[2]

---

[1] BEAUMANOIR, quoted CARLYLE, op. cit., vol. III, p. 49n.

[2] The most familiar example of this procedure is the conflict between John of England and his barons, which resulted in Magna Charta. The feudal king, having broken the feudal rules, or, if it paid him better, twisted them into an instrument of extortion, is overcome by a majority of magnates of his realm and forced to make concessions of a feudal nature, which are afterwards interpreted in another context in a wider and non-feudal sense. Typically, the baronage of the Charter were hard put to it to enforce their bargain; all they could do was to assert their right to make war on the king if he broke his word, a clumsy expedient. There was no *sovereign* authority on either side.

Such, then, were the ideas behind feudal society, which, cosmopolitan in its higher ranks, provincial in its lower, and superimposed on an agricultural peasantry, dominated western Europe by the twelfth century. These ideas were naturally antagonistic to centralized government and bureaucracy, but they embodied a rudimentary sense of obligation and mutual loyalty, a habit of consultation with 'peers', and a respect for the rules of feudal honour and feudal law. The idea of the mediaeval realm as a balance of interests, working together and taking counsel together, owed much to feudal tradition.

§ I I I

The pivot and centre of the mediaeval realm, the mediaeval king, disposed of certain sources of strength of an entirely unfeudal kind. In the first place he was the hereditary ruler of the Folk, with a sacred prestige and a divine descent going back to tribal and pagan times. In the full panoply of battle, with the great crest of painted horn and wood towering on his helmet, mounted on a charger bedizened with the colours of the royal house, with his war pennon fluttering above him, the feudal monarch, as he turns heavily in the saddle to survey the assembled host, is something more than the greatest of feudatories; he is the mascot and the leader of the Folk. And when, in formal posture, upon the canopied dais, he dispenses the justice to which all his folk have access by customary right, he is fulfilling an immemorial duty and renewing an ancient tie.

Indeed, he had need of all the prestige he could get; his was no easy task in the face of the difficulties presented by feudal arrangements to centralized government, added to the heavy enterprise of shaping an illiterate rural society not far removed from barbarism. Throughout feudal times there was a sense that the king was a public figure whose rights and obligations were undefined and extensive. From the French *Couronnement de Loois* comes the fine phrase, '*Deus fist roi por peuples justicier*'.[1] The German *Sachsenspiegel* of the middle thirteenth century insists on his obligations to 'do right'.[2] In his presence local custom is abrogated; he is the embodiment and the servant of a wider Law.

[1] Quoted by CARLYLE, op. cit., vol. III, p. 32.
[2] 'Unde sveren dat he recht sterke unde unrecht krenke.' *Vide* CARLYLE, op. cit., vol. III, p. 40n.

The royal coronation ceremony itself goes back, as has been seen, to Carloving times; the coronation oaths early accept a wide responsibility. For example, the Anglo-Saxon Aethelred the Redeless in the tenth century took the following oath, though he failed to live up to it:

'In the name of the Holy Trinity, three things do I promise to the Christian people my subjects: first that God's Church and all the Christian people of my realm hold true peace; secondly, that I forbid all rapine and injustice to all men under all conditions; thirdly, that I promise and enjoin justice and mercy in all judgements, that the just and merciful God of his everlasting mercy may forgive us all.'

'The oath of Aethelred', says Maitland, 'may be taken as the model of the oaths sworn by king after king in the days after the Conquest . . . the oath of Henry I seems to have been precisely that of Aethelred.'[1]

Later oaths are more elaborate; all assume a sacred trust. The king is to maintain justice and do right. By the fourteenth century Edward II of England promises to 'hold and keep the laws and righteous customs which the community of the realm shall have chosen (*les quiels la communauté de vostre roiaume aura esleu*)', and to 'defend and strengthen them to the honour of God'.[2]

These coronation oaths, with their roots in very ancient times, were to be assimilated into the legal theory of Bracton, who, trained in Italian method, was to systematize the political thought of the thirteenth century in England.[3] This conception of kingship at once focused the continuity and community of the life of the realm, and could link up with the main stream of the tradition of Roman justice and European order in its Christian interpretation. It was to persist into modern times.

§ I V

There were, thus, many elements in mediaeval thought which regarded the king as the symbol of the life of the community, a 'public power', and there were many cards in the hands of an able ruler. Further, in the struggle, the king had other allies. In England, in particular, with the intellectual and economic revival of the

[1] MAITLAND, *Constitutional History of England*, Cambridge University Press (1908), pp. 98-9 and ff.
[2] MAITLAND, ib.
[3] *Vide infra*, Bk. II, chap. v.

twelfth century, the idea of centralized government gained new backing. The growing complexity of administration, the greater wealth handled, the expanding scale of living, all demanded a literate bureaucracy. Government fell increasingly into the hands of professionals trained in the revived Roman tradition, whose interests narrowed to a systematic and technical building up and interpretation of a body of law. A tough legal tradition was coming into its own, although, of course, one must remember the intense conservatism of the mediaeval mind, their idea that law was the reduction of ancient custom to writing, their reluctance for any novel 'legislation' implying new laws.

A familiar example of this more constructive outlook is contained in the twelfth-century *Dialogue of the Exchequer*, attributed to Richard FitzNeal, Bishop of London. It gives a detailed insight into the minds of the new men; cast in the form of a dialogue between master and pupil, it is worth closer study than can be given it here. The conclusion sums up the mind of this pioneer in administration. Like many other men experienced in affairs, he realizes how little can be accomplished. 'I have followed indeed myself the worst of masters, but I have . . . done what I could without a leader and without a model. For I put my axe to a rude and untouched forest, cutting wood for rough edifices, to be planned by the tool of a more skilful builder. When, therefore, from this material the structure of the royal palace shall have arisen, let him who made the beginning merit the first, though not the chief thanks.'[1]

Here is a new level of purpose and foresight, of capacity for ordered routine.

To take another English example, we find the twelfth century has left a record of constructive political thought in a fully argued theoretical work. For it so happened that, while these developments were going on, in Angevin England, at the time the leading power in the West, dominating the British Islands and north-western France, fate threw a man of high intellectual calibre into the centre of great affairs. John of Salisbury,[2] by nature a discursive philoso-

---

[1] HENDERSON, *Historical Documents of the Middle Ages*, Bell (1925), p. 134.
[2] Born *c.* 1119 at Old Sarum, in Wiltshire. In 1132 he went to Paris and in 1137 studied at Chartres; 1140, a tutor in Paris; 1148, secretary to Archbishop Theobald of Canterbury; 1155, visited Rome. By 1159 he had written the *Policraticus* and the *Metalogicon*; 1162, secretary to Becket – he was with him in exile and at the time of his murder; 1176, Bishop of Chartres; died 1180. The *Policraticus* is dedicated to Becket, 'the most discriminating mind of our generation'. John's letters, also, are of particular interest and throw light on the politics of the twelfth century. The definitive Latin

pher, became secretary to Archbishop Theobald of Canterbury in 1148; later he occupied the same office in the household of Thomas Becket. Now at that time, with the advent of the young Henry II to the Angevin throne, and with the king still holding the brilliant chancellor in high favour, a phase seemed opening of new power and prosperity for the English realm. The twelfth-century intellectual renaissance was in full tide; it was natural that John's mind should turn to political speculation. The *Policraticus*, to give it the curious mongrel title coined by its author and typical of the age, had been written by 1159, when John was under forty and when Becket's quarrel with the king had not yet darkened the horizon. It is a work of political theory on a scale unknown since Roman times.

The book is concerned with the ideal ruler and the nature of the State; its central theme that the king is a 'public power'. If he rules in accordance with the Law, he is a just prince; if he breaks the laws, he is a tyrant and may be justly killed. The prince is the head of an organic commonwealth, ruled by 'reason . . . in accordance with the highest equity', subject to God. The book shows a new standard of critical judgement; it is the work of a civilized and learned mind, and it illustrates the mentality of an age less alien than is generally supposed.

The outlook of the *Policraticus* is foreign to the feudal world. Here is the revived voice of the Roman tradition of government speaking in mediaeval terms; the voice, too, of English common sense. The book displays a wide and co-ordinated learning. The author is familiar with Virgil, Plutarch, Suetonius, and Pliny, with Terence and Petronius and a whole range of other authors. He draws on an extensive, sometimes overwhelming, knowledge of Greek and Roman history and displays a realistic political judgement, a shrewd assessment of men and affairs, without the parrot-like quality and self-consciousness often apparent in mediaeval writing. The author's more general opinions are mainly contained in books I and III, and his political thought in books IV and VIII.[1] The ideal prince should,

---

[1] The contents are as follows: the first book in thirteen chapters, is concerned with the court and the contemporary fashion for hunting, gambling, and stage players. Book II, in twenty-nine chapters, deals with dreams, omens, astrologers, and crystal gazers.

edition of the *Policraticus* is by PROF. C. C. J. WEBB, Oxford (1909). There are two translations of selected parts of it: *The Statesman's Book of John of Salisbury*, edited and translated by DICKINSON, Knopf, New York (1927), and *The Frivolities of Courtiers and the Footsteps of Philosophers* (translation of books I and III and selections of books VII and VIII); edited by PIKE, University of Minnesota Press, Minneapolis (1938).

he says, be efficient, frugal, chaste, and learned. 'He shall keep the Law beside him . . . and he shall read it . . . but plainly he will hardly be able to do this if he is illiterate.' If he *is*, he will be *asinus coronatus*, but at least he can be read to. He should be affable, generous, and dignified. The sword of princely power 'smites without wrath', with due formality, thus consoling the victim, 'whose misery is mitigated by the calm reason of the words'. 'For the prince is responsible for all, since, having it in his power to correct all, he is deservedly regarded as a participant in the things he omits to correct. Being, as we said above, *a public power*, he draws from the strength of all and in order that his own strength may not fail he should accordingly preserve the soundness of all the members.'[1] The reward of the just prince is eternal life and the preservation of his dynasty, for the king is but the minister of the divine power.

John shows great admiration for the Romans, and in particular for Augustus and Trajan, whom he regards as worthy of preference before all princes. Of his own contemporaries, he praises Henry II. 'Destined to be the greatest king of the whole age among the British lands, he needs not to have me say how magnificent, how able . . . he has been from his very infancy.' When evils were multiplied in the days of Stephen, 'the valour of this boy took its stand against them, and shattered and broke the courage of the enemy'.

John well knew the difficulties of government, the demoralizing effect of success, and the folly of the court. Powerful men, blinded by fortune, surfeited with pleasure and business, lose integrity and grip.[2] Hunting and gambling, if carried to extremes, stultify their addicts. Hunting especially exasperates him; the pastime, he says, has a bad pedigree; those who pursue it come to bad ends. Ganymede was a hunter and came to little good; Actaeon was torn in pieces by his own hounds — 'a deplorable result of the training they

---

[1] Bk. IV, chap. xii.   [2] Bk. I, chap. i.

Book III, in fifteen chapters, deals with flatterers, the falseness of the rich (the rich, he says, are incapable of genuine friendship; familiarity with them, though seemingly advantageous, is often dangerous), and with the immorality of the times (chaps. x-xv). The fourth book, in twelve chapters, is concerned with the prince and the Law; how princes ought to behave and how they are rewarded; the fifth, in seventeen chapters, with the commonwealth and the administration of justice; the sixth, in twenty-nine chapters, with 'the armed hand of the State', with military problems, and the duty of magistrates. The seventh book is more general and contains many shrewd observations relevant to any age on the subject of ambition, careerists, and hypocrites ('they who seek to hide the stain of ambition under a false pretence of religion'), etc. The last book is mainly concerned with tyrants, their fate, and the rightness of tyrannicide.

had received'; Esau deserved to be cheated over his birthright; game preserves are a nuisance, and hunting interferes with the farmers.[1] Hawking is sillier than hunting, since less 'dependable'; betting and gambling, already a feature of English life, John thinks idiotic;[2] actors and jugglers are pests and generally immoral. Music he appreciates, though he distrusts it, particularly if overdone in Church services or employed to rouse passion after meals. In this kind of atmosphere, he says, the conduct of government is difficult.

Though unfamiliar with the *Politics* of Aristotle, John had evolved an organic conception of the State. The commonwealth is defined in terms of a crude simile. 'According to Plutarch . . . it (is) a certain body, endowed with life by the benefit of divine favour, which acts on the promptings of the highest equity and is ruled by what may be called the mediating power of reason . . . The place of the head is filled by the prince, who is subject only to God . . . the place of the heart by the senate, from which proceeds the initiation of good works and ill; the duties of eyes, ears and tongue are claimed by the judges and governors of provinces. Officials and soldiers correspond to the hands. Those who always attend the prince may be likened to the sides, financial officers and keepers may be compared to the stomach and the intestines, which, if they become congested through excessive avidity and retain too tenaciously their accumulations, generate innumerable and incurable diseases . . . The husbandmen correspond to the feet, which always cleave to the soil and need more especially the care and foresight of the head . . . They deserve protection all the more justly since they sustain and move forward the weight of the entire body.' The simile is difficult to work out fully, since there are so many of the last order, and, later on, the commonwealth is compared to a centipede. It is also compared to a hive. ' "Go to the ant, thou sluggard", says "Salomon", "That thou mayst get prudence", but the philosopher sends the political man to the bees.'

This commonwealth must be sustained by the Laws. Its hand 'is either armed or unarmed'.[3] The armed hand is employed only against the enemy — the unarmed is stretched out against the citizen also.

Here follows a long discussion of military affairs. Military service requires selection, science, and training; the secret of Roman success was 'to select the recruit who was quick of body and alert of mind, and, as has been said, to teach him the law of arms'. 'Singers,

[1] Bk. I, chap. iv.   [2] Bk. I, chap. v.   [3] Bk. VI, chap. i.

gamesters and fishermen' are unsuitable; recruits have to be tough, hardy, and enterprising. A small company of highly trained men will be more than a match for undisciplined valour. Strategy demands intelligence: 'The art of retreat, of attack, of surprise, is no mean one, for it provides the ability which enables one's soldiers to break up the enemy and inflict damage without at the same time exposing themselves to a counter-stroke. The practice of swimming is a great aid, for one can never foretell when necessity may require it, either on land or in a naval battle. Of great importance also is the use of missiles, by which the enemy can be damaged or thrown into a panic from a distance, while the exercise increases the strength of the muscles and cultivates the art and habit of hurling. The continuous practice of all these exercises results in making the men . . . self-reliant, bold and useful amid the confusion of war.'

The last book of the *Policraticus* discusses the right to kill tyrants. 'A tyrant is one who oppresses the people by a rule based on force, while he who rules in accordance with the Law is a prince.'[1] John relates at length the horrible ends of Caligula, Domitian, Severus, and Sardanapalus.[2] As for Commodus: 'He incommoded everyone and was finally murdered in the house of the vestals, having already in his lifetime been adjudged an enemy of the human race. And this is perhaps the best and fittest description of a tyrant; and as it is lawful to kill a condemned enemy of mankind, so it is to kill a tyrant.' All tyrants, he says, are miserable and come to bad ends — 'the exaltation of the impious is but the prelude to their heavier fall'.

He has no illusions about the holders of power. His conversation with Adrian IV, with whom he was on intimate terms, is of interest (book VI, chap. xxiv). He does not think the pope's position enviable. 'Although all defer to the supreme pontificate as the very apex of things, still in my own opinion I think that in so far as is consistent with the safety of religion a wise man ought to shun it rather than take it upon him. For, to speak truth from my own knowledge, it seems to me a most laborious and wretched post. Who then doubts that he is *servus servorum*? I call upon my lord Adrian, whose times may God make fortunate, to bear witness to this fact. He says that he wishes he might never have left his native soil of England . . . were it not that he dare not resist the dispensation of God.' Adrian he thinks sincere, but not the ambitious who pretend they have never

---

[1] Bk. VIII, chap. xvii.
[2] *Sardanapalus ille, vitiis multo quam nomine ipso deformior* – a dog with a bad name.

asked for promotion. 'For lo, to the end that some such men may be promoted, the Church is either coerced or cozened into saying, "Friend, go up higher". They feign naive amazement, shy off at the mention of dignity, even as a battering ram draws back that it may strike the harder; they decline advancement with sighs and groans and sobs interrupting their crocodile tears. For it is well known that promotion draws the unwilling irresistibly forward.'

Such is the range of John's political ideas. The conception of the prince as a public power, bound by Law; of the commonwealth as an organic whole; the shrewd assessment of political conduct; all, in spite of a mediaeval credulity, mark a new outlook. And, indeed, with the twelfth-century Renaissance, a new tradition has been assimilated from the South. Men are beginning to reason closely about matters hitherto taken for granted; a theoretical definition of kingly power, its duties and obligations, has been achieved.

In addition, therefore, to the feudal restraints on monarchy and the influence of Folk custom making for a conservative use of power, the king is regarded from another angle by the new clerical bureaucracy as the servant of the Law. This outlook is reinforced by arguments unknown to the baronage or to the Folk. The formidable array of classical texts is brought into play, appeal is made to a legendary Roman history interpreted strictly in terms of contemporary conditions. Little though John and his kind knew of the real facts of antiquity, they were opening windows on a wider world than their forebears for centuries had known. With increasing economic expansion and greater security, the fashion of this learning began to spread; its pervasive influence linked the great civil servants in a common freemasonry and touched the lay entourage of the king.

So by the end of the twelfth century a powerful monarchy is in being in England; the king has emerged from being *primus inter pares*, first among his feudal equals. From the limitations of the tribal leader of the Folk, he is beginning to take his place in the hierarchy of European Christendom, the trustee and the exponent of the tradition of the rule of Law.

CHAPTER IV

PAPACY AND EMPIRE: ST. THOMAS AQUINAS

§ I

THE distinctive civilization of the European Middle Ages contained elements unknown to antiquity and contributed a profound influence to the modern world. As we have seen, mediaeval political thought centred on the idea of a commonwealth of Christian men, working in a harmonious hierarchy under God; this ideal, though it naturally broke down in practice, in view of the elementary methods of government of the day and the limitations of human nature, left an uncompromising tradition of the moralization of power, which was to persist as one of the most valuable contributions of the Middle Ages. The idea of harmony and order is the essence, in particular, of Thomist thought, and it is with the political aspects of Thomism that we are primarily concerned, for in St. Thomas the Church produced the first mediaeval thinker of comparable range to the great thinkers of antiquity.

This ideal of harmony was riven and distorted by the conflict between clerical and lay power which echoes throughout the Middle Ages; yet both sides accepted the ideal of a Christian world order, the assumption that power is derived from divine sanction and carries obligations with it, a view incompatible with later theories of power as its own justification, and with the Renaissance idea of the State as an imposed creation of an individual ruler above the Law. The characteristic mediaeval tradition insisted that power derived from the whole community under God, having its place and justification in the divine order. As we have seen, even by the time of Gregory the Great, early Christian passivity towards government and the Augustinian dualism, which regarded the Church as a minority in a world in the main past redemption, had given place to a more responsible outlook; by the thirteenth century, with society predominantly Christian, that responsibility had been extended to all aspects of life. When, therefore, new knowledge appeared, the Church attempted to assimilate it, and following the twelfth-century Renaissance, the assimilation of Aristotle became the first task. It was the supreme object of Thomism to effect this reconciliation; but with the Aristotelian influence the value of the secular State was naturally enhanced, and in the event, classical knowledge broke the shell of mediaeval dogma, though political thought was still long expressed in scholastic terms.

Meanwhile Europe displayed the qualities of a healthy society inspired by beliefs shared by rulers and ruled. It had inherited and kept the ideal of a universal Christian order, spiritual and temporal, and it respected the rule of Law, inherent in the nature of things. The framework of Christian society is assumed; there is an all-pervading theoretical sense of order, surprising in such an age. Christendom, in spite of the barbarous aspects of the time, is regarded as a great community, sustained by an all-embracing purpose.[1]

This ideal of hierarchy under God, in which clerical and lay power harmoniously pursued their proper ends, implied no definition of sovereignty in the modern sense. Yet the exigencies of politics demanded an ultimate authority; pope and emperor both claimed such authority, and neither achieved it. In the end the defined sovereignty of lesser rulers proved the second best rallying point in the resulting breakdown.

The ultimate failure of this mediaeval moralization of power does not diminish its significance, and indeed the influence of that tradition is the most important political legacy of the time. The political aspects of Thomism demand, therefore, close attention; but before examining its essentials, some account must be taken of the background of papal power which conditioned it, and of the increasing and fatal assertion of papal claims to spiritual and finally temporal supremacy.

The Church had long embodied the memory of Rome, of civilization itself, and within the Church by the twelfth century the Papacy was increasingly influential. Of it, one of the leading authorities on the Middle Ages can write: 'The greatness of this European institution is apparent from an examination of the great mass of contemporary documents concerned with it; anyone examining it must be profoundly stirred to admiration of the machinery and organization of the Papacy; its enormous superiority, not merely as a religious centre, but as a centre of Law and government; its all-pervading activity, and finally the absolute and literal acceptance of it by the highest minds as the veritable oracle and tribunal of God.'

'On the other hand, there will be an impression, as deep, of the

---

[1] See GIERKE, *Political Theories of the Middle Age*; MAITLAND, Cambridge University Press (1913).

abuses, so unconcealed, yet so long endured, which ate into the very heart of the system; of the narrow selfishness and wholly political character of its most cherished aims . . . and, finally, of the growing bitterness and even outspoken invective which it aroused in all countries and all classes.'[1]

The theory of papal supremacy had already been foreshadowed, though not promulgated, in the ninth century in the *Donation* of Constantine, and in the eleventh by the claims of Gregory VII, who expressed the new drive of the Cluniac revival. Thus the Papacy emerged to its political culmination in the pontificates of Innocent III, Innocent IV, and Boniface VIII. Parallel with this development, the intellectual renaissance of the twelfth century culminated, in the thirteenth, in the writings of St. Thomas. Later, when the Papacy had over-reached itself, there followed the decline of the ideal of a united Christendom and a restatement of the papal and opposing positions in new terms.

§ 11

The eighth and ninth centuries had seen the consolidation of the papal power in Italy, originally the work of Gregory the Great. Following on the Carloving alliance and the defeat of the Lombards by the Franks, the Papacy developed wider ambitions, reflected in the famous *Donation* of Constantine.[2] Already the popes were dreaming of world power, their notaries providing the basis for later claims to temporal domination. It was long before reality began to corre-

---

[1] A. L. SMITH, *Church and State in the Middle Ages*, O.U.P. (1913).

[2] This celebrated document (devised c. 754-77), though not used to substantiate papal claims till the early twelfth century, shows the outlook of papal partisans as early as the eighth. It alleged that the Emperor Constantine had granted to Pope Sylvester the temporal domination of the West, and was generally accepted as genuine until the middle of the fifteenth century, when it was disproved by Laurentius Valla and, independently, by Reginald Pecock (see *The Repressor*, part III, chap. xii), in 1449. The legend from which the story of the *Donation* is derived is contained in a disreputable compilation of the early sixth century. It alleges that Constantine, who was suffering from leprosy as a punishment for persecuting the Christians, collected a number of newly born children to cure himself by bathing in their blood. 'A multitude of sucklings from all parts of the empire were collected for the ghastly purification, but with the babes came, of course, their mothers, who rent the air with such piteous cries that Constantine countermanded the massacre.' – HODGKIN, *Italy and her Invaders*, vol. III, chap. vii, Oxford University Press (1891). The emperor then fell back on Pope Sylvester, who had already won celebrity by chaining up a dragon in a cave under the Tarpeian Rock. The pope having baptized Constantine, the emperor was cured and converted. The anonymous author of the *Donation* based his mendacious construction on this tale. Gibbon remarks pertinently in this context: 'Fraud is the resource of weakness and cunning, and the strong though ignorant barbarian was often entangled in the web of sacerdotal policy.' *Decline and Fall of the Roman Empire*, chap. xliv, q.v.

spond to such ambition; the pope was not only a potential European power but also Bishop of Rome, at the mercy of the factions of the city, and the years before the Hildebrandine reforms were probably the period of worst decline. Rome itself was a wilderness of derelict palaces, baths, and public buildings, with the towers of the nobility, their stones quarried out of the desolate monuments of the past, placed at strategic vantage points among the ruins. The metropolitan city had no more economic life than the routine marketing of a low-grade agriculture; the aqueducts were broken and the bridges dilapidated; pilgrim traffic alone raised the economic life of the city above that of a second-rate provincial town; the nobility and their partisans fought one another in the streets, and the population was plagued by the fevers that haunted the dank purlieus of the river.

Against this background there emerged the notorious figure of Benedict IX, at whose accession the Papacy reached a nadir of degradation.[1] With the accession of Leo IX and Gregory VII (Hildebrand, 1073-85), the situation was transformed, a spiritual jurisdiction foreshadowed which was to culminate in the time of Innocent III. It was the world-embracing drive of the Hildebrandine Papacy that gave rise to the famous Investiture contest which determined and distorted so much of mediaeval political thought.

Gregory's pontificate marks the beginning of an attempt to create an 'imperium in imperio', a Church independent of secular society, cut

---

[1] Of this pope, Gregorovius writes with the fine gusto of the nineteenth century: 'In Benedict IX the Papacy reached the utmost depth of moral degradation. The existing conditions of Rome were apparently such as will cause us to modify our opinion even of the period of John XII, or, did we minutely compare one time with the other, would be found to surpass in wickedness the later times of the Borgias. Only an uncertain glimmer, however,' he continues, 'falls on those days, when the vicar of Christ was more boyish than Caligula and more criminal than Heliogabalus. We dimly see the captains of Rome conspiring to strangle the youthful delinquent at the altar . . . terror, however, produced by an eclipse of the sun perhaps prevented the deed; the design failed . . . Could a painter of morals but descend into the cloaca of these times, he would find sufficient material for depicting the crimes of the Roman clergy, and with this object in view, he might draw upon the *Gomorrhianus*, a book in which Peter Damian, a saint, describes the crimes of the priesthood with praiseworthy indignation but revolting artlessness' – *History of Rome in the Middle Ages*, vol. IV, part I, pp. 47, 73, 76. Sir R. Lane Poole, however, has since discounted the allegation that the pope was a boy, 'repeated by every historian who has ever written about him'. It rests on the sole testimony of Rudolf Glaber of Auxerre, an inaccurate and prejudiced chronicler, confused probably by a notice of Benedict's life, which states he had been pope for *twelve* years before his expulsion, and reading '*puer annos xii*' for '*per annos xii*' – *vide* R. LANE POOLE, *Studies in Chronology and History*, Oxford (1936). The Tudor antiquary Bale's lurid account of him, moreover, makes no such allegation, though doubtless he would have been glad to do so. He says merely that Benedict was strangled to death by a devil, and seen after death 'in a most ugly and gastefull shape . . . for his bodie was all rough and hairie like a beare'. BALE, *The Pageant of the Popes*, Englished by I.S. (1574), fol. 75, par. 87 ff.

off by celibacy and centralized: it provoked increasingly elaborate definitions of papal and imperial political ideas. But the beginnings were crude.

Both Gregory VII and Henry IV claimed divine sanction; as is well known, the result of the first crucial contest was the famous submission at Canossa.[1] The conflict is only an aspect of the expansion of a young and cosmopolitan society. Western civilization in the eleventh century was entering a phase of full vigour, foreshadowing the achievements of the twelfth. The crude vitality of the 'Gesta Francorum', the artistry of the Bayeux Tapestry, whose dandified figures swing their cloaks with a new elegance; the thick Norman pillars, striped and zig-zagged in bold relief, all are the expression of expanding enterprise.

It was an age, too, of economic revival. The great European trade routes began to pulse with a new tide: there was a steady colonization eastward in the Germanies. In Spain it was the age of the Cid Campeador and the beginnings of the Reconquista; southwards, of the Norman challenge to Byzantium in the Adriatic, of the consolidation of their power in Sicily. It was the century of the Chansons de geste, and the beginnings of Chivalry. Western Europe was again on the move; after Manzikert even the days of Byzantine pre-eminence were numbered.

The Hildebrandine movement was an aspect of all this vigour. Just as the cosmopolitan feudal world was asserting itself in the Crusades, when Europe for the first time since antiquity again took the offensive, coming to a new solidarity crystallized in the strange crusading principalities of the Levant, so the Church was developing

[1] The letter sent to Gregory on the emperor's behalf makes his position clear; *H. non usurpatione sed pia Dei ordinatione Rex, Hildebrando jam non apostolico sed falso monarcho* – 'Christ has called me to the empire, not you to the Papacy. Will you depose me, a blameless king who am judged by God alone, since the bishops left judgement even of an apostate Julian to God? Does not Peter, the true Pope, say, "Fear God; honour the king"? Because you fear not God, you honour not me whom God hath appointed . . . the curse of St. Paul touches you; the judgement of all our bishops condemns you and says, "Descend from the apostolic throne which you have usurped, that another may take it." . . . I, Henry, by God's grace King, with all our bishops, call upon you; descend, descend.'

Gregory replied by excommunication. Invoking St. Peter, he writes, 'Granted by heavenly grace, the God-given power to bind and loose in heaven and earth is mine; by that power and authority I abolish the dominion of Henry the King, son of Henry the Emperor (who with unheard of audacity has rebelled against Thy Church), over all the realm of the Germans and over Italy; and I absolve all Christian men from their oaths to him . . . and I forbid any man to serve him as King.'

This denunciation was effective. 'When it had got about among the common people that the king had been put under the ban,' writes a contemporary, *'universus noster Romanus orbis tremuit* – our whole world shook.'

out of its local particularism and coming to a more widespread sense of European community. The Investiture contest saw two conceptions of Christendom at odds; but both sides state their claims in European terms.

The episode of Canossa is a landmark in the development of the papal authority, which is conceived of as something of a different nature from feudal kingship altogether; it echoed the Imperial Roman traditions; Gregory, though he does not yet assert temporal sovereignty, has successfully stated a moral and spiritual claim.

The conflict was accompanied by a voluminous and obscure literature of controversy. It is beyond the scope of this chapter to investigate the writings of Manegold of Lautenbach, the papal apologist (*fl.* 1085), or the *Summa Gloria* of Honorius Augustodolensis (*fl.* 1125) who, following the famous Pope Gelasius, states, not very elegantly, that there are 'two swords; *unum spiritualem scilicet verbum Dei, quo sacerdotium utitur ad vulnerandos peccantes, alterum materialem, quo regnum utitur ad puniendos in malis perdurantes*'.[1]

It was in these terms that mediaeval controversy proceeded. The theory of the two swords, accepted by both sides, was never satisfactory, since it was impossible to define where spiritual and moral jurisdiction ended and secular jurisdiction began. The lurking problem of sovereignty was never solved.

Yet the Papacy, with its expanding organization, was bound to become increasingly involved in secular politics; the argument that the pope possessed spiritual jurisdiction over the emperor as a Christian was unanswerable, but the secular power could not admit the papal right to attack by excommunication the whole practical and legal basis of its position. The theocratic claim could hardly make for a healthy or an efficient conception of secular government, and the princes were right in combating it.

The imperialists fell back on the sacred character of monarchy, which derived, they insisted, in its own sphere, as directly from God as the papal power itself. It was the pope, therefore, who was the innovator, subverting the Divine order. Legal arguments were brought in to reinforce the theological; under the law, it was insisted, the emperor inherited his position from his ancestors, and legally the pope had no right to attack it. It was further argued that the spiritual

---

[1] 'Two swords, one spiritual, that is the word of God, which the Church uses to wound sinners; the other material, which the secular power uses to punish those persisting in their evil ways.'

power of all bishops was equal; that Rome had no jurisdiction over them, that the Church consisted not of the Roman hierarchy but of the community of all Christians.

The two positions were thus becoming clearly defined by the eleventh and twelfth centuries — on the one hand, the Papacy is on the way to assuming the overriding authority in the spiritual sense claimed by Innocent III, in the temporal by Innocent IV; and on the other, the secular power insists on its own divine right and is pushing back papal jurisdiction into the spiritual world. Both are worked out in detail in subsequent mediaeval political thought and largely determined it. Both, in the interest of an impracticable ambition, cut across the most valuable contribution of mediaeval thought, the derivation of power from the whole commonwealth under God.

With Innocent III (1190-1216) whose pontificate marks the climax of papal bureaucratic efficiency and economic power, the theocratic position is most clearly stated; he claims a direct authority from God in a way Hildebrand never dared to do.

'Every reader of Innocent's letters must be struck by his tremendous assertion of his exalted position; Gregory VII was content to be the Vicar of St. Peter; for Innocent the Pope was the Vicar of Christ.'[1]

In a sermon, probably preached at his consecration, he actually asserts a semi-divine status. He is 'midway between God and man ... *minor Deo, sed ultra hominem* — less than God, but more than man, the judge of all men, judged of none.' On another occasion, he compares the papal power to a two-edged sword, 'sharper than any other, which flashes from sea to sea as the eye sweeps over the sea at one view'. Characteristically, legalizing theological ideas, he argues he inherits the same jurisdiction as St. Peter; when Christ said 'Feed my sheep', he meant all of them, without distinction. Through James, the brother of the Lord, Peter received the government not only of the Church but of the whole world (*totum saeculum gubernandum*). Innocent thus takes responsibility for all Christendom, lay as well as clerical; for checking the behaviour of princes and for mitigating the horrors of war. For example, when attempting to impose peace on John of England and Philip Augustus, he writes: 'It is bad for Christendom for Christian rulers to be at war; We may not keep silent in such a necessity, like dumb dogs who cannot bark, lest the blood of so many of our people be required at Our hands.' Again, writing to the French king, he says: 'Your brother the king of Eng-

---

[1] CARLYLE, op. cit, vol. V, pp. 152-3.

land, complains *quod pecces in eum* (you are sinning against him).'
Thus, while here making no claim to direct temporal jurisdiction,
the pope maintains his authority even over princes. Further, as head
of the Church, his zeal against heretics is fierce; he calls them 'little
foxes who destroy the vineyard of the Lord'; to catch 'that kind of
beast' is his 'particular preoccupation, amid the press of business....'

With this theory behind him, Innocent III embarked on a great-
scale political activity unprecedented in the annals of the Papacy;
and indeed he was an administrative genius of the first calibre.
'Innocent's rescripts and decretals are classical models of legal judgement. In patient deliberation, in minute examination of every
relevant point, he excelled: 'Many learned men and jurisconsults
would frequent the Roman Church simply to listen to him, and
learned more in his consistories than they would have in the schools,
especially if they heard him giving judgement, for so subtle was his
statement of the case on either side that each party hoped for victory
when they heard his presentment of their position, and no advocate,
however skilful, appeared before him but did not acutely dread his
objections to the points pleaded.'[1]

A diplomat and a realist, he inaugurated a new bureaucratic
efficiency; elaborate precautions were taken against forgery and
comprehensive records kept. The papal court became the focus of
the greatest volume of legal business in Christendom.

'In the Roman curia men moved in a different world to that of
the State, a world where subtle distinctions were heard and delicately
shaded opinions expressed, the spiritual home of educated and
intelligent humanity. Moulded by this atmosphere, Innocent set himself to ensure the supremacy throughout Christendom of a cultural
life in all ranges of its activity, art and ceremony, Law, philosophy
and literature welded together in the synthesis of Religion.'[2]

Innocent III realized, indeed, a formidable power. At the Council
of the Lateran, held in the penultimate year of his pontificate, he
reached the summit of his temporal and spiritual prestige. The
Canons issued by the famous Council range over the whole field of
dogma and discipline: they make an uncompromising assertion of

---

[1] *Gesta Innocentii*, quoted in *C.M.H.*, vol. VI, p. 3.
[2] See *C.M.H.*, vol. VI, p. 36, for a detailed account of the Papal bureaucratic
methods. See also GIRALDUS CAMBRENSIS, *Autobiography, Selections*, Cape (1936), for
a first-hand account of Innocent and his court. The pope, in dealing with the tempera-
mental Welshman, displayed humour and kindness, but never let his feelings deflect
policy.

the sacramental function of the priesthood and of its monopoly of spiritual power; they insist on the regular reception of the Sacrament at Easter and upon auricular confession. Not only do they assume and assert the supremacy of the upper hierarchy of the Church, they attempt to raise the status and define the power of the whole priesthood all over Europe; the pope further insisted on regular and efficient preaching and on the maintenance and encouragement of a proper standard of learning and morality. Innocent III had laid down a great plan for a universal Church; for its dogma, its rites, its organization, its law. Besides this achievement, the political intrigues by which he was forced to maintain his position may seem insignificant.

Thus committed to temporal interests and involved in the finesse of diplomacy, the pontificate of Innocent III marks the crest of the wave of papal power before it broke. With Innocent IV (1241-54) the wave begins to topple into ruin. The conflict with the Hohenstaufen emperor, Frederick II, reached its climax under this pope. Though the Papacy broke him, it was at the cost of its own power; the effort exhausted its resources and rendered the Curia increasingly unpopular for exactions imposed all over Europe. At the Council of Lyons (1245) a crusade of annihilation was launched against the emperor and the conflict produced the extremest assertion of papal political theory. This pope definitely pushed the papal claim to spiritual supremacy into the temporal sphere as well.

Christ, it was argued, was *Dominus naturalis*; his successors, therefore, inherited jurisdiction through Natural Law. It would have been absurd, for example, if Christ, the ruler of the world, spiritual and temporal, had endowed his vicar with an impaired authority; as Christ was *Dominus* of all men, so was the pope. This assertion was reinforced by an historical argument. From the creation of the world to Noah God had governed the world directly; from Noah to Christ, by the patriarchs, priests, and kings of the Old Testament; Christ, again, governed directly; in the fourth and last phase, his authority was delegated to Peter and his successors. It followed that the papal authority embraced the whole world: *Omnes autem fideles quam infideles oves sunt Christi. Item Iudeos potest iudicare Papa.*[1]

The 'sheep' were equally pillaged by both pope and emperor. For Innocent IV was a power politician playing a ruthless military and diplomatic hand; Frederick a forerunner of the tyrants of the Italian

---

[1] CARLYLE, op. cit., vol. V, p. 323. 'All the faithful and the infidels as well are the sheep of Christ. The Pope has jurisdiction even over the Jews.'

renaissance. The two guardians of Christendom were thus tearing each other to pieces, and by the time of the death of Frederick in 1250, and of Innocent IV in 1254, the structure of Christendom was shattered. It was indeed a far cry from the fishermen of Galilee to Innocent III, *Gubernator Mundi*, and farther to the military adventures of Innocent IV. The concept of Christendom as an hierarchical commonwealth under God, in which each part works harmoniously for its proper end — the most valuable and fundamental aspects of mediaeval political thought — had been denied by both pope and emperor, each driven to assert a conception of sovereignty for which mediaeval thought had no place, and to assert it in an impracticable form.

The controversy was to continue into the fourteenth century. The best statement of the papal position will be found in the *De Ecclesia Potestate* of Egidius Romanus, on which the bull *Unam Sanctam* of Boniface VIII was probably based; the secular case is trenchantly argued in the *De Potestate regia et papali* of John of Paris (1302), and in the anonymous *Rex Pacificus* sponsored in the same year by the University of Paris at the instance of Philip le Bel.[1] Both these writers anticipate some of the arguments of Marsilio of Padua.[2]

§ 111

Meanwhile, though popes and emperors hurled their denunciations at one another, a vigorous civilization had come into being, capable of trenchant philosophical and political thought. While the Papacy was fighting its way to an attempted European supremacy, a steady intellectual development had been going on. The Italian universities concentrated their interest on law and medicine; the mind of the North ran free in elaborations of metaphysics and theology. The second half of the twelfth century saw the rise of the University of Paris, and already Oxford and Cambridge had begun to organize themselves. The next stage came with the development of the mendicant orders into an intellectual force of high calibre. By the middle thirteenth century the Franciscans had produced famous scholars; the Dominicans, founded in 1215, were primarily a preaching order; it was the Dominican St. Thomas Aquinas who was the dominant thinker of the Middle Ages.

The new contact with Byzantium, and through Byzantium with the Arabs, and Arab influence in Sicily and Spain, had enriched

---

[1] See ULLMANN, *English Historical Review*, vol. LXI, no. 240, May 1946.
[2] *Vide infra*, Bk. II, chap. vi.

Western knowledge and enlarged the bounds of speculation. The thirteenth century was thus able to produce a formidable statement of Christian political theory as part of the great scheme of thought, in which St. Thomas attempted to express a world outlook answering the fundamental questions of life.

For St. Thomas[1] made the most comprehensive statement of the mediaeval outlook, and the political implications of his thought are only one aspect of a great theological and metaphysical synthesis, comparable in range to the Hellenistic philosophies of antiquity.

The reinterpretation of the works of Aristotle in terms of Christian theology was the main intellectual preoccupation of the age. The works of Aristotle, including the *Ethics* and *Politics*, had become known in the West through Arab and Jewish transmitters by the middle of the twelfth century, though his writings were at first regarded with suspicion. The Dominican scholar Albertus Magnus (1193-1280), a Swabian of vast erudition, made it his life work to bring the science and philosophy of Aristotle to the understanding of his contemporaries. Aquinas was his pupil, and in 1263 Pope Urban IV commissioned him to make commentaries on the principal Aristotelian treatises; Aristotle was to be converted into a corner stone of orthodoxy, and later scholastic thought was dominated by his influence. In the political sphere the old organic conception of the *polis* and the Graeco-Roman conviction of the supremacy of Law are given a new interpretation.

St. Thomas wrote no separate full treatise on politics; his political thought is principally contained in the discussions of law and justice in the great *Summa Theologica*;[2] in passages of the *Summa Contra Gentiles*: in the *Commentaries on Aristotle's Ethics and Politics*; and in the authentic sections of the *De Regimine Principum*.

For an understanding of Thomist political thought a study of the original text is indispensable, and much tendentious modern inter-

[1] St. Thomas Aquinas, 1225-74; born at Rocca Sicca in South Italy, of noble family, which was partly of German and northern descent; 1231, sent to the Benedictine monastery of Monte Cassino. When the monastery was sacked by the emperor's soldiers in 1239, he removed to Naples. In spite of the opposition of his family, who shut him up in their fortress, he insisted on becoming a Dominican at the age of 18. He studied with Albertus Magnus at Köln; in Paris, 1245; in 1252 he became sub-regent of the Dominican school there; Doctor in Theology, 1257; 1263, commissioned by Urban IV to make a commentary on Aristotle. Died at Naples.

[2] There are short French translations of the relevant passages of the *Summa Theologica*, published by the *Revue des Jeunes*, Paris, 1931-5. For an admirable commentary, see PROFESSOR D'ENTRÈVES, *The Mediaeval Contribution to Political Thought*, Oxford University Press (1939). See also N. GRABMANN, *Thomas Aquinas, His Personality and Thought*, New York (1928), and M. C. D'ARCY, *Thomas Aquinas*, London (1930).

pretation would be avoided if the form and conventions of the original were understood. The principles enunciated were of great value, but it is a long road from the best thirteenth-century thought to the idiom of our own time.

In the space at our disposal it will be well to concentrate on the political sections embedded in the *Summa Theologica*; it is an enormous work in three parts, each a large book in itself, amounting in all to 769 *Quaestiones*, in over three thousand large pages in double columns of small print, running with its supplement well into a million words.[1] And this document is only part of the writings. The formula throughout is consistent and rigid; the *quaestio* is propounded containing the argument against St. Thomas's case. 'It is to be considered', he says, 'under three heads, first, second and third.' These are considered in turn under 'Articles', and the adversary's argument set out. Then comes the tabulated refutation: '*Sed contra . . .*' he continues. Finally, in the *Conclusio* of the *Quaestio*, he sums up the confutations in turn and propounds the definitive solution. All is as clear as a proposition in geometry, which it closely resembles. By the end of 769 *Quaestiones*, a gigantic work of reference has been compiled, an attempt at a complete answer to all the major problems of existence, an arsenal against heresy.

The setting of the passages relevant to political thought is highly significant and must be appreciated. The first part of the *Summa* contains 119 questions; it is metaphysical and theological — *De ipsa Sancta Doctrina; De Deo, an sit* — of God, whether He exists; of the Perfection, Nature and Will of God and the cause of Sin; of the Creation; and of the ordering of the world; of angels and men.

The second part is divided into two books; *Prima Secundae* and *Secunda Secundae*. *Prima Secundae*, in 114 questions, deals with the ultimate purpose of man in society, with Beatitude and Will. It is psychological and may be compared to the earlier parts of Hobbes's *Leviathan* which, in this aspect, follows scholastic method. It treats of good and ill will; of the passions; of pleasure and pain; of the effects of anger, which produce 'fury in the heart, impede the use of reason and cause taciturnity'. He discusses Original Sin and its effects, and significantly under this heading come the questions on Law (by which St. Thomas implies also political power), under 'external motives to actions impelling to good'. Here (1a, 2ae, qu.

---

[1] *Vide* the formidable one volume edition of Hunnaeus, Cologne, 1604. For a modern edition see the English translation by the Fathers of the Dominican Province. London 1911.

90-106) he deals with Eternal, Natural, and Divine Law, with the 'old Law' and the 'new Law' of the Gospel; there follow discussions on Grace and Merit. 'Law' is thus comprehended in the book dealing with psychology and morals.

The second part of the second book contains 189 *Quaestiones*, and treats antithetically of virtues and vices, of Faith and Blasphemy, Charity and Hatred, Concord and Discord, and of their internal and external effects (of War, Riot, Sedition, etc. — qu. 40-3). A discussion of wisdom and prudence leads up to the second important section dealing with politics. 'Of Justice and Injustice' and like problems, and that justice should proceed by written laws (2a, 2ae, qu. 57-81). He proceeds to examine homicide, *contumelia*, *detractio*, fraud, etc. The important question of obedience comes under oaths (qu. 104), and leads on to discussions of gratitude and ingratitude, bravery and cowardice, 'magnificence' and patience. There follow questions on Sobriety and Drunkenness (qu. 151), chastity and luxuria (qu. 153-4 — Isidore says *Luxuriosus aliquis dicitur quasi solutus in voluptates*) — the latter, in its detailed and exact assessment of the degrees of sin, curious to the modern mind and interesting to the psychologist. There follow questions on modesty, pride, and curiosity, and how to recognize a true prophet; on the status of man and the diversity of religions.

The third part, in 90 questions, is entirely theological. It covers the Incarnation, the Trinity, the Nature of Christ; the Immaculate Conception, the Nativity; Baptism, Transfiguration, Descent into Hell and Resurrection. There follows an explanation of the nature and efficacy of the Sacraments; of Penance and the Remission of Sins.

Such is the encyclopaedic structure in which the sections on Law and Justice are contained; in the first, in the discussion of Law, or, as we might say, power, the 'unbridled rationalism' of St. Thomas is revealed. The argument is geometrical, its roots deep in the past. In the Dark Ages this type of argument had its beginning; it had been the answer of crude minds to surrounding chaos; in a world of doubt and confusion here was the plain answer which alone could give certainty and power;[1] it is significant that St. Thomas quotes Isidore nearly as often as Aristotle.

This clear-cut 'ratio' — the defined process of reason as opposed to blind impulse — reflects a Divine order and the world is accordingly intelligible: here is the key to Thomist thought.

[1] *Vide supra*, p. 147.

The questions on *Lex* follow a discussion on venial sin, 'whether a good or bad angel can sin venially, and whether the first impulse of sensuality in infidels is mortal sin'. Law, he insists, is rational; the 'external principal inclining to evil' is the Devil, the 'external principle inclining to good' is God, who instructs us by 'laws' and helps us through 'Grace'[1] — the two supplementing, not contradicting, each other. The adversary argues that the Law is not something rational — *aliquid rationis*; if it were simply rational it would not exist during sleep; therefore it pertains to Will, and moreover *Iurisperitus* says, 'What pleases the prince has the force of Law'.

Here is a fundamental problem. It will be seen how strangely the question is brought in; if St. Thomas gives what we may feel is a right answer, it is for reasons odd to modern ways of thought. For he refutes the argument that Law is Will, 'because it belongs to Law to order and forbid; but to order is rational, as argued above — *ergo Lex est aliquid rationalis'*. Finally, he concludes, Law is a 'certain rule or measure of acts, according to which someone is induced to do something or stop doing something'. *Dicitur enim Lex a ligando*, from binding, because it compels to action; but the rule — *regula* — of action is *ratio*, and the philosopher says it is in nature to order things to an end (*finis*): therefore Law is rational.

After this strictly logical argument, St. Thomas raises the cardinal question whether Law is always for the common good, again stating fundamental principles in a strange context.

The adversary argues that if Law is reason, it is not confined to the common good, but extends to the private good of the individual (*unius*), although, indeed, Isidore says that Law is *pro communi utilitate civium conscripta* — 'for the common use of the citizens'. St. Thomas answers by comparing Law to a fire which radiates warmth impartially, since God ordained Law for the common good. The conclusion states 'Law belongs to that which is regulation and measure; felicity and beatitude are the ends of human life and all parts are ordered to the whole as the imperfect to the perfect'. It follows that a man is part of a perfect community; and it is necessary that Law makes for the felicity of the whole; hence the philosopher in the fifth book of the *Ethics* says that 'just laws make and preserve felicity — *Perfecta enim communitas civitas est* — and God ordains all laws to the common good'. Law is not then related 'generically' to the community, but is its final cause, since the common good is *finis communis*.

[1] Ia, 2ae, qu. 90.

The third goes equally deep. Can a man make his own Law? Isidore says 'Law is *constitutio populi secundum quam maiores natu simul cum plebibus aliquid sanxerunt*'. It follows, says St. Thomas, '*non est ergo cuilibet facere legem* — a man may not make laws for himself'. It will be seen he constantly quotes Isidore for key passages, and was doubtless happy to do so: for the thirteenth-century authority was more convincing than a new argument. He goes on to say that since Law aims at the good of the whole community, to 'order' it is the responsibility of the whole multitude (*totius multitudinis*), or of someone acting on their behalf; it belongs to 'a public person who has charge of the whole multitude, because to order anything to a given end belongs to him who is best fitted to do so'. Here is a straight derivation of power from the community within the framework of Thomist order; no assertion of popular sovereignty, but an important assertion of the moralization of power. Only the multitude or their representative ought to enforce Law; they alone have the coercive *vis*. Just as a man is part of the house, he concludes, and the house part of the *civitas*, and *civitas* is *communis perfecta*, so government is not for the good of one man but for the good of all; the individual cannot therefore make Law, though the *paterfamilias* may regulate it. Here is a vital principle, destined to persist outside the framework of Thomist thought.

Law, he further insists, must, in order to have its 'virtus', be promulgated:[1] it is a 'rational ordinance for the common good promulgated by whoever has care of the community'. God promulgated the Law of Nature by making it part of man's cognition; Isidore (contradicting his previous derivation from *ligando*) says in *Etymologia*, '*quod Lex a legendo vocata est* — because it is written'.

These necessarily brief but representative quotations[2] show the idiom of Thomist thought; the fundamental statement that political power derives from a supernatural order, that it derives from the community within that order, and that the good of the individual can only be perfected through the commonwealth.

In spite, therefore, of the tortuous and alien context of the original, here are vital principles, fundamental to the western European tradition, stated in terms intelligible to the mediaeval mind, and capable of transmission into modern terms. The sense of the trustee-

[1] ib., Art. 4.
[2] For a more detailed discussion of the upshot, the complexities and the contradictions of the Thomist political position, see D'ENTRÈVES, op. cit.

ship of power and of the worth of secular government are stated with uncompromising clarity.

This facet of Thomist thought must be set against the wider horizons of the scholastic outlook. The structure of Thomism, as already apparent, is built on man's relation to God. Man is held to be God's image, and his ultimate end to apprehend an 'increate good, to wit God . . . who alone of His infinite goodness can perfectly fulfil the Will (*voluntas*) of man'. 'Beatitude' is man's ultimate perfection and results from the intellectual apprehension of truth; *Beatitudo est gaudium de veritate*, Beatitude is joy in truth. The *visio Dei* of St. Augustine is here intellectualized. Since intellect is man's highest faculty, it follows that Beatitude is attained through it. Aristotle's statement that man aims at the highest good is interpreted in terms of Catholic Christianity, though there is little similar religious consciousness apparent in the original. At the same time, Aquinas believes it is not through intellect alone that man can apprehend God; the radiance of the Divine Being is such that the human mind is dazzled by it 'as the sun may not be seen by a bat'. He admits the limitation of intellect, which, as Hume argued centuries later, is incapable of apprehending reality by analysis and strictly bound by the biological conditions amid which it has evolved. It follows that this limitation of the mind must be supplemented by Grace and by Faith; if it were not so, the created intelligence would be incapable of apprehending God, which it desires passionately to do. If it cannot so apprehend God, 'an inane desire must be ascribed to Nature'. This, St. Thomas maintains, is absurd. For perfect Beatitude, the intellect must attain the 'very essence of the first cause and then it will have its perfection through union with God as its object'.

The material world, the body, and of course society, are subservient to this end; 'for the perfection of contemplation, soundness of body is needed, to which all the arts of living are directed'. So the full force of personality, focused in intellect and sustained by love, inspired by faith and disciplined by dogma, strives for apprehension of the supreme reality. Full Beatitude will not, of course, be attained in this life. Even as the intellectual vision by which Aquinas sets supreme store, and which brings men nearest to the knowledge of God, must be supplemented by faith which cannot be proved 'save by authorities', so the limited experience of temporal life will be explained and justified by the revelation of eternity. The angels, he argues, have a fuller vision of God than men, since they are devoid of human passions. They directly assist man, the 'viator'; for, says St. Thomas, each man has his guardian angel, and archangels look after communities.

The world is thus governed by God's Law, which rules at different levels in the cosmic hierarchy. Eternal Law transcends human experience altogether; next, Divine Law is embodied in the revelation of the Scripture and in the dogma of the Church; Natural Law rules the material and animal creation, including all men, while Human Law is assigned specifically for the regulation of society. It may take different forms in different places, but is the reflection on its own plane of the general pattern of Natural Law, whereby every creature fulfils its natural aim, the fullness of its own life within the Divine order. The whole creation is informed by purpose; the Aristotelian maxim that the end of the State is the good life, and the Hellenistic concept of universal Natural Law, are brought into the service of scholastic systematic theology.[1]

Thus Thomist political theory is expressed in a vast and rationalistic structure, which, in its majestic sweep, brought the function of government into a coherent plan, and explained the whole of human experience in the light of Catholic Christianity. It is remarkable that an age still so relatively backward could have produced so massive and comprehensive a structure of thought. The huddle of scholastic controversy, of shaven-pated, uniformed religious in the tortuous ways of the mediaeval cities, produced minds which could twist the legacy of the alien Greek genius to their own ends, and impose between the outlook of antiquity and the Renaissance a web of thought which conditioned speculation until well into the seventeenth century. St. Thomas represents the scholastic outlook at its climax; it is significant that his life coincided with the greatest period of mediaeval architecture; the clean lines of Lincoln, of Chartres, of Salisbury, which stand between the solid Romanesque and the elaboration of later mediaeval architecture.

§ I V

And so the climax of scholastic thought and of papal temporal power was reached in the thirteenth century. Europe was presented with a complete plan of intellectual, spiritual, and political order; the political theory of Catholic Christendom had come to its logical

[1] Averroes, on the other hand, interprets Aristotle in a sense hostile to the Thomist scheme.

development in a clear and universal ideal, expanded by the philosophic grasp of Thomist thought — the rigid and detailed argument, unanswerable, given its premises, the contradictions of the partially assimilated Aristotelian learning not yet apparent.

The contribution to political thought made by the papal and scholastic sides of mediaeval society was thus twofold. In the first place, the Papacy had to a great extent realized the dreams of the papal apologists of the eighth century. The tradition of Rome had gone on; the programme already implicit in the days of Gregory had been driven through, the unity of western Christendom preserved. From Gregory, through Hildebrand to Innocent III, transcending the setbacks and the corruption, the inefficiency and bickering of a small-scale Italian state, the steady purpose had been achieved; the prestige of papal power dominated all Europe.

The papal court set the highest standard of administration; the example of Canon Law contributed to the practice of secular government; the financial exactions of the papal bureaucracy, though bitterly unpopular, secured an immense revenue. This income, along with its spiritual disadvantages, assured a standard of civilized living for the great princes of the Church, and made them the patrons of the best artistic, literary, and speculative talent of the age. The habit of Christian order was preserved; men still thought as in the days of antiquity, as Europeans. But it was difficult to combine such worldly commitments with spiritual force. At the moment of its greatest triumphs, the Church was undermined from within, and the fourteenth and fifteenth centuries saw the ebb of the tide.

On the theoretical side, scholastic thought, too, had preserved the tradition of antiquity. Human society, under God, is governed by Natural Law; political power is moral so long as the secular arm fulfils its duty in its proper station. Both papal and imperial controversialists unite in an appeal to the authority of God; power can only be justified by service. This great Christian principle reinforces the originally pagan concept of Natural Law; it links up with the feudal and tribal idea behind mediaeval kingship. There is thus no question either of a merely pedestrian sanction for government, which says that whatever works satisfactorily is right, and looks no further; or of a totalitarian lay power. The great family of Christians, under the Fatherhood of God, unite for the realization of an ordered and static society. All have their place, all have their contribution, all are assigned their several privileges and obligations.

But not only was this society static, with its streak of fatalism and caste; it was alien to our own in two ways. First, the priests claimed the monopoly of spiritual power; the Christian doctrine of spiritual freedom was subordinated to a great organization claiming for itself alone the revelation of God. The price of the imposing edifice of scholastic thought and papal power was paid by the weaker heretics weeping at the confessional and the stronger heretics shrivelling at the stake. As in the State of Plato's old age, the State of the *Laws*, there is an answer for everything and little mercy for the rebel. It is the old response to the perennial whisper, 'Most men are fools and all men are sinners; they have opinion but seldom knowledge; they must be saved from themselves'. Only authority can do it, the authority of the wary and able few, authority backed by faith. And the majority of men believed. Mediaeval civilization was one of the most vital in history.

The second aspect of mediaeval thought, alien to our own, is an indifference to practical knowledge. There was no recognition of the possibilities of knowledge as power; they were not interested in that. The scientific outlook of observation and experiment had no hold on their minds; the literary and rhetorical tradition of their education made that impossible. The resulting practical incompetence and acceptance of disorder, famine, and disease as an integral part of the mediaeval outlook are paralleled to-day in the older traditions of the East. It may well be that these two aspects of mediaeval thought were the cause of the comparatively short-lived success of this civilization. Thwarted intellectual initiative and practical breakdown resulted in the decline of the mediaeval synthesis of thought and action. As the Papacy, enmeshed in its worldly commitments, became increasingly an Italian state, critics and rebels grew within the fold. The administrative inefficiency of the old way of government, cosmopolitan bishop and auxiliary secular arm, became increasingly apparent. The remedy was in the seizure of power by the new monarchy and the new bureaucracy.

Yet the mediaeval Papacy and the scholastic renaissance made their original and distinctive contributions to European thought; on the one hand, the authoritarian tradition of Rome had been carried on, in its new interpretation; on the other, the tradition of universal law, of a moral sanction behind political power, had been reinterpreted and reinforced in the light of the intellectual and spiritual beliefs of Catholicism.

CHAPTER V

THE MEDIAEVAL REALM

§ I

THE administrative progress of the Church was paralleled and reflected in the development of secular government. The thirteenth century saw a widespread elaboration of political theory and practice, and in particular the development of representative institutions, transmitted as an original legacy to modern times.

The theory of the mediaeval realm assumed the co-operation of all classes under the rule of Law; just as the 'realm' was part of the *Universitas* of Christendom, so theoretically the 'estates' and 'guilds' took their place in the community of the kingdom. The tradition of self-governing bodies within a commonwealth was to prove one of the most important contributions of the Middle Ages. In the light of Divine and Natural Law the realm appeared as a great 'foundation', with the king at its head, holding sway over the balanced interests of a *communitas regni*.[1] As the civilization of the high Middle Ages unfolded and came to its climax, the simplicity of the twelfth century is left behind; but before mediaeval society went into liquidation, it had evolved a complete theory, and some realization, of a community living under the reign of Law; and it had developed the representative institutions which later, in the West, and particularly in England, served as a precedent and framework for resistance to absolute monarchy in the seventeenth and eighteenth centuries.

It was indeed in England that these ideas and institutions found their fullest and most lasting expression; in this important corner of Europe the mediaeval tradition dug itself in. The constructive political sense of the Middle Ages, already described as the emphatic assertion of the rule of Law over unbridled power, is best embodied in English parliamentary institutions and defined by English political thinkers, the most representative writers of this important aspect of their time.

The movement was, of course, European. By the thirteenth century there are provincial and civic representative bodies in being

[1] This comparison of the realm to a college with the king as its founder is specifically made by Fortescue, the most eminent English constitutional writer of the late Middle Ages, *vide infra*, p. 228.

in Northern Spain, in France, and in the Germanies; in Switzerland popular assemblies early developed and long persisted; in the Germanies the weakness of the emperor and the prosperity of the Rhineland and the south encouraged the development of independent cities. The fierce and prosperous communes of the Low Countries defied their bishops and treated on equal terms with regal and ducal power; in France the great provincial cities exercised a formidable influence; but in none of these countries was civic independence and economic enterprise united with much sense of a common national interest, while the brilliant civilization of the Italian cities solved no better than Greece the problem of interstate war. In England, on the other hand, the central power was strong, though not despotic; based on the organic foundation of shire and borough, brought to some degree of discipline by a strong monarchy, the English third estate began a routine participation in government, and representative institutions began to develop on a solid national scale. In England, therefore, the more lasting and influential effects of this aspect of mediaeval secular political theory are to be found, and it is upon English writers that we will concentrate our attention in this chapter.

The theory behind this development is best expressed in the writings of Bracton[1] in the thirteenth century, and Fortescue in the fifteenth, for though the tradition of mediaeval self-government persisted in many areas of the Continent, it was not, as in England, integrated with national government on a large scale — the great states of the Continent being ultimately formed round a nucleus of absolutism.

Bracton asserts the supremacy of the Common Law and raises some of the deepest problems of political thought; he appears even to attempt to reconcile the clear-cut mediaeval theory of the State with the exigencies of business. Fortescue, in his *Governaunce of England* and his *De Laudibus Legum Angliae*, expresses a new economic sense and a new patriotism. Narrowed down to a national compass, the tradition of the supremacy of Law, the obligations of power, and the representative character of the ruler had come through.

[1] Bracton, Henry of Bratton, born in Devonshire, *c.* 1214; Justice of the King's Bench, 1248-57; Rector of Bideford, 1261; Archdeacon of Barnstaple and Chancellor of Exeter Cathedral; died 1268. Kantorwitz's attempt to deny Bracton's authorship of the *Treatise* would seem sufficiently refuted by the evidence of the text; for the whole controversy, see McILWAIN, *Harvard Law Review*, 1943, vol. 57, pp. 220-37. There is, however, general agreement on the need for a definitive emendation and a fuller investigation of Bracton's sources, *vide infra*, PROFESSOR SCHULZ, p. 216, note.

Bracton's *De Legibus Angliae* combines theoretical grasp with legal precision.[1] He is the greatest of English mediaeval jurists, the first trained administrator to summarize native custom and administrative practice within the framework of centralized government built up in Norman and Angevin times. The first ten chapters of this immense work, in particular, though sometimes confused, go a long way to define the political theory behind it.

Bracton was educated in the Italian tradition of the Law Schools of Bologna, of the glossators on Justinian's *Digest*, of the *Summa Asonis*, though his primary objective was to restore and collect the decisions of English judges given in the great days of Henry II. He had thus the ability and the desire to codify the practice of English Law, and his administrative experience and empirical mind would seem to have modified the static and absolutist outlook of the revived Roman Law whereby he had been influenced. The great bulk of his work deals with criminal and property Law, being probably designed for the use of the judges of the *Curia Regis*, but he systematically invokes custom and the judgement of the whole realm as the sanction for Law.

'Two things', he begins, 'are necessary for a king . . . arms and Law . . . if arms should fail, the realm will so be without defence, but if laws should fail, justice will be thereafter exterminated, nor will there be anyone to render a righteous judgement.'[2] 'Whereas', he continues, 'in almost all countries they use laws and written right, England alone uses . . . unwritten Law and custom. In England, indeed, right is derived from what is unwritten and that which usage has approved. But it will not be absurd to call the English laws . . . laws, for everything has the force of Law whatever has been rightfully defined and approved by the body politic (*reipublicae commune sponsione*), the authority of the king or the prince preceding.'[3]

Bracton would thus seem to put the sanction of the whole realm

---

[1] HENRICI DE BRACTON, *De Legibus et Consuetudinibus Angliae*, Libri Quinque, edited T. Twiss, Rolls series, 4 vols (1878). The book is divided as follows: (i) *De Divisione Rerum*, 12 chapters; (ii) *De acquirendo Rerum Dominio*, 50 chapters; (iii) *De Actionibus*, 37 chapters; (iv) *Novel Disseizin*, 50 chapters; Assize of Darrien Presentment, 9 chapters; *Mort d'Ancester*, 19 chapters; of *Consanguinity*, 7 chapters; *Assize Utrum*, 8 chapters; *De Dotis*, 20 chapters; (v) Treatise about writs of Right, 6 chapters; of Essoins, 17 chapters; of Defaults, 12 chapters; of Warranty, 17 chapters; of Exceptions, 33 chapters. The *Treatise* is generally thought to have been written *c.* 1250-9. For a modern text, see PROFESSOR WOODBINE's edition (1915-42).
[2] I, 1.   [3] I, 2.

behind the laws; he echoes John of Salisbury, whose book he had certainly read; he anticipates Fortescue in the fifteenth century, who regards the will of the realm as the basis for conservative change. The tradition that the king interprets and declares custom, with the advice of his wise men, is defined and organized by Italian method; it begins to expand into the idea of a growing body of Law, expressing the will of the whole community.

This conception was difficult to reconcile with the rigid scholastic outlook in which Bracton had been trained; as an administrator he was probably hard put to it to dovetail the exigencies of government into the rigid framework of scholastic political theory. How came the theory of Natural Law to be reconciled with the authority of custom, with the fact of serfdom, with the effectiveness of the king's power, with the rights of property? In attempting to find an answer, Bracton raises some deep problems of political thought, though it is necessary to beware of reading too much into his mediaeval argument. A recent authority[1] has, indeed, emphasized this limitation by analysing the sources of an important section of Bracton's text, which he has proved to be 'an artificial tissue of quotation', though the 'tissue is based on Bracton's own work'. Bracton's doctrine, he believes, is 'artificially woven with threads of various kinds and various provenances. Like his age, he was dependent on a traditional stock of formulae which he tried to harmonize'. Hence the contradictions of the work, notably of his views on kingship: 'To set forth his opinion with perfect clearness was apparently beyond his power.'

But Bracton is careful to set his theory in its place in the scholastic framework. He intends, he says, 'to write concerning Right, that the rude may be rendered subtle, the subtle more subtle, and bad men be rendered good and good men better . . . the end (*finis*) of this thing being that quarrels may be appeased and vices warded off and that peace and justice be preserved in the realm . . . and it ranks under *Ethics* as the science of morals, because it treats of habits'.[2]

'Justice' is God's will 'to award each his right, not as regards result but as regards intention', but jurisprudence is a 'science'. Law is both the expression of justice, which, as St. Thomas might have said, is 'in the Creator', and the 'common precept of prudent men in council'.[3] Custom also is 'sometimes taken for Law in parts where it has been approved by habitude and usage, and it fills the

---

[1] *Vide* SCHULZ, *English Historical Review*, May 1945, q.v. in particular p. 175.
[2] II, 5.   [3] III, 1.

place of Law, for the authority of long usage and custom is not slight'.[1]

Following Isidore and mediaeval legal theory, he then divides Law into three kinds: Natural Law, the Law of Nations, and Civil Law, under which he includes custom.

'Natural Law is that which nature, that is to say God Himself, teaches to all animals . . . a certain regulated impulse arising out of the nature of a living thing, whereby a particular animal is impelled to do something.' Each particular creature follows the Natural Law of its own being: 'If we have to give names to right', there is 'one right as regards horses, another as regards asses, another as regards vines . . . another as regards cattle, another as regards man.' 'Public right is what regards the state of the body politic and consists in sacred things, in sacred persons *and* in magistrates'; it is the Natural Law of human society.

Further: 'It is in the interests of the State to have churches in which men should petition for pardon for their sins; it is expedient that there should be constituted magistrates of the State . . . it is useless to have a State unless there be persons competent to administer it.' The mediaeval realm, with the Church at its head, forms the pattern of human society, and expresses the Natural Law behind it: the similarity to Thomist political theory is plain.

While Bracton tries thus to reconcile Natural and Human Law, he is shrewd enough to see the difficulties. The animal is not necessarily impelled by natural instinct to behave morally; in certain aspects, Natural Law, as Hobbes and Spinoza were afterwards to insist, was not always compatible with social values. Bracton raises but evades this issue: 'Our first impulses', he says, 'are not under our own control, but our second impulses are', therefore if the matter proceeds as far as delight and pleasure only and no further, we commit only a 'venial' sin . . . but if it 'goes further' and is 'planned and premeditated', the sin becomes 'mortal'.

As well as attempting to reconcile Natural and Human Law, Bracton faces the grave conflict between individual and society, in which both sides appeal to natural right. 'Private right pertains to the interests of the individual and pertains in a secondary manner to the State, whence it is said that no one should misuse his substance, and so, reciprocally, that the State should in a secondary manner regard the interests of individuals.' The conflict is resolved by an

[1] III, 2.

appeal to mutual interest in the conservation of property; like Fortescue, and Locke and Burke after him, Bracton would seem to want to preserve the realm on a basis of conservative mutual advantage.

Further, he attempts to relate Natural Law to the Law of Nations, the *Ius gentium*. 'The right of nations is what all nations observe, which proceeds from natural right, inasmuch as Natural Law is common to all. Likewise, since nature has established a certain relationship between men, it follows that for man to plot against man is wicked.'[1] Both the Law of Nature and the *Ius gentium* enjoin men to obey their parents and their *patria*, and force employed in resisting aggression is legitimate.

Bracton finds it more difficult to reconcile civil and customary right with Natural Law. Thirteenth-century society was organized in a rigid framework of social distinctions, based on the economic foundations of the manor and sustained by serfdom. How can serfdom be reconciled with natural rights? Bracton answers that while serfs are free under the *Ius naturale*, they are serfs under *Ius gentium* and *Ius civile*, which in this case 'detract' from the Law of Nature. Before God there are no slaves or free, and the first shall be last and the last first, but before man there must be inequality. The hierarchy of the Church witnesses it; likewise, in temporal matters, there are emperors and kings and great lords; they have 'swords to govern with' and 'belts to guard them from wantonness'. Over all is the king, who has no peer, but who is subject to God and the Law. He is *sub deo et sub lege; non est enim rex ubi dominatur voluntas et non lex*.[2] Christ and His Blessed Mother deliberately submitted to the Law. Yet it would be 'superfluous' to make laws with no one to enforce them,[3] and the king must therefore have proper power; but let him 'apply the bridle of moderation', for a king 'can do nothing on earth except what he may do of right'. Although, following Justinian's *Digest*, it is laid down that *quod principi placuit legis habet vigorem* (let the prince's pleasure have the force of Law), only if he does justice does the prince represent God; if injustice, the devil. '*Dicitur enim rex a bene regendo et non a regendo*', Bracton says, quoting Isidore — 'He is called King for ruling well, not merely from ruling'.

Bracton, however, will not in practice risk any diminution of the

[1] V, 7.
[2] III, 5. Under God and the Law . . . for he is not a king when he rules by will and not by the Law.
[3] III, 9.

royal authority, in his day the only hope of efficient government.
If the king contravenes the Law, he can only 'amend his own act',
since a writ does not run against him, 'which, if he omits to do, it is
sufficient for his punishment that he await the vengeance of God.
Let no man presume to criticize his actions (*nemo quidem de factis suis
praesumet disputare*)'. He, indeed, may be said in some sense to
anticipate the idea of the king's sovereignty, ignoring the imperial
claim to a European authority, when he remarks that the King of
England *non habet superiorem*.[1]

He is next concerned to reconcile the precepts of Natural Law
with the rights of property; to define where property begins. 'Of
natural right all these things are common; running water, air, the
sea and the seashore as giving access to the sea', except where
property has been built upon it. All rivers and harbours and the
right to fish in them are public, as is the use of the banks and of the
river itself. 'It is free to every person to moor a boat to the banks and
to fasten ropes to the trees growing upon them.'

How soon does property begin? 'Pursuit does not make a thing
mine, unless I capture it . . . if a wild boar falls into a net which I
have spread for hunting and I have carried it off — having with
much exertion extracted it from the net — it will be mine unless
custom and privilege rule otherwise.' *Occupatio* has been established.
Occupatio also includes shutting up: 'As in the case of bees, which are
wild by nature, for if they shall have settled on my tree they are not
mine until I have shut them up in a hive and, if another man take
them, *earum dominus erit* — he will be their owner.' A swarm out of
my own hive is mine so long as I can see it and 'overtaking' is
possible.

Bracton proceeds from this analysis of property, Law, and custom,
to a long detailed account of the laws regarding marriage, relief,
heirs and death duties, and of the methods of criminal justice.
Together, these topics make up the bulk of the five volumes of the
De Legibus, but only the first three books, which contain the theory
behind Bracton's practice, are here our concern. They seem to show
a characteristic English compromise between theory and expediency,
though one must beware of putting too modern an interpretation on
the mediaeval mind. His outlook and arguments illustrate both the
mentality of his age, and his contribution to the main stream of
English thought. Bracton bases Law on custom and practice, on the

[1] *Vide* SCHULZ, op. cit.

authority of the king and the magnates of the realm, not on immutable written edicts. He reconciles natural and public rights in the common interest that 'substance be conserved'. Natural Law may make all men equal in the eyes of God, but society must carry on; though no writ can run against the king, he is *Sub Deo et Sub Lege* — under God and the Law. He thus asserts the fundamental principle of the rule of Law and foreshadows a sovereign power based on the will of the whole realm; it is significant that, with Fortescue, Bracton was the authority most constantly quoted by the parliamentary opposition in the seventeenth century. His influence contributed directly to the victory of the Common Law against the Crown, for more than any other writer he had rendered individual case Law impervious to absolutist Continental influence.

§ III

Bracton wrote with a degree of stable administration behind him; by the second half of the thirteenth century the English realm was coming to its full development. The next step was the evolution of representative institutions, later to be revived and adapted to wider purposes and greater occasions. As mediaeval civilization expanded into the cultural and economic progress of its greatest age, the smaller nobility and the merchants, as well as the lawyers and civil servants, began to play their part in government, to influence policy in directions other than those congenial to the fighting baronage. The central power, for administrative convenience, called in representatives of corporate bodies within the realm; and by the second half of the thirteenth century the English crown, in particular, was strong enough to break away from the limitations of the feudal council of magnates.

Based on the work of Henry II and his officials, the reign of Edward I saw a phase of comprehensive legislation, carried through by the king, on a theory of prerogative power. This policy was realized through the King's Council, which, at its convenience, consulted representatives of the magnates and of the towns and shires, called not to decide policy but respectively *ad colloquium et tractandum* and *ad audiendum et faciendum* — 'to consult and debate' and 'to hear and to carry out'.

These representatives were summoned only for short periods and for particular occasions; they were concerned primarily with legal business. The term *Parliamentum* means what it says; it is a *colloquium*, a consultation of the king in council with representatives of the communities of the realm. The parliament of Edward's reign thus grew out of the need of centralized kingship to govern effectively; called into being for the king's convenience, providing at once information and reflecting generally through petitions and opinions of the substantial elements in the realm. In France, by the same period, the great provincial estates were growing up, but not in the same close and continuous relation to the Crown. In England the fifteenth century saw a fuller definition of parliamentary institutions; by the later years of Henry VI, parliament is defined as 'the King and the three estates of the Realm', and such a conception is assumed by Fortescue.

As we have emphasized, parliamentary institutions, most highly developed in England, are only an advanced and lasting aspect of a European movement. In Spain, for instance, the Cortes are effective by the early fourteenth century; the *Cavalleros e hombres beunas* of Castile, Leon, and Estremadura are already asserting their right to consultation and a degree of financial control. The towns and 'villas' are represented; political authority is, in theory, the expression of the life of the whole realm. The sessions of the Cortes ought, they insist, to be regular, freely elected, representing the bourgeois as well as the grandees. Again, in France, the Estates General both of the realm and the provinces go back a long way. Philip the Fair, in 1302, convoked the Estates General to assist him in liquidating the Templars. In 1363 they were convoked to discuss the defence of the realm against the English. These assemblies include clergy, nobility, *bourgeois et autres.*

None the less, both in England and elsewhere, little initiative came from the third estates in the fourteenth and still less in the fifteenth centuries.[1] Generally speaking, it became increasingly packed and terrorized by political factions, a façade before dynastic feuds; but

---

[1] 'The estates were approaching their final form, but there can be no more fruitful source of misunderstanding as to the nature of the fifteenth-century parliament than to seize upon each anticipation of modern parliamentary practice as it appears and take it as a victory for popular government. To do so is to read into the second century of parliamentary history the common will and purpose, the reasoned jealousy of its rights and powers, the fuller sense of its place in the constitution, which only came into parliament after it had fought its way to predominance against the Stuarts. The parliaments of Lancaster and York were still ancillary to the Council.' JOLLIFFE, *Constitutional History of England*, p. 441.

the theory and practice of representation are there to form a precedent in later times.

Meanwhile, over most of western Europe, the guilds and universities had long evolved methods of self-government. The merchant guilds have a very old pedigree. The growing volume of European trade had created a new mercantile class within feudal society; such a class was anomalous within the agricultural and military setting of the earlier Middle Ages, and at first stood at a disadvantage. The merchants therefore combined, both for mutual protection and to buy themselves out of the feudal obligations which crippled their enterprise and cramped their position; hence the appearance of merchant guilds and the development of urban communes, generally at odds with their feudal over-lords.

The kings in the West, from the beginning, tended to strike an alliance with the merchant interest, on advantageous terms. The Jews, who had largely held the monopoly of monetary transactions in the early Middle Ages, were alternately protected and persecuted by government. They afforded useful means of revenue, since they absorbed 'like sponges' the available wealth of the land; and as the 'King's Jews' they could be squeezed at the royal pleasure. With the advent of Gentile enterprise and a more solid basis of mercantile power, the central government continued its amicable if exacting relations with the urban interest, and by the thirteenth century the burgesses are a power to be reckoned with. There had grown up a cosmopolitan mercantile organization, focusing on the yearly cycle of fairs and markets, and a tradition of solvency in the world of feudalism and peasant routine. In England this element was called upon to send its representatives to take part in the deliberations of the estates of the realm; it developed a habit of responsibility, a degree of public spirit within the range of its own interests. Its influence is reflected in later English mediaeval political theory; in a realism and freedom from scholastic idiom which foreshadowed and contributed to the outlook of the Renaissance.

§ I V

The outstanding English political writer of the later fifteenth century is Fortescue. Like Bracton, a lawyer, he expresses a new and secularized outlook; he writes for a wider audience than Bracton, and he is alive to the economic aspects of government. Moreover, he writes one of his works in English, not in Norman French or Latin, the *lingua franca* of the clerical bureaucracy.[1]

His *Governaunce of England*[2] is the first constitutional treatise in the English tongue; it is notable for pithy expression and sound sense. The *De Laudibus Legum Angliae* is more specifically legal, the *De Natura Legis Naturae* more abstract, though similar ideas run through all three works.

The *Governaunce of England* is concerned, as well it might be in the fifteenth century, with the best way to make the king's rule effective. The contrast is drawn throughout between the inefficiency of the French monarchy, with its pretentions to unbridled power, its weakness and insolvency, and the relative efficiency of the limited monarchy of England, based on the common consent of the Estates of the Realm. Fortescue argues that no king can govern properly if he is insolvent; that the king ought to live of his own, but is prevented from doing so by the expense of government and war and the claims of his subjects for reward. He is therefore forced to alienate land, to the 'dilapidation of the Crown', and there ought to be a 'worshippefull and notable counsell' representing the whole realm, to protect his interests.

In some degree, Fortescue anticipates the renaissance outlook of Machiavelli and Sir Thomas More; but where Machiavelli regards despotism as the necessary price for efficient rule and More sketches an imaginary Utopia, Fortescue implies a sensible co-operation between men of goodwill. He appeals to the interests of property and order, to the classes with a stake in the country; he carries on a tradition going back to Anglo-Saxon and Danish times and anticipates Locke.

The *Governaunce of England* is a constructive programme for a reformed administration, and contains the essence of Fortescue's thought, but the earlier *De Laudibus*, designed for the education of

[1] Sir John Fortescue (1394-1484) came of a Devon family. Lord Chief Justice, 1442-61. He took the Lancastrian side in the Civil War and wrote the *De Laudibus Legum Angliae* when in exile in France, for the instruction of Henry VI's son, Prince Edward. The prince was killed and Fortescue captured at the battle of Tewkesbury. The *Governaunce of England* was written during the last decade of his life, which he spent in retirement in Gloucestershire. The translation of the *De Laudibus* here quoted was published in London in 1775 and illustrated with admirable notes by Selden. For a modern edition and introduction, see CHRIMES, *De Laudibus Legum Angliae*, Cambridge University Press (1942). For his *De Natura Legis Naturae*, see Clermont's edition (1869).

[2] The '*Governaunce of England*', *otherwise called the Difference between an Absolute and a Limited Monarchy*, edited PLUMMER, Oxford (1885). It is a short book of 48 pages in 20 chapters; the first printed edition appeared in 1546.

Prince Edward, leads up to the other and is also a rewarding document.

It opens with an account of the diversions of the prince, son of Henry VI, during his exile in Berry. 'The Prince, being mounted on fiery and wild horses . . . made it his diversion to attack and assault the young gentlemen his attendants . . . which a certain grave old knight, his father's chancellor, observing, he exhorts him to study Law as well as military exercises.' At this, 'looking very intently at the old knight', the prince replies, rather out of character, by 'drawing a distinction between Divine and secular Law'.[1] Whereupon Fortescue explains that human laws are 'the rules whereby the perfect notion of justice can be determined . . . Neither morning nor evening star is so bright and lovely as this. This justice is the subject of the royal care, without which a king cannot act in his judicial capacity as he ought to do'.[2] Just as 'a carpenter teaches his son to handle the axe, the smith brings up his to the anvil, so it becomes a king to have his son, who is to succeed him, instructed in the laws of his country while he is yet young; which rules, if kings would but observe, the world would be governed with a greater equality and justice than it now is'. It will take many years, objects the prince, to master such a subject; but Fortescue, anticipating a proper Oppidan tradition of Henry VI's foundation, reckons a year's study enough to give him knowledge 'sufficient for his high quality'.

Next he proceeds to the fundamental distinction between two kinds of government, which runs through both the *De Laudibus* and the *Governaunce of England*. There is 'political' government which fulfils justice and the Law of Nature, 'the mother of all human laws', and 'regal' government, or despotism, based simply on force. It follows that a king of England cannot, at his pleasure, alter the laws, for the nature of his government is not only regal, but political (chap. ix). Had it been merely regal, he might govern arbitrarily, but since it is political, he can 'neither make any alteration or change in the laws of the realm without the consent of the subject, nor burden them, against their wills, with strange impositions, so that a people governed by such laws as are made by their own consent and approbation to enjoy their properties securely and without the hazard of being deprived of them either by the king or by any other'.

Here is the characteristic English emphasis on property and

[1] Chap. ii.   [2] Chap. iv.

security, afterwards worked out by Locke. Fortescue is already adopting what comes near to Locke's position, putting property into the foreground and monarchy under the rule of Law. It is a most remarkable passage, and illustrates the continuity of mediaeval and seventeenth-century thought. 'Security and satisfaction', he goes on, 'will result from observance of these principles.'

After some account of the violent origins of regal dominion, Fortescue, defining the nature of the body politic, quotes St. Augustine's definition of a people as opposed to a mere mob. A people is an 'association of rational men, united in the pursuit of common interests'. This distinction between a people and a multitude is later used by Burke as the keystone of his argument against majority rule. The realm, says Fortescue, is like a living body; 'the heart is the first thing that lives', and the first thing that lives in the realm is 'the intention of the people'. The Law may be compared to the nerves and sinews, and since a body is useless without a head, and a 'mere trunk', some governing principle must represent the head; usually this principle is embodied in a king. The king's duty is to 'protect his subjects in their lives, properties and lands; for this very purpose he has delegation of power from the people' (chap. xiii). Here is Whig doctrine indeed!

On the prince inquiring if the laws of England work as well as the Civil Law of the Holy Roman Empire, Fortescue examines the nature of Statute Law, the use of witnesses and juries; torture and the abuse of it by the French government; the duty of sheriffs and county administration. The prince, by now convinced (chap. xxxiii) that the laws of England immensely excel, inquires why some English kings have attacked them. Fortescue replies that they 'have not been able to digest them' (chap. xxxiv), and have attempted an absolute regal power, such as the French kings exercise. He dilates on the disadvantages of the French way of government, thus beginning another long English tradition. The French king's troops live off the country (chap. xxxv): 'They usurp and claim the same privilege and custom not to pay a penny for necessities, either for themselves or for the women whom they always carry about with them in great numbers — *quas in magna copia secum semper vehebant.*' The result is a miserable condition of the peasantry, who wear 'little short jerkins made of canvas no better than common sackcloth; they do not wear any woollens except of the coarsest sort, and that only in the garment under their frocks (*froccas*), nor do they wear any trousers, but from the knees upwards'.[1] Such are the fruits of unbridled kingly power. Further, their diet is deplorable. 'They do not eat flesh, unless it be the fat of bacon and that in very small quantities, with which they make soup; as for their poultry, the soldiers consume them.' By contrast with this state of affairs, he compares the advantages of England. 'In England no one takes up his abode in another man's house without leave of the owner first had (chap. xxxvi), unless it be in public inns, and there is obliged to discharge his reckoning. Every inhabitant is free to use and enjoy whatever his farm produces.' Hence a substantial prosperity. They are not reduced, like the French, to drinking water. 'They drink no water, unless at certain times on a religious score, and by way of doing penance.' Everyone, according to his rank, has all things which conduce to make life easy and happy; they are arraigned only before the King's judges and according to the Law of the land. In France anyone is liable to get 'put in a sack by night and thrown into the river by the officers of the Provost Marshall'.

Such are the solid benefits of 'political mixed government'. As St. Thomas remarks, 'a king is given for the sake of the kingdom, and not a kingdom for the king'. A ruler, unable to protect his subjects from foreign incursion and the violence of each other, is 'weak', particularly if he be 'in so distressed a condition that he can't keep his hands off seizing on his subjects' property' (chap. xxxvii); but the wise and powerful prince can control his own passions and govern his people in 'the political way'. Finally, in an edifying conclusion, the prince eulogizes the laws of England, 'which are not only good but the best of laws for the particular constitution of England. And if at any time some of them want amendment, it may easily be done.' The English Law, he concludes, 'shall be ever dear to me, preferable to all other Laws in the world'.

It will be seen that though it owes something to the eighteenth-century translation quoted, the argument of the book is cogent, the distinction between legal and illegal government emphatic, reflecting the mediaeval doctrine of the supremacy of Law.

In his old age Fortescue was again to write upon the same theme; this time using the homely English of contemporary speech — to our ears at once trenchant and entertaining, still close to the village dialect of our own time.

The *Governaunce of England*, just as much as the *De Laudibus*, is

---

[1] *Neque caligis nisi ad genua, discoperto residuo tibiarum.*

designed for a specific end — this time the rehabilitation of regal power. Repeating the argument of the *De Laudibus*, Fortescue distinguishes between two kinds of government: 'There bith ij kindes off kyngdomes.' In a regal dominion the king is absolute, in a political and regal dominion, 'the kynge may not rule the people bi other Lawes than such as thai assenten unto, and therefore he may sett uppon thaim non imposition without their own assent'.[1]

The Jews, he says, were originally under a political and regal dominion, under God and the judges. When they clamoured for a king, God, after 'thondres and other gasteful thinges from the Heavens', allowed them to lapse into a regal dominion. This kind of government descends from 'Nimrod, *Primus tyrannorum . . . robustus venator coram Domino*', through 'Ninus, and after him other paynemes'. Political and regal dominion, on the other hand, descends from 'the fellowship that came to the land with Brute, willynge to be united and made a body politique called a Reawn . . . Then they chese (chose) the said Brute to be their hed and kynge'.[2] By contrast with this English tradition of political and regal dominion, the French monarchy has degenerated into a purely regal government.

'Seynt Lowes sette never Tayles or other imposition uppon the peple of that land without the assent of the three estates, but Ingelande men mad such warre in Ffrance that the three estates durst not come togeder.' In consequence, though the French 'yet dwellen in the most fertile reaum in the worlde', they are abjectly poor. 'Thai drinke water, thai eaten apples, with brede right browne made of rye.' 'But blessed be God,' concludes Fortescue, 'this land is ruled under better law.'

All turns on the solvency of the king: 'Euery raume is bonde to susteyne is kynge'; for poverty paralyses action, 'as the Philosopher[3] sayth in his Eythikes', and power depends in England on archers, who are very expensive. The king must be able to overawe over-mighty subjects; if not, government breaks down. 'The cronycles off every reaume, and in especial off Spayne and Denmarke, beth full of such ensamples.' Look, he says, at our own 'Herre the iijrd!'

How, then, best endow the Crown? Not by arbitrary taxation. 'Roboham' was expelled for overtaxing the Jews, 'of which departyng God sayde Himself afterwards "*A me factum est istud*" (I did that Myself)'. It is far better for the king to have adequate estates and for the estates of the realm to work together to sustain the public

---

[1] The *Governaunce of England*, chap. i.   [2] Chap. ii.   [3] Aristotle.

power in their own interest. *Ubi multa consilia . . . ibi salus.* But how can this 'worshippfull and notable counsell' be chosen? The old-fashioned council is concerned with its own interests, composed of the very men who fleeced the Crown, and incapable of transacting its business with secrecy. Fortescue outlines a royal council which is to work closely with the Royal administrative officers. There are to be twelve permanent spiritual and twelve temporal members, 'off the wysest and best disposed that can be ffound in all parties of this lande'. They shall be paid by the king, and take 'no rewardes off any man, like as the justices of the Kynges bench'. They are to be reinforced by four spiritual and four temporal members, chosen annually by the king; and there shall be a presiding head of this council — *Capitalis consiliarius.* Their agenda is to cover matters of high policy and economic affairs. 'How the going out off the money may be restrained, how bullyon may be brought into the lande, how also plate jewells and money late borne owt may be geyton ageyn . . . How our navy may be maintained and augmented . . . How also the lawes may be amendet in suche thynges as they neden reformacion in.' The civil servants of the exchequer and the office of Rolls 'may be off this council when thai be so desyred, and ellis not'. The routine of this procedure shall be regulated and 'putt in a boke, and that boke kept in this counsell as a register or a ordinarye, howe that they shall doo in every thynge' (chap. xv).

The Romans, says Fortescue, ruled the great part of the world when they had a senate; but when 'ill disposed emperours, as Nero, Domitian and other had slayn grete parte of the senators . . . the estate of the Romans began to fall downe' (chap. xvi). If the king rules on the advice of such a council and rewards his servants not with land but with offices; if all officials refuse other payment and swear loyalty to the king alone; and each man hold only one office, except the king's brothers, who may hold two, then stability and order will be achieved. The result will be a renewal and establishment of proper government. The king will have 'goten ageyn his lyuelihod', so as it may never be alienated without the assent of his parliament. There will thus be a new 'foundation' of the Crown, and the king will become the 'greatest founder' of the world, 'for as other kynges have ffounded byshopricks, abbeys and other howses of religion, the kyng shall then have ffounded an holl reaume' (chap. xix). His prerogative will be thereby increased and the country will be like a 'collage, in whiche shul synge and pray for everymore al the men of Ingland, spiritual and temporal, and ther song shal be suche among other anthemes, "I blissed be oure Lord God, for that he hath sent Kyng Edward the iiij to reign upon us. He hath don more for us than ever did kyng of Ingland"'.

The pithy good sense of these observations; the solid prosperity at which the writer aims; the sober pride he feels for English institutions and ways of living, these things are more characteristic of Tudor England than of the later Middle Ages. Yet the moral conviction, the vision of order and community, is mediaeval: Fortescue marks a transition from a mediaeval to a modern outlook.

§ v

Looking back, then, over the secular contribution to the theory of government made by English writers in the Middle Ages, destined to form the basis of the most successful challenge to absolutism in the seventeenth century, the inspiration of the American constitution and a foundation of modern democratic government, it will be seen that their constant theme, like that of Thomism, is the subjection of kingly power to Law. The monarchy focused the conceptions of the realm as a hierarchy of estates; the clergy, nobility, and commons, working, at least in principle, with the consent and advice of a parliament, which is not the legislative power, but which assists the work of legislation and registers the acts of government.

Bracton in the thirteenth century, amplifying John of Salisbury, had asserted the rule of Law, this time based on the custom and consent of the whole realm; Fortescue, in the fifteenth, assumes that substantial elements in the kingdom co-operate to assist the delegated power of the king. Thus, in England, in a comparatively small area, where provincial and civic patriotism was not too strong, a measure of self government through common consent was achieved, in spite of the setbacks of the later Middle Ages.

In general, on the Continent mediaeval society declined through excess of civic and provincial liberty. The great cosmopolitan orders, ecclesiastical, mercantile, aristocratic, went their way regardless of the necessities of central government; the resulting chaos produced as its remedy the unbridled power of the National State. The valuable traditions of the rule of Law, of the trusteeship of kings, and the balance of interests within the commonwealth were jeopardized, and most of Europe passed through a phase of monarchial absolutism.

In England that phase was to come, but it was brief and moderate; the parliamentary tradition never died, the rule of Law went on. The mediaeval legacy was preserved, and England, after 1688, offered to a Europe stricken with the paralysis of despotic power the alternative of a prosperous and stable community which combined stability with initiative, order with consent.

CHAPTER VI

THE DISRUPTION OF CHRISTENDOM

§ 1

WHILE these constructive secular developments had been going on, reaching their most lasting expression in England, the thirteenth and fourteenth centuries had seen the climax of mediaeval civilization. The far-flung majesty of the Catholic Church; the intellectual brilliance of the universities; the re-establishment of some degree of legal order and a routine of bureaucratic efficiency, marked the assimilation of the old tradition by the new elements contributed by the Northern peoples. Europe had again found its feet, and the North had been brought decisively into the orbit of the Mediterranean world in a way antiquity had never known. Further, an economic revival coincided with the emergence of powerful kingdoms out of the welter of later feudalism.

But the surging vitality of the new Europe was not destined to remain within the confines imposed by the old theology and world outlook. It may be the worldly commitments of the Church increasingly weakened the vital elements which had been its inspiration and its power; resentment at the attempt to impose a theocratic order by temporal means was certainly growing among thinkers and peoples, and the practical incompetence of the mediaeval outlook could not hold the forces of change.

In the realm of theory the non-Christian influence of the revived Greek learning pointed the way to a new outlook; and mediaeval thinkers, for all their efforts, failed to assimilate Aristotle into the framework of their thought. And, indeed, the adventure had to be made; the European mind break out of the framework dominant for a thousand years. A growing economic enterprise, forming the basis for a new sophistication, is already apparent by the twelfth century. The city as a cultural unit began again to emerge, and with it a return to a secular rather than a theocratic tradition. The main stream of civilization was beginning to flood in again, coming down from antiquity and the cities of the Near East; the mediaeval phase was over.[1] The city was the best ally of the new monarchy; the bour-

[1] See J. DE LAGARDE, *La Naissance de L'Esprit Laique au Fin du Moyen Age*, Paris (1934).

geois and the kings were going to supersede the feudal baron, the bishop, and the monk. Thus these two enemies of the feudal order combined; ultimately they were to create a new civilization, assimilating and superseding the mediaeval achievement.

As we have seen, the rift came in the very foundations, in the Papacy itself. After Innocent III and St. Thomas, the synthesis, political and intellectual, began to break down. The conflict of Frederick II with Innocent IV, between Philip the Fair and Boniface VIII, between Ludwig the Bavarian and John XXII, the Avignon 'captivity' — all combined to weaken the mediaeval order.

Of course they were attempting too much; the struggle ate like dry rot at the structure of Christendom. The political and spiritual conflict became so acute that the very conception of a spiritually united Europe, which all the controversialists assumed, begins to disintegrate. From Aquinas, through Dante, to Marsilio and Cusanus, the process works itself out, with Machiavelli waiting at the end, spiritually bankrupt, but practically efficient, and Cartesian scientific method offering the material mastery of the earth. Meanwhile the old order put up a formidable resistance; it took centuries for the tradition to swing over to the new outlook. The failure of empire and Papacy conflicted in the minds of later mediaeval writers with the knowledge that the things they stood for had been right, with the incapacity to see a way out, to think in new terms; and indeed it was a desperate venture, to leave the well-charted, land-locked sea of the old order for the uncharted ocean of the modern world.

Political theorists of the fourteenth century are predominantly hostile to the Papacy, but all are trying to preserve the idea of Christendom. St. Thomas assumed the papal supremacy; Dante finds his solution in an idealized Holy Roman Empire. He is still profoundly mediaeval in his attempt to relate politics to a religious world-embracing ideal. He sets out to define the goal of civilization and impose a philosophically conceived unity on the diversity of political facts.

Marsilio of Padua is more practical. With him the scientific outlook of his master Aristotle begins to find its natural expression, and the high theoretical argument of Dante is followed by a more deadly attack. He is concerned with the good government of a City State and is willing to push the theocratic influence out of politics to attain it. In the *Defensor Pacis* Marsilio tries to undermine the whole papal position by relegating the spiritual power to the next world and regarding the clergy simply as interpreters and advisers, a branch of secular society. It seems that the whole theocratic development in his view was wrong; he cites the poverty and simplicity of Jesus in contrast with the power and corruption of the Church; the clergy ought to go back, he argues, to reliance on their spiritual power, and on that alone. He sometimes appears to set out, along with much practical wisdom about government, what has been represented as in some degree a Protestant position, though he is anxious to maintain the unity of Christendom and ready to sanction the punishment of heresy.

Finally, in view of the manifest collapse of the moral authority of Rome, Cusanus, in the fifteenth century, attempts to devise a spiritual authority which shall control the pope. Christendom is to be rehabilitated by a Council which can take over the spiritual powers of an unworthy Papacy. In the constitutional expedients advocated, the Conciliar movement contributed to subsequent theories of self-government.

All these three thinkers attempted to make the best of the palpable failure of Papacy and empire. None succeeded, for all were too closely identified with the old outlook and enmeshed in scholastic conventions which cut them off from the laity. The men of action in the political and economic spheres went their way without them; for good or ill they were getting too firm a grip on the world by the fourteenth and fifteenth centuries to be the docile children of the Church.

§ 11

Dante's political thought is expressed in his treatise, the *Monarchia*,[1] and, as is well known, his absorption in the politics of his day is reflected in his poetry. The *Monarchia* is a clear and angular scholastic argument, at first sight rather arid, for all the sweep and rightness of its thought. There are, Dante maintains, two purposes of life:

---

[1] It is divided into three books, containing 150 pages of the English edition; it was probably written about 1309 though some authorities place it earlier. The first book, in 16 chapters, constructs the metaphysical argument, justifying a single ruler over all human society. In book II, in 13 chapters, Dante demonstrates from the history of Rome, the miracles that attended it, and the failure of other attempts at empire, that the Romans realized this ideal rule. The book concludes with the argument that Christ acknowledged the Roman power by submitting to be executed by it. Book III, in 16 chapters, sets out to prove that the imperial power is derived from God and to refute the arguments for papal supremacy (notably that based on the *Donation* of Constantine). Dante concludes that the emperor should reverence the pope but should be independent

'*Beatitudo vitae quae in operatione propriae virtutis consistit.*'[1] This is the earthly aim, which leads on to eternal life, the heavenly paradise. The goal of humanity is 'to keep potential intellect constantly actualized', first in speculation, secondly in action.[2]

In the first chapter of the *Monarchia* Dante gives his reasons for writing it. He says: 'Lest I should one day be convicted of the charge of buried talent . . . I long to bear fruit for the public advantage and set forth truths unattempted by others . . . And inasmuch as amongst other unexplored and important truths the knowledge of the temporal monarchy is most important and least explored, and, for that it stands in no direct relation to gain, has been attempted by none, therefore I am minded to extract it from its recesses.'

In the second chapter he defines what temporal monarchy means: it is 'a unique princedom extending over all persons in time'. He proceeds to consider the goal of human civilization and refers to Aristotle's *Ethics*, saying that each form of society has its own end and the supreme end is an ultimate goal embracing all human society. God and nature 'make nothing superfluous', he says, quoting Averroes on Aristotle. From these premises the scholastic argument proceeds rigorously to its appointed end. The aim of civilization is the fullest awareness of those who compose it. And here, indeed, Dante is expressing in the language of the fourteenth century a truth valid for any age.

He goes on to argue that only in peace can this realization come about: 'whence it is manifest that universal peace is the best of all things . . . and that is why there rang out to the shepherds from on high not riches, not pleasures, not honours . . . but peace'. The role of temporal monarchy is to keep this peace; as God is the monarch

---

[1] 'Beatitude of life which consists in the fulfilment of its own being.'
[2] I, 4.

of him. The correct title is *Monarchia*, not *De Monarchia*; see *Opere di Dante*, Barbi's introduction, p. xviii, Firenze (1921).

There is an excellent account of Dante's Florentine environment and the relation of his poetry to his political thought in DEAN CHURCH'S *Dante and Other Essays*, Macmillan (1888). The article on Dante in PROFESSOR HEARNSHAW'S *Social and Political Ideas of the Middle Ages* is not to be recommended. The most convenient translation of the *Monarchia* is contained in the Temple Classics, *Dante's Latin Works*, translated by WICKSTEED, Dent (1934). Dante has been credited with a sentiment of Italian nationalism, but though he had a keen and noble sense of Italy as a linguistic and cultural whole there is little evidence that he translated it into political terms. He looked to a Roman empire in the past and naturally had no conception of a Nation State. The whole question is fully argued in *Dante and the Regnum Italicum*, by B. H. SUMNER, in *Medium Aevum*, published by the Society for the Study of Mediaeval Languages and Literature (1932).

of all creation, so the emperor is the monarch of temporal things. In chapter x he argues that there is bound to be an ultimate judge of political questions; therefore monarchy is necessary for the world. He quotes Aristotle to support his argument.

Justice, he continues, quoting Virgil, is only realized under a universal authority. Finally returning to Aristotle, he says: 'Under a perverted government a good man is a bad citizen, but under a right one a good man and a good citizen are the same thing.' After further argument, Dante concludes that, 'for the well-being of the world, it is necessary there should be a monarchy' (I, 15), and he drives home this point by stating that Christ chose to be born under the rule of Augustus 'when there was a perfect monarchy'.

In book II he maintains that the Roman people was ordained by nature to command, and the Roman power ordained by God. 'Now I have pierced with the eyes of my mind to the marrow of it and have seen by the most convincing signs that it was divine providence that effected this.' The Romans were the noblest, he says, of all peoples, and he argues, from the miracles in Roman history and their over-coming all competition, that 'in subjecting the world to itself, the Roman empire contemplated the public good' (II, 6). 'Further, if the Roman empire was not of right, the sin of Adam was not punished in Christ . . . If then Christ had not suffered under a qualified judge, that suffering would not have been a punishment. And the judge would not have been qualified had he not had juris-diction over the whole human race . . . that was to be punished in the flesh of Christ, and Tiberius Caesar, whose vicar Pilate was, would not have had jurisdiction unless the Roman empire had been of right' (II, 13).

In book III Dante admits he is treading on dangerous ground in maintaining the imperial authority independent of the Papacy, but nerves himself by quoting Isaiah: 'I will enter upon the present wrestling-ground, and by the arms of Him who delivered us from the power of darkness by His blood, I will hurl the impious and the liar out of the ring.' He attacks the papal apologists with vigour, and though accepting the False Decretals, refutes the argument based on them by denying the right of Constantine to alienate the empire (III, 10). Tackling the analogy of the Sun and Moon, already well worn by the early fourteenth century, he argues that, though the Moon is dependent on the Sun for most of its light, it is not itself derived from the Sun and exists independently of it. Moreover, 'she has a certain light, as is manifest in her eclipses'. Dante next investigates Old Testament history as to the status of Samuel and proceeds to an attack on the papal power, *ligandi et solvendi* (to bind and loose), and on the doctrine of the Two Swords (IV, 8, 9). After further argument, he concludes: 'And now I have sufficiently reached the mark I set before myself, for the truth of that question has been searched out, whether the office of monarch is necessary for the well-being of the world.' As for the pope and emperor: 'Let Caesar observe that reverence to Peter which a first-born son should observe to a father, so that . . . he may with greater power irradiate the world over which he is set by Him alone who is ruler of all things spiritual and temporal.' Dante thus implies that the imperial authority comes direct from God, not through the Papacy.

From the above quotations, the philosophic grasp of the *Monarchia* is apparent; within its assumptions the trenchant argument is unanswerable. Driving to the centre of the problem, Dante argues in effect, that men 'should have life and have it more abundantly', in 'the realization of that fullness of life which consists in the fulfilment of our being'. Even if deprived of its Christian context, the argument remains valid; it is a clear statement of political aim facing the fundamental question of sovereignty in Christendom and the world. That peace is the condition of such a fulfilment and can only be attained by the authority of a supreme power is a truth reinforced by modern experience. For all the alien context and idiom of his thought, this mediaeval genius, stating the supreme political problem of his day, has left a trenchant statement of principles applicable to our own time on a world scale, and reflecting a fine synthesis of classical and mediaeval thought.

§ III

Where Dante was a universal poet and a philosopher, Marsilio of Padua, in the *Defensor Pacis*, sets out a theory of politics already to a great extent Italian, practical and secular, though still touched by the idealism of the Middle Ages and expressed in scholastic terms. It is based on an interpretation of Aristotle on lines more in sympathy with the original than can be found in the writings of St. Thomas or of Dante. Marsilio, in his concluding chapter, explains the book's title, '*Vocabitur autem Tractatus iste Defensor Pacis*'. — 'This Treatise will be called the *Defender of Peace*, for in it cases of peace and order are particularly examined, and also the obstacles to them.' His object is to 'define the essential elements of *Tranquillitas*.'[1] 'If', he adds, 'these things are understood and remembered, the realm will be saved.'

Marsilio was originally a physician, but he also had extensive political experience.[2] The book may have been influenced by John of Jandun, an Averroist Aristotelian, who was probably sceptical of the whole Catholic position.

Though there is danger, as in studying any mediaeval thinker, in reading too modern an interpretation into Marsilio's thought, Marsilio's outlook is eminently reasonable. He derives much of his thought from Aristotle and looks forward to Machiavelli. They both show the same hatred of the Church for the same reason — it interfered with the establishment of efficient government in Italy. But Marsilio, with his strong scholastic discipline, builds up a clearer structure of thought. Though driven to much the same conclusion, that the only way out is a strong sovereign power, he attempts to base that power on a modified popular consent and to circumscribe its exercise. The atmosphere of the book is therefore more attractive than that of the *Prince* or *Discorsi*.

Marsilio first examines the nature of the State and defines the object of his book. Starting with a conventional quotation from Cassiodorus, that the desire of all kingdoms should be 'peace, the seemly mother of all good arts', Marsilio insists that the object of government should be to ensure it. He proceeds to a definition of the State as *perfecta communitas*, in which men *non solum vivunt, quod faciunt bestiae aut servi, sed bene vivunt*.[3] It is a 'congregation', having its own sufficient *finem*. Here, in a mediaeval setting, is the unanswer-

---

[1] Bk. III, chap. iii.

[2] Marsilio of Padua, born. 1278; son of a notary to the University of Padua. Qualified in Medicine, 1311; studied in Paris, 1312; Canon of Padua, 1316; Counsellor to Can Grande della Scala, Lord of Verona, 1317. Afterwards in the service of Matteo Visconti of Milan, his academic and medical experience being thus supplemented by a thorough training in the ways of the world. Returned to Paris, 1320. Completed the *Defensor Pacis*, 1324. 1326, went to Nuremberg, accompanied by the Averroist John of Jandun, to the court of the German Emperor Ludwig IV. Cited as a heretic, and condemned by John XXII; Ludwig IV is said to have made him Archbishop of Milan, though he never got possession of the see. He died in Bavaria, 1343. His book is divided into three parts. The first *Dictio*, in 19 chapters, examines the object and nature of the State; the second, a long one in 33 chapters, the claims of the Papacy to spiritual dominion; the third, in three short chapters, recapitulates the argument of the whole book and its conclusions under 42 short headings and ends by giving the reason for the title chosen. *Vide* the *Defensor Pacis* of Marsilio of Padua, PREVITÉ-ORTON, C.U.P. (1928).

[3] 'Not only exist, as do animals and slaves, but live well.' *Vide* D'ENTRÈVES, op. cit., chap. iii, pp. 44-5.

able Aristotelian definition, that the end of the State is the good life
Marsilio, unlike many scholastic writers, appears to accept it fo
what it means.

He proceeds to an admirable analysis of the State on Aristotelia
lines. Born and bred in an Italian City State, he knew what Aristotl
was about; he seems to show the psychological insight which might b
expected from a doctor by classifying men according to their *habitu*
animae: some are apt for speculation, some for Law, some for agricul
ture. He simplifies his definition of Law by distinguishing betweer
the Divine Law and the laws and institutions of states, *quae immediata*
praeveniunt ex arbitrio humanae mentes. His conception of legal sove
reignty is clear and remarkable.

It is in this secularized concept of Law that Marsilio was most
revolutionary. 'Clearly', writes Professor d'Entrèves, 'we have a
notion of the sovereignty of the "general will" which reminds us
even more of Rousseau than of Bodin or of Austin. However that
may be, we are certainly in an entirely different world from that of
St. Thomas. There is nothing left of the Thomist idea that the State,
however "sovereign", is subject to an eternal and absolute order of
values, expressed in the body of Divine and Natural Law. The State
is the source of Law and its Law has to be obeyed not only because it is
the only rule to be endowed with coercive power, but because it is in
itself the expression of justice.'[1]

The legislator, or *causa legis*, says Marsilio, is ultimately the *popu-*
lu seu civium universitas; it is derived from the community and not
God. This apparently modern conception is probably brought in
against the claims of the Papacy and Canon Law, though Marsilio's
own judgement of politics may have suggested it was best for government to be based on a degree of popular consent. He qualifies this
view by saying that decisions ought to be based on the will of the
'more influential', so cannot be said to sanction the doctrine of
democratic popular sovereignty (*valentiorum per suam electionem seu*
voluntatem in generali civium congregatione expressam). The executive
power is exerted by the *pars principans*, which, be it wielded by one
man or several, must have overwhelming force at its disposal, but
it is a 'public force', not the private troops of a tyrant. Marsilio
still believes this disinterested attitude might be possible. Machiavelli did not. The Italy of the early fourteenth century was ferocious
enough; Machiavelli came after nearly a century and a half of further

[1] Op. cit., p. 63.

political crimes had poisoned the atmosphere, and Marsiglio is still scholastic.

Having thus given a definition of what a state ought to be, Marsilio proceeds to the main part of the book (*Dictio* II) — a devastating attack on the Papacy and the Canon Law. He knows he is on dangerous ground; 'May God be my help', he says, 'and I will not fear what man can do unto me' (*Dominus mihi adjutor et non timebo quod mihi faciat homo*). We will admit, he says, that those who claim spiritual and temporal power have 'just as much power and authority from Christ as we can believe from Scripture was handed down to them, and no more' (II, 5). Christ did not come into the world *dominari hominibus* or *principari temporaliter*. Marsilio quotes the Gospels accordingly. Christ could have commanded the angels; he deliberately refrained. Further, he conferred no such power on the apostles; the priests, who are in succession from them, cannot claim temporal power; in spiritual matters they are simply experts and advisers, 'doctors of the soul' — *medicus animarum, sacerdos scilicet*. Just as doctors can diagnose a case and advise on it *propter sanitatem conservandam*,[1] so the priest can exhort and advise, but no more. The priest, again, is *tamquam claviger* — 'like a turnkey' — who lets the prisoner out or shuts him up, but whose action is merely the result of the judge's decision on which he has no influence. Marsilio also attacks the validity of Canon Law by making an ingenious distinction between the Law of Christ, which is enforced in the next world, and purely Human Law, which is concerned with society. The wicked, he suggests, will be dealt with as they deserve in God's good time. It is no wonder he was regarded as a particularly dangerous heretic.

Turning from the theoretical to the immediate, Marsilio insists that his demonstration, *a priori* from Scripture, that the Church ought not to have coercive power, is reinforced by the spectacle of the behaviour of the clergy. 'Now', he says, 'we will declare it by manifest signs', and proceeds to do so in many chapters. Attacking the wealth, pride, and avarice of churchmen, he declares that they have no right to possess property at all, but are at best trustees of it. Christ and the disciples were poor *viatores*; they had nowhere to lay their heads. '*Nolite possidere aurum, neque argentum, neque pecuniam in zonis vestris*', said the Master. Moreover, the disciples were all equal. Christ sent them all out into the world together. He did not tell Peter, 'Go and send the others' (II, 16). Further, he said, 'I *will*

---

[1] To preserve health.

give you the keys of earth and heaven', not 'I *am* giving you' (*tibi dabo non tibi do*). It follows that the Bishop of Rome has no superior power to any other ordinary priest. Who, then, is to decide the affairs of the Church? A general Council, he answers, consisting of elected priests and laymen who will express the will of all Christians. This Council will be the *legislator humanus*. But he never makes a satisfactory answer to the question which arises, then as now, who is to be its *pars principans* and enforce its decisions?

Here, then, is an extremely able attempt to outline a theory of the State, in essentials secular, and in which the clergy are regarded as only part of an organic social structure. 'Marsilius of Padua, bred in an Italian commune, hating the ecclesiastical power which put it out of gear, is anxious to combine the sharply bound and compact unitary State he loved with a kind of society of Christendom guided by its elected advisory general council.'[1] The way in which the problem is attacked, the conclusions argued, set out and recapitulated, the objective clearly stated, show a power of exposition and grasp of general principles of refreshing scope. Apart from its historical interest, it is even relevant to the international problems of our day. Like the *Policraticus*, the *Defensor Pacis* is eminently sensible, but far more business-like and formidable, based on the assimilated *Politics* of Aristotle, which John of Salisbury never knew. It drives to the clearest conclusions and well illustrates the bracing effect of the best scholastic methods on the mediaeval mind, though its arguments are incompatible with the Augustinian world view, and indeed with Thomism. It will be seen that, though his arguments are devastating to the pretensions of Rome, Marsilio still assumes a united Christendom. The edifice is rocking, but he still attempts to support it on a Christian laity; he has not yet got to the stage of taking an immoral world for granted. He recognizes and defines the tendencies of his day towards centralized government, both in monarchies and cities, but he still attempts a compromise between efficiency and the old order. Marsilio's conception of society remains, it should be remembered, totalitarian; the persecution of heretics, for example, and their loss of civil liberty, is not criticized — it is merely handed over to the *pars principans* rather than the Church.[2] Yet though one must be careful not to read too

---

[1] See PREVITÉ-ORTON, op. cit., Introduction.

[2] *Vide* D'ENTRÈVES, op. cit., p. 79. 'That a system such as the one which I have described may have appeared to contain an anticipation of religious liberty, I confess is to me a cause of bewilderment. It seems to me essentially incompatible with the theory and practice of religious, and indeed of political liberalism.'

much into him, the contribution of Marsilio to political thought is not the least of mediaeval intellectual achievements.

§ I V

As is apparent from Marsilio's book, by the end of the fourteenth century the political bankruptcy of the Papacy was to lead to a concerted European effort to affirm once again the unity of Christendom through the Conciliar movement. This movement failed, and the disintegration already on the way was accelerated; the Protestant revolt and the Counter-Reformation were the sequel. Further, the decline of the Papacy encouraged the tendency to local absolutism, already apparent in the monarchies emerging out of later feudalism.

In the light of the political programme of the Conciliar movement as set out by the Councils of Constance and Basel, the view of the State and of a European order envisaged by Marsilio is worked out by Nicholas Cusanus[1] in the *De Concordantia Catholica*. The work of Nicholas has been described as 'the last sunset glow of mediaeval constitutional theory'; he is the last and one of the most effective exponents of the old order. Although, immediately, the Conciliar theorists failed, they stated principles of subsequent resistance to absolutism which were transferred from the ecclesiastical to the lay sphere.

It was argued that since the pope's authority led men to damnation, Natural Law and *salus populi* could be invoked against him, and Cusanus maintains that if the pope becomes *tyrannus*, he should be resisted; indeed resistance is essential to salvation. If necessary the papal power must be put in commission and vested in a council. The struggle between pope and emperor further led to the assertion that the emperor had been elected by the 'common consent of all the Germans and of others who were under the empire', not appointed by the pope, whose authority does not run in any *provincia* of Christendom without its consent. This leads to an invocation of Natural Law as justifying the right of free election. But Cusanus goes beyond the old papal-imperial controversy; some of the ideas

---

[1] Nicholas of Cues, born at Cues on the Moselle, 1401. Educated for the Law at Deventer and Padua; Archdeacon of Liége, took part in the Council of Basel, the occasion of the composition of the *De Concordantia*; papal Legate in Germany and Cardinal Bishop of Brixen, 1450; died Lodi, 1464. In certain aspects his writings anticipate the humanism of the Renaissance; he was the greatest German thinker of his age.

behind the Conciliar movement, for all its different context, were not
unlike those which brought about the League of Nations, and seem
to represent the attempt of 'men of good will' to deal with a situation
which had in practice deteriorated beyond such a remedy. The
political facts made the Conciliar assertion of the limits of Christendom belated, its administrative realization impossible. When feudal
society was already in decline, Conciliar theorists tried to apply
feudal ideas of representation and balanced interests to the ecclesiastical government of Europe. The significance of their work lies not in
their immediate failure but in their identification of Law, failing the
acceptance of papal or imperial sovereignty, with the common will
of the community. Cusanus asserts that power is sanctified *quando per
concordantiam communem a subjectis exoritur*, when it derives from the
subjects through their common agreement.[1] *Principatus* derives from
the community; only through consent and election can authority
be valid. Power is justified only when directed to the common good
in accordance with the will of the governed; a man will obey the Law
which he has himself made. Cusanus is only one and the most lucid
of many examples of mediaeval writers who thus assert the supremacy of Law in a new way and are driven by the failure of the great
European institutions — Papacy and Empire — into invoking some
measure of popular consent as a sanction for government. These
writers provided a store of arguments which were employed at the
Reformation, and, gradually secularized, were later used to curb
the power of the absolute State. This development ran parallel
with the local English secular assertion of representative institutions
and the rule of Law already described.

There are other and important thinkers of the later Middle Ages
whose contributions it is impossible here to describe; Pierre Dubois,
William of Ockham, Wycliffe, all are trying to preserve and adapt
the tradition of Christendom to the facts of their day. Yet the tide
was against them, and the failure of the Conciliar movement opened
the way to the National State, recognizing no spiritual or temporal
Law, and ultimately to the international situation Grotius was
to attempt to assuage. The Papacy was in the forefront of this development, and Jesuit theory becomes a state among and within
other states. Thus gradually the idea of united Christendom was
abandoned both by secular and spiritual power.

It was a considerable tragedy; the mediaeval view of European

[1] *De Concordantia Catholica*, iii. Quoted by CARLYLE, op. cit., vi, 170.

order had become involved with rigid and limited ideas and the theocratic claims of a discredited Papacy. All the new ideas and the scientific outlook of the Renaissance were bound to be against it. Political wisdom seemed to point to the absolute prince as the only way out; Machiavelli, Bodin, Bacon, and Richelieu, all the practical men, were bound to take this view; and by their lights they were right. But the sovereign National State brought its own nemesis; the mediaeval vision of co-operative order, though tied up with an obsolete terminology, was in fact superior both on grounds of ethics and common sense. It was discarded by the practical men and its failure meant a political retrogression in European order to the national Leviathan, which engulfs the smaller communities within the State and which, in relation to its own kind, lives in a 'posture of warre'.

Yet, though the period is one of political failure and, the late fifteenth century in particular, an age of superstition, violence, and often of despair,[1] mediaeval civilization had been brilliant. Ten centuries had passed since the decline of Rome, the effective duration of whose empire had been at most four hundred years. During that millennium, what an achievement confronts the historian! From the sub-Roman relics of fifth-century culture and the crude beginnings of the Carloving empire; through the solid building of Norman and Angevin administration and the spiritual fires of the Hildebrandine Papacy; to the thirteenth-century climax of papal imperialism and the far-flung, if shallow, glories of Barbarossa's empire; to the intellectual brilliance of the universities and the spectacular elaboration of later chivalry! And, as the undertone to this civilization, can be heard the plodding footsteps of the European peasantry, clearing the forest, draining the marsh, wresting an increasing harvest from the European lands, settling in, generation after generation, to the homes of their forebears; founding a civilization strong enough to bear the strain of Renaissance initiative, strong enough to dominate the world.

The eighteenth-century legend of a 'Gothick' age too long influenced the beneficiaries of this culture; the contribution of the Middle Ages, though it cannot be ranked with the contribution of antiquity, is a great and decisive factor in the development of Europe. This tradition was never without aim. In their different ways the minds of Aquinas, of Dante, of Marsilio are set on one thing: the integration of Christendom under the purpose of God. Here then, for all

---

[1] *Vide* Huizinga, *The Waning of the Middle Ages*, London (1924).

its failures, is a healthy society, with initiative in the hands of its *élite*, with the masses believing in the mythos of their culture, with a concerted drive towards an intelligible objective; hence, in spite of so much practical incompetence, their remarkable artistic and architectural achievement.

Yet, in history as in life, all things pass, and the elaboration of one theme cannot indefinitely continue. By the close of the Middle Ages it would seem the time was ripe for a new and more ambitious phase in the development of European civilization. Scientific humanism, the Renaissance outlook, was destined to explore a world whose physical and intellectual horizons dwarfed those of antiquity and the Middle Ages. The sequel to this initiative was an age of political expansion which has not yet stabilized, and of which the political price was the disintegration of Christendom and the emergence of the National Sovereign State.

BOOK THREE

THE POLITICAL THOUGHT OF THE RENAISSANCE AND THE AGE OF RATIONALISM

CHAPTER I

THE RENAISSANCE

§ I

THE Italian Renaissance begins the most important period in Western thought since the great age of Greece; it marks the re-emergence of the humanistic and, later, the scientific outlook which is peculiarly European. The interpretation of this originally Italian attitude by the thinkers of France, England, Germany, and the Netherlands, created the intellectual climate of the modern world. The social revolution it implied has not yet been worked out.

But where the Greek thinkers were untrammelled by an over-whelming legacy of the past, and made their speculations in the dawn of thought, the men of the Renaissance and the seventeenth century were over-shadowed by the legacy of the Middle Ages, and by the dynastic power politics of the emerging nation state. The idiom of political thought remains semi-mediaeval until the time of Hobbes, for Erasmus, More, Bacon, and Descartes were deeply influenced by scholasticism. With the break-up of mediaeval Christendom and the economic revolution of the time, the second half of the sixteenth century and the first half of the seventeenth were dominated by religious warfare; not only did the better mediaeval tradition survive, but the legacy of mediaeval controversy and doctrinal passion expressed itself with a fanaticism unparalleled since the time of the early Fathers. Luther, Calvin, and Milton are as savage in controversy as Tertullian, Athanasius, or Jerome, and the devastation caused by the Counter-Reformation in the Netherlands, the Huguenot wars in France, and the Thirty Years War in Germany, surpasses anything in the Middle Ages, because the protagonists were better equipped.

Splendid as this mediaeval ideal had been, it took over one and a half centuries for the virus of decadent mediaevalism to work itself out of the European system, and the thought of the sixteenth and seventeenth centuries suffered no less than the politics. The goal of religious toleration, without which there could be no intellectual and political advance, and which the Greeks took as their birthright, was hard come by. In the well-known words of Figgis: 'Political liberty, as a fact in the modern world, is the result of the struggles of religious organisms to live.'[1] It is not till after the tempest of the religious wars that the voice of humanistic common sense could effectively make itself heard, for the first time since the best of Graeco-Roman civilization foundered in the fifth century.

It was in Italy that the first widely influential political expression of this common sense occurs in the writings of Machiavelli;[2] but it is not yet humanitarian. It combines the objectivity of the new outlook with the realism of the Italian urban environment, expressed by Marsilio of Padua in the fourteenth century. Machiavelli is in the same tradition, but his thought is unredeemed by the Christian principles which inspire Marsilio, and conditioned by the limitations of its setting.

In spite of the strain of republican idealism expressed in the *Discorsi*, the *Prince* is devoid of the idealism which inspired Sir Thomas More's *Utopia*, in which Renaissance common sense, combined with the best mediaeval tradition, is touched with humour and kindliness. The sweeter sanity of More is of course as typical as Machiavelli's pessimism of the nascent Humanist outlook, which did not necessarily lead to such conclusions.

To turn first to Machiavelli. It is plain that the still small and

[1] FIGGIS, *From Gerson to Grotius*, Introduction, p. 5. Cambridge University Press, 2nd edition (1923).

[2] Machiavelli. Born in Florence, son of a lawyer of good family, 1469. Entered the service of the Republican government in 1494, the year of the expulsion of the Medici. From 1498 to 1512 he was secretary to the Chancellery, an important post concerned with diplomatic, military, and administrative affairs. In 1500 he went on a mission to Cesare Borgia, whose methods he studied and admired. From 1503 to 1506, in addition to further diplomatic activity, he was trying to substitute a reliable Florentine citizen militia for the mercenaries generally employed, and in 1506 was appointed to put his scheme into operation. In the same year he was sent to Rome as ambassador to Pope Julius II; in 1507 he was envoy to the German Emperor Maximilian at Bolsano. He thus had the opportunity of studying the French, Roman, and German courts at first hand, and obtained an insight into the workings of foreign governments.

But in 1512 his career was broken. With the return of the Medici, backed by Spanish arms, Machiavelli fell into disgrace. In November, 1512, he was deprived of his office; in the spring of 1513 put into prison and tortured. He was finally released on the condition that he retired to his farm in the country and took no further part in public affairs. Here he lived until his death in 1527, and here he set himself to write books that made him famous. The *Principe* was completed in 1513. The *Discorsi* – Discourses on the first ten books of Livy – is a longer work, begun before the other and completed after it (1520). Machiavelli also wrote a book on *The Art of War* (1520), a *History of Florence* (1520-7), a cynical and revealing comedy called *Mandragola*, and a scurrilous novel called *Belphegor*. He further wrote numerous and very able dispatches, reports on his diplomatic missions and on the political situation in France and Germany, and a number of familiar letters which have survived. In one of them, quoted by PROFESSOR TOYNBEE in his *Study of History* (vol. III, p. 371) Machiavelli describes his way of life on his farm and the occasion of writing the *Prince*.

huddled world of the Renaissance, with its relative technical incompetence, was untouched by the commanding optimism and humanitarian good sense of the more prosperous and stable eighteenth century. Where Voltaire is a crusader in the cause of reason and humanity on a universal scale, whose influence swept over the world, as did the influence of the great philosophers of antiquity, Machiavelli merely reveals plainly the squalid secrets of power politics. His outlook is objective but with a bitter and limited objectivity, the fruit of disillusionment.

There is little new in Machiavelli's *Prince*; any decently efficient tyrant or demagogue of the fifth and fourth centuries B.C., knew the tricks. Take, for example, Thucydides' well-known account of the Athenian negotiations with the Melians.[1] The outlook is purely 'Machiavellian'; it finds its parallels in the political practice of any age, ancient or modern, while Aristotle anticipates the most important of Machiavelli's observations. But what is notable in the *Prince* and the *Discorsi* is the abandonment of religious faith, and the absence of the moral framework in which the City State was set by Aristotle or the community of Christendom by Aquinas.

Yet it would be wrong to regard Machiavelli as a scoundrel who delighted in evil for its own sake, a view which is too often taken of him.[2] Like Dante, he was a patriot and passionately admired the Romans; he regarded a republican form of government as the best, as is apparent from the *Discorsi*; and he idealized Swiss and even German institutions. He was essentially a diplomat, and an administrator, not a speculative theorist; a craftsman of politics, not a philosopher, with no intention of expanding the political maxims and advice which his handbooks to politics contain into wider principles of action. It was the German philosophers of the nineteenth century and their followers who translated the political expedients suitable for a decadent phase of Italian politics into a theory of international conduct applicable to great nation states.

At the same time, Machiavelli's objective analysis shows a singular obtuseness of moral perception, such as might be expected from anyone who had seen the hectic and sanguinary political games of Renaissance at close quarters.[3]

---

[1] See THUCYDIDES, V, p. 85. Everyman translation.
[2] See MARLOWE, Prologue to *The Jew of Malta*: 'Albeit the world think Machiavel is dead, . . .', etc.
[3] e.g., He regards Castruccio Castracani as a 'great examplar to men'. After tracing the career of this brigand through its catalogue of crime to its deserved end, Machiavelli

His political realism was, indeed, based on a cynical view of human nature, expressed in the following well-known passage, in which he argues that it is safer for a ruler to be feared than loved: 'Because it is to be asserted in general of men that they are ungrateful, fickle, false, cowards, covetous and as long as you succeed they are yours entirely; they will offer you their blood, property, life and children, as is said above, when the need is far distant, but when it approaches they turn against you.'[1]

Such a view of human nature, excusable perhaps in any age, was natural in the Italy of Machiavelli's time. It was a society which combined many vital elements: the old pagan life of the south, of the piazza and the Forum, which went back unbroken to antiquity (the population of Italy in the Middle Ages never fell as did the population of the North), had been reinforced by the economic expansion of the Italian cities, particularly in Lombardy and Venetia, since the twelfth century.[2] Lombard banking had long devised its technique, when in the North the money transactions that survived were in the hands of ostracized Jews. The Italian nobility had remained urbanized and intelligent while the northern barons cared only for war and hunting. The Papacy, though it was politically a stumbling block to Italian unity, had always been a centre of artistic, financial, and legal activity. In the South, the Emperor Frederic II had blended the culture of the Saracen, Byzantine, Greek, and Latin worlds, while the law schools of Bologna, Padua, and Milan had long been flourishing.

In face of this intellectual and artistic achievement, the Italian political failure was deplorable. Italy was hopelessly divided, the battleground and victim for the armies of France, Spain, and the Empire. The new states of the North, educated by Italian thought and method, were now bringing their vastly greater resources to bear to swamp the Italians.

The world of which Machiavelli wrote, both in Italy and beyond,

---

[1] *Prince*, chap. xvii, Everyman edition.
[2] See PIRENNE, *Social and Economic History of Mediaeval Europe*, London (1936).

remarks, 'But Fortune growing envious of the glory of Castruccio, took away his life just at the time when she should have preserved it' – for further 'glory' – and laments that the hero should have been prevented from doing any more harm by the undignified agency of a chill, caught after he had exposed himself when 'over-heated' from battle to the 'wind which often rises at midday on the banks of the Arno' and 'which is often very unhealthy'. See also his admiring account of Cesare Borgia's calculated treachery. (Description of the Methods adopted by the Duke Valentino 'when murdering' Vitallozzo Vitelli, Oliverotto da Fermo, the Signor Pagolo, and the duke di Gravina Orsini.)

justified, therefore, a pessimistic view of human nature; and indeed the political situation generally in Europe in the early sixteenth century could not have appeared to thoughtful contemporaries a good one. Everywhere the mediaeval order was breaking up: the economic revolution, resulting from the discovery of the New World and the Far East, was beginning to rock the social fabric of Europe; the new national rulers had no sooner struggled out of the feudal background of the later Middle Ages than they began to dissipate their hard won resources in war. Charles VIII of France no sooner finds himself secure at home than he needs must pour his troops into Italy; Francis I and Charles V are locked in a dynastic struggle by the twenties of the new century; Henry VIII uses the capital left by his father in intrigues and campaigns abroad. The new national political units, the great 'States'—it is Machiavelli who first popularizes the term, which means originally no more than the entourage of the prince—had a bad pedigree. Schooled in violence and cunning, they had fought their way out of the later Middle Ages: the survivors of a murderous conflict, they could only go on playing the old game.

In Italy the political scene had long been desperate. In such a *milieu* it was only the most efficient rulers who survived, and the elegant cruelty and diplomatic cunning of these often self-made tyrants can be sensed from their portraits; for no men were better served by the artists they patronized.[1]

In their context, Machiavelli's ideas were natural; in a corrupt society despotic power is the only way out, and ruling becomes a hunt for security, with no time for idealism or any vision of a fine scheme of things. That scheme has disintegrated and only the short view counts — and Machiavelli is, of course, thinking throughout in terms of the government of city states.

The *Prince* is a short book in twenty-six chapters, like the *De Civitate Dei*, a *livre de circonstance*, written to win favour with the new government that had banished Machiavelli from political life. In the dedication he writes: 'It is not possible to make a better gift than to offer you the opportunity of understanding in the shortest time all that I have learned in many years with so many troubles and dangers.' It is the result of accumulated experience, 'digested into a little

---

[1] *Vide* BURCKHARDT, *The Civilisation of Renaissance Italy*, Phaidon Press (1937). Both text and illustrations are invaluable: See plate 8, Sigismondo Malatesta, Tyrant of Rimini; 41, Francesco Sforza; 71, The condottiere Colleoni; 100, Lorenzo de Medici; and 356, Borso D'Este, with his court jester – a more genial aspect.

volume'. The dedication ends: 'If your magnificence (Lorenzo de Medici) from the summit of your greatness will some time turn your eyes to these lower regions, you will see how unmeritedly I suffer the great and continued malignity of fortune.' Here is probably Machiavelli's principal motive for publication.

In the second chapter he remarks: 'I will leave out all discussions of republics, inasmuch as in another place I have written of them at length.' He refers to the *Discorsi*, which are not dedicated to any Prince, and show his admiration for republican government, to which, after all, he owed his phase of success. The *Prince* ought not, therefore, to be taken as representing Machiavelli's ideal of government. It is merely evident, that since the political situation in Italy had deteriorated to such an extent, he regarded republican government as impracticable, with dictatorship as the only way to create any sort of stability, and that he was anxious to ingratiate himself with the new rulers of Florence.

The first part of the *Prince* discusses the best method of winning and holding a principality. Dismissing hereditary principalities as easy to keep, Machiavelli says that 'newly acquired' ones present many problems. First, the Prince is certain to have made enemies in acquiring them, and will have disappointed some of his supporters of reward. If his new subjects talk the same language as his own, he must merely destroy the family of the previous prince. His own followers will then be able to fraternize with the inhabitants. When dealing with alien people, he should go and live on the spot, and so crush disorders. Another method is to send colonists to key places in the new state. This is preferable to keeping garrisons there, an expedient, which is expensive and reminds the conquered people of their servitude. He sums up as follows: 'Whenever those states which have been acquired as stated have been accustomed to live under their own laws and in freedom, there are three courses for those who wish to hold them. The first is to ruin them; the next is to reside there in person; the third is to permit them to live under their own laws, drawing a tribute, and establishing within it an oligarchy which will keep it friendly to you.' But he concludes that on the whole the safest way 'is to destroy them or to reside there'.

Further, it is best to govern newly acquired cities by ruthless agents who are afterwards broken. For example Cesare Borgia in the Romagna 'promoted Messire Ramiro d'Orco, a swift and cruel man, to whom he gave the fullest power. This man in a short time restored peace and unity with the greatest success'. Afterwards, to exonerate himself from his agent's actions, Borgia 'one morning caused him to be executed and left on the Piazza at Cesaria, with the block and a bloody knife at his side. The barbarity of this spectacle caused the people to be at once satisfied and dismayed'.

Fascinated by the subject of Borgia, Machiavelli dwells on his misfortune in falling ill just when his father, Alexander VI, died. Having provided for almost every contingency, he was ruined by sheer ill fortune: 'he told me that he had thought of everything that might occur at the death of his father, and had provided a remedy for all, except that he had never anticipated, when the death did happen, he himself would be on the point to die'. 'When all the actions of the Duke are revealed,' concludes Machiavelli, 'I do not know how to blame him, but rather it appears to me, as I have said, that I ought to offer him as an imitation to all.'

Dealing with those who have obtained a principality by wickedness,[1] it is best, he says, to strike mercilessly, all at one blow. 'Men ought to be either well treated or crushed, because they can avenge themselves of lighter injuries, of more serious ones they cannot; therefore the injury that is to be done to a man ought to be of such a kind that one does not stand in fear of revenge . . .' Again, 'injuries ought to be done all at one time; benefits ought to be given little by little, so that the flavour of them may last longer'.

The State must of course be adequately fortified and provisioned. A prince who 'has a strong city' will not be attacked; or, if he is attacked, the aggressor will be driven off in disgrace.

Machiavelli now turns to military matters. Power based on mercenaries is precarious:[2] good ones are untrustworthy; if they are not skilful 'you are ruined in the usual way'. Mercenaries are 'disunited, ambitious, and without discipline; unfaithful, valiant before friends, cowardly before enemies — they have neither the fear of God nor fidelity to men'. The ruin of Italy has been caused by nothing else than by resting all hopes for many years on mercenaries. When the foreigners came, these hirelings showed what they were worth; they have brought Italy into slavery and contempt. 'Auxiliaries are little better; Borgia tried them, but, finding them doubtful, unfaithful, and dangerous, he destroyed them. A wise prince trusts his own arms and his own citizens.' Further, the successful prince must personally study and practise the art of war, or else his soldiers look down on

[1] Chap. viii.   [2] *Prince*, p. 98.

him. In peace time he must keep his eye in by constant hunting. 'He must follow the chase, by which he accustoms his body to hardship, and learns something of the nature of localities, and gets to find out how the mountains rise, how the valleys open out, how the plains lie, and to understand the nature of rivers and marshes, and in all this to take the greatest care.'[1] If he knows the geography of his own country, he will be able to master that of another.

The next and most notorious part of the book starts with the prince's behaviour towards his 'subjects' and 'friends'. To hold his own, he must 'know how to do wrong'; yet however bad his character, he ought to be sufficiently 'prudent' to avoid getting too bad a reputation. For example, it is a good thing to be thought generous, though actually it is best to be mean. It is impossible to be generous without over-taxing your subjects, and though there is a way out — being liberal with the property of conquered aliens — this cannot last. On the whole, Machiavelli concludes, it is safer to be mean. 'We have not seen great things done in our time except by those who have been considered mean; the rest have failed.'

Again, when two powerful neighbouring states go to war, it is best to come out boldly on the side of the one you think likely to win. 'Irresolute princes who follow a neutral path are generally ruined. But when a prince declares himself gallantly in favour of one side, if the party with whom he allies himself conquers, although the victor may be powerful and have him at his mercy, yet he is indebted to him.'

The seventeenth chapter, 'Concerning cruelty and clemency and whether it is better to be loved than feared', contains the cynical estimate of human nature already quoted, which is the basis of all Machiavelli's thought. This leads to discussion if princes ought to keep faith. They are, he concludes, absolved from all the ordinary restraints of morality. Theirs is the law of the jungle; the prince must combine the qualities of the lion and the fox,[2] and the morality of the State is sub-human. At the same time the prince must always remember to appear merciful, faithful, humane, upright, and religious.

The nineteenth chapter is concerned with the obvious point: 'That one should avoid being Despised and Hated.' To avoid this, it is best not to be a violator of the 'property and women' of one's subjects. 'When neither their property nor honour is touched, the majority of men live content, and one has only to contend with the

[1] p. 116.   [2] p. 142.

ambition of a few.' The prince must, of course, be a good judge of men. The first opinion one forms of a prince is by observing the men he has around him. He must know how to recognize the capable and keep them faithful.[1] Flatterers should be avoided; this pest is an ever-present handicap to a prince.[2]

Such are the main points of Machiavelli's advice to tyrants. It will be seen that the lot of the prince is strenuous. The price of power self-control, eternal vigilance, an unsleeping cunning; one slip and the game is up. It is a hard one, which few can play.

Machiavelli acknowledges this fact, and in the twenty-fifth chapter qualifies the conclusions of the whole book. Is it not best, he asks, to let things take their course: since 'Fate governs all'? 'There are those who maintain it is unnecessary to labour much in affairs, but let chance govern them' . . . 'Sometimes, pondering all this', he admits, 'I am in some degree inclined to their opinion. Nevertheless, . . . I hold it to be true that Fortune (or Fate, we should say) is the arbiter of one half of our actions, but she still leaves us to direct the other half or perhaps a little less.' All the feverish scheming can only be within these limits; time and chance determine the rest.

The *Prince* concludes with an 'exhortation to liberate Italy from the barbarians'. 'It appears to me', writes Machiavelli, 'that so many things concur to favour a new prince that I never knew a time more fit than the present. Italy waits for him who shall yet heal her wounds and put an end to the ravaging and plundering of Lombardy, to the swindling and taxing of the Kingdom and of Tuscany.'

'Look', he says, 'how expert and subtle Italians are at duels and hand to hand contests', yet in the last thirty years, when there has been an army wholly Italian, it has always given a poor account of itself. The reason, he maintains, unconvincingly, is bad leadership. He concludes with an appeal to Lorenzo and the Medici family to save the situation.

It will be apparent that Machiavelli, besides taking a one-sided view of human nature, shows little interest in economic, emotional, or religious motives, which in practice are extremely influential. Actually he misjudges the politics of his own age, for the forces which were largely to control the sixteenth century were religious — the Reformation and the Counter-Reformation. Blinded by an over-insistence that political power alone is the end of the State, his view of government is too much that of the professional diplomatist.

[1] p. 185.   [2] p. 191.

The *Prince* is a book of great ability and much of its advice is sound, but the impression given by it is of meanness and limitation. It became notorious because Machiavelli said the obvious thing, that everybody knew and more or less acted on, in a plain manner. Such an outlook is implicit in a milder form in other books of the period; notably in Commines' memoirs, which describe the building of the French state by Louis XI, or, for that matter, in the English Paston Letters, which depict the small-scale struggles of a Norfolk family in the second half of the fifteenth century. The moral sense of Machiavelli, Commines, and the Pastons is numbed by the political situation with which they have to deal.

The *Discorsi*[1] are less notorious than the *Prince*; in some aspects they reinforce the conclusions of the earlier work, but they express also the republican idealism fashionable in Renaissance Italy: they indicate not only what the author regarded as expedient but also what he admired. Significantly Machiavelli dedicates the book to two men of intelligence, without any wide political influence.[2]

He has no illusions about the lot of original thinkers; in the preface to the first book he writes: 'Albeit the jealous troupe of mankind, ever more disposed to censure than to praise the work of others, has constantly made the pursuit of new methods and systems no less perilous than the search after unknown lands and seas; none the less . . . I enter into a path, which, being hitherto untrodden by any, . . . may yet win me thanks from those who judge my efforts in a friendly spirit.' The example of the ancients is followed in matters of art, literature, law, and medicine: 'yet in maintaining states and governing kingdoms . . . we find no prince who resorts to this example . . . Desiring to rescue men from that error, I have thought fit to note

---

[1] *Discourses on the First Decade of Titus Livius*, by NICCOLO MACHIAVELLI, citizen and secretary of Florence, Translated, N. H. Thompson, Kegan Paul (1883). Finished *c.* 1520 and dedicated to Zanobi Buondelmonti and Cosimo Rucellai. Divided into three books, the first containing 40 chapters, the second 33, and the third 49. The whole occupies 485 pages of the English edition. The first book ranges over the history of Rome; this survey gives an occasion for Machiavelli's own views of the merits of a republic as a form of government to be emphasized; the second book outlines the causes of the expansion of Rome and of wars in general; the third, still keeping to the thread of Roman history, diverges more widely into general political observations of great interest. The influence of Polybius is apparent in the book.

[2] It is instructive to compare the dedications of the two books: 'I send you a gift, which if it answers ill the obligations I owe you, is at any rate the greatest which Niccolo Machiavelli has it in his power to offer. For in it I have expressed what I have learned or have observed for myself, during a long experience and constant study of human affairs . . .' He has departed, he says, from the hackneyed custom which leads many authors to inscribe their works to some prince '. . . to avoid which error I have chosen not those who are, but those who deserve to be princes'.

down with respect to all those books of Titus Livius which have escaped the malignity of Time, whatever seems to me essential in the right understanding of ancient and modern affairs.'

This programme is expanded in the light of the author's own political experience, constantly applied to the interpretation of Roman history.

In many aspects the *Discorsi* show the same static and disillusioned view of men and affairs as appears in the *Prince*: 'Since the desires of men are insatiable, nature prompting them to desire all things and fortune permitting them to enjoy but few, there results a constant discontent in their minds, and a loathing of what they possess.'[1] But Machiavelli, though he takes a low view of human nature, is not paralysed or shocked by it: he has got beyond that. He accepts the situation and sets out to discover the best means of dealing with it. He is not so far disillusioned as to abandon the world altogether; government may be *magna latrocinia*, but he does not retire into a religious or metaphysical escapism: on the contrary, he still respects certain sides of human nature and the institutions which embody them.

His admiration for the Romans is apparent throughout the book, which is a panegyric on their political virtues; he looks back to an aristocratic republican regime which never effectively existed in Rome, and praises the practical sagacity of Roman administration. Defending himself against the charge of 'rendering excessive praise to the ancient times of the Romans while I censure my own', he writes 'and were not the excellence which then prevailed and the corruption which prevails now clearer than the sun, I should proceed more gradually in what I have to say'.[2] Dante, in the *Monarchia*, shows the same attitude.

Machiavelli also respects not the French but their institutions, because they are united and governed by a king who reveres the laws. He thinks well, too, of the Germans: 'among the last-named people a great show of the ancient excellence does in truth still flourish I shall show by an example similar to that which I have above related of the senate and people of Rome'. They are comparatively cut off from their neighbours, economically self-sufficient and therefore uncontaminated by 'the manners of the French, the Italians, and the Spaniards, which three nations are together the corruption of the world'. Machiavelli, like Tacitus, has his romantic side, though it is generally well concealed. Like Rousseau, he thinks

[1] Bk. II, Preface.   [2] Bk II, Preface.

well of the Swiss, 'the only people who to this day, both as regards religion and military discipline, live like the ancients', though he believes they would soon be contaminated by the 'Court of Rome', if there were any man powerful enough 'to transplant it into Switzerland'.[1] His loathing of the Papacy was similar to Marsilio's; he regarded it as the chief cause of Italian political failure. 'Through the ill example of the Roman court, the country has lost all religious feeling and devoutness . . . To the Church therefore and to the priests we Italians owe this great debt, that through them we have become wicked and irreligious. And a still greater debt we owe them for what is the immediate cause of our ruin — that by the Church our country is kept divided. For no country was ever united or prosperous which did not yield obedience to some one prince or commonwealth, as has been the case with France or Spain.'[2]

Machiavelli, then, had his standards, though they were obscured by his extreme shrewdness in summing up an immediate situation on a short view; and he believed there were phases in human history in which men had not been 'corrupt'.

'I am persuaded that the world, remaining continually the same, has in it a constant quantity of good and evil; but this good and evil shift about from one country to another. . . .' The good focused on Rome at the time of her greatest power, and 'although after the Roman Empire none has followed which has so long endured, or in which the world had centred its whole excellence, we may never the less find that excellence diffused among many valiant nations, the kingdom of the Franks, for example, that of the Turks, that of the Soldan and the states of Germany at the present day'.

Machiavelli thought that Italy had more than its share of the constant 'quantity of evil', and most of the book is concerned with Italian conditions. As in the *Prince*, he is constantly concerned as to the right way of building up a strong state, and reviews the various elements in society favourable or unfavourable to this aim. His only immediate remedy is the strong prince, deliberately using force, religious sanctions, and propaganda to keep his place. Further, it is wise 'to create new magistracies with new names, confer new powers, to exalt the humble and depress the great'. Moreover, the prince must 'pull down existing towns and rebuild them, removing their inhabitants from one place to another and in short leave nothing in the country as he found it'.

[1] Bk. I, chap. xii. [2] Bk. I, chap. xii.

258

As for the common people, they have little gratitude or political judgement; they must be kept constantly deceived, for their own good. Often, indeed, they become suicidal. 'A people, deceived by a false show of advantage, will often labour for its own destruction . . . and unless convinced by some one whom it trusts that the course on which it is bent is judicious, . . . will bring danger to the state. And should it happen, as is sometimes the case, that, having been deceived before . . . there is none in whom the people trust, their ruin is inevitable.'[1]

The people are at once dangerous and incapable. 'There is nothing more terrible than an uncontrolled and headless mob; on the other hand there is nothing more feeble.' None the less it is well to be generous to them or appear to be so, particularly in difficult times. But the people are no worse than most rulers: 'I maintain that this infirmity with which historians tax the multitude may with equal reason be charged against any individual man, but most of all against princes.'

Since force and fraud are the best means of governing the people, Machiavelli, as in the *Prince*, devotes many pages of the *Discorsi* to the discussion of correct and incorrect military tactics.[2]

Fraud is fair in war — a reasonable conclusion. 'Although in all other affairs it is hateful to use fraud, in the operation of war it is praiseworthy and glorious.' False sentiments of honour, too, must go by the board: 'For when the entire safety of our country is at stake, no consideration of what is just or unjust, merciful or cruel, praiseworthy or shameful, must intervene. On the contrary, every other consideration being set aside, that course alone must be taken which procures the existence of the country and preserves its liberty.'[3]

In spite of the author's admiration for republics, here is the classic definition of a political morality which sees no further than the

---

[1] Bk. I, chap. xvi.

[2] He discusses whether it is more important to have a good leader or a good army: 'the effect produced in battle by strange and unexpected sights or sounds'; the need for confidence between officers and men. He has a low opinion of the fighting qualities of the Renaissance Italians. 'Armies', he says, 'are of three kinds. In one you have discipline with bravery and valour in consequence . . . armies of the second sort, namely, those which have impetuosity without discipline. In armies of the third sort both natural spirit and trained valour are wanting; and to this class belong the Italian armies of our own times, of which it may be affirmed that they are absolutely worthless, never obtaining a victory, save when, by some accident, the enemy they encounter takes to flight.' Chaps. xiii and xiv.

[3] Bk. III, chap. xli.

interests of one state and which recognizes no political or ethical framework or laws beyond the State. Its appearance foreshadows the contests between great nations, wielding unbridled sovereign power, which were to reach their climax in the twentieth century. It marks a tragic falling off from the ideals of Christendom and indeed of antiquity.

Thus Machiavelli makes his diagnosis and suggests methods whereby political disaster may be staved off at the price of unsleeping vigilance and moral iniquity. Knowing all too well the way of the world, he still thought it 'the duty of a good man to teach others those wholesome lessons which the malice of Time and Fortune has not permitted me to put into practice; to the end that out of many who have the knowledge, some one, better loved of Heaven, may be found to carry them out'. Machiavelli, though battered, is still capable of this bitter hope.

Such, then, are the conclusions of the *Prince* and the *Discorsi*. Though touched by a vague republican idealism, the author's outlook is devoid of religious faith and reflects flatly the political bankruptcy of Renaissance Italy. It must be said for Machiavelli, however, that he achieves a non-mediaeval objectivity in the true Aristotelian tradition, though without Aristotle's moral and intellectual standards. The *Prince* and the *Discorsi* are both business-like documents, highly characteristic of their age. Just as Leonardo da Vinci was as much interested in engineering and scientific observation as in painting, so Machiavelli, within his narrower limits, is practical. In this quality he was in tune with the political developments of his time, not only in Italy but in the North.

§ 11

Beyond the Alps the new monarchies had consolidated their power, slowly, with difficulty. The steps whereby the mediaeval kings of France and England had fought themselves out of the feudal world of the eleventh and twelfth centuries have already been indicated. But the fifteenth century had seen a set-back in the development of centralized government owing in part to the mutual exhaustion of France and England by the Hundred Years War, that premature movement of misdirected nationalism, and in part to the threat to government from within the royal families themselves, the dynastic family feud. Where the early feudatories are out to shake off centralized government altogether, Yorkists and Lancastrians, Burgundians and Armagnacs, are attempting to seize and terrorize a machinery of government already in being. This kind of bastard feudalism was encouraged by the apparent wealth which was at the disposal of the aristocracy of the later Middle Ages — witness the splendour of the court of Burgundy or of Edward III, and by the fashionable traditions of military glory prevalent in the later mediaeval courts. But the dying splendours of decadent chivalry were extremely expensive, though picturesque, and the later Middle Ages witnessed the bankruptcy, intellectual, moral and practical, of the old-fashioned rulers and aristocracy. The beneficiaries of this carnival of arrogant incompetence and romanticism were the bourgeoisie and the surviving kings, who were driven into an alliance which proved more than a match for the great feudatories. The triumph of Louis XI over Charles of Burgundy and the business-like efficiency of Henry Tudor are landmarks in the history of political development, for all the limitations of the nationalism towards which they worked.

Business methods and a disregard for the conventions of the old chivalry mark both these architects of national government. The unbridled militarism of the late Middle Ages had brought its own nemesis; a comparison between the tone and atmosphere of Joinville, who described the exploits of St. Louis in the thirteenth century, and Froissart, who chronicled the glories of Edward III, with Commines, who witnessed the deadly struggle between Louis XI and Charles of Burgundy, tells its own tale. Again in Germany it is the same thing; Hohenstaufen and Wittelsbach go their spectacular and fatal way; it is the plodding Habsburg who reaps the harvest.

Parallel and consequent to this development, the military technique of the later Middle Ages became increasingly brutal; and dynastic blood feuds wiped out the old fashion of chivalry as practised within the feudal class. The superiority of pikemen and archers to cavalry reversed the battle tactics of the earlier period, while the growing efficiency of artillery dealt the structure of tottering feudalism its *coup de grâce*. The kings and the kings only, in alliance with the wealthy towns, could afford the professional armies necessary for successful war, while the siege train, by blowing in the castle defences, made the resistance of the great lords crumble before the superior resources of the central authority. This alliance of the kings with the towns goes back, we have seen, very far into the Middle Ages; it was a principle foundation of the power of the French, English, and Spanish monarchies. The new national states in the North and in Spain were thus built up by common-sense methods backed by the resources of cities with an interest in strong government.

Diplomatic ability and financial system were characteristic of both Henry VII of England and Louis XI in France, and both rulers deliberately employed ministers drawn, solely for their efficiency, from the middle or lower middle class. The typical Renaissance monarch, Henry VIII, employs Wolsey and Thomas Cromwell, the one the son of an Ipswich merchant, the other of a fuller at Putney, both parvenus of outstanding ability, ultimately broken by the power that made them. It is a pedestrian development, and must have appeared deplorable to men brought up in the tradition of the old aristocratic Catholicism. Economic change had long dislocated the attempt at the balanced commonwealth of later mediaeval thought. Religious schism and dynastic war broke up the remaining unity of Christendom.

§III

There were thus thinkers in the period highly critical of the drift of events, and where Machiavelli aided and abetted the power politics of Renaissance Italy and the great states of the North, Sir Thomas More and Erasmus are of a finer sensibility. More[1] represents the integrity of the best Catholic tradition and died for his opinions; Erasmus, who was personally careful to keep out of trouble, expresses a reasonable humanism which deplores the fanatical excesses of the men of action of his day. More ought to have lived in the twelfth century; Erasmus would have been happy in the eigh-

---

[1] Sir Thomas More, born 1478, son of Sir John More, a Judge of the King's Bench, whose father, John More, had been Steward of Lincoln's Inn. Sir John married Agnes, daughter of Thomas Graunger, a well-to-do merchant who was Sheriff of London in 1503. His son was educated at St. Anthony's in London and in the household of Archbishop Morton, then Lord Chancellor. He was at Oxford in 1493, at Canterbury College (the Benedictine foundation then on the site of Christ Church). In 1496 he was admitted to Lincoln's Inn; made friends with Erasmus and Colet, and studied Plato at a time when knowledge of Greek was rare. 1504, a Burgess of Parliament. He wrote in 1513 *A History of Richard III*; in 1516 the *Utopia* in Latin (English translation by Ralph Robynson, 1551); 1518, entered the service of Henry VIII, through Wolsey's influence; 1520, settled in Chelsea; 1521, Under Treasurer and knighted; 1523, chosen Speaker to the Commons; High Steward of both Oxford and Cambridge; 1529, Lord Chancellor; 1532, resigned in opposition to Henry's religious policy – 'The King's servant, but God's first'; 1534, Bill of Attainder against him brought in by Thomas Cromwell; executed 1535. See R. W. CHAMBERS, *Thomas More*, Cape (1935), for a good account.

teenth. Both men, born out of their time, made their protest, the one uncompromising, the other more discreet, against the public life of their age. Erasmus had the tide of events with him and knew it; his great achievement was in the sphere of scholarship, not of politics or political thought. That keen profile bears a striking resemblance to Voltaire, another witty and redoubtable champion of reason and intellectual freedom, though Voltaire was of even more formidable calibre.

More brings to political speculation the practical mind of late mediaeval England, articulate through the new knowledge. His most famous work is the *Utopia*, a sketch of an ideal commonwealth; in calibre and influence it cannot compare with Machiavelli's writings, but it presents none the less an important and contrasting aspect of Renaissance thought. The downright style of the translation of the Latin original, though made half a century later, does full justice to his shrewd, homely good sense — it is the Paston outlook humanized and retaining the values of the essential mediaeval tradition. The *Utopia* imitates the form of Plato's *Republic*; it is a protest against the economic tendencies of the time, and it also attacks that fundamental weakness of the nation state, the international anarchy to which the egoism of its foreign policy must lead. More, therefore, tackles, in his own context, the two major problems of the modern world: economic dislocation and war. He also puts his finger exactly on the weakness of the Protestant attack on papal authority and the absurdity of the attempt to define religion by Act of Parliament to which the English Protestants were ultimately driven. 'I will put you this case', he said at his trial, 'suppose the Parliament should make a law that God should not be God, would you then, Master Rich, say that God were not God?'

The *Utopia* is a miniature, in a Tudor setting. It is quite short, occupies little more than a hundred pages, and is divided into two books. Most of it was written when More was on an embassy to Flanders, and very well reflects the atmosphere of Bruges and Antwerp, the trim gardens and well-built houses, in the full tide of prosperity, when, as he writes, 'the most victorious and tryumphant Kynge of Englande, Henry the ight of that name . . . sent me ambassadour into Flaunders'.

The book opens with an account of 'Raphael Hithloday, a portugall borne . . . A man well stricken in age, with a black sonne burned face, a long beard and a cloak cast homly about his shoulders, whom by his favoure and apparell I judged to be a mariner.' Hythloday narrates his experiences in England, where he had known Cardinal Moreton, and remarks on the state of the country, then suffering the impact of the new capitalism. To More's suggestion that he should attach himself to the court of some prince, so that his 'good consells shall greatly help and further the common wealth', he answers that princes do not attend to philosophers, 'which thynge Plato himself proved with King Dionyse'.

Having raised the problems of contemporary economic dislocation and war, More and the stranger debate various remedies. This leads the latter to refer to Utopia. 'If you had been with me in Utopia and had presently seen their fashions and Laws as I did . . . then doubtless you would grant that you never saw people well ordered but there.' More then asks him to describe the country and the traveller gives the account contained in the second book.

More's shrewd criticism of the existing order is thus mainly concerned in the first part of his work, and before examining the striking remedies he suggests in the second part, it will be well to glance at his view of contemporary England and contemporary power politics. The economic and social situation of the time disturbed him and he criticizes it through Hythloday. The expansion of the wool trade had led to large-scale capitalist ventures in sheep farming, which caused depopulation and unemployment. 'Your shepe that were wont to be so meke and tame and so small eaters, now as I heare say, be become so great devowrers and so wylde that they eat up and swallow downe the very men themselves. They consume, destroy and devoure whole fieldes, howses and cities.' Landowners, 'yea and certain abbotts . . . leave no ground for tillage, thei enclose all into pastures: thei throw down howses, thei plucke down townes and leave nothing standing put leave only the church to be made a shepe howse' (p. 24). The husbandmen are 'thrown out of their own'; there is a riot of superfluous luxury on the one hand, destitution on the other.

More gives a shrewd picture of the internal social problems of his time: in the sphere of foreign politics he is also without illusions. It is ridiculous, he says, to suppose that princes will listen to the advice of philosophers. Look how they behave. Philosophers 'be not so unkind' but they would gladly give them counsel; but the last thing princes will do is to take any notice; they are far too much concerned with the pride and glamour of power. 'Suppose I were with the

French kynge and there sitting in his council, whilst in their moost secret consultation . . . they beat their brains and searche the very bottoms of their wittes to discern by what craft and means the kynge may styll keep Myllane, and draw to him again fugitive Naples, and then howe to conquer the Venetians and how to bring under his jurisdiction all Italy, then how to win the dominion of Flaunders, Brabant and of all Burgundie . . . here, I saye where so great and heyghe matters be in consultation, where so manye noble and wyse men counsel their kynge only to warre, — here yf I, selie man, should rise up and will them to turn over a new leafe and learn a new lesson, saying that my counsel is not to meddle with Italie, but to tarry still at home, and that the kingdom of Fraunce alone is almost greater than that it may well be governed by one man, so that the king should not study howe to gette more . . . this mine advice, Maister More, how think you it would be harde and taken? "So God help me, not very thankfully", quod I.'

This is a classic passage: it is with a sound assessment of the contemporary scene that the book is written.

Perhaps this realism made the compensating fantasy more exact. The *Utopia* is planned to the last detail. It is an attempt to realize a scholar's values. The discipline of such a community would in practice be irksome, at any rate for the young. But the stability More envisages and the social organization he suggests would tap and give scope for intellectual ability, though it would probably be too static to contain it in full freedom. More sets great store by the family — here he is too homely and English to follow Plato — although they 'dine and sup in common halls', private property is strictly limited and money is used only for external trade.

Utopia is alone a true commonwealth, 'for in other places they speak of the commonwealth, but every man procureth his own private wealth. In other countries, who knoweth but that he shall starve for hunger unless he make some several provision for himself, though the commonwealth flourish never so much in riches? In Utopia, though no man hath anything, yet every man is rich'. Their production is carefully planned according to the needs of the several districts: 'all are partners equallie; the whole island is as it were one familie or household'. And having satisfied their domestic needs, they plan a large export trade, which makes them rich.

Like the Temple State of early civilization, Utopia is a communal enterprise; to show their contempt of gold, they make their 'chaumber potts' out of it. They never make predatory war, but in matters of defence are particularly intelligent. 'Warre or battel as a thinge very beastely they do deteste and abhorre . . . They count nothing so much against glory as glory gotten in warre.' They use economic warfare, and overcome by 'might and puissaunce of witte', being ashamed to achieve victory with much bloodshed. They set a price on the heads of the enemy's leaders and pay it: they use highly paid mercenaries and rely on volunteers from their own men, for 'they thrust no man into warre against his will'. Picked men volunteer to destroy the adversaries' captain. They use novel and secret weapons and refrain from making war against the civilian population: 'they hurt no man that is unarmed, onless he be an espiall. All the weake multitude they leave untouched'. When they fight they carry the war into enemy territory. 'They meet him incontinent out of his own borders.' And when they have won, they exact, with a cheerful disregard for economics, swingeing reparations 'to be paid unto them yearly for ever' (pp. 91-9).

In religious matters they are tolerant. For the truth by 'its own innate force', will come to light, and every man will follow the religion he will 'so that he do it peaceably, gently, quietly and soberly': an admirable provision, not borne out by More's countrymen of his own and the seventeenth century. He advocates toleration, so long as the immortality of the soul and the existence of Providence is not denied; only those of 'exceeding holiness' become priests, who are therefore 'very few'. 'The most and the wysest part . . . believe that there is a certain godlie power unknowen, everlasting, incomprehensible, inexplicable, far above the capacitie and reche of man's witte . . . Him they call the Father of all . . . whom they all commonly in their country language call Mithra.' When they heard of Christianity, 'with gladde mindes they agreed to the same';[1] particularly because, according to Christ's teaching, they thought Christians had all things in common.

In the matter of marriage they are sensible, though pedantic. To avoid disillusionment, 'a sad and honest matron showeth the woman, be she maide or widowe, naked to the wowere; and likewise a sage and discreet man exhybiteth the wowere to the woman'.

'Matrymonie is there never broken but by death; except adulterie breake the bonde or else the intolerable waywarde manners of either partie.' This comprehensive proviso is enforced as follows: 'But now

[1] *Of the Religions of Utopia*, p. 101.

and then it chaunceth that whereas a man and a woman cannot well agree between themselves, both of them finding other with whom they hope to live more quietly and merrily, that they, by the full consent of them both, be divorced asonder and newe married to other. But that not without the council, which agreeth to no divorces before they and their wyfes have diligently tried and examined the matter; yea and then also they be loth to consent to it, because they know this to be the next waye to breake love between man and wyfe to be in easy hope of new marriage.'

More has little use for lawyers, though he was to be Lord Chancellor. 'They utterly exclude all proctors and serjeants of the law, which craftily handle matters and subtily dispute the laws, for they think it most meet that every one should plead his own matter.'

The *Utopia* is full of precise practical detail. The author has the close observation of a Flemish painter, and it is all very agricultural and traditional. In Utopia there are 'very few horses, nor none but very fearce ones for warre and exercise. For oxen be put to all the labour of ploughing and drawing, which . . . be not so good as horses at a sodaine brunt and, as we say, at a dead lift, yet they holde opinion that oxen would abide and suffere much more labour than horses will'. He even describes the Utopian method of chicken-farming. 'They brynge up a great multitude of pulleyne, and that by marvellous policie, for the hennes dooe not sytte upon the eggs, but by keeping them at a certain equal heate they bring life into them and hatche them' (p. 50). Further, the inhabitants 'kepe the wind out of their houses with glass, and somewhen also with fine linnen cloth dipped in oyle or amber, for by this means more light cometh in and the wind is better kept out'.

Government is provided for as follows. Every 30 families elect a Syphograunte or Philarch, and every 10 Philarchs elect a Tranibore. There are 200 Syphograuntes, who 'by a secret election . . . name Prince one of the four whom the people before named unto them'. He is to rule for life, but can be deposed for tyranny. There is also — and here Plato's influence is again apparent — an aristocracy of talent carefully selected, from which the rulers are chosen. They are limited to under 500 persons and exempted from manual work by 'a perpetual licence from laboure to learning'. If they do not live up to expectations, they are 'plucked back to the company of artificers'. But if a handicraftsman shows talent, he is 'taken from his handy occupation and promoted to the company of the learned'.

Further, 'every man is brought up to his father's craft, but if a man's minde stonde to any other, he is by adoption put into a familie of that occupation which he doth most fantasie'.

Such, in a short view, are the most striking aspects of More's *Utopia*. It will be seen that it is an admirable book, worked out on wise principles into the smallest detail. The essentials are what might be expected from a man of More's fine mind and sensibility: toleration; intellectual opportunity; decency and order; communal property, kindly administered by an aristocracy of talent. It is a dream touched with sarcasm and irony, combining a Platonic plan with Christian charity, the whole interpreted with sound common sense. It is all, of course, static. More plays for safety and his state might well be unenterprising to men of initiative. But what a contrast to the Machiavellian scramble for power! More's contribution to political thought, limited, practical and cheerful, is not the least of the achievements of Tudor England.

§ I V

Both Machiavelli and More, in their contrasting ways, mark a return to the objectivity of the Classical outlook — the one embittered by the evil environment of Renaissance politics, the other, in a political setting little less harsh, sustained by the Anglo-Saxon tradition of humour and good sense and inspired by a revived Platonism.

Both these Renaissance thinkers attempt to build up a stable society, the one in the immediate turmoil of Italian politics, the other as an ideal. Both keep closely to the facts: Machiavelli to an analysis of the technique of power; More to the two great problems looming out of the political development of the day, destined to haunt the subsequent political life of Europe, economic dislocation and war.

A new and constructive outlook, then, is implicit in Machiavelli's realism and More's good sense, though a true realism could not be content with the moral and political bankruptcy to which 'Machiavellianism' must lead, or with More's Utopian ideal, which had little influence on the world. But in both, as in the writings of Aristotle, political problems are stated plainly, without any superstructure of dogmatic assertion and without the conventional presentation of the old scholasticism. Political thought has been secularized. Thus, though the stark result in Machiavelli is unattractive, and More's *Utopia* was no more immediately effective than other books of its kind and harks back to a mediaeval ideal, the outlook of both writers has ceased to be mediaeval. They mark the revival of an attitude to politics lost since the days of antiquity. But before the voice of humanist Reason could emerge, Europe was destined to pass through a phase of violent religious conflict, before toleration and good sense could give the new outlook its full scope and intellectual justification. When that opportunity came, there ensued an expansion of thought and power which surpassed the achievements of antiquity and dominated the modern outlook.

CHAPTER II

THE REFORMATION AND THE WARS OF RELIGION

§ 1

BY the sixteenth century three new and vital developments are apparent in political thought. Two of them condition the whole of European civilization until our own day; the third is a short-term phase through which the long-term processes develop.

In the first place, the scientific humanist outlook, already foreshadowed in a limited way by the common sense of Machiavelli and More, with their respect for facts and secularized view of politics, gradually develops a greater confidence and range. By the first half of the seventeenth century, Descartes and Bacon formulate the idea of knowledge as power 'for the betterment of man's estate' in a way alien to the mediaeval world. The obscure beginnings of the scientific outlook in Renaissance Italy took, indeed, centuries to translate themselves into the minds of men of affairs; but by the seventeenth century the new point of view is affecting politics. There is a new confidence in reason and organization, a grasp of realities which had been absent from Europe since the days of antiquity.

In political thought this outlook is reflected in a restatement of Natural Law in secular terms as a basis for political authority. The Catholic adaptation of this originally pantheistic concept is modified by the majority of political thinkers, and Natural Law again interpreted in terms more akin to its Hellenistic origin. It is invoked both to justify the absolute authority of the new Great State[1] and also in support of the rights of the individual. The growing prestige of the scientific and humanistic outlook made it likely that the centre of political gravity would be defined in rationalistic terms, gradually divorced from theology. Finally, the idea of a transcendent Natural Law, reflecting eternal law and imposing a pattern on society, merges into a view of government as a convenience without which society would be impossible. Government is then justified because it works well, and retrospectively by the values an ordered civilization can create. In the second place, and creating the framework of

[1] *Vide infra*, Bk. III, chap. iii, *Richelieu's Political Testament*.

270

this development, the great national states, backed by an increasing economic expansion, continue to shoulder their way out of the wreckage of the mediaeval world and develop a new theory of absolute sovereign power both in relation to their 'subjects', a new term, and in relation to one another.

Both these fundamental long-term trends of thought will later be examined; the third, and more immediate phase, with which we are here concerned, and through which these basic ideas emerged, witnessed the conflict between Protestants and Catholics in terms of which the political problems of the time were formulated. The outlook of sixteenth-century writers was still profoundly dogmatic; salvation was what they cared about and to find a sanction for religious authority. In the process they assert Divine Right and Liberty of Conscience; secularized, these ideas later develop into Enlightened Despotism, and the assertion of the Rights of Man.

Thus the political theory of the later seventeenth century has its roots in the sixteenth, when political thought remained cast in theological terms and mass enthusiasm could respond only to religious ideas. Only doctrinal warfare could rouse men to the pitch of self-assertion which would later grow into a demand for liberty; the level of political consciousness still lit up mainly on the theological circuit.

Religious enthusiasm alone could have broken the authority of the mediaeval order. The new doctrines formed a fighting creed. 'What shall I do to be saved?' — the relentless question drove men to a supreme violence of self-assertion. So, in the first place, the Protestant revolt broke the power of the crumbling mediaeval order; in the second, it questioned the basis of all authority, and the con-flicting answers evoked must be related to the two general trends of political development already indicated, the secularized restatement of Natural Law and the establishment of the sovereign power of the national state. Generally speaking, the extremists on both sides, Calvinist and Jesuit, attacked the whole basis of secular authority, asserting the rights of conscience against the lay power. Both hanker for a theocratic order and regard secular politics with an Augustinian distaste. Milton's 'New Presbyter is but old priest writ large' gauges the situation shrewdly. The Calvinists, having found in the trans-lated Bible and their own consciences the basis of religious truth, outdo the thirteenth-century popes in theocratic ambition. Ordinary moderate opinion, on the other hand, sought stability in the assertion of the power of the secular State, as the only authority left to enforce true doctrine when found.

The failure of the Papacy indeed placed theologians in a difficult position. Assuming there is only one kind of religious truth, ascertainable and dogmatically expressed, and that it is extremely dangerous to get one's dogma wrong, the 'reformers' of the sixteenth century sought desperately for a religious authority to take the place of the discredited Papacy. The Protestant revolt was the sequel to the failure of the Papacy and of the Conciliar movement, itself, in its turn, a symptom of the decline of mediaeval civilization.

Meanwhile, coincident with the religious upheaval, economic and political conditions combined to foster a social revolution on a great scale. There had been heretics before Luther, and the Church had ultimately scotched them; doctrines similar to those of the Reformation had been canvassed in the thirteenth and fourteenth centuries without effect; but now the political and economic situation reinforced the Protestant revolt. The rising bourgeoisie and the new princes allied themselves with the Reformers against Rome.

For the Catholic Church the effect was devastating: the Teutonic, Scandinavian, and Anglo-Saxon peoples were largely lost to the Papacy: transalpine Europe, in revolt against the Eastern and Mediterranean aspects of Latin Christianity, returned nearer, perhaps, to the outlook of its forebears. The sturdy independence which has been noted in the early literature and institutions of the North combined with the influence of the translated Old Testament to produce the redoubtable sectaries of covenanting Scotland and Cromwell's East Anglian Ironsides. Southern English common sense and compromise came into its own with the Anglican Church; through the organizing genius of Calvin, the legalistic Northern mind put method into heresy, while in Germany the surge of Teutonic vitality found voice in the torrent of Luther's eloquence. With the Reformation the Puritan element in the North asserted itself against the traditional authority, the emotionalism, and the image worship of the Mediterranean world.

So the Protestant revolt broke the unity of Christendom, already stricken by the middle fifteenth century; asserted the Northern point of view against the South, and raised fundamental questions of the basis of religious and of secular authority.

In response to the Protestant attack, the Catholic writers of the Counter-Reformation invoked Natural Law and rights of resistance against Protestant rulers, together with the balanced conception of a Commonwealth characteristic of the mediaeval realm. Further, they re-stated the position of the Papacy, asserting for it the headship of the Church, a state within the European community of states, rather than the mediaeval supremacy over all Christendom. The writings of the Jesuits Mariana and Suarez are extremely able, and formulate political concepts which deeply affected subsequent thought. On the whole, the influence of Jesuit ideas tended to the assertion of natural rights against the absolute ruler; in the course of their attack on Protestant heretical sovereigns and their attempt to dominate the Catholic rulers in the interests of the Counter-Reformation, they raised arguments which afterwards sanctioned thought profoundly alien to their own.

It will be well, then, to examine the arguments, first of the Protestants and secondly of the Catholics, and to distinguish the ideas which make for liberty of conscience and ultimately for a democratic theory of the State. The Protestant influence is expressed through the political doctrines of Luther and Calvin, the Catholic through the Jesuit writers Suarez, Mariana, and Bellarmine.

Finally, both sides had to acquiesce in a toleration they equally loathed, but neither side could envisage a neutral lay power holding the balance between independent Churches. Such an idea would have appeared blasphemous in the sixteenth century; it was not until the results of religious warfare had combined with the new humanism to bring home the need for compromise that the idea of toleration could make headway at all.

§ 11

Luther and Calvin, then, made the initial break with Rome: both assert the freedom of individual conscience, though both were temperamentally conservative. Lutheranism grew up under the protection of the Protestant princes in Germany, but Calvinism in France, England, and Scotland found itself in political opposition. Out of power, the Calvinists increasingly put conscience before civil obedience; they aimed at best at an oligarchical democracy, at worst at a tyrannical rule of the saints. Further, the Calvinists practised a habit of discussion and a measure of representation in their congregations and conventicles, which was later translated into political practice.

Both Luther and Calvin asserted the rights of individual conscience, the 'spiritual priesthood of all believers', though it was far from the intention of either to produce the social disruption which in practice their doctrines entailed. Luther's teaching in some sense anticipates the Anglican theory of passive obedience which later developed into the assertion of Divine Right. Calvin's views, which were the more influential, developed through Knox and Languet, the supposed author of the *Vindiciae contra Tyrannos*, into open advocacy of the right of rebellion and even of tyrannicide against Catholic rulers.

The two reformers unite in hatred of Rome; where Luther struck his tremendous blow with the weight of awakening German nationalism behind him, Calvin provided in the *Institutes* a clear and grim definition of Protestant doctrine, and in the Genevan government a model of the organization which was to make the Protestant movement indestructible.

Luther was a fine poet — as his hymns witness — a man who saw life in immediate human terms; here he contrasts with Calvin, the theologian and organizer. Endowed with a boisterous temperament, for all his brutality he discerned the spiritual content of ordinary things, and set high the value of family life. The core of the Lutheran doctrine is in the 'Priesthood of Christian men': in this sense he is in line with Marsilio of Padua and the apologists of the Conciliar movement. The Church, he insists, is made up of laymen as well as of priests, and the authority of the Church officials is a matter of convenience. If the Catholic episcopate proves unworthy of its task, the lay princes must take over their responsibility; they become 'bishops by necessity'. Though they speak as laymen, it is with a new authority. The distinction between the 'spiritual' and the 'secular', so clear in Augustine and Calvin, is repellent to Luther. Hence, in part, his attack on the monasticism which he had experienced, taken with desperate seriousness, and ultimately loathed. It follows that, since Luther was in tune with ordinary life and people, he attacked the spiritual monopoly of the Roman priesthood, and by implication thought of the 'lay' government as something more than a 'secular arm'. He is on the side of those who regard secular society as possessing a spiritual value of its own, and not as a mere 'brigandage'.

The 'secular arm' took full advantage of the doctrines of the reformer; Protestant zeal was often made to serve political ambition.

Thus the usual competition of power politics was reinforced by a *motif* which added popular support to the game. It is, indeed, sad to remark what fuel can be flung on the ordinary flames of self-interest and avarice by individuals of religious genius, preoccupied with ideas largely unintelligible to ordinary men, so that the flames, from their usual mean smouldering, blaze up into full conflagration.

So Lutheranism made for the creation of national churches, for the disruption of that unity of Christian men which Luther taught. Further, Lutheranism was introspective: concerned with the struggle within the individual soul. This emphasis on faith rather than on works made it a more inward-looking religion than the comparatively extravert Calvinism. Luther takes up a very usual position for a German intellectual: he is concerned, as well he might be, with the inner processes of his own mind, and does not regard it as his business to tackle problems of organization and policy. The spiritual agonies of the reformer make interesting reading: imprisoned in the cage of sixteenth-century theology, Luther, who is a sympathetic, if coarse character, with a streak of profound spiritual power and insight, hurls himself this way and that like a tormented bull, bellowing his doubts and terrors to the world or drowning them in good living and overwork. 'If the Devil should come and torment you by filling your minds with gloomy thoughts, just go and have a drink or crack dirty jokes.' The doubts were often fundamental: 'Often the Devil says to me, "And what if your doctrine condemning the Pope, the Mass and the monks is false?" He torments me until the sweat runs down my brow and at last I reply, "Go and discuss all that with God!"'

His political opinions were violent. Take his attitude to the Peasants Revolt in 1525: 'Our princes must in the circumstances regard themselves as the officers of the Divine Wrath which bids them chastise such scoundrels . . . A prince who in such circumstances avoided bloodshed would be responsible for the murders and all further crimes these swine commit . . . they must be made to understand their duties by means of the arquebus.'

Luther had a thoroughly German respect for the official classes, and, though he could and did hate individual rulers, he was consistently on the side of authority as such. 'I would rather', he writes, 'suffer a prince doing wrong than a people doing right.' This aspect of his movement was to prove politically disastrous for

Germany. The Reformation never linked up with the ancient traditions of German mediaeval liberty and the promise they contained of the capacity to self-government. Luther's submission to authority marked a disastrous turning point in German development, a failure of leadership with adverse repercussions on the future. Like the great majority of German thinkers, Luther was not interested in the rule of Law, he 'thought with the blood'. Like his contemporaries, as we have noted, he was primarily concerned with salvation, with an attempt to get back to the essentials of the Faith: he is both a religious genius and profoundly German, with his German earnestness and humour, romanticism and brutality. He asserted both the independence of the individual and the German dislike of the Italian tradition. The frivolity of the Italians shocked the serious young monk who went to Rome; the luxury, cynicism, and finesse of the Princes of the Church, the whole inheritance of Mediterranean paganism interwoven in the Catholic outlook. In this aspect his movement was negative, an assertion simply of German independence and violent romanticism against the discipline and realism of the South.

Luther, then, as a religious genius and as a medium of the German protest against an alien influence, had little direct concern with larger political issues; his political views are immediate and often inconsistent, and he left little effective organization behind him. Politically, Protestantism, so long as it was restricted to Germany, was mainly destructive; it became a constructive force only on entering Britain and France, the Netherlands and Scandinavia.

At the same time Luther's assertion of the spiritual value and freedom of the lay believer was of great significance; in common with Calvinism, Luther's doctrine proclaimed the importance of the spiritual life, to be tried out in the world, no longer cloistered in the confines of monastic institutions and chastened by Catholic discipline. This acceptance of life, of the marriage of the clergy, of the pleasures of the table, of the knockabout humour and banality of sixteenth-century Germany, marks a weakening of the ascetic temper and an important breaking down of barriers between the clergy and laity. Further, Lutheranism is a landmark in the transference of authority from institutions to persons. Luther has little use for theories of Natural Law and no understanding of the traditions of European order. He goes straight for the prince's authority and pins his faith to that. His assertion of spiritual freedom is thus compatible with that docility to persons and political irresponsibility often characteristic of his race.

The Calvinist movement was better organized: the influence more direct, and Calvin defined his doctrines and political views with precision in the *Institutes*.[1]

The immediate occasion for their composition was as follows. In the year 1535 Francis I had published an attack, probably written by du Bellay, on the Protestants in France, whom he identified with the German heretics and denounced as international public enemies. Calvin's book was written to justify and to rally these French Protestants. He writes: 'Cependant que je demeuroya a Basle, estant là comme caché et cognu de peu de gens, on brusla en France plusiers fidèles et saincts personages, et le bruit en estant venu aux nations estranges, ces bruslements furent trouvés fort mauvais par une grande partie des Allemans' ... To meet this criticism, says Calvin, the French authorities had maligned the heretics, representing them as criminal revolutionaries, and he sets himself to defend his Protestant countrymen by defining Protestant doctrine. He asserts its dignity and right to exist. Between 1536 and 1564, when he died, Calvin never altered his book in essentials, though he expanded it into a large work of systematic theology.[2]

Cast in the orthodox forms of instruction of the day, and written in Latin, the first edition of the *Institutes* sold rapidly; in 1540 Calvin translated it himself into French, with a preface addressed to the 'Trés-chrèstien Roy de France, Françoys premier de ce nom; par

---

[1] *Institution de la réligion Chrétienne*, published 1536 in Latin; 520 pp., small octavo. French edition, 1541, a landmark in French style and clarity. He published it at 26, having begun to write it at Angoulême in 1534. He explained his motives as follows: 'Lors moy ... il me semble que sinon que je m'y opposasse vertueusement, en *tant qu'en moy estoit*, je ne pouvoye m'excuser qu'en me taisent que je ne fusse trouvé lasche et desloyal. Et ce fut qui m'incita a publier *mon Institution de la religion Chrétienne*.' It was originally designed as a 'petit Livret ... contenant sommairement les principales matieres, et non a autre intention, sinon afin qu'on fust adverti quelle foy tenoient ceux lesquels je voye que ces méschants et desloyaux flatteurs diffamoisent vilement et malheureusement'.

[2] *The Institutes of the Christian Religion* are divided into four books, of 18, 17, 25, and 20 chapters respectively; the first is entitled 'Of the knowledge of God the Creator'; the second 'Of the knowledge of God the Redeemer in Christ, as first manifested by the fathers under the law and, thereafter, to us in the Gospel'. The third book is concerned with 'The Modes of obtaining the Grace of Christ, the Benefits it confers, and the effects resulting from it', and the last 'Of the external means and helps by which God allures us into fellowship with Christ and keeps us in it'. The sections immediately concerned with politics are xv and xvi, 'Of Ecclesiastical Power and Civil Government', but it is necessary to understand Calvin's theological standpoint to follow his political conclusions. For the best exposition of Calvin's thought see P. DOUMERGUE, *Jean Calvin*, 5 vols. (Lausanne, 1899–1916).

laquelle ce present livre lui est offert pour confession de Foy'. In his preface Calvin emphasizes that he is particularly writing for Frenchmen, of whom 'there are many that hunger and thirst for Christ, and very few who have understood him rightly'. The Protestants, he insists, have been vilely misrepresented: 'Car entre le populaire sont semez contre icellez horribles rapports, lesquelz s'ils estoient véritables, à bon droit tout le monde la pourroit juger avec tous ses auteurs, digne de mille feuz et mille gibbetz.'

The first chapter of the *Institutes* opens with the contrast between the omnipresent splendour of God and the abject condition of men; 'their imbecility, misery, vanity, and wickedness', which lead us to 'despair, self-hatred, and loss of faith', and afterwards 'inflame us with the desire to find God, in whom reposes all our good'.

Calvin, like Augustine, sees the human race as subject to God's 'fearful vengeance' for the sin of Adam. But he regards Adam's sin as rebellious pride. 'It is unnecessary to confine the corruption to what is called "sensual motion".'[1] Adam not only 'committed apostasy through pride', but it was accompanied by 'foul insult to God'.[2] 'Corruption', beginning in Adam, is by 'perpetual descent' . . . '*before we behold the light of the sun, we are polluted* . . . But if the whole man is subject to the dominion of sin, surely the Will, which is its principal seat, must be bound by the closest chains.'

Since the whole creation is damned from the beginning, Calvin makes the atrocious statement that it 'no longer belongs to its creator' . . . 'except in so far as Grace rescues some, *not many*, who would otherwise perish,' while he leaves the world to the destruction to which it is doomed'.[3] This interpretation is strangely justified by the quotation of the words of Jesus, 'I pray not for the world, but for them which thou hast given me, for they are thine'.[4]

It follows, therefore, that 'all are not created on equal terms, but some are predestined to eternal life, others to eternal damnation. This God has testified . . . We say, then, that scripture clearly proves this much, that God, by his eternal and immutable Counsel, determined once and for all those whom it was his pleasure to admit to salvation, and those whom, on the other hand, it was his pleasure to doom to destruction; we maintain that this counsel, as regards his Elect, is founded on his free mercy, *without any respect of human merit*. While those whom he dooms to destruction are excluded from access to life by a just and blameless but at the same time incomprehensible

[1] Bk. II, i, 9.   [2] Bk. II, i, 6.   [3] Bk. III, xxii, 7.   [4] St. John, xvii, 9.

decree. In regard to his Elect, we regard Calling as the evidence of election and Justification as another symbol of its manifestation.'[1]

It follows that the world is divided between the elect and the reprobate. Once the 'state of grace' has been rightly experienced it can never be effaced, and if the regenerate man still feels temptation it is God's way of keeping him alert. If He afflicts the Elect, it is to try their patience, and they ought to show 'a pure and frugal use of worldly goods, and a patient endurance of want'.

The merits of conscious humility and self-denial, so characteristic of Protestant nonconformity, together with a sense of being a 'peculiar people' in a world hopelessly damned, are constantly stressed by Calvin's followers.[2] The resulting introspection and repression — could they always be certain that they were the Elect? — resulted often in vicarious unkindness and domestic tyranny.

Politically Calvinism, if in alliance with the lay power, was bound to be authoritarian, but it insisted that spiritual authority be exercised by the elders of the Church. Calvin denies that Protestants are rebels, except, and it is a large exception, against 'a usurping power which overrides private conscience'. Government ought not to 'compel consciences in matters which have been set free by Christ' or force them to deviate from the 'only law of liberty' which they must obey if they are to remain in a state of Grace. Thus although 'order, discretion, and modesty' are the aim of civil society, Calvin gave his followers the strongest possible motive to resist an authority of which they disapproved. Calvin constantly quotes the example of the Old Testament prophets to justify the authority of their successors, the elders of the Reformed Church, whom he calls 'les bons gens d'armes de Dieu'. Their task is to 'destroy the Councils' and all authority which prevents the true understanding of God, to see that God is obeyed, and to punish defaulters; they are his shepherds who not only protect his sheep but 'kill the wolves'. Civil magistrates, under God, are the indirect ministers of Divine Justice; and may kill and punish the perverse, for the rebel brings the calamity on himself; but if the civil power becomes 'intolerable', the Elect have been bought so dearly by Christ that they 'ought not to

---

[1] Bk. III, xxi, 5-7.
[2] The distinction between the reprobate and the elect is a difficult problem. Calvin held that even if the reprobate sometimes experience a degree of faith it is only because God, 'the better to convict them', instils into their minds 'such a sense of goodness as can be felt without the spirit of adoption'. A cat and mouse game.

hand themselves over as serfs to the wicked cupidity of men, and still less, to impiety'. Thus, although Calvin himself enjoins obedience to the civil power, the Calvinist political outlook approximates in the long run to that of the extremer Catholics; they hanker after a theocracy, naturally enough in the light of the theological structure they have built up.

Such then was the interpretation of the Gospels made by Calvin. As a fighting creed it was formidable and well organized; its widespread popularity is a psychological question of great interest. The doctrine took deepest root in Switzerland and Scotland, both threatened by Catholic power, under the indifferent stare of the great mountains round Geneva and where the east wind whistled round the granite purlieus of sixteenth-century Edinburgh and Aberdeen. It was a religion of wrath and fear, which made those tough enough to thrive on it formidable competitors in business, while the social ostracism with which the 'world' revenged itself on them concentrated their minds on their counting-houses and increased their solidarity. And, indeed, it is remarkable how men will thrive on the most unpromising disciplines. The theology of Calvinism should not, however, obscure the value of the methodical routine it fostered and the contribution made to practical invention and material progress by men brought up in its tradition of earnest enterprise and fierce moral purpose.

As long, then, as the secular arm was willing to obey the theocracy, Calvin is on the side of authority, but where the government was hostile, Calvinism developed an attack on the secular authority. It reinforced the middle-class attempt to throw off the control of the French monarchy and to break the power of the Catholic and aristocratic minorities in Scotland; it toughened the resistance of the Elect and made the Scots more ungovernable than they were before. In contrast to Lutheranism, which made for docility towards the lay power, Calvinism, in spite of its founder's arguments, put conscience before obedience, and, like the mediaeval Papacy, asserted a moral jurisdiction which included the political sphere. In the widest view, the Calvinist assertion of the spiritual liberty of the Elect was bound to diminish the value of the State. In common with Lutheranism, Calvin's doctrine is hostile to the great European institutions, Empire and Papacy, which claimed, so inadequately, to represent the Thomist order of Christendom. 'The spirit bloweth where it listeth', and the function of the State is to protect the liberties of the congregations within it, not itself to fulfil the spiritual development of its constituents. The best things in life are not in the State's province at all; they are realized in the homes and meeting houses of the elect.

This position is already asserted by the early Christians and by St. Augustine, but Calvinism put drive method and exclusiveness behind it. Calvinism is the Augustinian position as interpreted by the judicious, hard-minded, practical North; here again is the independence of the Icelandic sagas, the legal ability and mercantile enterprise, the tough intellectual tradition. And as the theological discipline of Calvinism gave place to a less dogmatic outlook, Puritan inspiration could live on in the militant agnostics of the nineteenth century. The refusal to be interfered with, so characteristic of British and North American Puritanism; the patriarchal assertion of family authority, unmitigated by the priest or the confessional; the strict morality and intellectual discipline of sermon and Sabbath; all contributed to the strength and the success of the Protestant democratic tradition. It is significant that Puritanism was so hostile to the finery in dress which had hitherto been a normal assertion of masculine prestige. The Puritans were remarkable in their indifference, and indeed hostility, to fashion and colour. This impatience with the florid pomp of secular society and hatred of the elaborate ritual of Catholic Christianity, this distrust of beauty and its 'deceits', made their contribution to British and North American civilization, and, indeed, perhaps the picturesque qualities the Calvinists disliked sometimes implied amateurishness, frivolity, lack of method and of fibre. Calvinist reliability and seriousness could not abide the morality of such a world; the tradition of modern bureaucracy and administration, so different from the casualness of the seventeenth and eighteenth centuries, is in part Calvinist in descent.

§ III

The writings of John Knox, of Languet, and Buchanan mark the stages whereby Calvinism worked out to its logical conclusion and linked up with ideas of Natural Law. Knox broke away from Calvin's doctrine of provisional obedience and asserted the right and duty of resistance against a Catholic sovereign. Languet, in the influential *Defence of Liberty against Tyrants*, invoked a theory of contract between God on the one hand and the prince and people jointly on the other. Both people and king are responsible for the observance of the correct form of worship; if the king defaults, the people have a duty to coerce him. They are guilty in the eyes of God if they do not oppose a prince who is in error, and are liable to Divine wrath if they shrink from doing so. The common man is thus caught between two fires.

The author of the *Vindiciae* further invokes Natural Law and quotes mediaeval definitions of its superiority to the ruler. It follows that the king may be called to account by his people and that if he breaks the law he becomes a tyrant, when it is right to resist through the proper channels. General rebellion, however, is never legitimate: it is legalized rebellion of estates or corporations on mediaeval lines which is advocated. The book is a Huguenot assertion of the old principle of limited kingship.

In 1579 Buchanan wrote his work, *De Jure Regni apud Scotos*, for the benefit of his pupil James VI and I. He, too, invokes Natural Law, justifies tyrannicide — a doctrine particularly hateful to that monarch — and asserts the right of popular rebellion. The book, which is written in Latin, is cast in dialogue between the author and 'Maitland' (Maetellanus). Buchanan argues that the Law of Nature is implanted in all men by God, that the ideal prince would hold his authority by natural superiority, but since kings are fallible and grow 'proud' they must be controlled by the law. Who then shall be 'pedagogue' to the king? No one but the people, whose will is behind the law. The judgement of the people is generally wiser than that of any individual. *Multitudo fere melius quam singuli de rebus omnibus iudicat*. Here is democratic doctrine indeed![1]

The king's hereditary right is conditioned by the law as much as if he were elected, and he is bound by his promise to administer the law justly. If he breaks this promise, he breaks his 'contract' with his subjects and their obligations to him lapse. St. Paul, 'Maitland' argues, instructed Christians to pray for their rulers, but this need not preclude resisting them: it is, indeed, possible to do both at once. Christian authority, Buchanan insists, comes from service; the king is a 'minister' and retains his power only so long as he does his duty. He cannot legislate by himself; legislation should be in the hands of the king and his council and their decisions ratified by the people.

Thus Buchanan has come a long way from Calvin's political position; the implications of Calvinism have been worked out and

---

[1] 'The people generally judge better in all things than the individual.'

linked up with a respectable mediaeval ancestry. So the Calvinist writers combined to set limits to the power of the Great State which threatened them: like the Jesuits, they were fighting a losing battle, but they helped to keep the tradition of the supremacy of the whole commonwealth and the rule of law alive, when the tide of the world was set full against them and the future seemed with Leviathan.

Meanwhile the religious feuds waxed fiercer. In face of the Protestant challenge, the Catholic Church struck back, and not only was the Protestant attack held, it was driven from some of the ground it had won. The intellectual champions of the Counter-Reformation were the Jesuits, who attempted to retrieve the appalling prospect of European disintegration by a re-statement of the papal position in the light of the new situation. The power behind the Counter-Reformation was the military and naval might of Spain, backed by the wealth of her enormous colonial possessions, by a dynastic network flung across half Europe. The authors of the two most important Jesuit works of political theory, Mariana and Suarez, are both Spaniards; both quote mediaeval doctrine against heretical princes.

Mariana, who published his *De Rege et Regis institutione* in 1599, became notorious for his advocacy of tyrannicide. He held that it was permissible to kill legitimate kings so long as the method employed avoided poisoning their food or drink, which would involve the tyrant in suicide and thus prejudice still further his chances of salvation. Hitherto the general opinion had been that it was only legitimate to kill sovereigns whose dynastic claims were not legally recognized. For example, on the more moderate view, the murder of Queen Elizabeth, who was never recognized by the Catholics as legitimate, would have been justified, but the assassination of Henry III of France could not be condoned, though Mariana goes further and justifies that.

Mariana takes an historical approach to political problems and derives the social order from a state of nature. Government, he argues, was evolved gradually to provide for the needs of civilized life and to protect property; it follows therefore that the interest of the whole community ought to be paramount and not subordinated to an absolute ruler.[1] The end of the State is the worship of God

---

[1] 'Constricto Legibus principatu nihil est melius: soluto, nulla pestis gravior', op. cit., i. 2. 'Nothing is better than a princedom controlled by law; uncontrolled there is no worse pest.'

and the establishment of Christian living in accordance with the doctrines of the Church; government is only justified if it furthers that end. Thus the Jesuits, in their rehabilitation of papal authority, take the old view that secular government is non-moral and incapable of commanding a spiritual loyalty, unless it is sanctified by the approval of the Church. In order further to undermine the position of heretical monarchs, they maintained in addition that ultimate power derives from the people.[1]

Another Jesuit thinker, Bellarmine,[2] following Thomist doctrine, asserts that the end of the community is spiritual, that the pope alone can wield spiritual authority, and that though he has a limited voice in secular affairs, his religious power can ultimately supersede the rights of any secular government. The pope can therefore absolve the subjects of an heretical prince from their allegiance — a far-reaching doctrine.

Suarez[3] asserts that all power comes from the community (*hominum communitate*): men are born free (*omnes homines nascuntur liberi*) and society is ordained to ensure order. The community is not, therefore, simply a multitude, but a body based on common consent. It follows that power may be transferred to a man or a governing authority but it does not come directly from God to the ruler; the community alone can sanction it. Though the prince may legislate, he may be deposed if he becomes a tyrant, and his subjects may rebel against him. Even if a king succeeds by ancient hereditary right, his ancestor, who founded the kingdom, took over the kingship with definite limitations, and these limitations his descendant inherits.

This is a remarkable development of a mediaeval position, and it is notable that it should be asserted so emphatically by the Jesuits. The Society of Jesus was extremely influential: it recognized no national boundaries. Its highly trained initiates took their dedicated lives in their hands, into countries whose governments were their sworn enemies. Living under a quasi-military discipline, educated in the latest thought of their age, sophisticated, able, they suffered exile in Europe and in the mission field overseas; as a matter of course they

---

[1] 'Leges quibus constricta est successio mutare nemini licet, sine populi voluntate, a quo pendent iura regnandi', i. 4. 'No one may alter the Laws by which the succession is bound, unless in accordance with the will of the people, on which the right to reign depends.'
[2] *De Potestate summi Pontificis* (1610).
[3] *De Legibus ac Deo Legislatore* (1619).

risked the hideous death of disembowelment and the stake. Such conviction and such exploits equal the sternest achievements of Calvinism; and, like the Calvinists, these men had the toughness to hold to their tradition and to defy the increasing and to them immoral power of the secularized great state.

Naturally, in defining the papal position in Europe, the Jesuits were realists; they abandoned the papal claim to sovereignty over all princes in a European commonwealth, and confined it to the headship of the Church, which admittedly did not comprehend all states. The pope becomes a sovereign on a level with others, and negotiates with them for the benefit of their Catholic subjects on equal terms. A great part of the later mediaeval position was therefore sacrificed to the necessities of the sixteenth century.

So the Jesuit thinkers of the Counter-Reformation asserted the mediaeval doctrine of the authority of the community and the place of human law in the Divine order; but they also adapt themselves to their time by claiming liberty of action within the national state for the spiritual society which they represent. Their position therefore links up with that of the Protestants in this latter aspect, since both have to recognize the accomplished fact of the new great state, whose rulers may hold a religious position different from their own. Both are working outside the assumption of a united Christendom.

§ I V

So the civil war in Christendom provoked widespread and passionate discussion of the basis of religious and political authority; the attempt at a total integration of Christian society was gradually abandoned. That experiment had failed; Empire and Papacy both were discredited. Men were left groping for a new sanction for religious and political authority among the relics of mediaeval thought. Consistently, Protestant and Catholic alike strove to keep a moral sanction behind political power; both sides appeal to the authority of what is, in effect, the Thomist tradition. Neither Calvinists nor Jesuits can tolerate the transference of power from law to persons, the naked power of Machiavelli's tyrant. Both invoke Natural Law, popular consent, the obligation of service which makes the king the people's minister.

The religious struggle, then, had four important results. First, it dealt the *coup de grâce* to the political and intellectual unity of

Catholic Christendom, and opened up a whole range of speculation, outside Catholic assumptions, which the Middle Ages had never compassed; secondly, in the course of the conflict, extremists of both sides canvassed and elaborated the old ideas of Natural Law and popular rights, later to be used in the struggle for individual liberty against the State. The demand for freedom of conscience was later translated into the assertion of the secular rights of man. In face of persecution by the non-moral Leviathan, the new Absolutist State, Calvinists and Jesuits alike kept the tradition of liberty alive. Only in religious terms could it have come through. Thirdly, moderate opinion, out for order at any price, veered towards the new centre of political power, the new 'sovereignty'. Machiavelli had used the term 'State'; Bodin was to coin the term 'maiestas', sovereign power, the absolute authority of the secular ruler, who alone, in default of Papacy and Empire, can enforce spiritual and political order. Finally, and inevitably, the bitterness of religious strife ended in a toleration of exhaustion.

European thought, then, in the sixteenth and early seventeenth centuries was still conditioned by the legacy of the Middle Ages, by the old high ideals of the trusteeship of power, by rival theologies, and by the swirling backwash of a foundering theocracy. The enmities of the new great state were made fiercer by religious passion; economic rivalry and theological hatred made the age one of the cruellest in history. And indeed it saw the death-throes of the old order. But in time the extremists fought themselves to a standstill, and the future was to be with the scientists and the philosophers who were quietly beginning to put their questions to nature; with the humanists who were coming to a deeper understanding of the best of the half-forgotten civilization of antiquity, whose outlook they attempted to revive.

Through theological controversies the path was being cleared for a secularized political theory which in time was to try to find its own sanction for the moralizing of power. Copernicus and Galileo, Montaigne, Descartes, and Spinoza, were the most significant representatives of their age; it is notable that Cervantes wrote his immortal masterpiece in 1605, expressing with a modern understanding and a Spanish irony the disillusion and the pity of a saner world.

So it was that the Protestant revolt indirectly encouraged the full and wide emergence of the scientific-humane thought of the Renaissance in the North. Though Luther and Calvin had far less in common with the humanists than Leo X, they were breaking the ice in the harbour in which the ship of European enterprise had long been bound. The individualism of the Renaissance, too, was reinforced by the individualism of the Protestant position, the assertion of the worth and liberty of the personal life. The humanistic spirit, in its turn, began to permeate the religious field also, attempting to get back to the sources of Christian inspiration by the free study of the Biblical text. For all the cruelty of Calvinism there is a spiritual freshness about the better kind of Puritanism which comes near to the Christianity of the Gospels.

So the short-term and agonizing phase of religious controversy saw the foundering of the mediaeval order and the birth of the modern world; it formulated and transmitted political ideas later to be re-stated in secular terms, in conformity with the long-term drift of the climate of European thought towards a scientific humanist outlook, expressed within the framework of great national states. The failure of the universal ideal of mediaeval Christendom, marked indeed, a moral retreat; but in the confusion the ideal of the rule of Law and the trusteeship of power came through; while gradually the rationalism of antiquity re-emerged, strengthened by scientific method, sometimes ruthless and immoral, sometimes inspired by the old ideals. The survival and reinterpretation of the concepts of universal law and justice, of the trusteeship of power, their conflict with the cynical outlook of the practitioners of naked force, and the attempt of the new rationalism to find a metaphysical justification, was to determine the course of political thought for the next two centuries.

CHAPTER III

SOVEREIGN POWER AND THE GREAT
STATE

§ 1

THE outstanding political fact of the sixteenth and seventeenth centuries is the emergence of the nation state, superseding the dynastic feudalism and city confederations of the later Middle Ages. The new states, which were built on a scale unequalled in the West since the Roman Empire, claimed a 'Sovereignty' of novel and absolute completeness. Political theory from the seventeenth to the nineteenth century is set in the rigid framework of the national great state. Just as in Greece the thought of Plato and Aristotle is in terms of the 'polis', and fails to get out of them, so the speculations of most European thinkers of this period never squarely tackle the problem of European order; and when they do tackle it, as did Grotius, they are comparatively ineffective. With the emergence of the nation State international anarchy had begun; modified by the Balance of Power it did not reach its logical conclusion until the twentieth century with the full force of popular nationalism behind it. The European 'period of the warring states', to borrow a phrase coined by historians of China, has its beginning in the sixteenth century.

The dominance of the nation state marks an increase in centralized efficiency but a failure of the tradition of European order; the waning of the mediaeval conception of universal empire; the incapacity of the Italian and Flemish cities to achieve any stable federation; the break-up of Catholic religious unity; left the way open for an international moral retreat in a time of unparalleled intellectual, social, and technical advance. As Alexander's empire broke up into separate and antagonistic kingdoms, so western Christendom developed into separate and competing successor states. It was in France that this type of state, centred on a bureaucracy and organized for aggression, first most powerfully emerged. Three books may be taken as typical of the new theory of the State, reflecting and determining this situation. First the *Six Books of the Republic* by Bodin, who formulates the full doctrine of sovereignty; secondly

Grotius's *Of the Law of War and Peace* (*De Jure Belli ac Pacis*), which, assuming the existence of sovereign states, attempts to regulate their conduct in accordance with a modernized Law of Nations; thirdly the *Political Testament* of Cardinal Richelieu, a book of no comparable influence, but revealing the mentality of the ablest seventeenth-century architect of the great state. All three lead up to Hobbes's *Leviathan*, the most complete expression of the new state theory and a turning point in political thought.

§ II

In face of the confusion of the Huguenot wars, Jean Bodin[1] saw the salvation of France in the rule of a central power. He is concerned to make the power of government so strong that it transcends the particular interest either of provincial autonomy, that perennial obstacle to the policy of the French crown, or even of religious belief. This realistic view anticipates the thought of the seventeenth century; and although it is wrapped up in a complex sixteenth-century erudition, it had a wide influence in its own day. He further emphasizes, as Locke emphasizes, the importance of property and the duty of the State to safeguard it. The aim of the State is order and only through absolute 'sovereignty' can order be brought about.

In the preface of *Les Six Livres de la Republique*[2] Bodin states the

[1] Jean Bodin, 1530-96: born in Anjou, studied and lectured at Toulouse; sat in Estates-General of the Loire. Came to England as secretary to Alençon on his visit to Queen Elizabeth. His intellectual interests were wide and his style attractive; he anticipated Montesquieu in an appreciation of the effect of climate on institutions and was a pioneer in the field of economics ('Discourse on the "extrème Chérité" en France', 1574, and '*Réponse au paradoxes du Malestroit*', on inflation. Among other works of general speculation he wrote *De la Demonomanie* (Paris, 1580). This work is divided into five books, and defines many popular beliefs. Sections VI and VII of the second book are particularly curious. Bodin's argument is clear and well arranged, his French lucid, yet the book is a monument of learned superstition. He takes immense pains in his investigation. All the best authorities, he insists, agree on the reality of the phenomena described; as St. Augustine says 'hoc negare impudentiae esse videatur'. In the sixth book (De la lycanthropie, et si les ésprits peuvent changer les hommes en bestes) he quotes innumerable authorities. Damiani believes that metamorphosed asses kept their human intelligence: 'Les cinqs inquisiteurs qui estoient experimentez en telles causes ont laissé par escript qui'l y eut trois socières près Strasbourg qui assaillerent un laboureur en guise de trois grans chats.' Discussing lycanthropy, he quotes Philo Judaeus, 'Rabin', and 'Moyse Maymon', and concludes that the transformation comes from eating children. It is most liable to occur at the end of December; 'les Alemans les appelent, "Wer Wolf" et les Francais "loups garou" qui veut dire 'gardez vous' '. He mentions many examples of this affliction, of men 'tournés en loups, courant d'une légèreté incroyable'.

[2] Published in French, 1576. 1222 octavo pages, 'par Jean Bodin, Angevin', and dedicated to Monseigneur de Faur, Seigneur de Pibrac; it went into 7 editions by 1579; in Latin, 1586; translated into English by R. Knolles, 1606.

T 289

aim of his book: 'Puisque la conservation des Royaumes et Empires et de tous peuples dépend, après Dieu, des bons Princes et sages Governeurs, c'est bien raison, Monseigneur, que chacun les assistera, soit a maintainir leur puissance, soit a éxécuter leurs sainctes loix, soit a ployer leurs suiets par dites et écrits, qui puissent réussir au bien commune de tous en général et chacun en particulier.'

When the ship of state, he says, is tormented by storms, the passengers ought to help; it is in danger of being 'froissé et brisé contre les roches périlleuses', and of a 'licentious anarchy which is worse than the most violent tyranny in the world'.

He then proceeds to his famous definition of the State, finding its characteristic quality to be 'Sovereign power' (maiestas), which holds together the various 'mesnages' which make up the community. 'The republic is the right government of several mesnages and what is common to them, and with sovereign power.' This sovereignty, he insists, is an 'absolute and perpetual power' . . . 'It is here necessary to define it, as no jurisconsult, no political philosopher, has done so. It is the essential point, and most necessary to be understood in a treatise on the Republic.'[1]

This sovereignty is inalienable. 'He is sovereign who recognizes nothing greater than himself save only Immortal God.'[2] 'The prince or people who possess sovereign power cannot be called to account for their actions by anyone but Immortal God — Princeps vero populusve in quibus maiestas inest rationem rerum gestarum nemini, praeterquam immortali Deo, reddere coguntur.'

Here is the charter of the modern state, a clear statement of absolute authority coming out of an experience of the French wars of religion. Yet Bodin is very much of the sixteenth century, and clothes his thought in a conventional garb; as we have noted his political speculations are embedded in volumes of curious learning. He was convinced that the courses of the stars influenced political events (bk. IV, chap. ii ff.). 'The great conjunction of the Scorpion coincided with the change of the Roman republic into Monarchy under the power of Caesar'; this conjunction occurred again in 1530 when there was a revolution in Constantinople. Bodin never believed in the fortunes of Henry III, that last and excessively degenerate representative of the Valois, because he was the 63rd of his family, and 63 is the product of the numbers 7 and 9, both notoriously fatal to princes. At the same time he is geometrically minded, and

---

[1] Bk. I, chap. i. [2] Bk. I, chap. ix.

anticipates the seventeenth-century idea of the mechanism and natural harmony of the world. The mediaeval cosmic vision is pulled down into a more practical imagery; Bodin in a sense formed a bridge between scholastic theory and Cartesian ideas. His interpretation of 'natural harmony' influenced Grotius, who attempted to base the beginnings of International Law on this unsatisfactory foundation.

Bodin was devoid of religious fanaticism, and the business-like quality of his thought anticipates the outlook of Richelieu, who was to put this theory into practice on a great scale. It was the remarkable achievement of Bodin to crystallize the conception of sovereign power, which is the basis of the development of the national state on a great scale.

This conception of sovereign power, still so much taken for granted, was new in the sixteenth century. 'The state was no longer derived from the Divinely ordained harmony of the universal whole . . . it was simply explained by itself. The starting point of speculation ceased to be general humanity; it became the individual and self-sufficing sovereign state; and the individual state was regarded as based on a union of individuals, in obedience to the dictates of natural law to form a society armed with supreme power . . . The word sovereignty becomes something in the nature of a magic wand which can conjure up the whole sense and content of the states' general power. From the quality of being simply the highest authority there is deduced the whole of that absolute omnipotence which the modern state claims for itself . . . The champions of popular sovereignty vie with the defenders of monarchism in exalting its claims.'[1] Thus was born the theory of the modern sovereign state which from the point of view of European order has reached its *reductio ad absurdum* in our own day, with power of life and death over the individuals who compose it and practising a subhuman morality in relation to others of its own kind. Both the classical Roman conception of a world order, and the ideal of a Christian society, formulated by St. Thomas and Dante, are abandoned, and Europe begins to move towards the Armageddon of the twentieth century. Meanwhile the technical limitations of the age kept this untamed power within bounds; Europe could still afford its inter-state warfare, and strong counter-currents of resistance made their appearance within

[1] GIERKE, *Natural Law and the Theory of the State,* edited by Sir E. Barker, C.U.P. (1934), vol. I, pp. 40-1.

the State. As a focus of order and administration the new concept of sovereign power was beneficent; it was supported both by practical men and theorists. Richelieu, as we shall see, justifies the power of the State by an appeal to God and Reason. He remains within the old-fashioned framework of a perversion of divinely sanctioned natural law: he has not come down to the Hobbesian justification of the State as a means of self-preservation, the purely utilitarian argument.

Though the long-term result of this disintegration of European order was to be disastrous, on the short view the only hope of efficient government was in the development of centralized power. Men took for granted the competitive and military inheritance of government. The majority of the thinkers of the sixteenth and seventeenth centuries, forced by the logic of events to take a realistic view of the function of government in restoring internal order, and so extending and defining it, do not face the problems of international politics. The situation had not yet become critical, though it was bad. The material resources at the disposal of a conservative agricultural society were very limited. Communications were slow and clumsy; coaches lumbered at a foot pace over atrocious roads behind their heavy horses; wooden ships, the equivalent on sea to the creaking farm wagons on land, were at the mercy of every change in the wind. Under these material handicaps, the greatest practicable political and economic unit was the nation state. Bad communication and difficulties of supply made war less destructive, the problems of international order less urgent.

Yet mediaeval Europe was materially no better off, and managed to formulate an ideal of a united Christendom; to create cosmopolitan institutions. In this respect the political thought of the Middle Ages was in advance of that of the seventeenth century. But in the short view, the contemporaries of Grotius were more practically minded men than their forebears, and preferred to work for some degree of efficiency on a small scale. At the same time, there is no doubt that deterioration of political morale had taken place. Take, for example, Bacon's complacent attitude to war, which he regards as the natural recreation of nation states. 'No body can be healthful without exercise, neither natural body nor politique, and certainly to a kingdom or estate a just and honourable war is the true exercise. A civil war is like the heat of a fever; but a foreign war is like the heat of exercise and serves to keep the body in health; in a slothful peace both courages will effeminate and manners corrupt.[1]

So the new absolute state overwhelmed men's minds and moral principle was sacrificed to the efficiency of this new unit of political power.

§III

There were minds, however, more sensitive than Bacon's, and the challenge of the new national state to the old tradition of European order was partially met by the definition of a new 'International' Law. Taking the national sovereign state for granted, Grotius[2] tried to bind Leviathan and legalize war between great states. He attributed to them a formal equality among themselves, so long as they conformed to certain standards of civilization which qualified them for membership of a comity of nations.

Grotius raises the fundamental questions: is war, ever justified, and what is the sanction for international order?

The *De Jure Belli ac Pacis*[3] is a famous and deeply learned work —

---

[1] *Essay of Kingdoms and Estates.* Compare Innocent III's view. *Vide supra,* Bk. II, chap. iv.

[2] Hugo Grotius, born at Delft in 1583; son of the Burgomaster of Leyden, who was also curator of the University. Came of a distinguished family of French-Dutch descent; Doctor of Law at sixteen; published a commentary on the works of Martianus Capella the next year and began his practice at the Bar. Appointed, 1603, Histriographer to the province of Holland; 1613, Pensionary of Rotterdam. Sent to England to negotiate between Dutch and English merchants over the East Indian trade. After the failure of Barneveldt's attempt to overthrow the house of Orange, he was arrested as a leader of the Republican party, and condemned to lifelong imprisonment. In 1619 he was confined to the Castle of Louvenstein, but by the contrivance of his wife, Mary of Regelsburg, he escaped from captivity in the following manner, disguised as a mixed cargo of washing and Arminian theology. This admirable woman 'having observed that the Guards, being weary of searching a large trunk full of books and linen to be washed at Gorcum, . . . advised her husband to put himself into it, having made some holes with a wimble in the place where the forepart of his head was, that he might not be stifled. He followed her advice and was in that manner carried to a friend of his at Gorcum . . . That good woman pretended all the while that her husband was very sick, to give him time to make his escape into a foreign country, but when she thought he was safe, she told the Guards, laughing at them, that "the birds were flown" . . . At first there was a design to prosecute her, but by a majority of votes she was released and praised by everybody . . . Such a wife deserved not only to have a statue erected to her in the Commonwealth of learning, but also to be canonized. . . .' *Life of Hugo Grotius,* London (1738).

Grotius escaped into France, where he remained for eleven years and where he composed the *De Jure Belli ac Pacis,* published in 1625. After a short return to Holland, he removed to Hamburg, and in 1639 accepted a post at the Court of Queen Christina of Sweden, who made him her Ambassador to the French Court. He died at Rostock in 1645.

[3] *Of the Rights of War and Peace,* in three books, wherein are explained the Law of Nature and Nations and the principle points relating to Government. Written in

the foundation of subsequent International Law.[1] The pith of the argument is contained in the famous Prolegomena — a short preface in 61 captions — and in the first and second chapters of the first book. The work is divided into three books, of 5, 26, and 25 chapters respectively; together with explanatory notes, it occupies over 700 pages of the eighteenth-century edition here quoted. Having established to his satisfaction the basis of his argument — that a Law of Nations exists, Grotius, in the second book, works out in detail the consequences of his conclusions with a wealth of historical example. The third book lays down precise rules for the conduct of a just war, for the treatment of prisoners, the taking of hostages, arbitration and surrender.

The work is dedicated to Louis XIII with all the fulsome flattery of the day. Enlarging upon the king's love of justice, Grotius compares him to a star of most benign influence: he deserves the title of most Christian King not only by inheritance but in his own right. His wars are undertaken only to bring about perpetual peace, and he may be destined to realize not only the cessation of inter-state warfare, but that even more difficult idea, peace between the Churches. Grotius concludes with a reference to the marriage of Charles I and the king's sister Henrietta Maria; this alliance he hopes will bring about lasting peace between England and France.

The Prolegomena opens by stating that though Civil Law has been fully dealt with by many authorities, 'none has methodically examined the Law which is common to many nations . . . though it is in the interest of mankind it should be done'. Many writers have argued that 'amongst the great the stronger is the juster side'. 'It is not only the opinion of the vulgar that War is a stranger to all justice, but many sayings uttered by men of wisdom and learning give strength to such an opinion.'[2] Grotius quotes Ennius, Horace, and Lucan among classical writers. Among Christian writers we find

---

[1] Many of the ideas in Grotius's great work are foreshadowed in his early *De Jure Praedae* written in 1604, and unpublished in his lifetime. The immediate occasion for its composition was the capture of a Portuguese galleon in the Straits of Malacca by a vessel of the Dutch East India Company, who had retained Grotius as their advocate. The company's right to make prizes was contested, and Grotius set himself to prove that under certain circumstances such action was lawful, and to assert the doctrine of the freedom of the seas.

[2] Pro. III.

Latin by the learned Hugo Grotius (1625) and translated into English, to which are added all the large notes of Mr. Barbeyrac. London (1738). For the best modern edition, see *De Jure Belli ac Pacis*, Text and translation by F. KELSEY. *Classics of International Law*, edited J. B. SCOTT, Washington (1913), Oxford (1925).

many sayings of the same kind: 'let that of Tertullian suffice for all, "Fraud, cruelty, and injustice are the proper basis of War.[1] If, then, there is no such thing as Right between Nations, it will be vain to treat of it." What, then, if any, are the foundations of international justice?'

Following Cicero, Grotius argues against Carneades, the Cynic, who asserts the relativity of all laws — that they are mere conveniences, and that Natural Law is a chimera. Grotius in reply takes up a significant position: he appeals not to Divine Law but to a Natural Law which would be valid without it. Man, he says, is an animal, 'but one of very high order', with '. . . a certain inclination to live with his own kind, not in any manner whatever, but peaceably'. Over and above this instinctive sociability[2] man has the gift of speech and of acting on general principles. This sociability, 'this care of maintaining society in a manner conformable to the light of human understanding is the fountain of right properly so called'. Here is the sanction of international morality — a rationalized instinct of sociability. Thus, says Seneca: 'Nature which has deprived men of teeth and claws makes amends by implanting in them an impulse to work together.' Now this property makes man 'abstain from that which is another's and obliges them to fulfil promises'. It would operate, say Grotius, even if God did not exist, 'though we should even grant that which cannot be conceded without the utmost wickedness, that there is no God or that He takes no care of human affairs'.[3]

It follows that the 'Mother of Natural Law is human nature itself'.[4] Indirectly of course it is sanctioned by God since it is his pleasure such principles shall be in us.

Now since the internal laws of states exist for the benefit of the citizens, so, Grotius argues, 'amongst all or most States, there might be, and in fact there are, some laws, agreed on by common consent, which represent the advantage of all in general . . . and this is what is called the Law of Nations; if those laws be observed all nations will benefit, and aggressors who violate the laws of nature and nations

---

[1] P. IV.
[2] Quoting Philo Judaeus on the sociability of animals, he cites in a footnote examples of mutual aid between storks, refers to Porphyry's remarks on pigeons, and to 'certain fishes' mentioned by Cassiodorus called 'Scari et Sauri' which show concern for those of their own species. His editor, Barbeyrac reinforces the argument by quoting Gronovius on the behaviour of hens 'the abstinence of hounds which bring game to their masters and the fervour with which bees . . . unite their labours for the good of the community'. P. VI, n.   [3] P. XI.   [4] P. XV.

break down the bulwarks of their future happiness and tranquillity.'

The Laws of Nations, like Civil Law, must be observed because the continuance of Society is impossible without it. Though great states may seem a law unto themselves, all are dependent on foreign alliances, political and economic: 'the moment we recede from Right we can depend upon nothing'.[1] It follows that war is justified against an aggressor who breaks these rules and so undermines the foundations of civilized life, though 'just' wars must be waged with care and integrity.

Such is the answer to the question whether war is justified, and the sanction of International Law; war can be just if undertaken 'solemnly', in defence of the conventions without which international order is impossible. The end justifies the means.

Gone were the days when the power of Rome imposed the habit of peace, when Christendom was to be united under pope and emperor. By the seventeenth century the one hope of order is that the nation states shall keep their contracts, and, if they violate them, that the French King — for that is what Grotius's argument amounts to in its context — shall coerce them to keep the law. War, he argues, shall only be undertaken as a last resort for this righteous end. That is why he is writing his treatise, having 'observed throughout the Christian World, a licentiousness in regard to War, a running to arms upon very frivolous occasions . . .', the spectacle of which 'monstrous barbarity brought many good men, among them our countryman Erasmus, to the view that Christians ought not to bear arms at all'.[2] All violence is iniquity, they argue, the end never justifies the means, and to gloss over the realities of war by these sophistries is wicked. They that take the sword perish by the sword.

Grotius dismisses this objection as unpractical. He writes, indeed, to confute such arguments and to regularize the conduct of war, there being nothing else left him to do, 'being unworthily banished'[3] from his native country.

Having explained the purpose of his book, he next describes how he wrote it, the arrangement of topics, the plan of its composition, and refers to the numerous and learned authors, classical and sacred, famous and obscure, from whose works he has liberally reinforced his argument. Lucidity, he says, has been his aim: 'to render the reasons for my decisions as evident as possible, to dispose the matters to be treated of into a regular method and to distinguish clearly

[1] P. XXII. [2] P. XXVIII. [3] P. XXX.

those things which might appear to be the same but were not'. He has followed, he says, as much as he could a concise way of speaking; finally, covering himself against all contingencies, he ends the Prolegomena with the proviso if there is anything in it contrary to piety, good manners or Christian doctrine 'let it be unsaid again'.[1]

So in a compendious form Grotius states his case; he proceeds in the first book of the main treatise, to enlarge upon it.

The first chapter discusses what War is and what Right is. The author plunges deep into a sea of classical and Biblical learning; text and footnotes extend themselves into the obscurer byways of patristic eloquence, into the more improbable stories of Pliny and Herodotus, into references to 'Strabo, Philo, Justine, Origen, Clemens Alexandrinus, Epiphianus, and Theodoret'.

The second chapter is entitled, 'Whether it is ever lawful to make War?' 'Among the first impressions of nature there is nothing repugnant to War.'[2] All animals defend themselves: Xenophon says 'that all animals know how to fight'. So in a fragment of Ovid's Halieuticon, or Art of Fishery, 'all animals naturally know their enemy . . .' and, in Horace, 'the wolves assault with teeth and the bulls with horns . . .'. But Lucretius has it more fully: 'every animal knows its own power — a calf is sensible of its horns and will push with its head when provoked, . . .' which Galen thus expressed: 'We see every creature employ his strongest part in his own defence.' Man also, though not born with weapons, has hands ready to make and grasp them. Right reason governs this instinct for self-defence. It prohibits, too, anti-social violence, 'for the design of society is that every man should enjoy his rights'.

Grotius then distinguishes between 'a solemn War which is also called Just' ('regular and compleat') and a war 'not Solemn'. There follows a long detailed examination of the views of the early Christians about War; he concludes an unconvincing argument by a quotation from St. Basil, 'our ancestors never accounted slaughters committed in war as murders, excusing them who fought for virtue and piety'. He then divides war into public and private — the latter is the more ancient — and proceeds to an historical account of the different kinds of war. The first book ends with a definition of who may lawfully make war.

'Every man has a natural right to defend himself and therefore were hands given us.' But, beyond that, common humanity ought to unite men in putting down wrong. If, he says, following Menander, 'Everyone would heartily engage in the defence of those who are insulted . . . the wicked would not become daily more bold and enterprising, but finding themselves watched on every side, and suffering the just punishment of their crimes, few or none would run the hazard of it.'

Since, then, the subjects of a state are as 'servants in a family', they may be lawfully employed by their Sovereign and naturally used for war. The clergy, however, he says, are generally exempt, quoting Josephus, Nicetas Choniates, the capitularies of Charles the Bald and Anna Komnena.

Having in five chapters of the first book elaborated the first principles outlined in the Prolegomena, Grotius, in the second, works out the implications of his theory in practice. It is impossible to do more than touch on some of the outstanding topics raised in these long, detailed, and often prolix, though important, chapters. What, he asks, are the causes of war? There can be only one just cause, 'injury received'. This he defines at length, with a wealth of historical illustrations, enlarging upon the various kinds of injury which justify self-defence. War undertaken to weaken a neighbouring power thought to harbour aggressive intentions, is unlawful, and all means must be used to avoid war by negotiation before resort to it. After an exhaustive examination of the nature and extent of property, running into nine chapters, Grotius raises the question of the validity of promises, particularly when Ambassadors exceed their instructions. He defines true contract, and the obligations of an oath, and how far treaties are obligatory on the successors of princes, and how far contracts with the heathen are binding. The status of ambassadors and their right of access are fully discussed in chapter xviii: they arise directly from the law of nations. Ambassadors, by a 'sort of fiction', are taken for the very persons whom they represent. Next, the right of burying the dead is examined; it is, says Grotius, quoting Josephus, and Isidore Pellusiota, a law of nature: Aristides, Lucan, Statius, Tacitus, and Lysias the Orator concur; Ulpian calls it 'an act of modesty and piety'; Modestinus terms it 'a memory of our mortal state'; Capitolinus 'an act of Mercy'; Euripides and Lactantius 'of Justice'; Prudentius 'of Liberty and Charity', while Optatus Milevitanus accuses the Donatists of impiety for denying burial to Catholics.[1]

[1] Bk. II. XIX. 4.

Next, he discusses the degree and proportions of punishment —
unjust and dubious causes of war, duelling and arbitration, and the
second book concludes with a justification of those who take up arms
by another's command for a righteous cause.

The third book is even more detailed and technical: it covers most
of the contingencies likely to arise in war. The first chapter contains
an interesting academic discussion of the use of fraud in war, which
expands into a discourse, in the manner of Burton's *Anatomy of
Melancholy*, on the whole question of lying. Many pagan authors
regard appropriate lying as an accomplishment of a just man: he
quotes Andronicus Rhodius, Quintillian, Isocrates, and naturally
enough, Herodotus.

The second chapter deals with the responsibility of subjects for
debts incurred by their prince; the next with the procedure for
declaring war, now frequently abandoned. The fourth chapter gets
down to essentials — 'the right of killing enemies and exercising other
violence upon their persons in a solemn war'. Grotius surveys the
common practice in this matter; a just war entitles men, strictly
speaking, to kill all their enemies, including women and children.
Such is the immemorial practice, says Grotius, giving many
examples.

He excludes the slaying of the women and children of Heshbon by
the Hebrews and the massacre of the Canaanites, as special acts
of God. 'That which is more proper to testify the common custom of
nations is that of the Psalmist' — 'Blessed is he that taketh and
dasheth thy little ones against the stones.'[1]

Germanicus and Titus massacred the Germans and the Jews
respectively, 'but these two Princes were never esteemed to be of a
cruel nature'. Grotius, while recording these practices, argues that
Christians ought to modify them. 'We ought not to attempt anything
which may prove the destruction of innocence, unless for some extraordinary reason and the safety of many.'[2] It has even been maintained, he says, that only those who resist with arms should be
slain; monks and priests, and some say farmers and merchants, ought
to be spared as being necessary to the public good. He, further,
draws the line at poison, at least among civilized nations; since wars
are become so frequent, 'this custom was established for the general
benefit, lest dangers should be increased too much'. Poison being

---

[1] Psalms cxxxvii, 9. [2] Bk. III. XI. 8.

more deadly to kings personally than arms, it paid them to discountenance its use. Poisoning the 'heads of darts', thus 'forcing death in a double way', is unlawful among the civilized nations, though, as John of Salisbury remarks, sometimes practised among infidels. 'The empoisoning of springs', is unlawful, though they may be made undrinkable. The employment of assassins is wrong, though often practised. The ravishing of women is sometimes permitted in war and sometimes not;[1] Grotius thinks it unnecessary to the efficient prosecution of a just war and therefore contrary to the law of Christian nations. He quotes Plutarch on Alexander's treatment of Roxana; 'he scorned to debauch her but married her, which was an action worthy of a philosopher'.

Spoil and rapine are treated of in the ensuing chapter, and the desecration of images and sepulchres. The rights of prisoners are next defined. Technically they are slaves, since in early times the victor spared his captives for gain; among Christian nations it is customary to hold wealthier prisoners to ransom. Escape is only justified if intolerable cruelty has forced men to it.

Chapter xxi treats of truces, safe-conduct, and the redemption of prisoners. The word 'induciae', truce, is not, Grotius doubtfully maintains, derived from 'inde uti jam', because, 'the moment it is ended, we may act as before' (Isidore probably had a hand in this derivation), nor from 'endoitus', entry, because we may then 'enter freely' into the lands of another, but from 'inde otium', because there will be rest 'from such a time'. Safe-conduct does not cease with the death of the authority who grants it; redemption of prisoners is a 'thing very favourable, especially among Christians'; St. Ambrose calls it 'the highest liberality'.[2]

Grotius concludes ('not that I have said all that might have been said') with the hope that he has laid the foundations on which a more stately fabric may be built, and a general admonition to princes to keep faith and avoid war. 'If faith be taken away, says Aristotle rightly, all human correspondence ceases' . . . 'Their practices cannot possibly prosper long which render man unsociable to man and hateful to God.'[3]

The only justification for war, he insists, is to win peace; it is a last resort, a gamble, and when peace has been established, rulers must observe it strictly, avoiding not only perfidiousness but 'whatsoever

[1] Bk. III. IV. 19.   [2] Bk. III. XXI. 23.
[3] Bk. III. XXV. 1.

may exasperate the mind'. 'May the Almighty,' he concludes, 'who alone can do it, impress these maxims on the hearts of Christian princes.'[1]

Grotius had thus defined a new law of nations, and laid a foundation for international law, but all within a framework of sovereign states.

But this attempt to moralize war naturally failed to arrest the drift of European disintegration: the period of the 'warring states' was fated to run its course; Grotius, however, by defining the principles of international law, helped to mitigate the horrors of war and to regularize the practice of diplomacy. So long as war was conducted by professional armies, officered by gentlemen, the conventions laid down by Grotius and his followers were often observed. So long as diplomacy was carried on by *diplomats de carrière*, with a common background of culture and conduct, treaties could generally be observed and undertakings kept, if interest did not upset the bargain. The eighteenth century, with a full quota of wars, saw fewer atrocities than those which marked the Thirty Years War in Germany; this was due in part to the decline in religious fanaticism, but in part to the observation of an accepted code.

In the day-to-day business between states, the international law defined by Grotius played a valuable part, but the fundamental problem remained: the unbridled sovereignty of the great state. After the French Revolution, when wars were fought by huge conscript armies and after the Prussians had made a science of war, the conventions of international law grew more threadbare, serving mainly to mask the savage realities of international politics, and right up to 1914, men, living on a volcano, were confident that 'the Powers would surely intervene'.

Grotius's remedy was indeed nothing but a palliative: given that the authority of Rome is dead, that the Holy Roman Empire has failed, that the order of Christendom is disrupted, that the new sovereign state is the only focus of power, there is one hope left; self-preservation will make Governments realize nothing is secure without the observation of covenants and they will band together against an aggressor. But such an alliance must be strong, and if states are strong they are the most liable to the temptation of aggression. Unless, therefore, one state subdues the rest and a revived empire imposes peace on Christendom, an uneasy 'Balance of Power' is all

[1] Bk. III. XXV. 8.

that remains, a balance shifting, unstable, as the circumstances and opportunities of the component states vary.

In practice, far from strong states combining to impose order, they combined only to prevent one power from dominating the rest. The price of the national variety, vigour, and enterprise shown by Western society in the eighteenth and nineteenth centuries, has been the recurrence of wars on an increasing scale, wars of local ambition expanding into wars of empire. Yet, within the national state, the standards of governments were going up; within its province Bodin's sovereign power was imposing decency and order. It was natural for Grotius, a great lawyer, versed in civil law, to be anxious about the cut-throat game of international power politics. Self-interest, he argues, will find the way out, will prove a basis for International as for Civil Law.

There is so much good in all this learning, with its weight of classical and Biblical knowledge; the solid scholar, with his method and erudition, looking out from his study, as from some calm Dutch interior, thought to establish European order out of the calculated aggression, the deadly cunning, the swift violence, of the rulers of seventeenth-century France, out of the bouncing militarism which was to culminate in the campaigns of Condé and Turenne.

None the less, Grotius has a just claim to greatness; the international law he defined increasingly regulated the routine business between states, so long as their 'vital interests' were not involved. The horrors of war were considerably mitigated until the advent of modern methods of destruction, and the contribution of international lawyers to the regulation of commerce encouraged economic development. Whole new fields of law were opened up by the enterprise of this great jurist. Further, his basic argument that law-abiding governments should combine in self-preservation to keep the peace, is obviously sound, though he naturally never advocates the merging of national sovereignties which is the only sure remedy, a remedy to which the world is now being driven only after three centuries of war and an Industrial and Atomic revolution.

§ I V

More in tune with the immediate realities of his day was the mind of the man responsible for French policy over the most critical years of the seventeenth century. Richelieu is an outstanding example of a successful power-politician who subordinated everything to the interests of the State. All personal feelings are sacrificed to the creation of a centralized government in France on a scale of unprecedented scope and efficiency. With remorseless lucidity he saw and remedied the problems which confronted him, and drove himself to death in pursuit of a ruthlessly willed end, a figure of sinister power and determination. A realist if ever there was one, he is psychologically an interesting study. He was driven from childhood by an unwavering ambition; the famous portrait, which shows within one frame the three aspects of his face, depicts a personality of inflexible power; the ill health which dogged him in a painful and humiliating form, set him out of the ordinary run of life and strengthened an already implacable will.

His object was to create out of the casual provincialism and religious animosities of seventeenth-century France the centralized structure of the kind of state Bodin defined, and having done so, to assert the power of France abroad. His outlook is realistic, systematic, limited, and in the short run successful: reviewing his difficulties, he faced them in turn and remedied them, if possible, without friction, if necessary, by force.

He had first to create an adequate military power. Under Henry IV France possessed a standing army of ten thousand men; by 1637 Richelieu had made it a hundred and fifty thousand, supplemented by defined quotas from the provinces, and he had organized proper provisioning, pay and accounts. Another potential instrument of power, the navy, had seldom been taken seriously by the French; Richelieu set to work to create an efficient fleet. He brought the separatist tendencies of the Church to heel; he founded the French Academy to extend the influence of the State over literature, and he created a secret inner committee of the Royal Council to be the instrument of his personal will. 'Nothing is more dangerous to the state', he wrote in his Political Testament, 'than diverse authorities on equal terms in the administration of affairs.'

This document,[1] which reveals Richelieu's mind, is of great

---

[1] The Political Will and Testament of that great Minister of State Cardinal Duke de Richelieu . . . Done out of the French, London (1695). The original was written between 1635-40 and dedicated to Louis XIII. Its authenticity has been questioned but never disproved. If it is not the work of the Cardinal himself (the internal evidence is strong for his authorship) it was written by one close in his confidence and steeped in his outlook and policy.

The book is divided into two parts. The first four chapters deal with the reformation of the Church, the control of the nobility and of the third estate. The fifth considers

interest. As his English translator well remarks: 'Most writers only reason after the fact and in their studies . . . They would be at a great loss themselves to overcome the difficulties of the least negotiation or the least dangerous intrigue; but the *Political Testament* is of a different nature; it is a Favourite and a First Minister of State, who has governed upwards of twenty-five years one of the most considerable kingdoms of Europe . . . who prescribes no counsel but what he has often practised himself. Therefore, there never was a work of more use to those who are called to the management of great affairs.'

Richelieu's theory of the State is contained in the opening chapters of the second part; and it will be well to deal with them first. The book is the work of an executive mind with little taste for metaphysical speculation, but Richelieu was near enough to the old tradition to combine a seventeenth-century common sense with a feeling for the intrinsic sanctity of government. 'The reign of God is the principle of the government of states, and indeed it is a thing so absolutely necessary that without this foundation it is impossible for any prince to rule well, or for any state to be happy' (Part II, chap. i). Reason, he maintains, properly exercised, reinforces this view. 'Natural knowledge convinces us that man being created reasonable, reason ought to be the guide to all his actions, since otherwise he would act against his nature and consequently against Him who is the Author of it.' It follows, 'that if a man is sovereignly reasonable, it is his duty to give reason an absolute empire, which does not only require his doing nothing without her but obliges him moreover to use his best endeavours to oblige those under his authority to reverence and follow it religiously. This consequence is the source of another; that, as we ought never to will anything but what is just and reasonable, so we must never will anything without putting it in execution and without exacting an entire obedience to our commands, since otherwise reason would not reign sovereignly' (Part II, chap. ii). A ruthless and far-reaching conclusion! Richelieu here comes near to

the 'state in itself', and the last three deal with the prince and his Council. The second part considers the purpose of the State (chaps. 1-3); and the method of successful government and negotiation (chaps. 4-8); the ninth, a long chapter, is concerned with the power of the king, and is divided into eight sections. It deals with the social, military, and economic structure of the State. The tenth chapter concludes the book with an exhortation to princes to live up to the exacting obligations Richelieu sets out. In the preface he writes: 'Two reasons oblige me to undertake this work; the first is the fear and desire I have of ending my days before the expiration of yours, the second is the faithful passion I have for your Majesty's interests.'

identifying his own will with that of God and natural reason. He goes on to say, 'that it is impossible for a people not to love a prince when they are sensible that reason is the guide of all his actions'. This very French remark might have been made in the eighteenth century; it is interesting that with all his experience and his evident contempt for the common man, Richelieu still retains this conviction.

The task of the prince, on whom everything depends, is a high and heavy one; he must set his subjects the best possible example and exercise unsleeping vigilance and intelligence in the craft of government. Richelieu constantly admonishes Louis XIII to live up to this ideal: 'we must sleep like the lion, without closing our eyes, to foresee the least inconveniences that may happen'. There are many hints and warnings to the lethargic king. 'Disorder reigns so universally in all your Majesty's household that there is no particular place free from it. Though all great princes are careful to have an equipage of great horses suitable to their Grandeur, your Majesty never had one in your great stable which you could use on occasions, though you are at a higher charge about it than any of your predecessors were.' He tactfully suggests that the king should cultivate a sense of proportion and stop fussing about trifles; that the rooms of the palace should be kept tidy and plates removed after meals.

The task of the administrator is hard and ungrateful. 'The more capable a man is, the more he is sensible of the weight of government which lies upon him. Public administration takes up all the thoughts of the most judicious; in so much that the perpetual meditations they are obliged to make to foresee and prevent the evils that may happen deprives them of all manner of rest and contentment, except that which they receive in seeing many sleep quietly (relying on their watchings) and live happily by their misery' (Part II, chap. iv).

Richelieu accepts the national state as the only possible kind of government and, taking for granted that it is reasonable, regards it as the pattern of God's will.

He has, of course, a rigid conception of the social order. 'This great kingdom can never flourish unless your Majesty takes care to keep the bodies that compose it in their order; the Church having the first rank, the nobility the second, and the officers which are at the head of the people the third.' None of the orders in the State will be a burden to the others if they remain in the place which their birth has assigned them. As for the common people: 'Unless they are kept under by some necessity, they will hardly keep within the bounds prescribed by Reason and the laws ... They may be compared to mules, which, being used to burdens, are spoiled more by rest than by labour ... but there is a certain point which cannot be exceeded without injustice, common sense teaching every man that there must be a proportion between the burden and the strength of those that bear it.'[1]

Richelieu has no illusions about popular education. 'As the knowledge of letters is absolutely necessary in a commonwealth, it is certain that they ought not to be taught without distinction to everybody. As a body having eyes in all its parts would be monstrous, a state would be the same if all the inhabitants thereof were learned; we should find as little obedience in it as pride and presumption would be common. The commerce of letters would soon destroy the nursery of soldiers, which increases more in the rudeness of ignorance than in the politeness of science. Finally, it would fill France with litigious persons.'[2]

His remarks on the putting down of duelling show a shrewd understanding of psychology of the French nobles. 'So many edicts have been made hitherto to no purpose that it is difficult to find out a certain way to put a stop to this rage. The French despise their lives so much that experience has taught us that the most rigorous proceedings have not always proved enough to stop their frenzy ... They value their honour more than their life. But the dread of losing the conveniency without which they cannot live happily in this world having a greater influence then the fear of dying without the grace of God, without which they cannot be happy in the next, the fear of losing their estates, their places and their liberty has proved more prevailing than the fear of losing their lives.' It is best therefore to confiscate their property rather than execute them.

Richelieu dislikes financiers. 'It is absolutely necessary', he says, 'to limit their encroachments, otherwise they will finally occasion the ruin of this kingdom ... The gold and silver they abound in affords them the alliance of the best families of the country', which 'are much bastardized by that means.' Even their looks deteriorate.[3] True, financiers can be used 'like sponges' 'but, in my opinion, it is an ill expedient'. His conception of economic welfare is thoroughly old-fashioned by contemporary Dutch or English standards. It is significant that finance was to be the Achilles' heel of the system he created.

[1] Part I, chap. iv, section i.   [2] Part I, chap. ii.   [3] Part I, chap. iii.

On foreign policy he is particularly interesting. Of war he declares roundly, 'states stand in need of it at certain times to purge their ill humours, to regain what belongs to them, to avenge an injury, to put a stop to the progress of a conqueror's pride . . . None but such as are deprived of common sense can be insensible how necessary it is for great states to have their frontiers well fortified'.[1] His comments on his own countrymen are significant. Though brilliant in attack, 'the subtle motions of the nation' make them unstable and not apt for the drawn-out endurance and method necessary for successful war. 'They run an hundred leagues to seek a battle, and yet would not expect the occasion of one a week.' They are liable to get feckless and bored when not in action. 'They are not afraid of peril, but will expose themselves to it without any pains, being destitute of phlegm, of patience and of discipline.'

Richelieu deals at length with military and naval questions. His conclusions are striking and worked out in detail. Antony Perez, he says, 'an old Spaniard consummated in affairs', had advised Henry IV of the importance of sea power. 'To proceed with order and method in this point, we must consider the Ocean and the Mediterranean separately . . .' There follows an elaborate survey of the whole maritime situation.

By the first half of the seventeenth century, then, the absolute state is taken for granted as the only effective unit of government and well enmeshed in large-scale power politics. Within its limits, Richelieu's analysis is brilliant; the *Testament* is a book of exceptional quality and should be more widely known. But the theory behind it is really that of the *Leviathan* of Hobbes, for all the conventional garb of God and Reason with which it is clothed. For Richelieu, power and the satisfaction of exercising it well were enough. The great man of action assumes the frame within which he works; within these limits he was immensely successful. What his success brought him we cannot know. His motives were disinterested, but he is the classic example of the power addict on a great scale.

It is indeed a curious picture which the contemporary accounts give. Surrounded by the complication of an enormous household, guarded night and day by pikemen and musketeers (the captain of his guard never left him), he lived in a calculated splendour of fabulous expense. In the middle of it all, in constant pain and generally unable to sleep, the parchment-faced, haunted, and all-

[1] Part II, chap. ix.

powerful minister sat through the elaborate meals his position demanded but which he was scarcely able himself to touch, or travelled in agonized discomfort in beds and litters on journeys made necessary by state affairs. He loved music but had no time for it; he expressed himself in the superb ceremony of his household and in the designing of great houses and gardens. There is a contemporary account of him at the end of his life, having killed one more of the conspiracies which constantly assailed him, journeying bed-ridden in full splendour down the Rhône in the heat of a Provençal summer. 'On the 24th August, 1642 Monseigneur the Cardinal Duc de Richelieu slept at Viviers. He was travelling down the River Rhône in a boat which had been fitted with a wooden apartment upholstered with scarlet velvet flowered with crimson, the groundwork being of gold . . . At the prow and stern of the boat were some soldiers of his guard wearing scarlet coats. His Eminence was in a bed adorned with purple taffeta. Monseigneur the Cardinal of Bichi and Messieurs the Bishops of Nantes and Chartres were there, with a large number of abbés and gentlemen in other boats. In front of them was an advance guard frigate, and behind came another boat filled with musketeers and their officers. When they came alongside some isle, soldiers were sent ashore to see if there were any suspected persons to be found and, not discovering any one, they guarded the banks until the two boats following had passed. These were filled with nobles and soldiers well armed. Then came the boat of his Eminence, to the stern of which was attached a small covered boat containing M. de Thou, a prisoner, and a dozen of his Eminence's guards. Behind the boats came three barges containing the wearing apparel and the silver vessels of his Eminence . . . When his boat came alongside the shore, a wooden bridge was fixed . . . after this was made secure, the bed on which the said lord lay was carried ashore. Six strong men carried the bed, but what astonished everybody was the fact that he entered the house by means of the windows, for before his arrival masons were brought who broke down the windows of the houses or made holes in the walls of the rooms where he intended to lodge, and then a wooden bridge was constructed stretching from the street to the windows or holes of his lodging. Thus in his portable bed he passed through the streets and was carried up the bridge and placed into another bed prepared for him in his room, that his officers had adorned with rose and violet damask and very costly furniture . . . His chamber was guarded on all sides, also the vaults and the roof of the building where he slept ... I saw him in his room; his aspect was very colourless. ...'[1]

His famous dying words are significant, 'Do you forgive your enemies?' he was asked. 'I have no enemies but those of the State.' Such was the mind and quality demanded by the seventeenth century, when ruling had become a craft, increasingly specialized and complicated; government in practice no longer depended on the king, but on the king's servants who came through the ruthless selection of the struggle for preferment. In all ages government has tended to be carried on by such artists in power; but the seventeenth century, perhaps, gave them the fullest scope and paid them the highest honour. Richelieu's career is paralleled by those of many contemporaries. In England Buckingham had the chance and lacked the ability to take it; Strafford tried and failed — efficiency was his goal, 'Thorough' his motto; Cromwell, among other things, was a cunning political realist; unlike Richelieu's his achievement was short-lived. The hard and watchful faces of the seventeenth-century great, so grim, so able, show the age as a time when the political gloves were off, when there was much to be done and the men to do it, no less than to build the new Leviathan, the national sovereign state, which, following the failure of pope and emperor in their over-ambitious attempt at European sovereignty, was the largest viable centre of authority, and destined, at a price of increasing international conflict, to realize within its own borders an efficiency which was to surpass that of the most powerful governments of antiquity.

[1] Narrative of J. de Banne quoted in BAILEY, *The Cardinal Dictator*, Cape (1936), p. 279.

CHAPTER IV

THE NEW RATIONALISM: DESCARTES: HOBBES

§ 1

WHILE the great statesmen were going their way of power politics and creating the framework of the nation state, an intellectual revolution had been going on. The new rationalistic outlook was peculiar to Europe; it is unparalleled in any other civilization and it was the work of a very few minds. The influence of this scientific humanism spread gradually, coinciding, as we have seen, with that other conspicuous development, the emergence of the modern great state. Both movements are based on organized common sense; the latter is an attempt at efficient planning within the limitations of national sovereignty. The idea of efficiency, characteristic of the Romans, but dormant since the decline of antiquity, returns to Europe with increasing power.

But the first architects of the new state — Machiavelli, Louis XI, Thomas Cromwell — were too short-sighted to be termed scientific and they were certainly not humane. They were realists struggling on a limited policy to keep their ships afloat; they went about their business with an unmediaeval respect for facts, but they had little theoretical grasp of scientific method. To find evidence for this, one of the most original contributions of Western civilization to the world, we must turn to the writings of Descartes, who formulates the principles on which a new approach to philosophical and practical problems can be made.

Following on the principles of Cartesian method applied to politics, Thomas Hobbes breaks away from the remnant of the old transcendentally sanctioned position, as interpreted by Richelieu, and depicts the State as a non-moral Leviathan, fulfilling the law of nature, which is the preservation of the race, and ingeniously invokes the rights of the individual in support of absolutism. This pessimistic view of human nature and society did not necessarily follow from the Cartesian premises; Spinoza was later to take a very different view.

It will be well first, then, to appreciate the unique and original significance of the new scientific outlook and relate it to its historical setting; then to proceed to a short view of Cartesian method, which, though not immediately concerned with politics, determines the background of European thought up to the nineteenth century; finally to examine the formidable contribution of Hobbes to political thought.

To turn first to the nature of the scientific outlook. The re-emergence of Greek scientific speculation in fifteenth-century Italy is the most important event in the history of European thought since the coming of Christianity. Professor Whitehead writes: 'The reformation, for all its importance, may be considered as a domestic affair of the European races . . . In every way the rise of modern science contrasts with the contemporary religious movement. The Reformation was a popular uprising, and for a century and a half drenched Europe in blood. The beginnings of the scientific movement were confined to a minority among the intellectual élite.'[1] The atmosphere of our civilization was profoundly altered, and, after the practical genius of the North had expanded and reinforced the Italian theoretical advance, the material basis of European power was transformed, so that applied scientific method in the nineteenth century was to give Europe and North America the domination of the world. This revolution was not easily made. The early scientists had to fight the organized opposition of orthodox opinion, they only won their freedom because rival religious theorists tore each other to pieces. Copernicus was imprisoned, Bruno burnt, Galileo forced to recant. To take account of facts and submit hypotheses to them was a revolutionary performance in the fifteenth and sixteenth centuries. Mediaeval learning, like classical learning, had been literary and rhetorical. The primitive respect for the 'scribe' — the literate man — and the corresponding degradation of the mechanic had run through European civilization from very early times. The Graeco-Roman aristocracy never dreamt of experiment as a fit occupation for a gentleman, and in the Middle Ages the tide was all the same way; Charles II of England, collecting clocks, fitting up a laboratory and patronizing the Royal Society; Peter of Russia, learning to build ships in Holland, represent a revolutionary departure. For the scientific speculations of the Ionian and Alexandrian Greeks never had the backing of professionalized skill and of the natural resources of coal and iron available in northern Europe. The slave basis of

[1] *Science and the Modern World*, pp. 1-2. C.U.P. (1926).

Hellenistic society prevented the expert attaining the respect and influence he has achieved in modern times, while the lack of instruments of precision, adequate microscopes and accurate measurement, handicapped the civilization of antiquity from attaining the command over its environment which might have been expected of it. The invention and perfection in Italy and Holland of telescopes and lenses is a landmark in the history of material progress. It is certainly strange that the Romans never developed the power of steam; the railway and the internal combustion engine would have appealed to them, and it is more extraordinary that, with all the opportunities for finding it out, the principle of the circulation of the blood was not discovered until the seventeenth century.

The Renaissance and the seventeenth century initiated a new advance after invention had been almost at a standstill since the great ages of material progress in the river valleys of Mesopotamia and Egypt; in the history of civilization, it would seem, inventive genius proceeds unevenly.

The diffused common sense which begins to permeate the European mind under the influence of the new ideas, and the conviction, reinforced by empirical knowledge, that there is a natural order which can be understood and mastered, began to create a new confidence and a new optimism about the aims and future of society. Granted that the moral order of the world as interpreted by Catholicism was broken, it did not follow that the scientific outlook led to bankruptcy. Mediaeval Catholicism had, it seemed, no monopoly of political wisdom, for all the immediate retrogression; it owed its conception of Natural Law largely to Hellenistic sources; the thinkers of the Renaissance were taking up and expanding the heritage of Classical Antiquity enriched by the humanitarian tradition of Christianity. The old outlook was gradually swept away and the aims of the State were to be reinterpreted in a new form, not necessarily immoral. From the tentative beginnings, within an increasingly efficient framework of government, the seventeenth century saw a growing confidence in a clear and distinct mathematical analysis of social problems and a conception of knowledge as power alien to the mediaeval mind. In reaction from scholastic thought, the new knowledge swung over to a fine confidence in the power of reason in human affairs and in the good sense of human beings. There runs through the thought of this period the assumption that there are laws of human behaviour, like the laws of physics, which have only to be ascertained to be acted on; that society is made up of intelligent individuals acting deliberately on general principles, who make their 'social contract' with the great state and 'consent' to the bargain of government.

What Newton achieved in cosmology, political theorists tried to do for society, and individuals were regarded as the hard little entities of a mathematical equation. The Protestant emphasis on personal judgement, independence, and perfectability further encouraged this individualism, while the prosperous background of the rising middle classes created a habit of enterprise and self-reliance. Such confidence helped to free thought from mediaeval limitations and produced a strong fighting spirit, but it led in the long run to a certain cocksureness of judgement which often becomes exasperating in the eighteenth century. For all that, the hard-bitten common sense of the seventeenth and eighteenth centuries laid the foundations of European power and prosperity and created the framework of a later and broader rationalism; it was, as it had to be, a fighting creed, and if its assumptions were sometimes thin, they were penetrating as a rapier.

The outlook of the seventeenth century is clear, reasonable, and mechanical. The triumphs of applied science and, above all, mathematics were reflected in an analytical approach to political thought.

§ II

The most famous pioneer of the experimental method is Descartes,[1] whose writings revolutionized the philosophical and practical outlook of his time, and although he wrote no treatise on political theory, he profoundly influenced it.

Descartes makes a cautious, laborious, and systematic investigation of experience in the light of the clear-cut principles defined in his *Discourse on Method* (1637). He was educated on orthodox lines, and to the end of his life shrank from the conclusions to which his thought led him. 'Trained by the best educators of the seventeenth century,

---

[1] Descartes, 1596-1650. Born at La Haye, near Poitiers, of good family; educated at the Jesuit College of La Fleche, in Maine, 1604-12; 1612-19, served under Prince Maurice of Nassau in the Low Countries, and 1619-21, under Maximilian of Bavaria on the Danube. Here he made his famous definition of Cartesian method. 1628, settled in Holland; 1637, published the *Discours sur la Méthode*; 1641, *Méditations*; 1642, *Principles of Philosophy*; 1649, went to Stockholm to instruct Queen Christina of Sweden, where he died February 1650.

the Jesuits, naturally endowed with a dialectic grasp and subtlety which even they could hardly improve, and with a passion for getting at the truth which even they could hardly impair, Descartes possessed in addition a rare mastery of literary expression.'[1]

The famous *Discourse on Method*, in which he sets out the principles of his philosophy, is a short book, about sixty pages long, divided into six sections. The first comprises a history of his intellectual development: 'I was especially delighted with the Mathematicks, on account of the certitude and evidence of their reasoning.'

Having ranged over the fields of seventeenth-century knowledge, Descartes was not content with a purely academic study. 'I entirely abandoned the study of letters and resolved no longer to seek any other science than the knowledge of myself or of the great book of the world. I spent the remainder of my youth in travelling, in visiting courts and armies . . . in proving myself in the different situations into which fortune threw me. After I had been occupied several years in thus studying the book of the world, . . . I at length resolved to make myself an object of study.'

In part II of the *Discourse* he describes the circumstances in which he formulated his method. 'I was then in Germany . . . and, as I found no society to interest me, and was besides fortunately undisturbed by any cares or passions, I remained the whole day in seclusion in a room heated by means of a stove, with full opportunity to occupy my attention with my own thoughts.' He decided to sweep away all the assumptions he had hitherto been accustomed to make, and with laborious caution he proceeded on the following principles:

'The *first* was never to accept anything for true which I did not clearly know to be such; that is to say, carefully to avoid precipitancy and prejudice, and to comprise nothing more in my judgement than what was presented to my mind so clearly and distinctly as to exclude all ground of doubt.

'The *second*, to divide each of the difficulties under examination into as many parts as possible, and as might be necessary for its adequate solution.

'The *third*, to conduct my thoughts in such order that by beginning with objects the simplest and easiest to know I might ascend little by little, and, as it were, step by step, to the knowledge of the more complex . . . and the *last*, in every case to make enumerations so

[1] T. H. HUXLEY, *Essay on Descartes*, collected works.

complete, and reviews so general, that I might be assured that nothing was omitted.'[1]

These principles may have ultimately led philosophy into a blind alley; they are invaluable to practical affairs. The Cartesian statement of organized common sense is of cardinal importance to political thought. Here Greek rationalism emerges again, reinforced by experimental method. Descartes, 'like one walking alone and in the dark', helps to set the Western world on the road which was to end in the material mastery of the earth. He was well aware of the possibilities of his method and reluctant to publish his treatise because the Catholic authorities had condemned Galileo. But he conceived it his duty not to keep his principles concealed 'without sinning grievously against the law whereby we are bound to promote the general good of mankind. For by them I perceive it to be possible to arrive at knowledge highly useful to life, and in room of the speculative philosophy usually taught in the schools, to discover a Practical, by means of which . . . we *might render ourselves the lords and possessors of nature*'.[2]

Descartes's method and its success made for an increasing confidence in the power of rational analysis. In terms of political theory, this rationalistic outlook could be linked up with the concept of a secularized Natural Law. Politically the Cartesian method was neutral; and, just as Natural Law was invoked both by the defenders of despotism and the pioneers of democracy, Cartesian analysis might reinforce either interpretation. Political thought was certainly clarified by it, and attained a new efficiency and a new impartiality,

---

[1] *Discourse on Method*, Everyman edition (1912), edited by A. D. LINDSAY.

[2] A link between the short-sighted common sense of Machiavelli and the theoretical approach of Descartes may be found in Francis Bacon, Lord Verulam, at once a realist statesman and an amateur scientist, who followed up the new conception of knowledge as power, which Descartes throws off as it were incidentally. Unlike Descartes, who was a speculative type, and careful to keep out of trouble, Bacon was a man steeped in the experience of politics, a lawyer who over-reached himself on the pinnacle of worldly success. His portraits show the shrewdness of what Aubrey calls his 'viper eye'. Thoroughly at home in the world, his rather flat maxims of conduct are expressed with a profundity to which the superlative English of his time contributes a good deal. But he had the vision, which Descartes shared in a superior form, of knowledge as power, and he displayed a rationalistic disgust with religious fanaticism. It was well for him that he never lived to see the English Civil Wars and the phase of the Puritan domination.

He writes: 'Lucretius the poet, when he beheld the act of Agamemnon that could endure the sacrificing of his own daughter, exclaimed "Tantum religio potuit saudere malorum". What would he have said if he had known of the Massacre in France, or the Powder Treason in England? He would have been ten times more epicure and atheist than he was' (Essay on *Unity of Religion*). See his *Advancement of Learning, Essays, Novum Organum*, etc.

but this neutral method alone could not ultimately give any but a utilitarian sanction for government.

Such, then, is the revolutionary outlook formulated by Descartes, which in its application was to give the world all he claimed for it. Its effects on political development had one particular disadvantage: on the theoretical side, it made for an artificial distinction between the State on the one hand and the individual on the other, and for a mechanical view of their relationship, at variance with the facts. As in the philosophical field, where the Cartesian method led to the 'fallacy of misplaced concreteness', so in the political sphere the organic totality of the political relationship tended to be lost, and the moral justification of power confused.

§III

The application of Cartesian method to political thought finds its moral expression in Spinoza and its immoral expression in Hobbes. In the seventeenth century the latter was by far the most influential. Spinoza's contribution is only beginning to be appreciated. The writings of both men mark a radical break with the past; reading their books we sense fully for the first time the atmosphere of the age of rationalism.

Both abandon the *a priori* approach to political theory; both ultimately appeal not to a Divine purpose or an imposed Natural Law which is the expression of eternal values, but to the sanction of utility, which in Spinoza's view is ennobled by the intellectual and spiritual progress it makes possible. But where Hobbes is content to cast a depraved humanity into the shackles it deserves, sacrificing liberty and initiative for order, content with the reality of a power which works, Spinoza insists that the State ought to ensure liberty of mind and education, that it must rest on the consent of the majority, and that an expanding 'fullness of life' is the end and justification of government. His political writings, chronologically later than those of Descartes and Hobbes, will be examined in a later chapter.

While Descartes was in the full tide of his thought, the English civil wars had wrecked the immediate chances of a contemplative life for a philosopher of genius, who was forced by the tide of events to turn his mind to the theory of government and to fly into France.

NEW RATIONALISM: DESCARTES: HOBBES

Thomas Hobbes[1] worked out a justification of the utilitarian power

[1] Thomas Hobbes, 1588-1678. There is a full account of his life by one of the most observant English biographers. Aubrey's life of him is the most elaborate of the *Brief Lives*; and in the full text one of the most representative of the biographer's method. I quote the main gist of it.

'Thomas Hobbes, Malmesburiensis, philosophus', was the second son of Mr. Thomas Hobbes, vicar of Westport juxta Malmesbury, who married – Middleton of Brokinborough (a yeomanly family). Thomas, the father, was one of the ignorant 'Sir Johns' of Queen Elizabeth's time; 'could only read the prayers of the church and the homilies'. Thomas was educated by his uncle, by profession a glover, 'which is a great trade here, and in times past much greater. His mother fell in labour of him in fright of the invasion of the Spaniards . . . His hair was black, and his school-fellows were wont to call him "Crowe".' In 1603 he 'went away a good schoole-scholar to Magdalen-hall, in Oxford' . . . 'where he took great delight there to goe to the booke-binders' shops, and lye gaping on mappes'.

In 1607 he entered the service of the Earl of Devonshire, and served Bacon as a personal secretary. 'His lordship . . . was wont to contemplate in his delicious walkes at Gorambery . . . His lordship would often say that he better liked Mr. Hobbes's taking his thoughts than any of the others, because he understood what he wrote. . . .'

He was also much 'addicted to the mathematiques', but was over forty years old before he looked on geometry, 'which happened accidentally. Being in a gentleman's library, Euclid's Elements lay open, and 'twas the 47 El. lib: I. He read the proposition. "By G——', sayd he, "this is impossible!" So he reads the demonstration of it, which referred him back to such a proposition; which proposition he read. That referred him back to another, which he also read. *Et sic deinceps*, that at last he was demonstratively convinced of that trueth. This made him in love with geometry . . . He would often complain that algebra, . . . though it did rarely well and quickly and easily in right lines, yet 'twould not *bite* in *solid* like geometrie.'

During the civil war he wrote 'a little treatise in English' (afterwards the *De Cive*), defending the king's prerogative, and 'withdrew into France', where he wrote the *Leviathan*; 'the manner of writing which booke', says Aubrey, 'was thus. He walked much and he had in the head of his staffe a pen and inke-horne, carried always a note-booke in his pocket, and as soon as a thought darted, he presently entred it into his booke, . . . thus that booke was made.'

Of his general characteristics Aubrey says: 'In his youth unhealthy; of an ill yellowish complexion . . . and trod both his shoes the same way. From forty, or better, he grew healthier, and then he had a fresh ruddy complexion. Head: in his old age he was very bald (which claymed a veneration); yet within dore, he used to study and sitt bare-headed, and sayd he never tooke cold in his head, but that the greatest trouble was to keepe off the flies from pitching on the baldness. Ample forehead, whiskers yellowish-redish, which naturally turned up . . . He had a good eie, and that of a hazell colour. When he was earnest in discourse, there shone (as it were), a bright live-coale within it. He had two kind of looks: – when he laugh't, was witty, and in a merry humour, one could scarce see his eies round . . . He was six foote high, and something better, and went indifferently erect, or rather, considering his great age, very erect . . . He had a curious sharp sight, as he had a sharpe witt, which was so sure and steady that I have heard him often-times say that in multiplying and dividing he never mistooke a figure: and so in other things.'

Aubrey ends his classic biography with an account of Hobbes's very curious habits: 'Besides his dayly walking, he did twice or thrice a yeare play at tennis (at about 75 he did it); then went to bed there and was well rubbed . . . At night, when he was abed, and the dores made fast, and was sure nobody heard him, he sang aloud (not that he had a very good voice) but for his health's sake.' Hobbes himself thought better of his voice; *ipse quoquam carmen eructavit, nec (ut plurimi judicabant) infeliciter*, he says in his autobiography.

Such is John Aubrey's picture of this man: a real *character*, in the old sense of the word. *Vide* AUBREY's *Brief Lives*, ed. Andrew Clark, vol. I, O.U.P. (1898). Also LESLIE STEPHAN, *Hobbes*, London, 1928. For a good edition of the *Leviathan* see W. G. Pogson Smith, Oxford, 1909.

of the sovereign state which was more elaborate and trenchant than any hitherto made. On the assumption that men are at once reasonable and predatory, he constructs an argument for the absolute authority of the sovereign, whether it be monarch or assembly, and puts the ecclesiastical power firmly under it.

The book is characteristically English in its pedestrian common sense, its ironical humour and lack of understanding for apparently unpractical idealism. Hobbes wants *security*, of person and property, from civil war and external attack; he is willing, in his 'realistic' disillusionment, to pay a heavy price for it. In the course of his argument Hobbes faces the deepest questions of politics and the *Leviathan* is one of the great books of political theory. It contains the most comprehensive statement of Hobbes's position; but for a full understanding of his thought his other works ought to be studied,[1] notably the *De Cive*, the *Tripos*[2] and the *Philosophical Rudiments*,[3] and *Behemoth*.[4] His translation of Thucydides, whom he admired above all other historians, throws much light on the development of his mind. It is impossible in a work of this scope to do justice to these books. But the reader is strongly recommended to study them; all Hobbes's English works are written with the same trenchant power of thought and expression as is apparent in the *Leviathan*.

The *Leviathan*, 'my discourse of Civill and Religious Government occasioned by the disorders of the Present Time', was published in 1651, dedicated to Mr. Francis Godolphin. Hobbes is slightly apologetic about the book, and seems to expect it will be found shocking, ending the dedication rather lamely, 'If not withstanding this, you find my labour generally decried, you may be pleased to excuse yourself and say I am a man that love my own opinions and think true all I say. . . .'

The top half of the title-page of the *Leviathan* contains a landscape depicting a neatly planned town with a background of open country. Towering over the scene, there stands the crowned figure of a huge

---

[1] See *Hobbes' Works*, edited Sir W. MOLESWORTH. English, 11 vols.; Latin, 5 vols. Bohn (1840). See also STRAUSS, *Hobbes' Political Philosophy*, Oxford University Press (1936).

[2] *Tripos: in three Discourses.* 229 pp.
    i. Human Nature, or the Fundamental elements of policy.
    ii. De Corpore Politico, or the elements of Law.
    iii. Of Liberty and Necessity.

[3] *Philosophical Rudiments of a Free Citizen.* Of Liberty, pp. 1-59; of Dominion, pp. 63-182; of Religion, pp. 201-98.

[4] *Behemoth.* The history of the causes of the Civil Wars of England.

man, shown from the waist upwards, with the arms stretched out protectively, grasping in his right hand a great sword and in his left a crozier. The body of the figure is made up of a swarm of little people, with their backs to the reader and their eyes fixed on the figure's expressionless face. Beneath this picture is the title — 'Leviathan, or the Matter, Forme and Power of a Common-wealth Ecclessiasticall and Civil. By Thomas Hobbes of Malmesbury', framed by the emblems of civil and ecclesiastical power.

The book is divided into four parts. The first, entitled 'Of Man', comprises 16 chapters, of which the first 10 are a typically seventeenth-century investigation of human knowledge and psychology. Chapters xiii to xv are concerned with the 'Lawes of Nature' and the origins of the social contract. The second part, 'Of Commonwealth', contains, in chapters xvii to xxxi, the most essential part of Hobbes's political thought. Part III is entitled 'Of a Christian Commonwealth'; chapters xxxii to xliii contain Hobbes's religious views; the fourth and final part, 'Of the Kingdom of Darkness', in four chapters, is concerned with interpretations of scripture, daemonology and an attack on the Catholic Church. It is followed by a short final review and conclusion.

The geometrical quality of seventeenth-century thought is well illustrated in the *Leviathan*. Fundamentally, Hobbes is convinced, the problem is simple, the truth ascertainable. 'The skill of making and maintaining Common Wealths consists in Certain Rules, as doth Arithmetique and Geometry; not (as Tennis play) in practice only ... which rules neither poore men have the leisure, nor men that have had the leisure have hitherto had the curiosity, or the method, to find.'[1]

The *Leviathan* attempts to expound a theorem of politics; the word 'method' is significant; the thought is plodding, angular, trenchant, as in Descartes's *Discourse*. Such an effort was doubly congenial to the keen-minded North Wiltshireman, with the harsh rapid speech, who looks out of the contemporary portraits with such a wary eye. It is highly instructive to watch Hobbes sailing near the wind in matters of theology; to note the cunning with which the heterodox opinions are quietly inserted, the advance towards conclusions which torpedo the whole conventional position headed off just in time, the luffing to and the swing over on a new tack.

Hobbes writes in a homely vigorous English, which comes straight

[1] II, 20.

from the country dialect, enriched with a well digested Latinity. The ironical similes go home and stick.

'It is with the mysteries of our religion as with wholesome pills for the sick, which swallowed whole have the virtue to cure, but being chewed are cast up again without effect'; universities which 'yet retain a relish of that subtle liquor wherewith they were first seasoned against the civil authority'; men that 'stick their corrupt doctrine with the cloves of other men's wit'.

Hobbes had one illusion: it is the old one of the philosopher king . . . 'Neither Plato nor any philosopher hitherto hath put into order, and sufficiently, or probably proved all the Theorems of Morall Doctrine, that men may learn thereby, both how to govern and how to obey; I recover some hope that, one time or other, this writing of mine may fall into the hands of a sovereign, who will consider it himself (for it is short and I think clear), without the help of any interested or envious Interpreter; and by the exercise of entire Sovereignty in protecting the Publique teaching of it, convert this Truth of Speculation, into the Utility of Practice.'

He believes it possible to demonstrate the cogency of his views, and put them into effect by education. 'The common people's minds are like clean paper, fit to receive whatsoever by Public Authority shall be imprinted on them.'

The seventeenth century was innocent at any rate in its belief in the power of reason in human affairs. Here, then, is the flaw in the armour of Hobbes's disillusionment: he believes that men are consistently reasonable, if vulpine beneath the veneer. He also believes that society can be static. Once the 'theorem' has been demonstrated and the structure of Hobbes's absolutism imposed, there is an end of it. There is here no conception of organic change, the thing is fixed and immutable.

Hobbes further reduces the State to an artificial contrivance for better furthering the interests of the individuals composing it. He therefore anticipates the Utilitarian view of the functions of government, and he puts man into society, not organically and inevitably, but by artifice.

It follows that the State is a morally neutral and mechanical thing; but Hobbes does not follow out the logic of his conclusions and reduce its function as much as possible. This course is a luxury which can only be afforded in securer times than the seventeenth century. The *Leviathan* retains all the coercive powers necessary for the preservation of order. Further, Hobbes's view of human nature is pessimistic: the natural condition of men is war.

'If', says his able adversary, Dr. Bramhall, 'men had sprung up from the earth in a night, like mushrooms or excrescences, without all sense of honour, justice, conscience or gratitude, he could not have vilified the human nature more than he does.'[1]

This pessimistic outlook colours the whole book. In chapter xiii of the first part, Hobbes insists that nature 'hath made men so equal in faculties of body and mind . . . when all is reckoned together, the difference between man and man is not so considerable as to prevent competition between them'. Hence the natural condition of man is unending strife, and 'men have no pleasure (but on the contrary a great deal of grief) in keeping company where there is no power to overawe them all' . . . 'So that in the nature of man we find three principall causes of quarrel. First, Competition; secondly, Diffidence — (by which Hobbes means fear) — thirdly Glory.'

The result is a 'condition which is called Warre' . . . 'Whatsoever therefore is consequent to the time of Warre when every man is Enemy to every man; the same is consequent to the time wherein men live without other security, than what their own strength and their own invention shall furnish them withall. In such condition there is no place for Industry; because the fruit thereof is uncertain: and consequently no Culture of the Earth; no Navigation, nor use of the commodities that may be imported by Sea; no Commodious Building; no Instruments of moving and removing such things as require much force; no knowledge of the Face of the Earth; no account of Time; no Arts; no Letters; no Society; and which is worst of all, Continuall Feare, and danger of violent death; and the life of man solitary, poore, nasty, brutish and short.'[2]

Hobbes reinforces this pessimistic view of 'natural' society by a glance at the behaviour of contemporary 'Kings and persons of Sovereign authority', who, 'because of their independency, are in continuall jealousies and in the state and posture of gladiators;

---

[1] An answer to a book published by Dr. Bramhall, late Bishop of Derry, and called the *Catching of the Leviathan*. *Hobbes's Works*, English, vol. IV, p. 279. MOLESWORTH, op. cit.

Bramhall puts the case against Hobbes cogently: Men are naturally religious, he argues: 'This is acknowledged by T. H. himself in his lucid intervals' . . . 'He inserteth gratitude to man as the third precept of the Law of Nature, but of the gratitude of mankind to their Creator there is a deep silence.' The full text of Bramhall's extremely able attack will be found in his *Collected Works* (Library of Anglo-Catholic Theology, 5 vols., Oxford, 1842). It is worth careful study.

[2] Part I, chap. xiii.

having their weapons pointing and their eyes fixed on one another; that is their forts, garrisons and guns upon the frontiers of their kingdoms; and continuall spies upon their neighbours, which is a posture of war'. He then remarks that 'because they uphold thereby the industry of their subjects there does not follow from it that misery which accompanies the liberty of practical men', thus showing himself resigned to the problems Grotius attempts to tackle, for it is beyond the scope of the *Leviathan* to face the problem of international order: it is concerned with the establishment of order within the national state.

It follows, then, that to avoid the primitive condition of perpetual war, men must submit to a common authority, and Hobbes invokes natural law in support of this view. But he interprets it in a new way. Since the law of nature is self-preservation, it follows that men are obliged to transfer to a common power the rights, which, if retained, 'hinder the peace of mankind' (Part I, chap. xv), since if peace be 'hindered' the law of self-preservation will be void. He thus calls in his version of Natural Law to put man under authority, taking the interpretation clean contrary to the outlook which invokes it to justify the rights of the individual. It is an ingenious and characteristic argument.

Further, it is a natural law that 'men perform their covenants made', and this law is the 'fountain and originall of justice'. Yet it is invalid without power to enforce covenants; 'before the names of just and unjust can have place there must be some coercive power'. Since, then, 'the final cause, End or Design of men' is 'getting themselves out of the miserable condition of warre which is necessarily consequent (as has been shown) to the naturall passions of men, where there is no visible power to keep them in awe and tye them by fear of punishment to the performance of their covenants' (Part II, chap. xvii), it follows that 'they ought to set up such a Common Power as may be able to defend them from invasion by Forraigners and the injuries of one another and thereby to secure them in such sort, as that by their own industry and by the fruits of the earth they may nourish themselves and live contentedly'. They therefore 'conferre all their power and strength upon one man, or upon one assembly of men that they may reduce all their wills . . . to one will . . . which is as much as to say, to appoint one man or assembly of men to *beare their Person*'. There follows a real 'unitie of them all', and 'the multitude so united in one person is called a commonwealth, or in Latine civitas. This is the generation of that great Leviathan . . . or rather of that mortal God to which we owe, under the immortal God, our peace and defence.' The Leviathan 'is said to have Sovereign Power, and every one besides is his Subject'.

Hobbes is thus in line with Bodin and Richelieu, regarding sovereign power as the only basis for effective government, and owing to his superior theoretical ability, he provides the accomplished fact with an able and highly sophisticated argument. Once the sovereign power is imposed for men's own good, Hobbes goes on to clamp it down on the subjects in perpetuity. He turns the idea of contract, so often quoted as a justification for the renouncement of obedience, into an argument for it. Having once made the covenant, the subjects cannot make a new one without the sovereign's permission, 'and therefore they that are subjects to a Monarch, cannot, without his leave, cast off Monarchy and return to the confusion of a disunited Multitude'. He tries to stop the loophole, so widely used in arguments for resistance, of an appeal to God or conscience, by arguing that there can be no covenant with God but by 'Mediation' of some body that represents 'God's person; which none doth, but God's Lieutenant, who hath the sovereignty under God'.

This unconvincing case against an appeal to conscience is reinforced by invective, as though Hobbes was not too happy about it. 'But the pretence of Covenant with God', he says, 'is so evident a lye, even in the pretender's own conscience, that it is not only the act of an unjust but also of a vile and unmanly disposition.' Naturally no kind of man could be more uncongenial to Hobbes's practical mind than the religious visionary. He goes on further to consolidate the sovereign's position by another ingenious argument. Since the sovereign was only put there by a contract of subjects between one another, there never arose any contract between the sovereign and them: there is no contract, it follows, for the sovereign to break. Next, since the majority made the sovereign, he that dissented must now consent with the rest, for by 'entering into the covenant of them that were assembled' he implied he would stand by the majority's decision. He must either submit to their decrees or revert 'to the condition of warre he was in before; wherein he might without injustice, be destroyed by any man whatsoever.' (Part II, chap. xviii).

Hobbes goes on to assert that whatever the sovereign does it cannot be unjust, since 'he that complaineth of injury from his sovereign complaineth of that whereof he himself is author . . . It is true that they that have sovereign power may commit Iniquitie, but not Injustice of Injury in the proper signification.' It follows that 'no man that hath sovereign power can justly be put to death'.

The sovereign must control opinion, for the sake of peace, and 'examine the doctrines of all books before they be published'. He must not grant away the power of raising money or 'transferre the militia' — points highly relevant to the controversies of Hobbes's day. Concluding the definition of the scope of sovereign power, Hobbes admits that such strict government is unpleasant to live under, but argues that it is the lesser of two evils, life and men being what they are. The disadvantages of a powerful state are 'scarce sensible' in comparison with 'the miseries, and horrible calamities that accompany a Civil Warre, of that dissolute condition of masterlesse men' (Part II, chap. xviii).

The xixth chapter of the second part deals with the different kinds of commonwealth, of which there are three — Monarchy, Democracy or popular commonwealth, and Aristocracy. The difference 'consisteth not in the difference of power, but in the difference of convenience'. Of the three he prefers monarchy, since the private interests of the monarch coincide with the public interest, he can consult whom he pleases, and 'cannot disagree with himself'. As for 'favourites', they are an inconvenience, but 'whereas the favourites of monarchs are few . . . the favourites of an assembly are many and their kindred much more numerous'. Sovereign assemblies have need of 'custodes libertatis', for they cannot dissent from the majority's opinion even if it be bad.

In attempting a definition of liberty (Part II, chap. xxi), Hobbes shows the mechanical outlook which was the fashion of his time, and, trenching on theological ground, comes near to denying free will. The liberty so often extolled in classical history is not, he maintains, the liberty of particular men, but the liberty of the commonwealth. 'It is an easy thing for men to be deceived by the specious name of liberty, and for want of judgement to distinguish, to mistake for their private inheritance and Birth Right, that which is the right of the Public only.' At the same time he denies the sovereign the kind of absolutism practised in Oriental societies, and he goes on to allow subjects rights which are not conceded by modern democratic states. If a man is ordered to perform some dangerous or dishonourable office, he is only bound to obey if the non-performance of it 'frustrates the end for which sovereignty was ordained; then there is no liberty to refuse, otherwise there is'. This far-reaching proviso is applied by Hobbes to the question of conscription; he concedes that the sovereign has the right to punish refusal by death, but if a man 'substitute a sufficient soldier' in his place, 'he deserteth not the service of the commonwealth'. There is 'allowance to be made for naturall timorousnesse, not only to woman (from whom no such dangerous duty is expected), but also to 'men of feminine courage'. The seventeenth-century Leviathan, in its small-scale operations, owing to the limited efficiency of its organization, did not attain the impersonal power of the modern state. The full implications of the unbridled sovereign state were not worked out until it became reinforced with modern technique, but Hobbes is careful to insert the clause that 'when the defence of the commonwealth requireth at once the help of all that are able to bear arms, every one is obliged'.

The next chapters are devoted to examining problems of executive government and to the position of the sovereign as legislator, to the definition of crimes and the comparison of their gravity (Part II, chap. xxvii), and to questions of punishment. The twenty-ninth chapter examines the causes of the dissolution of commonwealths, of which one of the most powerful is the undermining of the civil authority by the 'ghostly authority' or Spiritual Power. Either the one or the other must be supreme. The spiritual power, 'because the fear of Darkness and Ghosts is greater than other Feares, cannot want a party sufficient to trouble and sometimes to destroy a Commonwealth'. He compares the result to epilepsy. He also ascribes rebellion to the 'Reading of the books of Policie and Histories of the Antient Greeks and Romans', which encourage regicide under the name of tyrannicide, concluding: 'In Summe I cannot imagine how any thing can be more prejudicial to a Monarchy than the allowing of such books to be publickly read, without present applying such correctives of discreet Masters as are fit to take away their venime, which venime I will not doubt to compare to the biting of a mad Dogge.' He thus strikes at liberty of thought and imposes a censorship on opinion.

Another cause of the decline of commonwealths is 'when the passage of money to the public treasure is obstructed, by the tenacity of the people'. This distemper he compares in detail to an ague: 'A great number of corporations are like wormes in the entrails of a naturall man', and 'we may further adde the insatiable appetite or Bulimia of enlarging Dominion. . . .'

The thirtieth chapter of the second part contains detailed proposals for educating the common people in the right principles of government and remedies for the problem of over-population. Encouragement of industry of all kinds is one remedy, and 'the multitude of poor yet strong people still encreasing, they are to be transplanted into countries not sufficiently inhabited', where they should 'court each little Plot with Art and Labour, to give them their sustenance in due season. And when all the world is overcharged with inhabitants', he concludes cynically, 'then the last remedy of all is Warre, which provideth for every man, by Victory, or Death' (Part II, chap. xxx). Hobbes thus anticipates many of the ideas of the totalitarian state: a subordinate Church, a controlled press, a doctrinaire education, ultimate war.

The concluding chapter of the second part proceeds, surprisingly enough, to invoke the Divine sanction for the commonwealth, in spite of its strictly utilitarian basis, and to outline the programme of the third part, of 'a Christian Commonwealth'. Hobbes sets himself to find out what the Divine laws are and states that God declares them in three ways: 'by the Dictates of Natural Reason, by Revelation, and by the voyce of some man, to whom by the operation of miracles, he procureth credit with the rest'. He then goes on to an analysis of the theological aspect of Natural Reason, and his chapter ends with the passage already quoted, in which he expresses the hope that his book will one day fall into the hands of a sovereign who will 'convert its doctrines into the utility of practice'.

The third and fourth parts of the *Leviathan* are mainly theological, full of intricate seventeenth-century argument; the latter book, entitled 'Of the Kingdom of Darknesse', being a devastating attack on the Roman Church.

Putting aside the arguments of natural reason, Hobbes deals with the laws of God as expressed by Revelation, 'not only the naturall Word of God but also the propheticall'. Here occurs the famous comparison already quoted of the 'mysteries of our religion' with 'wholesome pills for the sick' (Part III, chap. xxxii).

How can prophets be recognized, he asks, since often they do not even recognize one another? 'The prophet that was sent to prophesy against the altar set up by Jeroboam, though a true prophet, was yet deceived by another old prophet that persuaded him to eat and drink with him. If one prophet deceive another, what certainty is there of knowing the will of God by other way than that of reason?' Hobbes's sly answer is as follows: 'To which I answer out of Holy Scripture that there be two marks by which, together and not asunder, a true prophet is to be known. One is the doing of miracles; the other is not teaching any other religion than that which is already established.' Hobbes has little understanding for 'the spirit that bloweth where it listeth'.

He then proceeds to discuss the books, writers, scope, and authority of the Bible; he worries at the question whether Moses wrote the Pentateuch, and concludes that he only wrote part of it; he examines the dates of the books of Joshua and Chronicles, of Ezra, Nehemiah, and Job, and debates in detail the exact nature of angels and of inspiration.

He next concerns himself with eternal life, hell, and salvation. He argues strongly that the Kingdom of God will be realized on earth, not in any remote part of the Universe beyond the stars. Adam, had he not sinned, would have enjoyed his life everlastingly in the garden of Eden: 'if, as in Adam all die, that is have forfeited Paradise, even so in Christ shall all be made alive. Then all men shall be made to live on earth, for else the comparison were not proper'. The Kingdom of Heaven, where there is no marriage or giving in marriage, will repeat the conditions of the original Eden, where, so long as Adam and Eve were immortal, marriage was impracticable, 'for if immortals should have generated as mankind doth now, the earth in a small time would not have been able to afford them a place to stand on'. The kingdom is to be a civil commonwealth created at the Second Coming, 'in which Our Saviour is to reign actually'. Having made his own position clear, Hobbes is careful to deny that he propounds the truth of this proposition, leaving it, according to his principles, to be decided by whichever authority becomes sovereign by winning the Civil War — 'that dispute of the sword not yet amongst my countrymen decided'.

Turning to the question of hell, Hobbes maintains that the bottomless pit could not be contained in the globe of the earth, 'which is not only finite but also, compared to the height of the stars, of no considerable magnitude'. Actually, the writers of Scripture do not mean 'a pit without a bottom, but that we should believe them there indefinitely . . . on whom God inflicted that exemplary punishment'. 'Utter darkness', again, 'does not signify how great but where that darkness is to be, namely without the habitation of God's elect. Hell fire, too, is metaphorical, and the terms Satan and Devil are not proper names; they are appellatives signifying an office or quality which 'ought not to have been left untranslated as they are in the Latin and modern Bibles, because thereby they seem to be the proper names of Demons'.

The forty-first chapter traces the Old and New Testament pedigree of the Church, and Hobbes defines ecclesiastical power as a power of persuasion, not coercion. Christ 'said not to his apostles he would make them so many Nimrods, hunters of men, but fishers of men'. God's ministers have no intrinsic power of compulsion, except in their civil capacity, when it is derived from the temporal power. If a man conform to the laws of his sovereign, contrary to his private conviction, the moral responsibility is on the sovereign; the subject cannot be blamed. This bland proviso evades many difficulties, and it would seem to follow that martyrdom is unnecessary. Hobbes answers this difficulty by dividing martyrs into two classes, those who bore witness to the Resurrection of the Messiah, 'which none can be but those that conversed with Him on earth', and those who are but witnesses of other men's testimony and are but 'second martyrs'.

He goes on to insist that clerical appointments should be in the hands of the civil power, since the sovereign is the supreme pastor *jure divino*; the clergy are only pastors *jure civili*. Thus 'bishops ought to put at the beginning of their mandates "by the favour of the King's Majesty, bishop of such a diocese", for in saying *Divina Providentia* they slily slip off the collar of their civil subjection' (Part III, chap. xliii). Hobbes then attacks the doctrines of Bellarmine in detail, and concludes the third book by recapitulating the arguments reconciling the laws of God with those of a Christian commonwealth.

The fourth part (chapters xliv–xlvii), 'Of the Kingdome of Darknesse', identifies the Papacy with the principality of Beelzebub. The dissensions of Christendom, 'such Diversity of ways in running to the same mark, Felicity', indicate we are 'yet in the dark'. Hobbes goes on to attack the doctrines of transubstantiation and purgatory and the relics of paganism perpetuated by the Catholic Church, notably demonolatry and image-worship. The term *Pontifex Maximus* is pagan, and signifies a power subject to the secular authority, while processions, candles, torches, and holy water are 'old empty

Bottles of Gentilisme fille up again with the new wine of Christianity that will not fail in time to break them' (Part IV, chap. xlv). He then attacks the errors of pagan philosophy, derived 'partly from Aristotle, partly from blindnesse of understanding'; he instinctively dislikes metaphysical abstractions, 'which would fright subjects from obeying the laws of their country with empty names, as men fright birds from the corn with an empty doublet, a hat and a crooked stick'. His mistrust of scholasticism, with which he mistakenly identifies Aristotle, blinds him to the natural affinity between his own mind and that of the philosopher.

The concluding chapter deals with the alleged errors of the Catholic Church and contains the following famous passage, an example of the superlative English of the seventeenth century. 'For from the time the Bishop of Rome has gotten to be acknowledged for Bishop Universall . . . their whole hierarchy . . . may be compared not unfitly to the Kingdom of Fairies; that is to the old wives' Fables concerning ghosts and spirits and the feats they play in the night. And if a man consider the originall of this great Ecclesiastical Dominion, he will easily perceive that the Papacy is no other than the Ghost of the deceased Roman Empire, sitting crowned upon the Grave thereof; for so did the Papacy start up on a sudden out of the ruines of that Heathen Power' (Part IV, chap. xlvii).

The *Leviathan* ends with a short review and conclusion in which Hobbes amplifies certain points made in his discourse and rounds it off by recommending that it be taught in universities, because the universities are 'Fountains of civill and morall doctrines, from which the preachers and the Gentry, drawing such water as they find, use to sprinkle the same upon the people'. 'Great care', he says, 'ought to be taken to have it pure both from the venime of heathen Politicians and from the incantations of deceiving Spirits.' He concludes, 'and thus I have brought to an end my discourses on civile and ecclesiastical government occasioned by the disorders of the present time'. 'I cannot', he says, 'think it will be condemned . . . by any that desires the Publique Peace, and in this hope I return to my interrupted speculation of Bodies Naturall.'

Hobbes had, indeed, made his contribution, clear, geometrical, and one-sided: he was right in his apprehension that it would be ill received. Clarendon hated the doctrine of this dangerous ally, for Hobbes had set up a new standard by which government was to be judged and tried to destroy all others. It was a thoroughly modern argument in the seventeenth century. Where Bodin is obsessed with astrology, Hobbes brings political thought into line with the Cartesian outlook; he is thoroughly up to date in his age. Hobbes's thought, like Richelieu's, is relentlessly clear, and he builds his theory upon a psychology which follows from his ideas of physics; he rules out abstract notions of justice and bases the morality of the State simply on what is useful. He interprets the Law of Nature as an instinct for self-preservation, driving all creatures to the fullest realization of themselves. He rightly argues that society ought to further this end, that only in peace and security can such realization be brought about. But he goes on to assume that human motives are uniformly selfish and predatory and the natural condition of men a war of all against all.

To remedy this state of mutual conflict, Hobbes imposes an absolute sovereign in perpetuity as the lesser of the two evils, and the only way to secure peace. He despairs of self-government and ordered freedom, and he rejects any doctrine of natural right or a 'city of God'. His state is justified because it benefits those who compose it, his outlook is utilitarian. He is a forerunner of one aspect of the Benthamite school of the early nineteenth century, with their isolation of the calculating, one-sided and rational man, and their passion for efficient government. He ignores the side of men which is naturally co-operative, the binding debt and dependence of all men in practice on their society and environment, the power of tradition and instinctive loyalty. This individualism is also apparent in his contempt for institutions which come between the individual and the State; he sweeps away the 'mesnages' which Bodin admits. The sovereign power is not a mediator and a referee between other institutions within the State; it has no room for them.

Thus England produced a thinker who, following Cartesian method, worked out the full implications of Bodin's thought and provided an up-to-date justification for Richelieu's practice. But Hobbes did more than that. He set up a new standard by which all institutions could be judged; the common-sense standard of utility. His fundamental assumption is the natural depravity of human nature, and the practical aims of the State, which by saving man from himself fulfils the object of the law of nature, which is self-preservation.

'The greatest part of those men who have written aught concerning commonwealths either suppose or require us, or beg of us, to believe that man is a creature born fit for society. The Greeks call him "ζωον πολιτικον",[1] but in truth men are actuated not by good fellowship but by ambition and selfishness. If they meet for "traffic", a "certain market fellowship is begotten which hath more of jealousy in it than true love": if they meet for pleasure, they delight to ridicule other men's defects for their own "vainglory". If one begins to talk about himself, "instantly everyone of the rest greedily desires to speak about himself too". It follows that all society is either for gain or for glory. All men can kill each other and all are therefore equal, since they can do "the greatest thing, namely kill".[2] A "mutual will of hurting" pervades society, for many men at the same time have an appetite for the same thing.'[3] Here, in a less famous context, are the fundamental assumptions behind Hobbes's thought.

It was understandable: Hobbes was not only a mathematician and a philosopher, he had consorted with the great ones of the earth as well; he knew the wickedness of state business, he had not been secretary to Bacon for nothing. Thus the geometrical seventeenth-century thought went along with the disillusionment of the intellectual: when it was not fear which actuated men, it was pride. It is an old, amoral, and hard-bitten philosophy, and Hobbes's writings are probably the most effective exposition of it.[4]

So the *Leviathan* of the seventeenth century came into its own in theory as well as practice. The price of order and security was the naked power of the Great State: the natural depravity of man asked and deserved this totalitarian answer. The new scientific outlook had defined its method in Descartes's *Discours* and foreshadowed a pessimistic conclusion in the writings of Hobbes. 'Never to accept anything for true which I did not clearly know to be such; that is to say, carefully to avoid precipitancy and prejudice. To comprise nothing more in my judgement than what was presented to my mind so clearly and distinctly as to exclude all ground of doubt.'[5] Neither of these scientific principles necessarily implied Hobbes's bitter conclusions. Nor were these conclusions as realistic as Hobbes believed: the *Leviathan* as a political programme is impracticable. It is static, rigid; the work of a man of the study rather than a man of affairs.

[1] *Philosophical Rudiments*, I, 2.
[2] ib., I, iii.
[3] ib., I, vi.
[4] See R. H. COLLINGWOOD, *The New Leviathan*, Oxford University Press (1942), for a brilliant attempt to bring Hobbes's conclusions to bear on modern society.
[5] *Vide supra*, 314; DESCARTES, *Discours*.

As Clarendon, bringing the judgement of a statesman to bear on Hobbes, remarks: 'his solitary cogitations, how deep soever, and his too peremptory adhering to some philosophical notions, and even rules of geometry, had misled him in the investigation of policy'.[1]

None the less, in Hobbes as in Descartes, here is the voice of a modern outlook, objective, wary, peering out into the world with a new disillusioned appraisement. Descartes, with the seamed forehead and black arched eyebrows, the fierce profile, the great nose and chin, a portent if ever there was one — Hobbes, with the gimlet eye and massive brow; both gaze down out of Time, two of the makers of the modern world.

---

[1] *A Brief View and Survey of the Dangerous and Pernicious Errors to Church and State in Mr. Hobbe's book Entitled Leviathan.* By Edward, Earl of Clarendon. Oxford (1676), 2nd edition, p. 322.

CHAPTER V

ENGLISH PURITANISM

§ 1

SUCH, then, were the political ideas predominant over most of Europe during the seventeenth and eighteenth centuries, as defined by Bodin, practised by Richelieu and his like, and given theoretical justification by Hobbes; they form the pattern of despotic government which was to be realized to its fullest extent by Louis XIV and to be given a more humane interpretation by the 'Enlightened' despots of the ensuing century.

But while the hard high policies of great states were conducted internally and externally on these terms, and mediaeval ideas of European order and of local community widely abandoned, there remained two traditions strong enough to modify and outlast this imposing shift of power — the Protestant tradition of spiritual independence and the ancient tradition of the rule of law and the trusteeship of power. Both these movements found their most influential expression in England, and thence spread abroad to form the inspiration of the modern democratic state. While bearing in mind, therefore, that the predominant form of European polity in that epoch was despotic, following Hobbesian lines, it is necessary to examine shortly the ideas of the English Puritan movements which expressed the politically more radical aspects of the Reformation, and gave rise, not only to notions of radical democracy, but of rudimentary communism as well; secondly, and more fully, the Whig theory of government which reflected the main drift of English development, more powerful and more successful, expressive, too, of the deeper genius of the country. This developed mediaeval tradition, coming down from Bracton and Fortescue through Hooker to Locke, stands for the rule of law and the trusteeship of government. Both these movements were destined to expand from a national to a world influence, the latter dominating in particular the political evolution of North America and the British Commonwealth.

If we turn first to Puritan Radicalism, we find that in spite of the predominance of doctrinal controversy and religious war, the seventeenth century saw the beginnings of modern public opinion,

333

the diffusion of a wide range of proletarian and democratic political ideas, and a new freedom of thought and speech. The English civil wars, in particular, occurred when the printing press had widened the area of political controversy, when our language was in one of its most forceful and eloquent phases, and when familiarity with the translated Bible had brought home the habit of religious and political thought.

The social upheaval of the time gave rise to a vast literature of tracts and pamphlets, generally embellished with titles of a startling kind. It has been rightly said that 'in the politics of the nineteenth and twentieth centuries there is scarcely a speculation which the seventeenth century has not already anticipated'.[1] Though the Commonwealth was politically a failure and Leveller thought driven underground until the late eighteenth century, Radicalism and Socialism have their roots in the religious and economic struggles of the period: the rumblings of proletarian discontent, hitherto confined to slogans and petitions devised by ephemeral leaders of local rebellion, became articulate in the writings of the Levellers and in the debates of the Cromwellian army.

The rift between the king's government and elements of the class Elizabeth had been careful to conciliate, the doctrinal feuds cutting across class solidarity, the recourse to arms, opened the way for a period of proletarian unrest, for a threat of subversion to the Anglican social order. The masses stirred uneasily; there was a menace of revolution in the air; strange and desperate political ideas found their expression. Then the Puritan leaders, carried away by forces they could not control, smashed their way out into a decade of sword government. The king, scorning the 'gentlemen's agreement' Cromwell would have offered him, had died for the principles of the old monarchy. Driven thus far, Cromwell, aware of the chasm opening beneath him, swung over, after a series of vain experiments, into dictatorship. Such was the course of the English Revolution, paralleled by many others. Its political thought is worth examination.

The Cromwellian period is now regarded in a more sober light than was fashionable in the time of Carlyle or even Gardiner.[2]

---

[1] TANNER, *English Constitutional Conflicts of the Seventeenth Century*, Cambridge University Press (1928), p. 213.

[2] G. M. YOUNG, *Charles I and Cromwell*, Davies (1935), p. 146. 'Gardiner's industry, his accuracy, his learning, were such that every future interpretation of the period must be in the main a reinterpretation of his material, but he was dominated not by

The Commonwealth and Protectorate cut across the normal trend of English development; it left the country with an abiding hatred for military dictatorship and Nonconformist tyranny. With the murder of the king, in the words of a modern historian, the Puritan cause 'gained ten years of domination and lost its own soul. In defying the law which guarded both Parliament and king, it defied the ancient and inbred integrity and piety, good sense and good humour of the people of England':[1] increasingly research supports this judgement.

Contemporary evidence reveals also the divergence of ideas and interest between the Radicals and the Whiggish outlook of the army leaders, who were driven, in the effort to save their own skins and preserve social order, into desperate courses which brought their party to ultimate disaster.

How serious was the threat to security and tradition is clear. The army debates show the clash of opinion between the generals and the 'Agitators' or 'Agents', representing the regiments, who were often aided by civilian politicians. The 'Levellers' represented the interests of the men, but it is doubtful if their ideas had a wide following; the concern of the rank and file, as in most armies, being with matters of pay, service abroad, and demobilization.

According to an inquiry into army morale made in 1647, the men wanted indemnity and arrears of pay, and to postpone or avoid service in Ireland.[2] 'To speak seriously', says this account, 'many of them did not know what they did, for many of them cried out "Indemptnity, Indemptnity" and afterwards asked what it was.' The problem of the moment was to keep the army solid behind their leaders; to thrash out some agreed programme and policy which could be put forward both to king and Parliament. Cromwell succeeded in his immediate aim; not before the extremity of the Levellers' view had become apparent. Yet their views reflect an element in English life later to become powerful. The significance

---

[1] Ib., p. 144.

[2] Heads of Proceedings in Walden Church, May 16th, 1647. (*Clarke Papers*, selections from the papers of William Clarke, Secretary to the Council of the Army 1647-9. Edited FIRTH, Camden Society, 1891, vol. I, p. 66.) 'Col. Hewson; I moved about the Irish affair: they seemed to be utterly unwilling to stirre in thatt untill such time as they had some satisfaction.'

Carlyle indeed, but by the atmosphere which Carlyle created, an atmosphere which had a peculiar influence on safe living Victorian Liberals, bearing witness from the security of their pulpit, their desk or their counting house, against the short-comings of the gentry and the Church, lashing themselves to imaginary stakes and glowing in the flames of property bonfires.'

of the Levellers, then, lies not in their generally raw and impracticable doctrines, but in their politically premature assertion of the political responsibility of the common man.

Another and more distinguished contribution of Puritan thought is to be found in Milton's famous vindication of freedom of speech and his advocacy of vigorous local government and education. Milton's first-hand experience of government led him to a cautious view of the political capacity of the people. He was concerned, as was proper to a great poet, to vindicate intellectual freedom, to maintain intellectual values; the famous *Areopagitica* is a lasting monument to his genius, a classic achievement of seventeenth-century prose. *The Tenure of Kings and Magistrates* and the *Ready and Easy Way to Establish a Free Commonwealth* express some of his views on contemporary politics. Yet the sectarian oligarchy Milton delineates as the best government for a free people could never have struck roots in seventeenth-century England; his censorious hatred of king and court, the bitterness of his invective, and the rancour of his religious feuds are inseparable from the integrity of purpose and splendour of language which clothe all his thought.

As the Levellers represented the proletarian wing of Puritanism, so Milton represents the intellectual side of the movement; the crudity of the former and the intolerance of the latter show what a deliverance was wrought for England at the Restoration, but both contributed to an important stream of political ideas.

§ 11

Turning first to the Radical theorists of the Civil War, we find a cross-section of Leveller opinion recorded in the proceedings of the Council of Officers at Putney on October 28th and 29th, 1647, set out verbatim in the Clarke Papers. The contrast of the outlook of the leaders, representing a powerful section of the classes who had done well out of the Reformation, with the view of the Radicals is pungently expressed.

The Levellers show a forthright eloquence and honesty; they voice in a new way the discontent of the classes depressed by the economic changes of the age. Swept under by the tide of events, outmanœuvred and gulled, they command sympathy; yet they show little sense of what is possible, no political finesse. Their crudity and violence, the probable effect of their doctrines on the rank and file, their subversion of discipline, made them a real menace. For the propertied and educated classes the situation was highly dangerous. Many of the soldiers were illiterate; they were fanatical and they were armed. It must be remembered that contemporaries took a poor view of the Puritan army, having seen them at close quarters, stabling their horses in the cathedrals, hacking off the hands and noses of ancient effigies, and destroying windows which were a glory of our mediaeval inheritance. There is full evidence that they left a bad impression on the common people of England, that the Restoration expressed the will of the nation. Nonconformity, good and bad, remained under a cloud for many generations. 'I am engaged', said General Monk on the eve of the Restoration, 'in conscience and honour to free England from that intolerable tyranny of a sword government.'

It should be remembered that the Leveller movement was not unique. The spontaneous popular uprisings of the Clubmen in the southern and western counties, who objected to their farms being fought over by either side, form an interesting parallel to the Leveller movements, actuated by similar ideas, equally democratic and more constitutional. They were ruthlessly put down by the Puritan government; their protests, though less well known, are in a more direct English tradition, seeking redress for grievances within the existing social order. For example, the Declaration of the County of Dorset, made in June 1648, is a remarkable document. The 'surviving' inhabitants of the 'much despised and distressed County of Dorset, having, like the rest of the Kingdom, long groaned under the oppressing tyranny of those whom we reputed our redeemers', make their demands as follows: 'That the common birthright of us all, the Laws, may be restored to their former purity, and that we may enjoy them without corrupt Glosses and Comments of their Arbitrary Power, or unequal Ordinances and practices, between them and their Committees.' They petition that these things be granted: 'That we may no longer subjugate our necks to the boundless lusts and unlimited power of beggarly and broken Committees, consisting generally of the tail of the gentry, men of ruinous fortunes and despicable estates, whose insatiate desires prompt them to continual projects of pilling and stripping us; and that we be not awed by their Emmisaries — generally the most smirking and cunning beggars that can be picked out of a County.'[1]

[1] BAYLEY, *The Great Civil War in Dorset*, Wessex Press (1910), pp. 351-2.

Here is a trenchant and convincing parallel to the political ideas expressed by the Puritan soldiers.

The debates at Putney,[1] which throw such a clear light on the minds and motives of both elements of the army, turn on two major questions — the extent of the franchise and the obligation to obey the law. There are also subsidiary questions raised, notably the terms of a possible settlement with the king.

The Levellers' demands are put forward principally by Thomas Rainborough, John Wildman, Edward Sexby, and 'Buffecoate'. Rainborough, the son of a Wapping sea captain, brought up at sea, a violent and courageous character, perished in battle in the second Civil War.[2] Wildman, a civilian 'brought along' by the soldiers, later took to land speculation in a big way in forfeited royalist property, and survived, after dabbling in Royalist conspiracy, the Rye House Plot and the Monmouth Rebellion, to be knighted by William III.[3] Sexby, a Suffolk man, who had fought through the first Civil War, was destined to be cashiered for malversation of funds, to engage in conspiracy against Cromwell, and to die mad in the Tower.[4]

The case against the Levellers is argued by Cromwell and Ireton; by Cromwell with great shrewdness and volcanic eloquence; by Ireton with a more academic skill. In the background are various moderate men who suggest at intervals that if the debates last much longer 'the King will come and say who is to be hanged first', or that 'it is onlie idlenesse that hath begott this rust and gangrene among us' — 'Lett us go about the worke', they say, 'while in debate we doe nothing'.

The demands of the Radicals included manhood suffrage without

[1] 'Att the Generall Council of Officers att Putney . . . To consider the case of the army truly stated . . . together with the Mischiefs and dangers that are imminent, and some suitable Remedies, humbly proposed by the Agents of five regiments of horse to the respective regiments of the whole army.'

[2] Son of Wm. Rainborough, Master of the king's ship *Sampson*. Served in the Parliamentary fleet; raised a regiment from returned New England emigrants; fought at Naseby; took Berkeley Castle; M.P. for Droitwich 1645; Vice-Admiral 1648; killed at Doncaster in the same year.

[3] Educated at Cambridge; author of *Putney Projects, or the old Serpent in new form*; *Truth's Triumph*; *The Laws Subversion*; etc. etc.; Postmaster-General under William and Mary 1691; knighted 1692, in which year he died. For his speculative activities, see *Calender of Committee for Compounding*. Pepys says he was 'a false fellow to everybody', Macaulay that 'he had a wonderful skill at grazing the edge of treason'.

[4] Governor of Portland 1649-50; cashiered; secret agent in France; involved in the Rebellion of 1655; plotted against the Cromwellian Government in Spain; apprehended in England, on July 25th, 1657. 'It was reported that "yesterday Colonel Sexby (disguised in a very poor habit with an overgrown beard) was taken on shipboard going out of the nation; and after a short examination by his Highness was sent prisoner to the Tower".' (BAYLEY, op. cit., p. 381.) Sexby died in 1659.

property qualification; a revision of electoral districts; dissolution of the Long Parliament and religious toleration. The discontent of the soldiers was voiced by Sexby. What, he asked, had they got out of the war? 'We have been by providence put upon strange things, such as the ancientest heere doth scarce remember . . . providence hath been with us and yett wee have found little fruit of our endeavours.' 'Buffecoate' supported him. 'Wee desire that all carping uppon words bee laid aside and that you fall directly on the matter presented to you.'[1] They then confronted Cromwell with 'The Agreement of the People', a document containing the soldiers' demands.

The authors of the Agreement strike the same note as the leaders of the Peasants' Revolt in the late fourteenth century; they attack the rich but are anxious to remain respectable. Like the men of Dorset, they appeal to the rights of their ancestors; they claim to assert the ancient fundamental rights of the kingdom, and being seventeenth-century Englishmen, they are intensely patriotic.

The Agreement concludes: 'These things we declare to be our native rights and are agreed and resolved to maintain them . . . being compelled thereunto not only by the example of our ancestors, but by our own woeful experience, having long expected and dearly earned the establishment of these *certain* rules of government.'

Cromwell was taken aback by the demands; they implied, he said, 'very great alterations in the government of this kingdom . . . Would it not be confusion? Would it not be utter confusion? Would it not make England like unto the Switzerland country, one canton of the Switz against another?' Further, they are impracticable, and here speaks the statesman: 'Wee have to consider whether the spirit and temper of the nation are prepared to go along with it.' 'Faith', in this context, is not enough. 'Wee are very apt all of us' (and who knew better!) 'to call that Faith that perhaps may bee but carnal imagination.'[2] He will consider the paper, he concludes, but only in the light of existing engagements.

This proviso raised the second major issue of the discussion: how far are contract and the laws binding? Wildman denies that such engagements are valid. The whole question of political contract is hotly debated, and Ireton ably defends the orthodox position. 'To rule otherwise is a principle that will take away all government.' Rainborough on the other hand maintains that conscience comes before engagements, expediency before law, that if laws are 'not

---

[1] *Clarke Papers*, vol. I, p. 255.   [2] *C.P.*, vol. I, p. 238.

suitable to free men' they should be altered. 'Buffecoate' declares roundly that conscience comes before obligation, 'whatsoever hopes or obligations I should be bounde unto, if afterwards God should reveal himself, I would break it speedily, if it were an hundred a day'. Such was the attitude of the Levellers towards political obligation.

Cromwell, meanwhile, had seized on Rainborough's suggestion of a two days' adjournment to consider the proposals. He had climbed down, with a smooth answer. It was indeed 'sinful to keep un-righteous engagements'; for his part he says he is free of engagements to the king (with whom he was, in fact, deeply enmeshed in doubtful negotiations) but there are obligations to the parliament. He proposed an adjournment and a prayer-meeting 'that we may seek God together and see if God will give us a uniting spirit'. He concludes with a threat to resign his commission. At this Colonel Goffe supported the adjournment: 'We have wandered far from God. I speak it I hope from a divine impression . . . we should seriously set ourselves to seek the Lord, and I think to-morrow will be the best day.' Cromwell ends by pressing the agitators to join the prayer-meeting. 'Itt remains only for God to show us the way.'

Throughout the debates, it will be seen, Cromwell shows a hard grasp of the facts; he argues, he rants, with the best of them, and he pounces, like a pike, on the bare essentials, heading the dispute firmly towards his objective, a compromise that will keep the army solid behind him.

On October 29th the meeting opened at 8 o'clock, and they continued in prayer until eleven, Goffe testifying to them out of the Book of Revelations.[1] That evening there was again a long discussion on manhood suffrage, the Levellers maintaining that all inhabitants who had not 'lost their birthright' should have an equal voice in elections. Sexby argued hotly 'we have engaged in this kingdom and ventured our lives, and it was all for this, to recover our Birthrights and privileges as Englishmen . . . there are many thousands of us soldiers that have ventured our lives; we have had little propriety in the kingdom, yet we have had a Birthright. If we had not a right in the kingdom we were mere mercinarie soldiers . . . I am resolved

---

[1] It was also the habit of the Council to seek inspiration from outside sources. 'On October 7th they had given audience to a High German who pretended to be a prophet and would prescribe a way for a lasting peace.' At Whitehall December 29th, 1648, on the eve of the murder of the king, Elizabeth Poole of Abingdon testified before them 'that God was about to break the pottsheards of the earth, and declared the presence of God with the army'. Thus mediaeval practice persisted outside mediaeval discipline. C.P., vol. II, pp. 150-1.

to give my Birthright to none, whatsoever may come in the way, I
will give it to none . . . I do think the poore and meane of this kingdom have been the means of the preservation of this kingdom, and
their lives have not beene deare for purchasing the good of the
kingdom.'

Rainborough, raising both major issues, asserted the right of
participation of all in the choice of the government and the right to
renounce obligations. 'The poorest hee that is in England hath a
life to live as the greatest hee; and trulie, sir, I thinke its cleare that
every man that is to live under a government ought first by his own
consent to put himself under that government. And I doe thinke
that the poorest man that is in England is not at all bound in a strict
sense to that he hath not had a voice to put himself under . . . I
should doubt whether he is an Englishman or no that should doubt
of these thinges.'

But Ireton denies both principles, so subversive to property and
administrative order. 'It denies all Civil Right . . . a man must
have a permanent fixed interest in the Kingdom . . . That by a mans
being born here he shall have a share in that power that shall dispose
of the lands here, I doe not think it is sufficient ground.' As to the
second point, the laws are binding on all, whether or not they have
a voice in choosing the government; if men object to the laws they
can emigrate. 'If a man means by a birthright whatsoever he can
challenge by the law of nature . . . there is noe foundation for any
man to enjoy anything.'[1] For the poor to subvert the social order
would be 'to make a public disturbance upon a private prejudice'.[2]

At this point Cromwell weighed in to support him and to head
back the debate into some conclusion. He objects to Sexby's argument 'because it savours so much of Will . . . Lett us not spend so
much time in such debates as these are, but lett us apply ourselves
to such things as are conclusive'. All are agreed that 'the Representative might be amended', but 'I have not heard the Commissary
General (Ireton) answered, not in a part to my knowledge, not in a
tittle'.[3] If they cannot agree, and the extremists press their views,
he will 'withdrawe from the Army' and leave them to it. Rueful
apologies followed all round.

In conclusion the discussion turned on the terms of agreement
with the king, the Heads of Proposals[4] being compared with the

[1] *C.P.*, 325. [2] *C.P.*, ib. [3] *C.P.*, vol. I, pp. 328-32
[4] Heads of Proposals to the Army, August 1st, 1647.

Agreement on this question. Here again there was profound disagreement. Wildman insists that the soldiers may speak, not only as soldiers but 'as Englishmen they have as much right as any commoner' to express themselves. By the Proposals 'the Foundation of slavery is revetted more strongly than before'; the Agreement 'lays down the foundations of freedom for all manners of people'; the Proposals, with the negative voice left to the king, will enable the king's judges to 'Hang them all upp for what they did in the Warre'.[1]

Such were the fundamental and explosive ideas canvassed at the Putney debates, but the result of these and other meetings was a measure of compromise which left the conduct of policy in the hands of the Generals. The second Civil War put an end to such discussions, and the army held together out of common interest, through Cromwell's adroit management and apt use of force. His use of the prayer-meeting as a method of reconciliation was very effective.

The conflict of interest and political ideas between the landowning classes and the radicals displayed in the Putney debates is paralleled and amplified in many similar discussions and in a vast pamphlet literature. The best known theoretical exponent of Leveller opinion is John Lilburne,[2] whose stormy career and widespread popularity left its mark on seventeenth-century politics.

Meanwhile, besides the politically radical ideas canvassed by the Levellers, communist doctrines were in the air, though the direct attack on property itself was never formidable. The Diggers, whose communistic theories are expressed in the writings of Winstanley, have since received more attention than they commanded in their own day: their ideas, like the trickle of sand that marks the first shift of a landslide, represent a movement later to become far more powerful.

Winstanley[3] cannot be termed a statesmanlike writer, and the merits of his style have been exaggerated. He possessed, indeed, a

---

[1] *C.P.*, vol. I, p. 353.

[2] See his *The Work of the Beast*; *Jonah's Cry out of the Whale's Belly*; *Truth Justified*; etc. etc. See also, WOLFE, *Leveller Manifesto's of the Puritan Revolution*, Nelson (1946).

[3] G. Winstanley, born at Wigan 1609. He became a merchant tailor, but went out of business in 1640, when he 'left off trading by reason of the badness of the times . . . I was beaten', he says, 'out of estate and trade'. In 1648 took up with Everard, a well-known agitator, and like those of other broken men of his age, his thoughts ran on social reform. See his *A Watchword to the city of London and the Army* (1649), and EVERARD's *The True Leveller's Standard advanced, or The State of Community opened and presented to the Sons of Men*, of the same year. For a modern selection from his works, see *Selections from the writings of Gerard Winstanley*, edited HAMILTON, Cresset Press (1944).

fanatical zeal, but the fine phrases which occasionally redeem the wastes of a turgid rhetoric do not raise his writings to the level of the average run of seventeenth-century prose. It is difficult to see how any one familiar with the trenchant and pithy idiom of the time, can rate Winstanley's style very high in an age with such a standard of English. But he squarely defined important principles in a homely manner, principles later at the heart of communist doctrine.

Since he denied the doctrine of the Resurrection, Winstanley can hardly be described as a Christian communist; rather he was a Deist, who equated God with Reason, and believed in the manifestation of the Divine Spirit in nature. His mind combines the backwash of mediaeval heresies with anticipations of eighteenth-century rationalism, for he was afflicted with the old Manichaean dualism, attributing evil to natural instinct. He explained the ills of society by 'human flesh delighting in the objects of creation'; through this pride of life, resulting in 'selfish imagination', man had fallen into 'bondage of his own kind'.

'In the beginning of Time', he writes, 'the great Creator, Reason, made the Earth a common treasury, to preserve beasts, birds, fishes and Man, the lord that was to govern Creation . . . but not one word was spoken in the beginning that one branch of Mankind should rule another.'[1] For this idea Winstanley claimed Divine inspiration: 'The voice that hath made the Earth a common Treasury was showed us by voice in trance . . . "Work together; eat bread together; declare all abroad", . . . which voice was heard three times.'[2]

He further anticipates later communist theory by declaring that a 'A people thus united by common community into oneness' will become 'the strongest land in the world'.

Like other enthusiasts, he had been disillusioned by the outcome of the Puritan revolution: Oliver, for all his promises, had substituted one tyranny for another, outraging the liberties of England violated at the Conquest, 'reinforcing the yoke of the Norman *Colonels*'. He denounced, after the manner of his time, the 'Adams of the Earth' and the 'Pharaohs' who exploited the sufferings of the poor, but of the realities of government he had no sense. For all the subsequent importance of the ideas he defined, a study of his works, of which the above extracts are representative, does not invalidate the judgement of the soldiers sent to deal with him, who refused to take him

[1] HAMILTON, op. cit., p. 37.   [2] Op. cit., p. 41.

or his following seriously. His experiment on 'George's Hill' — Winstanley refused to use the term 'Saint' — ended in liquidation by the local freeholders, and the restoration of order by the military.[1]

The rift in the front of the propertied classes was, indeed, soon closed, first by the Protectorate, later by the Restoration. The period of licence had been brief, but the Levellers, in particular, had their day: they expressed fully, for the first time in England, the interest of the poor. Their demands, premature in the seventeenth century, were destined to return with greater power.

Meanwhile, to put conscience before obligation, to defy the law if God should reveal himself, to appeal to abstract natural right, was to run headlong against the predominant and gradualist tradition of English politics. To extend the franchise without property qualification was a revolutionary project in that day; the moderate Independents, the great majority, hastened to disown it.

Such, then, were the ideas and the circumstances of the Leveller and Digger movements. Were they simply another and more articulate protest against the conservative order, similar in kind to the Peasants' Revolt and to the popular movements on the Continent in the sixteenth and seventeenth centuries and destined to the same fate? Yet another ineffective protest against exploitation, the men anxious only for equality before the law, for some voice in the conduct of affairs, deluded and exploited by fanatical or self-seeking demagogues? There is truth in this interpretation of events, but not the whole truth. The Puritan revolution, indeed, let loose much wild speculation; the intense individualism of Hobbes is apparent in the ideas of his opponents, and this individualism, inflamed by religious strife, could lead only to anarchy. 'I tremble

---

[1] See the account of the officer concerned, doubtless representative of public opinion. 'Information of Henry Sanders: "That on Sunday sennight last there was one Everard, once of the army but now cashiered, who termeth himself a prophett, one Stewer and Colton, and two more, all living att Cobham, came to St. George's Hill in Surrey and began to dig that side of the hill next to Camp Close, and sowed the ground with parsenipps, and carrettes and beanes. On the Munday following they were there again, being increased in their number, and the next day being Tuesday they fired the heath . . . which is a very great prejudice to the town . . . They invite all to come and help them . . . Itt is feared they have some designe in hand." Later, Captain Gladman wrote to Fairfax, "According to your order I marched towards St. George's Hill . . . I cannot heare that there hath beene above twenty of them together since they first undertook this businesse. Mr. Winstanly and Mr. Everard have engaged to be with you this day; I believe you will bee glad to bee rid of them again, espeshially Everard who is no other than a madd man . . . Indeed, the businesse is not worth the writing nor yet taking nottis of; I wonder the Council of State should be so abused with informations. Jo Gladman, Kingston, April 19th, 1649".' *Clarke Papers*, vol. II, pp. 209-12.

at the boundless and endless consequences of it',[1] said Ireton, and he was right. Yet the mere fact of discussion was a portent, premature perhaps, but significant. Radical thought, though haunted with the individualism of its seventeenth-century origin, attempts to include the common people in the process of government; it indirectly foreshadows the view that government ought not to dictate opinion, but hold the ring for the free play of vigorous private and religious organizations within the State. On this view, the decisions of government, though in detail an administrative matter, should in principle reflect the emergent will of the community. That community in Leveller thought, is extended throughout the nation, and though driven underground and politically powerless for generations, the tradition continued and flourished in the Puritan settlements in America and revived in England at the close of the eighteenth century. Radical democracy in Stuart England could not be practical politics; Cromwell who could feel the pulse of opinion, knew that the nation would not 'go along with it'; but the proletariat was beginning to stir, and the Civil Wars mark a rehearsal of political ideas which were to become formidable and dominant after the Industrial Revolution in the nineteenth and twentieth centuries.

Meanwhile the gain brought about by the Cromwellian age was first that the threat of Absolutism on the Continental model was averted; second that the position of the monarchy when it returned reflected the shift of economic power, in the main to the families founded in the Elizabethan age; third that the threat of Presbyterian tyranny was destroyed and that a habit of free speech and writing became gradually accepted.

This last benefit was caused by the native vigour of a free and brilliant culture, reaping the full harvest of assimilated Renaissance learning. It was impossible to suppress a people who could produce within fifty years the bulk of Shakespeare's plays, the verse of Campion and Herrick, the Authorized Version of the Bible, Bacon's Essays and the Sermons of Donne: from the gossip of Aubrey to the splendours of *Paradise Lost*, the seventeenth century set its distinctive seal on the literature of a great age.

[1] Quoted by A. D. LINDSAY, *The Essentials of Democracy*, O.U.P. (1929), q.v. for a profound analysis of Leveller ideas and of the nature of Democratic Government. See particularly the introduction to the second edition.

No man did more for the cause of intellectual freedom than John Milton, whose political writings, in their outlook and limitations, may be taken as representative of educated Puritanism. His vindication of intellectual liberty is the most permanent contribution to the pamphlet literature of the Civil Wars; the famous *Areopagitica*[1] asserts values fundamental to the European tradition. His purely political writings are full of the dust of controversy. The *Tenure of Kings and Magistrates*[2] is a defence of tyrannicide on traditional lines, reinforced by Calvinist doctrine; it concludes with an attack on the Presbyterian clergy. Here Milton shows the disillusionment and bitterness natural to a visionary of acrid genius, immersed in the politics of a revolution. The work is of interest both for the force of its language and for its appeal to mediaeval tradition. A third notable work of political theory, *The Ready and Easy Way to Establish a Free Commonwealth*, was written amid the break-up of the Cromwellian Commonwealth, the ruin of Milton's hopes.[3] It is a constructive but academic programme of reform, designed to appeal away from the political stampede of the coming Restoration to good men in the future who may revive the tradition of 'Liberty'. Milton's hatred of the mob and his impatience with the realities of politics are apparent in this short and interesting work. He is left, a great and tragic figure, amid the wreckage of the Commonwealth.

The *Areopagitica* opens with an appeal to the Long Parliament to abandon the censorship on books, expressed in fulsome seventeenth-century terms. Milton exhorts Members to 'show their greatness by allowing intellectual liberty, to imitate the old and elegant humanity of Greece, rather than the barbaric pride of Hunnish and Norwegian stateliness'. Actually he argues, censorship is impracticable; all it can do is 'to hinder and crop' further discoveries in 'religious and civil wisdom'. It has a bad pedigree, coming down from the Roman Catholic Church, directly copied by the Anglican bishops from Rome. 'God and nature allow liberty, and virtue cannot be forced.' If censorship of opinion be imposed it must extend over all sides of life, over 'lutes, violins and guitars', over 'household gluttony', over

---

[1] *Areopagitica*: a speech for the liberty of unlicensed printing to the Parliament of England. See *Milton's Prose Works*, pp. 103-19, edited FLETCHER, Westley & Davis (1834).
[2] *Of the Tenure of Kings and Magistrates* (published 1649), pp. 232-46, op. cit.
[3] *The Ready and Easy Way to Establish a Free Commonwealth*, pp. 442-52, op. cit.

'garments', over 'mixed conversations' '. . . these things will be and must be, but how they shall be least hurtful, how least enticing, herein consists the grave and governing wisdom of a state'.

Further, men are naturally endowed with intellectual freedom and to destroy it is to subvert the purpose of God. He who destroys a good book 'kills reason itself . . . a good book is the precious life blood of a master spirit embalmed and treasured up on purpose to a life beyond life'. Opinion is knowledge in the making, and nowhere is freedom of thought more valuable than in England, where God reveals himself 'as his manner is, first to his Englishmen'. Beleaguered London is a hive of intellectual activity; England is rising to her true greatness before the challenge of war. 'Methinks', he writes, in a famous passage, 'I see in my mind a noble and puissant nation, rousing herself like a strong man after sleep, and shaking her invincible locks: methinks I see her as an eagle mewing her mighty youth, and kindling her undazzled eyes at the full midday beam, purging and unscaling her long abused sight at the fountain itself of Heavenly radiance, while the whole noise of timorous and flocking birds with those also that love the twilight, flutter about, amazed at what she means.' Let the Parliament but give Truth a fair field; she will hold her own. 'Let her and falsehood grapple; who ever knew Truth put to the worse in a free and open encounter?' A 'gross conforming stupidity' will never discover truth. Milton's conception of knowledge is progressive; diversity of opinion sharpens truth, which is often manifested through strange channels. He concludes that printing ought not to be confined to a small circle of licensed printers, but that liberty to publish should be accorded if the name of the printer be registered; mischievous and libellous books can be dealt with by fire and the executioner.

The *Areopagitica* strikes the authentic note of bold seventeenth-century thought: though passionately concerned with religious issues, Milton falls into line with the great minds of his century, with Descartes, with Spinoza, with Locke. Here is a permanent contribution to the European tradition, transcending the religious controversies which were its occasion.

The Tenure of Kings and Magistrates, published in 1649, was written in part to justify tyrannicide. It opens with a disillusioned statement 'that since the majority of men are slaves within doors', blinded by customs and passion, impervious to reason and 'naturally servile . . . Tyrants particularly loathe men of virtue and true worth'.

Having appeared patriots, though actuated in truth by their own grievances, they have clamoured for extreme measures but drawn back, leaving just men in the lurch. 'It is true', further, 'that most men are apt enough to civil wars and commotions as a novelty',[1] but leave reconstruction 'to be laboured out amidst the throng of vulgar and irrational men'. They quibble over 'privileges, customs, forms and that old entanglement of iniquity, their gibberish laws'. Milton complains of their 'levity and shallowness of mind, their carnal admiring of worldly pomp'. Here is a devastating and understandable impatience with the instinctive loyalty, the customary ritual, the normal ideology on which society must depend.

There follows a savage attack on 'apostate scarecrows and dancing divines'. Milton inveighs, with singular lack of humanity, against preserving the 'mere useless bulk' of the king's person, and proceeds to an account of the origins of tyranny, 'fetched out of the midst of choicest and most authentic learning, and no prohibited authors, nor many Heathen, but Mosaical, Christian, orthodoxal . . .' All men naturally were born free until Adam's transgression, then, falling into violence and 'foreseeing that such courses must tend to the destruction of them all', they entered into a contract, the foundation of civilized life. Kings and magistrates thus originally disposed of a delegated power; when they abused it they were bound by oaths and bridled by Councillors and Parliaments. Their power is only derivative from the people, from whom it cannot be taken 'without a violation of their natural birthright'. Milton develops the orthodox mediaeval argument, quoting Aristotle, that 'monarchy unaccountable is the worse sort of tyranny and the least to be endured by freeborne men'. Hereditary title is not enough, for the king to claim responsibility only to God subverts all government. He embarks on an account of tyrannicide in classical times and in the Old Testament. Tyrants have ever been the enemies of the Church — Jesus called Herod 'that Fox'. A tyrant is a 'common pest'; he cites Knox's opinion that subjects ought to execute God's judgements upon their king, quoting the example of Jehu. Further, the Scots deposed Queen Mary; the Dutch, Philip of Spain; and having 'hunted and pursued' the king about the kingdom with fire and sword, it is hypocrisy to shrink from killing him. He quotes examples of the treachery of rulers, of the Emperor Maximilian at Bruges; of Charles IX and the massacre at Paris; finally, he marshals the

[1] Op cit., pp. 231-46.

authority of Luther, of Zwingli, of Calvin, of English Puritan writers, quoting their denunciations of tyranny, attacking 'greedy church wolves' who 'feed on pluralities, advowsons' and 'the hot scent of double livings'. The significance of this tract is twofold: first it shows Milton's impatience with the common man, and his uncompromising rigidity of mind; second it shows how closely the Calvinist tradition was bound up with mediaeval thought, and transmitted some of its most valuable legacies.[1]

The other pamphlet is more constructive but equally academic. Milton begins *The Ready and Easy Way to Establish a Free Commonwealth* with the hope that 'before so long a Lent of servitude, a little shroving may be permitted wherein to speak freely and take our leaves of liberty'. After the achievements of the Commonwealth, it would be 'a miserable thing to creep back so poorly, as it seems the multitude would, to their detested thralldom of Kingship'. This would be to have built a tower of Babel and bring upon England 'the common laughter of Europe'. A Restoration would bring back a dissolute and haughty Court, expense and luxury, masks and revels, 'debauches of our prime gentry both male and female'; further, there will be a Queen 'of no less charge: in most likelihood outlandish and a Papist'.

He compares a kingdom unfavourably with the community of industrious ants, 'who set example to imprudent and ungoverned men of a frugal self governing democracy or commonwealth'. Running on for some time in this unsympathetic vein, displaying the censorious and gloomy outlook which made the Puritans so detested and which was one of the major causes of their political failure, Milton proceeds to outline his constructive proposals for a society under which a man 'may serve God and save his own soul'.

First, there should be a general Council of the ablest men, chosen by the people: this Grand Council will possess a delegated sovereignty 'committed to them for the preservation of common peace and liberty'. This Council, like Plato's Nocturnal Council, 'will be perpetual since it is the main pillar of the whole state and to remove pillars . . . cannot be safe for the building'. He objects even to a changing of one-third of the senators by partial rotation yearly, and concludes that they ought to be removed only by death or by conviction of crime. He quotes precedents from the Jewish Sanhedrin, the Spartan Ancients, the Roman Senate, and the Venetian oli-

[1] *Vide supra*, p. 282.

garchy; Englishmen, he suggests, are naturally fickle, owing to their watery situation, and they ought to correct this defect. To prevent mistrust of the 'chosen patriots' of the Council, assemblies should be held in the chief towns of every county; this would have the advantage also 'of annihilating the odious power and name of committees'. These Assemblies would be recruited by rotation. This form of Government, centred on the Grand Council, Milton hopes would continue prosperously until the second coming of Christ.

It is a 'plain easy and straitforward way', he says: it does not attack property and implies no exotic ideas. Strangely enough, Milton, with all his political experience, regarded the attainment of this rigid constitution with no organic roots in the country, as an easy project. Such a 'free' commonwealth, he continues, would allow liberty of conscience, confident of its own 'fair proceedings'. The alternative, he argues, is the re-establishment of the Church of England and the suppression of the Presbyterians and Independents.

Advancement according to merit, too, he maintains, will be provided by such a commonwealth; this is best obtained by a vigorous regional life in every county. Subordinate commonwealths, local nobility and gentry and men of substance will conduct local government, including the execution of justice by elected judges without appeal in matters of civil law. These local assemblies will be in touch with the Grand Council and subordinate to it; Milton it seems, is suggesting a form of Federal Government. In addition, a vigorous local education should be developed, 'not in grammar only, but in all Liberal Arts and exercises'; this would revitalize the whole nation, 'communicating the natural heat of government and culture to all extreme parts which now lie numb and neglected'. Thus would be achieved a high-spirited, free, and prosperous nation, composed of 'many commonwealths under one united and trusted sovereignty'.

In conclusion, he insists that the way out is clear. The populace argue that a Restoration will revive trade, not remembering that under Kingship plague infested the city, 'such as through God's mercy we have never felt since'. Trade too flourishes best in the free cities of Italy, of Germany, of Holland. In any case we cannot sacrifice our religion, liberties and honour to 'keep up trading'.

Milton finally forewarns his countrymen that what he has spoken is the language of the 'good old cause'; it may be the last words of our expiring liberty. He still hopes the country may 'stay these ruinous proceedings, justly and timely fearing to what a precipice of destruction the deluge of this epidemic madness would hurry us, through the general defection of a misguided and abused multitude'.

Here is a detailed but impracticable programme of reform, destined to failure, since out of harmony with the political and economic forces of the day. The aristocracy of character and intellect through which the poet would govern would be hard to come by, but naturally Milton was loyal to his own kind. He was, after all, a creative genius of the first order, one of the outstanding minds of his own or indeed of any age. The energy behind his writings is apparent in the volume of his prose works, in the untiring vigour with which he manipulates the complexity of his Latinized style. The depth and range of his scholarship marks the full assimilation of Renaissance and Patristic learning. Milton was indeed a man of the mature Renaissance, but here is no balanced humanism; he is deeply and savagely fanatical, steeped in the controversial literature of his age. The seventeenth century was a period of intense ideological warfare, the venom and fury of religious strife here overcomes the humanistic tradition.

Not since the patristic age had the volume and the ferocity of religious controversy reached such formidable proportions; the memories of '88, of the massacre of Paris, of the Gunpowder Plot, the martyrdoms inflicted on Jesuits and Protestant alike, the intolerance, the century-old tale of wrong and persecution, obsessed the minds of even the ablest men. The generation which saw the Civil Wars were the children and the grandchildren of Elizabethans and they had about them something of the Elizabethan violence and extremity. Life, moreover, was a hard struggle for property and preferment; only the most tenacious foresight and contrivance could hope to build up the accumulation of land and treasure which was the goal of contemporary ambition. The level of education was high, the discipline of legal learning widespread; the Stuarts found the English Puritans tough opponents and in the arena of political controversy no quarter was asked or expected. The style of their writing was oratorical, as might be expected of an age so critical and so appreciative of extempory sermons and spectacular speeches from the scaffold; they were trained and brought up on oratory. When Milton descends into the political arena, coming down like Dante 'into the ring', he uses all the violence, all the ferocity, characteristic of his age. In this sense he is one of the last of the Elizabethans, his style so different from the hard-hitting lucidity of Dryden and Halifax, in the second half of the century. For all his genius of thought and expression, his political judgement is warped by the circumstances of his age; it lacks the objectivity of statesmanship. Like Dante, Milton was passionately partisan. His constructive proposals, like those of Plato, are those of an intellectual who would see government in the hands of an oligarchy of just men, but of one who cares passionately for intellectual freedom. It is here, on his own ground, his greatness appears, the trammels of political strife sloughed off and his mind soaring into the world of permanent values native to it. The controversies of the age had cramped Renaissance intellectual enterprise and judgement, yet Milton at his greatest could rise above the rage of controversy and make his contribution to the cause of intellectual freedom. And, indeed, it was this increasing intellectual range, this deep assimilation of a civilized inheritance harking back to antiquity, which was to determine to a great extent the political progress of the seventeenth century in the most dynamic states of the age.

For the freedom Milton defends implied a religious toleration he could never compass, a moderation in politics which the Puritans — both the Levellers at one extreme and Milton at the other — could never display. Yet, after 1660 and 1688, Protestant England with all its widening influence in the world, turned to the statesman-like Whig interpretation of that tradition of mediaeval freedom and sense of disciplined power, of community and the rule of Law, which, abroad in jeopardy before the rise of the Absolute State, was to find so lucid and so powerful a vindication in the writings of John Locke. It is this second and predominant stream of English political thought which now demands our investigation.

CHAPTER VI

THE WHIG TRADITION: HOOKER: LOCKE: HALIFAX

§ I

THE Protestant tradition of spiritual independence, expressed in the radical doctrines of Puritanism, was destined to a great future, but the immediately most powerful expression of English political genius, better able to cope with the realities of politics at that time, is found in the Whig assertion of the supremacy of Law and the rights of property; of government's responsibility to the governed. This movement of thought came down from the mediaeval ancestry already described, itself in part a reflection of the best political thought of antiquity. Summing up, as it did, centuries of political evolution, it was reinforced by success, forming a pattern of ideas in harmony with the most powerful economic tendencies of the day. Whig doctrine, politically mature, yet up to date in its age, was strong enough to challenge the predominant power of dynastic absolutism, the logical expression of the thought of Bodin and Hobbes. Its strength lay in a close reflection of the practical sagacity of the time, combined with a growing humanitarian common sense and a growing intellectual toleration. Shorn of metaphysical abstractions, limited perhaps in consequence, it was able to grapple with the close tangle of immediate business, with the massive problems of political life. In due course, Whiggism was both to be reinterpreted on a cosmopolitan and more abstract scale, and broadened by revived radical influences. Throughout, moderation was its keynote, for after the Revolution of 1688 England returned to an older tradition of religious and political compromise. The threat of absolutism had been destroyed, and after the settlement, the Crown was financially in the hands of Parliament. The Commonwealth and Protectorate had demonstrated that the rule of the sword had never reflected the political instinct of the nation. In political theory also, continuity was never broken; Locke, who voices the outlook of the classes dominant in 1688, reflects closely the ideas of Hooker, who wrote in the closing years of Elizabeth and who was deeply influenced by mediaeval thought.

z   353

At the Restoration the wind had seemed set fair for the Stuart dynasty, but James II thought the game not worth his convictions; his fall cleared the way for the English assertion of political and commercial power in the reign of Anne. By the first decade of the eighteenth century, England had preserved her liberties and asserted her economic, maritime, and commercial power; the tough oligarchy of the 'Glorious Revolution' had led the country to a position of unprecedented influence in Europe. In face of this prestige and the political and intellectual liberty that went with it, Continental thinkers began to conceive an admiration for English political thought and institutions, and the influence of Locke profoundly affected the development of French and American thought and practice.

Thus English political development never lost its continuity: the tradition of John of Salisbury, Bracton and Fortescue, and indeed of Anglo-Saxon and Scandinavian good sense, had carried on unbroken and unimpaired.

Three great political thinkers reflect this steady unfolding of thought and power. First, the 'judicious' Hooker, born near Exeter[1] in 1553, a man of peace, the master of a lucid and orderly prose, whose *Ecclesiastical Polity* remains one of the classics of the English tongue. An exponent of reason and compromise, he translated the high foreign Thomist doctrine of Divine order and Natural Law into homely terms. Next, John Locke turned the force of a great philosophical intellect 'to justify to the world the people of England', to work out a closely reasoned argument which combined the utilitarian sanction for government with the traditional assertion of popular rights and Natural Law. Locke, who believed in human nature, who assumed a vital and enterprising society for which government should be a 'hedge', who, in contrast to Hobbes, thinks well enough of men to advocate free speech and ordered liberty — Locke, so up to date in his age, with his interest in economic affairs, the defender of property, the prophet of toleration — he makes a striking contrast to Richelieu, with his dislike of the commercial interest, his aristocratic disdain for financiers, and his censorship of speculation.

Finally, Halifax represents the dynamic leadership which made all

---

[1] It is notable how large a contribution the West of England has made to English political thought. Hooker, Bracton, and Fortescue from Devon; Hobbes and John of Salisbury from Wiltshire; Locke from Somerset.

this success possible; he is one of the most brilliant of politicians and expresses the racy good sense of his age. His maxims of state policy, so pithy, so modern, strike deep to the foundations of political practice in all times. He reflects the hard-hitting realism of the generation which had grown up under the shadow of the Civil Wars, who had known outlawry, and transportation, their patriotism sharpened by the sad expedients of indigence and exile. When Halifax and his like took over the helm in 1688, they knew the tricks of the game, and the English state, like one of the Great East India-men of the age, with sails set and ensigns billowing from peak and stern, turned to run before the steady trade wind of the eighteenth century, pitching into the blue seas of a new greatness, of an imperial future.

§ 11

Hooker's[1] *Of the Laws of Ecclesiastical Polity* sets out to defend the Elizabethan religious settlement against extremists of both camps. In particular against the Puritans who appealed to biblical authority

[1] Richard Hooker. Born at Heavytree near Exeter, 1553, of yeoman stock. As a child, says Walton, Hooker was 'quietly inquisitive', 'a little wonder'. Through the good offices of his uncle and of Dr. Jewell, Bishop of Salisbury, he was sent to Oxford. Walton tells a pleasant story of how Jewell lent the boy his own staff, which he had himself used in Germany in his youth. Hooker was making a journey on foot from Oxford to Exeter, 'to satisfy and see his good mother, being accompanied by a country-man and companion of his own college . . . so on foot they went and took Salisbury on their way, purposing to see the good bishop'. It is all in a good old tradition, coming down unbroken from the days of Bede. In 1573 Hooker was elected a founda-tion scholar to Corpus Christi, Oxford, and in 1577 became a fellow of the college.

In 1584, he was presented to the living of Drayton Beauchamp near Aylesbury, and was made Master of the Temple in March 1585, through the influence of Arch-bishop Sandys. He became involved in the religious strife of the day and designed the *Ecclesiastical Polity* as an answer to a rival whom he had displaced. But Hooker disliked controversy, being of a retiring and peaceful disposition. 'I am weary', he wrote, 'of the noise and opposition of this place', and in 1591 he took the living in Wiltshire where he settled down to compose four of the eight projected books of the *Ecclesiastical Polity*. 'About this time the parsonage and rectory of Boscum in the diocese of Sarum, and six miles from that city, became void.' Boscombe carried with it a minor prebend of Salisbury Cathedral, Netheravon, five miles north of Amesbury. At Boscombe, with its tiny church, in which the sixteenth-century pulpit and wood-work are yet intact, on the edge of the Salisbury Plain, where he could 'see God's bounty spring from the earth and be free from noise', he settled down to write 'a treatise in which I intend a justification of our Laws of Ecclesiastical Polity'. In the next three years he finished the first four books of his work, which were published in 1594. In 1595 he was presented to the substantial living of Bishopsbourne in Kent, three miles from Canterbury, and his fifth book appeared in 1597. His reputation was considerable in his lifetime, and his lucid exposition of Natural Law, translated into Latin, was admired in Rome. He remained modest and obscure. 'His poor parish

and their own conscience against Church and State. It is a long book in six volumes, but Hooker's contribution to political theory is mainly contained in the first. He is concerned, he says, to examine the foundations of government, and to set the Church in the general frame.

Hooker attempts to reconcile the Thomist theory of Eternal and Natural Law, of a God-given social order, with the demands of utility and common sense. He expresses the sober Anglican outlook; there is nothing disconcerting or violent about him. The 'admirable child', the 'little wonder', had grown into a simple and kindly man with a fine sense of proportion and a rare clarity of expression. He translated the mediaeval tradition into a form congenial to English minds, and his work achieved widespread and immediate popularity.

Government, he says, is a hard business; men do not realize the 'secret lets and difficulties which in public proceedings are innumerable';[1] they notice the 'stateliness of houses and the goodliness of trees', not the foundations and the roots. He therefore sets out to explain the foundations of government, as a preliminary to the main argument of his book, which is concerned with 'that politic society which is the Church'.

Behind the whole cosmic order is Eternal Law, 'the admirable frame' from which 'shinest in perfect beauty the countenance of God.' Man apprehends Eternal Law through Natural Law, the 'participation of the rational creature in the Divine'. 'Obedience of creatures to the Law of nature' is 'the stay of the whole world'.[2] Such law is obligatory to all men:[3] 'the laws which have been hitherto mentioned do bind men absolutely as they are men, although they never have any settled fellowship, nor any engagement among them-

---

[1] Chap. i, Concerning laws and their several kinds in general.
[2] I, iii, 2.
[3] For an anticipation, in the clumsy and vigorous English of the fifteenth century, of Hooker's defence of Natural Law, see BISHOP PECOCK'S *Repressor of Overmuch Blaming of the Clergy, c.* 1449, written against the Lollard appeal to Biblical authority. (Rolls Series, 1860. Edited Babington. Vol. I, part I in particular.)

---

clerk and he did never talk but with both their hats on or both off at the same time.' He was short-sighted 'and where he fixed his eyes at the beginning of his sermon, there they continued till it was ended'. He died comparatively young in 1600, leaving a tolerable fortune, the great part of it being in books. Hooker's mild tenacity and self-effacement is typical of a sound Anglican tradition.

A complete edition of his works was edited by KEBLE, O.U.P. (1836). The Preface to the *Laws of Ecclesiastical Polity* is particularly revealing of Hooker's attitude to the Puritans, whose doctrines he designed to confute.

selves what to do or not to do'.[1] Natural Law exists in its own right as the reflection of God's eternal law. Hooker here adopts the ordinary Thomist position.

How, then, has government come about? It is a convenience, the price of civilized society: 'all public regiment seemeth to have arisen from deliberate advice, consultation and composition among men . . . finding it convenient and behoveful, there being no impossibility in nature considered by itself but that men might have lived without any public regiment'.[2] The words 'convenient' and 'behoveful' are significant; Hooker had St. Thomas's theory behind him, but he has Locke's desire for well ordered living; the fierce ascetic vision of a Hildebrand or a Dante, the Roman splendours of Innocent III, make no appeal to him: he goes for the ordinary, the seemly, the simple interpretation.

'Howbeit', he continues, 'the corruption of our nature being pre-supposed, we may not deny but that the law of nature doth now require of necessity some kind of regiment, so that to bring things unto the first course they were in, and utterly to take away all kinds of public government in the world, were apparently to overturn the whole world.'[3]

Natural rights cannot therefore justify anti-social behaviour. To avoid penury we must have 'implements' and 'arts mechanical discovered in the very prime of the world'; similarly, a life 'fit for the dignity of man' needs ordered society. 'We all make complaint of the iniquity of the times, not unjustly for the days are evil', but before 'public regiment' there were 'not above eight persons righteous living upon the face of the earth'.

There are thus 'two foundations . . . that bear up public society': the first is natural inclination, 'whereby all men desire social life and fellowship', the other 'an order . . . agreed upon touching the manner of their union'. This order must assume the worst. 'Laws politic are never framed as they should be unless presuming the will of man . . . to be obstinate, rebellious and averse from all obedience . . .'; they must direct 'nature depraved to a right end'. The form of Government may vary: 'the kinds thereof being many, nature tieth not to any one, but leaveth the choice as a thing arbitrary', but 'the

---

[1] I, x. Compare Pecock, 'Doom of Natural Reason which is clept Moral Lawe of Kinde, and not Holi Scripture, is the ground of the said governaunce . . .' etc., and that 'a man should love himself and his neighbour as himself, though not [sic] so miche as himself'. Op. cit., Part I, cap. II.
[2] I, x, 5.　　　　　　　　　　[3] ib.

case of man's nature standing as it now doth, some kind of regiment the law of nature doth now require'.[1] Humanity needs and demands government.

Hooker, then, puts men into society by natural agreement, for the betterment of man's estate; since the Fall, Natural Law is not enough. But society is only the fulfilment of Natural Law in the prevalent conditions in the world; human law reflects Natural Law, which in turn is the reflection of a Divine reality. Against this background 'Somewhat over and beside', the laws of nature and reason is further necessary, 'namely human and positive law, together with that law which is of commerce between grand societies, the law of nations and of nations Christian'.

Hooker held the mediaeval Aristotelian view of the importance of the community, the commonwealth. He quotes the time-honoured definition of a tyrant: 'Power belongs not to any one individual but to the community under the law.' 'By the natural law, where unto He (God) hath made all men subject . . . the power of making laws to command whole political societies of men belongeth so properly unto the *entire society* that for any prince to exercise the same of himself, and not rather by express commission immediately and personally received from God, or else by authority derived at the first from their consent upon whose persons they impose laws, it is no better than a mere tyranny.' Quoting Bracton, he concludes: 'Laws they are not therefore, which public approbation hath not made so.'[2]

On this manner, though he makes a compromise in the matter of the prince 'personally' commissioned by God, Hooker states the mediaeval doctrine of the supremacy of the commonwealth. He anticipates Locke's conclusion that governments derive their authority from their subjects' consent. Laws are devised by 'wise men', but they are sanctioned by the whole community. 'Lex fecit regem', he asserts; our kings have this truth impressed on them in the 'very ceremony of coronation'.

Further, the king exercises a power freely delegated to him by parliament, which is 'even the body of the whole realm'.[3] 'The Parliament of England, together with the convocation annexed thereunto, is that whereupon the very essence of all government within the kingdom doth depend.'[4] The king's authority is 'a power which the whole body of the realm being naturally possessed with,

[1] I, x. 5.   [2] I, x, 7-8.   [3] VIII, vi, 11.   [4] ib.

hath by free and deliberate assent devised unto him that ruleth over them'.[1]

Here again is a clear assertion of the sovereignty of the commonwealth through Parliament, one of the foundations of Locke's thought and, indeed, of the whole English Whig tradition. Hooker had done his work well, and since he wrote about the position of the Church, a problem which held men's minds more closely than any political issue, his views were widely canvassed, discussed, and, since his argument justified the Anglican position, accepted. His contribution to English political thought was extremely important: he put mediaeval social theory into just the simple, ordinary form which appealed to the substantial elements of the country. All was well, all was 'seemly', all was 'convenient', all for the best. The Elizabethan settlement represented the Divine order.

The ugly expedients of government are redeemed by this lucid picture of ordered good sense, and Hooker drives home the argument by a homely simile. Take, he says, the matter of food. By Natural Law, common to beasts, we know food when we see it; 'and the law of reason adds thankfulness'. Next, 'lest appetites should lead on beyond that which is meet', we 'owe obedience to the law of reason which teacheth mediocrity in meats and drinks'. Public law relating to food varies in different countries, but yet reflects these fundamental principles. Finally, 'in the Eucharist, food touches Divine law'. So the self-same thing is reflected through many laws, in the admirable order of the world. All is order, moderation, seemliness; it is very English, very dependable, and Hooker concludes his argument with a paean in praise of law. 'Wherefore, that we may briefly end: of law there can be no less acknowledged, than that her seat is the bosom of God, her voice the harmony of the world; all things in heaven and earth do her homage, both angels and men and creatures of what condition so ever, . . . all with uniform consent admiring . . . the mother of their peace and joy.'[2]

Here is a note of innocent confidence; it harks back to the Anglo-Saxon ideas quoted in an earlier chapter,[3] the vision of reward . . . 'for the happy ones, peace without strife for friends happy in heaven'.

So Hooker's serene vision expressed the good sense, the kindliness, if perhaps the limitation, of the Anglican mind. 'Judicious' he was called; they could not have paid a higher compliment to 'Mr. Hooker, that writ the books of Church polity'.

[1] ib.   [2] I, xviii, 8.   [3] *Vide supra*, Bk. II, chap. i.

In spite, then, of the strident assertions of seventeenth-century radicalism and the uncompromising conservatism of royalist political theory — which, since it had little future, cannot be examined in a work of this scope — the stream of Anglican doctrine still flowed clear and strong in the influential works of Hooker, whose popularity lasted right through the seventeenth century and beyond.

§ III

The political theory inherited by Hooker from the Middle Ages — and the more one studies the forerunners of Hooker the more direct this inheritance appears — was given a more business-like and even more influential interpretation by John Locke, the prophet of the English business Commonwealth, of the rule of law and toleration. Before examining his wide ranging thought, which summed up and modernized the old tradition, it would be well to glance at the social background of his age.

It has been already emphasized that the predominant trend of English development was not towards the sterile glories of monarchical absolutism, or towards radicalism or the rule of the Saints, but towards a new kind of Commonwealth, in which individualism and relative toleration allowed a new outlook to develop. The focus of central government remained firm, but the flexibility of ideas and the lack of bureaucratic control allowed a vigorous intellectual and economic life. Within the framework of the nation state and within its limitations, there developed a new kind of polity, the business commonwealth. The two most successful examples of this state were the British constitutional monarchy and the Dutch republic. In England the phase of centralized power had been efficient and brief: the Tudor dynasty did its work well, and the landowning and commercial interest it fostered soon stopped Charles I and Strafford going the way of Louis XIII, Richelieu, and Mazarin. Henry VIII and Elizabeth, moreover, emancipated the Anglican Church from Rome, while James II's attempt to restore Catholicism resulted in his expulsion. The thread of politico-clerical absolutism in England was thus destroyed and English thinkers of the Age of Reason did not have to reckon with the structure of privilege, clerical influence, and censorship which Voltaire had to attack in France; anti-clericism is not widely apparent in England till the nineteenth century and then in moderation. In the Netherlands the successful struggle against the Spanish domination also allowed a business-like people to achieve a financial and colonizing progress, and made Holland a pioneer of religious toleration and intellectual enterprise.

It was from the political speculation of Locke[1] and the actual working out in England of the principles of toleration and limited monarchy, that the French thinkers of the Enlightenment drew their inspiration. In their turn, they reinterpreted and generalized the more liberal aspects of English thought, so that it was translated from a local into a world influence.

The prosperity of the English and the Dutch was a long-term result of the change of economic scale and the shift of economic power from the Mediterranean to the Atlantic, following the discovery of America, and the development of trade with the East Indies and India.[2] The politics of the nation state had been increasingly decided by trade rivalries rather than by religious and dynastic feuds; for example, in the sixteenth century, the English attacks on the Spanish sea routes coincided with religious and dynastic rivalry, but the Cromwellian wars with the Dutch cut across a common political and religious interest in the pursuit of economic advantage. The effect of the increase of wealth and the growing mercantile influence on government in the two states which were the leaders of European enterprise, made for a growing emphasis on the importance of property and freedom for individual business initiative, which is conspicuously apparent in Locke.

Further, although the Whig advocacy of government with the consent of the governed did not extend far outside the pale of the propertied classes, Locke held the view that government ought to trust its subjects and reflect their interests, and he demanded wide

[1] John Locke. Born at Wrington, in North Somerset, 1632; spent his childhood at Pensford, near Bristol, his father a lawyer of Roundhead sympathies. 1645, went to Westminster School; 1652, proceeded to Christ Church; 1659, Senior Student. In 1666 he began to study medicine, made friends with Boyle, the physicist, and obtained the patronage of Anthony Ashley Cooper, Earl of Shaftesbury. 1672, secretary of Ecclesiastical Presentations to Shaftesbury when he was created Chancellor. 1673, secretary to Board of Trade and Plantations. In 1684 he was exiled owing to his connection with Shaftesbury. Took refuge in Holland. 1689, returned to England, where William III made him Commissioner for Appeals. Settled in Essex. Died 1704. Locke was physically frail, as is apparent from his portraits, but of great intellectual power and tenacity. A member of the Royal Society, 1668. Primarily a philosopher, his political theory is contained in *Two Treatises of Civil Government* and his *Letters on Toleration*. He probably owed a good deal to PHILIP HUNTON'S *Treatise of Monarchy* (1643). For good modern edition see J. W. GOUGH'S volume in Blackwell's Political Texts, 1946.

[2] The best general account of this economic crisis and its effects on political and religious thought is still R. H. TAWNEY'S well-known *Religion and the Rise of Capitalism*, though Professor Tawney goes rather further than more recent authorities in equating 'capitalistic' with 'Puritan' enterprise.

toleration in matters of religion. He combines the traditional mediaeval view held by Hooker that government is a delegated power
responsible to the whole community of the realm, with the new
individualism of the seventeenth century: and his emphasis on
property and the importance of a healthy economic life picks up
and develops the argument foreshadowed by Fortescue.

He voices, indeed, the common sense of an age tired of the conflicting enthusiasms of the English Civil Wars and anxious to be
allowed to reap the harvest of prosperity which stretched out into
the long horizons of the eighteenth century. The colonial expansion
of England, the creation of a modern system of banking, the advent
of a Dutch Protestant king, the rise to full power of the commercial
landowning interest, and the gradual stabilization of party government, all demanded a political theory which should safeguard the
institution of private property and provide a basis of sovereignty
other than that of monarchy by Divine Right. The immediate
occasion of Locke's famous book is a refutation of the monarchical
theories of Filmer, a writer whose *Patriarcha* (1680) was representative of an influential body of opinion. Locke was writing to justify
a change in dynasty which had little justification in theory, though
plenty in practice.

The full title runs: '*Two Treatises of Government.* In the former the
false Principles and Foundations of Sir Robert Filmer and his
followers are detected and overthrown. The Latter is an Essay concerning the true original extent and end of Civil Government . . .
Salus populi suprema Lex esto.'[1]

The finely written preface states the immediate purpose of his
book: 'Reader, thou hast here the beginning and end of a discourse
concerning government; what fate has otherwise disposed of the
papers that should have filled up the middle and were more than
all the rest, it is not worth while to tell thee. These which remain I
hope are sufficient to establish the throne of our great restorer, King
William, to make good his title, in the consent of the people, which
being the only one of all lawful governments, he has more fully and
clearly than any other prince in Christendom; and to justify to the
world the people of England, whose love of their just and natural
rights, with their resolution to preserve them, saved the nation when
it was on the very brink of slavery and ruin.'

---

[1] 'Let the safety of the people be the supreme law.'

Locke's refutation of Filmer in the first treatise, though interesting in the light it throws on the mentality of the day, and regarded by Locke himself as important, contains little that is original. Seven out of eleven chapters are devoted to a confutation of the argument that sovereign power descends from Adam and that monarchical power inherits it.

In the second and more important part of the book Locke concentrates on two problems: the origin, extent, and limitation of civil government, and of the rights of property.

In the face of the Catholic attack developed by James II under the influence of the Jesuits, the Lords and Commons of England replied with a practical assumption that the business of government was not the spiritual salvation of the governed but their interest and material well-being. Locke and the England he represents had no need to shut their eyes to the visions and splendours of the counter-Reformation; they were firmly unaware of them. Unable to be bothered with such abstractions, Locke works out his case on his own plane.

We will first examine Locke's views on civil government, and, secondly, on private property. In the first chapter of the second treatise, he defines the nature of political power: 'Political power, then, I take to be a right of making laws with penalties of death, and consequently all the penalties for the regulating and preserving of property, and of employing the force of the Community in execution of such laws, and in the defence of the Commonwealth from foreign injury; and all this only for the public good.'[1]

Following the conventions of his day, he assumes that men in a state of nature are equal: 'The equality of man by nature the judicious Hooker looks upon as evident in itself . . . But though this be a state of liberty yet it is not a state of licence . . . the state of nature has a law of nature to govern it . . . Men are God's property, made to last during his, not another's pleasure.'

Locke further argues that the end of civil society is to avoid the 'inconveniences of the state of nature' which follow from every man being a judge of his own case, by setting up a known authority to which everyone may appeal and which everyone ought to obey. The absolute prince, he says, cannot fit into such a society, for he admits no superior and is therefore outside the rules; he has, in fact,

---

[1] Chap. i, 3.

never got beyond the state of nature, 'increased with power and made licentious by impunity'.[1]

'No man in civil society can be exempted from the laws of it.' There can be no place in a civilized community for anyone who declares that the laws are in his own breast. Once the community has been formed, decisions must be made by the will of the majority, otherwise it will defeat its own end and break up. 'Any man, by consenting with others to make one body politic, under one government, puts himself under an obligation . . . to submit to the determination of the majority . . . else this original compact would signify nothing.'

Men are willing to do this because 'the great and chief end of men's uniting into commonwealths and putting themselves under government is the preservation of their property'.[2]

Locke, here, agreeing with Hobbes, insists that the law of nature is not enough and men are driven into society. This is the basis of legislative and executive power, and nothing else. It follows that the power of society can never be suffered to extend further than the common good; it is therefore bound to govern by 'established standing laws, and not by extemporary decrees; by indifferent and upright judges, who are to decide controversies by those laws, and to employ the force of the community at home only in the execution of such laws, or abroad to prevent or redeem foreign injuries, and secure the community from inroads and invasion. And all this is to be directed to no other end than the peace, safety and public good of the people.'[3]

Locke thus curbs the power of government and maintains it must act in accordance with the interests of its subjects, in conformity with the fundamental 'law of nature', which is the preservation of mankind. It follows, therefore, that if a government is pillaging and impoverishing its own subjects they have a right to resist it.

Moreover, 'whatever form the Commonwealth is under, the ruling power ought to govern by declared and reasoned laws', so that both people and rulers will know where they are.[4] Finally, the supreme power cannot take from a man his property without his consent. In the army, 'neither the sergeant that could command a soldier to

---

[1] Chap. vi, 90-3.   [2] Chap. ix, 124.   [3] Chap. ix, 131.
[4] Compare Isidore. 'A law . . . shall be necessary, useful and clear, and not containing any obscure expression to deceive anyone.' *Vide supra*, p. 153.

march up to the mouth of a cannon . . . can command that soldier to give him one penny of his money'. 'It is fit that taxes should be laid, but only by consent' — the ruler who claims the right to levy arbitrary taxation invades the fundamental law of property and subverts the end of government.

Locke is deeply concerned with the preservation of property. He inquires how the right of property comes about. 'Every man has a property in his own person. This nobody has any right to but himself. The labour of his body and the work of his hands, we may say, are properly his. Whatsoever he removes out of the State that nature hath provided and left it in he *hath mixed his labour with*, and joined to it something that is his own, and thereby makes it his property.' He illustrates this with a homely instance: 'Even among us, the hare that anyone is hunting is thought his who pursues her during the chase, for being a beast that is still looked upon as common . . . who ever has employed so much *labour* about any of that kind as to find and pursue her, has thereby removed her from the state of nature, wherein she was common, and hath *begun a property*.'[1]

God gave the land for the use of 'the industrious and rational (and labour was to be the title to it), not to the fancy of the quarrelsome and contentious'. In primitive conditions, Locke maintains, no one needed an amount of property which would prejudice the rest of mankind: it was the invention of money which 'introduced, by consent, larger possessions and the right to them'.[2]

Locke goes on to emphasize the benefits conferred on the community by the cultivation of landed property, 'for I ask whether in the wild woods and uncultivated wastes of America left to nature . . . a thousand acres yield the needy and wretched inhabitants as many conveniences of life as ten acres of equally fertile land in Devonshire, where they are well cultivated?' It is labour, then, which puts the greatest part of value upon land, without which it would scarcely be worth anything: 'Man, being proprietor of his own person and the actions of labour of it, had still in himself the great foundation of property.' 'By money men found out a way how a man may fairly possess more land than he himself can use the product of, by receiving in exchange for the overplus gold and silver.'

The implications of Locke's attitude to property are very far-reaching; ultimately they might well cut across his political principle that the well-being of all is the test of good government, for to give

[1] Chap. v, 30.   [2] Chap. v, 37.

carte blanche to the property-holders may well produce an oligarchical society in which the interests of the few may be thought to supersede those of the majority. But Locke, like nearly all his contemporaries, naturally took the inequalities of the economic and social structure of the time for granted; 'general interest' coincided with the interest of the possessing classes.

Locke's individualism about property is one with his individualism in the constitutional sphere; though he carried on the mediaeval idea of corporate life, expressing itself in a balance of institutions, he assumes, like Hobbes, the separation of individuals on the one hand and the State on the other. The binding force between them is not that of an organic community but of a nexus of legal and economic interest, which touches only the immediately practical aspect of their lives. This view was later developed into a one-sided outlook by the Utilitarian thinkers who were the heirs of Locke, who further diminished the function of the State. Though there were obvious dangers in this individualism, the traditions of self-reliance and enterprise fostered by Locke were fundamental to the success of liberal civilization, and reflected the best tradition of antiquity. The confining of the function of government to the enforcement of 'known standing laws', the subordination of the interest of government to the interest of the governed, and the separation of political and economic power, were to produce a society of unusual vigour and resilience. For conservative as was the Whig tradition, with its roots in mediaeval thought, its principles were revolutionary when set against the predominant absolutism of the time; in formulating his ideas in the context of his age, Locke exercised an influence as important and salutary as that of the greatest masters of political thought.

This mediaeval background made Locke more cautious than his later Continental admirers, particularly on the essential question of majority rule. Mediaeval writers, when they spoke of the rights of the majority, were careful to qualify it by asserting that the 'prevalent part' of the community ought to have the last word. Further, the theory of the State transmitted by Hooker assumes a graded social order with the more substantial elements predominating; Burke's view of the society is much nearer Locke's mind than the outlook of the exponents of the Rights of Man.

It is, indeed, in his championship of the cause of intellectual liberty that Locke went farthest along the liberal road; such was always to be the Whig tradition, the tradition of Charles James Fox and Holland House. One of the strongest objections to James II's attempt to restore the Catholic religion was the close censorship on education and political discussion which would have come in with it. The brilliantly written pamphlets of the age, the increasing habit of association in clubs and coffee houses, the widening literacy of the general population, all made a return to the traditional controls unthinkable.

When Locke wrote his great work on Toleration, in this aspect carrying on Milton's tradition, he was asserting one of the fundamental doctrines of later democratic theory. Further, in his *Thoughts Concerning Education*,[1] he states another fundamental principle of liberalism, the need for freedom and variety in the training of the mind. He takes the psychological approach to education which might be expected from his philosophy, and in this valuable treatise, which should be better known, makes a real contribution to an important study. Parents, he insists, have a right to be 'so irregularly bold as that they consult their own reason in the education of their children, rather than rely wholly on old custom'. Different minds have different aptitudes, and individual initiative ought to be encouraged.

In his *Letters Concerning Toleration*, Locke argues, in the preface to the first letter, that 'although no nation under heaven has said so much upon this subject as ours', the argument has hitherto been too narrowly conducted. 'Our Government has not only been partial in matters of religion; but those also who have suffered under that partiality' have generally argued along sectarian lines. 'We have need of more generous remedies than what have yet been made use of in our distemper.' Declarations of indulgence are not enough: 'Absolute Liberty', he argues, 'just and True Liberty, equal and impartial Liberty, that is the thing we stand in need of.' He has therefore translated his treatise out of the original Latin, for the perusal of his countrymen.

He insists that the principles of Christianity demand toleration: 'No man can be a Christian without charity, and without that faith which works not by force but by love . . . Now I appeal to the consciences of those who persecute, torment, destroy and kill other men upon pretence of religion, whether they do it out of friendship

[1] Published 1690. *Vide Works*, vol. VIII, pp. 1-204. London (1796).

and kindness to them or not.'[1] 'Toleration . . . is agreeable to the Gospel of Jesus Christ, it is also dictated by the general reason of mankind.'[2] Persecution is generally the result of lust for power and jealousy masquerading as religious zeal. The Church, he argues, should be a free voluntary association: 'nobody is born a member of any Church; otherwise the religion of parents would descend to their children by the same right of inheritance as their temporal estates'.[3] Differences of religious belief ought not to affect civil right, 'no private person has any right . . . to prejudice another person in his civil enjoyments because he be of another church or religion. All the rights and franchises that belong to him as a man . . . are not the business of religion, no violence or injury is to be offered him, whether he be Christian or Pagan[4] . . . the care of each man's salvation belongs only to himself'.[5]

These principles, which run directly counter to the predominant mediaeval and sixteenth-century theological outlook, and which have been taken for granted by liberal thought for many generations, were advanced in Locke's day; they are fundamental to the traditions of freedom.

Locke's statement of Whig principles were to have a wide influence not only in England but in France and America, where his views were further developed and broadened out. The vital achievement of Locke is, first, his statement that sovereignty residing ultimately in the commonwealth as a whole, government derives its authority from the governed; that it is responsible to them and holds its title only so long as it does its duty by them. Secondly that government must exercise its authority through clearly defined laws and impartial judges, that arbitrary taxation and imprisonment without trial are illegal. Third, that within limits, government must allow freedom of discussion and worship. Thus, and thus only, a healthy and truly Christian society can be achieved; men can and ought to be trusted to work out their own spiritual and intellectual salvation within a framework of ordered liberty; he assumes that society, if left to its own development, will produce a varied and healthy community, of which government is the guardian but not the despot.

---

[1] Op. cit., p. 6. Compare Halifax's view, 'Partiality to ourselves makes us often mistake it for a duty to fall hard upon others . . . and being pushed on by self conceit, we strike without mercy, believing that the wounds we give are meritorious and that we are fighting God Almighty's quarrel, when the truth is we are only setting out ourselves' (Advice to a Daughter). *Vide* note, *infra*, p. 370.
[2] Op. cit., p. 9.   [3] Op. cit., p. 13.   [4] Op. cit., p. 17.   [5] Op. cit., p. 41.

Such, then, was the political theory of the business common-wealth, the Whig interpretation of the tradition of Natural Law. Appealing to the law of nature and seeking security, Locke, unlike Hobbes, finds it in the rule of the majority of the propertied class, in the rule of law and in toleration of opinion. This tradition of ordered liberty and respect for law is at once mediaeval and modern; mediaeval in its aim of a balanced community, modern in its assumption of progress, harking back, too, to the best Roman and Hellenistic thought.

Fortunately Locke's thought was immensely influential. He summed up and modernized the aspects of the classical and mediaeval tradition which were to be most congenial to the eighteenth-century mind. He represents also the hard-bitten common sense of late seventeenth-century England; his reasoning is closely knit, his prose sober but trenchant, and he takes short views. He gets down to essentials, but does not, in his political writings, follow up the metaphysical and religious implications of his thought. This narrowing of the field, this distrust of generalization in a political context, gave his books the greater appeal to practical men.

§ I V

Locke's outlook, for all its powerful and far-ranging thought, is cautious and pedestrian. A more high-spirited version of this common sense is found in the writings of Halifax,[1] an experienced and successful statesman, who played a considerable part in arranging the settlement of 1689. Like John of Salisbury, far back in the twelfth century, Halifax knows how government really works and takes account of the circumstances and limitations which are bound to condition it; he has a brilliant insight into human nature and he is a master of English prose.

It is rare that an aristocrat of Halifax's position is both sufficiently articulate and sufficiently energetic to write out his thoughts about matters he takes for granted. Halifax speaks for a good many statesmen who have held similar responsibilities and possessed a similar background; men who have casually and effectively under-taken the duties of government, not as a career, but as an obligation, and who have preferred the company of their mistresses and their

---

[1] For a full account of Halifax's life, see *The Life and Letters of Sir George Savile, Bart., First Marquis of Halifax*, by H. C. FOXCROFT, 2 vols., Longmans (1898).

racehorses to the routine of office. Among political theorists the influence of such men is salutary, for they regard public life with humour and detachment, qualities often invaluable in the making of great decisions; further, their writings are free from pedantry and self-righteousness.

The political wisdom of Halifax is contained in two volumes,[1] published after his death: first, the *Miscellanies*, which include the 'Character of a Trimmer', 'Cautions for the choice of Parliament men', and a 'Rough Draft for a New Model at Sea'; second, the *Character of Charles II, and Political, Moral and Miscellaneous Thoughts and Reflections* (1750).

The Trimmer bases his political maxims upon 'Veneration for Laws' . . . 'he looketh upon them as the Chains that tie up our unruly Passions, which else, like wild beasts let loose, would reduce the world into its first state of Barbarism and Hostility . . . All Laws flow from that of Nature . . . by this Nature is not meant that which fools and madmen misquote to justify their excesses, it is innocent and uncorrupted nature, that which disposes men to chuse vertue, without its being prescribed. . . .'

Monarchy is a more popular form of government than a commonwealth, 'since the rules of a commonwealth are too hard for the Bulk of mankind to come up to . . . Monarchy is liked by the People for the Bells and the Tinsel, the outward Pomp and Gilding, and there must be milk for Babes, since the greater part of mankind are and ever will be included in that list'.

But monarchy must be restrained by laws, for 'there is a wantonness in great power that men are generally apt to be corrupted with'. The king and kingdom 'ought to be one creature . . . and when either of them undertakes to act apart, it is like the crawling of worms after they are cut in pieces, which cannot be a lasting motion, the whole creature not stirring at a time'. There cannot be mutual trust without a 'principle of love'.

Rule based on force results in rebellion by force; Halifax wants a compromise between liberty and order. 'Our Trimmer owneth a

---

[1] *The Complete Works of George Savile, First Marquis of Halifax*; edited with an introduction by WALTER RALEIGH; comprising Miscellanies (1700) and A Character of Charles II, Oxford (1912). The Trimmer covers 53 pages of this edition; it is divided into sections dealing with laws and government, the Protestant religion, the Trimmer's opinions concerning the Papists, in relation to things abroad, and the conclusion. The introduction is of particular excellence. The term 'Trimmer' is used not in the sense of 'trimming one's sails', but of 'trimming a boat' to keep it on an even keel, a simile to which Halifax often recurs.

passion for Liberty', which he compares, in a characteristic simile, to a mistress . . . 'if she was not a Beauty the world would not run mad for her'. Dominion and liberty must be 'balanced and regimented'. 'Our Government is in a just proportion . . . Our Government is like our climate, there are winds which are sometimes loud and unquiet, and yet with all the trouble they give us, we owe a great part of our health to them.'

Halifax's racy description of a tyrant is in the best tradition. 'Let us imagine a Prince living in his kingdom, as if in a great galley, his subjects tugging at the oar, laden with chains . . . that they may gain him imaginary laurels . . . wallowing in his soft bed of wanton and unbridled greatness, blown up with an ambitious dropsy, never to be satisfied by the conquest of other people or by the oppression of his own; by aiming to be more than a man he falleth lower than the meanest of 'em, a mistaken creature, swelled with Panegyricks and flattered out of his senses, not only an encumbrance but a *nuisance to mankind*, he groweth great by other men's miseries; an ambitious Ape of the Divine Greatness . . . and, with all his pride, no more than a whip in God Almighty's hand to be thrown into the fire when the world hath been sufficient scourged by it.'

Halifax's view of religion is devoid of fanaticism; he emphasizes its practical side. 'Religion is the foundation of Government; without it man is an abandoned creature, one of the worst beasts Nature hath produced.' The clergy should steer a middle course between the 'overdoeing' of the Dissenters and the apathy of the conventional clergy, who are like 'old warders in the Tower who do nothing in their place but receive their wages for it'. The clergy ought to be on their mettle in a critical age, 'and therefore, tho' in some dearly beloved audiences *Good Resolute Nonsense* backed with Authority may prevail . . . now the world is grown Saucy and expecteth Reasons, and good ones too'. Dissenters ought to have more toleration, 'a veil thrown over an innocent and retired conventicle'.

His attack on the Catholic Church is characteristic and biting. 'I can not hinder myself from a small digression to consider with admiration that the Old Lady of Rome with all her wrinkles should yet have charms able to subdue great princes, so painted and yet so pretending.'

The best way to assuage the legacy of religious rancour inherited from the Civil Wars is toleration. When men by 'fair usage' are put into their right senses . . . 'A lay Papist will first consider his Abbey lands, which, notwithstanding whatever hath or can be alledged, must sink considerably in the value, the moment that Popery prevails'.

In the passage concerning the Catholics, Halifax administers a swingeing dose of common sense to those whose faith still induced them to put up with the social disadvantages of Catholicism in England, enumerated with shrewd and detailed observation; he is indeed incapable of understanding that anyone can really put faith before interest.

Turning to foreign affairs, the Trimmer affirms a proper patriotism. 'Our Trimmer is far from Idolatry in other things; in one thing only he cometh near it, his country is in some degree his Idol . . . for the *Earth of England* . . . to him there is Divinity in it and he would rather dye than see a spire of English grass trampled down by a Foreign Trespasser.' He attacks the king's pro-French policy as contrary to the true interest and dignity of the country, which demands that no one power should dominate Europe. 'To look like the Kitching Yacht to the Grand Louis is but a scurvy figure for us to make on the Map of Europe.'

Summing up, Halifax defends his moderate position; he has grounded his opinions, he says, on truth, 'which equally hateth to be under the oppression of wrangling sophistry on the one hand, or the short Dictates of mistaken Authority on the other'.

He concludes: 'Our Trimmer therefore . . . thinketh fit to conclude with these assertions, that our climate is a Trimmer, between that part of the world where men are roasted and the other where they are frozen — that our Church is a Trimmer, that our Laws are Trimmers, between the excess of unbounded power and the extravagance of liberty not enough restrained, that true virtue hath ever been thought a Trimmer and to have its dwelling in the middle between the two extremes; that even God Almighty himself is divided between his two great attributes, his Mercy and his Justice. In such a company our Trimmer is not ashamed of his name. To conclude, our Trimmer is so fully satisfied of the Truth of these Principles, by which he is directed in reference to the Publick, that he will neither be Bawled, Threatened, Laught nor Drunk out of them.' It is an admirable conclusion.

Halifax's insight into politics and human nature is further shown in the detailed 'Cautions offered for the consideration of those who are to Chuse Members to serve for the ensuing Parliament'. 'A very extraordinary earnestness to be chosen is no very good symptom.'

'Great drinkers are less fit to serve in Parliament than is apprehended . . . nothing is more frail than a man too far engaged in Wet Popularity. It is seldom seen that any Principles have such a root as that they can be proof against the continual droppings of a Bottle. Nothing, sure, is a greater enemy to the Brain than too much Moisture; it can the least of anything bear the being continuously steeped. . . .'

Petty-minded men, too, 'merchants of small conceits', are unfit for State business, which requires 'a deliberate and an observing wit that takes greater pleasure in mending a fault than in finding it out'. The 'Blockhead who is apt to pretend that his heaviness is a proof of his judgement' is indeed liable to obtain political advancement through his apparent gravity, but such men are useless for public business; they possess a 'True Heart of Oak Ignorance that will never yield, let Reason beat never so hard upon it'.

Halifax ends his 'Cautions' as follows: 'In the mean time, after having told my opinion who ought not to be chosen; if I should be asked who ought to be, my answer must be "Chuse Englishmen"; and when I have said that, to deal honestly, I will not undertake that they are easy to be found.'

As is well known, Halifax was alive to the importance of sea power, and displays much wisdom about naval matters in his 'Rough Draft of a New Model at Sea' (1694). 'It may be said', he writes, 'to England; Martha, Martha, thou art busy about many things, but one thing is necessary. To the question, What shall we do to be saved in this world? there is no other answer but this — Looke to your Moate.[1] The first article of an Englishman's Political Creed must be that he believeth in the sea, etc., without that there needeth no General Council to pronounce him incapable of salvation here. We are in an Island, confined to it by God Almighty, not as a Penalty but a Grace . . . Happy Confinement, that hath made us Free, Rich and Quiet; a Fair Portion in this world and very well worth the preserving. . . .'

---

[1] Dealing with the question whether naval officers ought to be selected from the 'Gentlemen' or 'Tarpaulins', Halifax concludes, very properly, that the Gentleman must qualify for his preferment by proving himself equal to the Tarpaulin at his own game; then his birth will give him an additional advantage, and he will make the better officer. He must 'smell as much of Pitch and Tar' as 'those that were swaddled in sail Cloath'. 'When the undistinguished Discipline of a ship hath tamed the young Mastership, which is apt to arise from a Gentleman's birth and education, he then groweth proud in the right place and valueth himself first upon knowing his Duty and then upon doing it.'

The *Political Thoughts and Reflections*, posthumously published half a century later, contain a more bitter wisdom, and in spite of their sententious form, retain the racy quality of the earlier work. In political life the need to conceal ability is wisely stressed. 'It is thought an unsociable Quality in a Court to do one's Duty better than other men. Nothing is less forgiven than setting Patterns Men have no mind to follow.' He has no illusions about the art of government. 'State Business is a cruel Trade; good nature is a Bungler in it.' Further, the carping and grumbling of inferior subordinates must be tolerated. 'The lower sort of men must be indulged in the Consolation of finding fault with those above them; without that they would be so melancholy they would be dangerous, considering their numbers.'

He dislikes the stupidity and beastliness of the mob. 'There is an accumulative cruelty in a number of men though none in particular are ill natured. The angry Buzz of a multitude is one of the bloodiest noises in the world.'

His judgement of the clergy is cynical: 'If the clergy did not live like temporal men, all the Power of Princes could not bring them under the temporal jurisdiction.'

The catalogue of disillusionment ends with the remark that 'old men have in some degree their Reprisals upon younger, by making nice observations upon them by virtue of their experience'.

Yet in spite of his preoccupation with politics, Halifax retained an aristocratic detachment. 'The serious folly of Wise Men in over-valuing the world', he says, 'is as contemptible as anything they see fit to censure'; he even puts the art of government in its place with the unanswerable reflection that 'the Government of the world is a great thing, but it is a very coarse one too, compared with the Fineness of Speculative Knowledge'. Halifax's intellectual enthusiasm is so great that he pays knowledge the highest compliment in his vocabulary: 'the struggle for knowledge hath a pleasure in it like that of wrestling with a fine woman'.

Such is the contribution of Halifax to English political thought. He was a successful and powerful politician, and a shrewd if insular observer of life. Raleigh says rightly: 'The Aphorisms of Halifax are a better guide to the world than all the brilliance of his epigrammatic French contemporaries.' And indeed there is no trace of thwarted ambition in these objective statements.

Halifax, then, sums up the practical if limited Whig tradition which combines political and business ability with a fine, if cynical, sense of toleration and public duty. He is also highly patriotic, with all the self-confidence and gusto of his age; contemporaries of his stamp were carrying on the Elizabethan and Caroline beginnings of colonial enterprise on a bigger scale, creating a brilliant literature, building, within the nationalistic framework of the day, the foundations of modern scientific power.

Hooker, Locke, and Halifax, then, express three aspects of the English character. Hooker, mild and kindly, with an ordered lucidity of mind, explains the Thomist tradition of liberty and godly order in plain terms; Locke, also with his roots in mediaeval thought, but taking a political and economic approach, voices the good sense and the interest of the new business Commonwealth, and insists on the supremacy of the rule of law. His writings, immensely influential, were to inspire not only the Whig but the American tradition, which thus harks back directly to mediaeval and classical influences. Further, he advocates religious and intellectual toleration, and tends to confine government to a framework within which a naturally healthy society can be trusted to expand. Halifax, more high-spirited, cynical, and worldly than the other two, stands for the 'attack' and enterprise which were to make England an imperial power. These three elements combined, both in their English and American expression, to draw the admiration of the French thinkers of the Enlightenment, to whom, in the eighteenth century, passed the major initiative in the field of political thought.

CHAPTER VII

SCIENTIFIC HUMANISM: SPINOZA: VICO

§1

BEFORE tracing the influence of English political thought on the brilliant culture of eighteenth-century France, it is worth turning to examine the writings of two original and important thinkers, who, though they had little effect on the minds of their contemporaries, anticipated to a remarkable degree the outlook of modern Scientific Humanism.

The criticism of Hobbes, implicit in the doctrines of Puritan radicalism and in the more powerful Whig tradition expressed by Locke, was reinforced with a profound philosophical argument in the political thought of Spinoza. Employing the same Cartesian method as Hobbes, Spinoza comes to morally opposite conclusions; like Locke, he takes a utilitarian view of society, but puts a new sanction behind it. His political writings, an aspect of his general philosophy, demonstrate that the new scientific outlook was not necessarily pessimistic, but compatible with deep moral insight. His books, indeed, had little contemporary influence, but they foreshadow a great tradition, now finding a wider fulfilment. Religious toleration, liberty of thought, responsibility of government to the governed, these Whig principles were emphasized by Spinoza, and he gave them a philosophic basis, a mystical and original interpretation, which looked out beyond his own age. This Jewish philosopher, too little appreciated now as in his own time, is a political thinker from whom the world still has much to learn.

While Spinoza's secularized thought, accepting the principles of scientific method, and informing them with religious understanding, reflects the anthropocentric tendencies of the Cartesian world view, the curious speculations of the Italian Vico adumbrate a new historical outlook. His original philosophy of history, long neglected, shows a psychological insight and an historical sense unique in his day. He is the first modern thinker to view history in terms of the changing consciousness of mankind, and to interpret the past by a deliberate effort of intuition. Though long unappreciated and premature in its original and tortuous thought, Vico's *Scienza Nuova* marks a new departure. As much as the ideas of the Levellers, it deserves consideration, for it marks the beginning of a movement later to become formidable.

Spinoza in the Netherlands, and Vico in Naples, worked out their thought against very different backgrounds, but both were united in a common modernity and range of mind. That such an objective and imaginative outlook was beginning to appear in Europe had profound significance for the future. Though Vico cannot compare in philosophical stature with Spinoza, both were deeply influenced by the Cartesian outlook. Neither were content with its limitations. Spinoza, in particular, unlike Hobbes, believed it possible to combine realism with morality. By the later seventeenth century, a new way of thought was becoming predominant, based not on revelation but utility. The aim of government was to be security and freedom, whereby the development of the human spirit, and with it the mind of the universe as far as man can apprehend it, could be realized. Spinoza attempts to find a moral answer within the Cartesian framework; and his aim is to understand men as well as things. An ordered society can achieve control over environment; it can achieve stability if based on majority rule; it can achieve moral progress by religious and intellectual toleration. Vico, a pioneer of modern sociological method, broke away from the atomistic Cartesian tradition and by a series of brilliant hypotheses, set out to construct a secular philosophy of history. Like Spinoza, he attempts to understand men in a spirit of tolerant inquiry; going further than Spinoza, he tries to discover the 'Laws of the development of nations'.

Both these great thinkers were outside the immediate tradition of their day, but their writings form a landmark in the development of the modern outlook, and as such are of more importance on a long-term view than those of many writers of more immediate influence.

§11

Where Hobbes, facing the implications of Cartesian thought, comes to a pessimistic conclusion, Spinoza, equally up to date in his age, attempts to combine realism with an affirmation of spiritual and intellectual values.

Spinoza assumes that the Divine order is not a geometrical pattern 'laid up in Heaven'; he admits that the order of nature does not reflect human standards, and, like Hobbes, he justifies sovereign power as the price of order. Men obey it not because they instinctively do their duty by the light of natural law and right reason, but because they must unite to get themselves out of the state of nature in which no civilized values can live. But with his pantheistic outlook and strong sense of community, Spinoza combined scientific detachment and analytical power with a sense of the organic quality of the State alien to the prevailing fashion of the time. He is determined to preserve intellectual and political liberty within the framework of a utilitarian state, and unlike Hobbes, he does not despair of humanity. Mutual aid as much as pride and fear is natural to men; the aim of society is the extension of human awareness and power. His philosophy is progressive and more truly scientific than the static pessimism of Hobbes.

Spinoza[1] complains that philosophers 'conceive men not as they are, but as they would wish them to be'. 'Homines namque, non ut sunt, sed ut eosdem esse vellent concipiunt: unde factum est ut plerumque pro Ethica satiram scripserint — they write satire instead of ethics.'

He then states, with excellent brevity, that he intends 'humanas actiones non ridere, non lugere, neque detestare, sed intelligere — not to laugh at men or weep over them or hate them, but to understand them'.

Here, in the same century as the Thirty Years War, is the voice of detached scientific toleration. It is true that Spinoza's influence

[1] Baruch de Spinoza, born 1634, at Amsterdam, of a well-to-do Portuguese Jewish family. Highly educated in the rabbinic tradition and an accomplished linguist, he studied science and optics and was deeply influenced by Cartesian thought. In 1656, he broke with his family and the Jewish community and removed to Leyden, where he practised as an optician. He was excommunicated from the synagogue and cut off from his inheritance. In 1663 he published the *Principles of Cartesianism geometrically demonstrated*, and in 1670 settled at The Hague, where he published anonymously the *Tractatus Theologico-Politicus* in the same year. The book was banned by the Dutch authorities and the Catholic Church. *The Ethics* and *Tractatus Politicus* were published after his death.

Spinoza led a frugal and well-regulated life and appears from his letters to have been an attractive and kindly character with numerous friends. 'He was of middle size; he had good features in his face, his skin somewhat black, black curled hair . . . so that one might easily know by his looks he was descended from Portuguese Jews . . . He was never seen very melancholy nor very merry . . . he was, besides, very courteous and obliging.' KOHLER'S *Biography*.

He spent his life in study and speculation, following an equable routine. He died of consumption in 1677. There is a modern translation of his works by R. H. ELWES, Bell (1891).

on his contemporaries was negligible: the 'God-intoxicated man' was denounced by his own age as an atheist; he extended scientific method to the study of the Scriptures and horrified orthodox opinion by rejecting the reality of miracles. Yet the kind of detachment he displays marks not only a new scientific outlook but an extension of that outlook to include all human activities. Geometrical as may be the structure and presentation of his thought, he is yet studying the immediacy of action in all its complex variety. He does not, like Hobbes, whose writings suffer from the defects of Cartesian method applied to politics, attempt to impose a static pattern on events; he revives the truly scientific attitude of Aristotle and anticipates the outlook of modern sociology, although his evil reputation in his own day — 'Spinoza's hideous hypothesis' — circumscribed his influence and he was in the main unappreciated until the nineteenth century.

Spinoza's two political treatises form a closely-reasoned attempt to fit the political structure into an ethical framework, to find out what principles spring from men's nature, impartially studied. Without attempting 'to discover anything new or unheard of', he inquires what actually happens.

Man, he argues, can only realize his higher qualities when co-operating for some higher good; the community alone is the medium through which this can be done. Following 'the common order of nature', man cannot stand alone. Spinoza's conception is unusual in the seventeenth century; he does not regard man as an autonomous, self-contained individual, but rather, following Aristotle, anticipates modern conclusions which place man intimately in their social group: he senses the wholeness of the social pattern. The full exercise of 'libertas animae', spiritual freedom, the development of the higher aspects of personality, alone can give the lasting concord which is the 'beatitude' of men. Spinoza assumes Aristotle's view that man is a social animal, though he does not appear to have been directly influenced by his writings, and it is likely that the scholastic monopoly of Aristotle repelled him.

Spinoza insists that the best means of attaining concord in society are not the baser appetites of interest and greed, rather that the higher faculties make possible and secure the existence of ordered government. Thus where Hobbes bases public authority on the need to restrain the natural wickedness of men and justifies it by invoking Natural Law which he interprets as self-preservation, Spinoza regards government as an expression of the impulse to

mutual aid instinctive to mankind. He defines the power of the
State as 'the power of the common people when they are led and
determined by a single mind', and he unites men, not through the
lowest common factor of fear and pride, but through sociable instinct for the furtherance of the good life of intellectual and spiritual
awareness, which can only be achieved where there is liberty and
security. His thought is indeed a landmark in the assertion of
scientific humanist values, in the acceptance and glorification of life.

The aim of life and the State is the fullest realization of its own
being; the State's authority is valid only if it promotes the good of
its citizens. 'It follows', he writes in the *Tractatus Theologico-Politicus*,
'that the ultimate aim of government is not to rule . . . by Fear, not
to exact obedience, but to free men from fear, that they may live in
all possible security . . . No, the object of government is not to
change men from rational beings into beasts or puppets, but to
enable them to develope their minds and bodies in security and
to employ their reason unshackled; . . . in fact, the true aim of
government is Liberty.'[1]

This outlook is the antithesis of the fear of life apparent in Calvin
or St. Augustine. Though without illusions, Spinoza accepts evil as
part of the incomprehensible nature of things, he is not cowed into
a denial of life, into crying for salvation. 'No deity', he says, 'nor
anyone save the envious is pleased by mere want of power or inconvenience, nor counts as virtuous our tears, sobs, fear and other
signs of weakness; on the contrary, the more we enjoy, the more we
pass to a greater perfection, that is the more we necessarily participate in the Divine Nature.'[2] It follows that in the words of Jesus,
the aim of mankind is 'To have life and to have it more abundantly',
and the State must be directed to this clear end. It is impossible
here to follow up the great range of metaphysical and psychological
argument contained in Spinoza's *Ethics*, a highly technical book, but
a knowledge of it is necessary for a full understanding of Spinoza's
position. Meanwhile it must be sufficient to outline the main
argument of the *Tractatus Theologico-Politicus*, and of the *Political
Treatise*.

The *Tractatus Theologico-Politicus* is primarily a defence of
freedom of thought. The preface attacks 'superstition', the deliberate
'clogging of men's minds' by rulers seeking their own ends. Spinoza
also brings the light of impartial analysis to the study of the Bible,

---

[1] Chap. xx.   [2] *Ethics*, iv, 45.

'making no assumptions concerning it and attributing to it no doctrines which I do not find clearly set down therein'. Proceeding to the question of the nature and limitations of governmental power, he argues from a study of the Hebrew state that the sovereign power ought to have religious as well as secular authority; finally, he insists that the best security of the State lies in toleration of opinion and freedom of speech.

The preface ends by a plain statement that the book is not meant for the 'multitude'. 'Therefore the multitude, and those of like passions with the multitude, I ask not to read my book; nay I would rather that they should utterly neglect it than that they should misinterpret it after their wont.'

The treatise is divided into twenty chapters, of which the first ten are concerned with the Old Testament, with the authenticity of the books and the nature of miracles.[1] The 'Foundations of a State' are examined in chapter xvi, as subsidiary to the problem of the right extent of freedom of thought.[2] Spinoza examines what is meant by Natural Law. This he defines, in a way at once mediaeval and scientific, as the right of every individual 'to exist and act according to its natural condition'. For instance, fishes are naturally conditioned for swimming, and the greater for devouring the less; therefore fishes enjoy the water and the greater devour the less by sovereign natural right . . .' Men are not conditioned to live by reason alone, but by instinct, 'So that they are no more bound to live by the dictates of an enlightened mind . . . than a cat is bound to live by the laws of nature of a lion'.[3]

[1] Spinoza's approach to this problem is characteristic. He takes account of the kind of people who recorded the miracles and their object in writing. Much Scripture is written to 'impress the minds of the masses with devotion'. Further, in order to understand what actually took place, 'we ought to be familiar with Jewish phrases and metaphors . . .' 'Hence we must believe that when the Bible says that the Lord hardened Pharaoh's heart, it only means that Pharaoh was very obstinate; when it says that God opened the windows of heaven, it only means that it rained very hard, and so on . . .' He concludes that since the natural order is fixed and unchangeable, and 'God, in all ages, known and unknown, the same', the laws of nature are so perfect that nothing can be added thereto or taken therefrom and . . . miracles therefore only appear as something new because of ignorance.

[2] Chaps. xi to xv deal with Divine Law, the nature of faith and the relation of Reason to Theology. Chap. xvii is directly concerned with political theory and entitled 'Of the Foundation of the State'. The next chapter deals with the 'Hebrew Republic' and the lessons which may be derived from its success and failure.
Chap. xix maintains that 'Right over matters spiritual lies with the sovereign', and the final chapter is a defence of freedom of thought and expression. The part of the book directly relevant to political theory is contained in the last sixty-five of the 265 pages of the English translation.

[3] Chap. xvi.

It follows that the basis of political obligation is the desire for security, which is attained by a purely utilitarian compact. Thus Spinoza, in spite of his high moral purpose, throws over the whole classical and mediaeval assumption that imposed, transcendent, Natural Law sanctions human values and that men act morally within the framework of it according to their lights. Like Hobbes, he bases his social contract on self-preservation, which is the emergent law of life. As in the *Political Treatise*, where the thought is worked out more fully, Spinoza regards the sovereign state as the 'least of two evils'. Its authority only extends, as does the 'natural right' of the individual, so far as it has the power to enforce it, and the sovereign is encouraged to consult the public good in his own interest, since an unpopular government does not last — 'Violenta imperia nunquam continuit diu'. In a democracy 'the danger of irrational commands is less to be feared, since it is almost impossible that the majority of the people, especially if it be a large one, should agree on an irrational design'. Spinoza here shows a greater faith in human nature than is apparent in the posthumously published *Political Treatise*.

All depends on the aim of the State; if it aims at the good of the individual its authority is valid; if at its own good at the expense of individuals, invalid. Thus Spinoza, starting from Hobbes's premise that the basis of the State is a man-made compact, which rescues men from the inconveniences of a state of nature, comes to a different conclusion about the extent of its authority, and prefers democracy as the form of government most consistent with individual liberty and freedom of thought, which, unlike Hobbes, he is anxious to defend. Spinoza tackles the problem of how 'liberty is to live in the presence of Leviathan', the new great state; and he tackles it with greater success.

The sovereign power, he continues, should count all men rich and poor equal before it, for justice, he says, quoting the mediaeval definition coming down through Isidore from antiquity, 'consists in the habitual rendering of every man his lawful due'. Treason consists in being caught in the act of attempting to transfer sovereign power to oneself or to a power other than that existing; if one can acquire or transfer the sovereign rights before being caught, treason will not occur — a subtle view.

Following up the question of the limits of sovereign power, Spinoza shows himself more of a political realist than Hobbes. The power of the ruler is in practice limited by the fear he feels of his subjects; the extent of 'Dominion' is bounded by the degree in which it can persuade or compel men to obey it in practice, 'for it is the fact of obedience, not the motive of obedience which makes a man a subject'.[1]

The aim of the statesman is to 'frame our institutions so that every man, whatever his dispositions, may prefer public right to private advantage; this is the task and this the test'.

The book concludes with a detailed description of the Hebrew theocracy, which, at its best, fulfilled the conditions of a sound commonwealth, and with an investigation of the causes of its decline.

Spinoza's political thought is further set out clearly and shortly in his unfinished *Political Treatise*, of which the full title is as follows: 'Benedict de Spinoza's political treatise, wherein is demonstrated how the society in which Monarchical Dominion finds place, as also that in which the dominion is aristocratic, should be ordered so as not to lapse into a tyranny, but to preserve inviolate the peace and freedom of the citizens.'

The book is divided into eleven chapters: an Introduction and a discussion of natural rights, followed by chapters dealing with the basis of political authority, the functions of authority as 'the best kind of Dominion'. Two chapters follow on Monarchy, three on Aristocracy, and the final unfinished fragment is concerned with Democracy. The whole is contained in a hundred pages of the translated text.

As in the *Tractatus*, Spinoza sets little store by the power of reason in political affairs. Reason may to some extent 'moderate the passions', but 'such as persuade themselves that the multitude of men distracted by politics can ever be induced to live according to the dictate of reason, must be dreaming of the poetic golden age or of a stage play'.[2] Security is the aim of the statesman and 'a dominion whose wellbeing depends on good faith . . . will be very unstable'. Public affairs ought to be administered on principles which are fool proof and knave proof, and such principles can only be derived from the 'general nature and position' of mankind. Spinoza is concerned to find a plan of political action other than abstract Natural Law or Reason, existing in its own right; his scientific bent of mind leads him to deducing his principles from the facts.

[1] Chap. xvii.   [2] I, 5.

Following on his pantheistic view of the world, whereby Spinoza sees all nature as the manifestation of God, he argues, as in the former treatise, that every creature manifests Natural Law in fulfilling the impulse of its being to the utmost extent of its power. 'Whatever a man does after the laws of his nature, he does by the highest natural right and has as much right over nature as he has power.' Now since men are not actuated by reason so much as by appetite, it follows that Natural Law cannot be identified with reason alone, but with the drive of the whole personality, 'the natural impulse by which men strive to continue in existence'. That is the clue to the nature of things and the manifestation of God. Spinoza thus confines man's apprehension of God to His manifestation in terms of nature. He attacks the dualism which conceives 'that the human mind is produced by no natural causes, but created directly by God, and is so independent of other things'; experience, however, teaches us only too well 'that it is no more in our power to have a sound mind than a sound body'.[1] He insists that the doctrine of the Fall cannot explain man's unreasonableness, for if the first man had been sovereignly reasonable he would not have been deceived by the devil.[2]

He agrees with St. Thomas that reason is blind when faced with the full manifestation of Deity, but he rejects the Thomist view that revelation and Divine Law bring the beatitude of peace. On the contrary, Spinoza maintains that man's consciousness, for all its limitation, is the measure of all things and its only intuition of God through terrestrial experience. It would indeed be difficult for a scientist, following Cartesian principles, to take any other view.

Thus, when a man fulfils his own instinct, he follows the law of nature, 'which forbids nothing but what no-one wishes or is able to do, and is not offended at anything that appetite suggests. For the bounds of nature are not the laws of human reason . . . but other infinite laws which regard the eternal order of universal nature, whereof man is an atom . . . Whenever, then, anything in nature seems to us ridiculous, absurd or evil, it is because we have but a partial knowledge of things, and are in the main ignorant of the

---

[1] II, 6.

[2] 'But they say he was deceived by the Devil. Who then was it that deceived the Devil himself? Who, I say, so maddened the very being that excelled all other created intelligences, that he wished to be greater than God? For was not *his* effort, too, supposing him of sound mind, to possess himself and his existence as far as in him lay?'

order and coherence of nature as a whole, and because we want everything arranged according to the dictate of our reason.'

This relativity of human values in relation to nature is paralleled within human society itself. Every man has a right to fulfil his own being in so far as he has the power, and men have naturally authority over one another only in so far as they can impose it by force or persuasion; further no man need keep faith with another after he has judged it, rightly or wrongly, in his own interest, to break it '. . . he only made a present of words'.

Thus, if men follow Natural Law, they are in a condition similar to that depicted by Hobbes, and Natural Right 'which is special to the human race' cannot be conceived at all except if men combine to protect themselves, for 'without mutual help men can hardly support life and cultivate the mind . . . and if this is why the school men call man a social animal, I have nothing to say against them'.[1]

Thus moral values are a human creation, cultivated in an artificial garden. 'Wrong doing cannot be conceived of but under Dominion'; that is, in an ordered society, not in a state of nature.

Where, then, can we find the basis of obligation? Spinoza finds it in *the power of the majority*. Every man has the less right, the more the rest collectively exceed him in power. Given that all men strive to fulfil their own being, 'if two come together and unite their strength, they have jointly more power and consequently more right over nature than both of them separately, and the more there are, that dominion supersedes that of individuals' — the 'will of the commonwealth must be taken to be the will of all'. This sacrifice of individual freedom is not repugnant to reason, Spinoza argues, since so long as men are 'subject to passions', there can only be peace on these terms. The civil state, like Hobbes's Leviathan, is designed to 'remove fear', and exacts its price. It is the lesser of two evils. The best kind of state is that which pursues reasonable ends, since it is in the interest of all — really an individual on a greater scale. The sanctions of the State are 'rewards and threats', so that its power is limited. It cannot enforce belief or control a man's affections, and, as for religious opinions, 'everyone, wherever he may be, may worship God and mind his own business, which is the duty of a private man'. If the policy of the commonwealth causes 'indignation in the majority' to the extent that they conspire against it and break the peace, it loses its *raison d'être*, which is security. Thus Spinoza

[1] II, 15.

hedges about the authority of his sovereign and is not ready to concede a permanent power.

Having defined dominion and its limitations, he proceeds to discuss the best kind of state. The test of it is peace and security: 'that dominion is the best where men pass their lives in unity and the laws are kept unbroken . . . men are not naturally born for citizenship, but must be made so'.[1] That state is the most successful which best secures this end, which is not mere existence, but a 'human life, defined not by the mere circulation of the blood and other qualities common to all animals, but above all by reason, the true excellence and life of the mind'. He criticizes Machiavelli shrewdly as follows: 'But what means a Prince, whose sole motive is lust of mastery, should use to establish and maintain his dominion, the most ingenious Machiavelli has set forth at large, but with what design one can hardly be sure.'[2] He generously gives Machiavelli the benefit of the doubt by suggesting that he wished to warn a 'free multitude' against entrusting its welfare to one man.

The rest of the book (chaps. vi-ix), is concerned with forms of government, with Monarchy, Aristocracy, and Democracy. Men cannot dissolve their commonwealth and return to the state of nature; political discontent merely changes the form of government. Which, then, is the best and in what circumstances? Clearly that which best promotes unity of purpose and mind. The absolute power of one man may make peace, but not a dynamic peace; only one of desolation. There are indeed sharper quarrels between children and parents than between masters and slaves, yet it does not follow that a father's right should be 'changed into a right of property'.

Spinoza, then, in both books, adopts a similar position. The aim of the State, he maintains, is the fulfilment of man's power and awareness on the greatest possible scale. The State exists for man and not man for the State; its authority ought to be obeyed only so far as it promotes the fulfilment of life. It is a convenience, devised to bring about that security without which there can be no civilization.

Given the minimum security guaranteed by the State, and given liberty of thought within this framework, man can realize his own values, fulfil his own Natural Law, irrespective of the denial of human values in nature, which is none the less a manifestation of God. Spinoza has the Jewish sense of the incomprehensible omnipotence of God, combined with a scientific awareness of things as they are

[1] V, 1.   [2] V, 7.

which forbids him illusions. 'I am that I am' is the answer given through the vast process of nature, alien to the human mind. Man can only acquiesce in his limitations; he ought not to seek to impose his pattern of values on the unfolding of the universe. Echoing St. Paul, he compares men to 'clay in the hands of the Potter, who of the same lump makes some vessels unto honour, others to dishonour'.[1] Man comes nearest to God when he worships God in sincerity and attempts to control blind desire, but the mysterious power of God governs all. Man, fulfilling his own being and power, actuated by motives of mutual aid and sociability, thus combines order with intellectual liberty.

Spinoza's idea of the State is surprisingly dynamic for his age: he implies a progressive awareness, an expansion of spiritual and intellectual consciousness. Although he founds his social order on utility, it aims at fullness of life: the State, though utilitarian, is informed with a purpose to realize the highest values. Like the process of natural evolution, Spinoza's thought proceeds from small beginnings to great ends: human values are just as much a manifestation of God as any other, and by their realization God becomes manifest in the world in a new guise. Man, in making his own values and enjoying his intellectual and spiritual powers, comes nearest to God, may even be the instrument of God's self-realization in the world. Spinoza does not attempt to moralize politics by invoking either a transcendent Natural Law or theology; he constructs his moral law out of men's own nature. The utilitarian basis of the State, reflecting the will of the majority, thus becomes retrospectively sanctioned by the highest moral values. Taken all of a piece, intellectual and spiritual progress and the humble instrument of its realization — the rules of human society — are seen as one. Man thus fulfils his own emergent moral law for himself and wins communion with God in his own mind.

§III

Where Spinoza's objectivity and toleration foreshadows the outlook of modern scientific Humanism, the Italian thinker Vico,[2]

---

[1] *Tractatus Politicus*, xi, 22.
[2] Giambattista Vico was born in 1668, the fifth of eight children. His parents were poor, his home in the heart of old Naples. He was early educated by the Jesuits, but

writing in Naples in the first quarter of the eighteenth century, strangely anticipates the range and method of modern sociology.

This curious and original genius attempted to construct a secular philosophy of history, deduced, not *a priori*, but from a sympathetic study of the facts as known to his age. Vico had conceived a profoundly new idea. Human history, being a history of human institutions and man-made, can be understood only in terms of the laws and habits of the human spirit, and not of those of material nature. Man can know himself more profoundly and clearly than even Newton can grasp the laws of matter: consequently knowledge of history, being the story of human motives and their effects, can in principle be far more profoundly and minutely known than the external world, which is ultimately opaque. This outlook, so unorthodox in its day, was destined to bear its full fruit in the Romantic movement, from Herder to Hegel and down to Croce and the modern idealist interpretation of history.

Vico's brilliant hypothesis may not always have stood the test of modern research, but he is a writer of profound historical intuition; a poet as well as a scholar. He thinks himself back into the minds of primitive men, into the outlook of the poets and warriors of the Heroic Age; he is a philosopher with a deep historical sense, aware of the difficulties and the promise of a whole new field of research.

---

was forced by ill health to abandon orthodox study and largely educated himself. In 1684 he became tutor to the nephews of Dominico Rocca, at Vatolla, where he lived for nine years.

In 1694 he was elected to the Chair of Rhetoric in the University of Naples and retained the post until 1741. Apart from his *Lectures* (1699-1708) he published among other works, *De Antiquissima Italorum Sapientia* (1710), *Life of Caraffa* (1716), *De Universi Juris Uno Principio* (1720). By 1724 he had completed the first draft of his *Scienza Nuova*; to publish it he had to sell his diamond ring for printing expenses. It appeared in 1725, when it received a short and unfavourable review in a German periodical and was otherwise ignored. In the same year Vico wrote his autobiography – a remarkable and eloquent work. 'The invalid child', says his biographer, 'with Titanic intellectual pride, with a Faust-like mental energy and ambition, driven inward by the weakness of his physical condition, by the sensitiveness of his temperament and the depressing poverty of his family, yet working on in the subterranean mazes of a heroic self-education, compensating by lonely intellectual victories for the denial of conquest in the world of action and fame . . .' (ADAMS, *Life and Writings of Vico*, p. 177.)

In 1730 he re-wrote and expanded his *Scienza Nuova*; the third edition, incomplete, appeared in 1744. In 1735 Vico became Historiographer Royal. The mainstay of his later years was his own son Gennaro, who succeeded to the Chair of Rhetoric in 1741. Vico died in 1744, aged 77. He was a man beloved by his pupils and his family: 'he was of medium height, his nose aquiline, his eyes living and penetrating, and from their fire it was easy to conceive the power and energy of his vigorous mind'. His works are contained in the six-volume edition edited by FERRARI, Milan (1836). See also MICHELET, *Œuvres choisis de Vico*.

His contribution to historical science is too little known to the Anglo-Saxon world, though it has had wide influence in Italy, Germany, and France. By interpreting the past in terms of ideas, of poetry, of language, and of psychology, Vico has laid posterity under a debt which has been too little acknowledged. It was through Michelet, the French historian, that his organic and comprehensive interpretation of history had its first effect; Michelet in 1824 published and translated selections from his works and admitted his obligation to Vico.

It is here impossible to give more than a bare outline of his thought, and we must confine our analysis to his most important and lucid book, the *Scienza Nuova*, published in 1725.

It is a remarkable work. Vico, attempts to discover a secular philosophy of history, 'storia universale, certa e ragionata'. Like Plato and St. Augustine, he saw in history the realization of a divine idea; God, working through the mind of fallen man, manifests his providence in the cycle of human development. Vico, like Thomas Hardy, sought to trace the working of the Cosmic Will in the tide of time; unlike Hardy he claimed to have found evidence of constructive purpose, though not of divine interference. Under providence, he believed the cycle of human development works out deterministically, according to the laws of man's nature; in this determinism he had affinities with Hegel and Marx, who were influenced by him. Vico by modern standards was ignorant of pre-history, of biology, of evolution, yet his original genius interpreted history in terms of social origins. He believed that the mind projects its interpretation on the outside world, creating a realm of ideas appropriate to the stages of historical evolution, though we must beware of attributing to Vico the optimism of later thought.

He was a man unappreciated in his own age, fighting a battle for recognition in the provincial academic world of seventeenth-century Naples. His autobiography describes his struggle with poverty and ill health, and the obstinate inflexible faith which sustained him in bringing his magnum opus, the *Scienza Nuova*, to fruition. In spite of difficulties, Vico was certain of its greatness. 'Since I completed my great work', he writes in 1726, 'I feel that I am become a new man, I am no longer tempted to declaim against the bad taste of the age, because in denying me the place I sought it has given me time to compose my *Scienza Nuova* . . . I feel that I am seated upon a rock of adamant when I think of that law of God which does justice to genius by the esteem of the wise.'[1]

Vico was endowed with remarkable poetic imagination; he was a philosopher and a man deeply learned in law. The versatility of his mind, which ranged over the fields of metaphysics and history, philology, poetry and law, found expression in a sociology comprehending the whole panorama of human life, for he was never crushed by the orthodox education of his day, following his own bent in spite of all obstacles. Years before the publication of the *Scienza Nuova*, he had attacked the limitations of the Cartesian position, attempting a fuller answer to the problem of knowledge. As an historian he was deeply versed in Greek and Roman history, and as a poet steeped in the writings of Homer and Dante. He developed new and startling theories on the origins of the Homeric poems, similarly, in the study of law, he went deeper than his contemporaries.

Although in the eighteenth century Italy was politically backward; the tradition of legal learning had survived since the Middle Ages, when the universities of Naples and Salerno had been the centres of a brilliant culture. There was still a flourishing school of Jurisprudence at Naples, and Vico was led to the study of sociology through Roman Law. The ideas condensed in the *Scienza Nuova* are anticipated in the *De Universi Juris*.

Vico held the orthodox opinion that God rules the world by laws traceable in human affairs; but he believed, like Spinoza, not in a transcendent law, but in an immanent law, emergent in human institutions. Where Vico differed from the orthodox authorities, notably Grotius, Hobbes, and Puffendorf, was in his refusal to explain the origins of law in terms of rational contract. He was too good an historian to believe that under primitive conditions men were capable of a deliberate reasoned argument to obey the laws for their mutual benefit. Still less could he accept the view that elaborate legal codes could spring suddenly from the mind of a single legislator; on the contrary, he knew that rational law had grown up gradually out of primitive custom: that out of the mnemonic formulae of primitive law grew the elaborate structure of later times; that the legislators to whom codes are attributed were frequently mythical figures devised by later ages. Justice arose not from personal and rational planning but from the instinctive wisdom of custom.

Following the conventional scheme of his day, Vico starts his

[1] Quoted by FLINT, *Vico*, Blackwood (1884), p. 35.

hypothesis from the fall of man. Fallen humanity, no longer apprehending truth directly, is yet linked with God by the promptings of
instinct. Through the darkness, men and nations still perceive
glimmerings of the Divine purpose by a 'common wisdom', emergent
in response to the challenge of environment. Vico grasped the truth
that history must be interpreted in terms of psychology; here, in the
early eighteenth century, in an age of triumphant rationalism, is a
writer aware not only of the importance of human origins but of the
imaginative effort necessary to interpret them.

The *Scienza Nuova* was written, not in the conventional Latin of
his earlier works, but in vivid flexible Italian. It is entitled: 'Principi
di Scienza Nuova d'intorno alla comune Natura delle Nazioni.'[1]

In the dedication to Cardinal Corsini, the author states that many
learned men have speculated on the natural law of nations 'Diritto
Natural delle Genti', but that they have all of them been 'ultramon-
tani', foreigners. Now, for the first time, an Italian, writing in his
native tongue, in conformity with the orthodox teachings of the
Roman Church, is delineating a new science in accordance with the
nature of nations.

The work is divided into five books: the first, consisting of thirteen
short chapters, lays down the general principles on which the author
intends to proceed. The fall of man, he argues in the first chapter,
was due to curiosity, forbidden by the nature of things, whereby
men inquired into mysteries proper only to God. The Jews alone,
through their revealed religion, retained direct contact with God;
the rest of the human race were condemned to misery and death.

The 'Gentile nations', however, retained a certain 'common
wisdom' (sapienza vulgare) which grew out of two great principles
of truth, first that Divine Providence governs human affairs, and
second that man enjoys free will. From the second principle it
follows that men have a desire to live according to Justice.

There are three instincts, says Vico, common to the human race.
First, the belief in Providence; second, the recognition of parenthood;
third, the instinct to bury the dead. These instincts are reflected in
the customs of religion, marriage, and sepulture. Thus, by confining
direct revelation to the history of the Jews, he avoids various pit-
falls, and retains a free hand in speculating on Gentile history, which
after all, covers a wide field. The originality of this approach, which
emancipated knowledge from the framework by which even Spinoza

[1] VICO, *Opere*, vol. IV. Edited FERRARI, Milano (1836).

and Hobbes are bound, shows the measure of Vico's genius. The perspective is immediately altered; an objective analysis becomes possible.

Gentile man, though fallen from grace, is the master of his own fate under Providence, whose purpose he increasingly apprehends with the development of civilized life. Civilization is based on the three principles already defined, which no nations, however barbarous, have been known to violate. On this foundation, stabilized by religion and laws, is built the structure of Science and the Arts, and philosophic knowledge can supplement instinct.

In the second chapter of the first book, *Meditazione di una Scienza Nuova*, Vico asks how Gentile civilization emerges from primitive beginnings. How do nations attain their full development? Hitherto all the sciences and arts have been thought of in terms of perfecting the individual; no one has studied the principles of perfecting nations. This state of perfection is achieved, when, on the firm basis of custom, 'recondite wisdom' (Sapienza riposta de filosofi — The stored up wisdom of philosophy) joins hands with 'common wisdom'. Vico attacks the Stoics and Epicureans for ignoring this 'common wisdom', for their materialism, and their abandonment of free will. Plato alone transcends these errors, teaching that the proper duty of the philosopher is to live in conformity with the laws, according to the example of Socrates. None the less, even Plato falls into the 'learned error'[1] (eruditto errore) of deriving the laws from the deliberations of philosophers.

Vico proceeds to criticize the limitations of Grotius, of Selden, and of Puffendorf. The first book concludes, after a series of speculations on the origins of language and law, by stressing the extreme difficulty of building up the new science. 'Because of which harsh uncertainties and almost desperate difficulties involved in such a project, where we know nothing either of these first men or, in consequence, of those original places in the world from which the Gentile nations began to emerge, we, following in our thought the animal wanderings of such people, have as the heading of this work, put forward this first book of ours, the substance of which can be summed up briefly, in these words — "we wander ignorant of the men and the places".'[2]

[1] Bk. I, chap. iii, p. 16.
[2] Bk. I, chap. xiii, p. 41. 'Per le quali tutte aspre incertezze e quasi disperate difficoltà di si fatto divisamento, nulla sappiendo nè da quali primi uomini si fatti, nè'n conseguenza da quai primi luoghi del mondo le nazioni gentilesche cominciarono a provenire

Vico in the first book has thus stated his position clearly. Far from interpreting history in terms of revealed religion, the normal approach in his day, he has extricated himself from conventional limitations, while at the same time preserving his orthodoxy. The fallen Gentile world has achieved civilization through following its own instincts; in the course of history man has made himself. Here is a revolutionary approach to sociology, anticipating the predominant modern view.

How this process has occurred can be ascertained only through patient investigation and impartial study. Further, far from interpreting society in terms of individuals, Vico attempts to trace the development of nations, of communities, and to apprehend the pattern of their evolution.

The second book, in sixty-seven chapters, applies these philosophical principles to the study of history. 'The Divine Architect', he says, rules the Gentile nations according to the mandate of 'common wisdom', which is 'an instinct common to each people and nation'. The sum of this instinct is the 'combined wisdom' of the human race,[1] and through it God manifests his purpose, not by external intervention; like Spinoza, Vico holds the divine purpose to be immanent, not transcendent.

Tracing the origins of the Gentile nations, Vico maintains that after the Deluge the human race became divided into two kinds: on the one hand, men of normal size; on the other, idolatrous and bestial giants, living in the diluvial marshes left by the receding Flood. From these giants Gentile humanity descends, for in the process of time men reverted from the monstrous stature of these forbears to a proper size.

The first step towards civilization came through fear of thunder and lightning, whereby the giants were startled out of their brutish stupor: they began to feel shame. No longer daring to indulge their instincts in the open, they carried off their mates into caves and thus founded family life; hence the 'natural docility' of women and the 'natural nobility' of men, arising out of this first act of 'violent authority'.[2]

Vico, enforcing his argument, instances how often thunder is

---

[1] Bk. II, chap. ii, p. 46.   [2] Bk. II, chap. xiii, pp. 89-90.

noi, seguitando col pensiero l'error ferino di uomini così fatti, qui sopra nella Idea di quest' Opera, proponemmo questo Libro tutto raccolto in questo motto . . . "Ignari Hominumque Locorumque Erramus".'

made an attribute of Jove in pagan mythology. Far from dismissing this mythology as a fantastic rubbish heap, he subjects it to serious investigation. Old Testament references to giants are linked up with Greek legends and with the war of the Titans against the Gods. The first phase of human history is thus 'The Age of the Gods', in which the ancestors of men were 'disciplined'. During this age they devised the Gods personifying the sea, the sky, fire, and the crops; they achieved the rudiments of religion, family life, speech, and property, the last associated with the burial of the dead.

The next phase of human history was the Heroic Age, in which the fathers of families developed into heroic leaders and men were ruled by an aristocracy of virtue and ability.

In this age appeared two types of men,[1] 'una nobile perché d'intelligenti; un altra vile, perché di stupidi'. This nobility fulfils the purpose of God and realizes the full stature of men. The rest of humanity are their 'clients'. During the Heroic Age they remain subservient to their masters: later, with growing civilization, these plebeians assert themselves. Meanwhile, the heroic *élite* are responsible for the progress of arts and morals, agriculture, colonization, and industry; they protect the people from robbers, they guide and discipline the ignorant through an instinct of generosity and justice. Vico illustrates this theme from Classical history; like Dante, he regarded the Roman State at its apex,[2] as the highest achievement of humanity, and he devotes many chapters to its evolution. Though he disagreed with Machiavelli's conclusions, he probably owed much to the *Discorsi*. Vico admired the brutality of the early Romans[3] and the severity of their laws, an admiration of force characteristic of many Italian thinkers.

The third stage of history, he continues, is the Human Age, when civilized rationality has enabled the majority of men to participate in government, when an exact and comprehensive system of laws has been made and alphabetic writing invented.

It is an age of great material achievement, of prosperity and splendour, and, like all phases of history, it does not last. Men become over-civilized and decadent; luxury and class conflict occur; the end is dictatorship, ultimately conquest by more virile peoples, 'since he who cannot govern himself must be governed by another'.

[1] Bk. II, chap. xvi, p. 96.
[2] *Vide* chaps. xxxiv–xxxv on 'Heroic Republics' and the 'Regno Romano Eroico'. Bk. II.
[3] Bk. II, chap. xxxv, p. 123.

Such is the outline of Vico's historical analysis: not only can the development of classical history be traced according to this pattern, but a similar cycle of events, he maintains, has occurred since the Roman Empire. The Dark Ages may be compared to the original Divine Age; the Heroic Age of Antiquity is paralleled by the Middle Ages, with their chivalry and poetry; while the Renaissance begins a period of sophistication comparable to the later Roman Empire. Vico envisaged a process of cyclical recurrence, of 'corsi e ricorsi'. Each cycle might be on a greater scale and not always alike in detail, but the same theme runs through all. He ends the second book with a series of speculations on the chronology of early history[1] and on the geography of classical times; his reflections on the colonizing activity of the Greeks,[2] and its effect on their outlook, are interesting and suggestive. Finally, he sums up his closely reasoned argument, maintaining that his original hypothesis has been borne out by the study of history.

Reinforcing these general conclusions, the third book, in forty-one chapters, attempts to investigate the development of the human race by the study of language. Vico attacks the pedantry of contemporary scholars; philology, he argues, using the term in the Italian sense of the study of literature, can throw a searching light on to the most fundamental ideas; it is a branch of philosophy and a weapon of trenchant power. He is mainly concerned with the light thrown by mythology and poetry on the mind of primitive man.

Peoples who are in the depths of ignorance naturally interpret their surroundings by fables and allegories: the development of language corresponds with the development of society. During the Age of the Gods, when men were inventing speech, language was vague and poetical; the lapse of time was indicated by the number of harvests; the names of the gods symbolized the natural interests of food and agriculture; here Vico's literary speculation runs parallel with his historical hypothesis.

During the Heroic Age, men still communicated by symbols and heraldry.[3] The writings of Homer,[4] though dating from the close of an Heroic Age, yet display the noble characteristics of this society

[1] Bk. II, chap. vii, p. 58.   [2] Bk. II, chap. vii, p. 63.   [3] Bk. III, chap. xli.
[4] In the notes supplementary to his *Treatise on Universal Law* Vico investigated the origin of the Homeric poems. In the second, expanded edition of the *Scienza Nuova* (1730) he devotes a whole book to the question, concluding that Homer himself was a myth. The Homeric Poems, he argues, were the creation not of one individual, but of various authors writing during successive generations. Vico thus anticipated one of the major scholastic controversies of the nineteenth century.

in its full flower. Dante, again, is a poet of the heroic virtues, and both are superior to Virgil, for all his technical skill. Homer, indeed, depicts the virtue of an Heroic society in the *Iliad*, Achilles symbolizing the youth of the race; in the *Odyssey*, Ulysses expresses the cunning and wisdom of the human age. Having thus brought the development of literature into line with his philosophy of history, Vico concludes the third book by reverting to the theme of a dictionary of ideas common to the human race and the foundation of all language ('Dizionarii di voci, per cosi dire mentali'). The fourth book consists of a short recapitulation of the main argument, covering only three pages and a half: it knits up the themes of the previous books.

The fifth is divided into eleven chapters, followed by a short conclusion to the whole work. After a further general survey and recapitulation of his arguments, Vico attempts to prove and illustrate his thesis from the history of the Gentile nations. The second chapter draws a detailed parallel between Greek and Roman history; in it he maintains that all nations pass through the same inevitable phases of development. Chapter three deals first with the Age of the Gods, and next with Egyptian history, language, and religion. In the following chapter, reverting to his main theme and quoting from biblical history, he declares that social development follows from the three punishments inflicted on fallen humanity, the sense of shame, curiosity, and the need to work.

There follows an excursion into Antediluvian history,[1] and Vico goes on to review the history of the Assyrians, Phoenicians, and Egyptians, claiming that they have passed through the two first phases, an Age of the Gods, and an Heroic Age. Chapter seven is of particular interest; reverting to the Age of the Gods in Greece, Vico subdivides it into minor epochs, and going through the catalogue of the major Greek Gods, gives a full and remarkable account of their origins and the ideas they symbolize. For example, under the name of Jove, the earliest God invented by the Greeks, he groups ideas not only of justice and power, but of auspices and divination; he analyses the Myths very fully, and admirably illustrates the significance of each of the Gods, relating them to social development. Then follows a short dissertation on the similarity between the ancient Gentile nations; they had an Age of the Gods too. He draws parallels between Greek mythology and oriental legends, including the story of the Magi.[2]

---

[1] Bk. V, chap. v.   [2] Bk. V, chap. viii.

He proceeds to a long analysis of the Hero myths, bringing in the liberation theme, referring to Theseus and Minos, Perseus and Andromeda, the Trojan War and the Cadmus myths of expansion and colonization. Vico goes on to demonstrate from the Hercules legend the universality of the Heroic Age: in this lengthy chapter he interprets the legend of the Golden Fleece, and cites Romulus as the typical Hero founding a 'clientela'.[1]

The book, and with it the whole work, ends with a short chapter and conclusion. Vico claims that the stages of evolution he has traced are under the design of Providence. He will not accept the inadequate philosophies of Grotius and Puffendorf, still less the godless views of the Stoics and Epicureans. Though the evolution of history is self-contained, Providence, he insists, ultimately governs human affairs. The book concludes with a passage of notable eloquence and power. Without this overriding Providence of God, he insists, the world would be a silent wilderness and the human race long extinct.[2] 'Che era l'Idea dell'Opera, che tutta incominciammo da quel motto: "A Jove principium Musae"; ed ora la chiudiamo con l'altra parte: "Jovis omnia plena" ... che, senza un Dio Provvedente, non sarebbe nel mondo altro stato che errore, bestialità, bruttezza, violenza, fierezza, marciume e sangue; e forse, e senza forse, per la gran selva della terra orrida e muta, oggi non sarebbe genere umano.'[3]

It will be seen that Vico's presentment of his theme is overschematic; like many original thinkers, he is apt to fit the fact to theory. His thought is often repetitive; his intuitions of uneven value; yet, these defects pale beside the originality, the eloquence, the modernity, of his overmastering idea. With an imaginative range unparalleled in his age, Vico had constructed a secular philosophy of history. The modernity of his outlook is apparent first from his insistence that man, under Providence, makes his own history; second, from the historical sense apparent throughout his work. The concept of social evolution, dominant to modern minds, is foreshadowed in this remarkable book.

---

[1] Bk. V, chap. x.   [2] Bk. V, chap. xi.

[3] 'This was the idea of the work, at the very beginning of which we quoted the words "with Jove my lay begins" – (Virgil, *Eclogue* III, line 60) – and now we close with the other half of the line, "the world is full of Jove". For without a providential God there would not be in the world any condition but that of error, bestiality, brutality, violence, savage pride, corruption and blood – and it may well be perhaps, and we need not say "perhaps", the great wilderness of the world would be ugly and dumb, without a human race.'

It is in this modern, anthropocentric outlook that his affinity with Spinoza lies; both men, saving the artificiality of Vico's scheme, are objective in their treatment of facts. 'Humanas actiones non ridere, non lugere, neque detestare, sed intelligere' — not to ridicule human actions, or to weep over them or hate them, but to understand them. Both are outside the immediate stream of political and intellectual development — that was to be dominated by more politically minded, more practical thinkers. But Spinoza achieved a constructive refutation of Hobbes, and Vico an historical outlook of revolutionary scope. Their writings are among the firstfruits of a new and modern awareness.

CHAPTER VIII

THE AGE OF REASON

§ I

WE have seen how the main stream of political speculation, expressed in terms of Cartesian method within the framework of national states, and set against the background of predominant Continental absolutism, displayed its greatest vitality in England, where the mediaeval tradition of the rule of Law and the trusteeship of government was reasserted in contemporary terms in the writings of Locke. How, also, in Holland, the political philosophy of Spinoza, and in Italy the new historical sense of Vico, looked forward to a deeper understanding of the scientific outlook. With the eighteenth century, both these lines of thought were given a French interpretation; the political philosophy of Locke, in particular, becoming a world influence both in Europe and America, destined largely to undermine the *ancien régime*, still so imposing to the contemporary view.

Three great thinkers, Montesquieu, Diderot, and Voltaire, may be taken as representative of this French influence. A new confidence in the perfectibility of man and of institutions is widely apparent, and a remarkable faith in the power of reason in human affairs. But this rationalism was to have its reaction, and the wave of eighteenth-century thought culminates and breaks in the devastating conclusions of Hume, who, by strict rational analysis, demonstrated the limitations of reason itself, and further modified an ancient tradition of political thought already shaken — the faith in abstract natural reason, reflecting a transcendent Natural Law. None the less, with that hypothesis thrown overboard, empirical reason — the tradition of knowledge as power, proceeding on Cartesian lines — continued with growing effectiveness. Meanwhile the eighteenth century was the age of the triumph of abstract reason, and French thinkers were its prophets.

The situation in France at the beginning of the eighteenth century was paradoxical; the most brilliant and highly civilized nation in Europe, disposing of the largest population and the most extensive economic resources, was governed by a rigid and clumsy absolutism.

The military glories of Louis XIV were expensive and unsuccessful:[1] the financial incompetence of his ministers, natural in an age which was without reliable statistics; the religious bigotry which revoked the Edict of Nantes as late as 1687, when men were beginning to think of toleration, and imposed a heavy censorship on the wittiest and most articulate people since the fifth-century Greeks, were bound to provoke first an intellectual and later a political protest of formidable dimensions. Divorced from the temptations and restraints of executive responsibility, the French intellectuals of the Enlightenment were free to create a telling propaganda in the cause of 'Reason' which was to pervade European thought and set the tone of eighteenth-century society and literature. The most famous of the many exponents of this outlook are Montesquieu, Diderot, and Voltaire, and we will examine in turn their contributions to political thought.

This brilliant dogmatic crusade provoked its reaction, expressed by Rousseau in France and in their different ways by Hume and Burke in England. Both Voltaire and Montesquieu had spent impressionable years in England; both admired English political institutions, and both broadcast their interpretations to the world, Voltaire with the malign gusto of French urban wit and the verve of exasperated intelligence. Voltaire possesses Pope's bitterness and lucidity, with more than Pope's grasp of the realities of politics; Montesquieu brings to political speculation a scientific approach of surprising modernity.[2] They were both influenced by the increasing interest in savage peoples and alien civilization which colonial exploration had brought into Europe, and both wrote a French of unsurpassed vivacity and charm.

[1] Anyone who goes to Versailles and notes the martial decorations and the subjects of the tapestries displayed in the rooms inhabited by the Roi Soleil and his entourage, can take the measure of his mind.

[2] Montesquieu, 1689-1755. Charles de Secondat, Baron de la Brède et de Montesquieu, was born near Bordeaux in 1689. His maternal grandfather was President of the Parliament of Bordeaux, which office Montesquieu inherited. In his youth travelled in Italy, Switzerland, Holland, and was for two years in England. (He said that Germany was made to travel in, Italy to stay in, England to think in, and France to live in.) He spent most of his life at Brède or in Paris. He was a good musician. Published Lettres Persanes, 1721 (revised edition 1754); Considerations sur la grandeur des Romans et de leur decadence, 1734; Esprit des Lois published anonymously at Geneva, reprinted 1741. Died in Paris 1755. 'Entouré de quelques amis, et d'un plus grand nombre des spectateurs.' He had a wide reputation and many friends in England. The English Evening Post wrote the following characteristic obituary of him: 'His virtues did honour to human nature, his writings to justice. A friend to mankind, he asserted their undoubtable and inalienable rights with freedom, even in his own country, whose prejudices in matters of religion and government he had long lamented, and endeavoured, not without some success, to remove.

Montesquieu was lucky to be born in a time when the social sciences were opening out into a dazzling range, but were yet capable of simplification by an elegant amateur. The *Esprit des Lois* makes what is in effect an environmental and anthropological approach to political theory and social practice. Montesquieu has a sublime confidence in the beneficent order of nature. 'Je n'ai point tiré mes principes de mes préjugés mais de la nature des choses', he writes in his preface. This natural order extends also to human society. 'Les Lois, dans la signification la plus étendue, sont les rapports nécessaires qui dérivent de la nature des choses; et, dans ce sens, tous les êtres ont leurs lois; la divinité a ses lois, le monde matériel a ses lois, les intelligences supérieures à l'homme ont leurs lois, les bêtes ont leurs lois, l'homme a ses lois.

'Ceux qui ont dit qu'une fatalité aveugle a produit tous les effets que nous voyons dans le monde ont dit une grande absurdité; car quelle plus grande absurdité qu'une fatalité aveugle qui auroit produit des êtres intelligents?'

Montesquieu's confidence in the validity of Natural Reason simplified his problem; the minds of all men are capable of understanding it according to their setting in the world.

'Toutes les nations ont un droit des gens, et les Iroquois mêmes, qui mangent leurs prisonniers, en ont un.' Governments are adapted to the dispositions of their peoples and their environment; all are the expression of the same principle. Laws 'ought to be in relation to the physical structure of the country, to a cold, hot or temperate climate, to the quality of the soil, the situation and size, to the kind of life led by the inhabitants . . . their religion, instincts, customs and manners' (Bk. I, chap. iii).

Montesquieu believes that an examination of the structure of different societies will reveal 'what is called "L'Esprit des Lois" ' — the appropriate principle behind their government. This simplification is highly characteristic of the early eighteenth century; Montesquieu's thought tends to be geometrical and artificial in the Cartesian tradition. But he adds also the principle enunciated by Spinoza, that men ought to be examined for what they are. Newton had discovered the laws of the universe and Montesquieu is confident that he can find those of society; this scientific empirical bias conflicts with his *a priori* assumption of the validity of a universal law of reason, but Montesquieu's genius may be allowed its inconsistency.

He has a remarkable sense of how societies actually work and of the effect of environment: for example, he observes that monasticism is born in the hot countries of the East where men are less carried to action than to speculation: in Asia the number of dervishes and monks seems to 'increase with the heat of the climate; in India the place swarms with them' (Bk. XIV, chap. vii). He remarks on the hypersensibility of the Indians, whom, he alleges, tend to be at once soft and cruel. In the cold of the North he observes that people drink more, while the English, he alleges, are notoriously prone to suicide owing to their climate.

His outlook is cosmopolitan and humanitarian; he writes that if he knew of 'something which was useful to my country, but injurious to Europe and the human race', he would think it a crime to take advantage of it. The scope of his interests is world-wide, and ranges from China and Japan to South America, in a far-flung manner alien to the English outlook of Locke. His book is very long and sometimes swamped with knowledge, and his excursions into classical and Frankish history, though often entertaining, suffer from the limitations of the research of the day. He hates despotism — that disastrous expedient — and criticizes the French Government by thinly disguised observations on the state of China. At the same time Montesquieu, a discursive, urbane, arrogant, eighteenth-century gentleman, had no sympathy for republicanism and little sympathy for the poor; the existing social injustices in France are taken for granted.

Though the sociological aspects of Montesquieu's writings are the most attractive, and, in spite of a certain lack of historical sense, the most sound, it is his constitutional theory which has been most influential. Governments, he says, following the ordinary convention, are despotic, monarchical or republican. According to the fashion of the age he idealized the virtues of the Roman republic, he detested the despotism of the French Government, and he admired the English constitutional monarchy. In the eleventh book of the *Esprit des Lois* he attempted to analyse the British constitution, and he came to conclusions which, though rather wide of the facts, deeply affected the thought of the American and French revolutionaries of the late eighteenth century, and which were embodied in the Constitution of the United States and in the French declaration of the Rights of Man.

Montesquieu is concerned, rightly, with the problem of the control of power; he lays down the principle that there are three kinds in a well-ordered state: legislative, executive, and judicial. 'If the legislative power is united with the executive power in the hands of one person, or of any one body of officials, there can be no liberty, nor can there be any liberty if the power to judge is not separated from the legislative and executive powers.' In practice, the English constitution was never dependent on such a balance, in which the three elements would actually tend to paralyse one another.

Montesquieu gave the over-simplified interpretation of the complex, inarticulate, English political compromise which one would expect; in practice the sovereignty in England was tending to be vested in the King-in-parliament, and the evolution of party and Cabinet government was beginning to solve the problem, which had baffled the seventeenth century, of making the executive reflect the will of the legislature. The revolution of 1688 had, in effect, been a successful compromise of balanced interests, but it was not possible to obtain the benefits of instinctive common sense and political intuition simply by adopting a written constitution based on general principles worked out in legal form. This aspect of Montesquieu's influence is less attractive than his brilliant if reckless excursions into largely unexplored fields of world sociology.

In his method of approach Montesquieu was influenced by Aristotle, but profound as was Aristotle's observation, the range of his facts was comparatively narrow. Montesquieu, superficial as he often can be, is aware of the possibilities of a scientific approach on a world scale, and his sense of the effect of environment on society has been borne out by subsequent research.

The confidence and serenity of Montesquieu's writing recall the poise of the Hellenistic and Augustan Ages, but the French eighteenth century had about it an optimism alien to the thought of Antiquity. The idea of progress, absent from classical and mediaeval thought, pervades the minds of the writers of the *Eclaircissement*. As we have seen, the idea of the perfectibility of man is already apparent in Locke's thought, which assumes that if Government lets men alone they will order their affairs satisfactorily; this assumption was reinforced by the optimism of the day which was finding fresh fields of knowledge to conquer, and making knowledge much more widely attractive than it had been when expressed in terms of the ponderous learning of the sixteenth century and the Middle Ages.

This knowledge was systematized and given wide currency by the French Encyclopaedists. Diderot, the most influential of these writers, set himself to chart the bounds of a new outlook; of a new orthodoxy. He embarked upon an alphabetical classification of the whole field of contemporary knowledge. The great encyclopaedia, which took twenty years to produce, and which ran to seventeen volumes, with three supplementaries, proved one of the foundations of a new secularized French mentality, and, with that, of a new point of view for the polite world of Europe.

Diderot, a man of miscellaneous genius and immense energy, was endowed with an irrepressible vitality.[1] The finely produced first volume (1751) contains a Preliminary Discourse which shows how deeply its editors were influenced by English thought and Cartesian method. 'L'ouvrage . . .' they write 'a deux objects; comme encyclo-pédia il doit exposer autant qu'il est possible l'ordre et l'enchaine-ment des connoissances humaines; comme dictionnaire raisonné des Sciences, des Arts et des Métiers, il doit continuer . . . les principes généraux qui en sont la basse, et les détails les plus essentiales. . . .'

The work was designed to set out the 'genealogy and affiliation of our knowledge'; the 'Discourse' emphasizes the debt of the authors to 'François Bacon, l'immortel Chancellier d'Angleterre' whose 'Novum Organum' has influenced the order of their 'arbre encyclo-pédie'. Following the principles of Descartes, 'cet homme rare', they go back to the origin of ideas, maintaining the principle that 'la première chose que nos sensations apprennent . . . c'est notre

---

[1] Diderot, 1713-84. Born at Langres, and educated by the Jesuits, he became a literary adventurer in Paris. After various publications he was imprisoned by the authorities for his *Lettres sur les Aveugles* (1749), which satirized the old order. The encyclopaedia originated in a scheme for the translation of an existing English work, expanded by Diderot into his immense enterprise. It was composed under great difficulties and in 1759 was formally suppressed. His collaborator, D'Alembert, with-drew from the enterprise, and Diderot was reduced to secret visits to the workshops of artisans for his technical information, returning in the evening to write up the knowledge collected. In these circumstances Diderot made a poor enough living but achieved celebrity among a brilliant circle, his principal friend and patron being the Baron D'Holbach, the well-known writer. When he was forced to sell his library, the Empress Catherine of Russia bought it, gave orders that the books should remain in Paris, and appointed Diderot Librarian. The efforts of the authorities to suppress this persevering champion of intellectual liberty succeeded no better than they deserved, and Diderot lived to see his name famous. The full title of the work runs *Encyclopédie, ou Dictionnaire Raisonné Des Sciences, des Arts et des Metiers, par une société de gens de lettres, Mis en ordre et publié par M. Diderot et par M. D'Alembert*. Paris, M.DCC.L.I. avec approbation et privilège du Roi.

existence' — Descartes's well-known 'cogito ergo sum'. Locke, they continue, one can almost say, created modern metaphysics, as Newton created physical science.

On this metaphysical basis Diderot and D'Alembert proceed to the classification of external knowledge in the light of the Baconian view of knowledge as power and the Cartesian method of systematic analysis of all relevant facts. For this redoubtable marshalling of contemporary information they have sought out, they say, the collaboration of experts in every field, particularly from the 'nation Eclairé des Gens de Lettres'.

It may well be imagined the influence this Encyclopaedia, with its appeal not only to speculative minds but to those in quest of technical information, was to exercise in that day, for such an enterprise on such a scale was without precedent. Its appearance is a landmark in the development of the modern outlook, of that French rational orthodoxy which was to achieve so much, and which was later to develop an almost crushing elaboration. Here was something formidable indeed, with so wide a popular appeal; the beginning of a new professionalized competence which was to be at the back of most subsequent political thought.

Though some of the contributors allowed themselves a pretty wide liberty, the Encyclopaedia did not constitute a direct attack on the old ideas; rather it undermined them in a more deadly manner, by implication, or by citation of factual evidence.

The verve of Montesquieu's writing is surpassed by the brilliance of Diderot's most hard-hitting contributor. Voltaire's crusade against the obsolescent social and political regime of eighteenth-century France supplemented the influence of the encyclopaedia with a more direct attack.[1] Like Erasmus, Voltaire was a propa-

---

[1] Voltaire, François Marie Arouet de; born in Paris 1694; son of François Arouet a notary, and his wife Marie Margaret Daumart; both parents of Poitevin origin. Educated by the Jesuits. In spite of opposition he was determined to make literature his career. 1716, exiled from Paris for subversive political libels. 1717-18, in the Bastille; emerged having changed his name to Voltaire. His first tragedy, *Oedipe*, acted in 1718 with success. Employed on secret diplomatic missions to Holland. 1724, published the *Henriade*. Quarrelled with de Rohan, who had him beaten by his servants, 1725. Exiled to England, 1726-9. His successful stay there profoundly influenced his thought. 1733, *Lettres Philosophiques sur les Anglais*, a covert attack on French institutions. 1751, Went to live at the Court of Frederick of Prussia. 1753, *Siècle de Louis XIV*; *Diatribe du Dr. Akakia*, an attack on one of Frederick's officials. Quarrelled with Frederick. 1754, *Essai sur les Mœurs*. Settled near Geneva. 1758, bought Ferney. 1759, *Candide*. 1778, *Irène*. Triumphal visit to Paris where he died on May 30th of that year.

His *Dictionnaire Philosophique* is composed of articles contributed to Diderot's *Encyclopédie*; next to *Candide*, it contains his point of view most succinctly.

gandist, powerful just because he was not committed to specific political doctrines, but expressed a general point of view congenial to his audience. Voltaire accepted the social inequalities of his day: his outlook is not in the least democratic, though he loathed the conventional structure of the Catholic Church. In spite of his detestation of human folly, Voltaire's hard-boiled assessment of historical evidence leads him to a qualified belief in progress. Summing up the conclusions of his *Essai sur les Mœurs et L'Esprit des Nations*,[1] he decides that the industry of mankind is stronger than their fanaticism. It is indeed a great nuisance that Princes should keep so many professional soldiers, but at least the common people are not involved in the wars made by 'their masters', and in spite of the catastrophies brought about by 'fureur dogmatique'—('vous avez vu parmis les barbaries ridicules, les barbaries sanglantes des guerres de réligion')—and in spite of the monumental follies of superstition ('une Princesse idiote bâtit une chappelle aux onze vièrges') the human race has in fact multiplied — 'there is no lack of human beings'. In a passage of superb prose, with a fine cadence in the best French tradition — 'Que l'on considère depuis Petersburg jusqu'à Madrid, ce nombre prodigieux de villes superbes, bâtits dans les lieux qui étaient des déserts il y a six cents ans' — he marshals the unanswerable evidence for material progress and proceeds to compare the civilization of Europe favourably with that of Asia.

His survey of European development does not, indeed, possess the impartial understanding of a balanced historical judgement. Set out with all the seductions of a brilliant style and a barbed wit, Voltaire's history is a weapon of political warfare against an obscurantism that was still dangerous. He cannot think himself back into the mind of the eleventh century: he sees only its folly, its superstition. This limitation made his writings the more influential in spreading the new orthodoxy systematized by Diderot, for the majority of minds are glad to exchange one set of intellectual conventions for another, and a confident dogmatism does much to recommend a writer, particularly when he is endowed with literary genius.

Voltaire's history of his own time is more objective, with a deeper understanding: the well-known *Siècle de Louis XIV* remains a

---

[1] *Essai sur les Mœurs et L'Esprit des Nations, et sur les faits d'Histoire depuis Charlmagne jusqu'à ce que Louis XIII*. Remarques pour servir pour supplement. Œuvres, 19th vol. 1789 edition.

masterpiece in its own field; it is informed with the same rationalistic bias and the same clarity of mind.

But in all the seventy volumes of his collected works Voltaire's point of view is most strikingly expressed in the famous novel *Candide*, in which he scarifies the imbecility of militarism and superstition, and, indeed, the irresponsibility of nature. Against a background of cumulative catastrophe, rendered tolerable by the wit with which it is described and the intelligent gallantry of the victims portrayed, Voltaire draws the conclusion, similar to that of Epicurus, 'il faut cultiver notre jardin'. Such a negative attitude would not seem, on the face of it, politically influential, but the tone of mind which it implied, the ability to see through institutions and the raillery with which the forces of stupidity are defied, were destructive elements of the first calibre.

The popularity of Voltaire's writings helped to spread an outlook always congenial to the French mind. This witty and tough individualism contributed a great deal to the breaking not only of the obscurantist hold over the French people, but also of the monarchical and aristocratic institutions which the revolution was to sweep away. Since many of the more intelligent of the French aristocracy ceased to believe in themselves, the citadel was undermined from within.

Voltaire kept, however, a fierce faith in the power of enlightenment. He undoubtedly believed that the triumph of reason would make existing institutions, after due reform, work in a flexible way; he may be ranged with those thinkers who held that reason can discern and put into action a right pattern of human affairs.

§ III

It remained for Hume[1] to push disillusionment deeper: carrying

---

[1] David Hume, 1711-76, a younger son of a good Scottish family. He was 'seized very early with a passion for literature'. In 1734, having attempted without success to adapt himself to business in Bristol, he went over to France, where he writes, 'I resolved to make a very rigid frugality supply the deficiency of fortune, to maintain unimpaired my independence'. He settled at La Flèche, in Anjou, where he wrote his *Treatise on Human Nature*, published 1739. 'Never literary attempt was more unfortunate than my *Treatise on Human Nature*. It fell dead born from the press. But being naturally of a cheerful and sanguine temper, I very soon recovered the blow and prosecuted with great ardour my studies in the country.' Published in 1741 the First Volume of *Essays*. 1744, tutor to Lord Annandale. 'I lived with him a twelvemonth; my appointments during that time made a considerable accession to my small fortune.' 1747, secretary to General St. Clair in Vienna and Turin. *Inquiry Concerning Human Understanding*, 1749. 'Found by Dr. Warburton's railings that my book was beginning to be esteemed in good company.' 1752, appointed Librarian to the Faculty of

the cool analysis of the eighteenth century to the logical and disconcerting conclusion of undermining the faith in transcendent natural reason which had remained, rather uncomfortably, behind the thought of Hobbes, Locke, Montesquieu, and Voltaire. The Platonic geometrical plan which haunts the minds of seventeenth-century political thinkers and harks back to the scholastic assumption of natural reason as part of divine design, seemed dissipated by Hume's philosophical analysis of the faculty of reason. Hume distinguishes mathematical certainty from empirical probability; he subordinates reason to instinct, thus denying that a quasi-mathematical science of politics is possible, and striking at the whole tradition of natural reason. Further, he anticipates many modern biological interpretations of social values by regarding them as rules designed for utility, or, as we should say, 'survival'. Society, he maintains, is held together by conventions which are merely relative and not 'eternal truths'. He distinguished between two kinds of

---

Advocates in Edinburgh. In the previous year had appeared the *Inquiry into the principles of Morals*. 'Which in my own opinion (which ought not to judge on that subject) is of all my writings, historical, philosophical or literary, incomparably the best. It came unnoticed and unobserved into the world.'

1752, *Political Discourses*, 'the only work of mine that was successful on first publication'. 1754-61, *History of England*. 1757, *Natural History of Religion*. 'Its public entry was rather obscure except only that Dr. Hurd wrote a pamphlet against it with all the illiberal petulance, arrogance and scurrility which distinguishes the Warburton school. This pamphlet gave me some consolation for the otherwise indifferent reception of my performance.'

None the less, by 1761 his reputation was made. 'I was become not only independent but opulent.' 1763, secretary to the Embassy in Paris. 'There is however a real satisfaction in living at Paris from the great number of sensible, knowing and polite company with which that city abounds above all places in the universe. I thought once of settling there for life.' 1765, Chargé d'affaires. 1767, returned to Edinburgh, 'very opulent, for I possessed a revenue of £1000 a year, healthy, and though somewhat stricken in years, with the prospect of enjoying my ease and of seeing the increase of my reputation'. But in the spring of 1775 he found himself seriously ill. 'I now reckon upon a steady dissolution . . . I consider besides that a man of 65 by dying cuts off only a few years of infirmities . . . It is difficult to be more detached from life than I am at present.' He could think of no excuse why Charon should not take him . . . 'I have done everything of consequence that I have ever meant to do.'

(The above quotations are taken from Hume's account of his own life.)

Dr. Johnson and Wesley, as might be expected, both profoundly disapproved of Hume . . . 'BOSWELL: I told him that David Hume said to me he was no more uneasy to think that he should not be after his life than that he had not been before he had begun to exist. JOHNSON: Sir, If he really thinks so, his perceptions are disturbed; he is mad; if he does not think so, he lies.'

Wesley asks: 'Did Mr. David Hume know the heart of man? No more than a worm or a beetle does. What think you now of Charon? At length you know it is a fearful thing to fall into the hands of the living God.' (Sermon on Deceitfulness of the Human Heart.)

See HUME's *Works*, edited T. H. Green and T. H. Grose, London (1895-8): in particular '*Of the Original Contract*'. But Hume is more original and influential as a philosopher, than by his direct political analysis, which has little new in it.

truth: formal truth, a logical pattern of ideas, coherent within its own sphere but not valid to interpret the totality of experience; and empirical truth, based on inferred probability but without formal necessity. Further, reason, formal or empirical, does not in fact guide conduct. It is morally neutral and merely 'obeys the passions'; it is determined by instinct and guided by inclination; rational values are therefore relative and not absolute. It follows that Natural Law and natural reason, reflecting a rational transcendent plan, are terms without meaning, for conduct is determined by conventions which have no absolute validity. There is, on these premises, no 'Right Reason'; it is indeed even doubtful if self-interest often determines behaviour, which is generally the result of irrational impulse, when fully analysed. Hume thus drives the trenchant analysis of Cartesian rationalism deeper, working out its full and philosophically self-stultifying conclusions and reinforcing them with the observed conclusions of a man of the world. There is according to this argument no evidence for a 'just basis' of political society; men live in societies because it is convenient to do so, and habit and instinct impel them; there is no 'legal' or contractual basis about it. He confines his idea of justice to a convention for the preservation of property, which keeps contracts valid; the authority of government is relative and depends on being accepted and working in a fairly satisfactory way.

Here is the antithesis of the view of Cicero and St. Thomas, who believed, as we have seen, that human society was the rational expression of a Divine design; but this is not surprising, since Hume regarded the existence of God as unlikely, and had little idea of emergent values.

Hume is therefore not ready to share the optimism of Montesquieu. 'I am apt', he writes, 'to entertain a suspicion that the world is still too young to fix many general truths in politics which will remain true till the latest posterity. We have not as yet had experience of three thousand years, so that not only the act of reasoning is impotent in this science, as in all others, but we even want sufficient material upon which we can reason.' Here is a dose of worldly common sense for the confident angular thought of the seventeenth and early eighteenth centuries.

'It is not yet truly known', he continues very justly, 'what degree of achievement either in virtue or in vice human nature is susceptible of, nor what may be expected of mankind from any great revolution in their education, custom or principles.' Here is an outlook which looks forward, which expects change, which is modern, as Spinoza's desire to understand men is modern, but without Spinoza's concept of emergent values.

Hume, as we have seen, by his criticism of the processes of reason, questioned the assumption that men are actuated by reasonable motives. It had always been apparent to statesmen such as Machiavelli and Halifax that the majority of men were impervious to argument, but the political theorists had long been loath to admit it; Hobbes is cynical enough in his views of human nature, but he attributes to men at least consistency in wrongdoing.

Yet Hume, of course, never destroyed the validity of the tradition of empirical reason, of the Baconian concept of knowledge as power, still less of emergent values; while denying that reason reflects a Natural Law outside experience, he admits that it proceeds on a basis of empirical probability, and this is good enough to give a prospect that limited planning for obvious ends will remain effective in politics, so long as the statesman takes account of the unreasonableness of the multitude. What, apart from his metaphysical analysis, Hume made clear and taught the political theorists, was that the statesman cannot count on a widespread response to the appeal to reason outside a tiny *élite*; armed with this knowledge, the statesman can proceed the more effectively. Not that Hume's analysis deflected the followers of Adam Smith and Bentham from attributing an exaggerated rationality to the 'economic man'; but the idea that reason somehow reflected a transcendent and eternal Natural Law, that assumption was gravely shaken by the self-confident and apparently unanswerable arguments put forward by this Scotsman who, by the end of his life, had 'done everything he had ever meant to do', though Hume never destroyed the concept of Natural Law as the law of self-preservation, nor the validity of the concept of the rule of law based on the consent of the governed.

Here, then, is an attempt to interpret political thought in purely relative and human terms, with no religious or metaphysical explanation behind it, save the idea of self-preservation. Naturally, on Hume's own premises, that men are guided not by reason but by instinct, his conclusions were rejected, though not disproved. A new emergent basis for value had to be sought which was to be outside the Catholic answer, still waiting intact, then as now, for anyone who could make the necessary act of faith. The result for those who could not accept Catholic dogma was a new departure in philosophy; its effect on political theory was to glorify the community, to exalt the will at the expense of reason, and to regard the historical process as something immanent, working itself out in time, creating its own values as it went along.[1]

But of course this open-mindedness of Hume was far too barren to be widely palatable; nor was its influence immediate. Just as when Hume in philosophy seemed to have brought speculation to a dead end, Kant reaffirmed the moral liberty of man by asserting the freedom of the 'good will', so in the political sphere this bland scepticism was not enough, and subsequent thinkers put in its place the organic conception of the State and the emergent conception of reason, to which Rousseau feels his way and which finds its sober expression in Burke and its exaggerated expression in Hegel.

Hume's analysis therefore marks a turning point in political theory of the first importance, as will be apparent if the reader casts back over the whole field surveyed. Hume reinterprets reason in terms of empirical probability, reinforcing it as an instrument of practical control, but gives up the claim that it reflects an absolute value. While empirical reason is thus reinforced, the idea that man is actuated by clear-cut rationality reflecting a transcendent Natural Law is abandoned as a basis of social order.

So the eighteenth century saw the development of a rationalistic outlook which reached its climax and, philosophically, but not practically, its nemesis in Hume. It not only undermined the belief in a divine plan for a social order; it also, with growing maturity, realized the limitations of reason in the conduct of human affairs. Both Natural Law and right reason are ultimately regarded as sub-jective fantasies created by the mind itself, without the objective validity constantly claimed for them by generations of political thinkers. But this apparent impasse was not reached before the destructive power of rationalistic analysis, on the plane of common sense, had undermined also the accumulated social wreckage left over, notably in France, from feudal decentralization and mon-archical absolutism.

Thus the utilitarian view of institutions, deriving from Cartesian method aiming to discover the means of mastering environment, was widely broadcast in the eighteenth century, and, reinforced by the professionalized knowledge of the nineteenth, was to prove the

[1] *Vide supra*, p. 81.

rallying point of a practical political outlook down to our own day. Although, therefore, the reaction which the full conclusions of 'enlightenment' provoked, and of which the principal champions are Rousseau, Burke, and Hegel, provided a political mythos which could give a psychological satisfaction eighteenth-century rationalism could never offer, the value of the tradition of empirical reason broadcast by the enlightenment was incalculable, and has yet probably its major achievements before it. Even if the theory of natural reason wore thin, the rationalistic approach was never discredited in the practical sphere; its weakness in its eighteenth-century interpretation was simply that it took too little account of irrational elements in society with which the empirical rationalist has to cope. This brittleness and cocksure quality of thought was only a symptom of crudity; with growing sophistication eighteenth-century rationalism was destined to grow into the wary, tentative, and increasingly effective outlook of modern evolutionary scientific humanism.

The spirit of impersonal inquiry and humanitarian pity which the eighteenth century contributed to political thought is one of the most valuable of European traditions; it has much in common with the best Greek thought, and, reinforced by the knowledge and power of modern scientific method, may yet show itself the most formidable and decisive element in human affairs.

CHAPTER IX

THE ROMANTIC REACTION:
ROUSSEAU AND BURKE

§ 1

THE late eighteenth century, as we have observed, saw the breakdown of the remnant of the old European political order, already long undermined by the individualism and scepticism of the seventeenth century, and superseded by the nation state; while the relics of feudalism, still embedded in the privileges of the aristocracy and long persisting in social usage, crumbled before the onslaught of empirical rationalism and before the economic and administrative demands of an expanding middle class. The transference of power to this new class, destined in our day to be paralleled by a transference of power to the masses, was the dominant political fact of the succeeding century.

The foundering of the old order, also a long-term result of the breakdown of mediaeval religious unity, took place in a time of expanding technical and speculative enterprise. Where the social structure of antiquity went down into the twilight of the Dark Ages, the decline of the eighteenth-century order coincided with a vast expansion of knowledge and industrial skill. Where the one was a symptom of decadence, the other was a long-term result of the Renaissance and applied scientific method. Where the social pattern of antiquity collapsed of its own accord, the eighteenth-century social order was broken by forces it could not contain.

Yet the rationalism which had riddled the structure of feudal, civic, and clerical privilege, left high and dry by the receding tide of popular loyalty and religious belief, was to provoke its own reaction. The outlook of Voltaire and Hume was too hard and too exacting to appeal to the minds of the classes now grasping power for the first time. The brutal rationalism of *Candide* was congenial to a disillusioned and hard-bitten aristocracy; it was too ferocious a creed for the generation which saw the beginnings of the romantic movement.

Moreover, as we have seen, Hume's analysis of the limitations of rationalism struck at the tradition of natural reason which went back to pagan Antiquity. Not only had the Catholic order long been undermined; now the ancient faith in transcendent Natural Law was shaken. Though the majority of practical men ignored the implications of Hume's thought, the Benthamite school in particular carrying on the tradition of empirical rationalism, and administration, following Cartesian method, achieving a new technique, there was a growing demand for a political theory of emotional appeal to take the place of the wavering certainties of revealed religion and Natural Law, for which the tentative beginnings of an emergent philosophy of history as yet could provide no substitute.

An answer was supplied in France by Rousseau, in England by Burke, and, later, in Germany by Fichte and Hegel. Rousseau, by his assertion of the reality of the general will, attempted to provide the State with a sanction the rationalism of the day had failed to find. The general will, he maintains, is 'always right'; it expresses the drive of the whole society. Further, Rousseau was a brilliant phrasemaker and his age gave him his opportunity.

For political theory had been hitherto confined to a minority of aristocratic, clerical, and academic writers, appealing to a limited and responsible audience; the collapse of the *ancien régime* in France and the falling off of Christian belief mark a new phenomenon in world history, the permeation of the masses by general ideas which are not religious. Rousseau's heady phrases 'caught on'; he came to be regarded as the prophet of democratic revolution.

Burke, on the other hand, though he shares with Rousseau an intense awareness of the community and the values it can realize, is profoundly conservative; he is determined to preserve the ancient structure of the State; he defined in memorable prose the best political traditions of eighteenth-century England.

§ 11

Rousseau is at once a famous political thinker and a disconcerting figure in the annals of political thought,[1] but his unconventional

---

[1] Jean-Jacques Rousseau, born at Geneva, 1712. His father was a watchmaker and dancing master, his mother a Savoyard. He was flung on the world at sixteen, when his father fled the country to escape his creditors. (See the *Confessions*.) He early showed literary talent and a capacity for imposing on women. At Paris, 1742. At Venice, 1743, where much struck by Italian music. 1749, won the prize offered by the Academy of Dijon. 1755, *Discourse on Inequality*. 1755, article on 'Political Economy' in Diderot's *Encyclopédie*. 1760, *Nouvelle Héloïse*. 1762, *Emile; Du Contrat*

habits and the vulgarization of ideas to which his writings contributed, should not obscure his remarkable ability. He was a neurotic genius, a musical bohemian, with a flair for generalization combined with flashes of brilliant statesmanship. Like Montesquieu, he was lucky in his age; he leapt into fame through a prize essay written for the academy of Dijon. Its theme was, 'Has the progress of science and art contributed to corrupt or purify morals?' Acclaimed by Parisian society, Rousseau set up as the prophetic genius which was the role the convention of the day cast for him; in the Middle Ages he would probably have been buried in a monastery or worn out his life in the obscurity of a mendicant order; in our own day he might have achieved influence in journalism and politics.

Rousseau, along with much political wisdom, formulated the middle-class revolt against the intellectual arrogance of the age of reason. His personality was the antithesis of all the age of Montesquieu admired; though shrewd and able he revelled in emotion; he was an exhibitionist, confessing and parading his vices and virtues to the world, devoid of self-control; haunted by a sense of sin, yet driven by the force of genius. Social circumstances played into his hands; the cult of sensibility, outside a religious framework — a new phenomenon in Christian Europe — was widespread in the cosmopolitan urban society of England and France in the later eighteenth century. The growing influence of women in French polite society, the security of the English 'home', the prosperous economic situation which sustained it, combined with increased leisure, makes the late eighteenth century the 'civilizing' century *par excellence*. The

---

Social. 1763, *Lettres du Montagne.* 1765-6, in England: *Projet de constitution pour La Corse. Considerations sur la Gouvernement de Pologne* (Posthumous 1782).

Professors Hearnshaw and Dunning vie with one another in their descriptions of his domestic life. First PROFESSOR HEARNSHAW (*French Thinkers in the Age of Reason*): 'He struck up an acquaintance, which soon developed into cohabitation, with an illiterate and sensual barmaid, Thérèse Lavasseur, by whom he had five children, which [*sic*] . . . were at once sent anonymously to the asylum for foundlings.' Professor DUNNING runs him close and refers to the 'coarse and unlovely woman with whom for a third of a century he lived in squalid and irregular domestic relations' (*History of Political Theory*, vol. III). Neither allows Rousseau any credit for the virtue of constancy, but both are surpassed by Burke, who probably started the tradition. 'Setting up', he says, 'for an unsocial independence, this, their hero of vanity, refuses the just price of common labour as well as the tribute opulence owes to genius . . . He melts with tenderness for those only who touch him in the remotest relation, and then, without a natural pang, casts away as a sort of offal and excrement the spawn of his disgustful amours . . . The bear loves, licks and forms her young' (See SIR THOMAS BROWNE, *Enquiry into Vulgar Errors*, Bk. III, chap. vi *passim*) – 'but bears are not philosophers'. Letter to a member of the National Assembly, 1791.

result was a softening of both the hard outlook of the seventeenth century, inured to civil war, religious persecution, and political instability, and of its early eighteenth-century reaction, 'good sense'. In Germany also this influence was to find its expression in the writings of Goethe and the German romantic poets. This softening of fibre coincided with the growing power of the middle classes, and Rousseau became their prophet. His attitude must be distinguished sharply from the fierce intellectual honesty of Voltaire, the aristocratic impersonality of Montesquieu, though he shares their anticlericalism.

Further, that other element of romantic escapism, the cult of the noble savage, usually apparent in highly sophisticated societies, is embodied in Rousseau's thought. Rousseau admires the average man: he wants to level out the actual inequalities of men by stressing moral intuition and character, often at the expense of disciplined intelligence. The healthy political framework, he rightly maintains, should be an organic community in which the 'chains' in which the natural man finds himself would be superfluous, for men would find their fulfilment, as Plato had long before maintained, in their citizenship.

Now, as Rousseau himself admits, such a resolution of individuality can only be found in small-scale political units, for example, the Greek city state, and Rousseau harks back to the Swiss communities he admired. His rehabilitation of the community is therefore not appropriate to the nation state, though in fact he greatly contributed to strengthen it. One of the functions of Rousseau's thought was to disintegrate the old order by setting up an impossible ideal, drawn from classical antiquity and romanticized savagery, at the disposal of revolutionaries.

Rousseau's inconsistency makes it difficult to give a short account of his political thought, which has been variously interpreted. It is best to admit that he did not trouble to be consistent,[1] and to emphasize that part of his writings which had the widest practical effect.

The *Du Contrat Social* is only a fragment of a larger work, destroyed if ever written. Describing its origin, Rousseau writes, 'I conceived the first idea of the book when I was at Venice (1743-4), and I had

---

[1] C. E. Vaughan, in his exhaustive and indispensable edition of the Political writings, carries, it may be thought, the attempt to impose a pattern on Rousseau's inconsistency too far; he is often reduced to using such phrases as 'when Rousseau is true to himself',

occasion to remark the defects of the much vaunted constitution . . .
I had come to see that in the last resort everything depends upon
politics, and that whatever men may do, no nation will ever be
anything but what the nature of its Government may make it'
(*Confessions, Liv. IX*).

It is a short work, divided into four books. The first is entitled
'How men developed from the state of nature to civil society and
what are the essential conditions of the social contract'; the second,
'On Legislation'; the third, 'On the Law of Politics: the form of
Government'; the fourth, 'The study of the Laws of Politics
continued and how the construction of the State may be
strengthened'.

Rousseau calls himself 'Citoyen de Génève', and had the usual
eighteenth-century admiration for the republics of classical antiquity,
and his thought is deeply conditioned by his early admiration for the
natural good sense of the Swiss peasants. 'When one sees groups of
peasants deciding their affairs under an oak tree and how sensibly
they always conduct themselves, it is difficult not to distrust the
refinements of other nations, who have made themselves illustrious
and miserable with so much artifice and mystery' (Bk. IV, chap. i).
This 'committee sense', which such small groups may well achieve,
is probably the basis of Rousseau's difficult conception of the general
or group will. His followers tended to interpret the politics of great
national states in terms of these organic smaller communities. Torn
from the environment in which it is psychologically natural, the
volonté général becomes the principle of the democratic nation
state — that principle, interpreted in terms of national sovereignty,
was destined to contribute to an increase in the political divisions of
Europe, which Rousseau himself deplores.

We have seen that the arid but formidable analysis of Hume had
apparently left the State without the religious sanctions of Thomism
or the mechanically determined purpose of Hobbes: there was
neither a divine plan nor an ascertainable theorem of politics.
Rousseau gets out of the political difficulty, as Kant gets out of the
philosophical one, by an assertion of the freedom and rightness of the
Will, which steps in to fill the void left apparently vacant by both
transcendent reason and religon.

But not only did Rousseau contribute to providing the national
state with a new justification, he also provided a new theoretical
basis for popular sovereignty. This second achievement is even more

important and influential than the first; the principle that consent
on the part of the governed was the basis of the State's authority
had already been clearly stated by Locke with the full force of
mediaeval tradition behind him, though, as we have seen, Locke's
attitude to property has prevented his theory being very 'democratic'. Rousseau develops the idea that consent is the basis of
obligation further than Locke, and in his general will tries to provide
an organic principle informing the State, which will make that
consent natural and assuage the conflict between individuals — who
are still thought of with the exaggerated individualism of the
eighteenth century — and the sovereign national state.

In the second chapter of the first book, Rousseau makes the famous
phrase, 'Man is born free, and everywhere he is in chains'. He here
states the conflict between 'romantic' individualism and the State.
But Rousseau was well aware that man, as Aristotle had said, is 'a
political animal'; — he can only fulfil himself in society, a dictum
fully borne out by modern knowledge of primitive communities.
Society, he well knew, is the natural medium to which personality
owes its development and in which alone it can find fulfilment: in the
realization of this truth he is in line with the greatest political thinkers.

Following on from this remark, he proceeds to examine the basis
of the State's authority. It is not simply force: 'might does not make
right'; the problem is 'to find a form of association which may
defend and protect with the whole force of the community the
person and property of every associate, and by means of which each,
coalescing with all, may nevertheless obey only himself and remain
free as before'.[1]

In contradiction with Rousseau's overriding organic conception
of the State, the immediate solution is found in the well-worn theory
of contract. Since individuals are helpless alone, they combine and
'each giving himself to all, gives himself to nobody' . . . 'each of us
puts in common his person and his whole power under the supreme
direction of the general will'. But how is the State to make sure the
individual will keep the rules? The 'particular will' of each member
of a society may well conflict with the general will, it may appear
to him that he makes a 'gratuitous contribution, the loss of which
will be less harmful to others than the payment of it will be burden-
some to him'.

Rousseau replies that the recalcitrant individual should be forced

[1] Bk. I, vi.

by the majority to obey the general will, or in a tendentious phrase 'forced to be free'. Moreover, the social contract makes men who are naturally unequal 'equal by convention and legal right'.[1]

He then tries to establish what he claims to be a moral basis for public authority, and proceeds to the curious assertion that the general will is always right. Naturally, since experience contradicts this view, he makes the difficult distinction between the 'will of all', which is the 'sum of particular wills' and may be deceived and therefore will wrongly, and the 'general will', which in a mystical manner cannot err. This general will is 'the sum of the differences' of conflicting private wills; but why it should be right remains obscure.[2]

Rousseau is thus on the way to creating the myth that the sovereign people is always right, an intoxicating doctrine which was to link up with the later theories of Hegel to endow the nation state with a quasi-divine sanction, and which provided democratic revolutionaries with one of their most powerful weapons. The democratic individual is to have his cake and eat it; he is obeying only himself, since the general will 'gives the force of self-love all the beauty of virtue'.

We have been so far mainly concerned with the highly theoretical aspects of Rousseau's writings, but there is a more practical side to him, the suggestions he makes about the actual functioning and structure of government. One sound principle holds good throughout and links up the two, that executive government is only a delegated power. 'The depositories of the executive power are not the masters of the people but its officers' (Bk. III, chap. xviii). Government, he says, is apt to usurp the sovereignty, and if it does so, then the ordinary citizen is not morally bound to obey it (Bk. III, chap. x). 'The principle of political life is the sovereign authority. The legislative power is the heart of the state; the executive power is its brain' (Bk. III, chap. xi). Theoretically all citizens should participate in the legislative action of the State. 'The better constituted a state is, the more do public affairs outweigh private ones in the minds of the citizens . . . In a well conducted city state everyone hastens to the assemblies . . . as soon as anyone says of the affairs of a state "of what importance are they to me?" we must consider the state as lost.' Obviously the conditions of a 'well conducted city state' are not reflected in the great national states of Rousseau's

---

[1] Bk. I, viii.
[2] The distinction was current in contemporary thought. See E. DE VATTEL, *Le Droit des Gens, ou Principes de la Loi Naturelle*, 1758, to whom Rousseau probably owed much.

time, still less of our own, and he was well aware of it, though his followers were not.

He dislikes the democratic expedient of representation. 'The idea of representatives is modern; it comes to us from feudal government, that absurd and iniquitous government, under which mankind is degraded and the name of man dishonoured. In the republics and even in the monarchies of antiquity the people never had representatives' (Bk. III, chap. xv). It seems clear that Rousseau, hankering after an antiquity which never existed, would have had little sympathy with the mass democratic institutions, to the success of which his writings largely contributed. He is, as we have seen, primarily concerned with the ideals of a small-scale community, and interpreted in this context his organic idea of the State is intelligible.

This idea, he maintains, is hostile to organized Christianity, which by 'separating the religious from the political system, destroyed the unity of the state, and caused the intestine division which has never ceased to agitate Christian nations. Now this new idea of a kingdom of another world having never been able to enter the minds of the pagans, they always regarded the Christians as actual rebels, who under cover of hypocritical submission, only sought an opportunity to make themselves independent and superior, and to usurp by cunning the authority, which in their weakness they pretended to reject. This was the cause of the persecutions. What the pagans feared came to pass. Then everything changed its aspect; the humble Christians altered their tone, and soon the pretended kingdoms of the other world became, under a visible chief, the most violent despotism on the world' (Bk. IV, chap. viii, 'Civil Religion').

Rousseau senses that the most uncompromising enemy of the organic conception of the State is bound to be a religion with its values outside temporal life, though he insists on the sublimity of the teaching of Jesus. At the same time he is aware that organized religion is a psychological and social necessity, and adopts the expedient of a 'Civil Religion'.

'Christianity is an entirely spiritual religion, concerned solely with heavenly things; the Christian's duty is not of this world . . . If the state is flourishing, he scarcely dares to enjoy the public felicity; he fears to take a pride in the glory of his country. If the state declines, he blesses the Law of God, which lies heavy on the people.'

'We are told that a nation of true Christians would form the most perfect society conceivable. In this supposition I see only one great difficulty — that a society of true Christians would be no longer a society of men.'

He then alleges that Christians, if they are true to their principles, will not be effective fighters: 'Suppose your republic opposed to Sparta or Rome, the pious Christians will be beaten, crushed, destroyed, before they have time to collect themselves, or they will owe their safety only to the contempt which the enemy may conceive for them.' Rousseau is here clearly flying in the face of the historical evidence.

'There is, however, a purely civil profession of faith, the articles of which it is the duty of the sovereign to determine, not exactly as dogmas of religion, but as *sentiments of sociability*, without which it is impossible to be a good citizen or a faithful subject. Without having power to compel anyone to adopt them, the sovereign may banish from the state whoever does not believe them; it may banish him not as impious, but as unsociable.' If he pretends to believe in them but acts against them, he should be put to death: 'he has committed the greatest of crimes; he has lied before the laws'. This ruthlessness comes strangely from Rousseau after his attacks on Christianity for intolerance.

Rousseau admired Montesquieu and took a number of valuable ideas from him; in the first place he has a statesmanlike awareness of the importance of habit in holding society together, and refers to 'particular regulations that are merely the arching of the vault of which manners, slower to develop, form at length the immovable keystone' (Bk. II, chap. xii). He further stresses the effect of climate and environment on institutions (Bk. III, chap. viii); each nation ought to have the legislation suitable for it; there is no absolute constitution; 'the more we consider the principle established by Montesquieu, the more we perceive its truth'. He goes so far as to state that 'Liberty is not the fruit of all climates, is not within the reach of all peoples'.

The most complete expression of this practical outlook, one of the soundest aspects of his thought, is the pedestrian measure to which Rousseau is reduced judging the goodness or badness of government: number and population is to be the test.

'All other things being equal, the government under which, without external aids, without naturalizations and without colonies, the citizens increase and multiply most, is infallibly the best . . . that under which a people diminishes and decays is the worst. Statisticians, to your business; reckon, measure and compare.'

This view may be regarded as an intelligent anticipation of realistic standards[1] or a confession of spiritual bankruptcy; it is difficult to square it with the cult of the general will and the burning patriotism of Rousseau's more emotional side.

In facing the economic problem, Rousseau states generally that legislation should aim at liberty and equality, 'no citizen should be rich enough to be able to buy another, and none poor enough to be forced to sell himself' (Bk. II, chap. xi). 'Tolerate neither rich people nor beggars.' This extremely comprehensive principle is thrown off, but not followed up; it served the revolutionary purpose of Rousseau's later interpreters, but it is not much emphasized in the text of the *Contrat Social*.

In the sphere of international politics, Rousseau has no illusions about the dangerous European situation: in the concluding paragraph of the *Contrat Social* he suggests that the appropriate sequel to a treatise on the State should be another dealing with its external relations, but remarks that this is 'too vast' a subject for his 'limited scope'. In his essay on the State of War (Neuchatel MSS.) he is wise and explicit on the dangers of European international anarchy. 'We live (internationally) in a state of natural liberty . . . Living at once in a social order and in a state of nature, we are subjected to the inconveniences of both; and have got into the worst possible state that we could.'

Rousseau's good practical judgement is shown both in this passage and in his analysis of the motives of rulers. Unfortunately, he says, truly enough, princes do not act for their real advantage. Their real interest lies in peace; but they think their interest is found in the condition of complete independence, which emancipates them from the rule of law to put them at the mercy of the caprice of fortune; 'like a crazy pilot who prefers to sail among rocks in a storm instead of casting anchor, in order to show off and order the sailors about'.

Actually, he argues, wars of conquest are unprofitable. Hannibal writes to the Carthaginians, 'I have defeated the Romans, send me reinforcements; I have held Italy to ransom, send me money. That is all the *Te Deums*, the *feux de joie* amount to'. Ministers of state, he suggests, profit by war since it makes them more important.

---

[1] PROFESSOR V. GORDON CHILDE, in *Man Makes Himself*, expresses exactly this view as the considered conclusion of a modern archaeologist.

What, then, is the remedy? 'If you could realize a European republic for one day, it would be enough to make it last for ever; everyone would find their own advantage in the common good', he writes of the Abbé St. Pierre's project of perpetual peace, and concludes that owing to the stupidity of mankind the project would imply too great a revolution to be practicable.[1]

How can this regime of sanity be brought about? Rousseau finds it in federation. 'We shall examine the kind of remedy men have sought against these evils in Leagues and Federations, which leaving each state master in its own house, arm it against all unjust aggression . . . we shall inquire what are the means of establishing a good form of federal association and what can give it permanence, and how far we can extend the rights of federation without touching on those of sovereignty.'[2] Here is a trenchant statement of a problem which has since become even more urgent. It is a pity that Rousseau never wrote the work at which he glances in the closing paragraphs of the *Contrat Social*.

In face of these views it is ironical that Rousseau's attempt to recapture the organic unity of the city should have contributed to the glorification of the great national state which swamps smaller communities, and that the prophet of liberty, and a man well aware of the need for European order, should have contributed so much to building the totalitarian state. Fichte's German nationalism and Hegel's expanding of the national community sense into time as well as space was to combine with the industrial revolution and the advent of mass democracy to render the European anarchy far more dangerous than it was in the eighteenth century, and to provide a justification for the State to crush the individual freedom of which Rousseau was often the prophet.

The preceding sketch does not pretend to do justice to the full complexity of Rousseau's thought: it has been necessary to simplify and to select, and to emphasize those aspects of his work which have had the most practical influence. These may be recapitulated as follows.

First, Rousseau reaffirmed that man is a political animal; that a healthy political community must be organic; and so broke away from the over-intellectualized tradition of the early eighteenth century. Secondly, he gave society a new theoretical basis in the

---

[1] *Political writings of Rousseau.* Edited C. E. VAUGHAN. Vol. I, pp. 365-88 ff.
[2] *Emile*, vol. V.

idea of the general will, and declared that executive government was only its servant. Thirdly, he provided revolutionaries with phrases which have rung round the world — for he was a phrase-maker of the first order — and played a vital part as the prophet of middle-class liberalism in undermining the structure of the *ancien régime*, although his thought is predominantly collectivist.

The inconsistency, the metaphysical confusion of Rousseau, are counterbalanced by the force of his practical insight, the sweep of his eloquence and the drive of his vitality; we are dealing, it is evident, not with a philosopher, not with a statesman, but with an original and unstable genius.

§ I I I

Rousseau's assertion of democratic sovereignty and of the general will, his rehabilitation of the community against the disintegrating influence of eighteenth-century rationalism, carried to its logical conclusion in the scepticism of Hume, is paralleled in England by Burke's eloquent assertion of the organic English national tradition, of the mediaeval doctrine of the trusteeship of power and the hierarchical nature of society in its Whig interpretation, backed both by the traditional religious sanctions and by a new romantic appeal to the sense of the historical development of the State.[1]

Both exalt the community as the ultimate sanction for government, but where Rousseau was highly critical of the existing regime and

---

[1] Edmund Burke, born New Year's Day, 1729, at Arran Quay, Dublin. His father, Richard Burke, was a Dublin Attorney. His mother came of an Irish Catholic family from Ballyduff, Co. Cork. Educated at Ballitore school outside Dublin; left in April 1744 for Trinity College, Dublin, where he won a Classical Scholarship in 1746. Took his degree, February 1748. Left Dublin for London to study the Law; formed friendship with William Burke, who was not a relative.

Published his first book, *The Vindication of Natural Society*, 1756. Married Jane Nugent, March 1757. Edited *The Annual Register* from 1759 onwards.

Private Secretary to 'Single Speech' Hamilton, 1759. Private Secretary and Chief Whip to Rockingham and M.P. for Wendover, 1765. Purchased estate at Beaconsfield, 1768. Wilkes Controversy. April 1770, *Thoughts on the Causes of the Present Discontents*. Visited Paris, January 1773. Speech on 'Conciliation with America', March 1775. Privy Councillor and Paymaster-General, 1782. Resigned July 1782.

February 1785, Speech on Nawab of Arcot's debts. Resolution censuring Warren Hastings, February 1786. Trial of Hastings began, February 1788. 'Letter to Monsieur Dupont' on French Revolution, October 1789. November 1790, *Reflections on French Revolution*. January 1791, 'Letter to a Member of the National Assembly'. Break with Fox. 1791, 'Appeal from the New to the Old Whigs'.

'Heads for the consideration of the Present State of Affairs', 1792. 'Remarks on Policy of the Allies', 1793. 'Thoughts and Details on Scarcity', 1795. 'Letter to a noble Lord', 1796. Died at Beaconsfield, July 9th, 1797.

appealed away from it to the democratic *volonté général* of the Swiss peasantry, Burke intensely admired the British Constitution as stabilized by the Settlement of 1689. Where Rousseau revelled in generalizations, Burke all his life attacked the 'nakedness and solitude of metaphysical abstraction'. This distrust of theory is apparent throughout his writings, from the early *Vindication of Natural Society* to the *Reflections on the French Revolution*, and *The Appeal from the New to the Old Whigs*. In the first he writes: 'The body, or as some love to call it, our inferior nature, is wiser in its plain way and attends to its own business more directly than the mind, with all its boasted subtlety.'[1] In the *Reflections*, published over thirty years later, he writes, referring to the Settlement of 1689: 'This policy appears to be the result of profound reflection or rather the happy effect of following nature, which is wisdom without reflection and above it . . . The science of constructing a commonwealth and of renovating or reforming it is, like every other experimental science, not to be taught *a priori*.'[2]

Burke is indeed the greatest prophet of the English conservative tradition. Like Rousseau, he was a phrase-maker of the first order, and more than Rousseau, a lord of language in the finest lineage of political thought. Yet, by origin and temperament, Burke was profoundly un-English. Racially he came of predominantly Southern Irish stock on both sides; temperamentally he was the antithesis of nearly all the English admire. A failure as an executive statesman, constantly insolvent, lured by a native generosity into lavish expenditure and feckless speculation, surrounded by a shady entourage of poor relations and hangers-on, Burke managed to win and retain the admiration and friendship of Goldsmith, Windham, and Dr. Johnson. He was a man of dazzling and exceptional charm, though he provoked, and occasionally deserved, the detestation of some of the best minds and characters of his age. But his Celtic intuition understood the political genius of England, which he made articulate in a regal splendour of language, destined to colour our political oratory for generations. Yet he was not generally an effective speaker; his delivery was often poor, his sense of an audience and of occasion faulty, and his hold on the House of Commons intermittent. But this Irish genius voiced a superb sense of the historical greatness of England, of the unfolding of parliamentary institutions, of the

[1] 'Vindication of the order of Natural Society', 1757, vol. I, p. 8, *Works*, Bohn, (1845). [2] 'Reflections', ib., vol. III, pp. 52 and 82.

power behind the statesman's office. A House of Commons man, and by origin an outsider, Burke, with his admiration for splendour and power, expresses the pride and confidence of the ruling classes of the eighteenth century. He is the exponent also of a new evolutionary historical sense.

But this sense, for Burke, was national: mediaeval political thinkers were part of a great European society and were bound together by the discipline and loyalty of the great religious orders. With the integration of the nation state, culture became more deeply rooted, more circumscribed, narrower but richer in its national context. It was a lay culture, no longer confined to universities and the clergy, more the affair of 'Society' and of the new leisured gentry in their comfortable setting of town and country houses.

Burke's England had seen two generations of security; the revolution of 1688 had set the stage for a steady unfolding of prosperity and power. The Fifteen and Forty-five had been disconcerting, but the position of the English oligarchy had never been seriously threatened. The atmosphere of society had changed; the Restoration era of savage political feuds and reckless morals, the *milieu* of Dryden and Halifax, was giving place to a more sedate and elaborate world. The tarnished finery of the Restoration, of the gipsy beauties of Charles II's harem, were outmoded by formal manners and a drilled sophistication. Sensibility became the mode; the more fashionable gentry affected a languid elegance and humanitarianism, which would have been properly scouted by their Restoration forbears. There was indeed a widespread genuine benevolence, very notable in Burke, a sense of obligation and a cheerful assumption of improvement. Meanwhile, the antiquaries, the eccentric clergymen and curious dons, were leisurely probing the mysteries of the national past, and Hume was writing his brilliant survey of English history, of the building of the English state.

All this is behind Burke, but there is another side to him as well. Beneath the veneer of sophistication, the English eighteenth century was an age of brutal indulgence, of administrative and financial corruption, of bitter personal animosities, while, outside the pale of polite society, unorganized by any efficient police or civil service, untutored by the conventional education of the day, was the mob which bayed round the Houses of Parliament in the Gordon Riots, and made a hero of the scoundrel Wilkes.

It was Burke's fate to be the defender of a national social order which had entered upon a phase of opulent but autumnal splendour. But it was a green and late autumn, with the shadows drawing in; and yet, such was Burke's genius, that though he was the prophet of a dying order, he made a permanent and elevating contribution to European thought, suffusing the political horizon with the glow of his eloquence and high purpose. Prejudiced, sometimes unbalanced, inconsistent, yet his works remain a mine of political and moral wisdom. And his influence on English politics has been justly compared to the influence of Wesley on English religion.

Burke's political thought is expressed in a series of speeches and pamphlets designed to meet particular occasions. He had not the philosophical grasp to build up a great structure of thought such as Hobbes built up in the *Leviathan*. He depended, like many artists, on external stimulus. His life is therefore divided into a series of crusades; on behalf of the American colonists; on behalf of the peoples of Ireland and India; against the doctrinaires of the French Revolution and their English admirers. Burke could think best at white heat; roused to a frenzy of anger and enthusiasm, his mind struck out flashing generalizations which transcended the immediate and important occasions of his eloquence. Though Burke was wrong-headed in his hounding down of Hastings, unreasonably prejudiced over the question of Ireland,[1] and broke all bounds of controversial decency over the French Revolution, these frenzies produced the lasting expression of his political genius. Burke's thought thus proceeds in a series of waves, occasioned by particular emergencies. His principles are never set out in any one work of theory, but embedded in volumes of controversial eloquence.

It will be well, therefore, to take his most important writings in order, and to trace the continuity of his emergent thought. His earliest work, published in 1756, the *Vindication of Natural Society*, is a slight but well written essay in political theory. He takes the fashionable eighteenth-century line, criticizing the 'artificial' contrivances of government, and maintains that if men used their 'Natural Reason' much evil would have been avoided.

'In considering Political Societies', he writes, 'their origin, their consideration and their effects, I have sometimes been in a good deal more than doubt whether the creator really intended Man for a

---

[1] A not unusual characteristic of politicians who have the courage to grasp that nettle. In assessing the generally disastrous influence of the two countries on one another's political life, it should not be forgotten that Eire gave the British Empire Burke.

state of Happiness.'[1] The development of civil society has exacted a great price in human suffering: 'The first accounts we have of Mankind are but so many accounts of their butcheries . . . all Empire has been cemented in blood.'[2]

Burke's youthful idealism veers towards the conventional eighteenth-century position that the state of nature may have been preferable to that of organized society. This outlook was quickly modified by age and experience, and is the antithesis of his later view. 'Has not', he asks, 'this Leviathan of Civil power overflowed upon the earth with a deluge of blood? . . . Political society in one form or another has been the means of murdering several times the number of inhabitants now upon earth, during its short existence, not upwards of four thousand years, in any accounts to be depended on.'[3] '. . . We are indebted for all our miseries to our distrust of that guide which Providence thought sufficient for our condition, our own Natural Reason.'[4] By 'Natural Reason', however, Burke implies not old-fashioned abstract rationality but the social instinct of the whole man. He has thus already taken the first step away from the orthodox position; the next step which came easily, as he made closer contact with the realities of politics, was to shake off the ideas that 'Civil Society' was built up by artificial contrivance and calculation and to regard it as the fulfilment of natural instinct. 'Art', as he was to say later, 'is Man's Nature'.[5] He thus ceased to identify the social order, which he passionately admired, with the abstractions he detested.

The book which brought Burke fame was his *Essay on the Sublime and Beautiful*, published in 1757. This abstract theme was not particularly congenial to his mind, but he won a considerable reputation by it; following it up in the same year with his *Account of the European Settlement in America*, and in 1758 by a *History of England*, from the earliest times to the reign of John. In 1759 appeared the first number of the *Annual Register*, a general survey of political affairs, national and international, and in the same year he became private secretary to William Hamilton, Chief Secretary to the Viceroy of Ireland. This appointment gave him the *entrée* to politics, and in 1765 his real opportunity occurred, which was to colour his thought for the rest of his career. In July 1765 Burke became private secretary to the new Lord of the Treasury, Rockingham, Party Whip to the Rocking-

---

[1] *Works*, vol. I, p. 8,   [2] ib., vol. I, p. 12.   [3] ib., vol. I, p. 50.
[4] ib., vol. I, p. 52.   [5] ib., vol. III, p. 425.

ham Whigs, and a Member of Parliament. Lord Rockingham's followers represented the more disinterested section of the Whig Party; they were affluent, they were secure, they were all the brilliant Irish parvenu admired. Burke became deeply loyal to his party[1] and determined to recall them to the obligations of aristocratic leadership, obligations which had worn thin during the long years of Whig power.

The Rockingham Whigs were great landowners, whose political interests were rather incidental to the normal routine of sport, gambling, and society. Burke attempted to recall his party to the obligations of aristocratic trusteeship, and to the expanding and novel obligations of Empire. In his *Thoughts on the Causes of the Present Discontents*, published in 1770, he defined the principles of an idolized Whig Party and embodied his own growing experience of the art of government. 'Nations are not primarily ruled by laws, still less by violence — Nations are governed by a knowledge of their temper and by a judicious management of it.'[2]

'It is the business of the speculative philosopher to mark the proper ends of government. It is the business of the politician, who is the philosopher in action, to find out the proper names towards these ends and to employ them with effect.'[3]

The authority of government comes from the whole community, he insists, echoing the best sense of the Whig tradition, and indeed of classical and mediaeval thought.

'Although Government is an institution of Divine authority, yet its form and the persons who administer it all originate from the people . . . The virtue, spirit and essence of the House of Commons consists in its being the express image of the feelings of the nation.'

Burke, who opposed the redistribution of parliamentary seats in accordance with the shift of population and industry, and supported the regime of 'rotten' boroughs, was not of course advocating democratic theory in the modern sense of the term: he held that the people were best represented by the existing structure of society, which it was the business of the House of Commons to reflect.

---

[1] His loyalty was proved in 1766 when after the fall of the Government, the Duke of Grafton, a statesman whose conduct of the American question has been excessively maligned, told Chatham that Burke's services ought to be secured for the new Administration; Burke preferred to remain with his Party.
[2] 'Thoughts on the Present Discontents', pp. 218-19, *Works*, vol. II, 1826 edition.
[3] ib., p. 74.

Burke appealed for disinterested government, no easy task in the eighteenth century. Quoting 'an old scholastic aphorism' which says, 'that the man who lives wholly detached from others must be either an angel or a devil',[1] Burke continues, 'In the meantime we are born only to be men; we shall do enough if we form ourselves to be good ones. It is therefore our business carefully to cultivate in our minds every sort of generous and honest feeling that belongs to our nature, to bring the dispositions that are lovely in private life into the service and conduct of the commonwealth.' This genuine good heartedness reflects the benevolence of many of those within the pale of eighteenth-century culture; it is a notable element in political affairs and contributes to the sense of obligation and trustee-ship apparent in Burke's conception of empire. It is paralleled, like so much of Burke's thought, in the sense of duty and 'pietas' of Cicero's dialogues.

Thus the *Thoughts on the Causes of the Present Discontents* sets out an ideal of representative and disinterested government within a frame-work of eighteenth-century society; *mutatis mutandis*, these principles apply to other forms of parliamentary organization in a wider con-text, and they express one of the deepest traditions of Western political thought.

Burke further defined his parliamentary ideals and the duty of representatives in the first speech at Bristol in 1774, in which he denied that the electors mandate confined his judgement on particu-lar issues; the interests of the nation, he insists, must come before the interest of the constituency. 'Parliament was not a congress of Ambassadors from different and hostile interests', but a 'deliberate assembly of one nation, with one interest'.

By 1774, then, the first phase in Burke's thought has been defined; he had expressed a memorable ideal, at a time when idealism was at a discount, and he had achieved comparatively young a maturity of reflection and a command of words which would have done credit to a great statesman at the height of his experience and power. The next phase was occasioned by the crisis over the American colonies; one of the crucial moments in the history of the world. Burke was defeated; the colonies were lost; for good or ill the States were to go their own way, to build their own different way of life. But in the controversy Burke set out a new conception of empire, destined to

[1] It is notable that the quotation comes naturally to his mind through this medium, not direct from Aristotle.

be the inspiration of the best British Imperialism, and later to bear its full fruit in the organization of the British Commonwealth.

This contribution to the Commonwealth's political evolution supplements Burke's salutary influence on home politics. His views on the American question are contained in the *Speech on American taxation*,[1] and the *Speech on Conciliation with America*.[2] Both are performances of the first order; the latter contains some of the most famous of Burke's phrases.

Burke attacked the pedantic methods which lost the American colonies: it was to be said, later, that England 'in a moment of absent mind had expanded into Empire'; and, indeed, eighteenth-century governments tended to regard the colonies as an embarrassment. Caught up in the new problem of imperial responsibility, Burke and his contemporaries were 'under the necessity of forming some fixed ideas concerning the policies of the British Empire . . . I really did not think it safe or manly', he declared, 'to have fresh principles to seek upon every fresh mail that arrives from America'. Burke undertook to supply the answer, and the great speech on 'Conciliation' is both in power of thought and artistry of language one of the major classics of English oratory. Not a word is wrongly placed, not a sentence but flows naturally and inevitably from the other.

As usual when deeply moved, Burke repudiates abstractions. 'Man acts from adequate motives, relative to their instincts and not on metaphysical speculation. Aristotle, the great master of reasoning, cautions us with great weight and propriety, against this species of delusive geometrical accuracy in moral arguments as the most fallacious of all sophistries.' Burke's peroration is a masterpiece. 'I do not know the method of drawing up an indictment against a whole people . . . My hold on the colonies is in the close affection which grows from common names, from kindred blood, from similar privileges, from equal protection. These are ties, which, tho' light as air, are as strong as links of iron . . . Slavery they can have anywhere. It is a weed that grows on every soil. They may have it from Spain, they may have it from Prussia: freedom they can have from none but you.'

He invokes the Spirit of the British Constitution, . . . the 'great contexture of the mysterious whole'. At home, he says, government rests on the consent and interest of the whole people. 'It is the love

[1] 1774.　　　[2] March 22nd, 1775.

of the people, it is their attachment to their Government from the deep stake they have in such a glorious institution' that inspires the loyalty of the country: without it 'your army would be a base rabble and your navy nothing but rotten timber'. The famous phrases follow one another, 'Magnanimity in politics is not seldom the truest wisdom, and a great empire and little minds go ill together'. Here foreshadowing the responsibilities of the nineteenth century, is the authentic rumble of imperial greatness.

The next occasion of Burke's thought was his crusade against Warren Hastings. There can now be little doubt that Burke was wrong in his indictment of one who ranks with Clive as the founder of British power in India, that his mind had been poisoned against Hastings by the influence of Sir Philip Francis, the author of the *Letters of Junius*. This eighteenth-century *cause célèbre*, which made such a stir at its inception, so that historians have vied with one another to paint the extraordinary scene, when most of English society crowded to the House of Commons to witness the histrionic performance of Sheridan and Burke, petered out ingloriously after seven years intermittent torment for most of those concerned. It is remarkable for two things: first, that Burke, who had no immediate knowledge of Indian conditions, based his attack on a superficial and romantic view of Indian civilization; and second, that, as usual, the excitement wrought Burke into a fury of prophetic utterance which incidentally asserted some of the most important principles of imperial trusteeship.

But the realities of the situation, which Hastings had to face, the appalling economic and political problems of eighteenth-century India, were submerged in the torrent of Burke's invective.[1] The whole force of his personality was flung into the attack on Hastings and the trial dragged out until Hastings's acquittal in 1785. But in the process Burke asserted, amid much rant, his conception of the reign of law. He attacked Hastings's assumption of arbitrary power — 'That', he maintained, 'is against the Rights of Humanity, anywhere in the world.' We have no arbitrary power to give, because arbitrary power is a thing which neither any man can hold nor any man

---

[1] His friend William Burke took a different view. He writes to Burke's son, Richard: 'We English here are a respectable, humane and friendly people, nor can I for the soul of me feel as your father does for the "Black Primates". Do say for me to your father that the Abstract Right of things in the East has scarcely an existence: all is usurpation and force.' See SIR P. MAGNUS's excellent *Edmund Burke*, Murray, London (1939).

can give . . . We are all born in subjection to one great immutable
pre-existent Law, prior to all our devices, prior to all our contrivances, . . . by which we are knit and connected in the Eternal frame
of the Universe . . . Those who give and those who receive arbitrary
power are alike criminal and there is no man but is bound to resist
it . . . whenever it shows its face in the world . . . it is wickedness in
politics to say that one man can have arbitrary power. In every
Patent of Office the Duty is included.'

Here Burke is reconciled to abstract principles, re-stating with
unusual explicitness the tradition of Cicero, of Aquinas, of Hooker,
of Locke. 'Man is born to be governed by Law, and he that will
substitute will in place of it is an enemy of God.' Burke leaves no
doubt as to his position in this ancient battle, and the trial of Hastings
witnessed his most convincing assertion of it.

The final and culminating wave of Burke's activity was occasioned
by the French Revolution. Burke realized fully the implications of
this event, and his defence of established society, together with his
denunciation of the revolutionary doctrines, are contained in his
Letter to Monsieur Dupont (1789), in his *Reflections on the Revolution in
France* (1790), in his *Letter to a Member of the National Assembly* and in
his *Appeal from the New to the Old Whigs*. He resented the French
claim that they were practising the principles of English freedom,
and it is upon this theme and upon the abstract nature of French
political thought that Burke concentrates his attack.

The hatred of doctrinaire abstractions which run through most of
his thought is expressed again and again in the writings on the
Revolution. 'I flatter myself that I love a manly moral regulated
liberty . . . but I cannot . . . give praise or blame to anything which
relates to human actions . . . on a single view of the object as it stands
in all the nakedness and solitude of metaphysical abstraction. The
circumstances are what render every Civil and Political scheme
beneficial or noxious to mankind . . . Am I to congratulate a high-
wayman and a murderer who has broken prison, upon the recovery
of his Natural Rights?'[1]

The immediate cause of Burke's wrath was a sermon by Dr.
Richard Price, a Nonconformist minister who had preached at the
Dissenting Meeting House in Old Jury. His 'very extraordinary

---

[1] 'Reflections on the Revolution in France, and on the proceedings in a certain
society in London relative to that event, in a letter intended to have been sent to a
Gentleman in Paris.' *Works*, Bohn, vol. III, p. 251.

miscellaneous sermon' had inspired the 'Revolution Society of London' to send a message of encouragement to the new government in Paris. Burke detected in this sermon 'a strain which I believe has not been heard in this island in any of the pulpits which are tolerated or encouraged in it since the year 1648'. He appealed to all the ancient prejudices; he identified Dr. Price with the regicides of the Civil War. That the sentimental doctor should dare to quote the English Settlement of 1689 as a precedent of the Revolution in Paris roused Burke to a frenzy of invective and to a detailed able analysis of the exact nature of the Settlement. Far from being founded on abstract Natural Rights, it was intensely practical; 'Drawn up by Great Lawyers and great Statesmen, and not by warm and inexperienced enthusiasts': it was concerned with an immediate objective, with 'settling' the succession of the Crown, not with 'delusive gypsy prediction of a right to choose our Governors'. The statesmen of 1689 'threw a politic well-wrought veil over every circumstance tending to weaken the Rights which in the ameliorated order of succession they meant to perpetuate, or which might furnish a precedent for any future departure for what they had then settled for ever'. The settlement was a triumph of cunning and detailed contrivance by shrewd administrators and statesmen conscious of their responsibilities; it was made to preserve our 'Ancient indisputable laws and liberties'.[1]

The 'Reflections' end with a defence of learning and property. The former, he maintains, in a democratic society, will be 'cast into the mire and trodden under the hooves of the swinish multitude'. Burke's prediction has not yet been justified. Finally, he shrewdly points out that such political sentiments as the 'Rights of man' are really incantations which reconcile the masses to the political action of a few realist politicians, and compares the French appeal to such sentiments to Henry VIII's allegations against the morality of the monasteries he had determined to dissolve for quite other reasons. Finally, like Fortescue, he insists on the alleged fecklessness of the French.

Burke's last major work, the appeal 'From the New to the Old Whigs',[2] is a justification of his views and conduct over many years; it defines the fundamentals of his position. He defends his support of the American colonists; his quarrel with Fox; his attitude to the

---

[1] Op. cit., p. 50.
[2] 'An appeal from the New to the Old Whigs' in consequence of some late discussions in Parliament, relative to the reflections of the French Revolution, 1791. *Works*, vol. III, pp. 333-457.

Revolution. Comparing himself with Diogenes, Burke calls on 'impartial men of the world' to judge between him and the Foxite Whigs. He appeals to the principles of 1689, which he claims to interpret better than Fox, with his over-generous idealizing of foreign revolutionaries, that persistent characteristic of English liberal thought.

Coming to the heart of the matter, Burke attacks the theory of the 'sovereignty of the people', the trump card of the revolutionaries. In a famous passage, he denies the right of rulers, or ruled, to denounce the obligations of the compact which makes a society as distinct from a 'mere multitude'.

'Neither the few nor the many have the right merely to act by their Will.'[1] Here he echoes the principles laid down in the speech against Hastings.

'If arbitrary power is to govern all, it will not be the people who will benefit; in that kind of game the people are sure to be the losers.' 'To flatter any man, or any part of mankind . . . that in engagements he or they are free, whilst any other human creature is bound, is . . . to subject the sovereign reason of the world to the caprices of weak and giddy men.'

It follows that the multitude are the last people who ought to rule unchecked, for their arbitrary power is the most difficult to tame.

All men, he insists, then, are bound by social obligations: 'Duties are not voluntary.' A man can only develop in the historical and social setting into which he is born, and though the original contract may have been voluntary, 'its continuance is under a permanent covenant, co-existing with the society, and it attaches upon every individual of that society, without any formal act of his own. This is warranted by the general practice arising out of the general sense of mankind . . . Men without their choice derive benefits from that association, without their choice they are subjected to duties in consequence'. Here is an evocation of the authority of the community in its own right defensible without abstract sanctions.

All, indeed, depends on a God-sanctioned moral law; if no God or Law exist there can be no appeal against the 'Right of Prevalent power'. But assuming God has 'marshalled us according to a Divine tactic, not according to our will but according to His . . . he has virtually subjected us to act the part which belongs to the place assigned to us'.[2] 'The presumed consent of every rational creature is in unison with the predisposed order of things.'[3] Further, the

---

[1] Op. cit., p. 414.   [2] Op. cit., p. 417.   [3] Op. cit., p. 418.

community extends in time as well as space: 'Our country is not a thing of mere physical locality, it consists in a great measure in the ancient order into which we are born.'

Burke now turns to analyse what precisely is meant by the 'People' whose authority is evoked by revolutionaries, and to attack their assumptions in a damaging way. The idea of a people is artificial, 'a legal fiction, made like other legal fictions by common agreement'. If the social order is broken up there can be no such thing as a people, only a number of 'vague loose individuals'. 'Amongst men so disbanded there can be no such thing as a majority or minority ... the power of acting by a majority has disappeared', for the idea of majority decision is highly artificial. Having dissolved society, and with it all rights, revolutionaries cannot have it both ways and claim legality for their acts. Moreover, he insists, a 'true natural aristocracy' is the fine flower of civilization. Man's 'reasonableness', he concludes, creates society; far from being artificial, it is the fulfilment of human instinct.[1]

It will be seen that this vindication of the community as an organic, hierarchical whole reflects closely the mediaeval and the Whig tradition, though it lacks the universality of Thomism. Further, though Burke invokes supernatural sanctions, he comes near to maintaining that the general sense of the community in space and time is valid in its own right. He thus contributed to the romantic cult of the will as a basis for right; to the tide of reaction against the artificial rationalism of the Cartesian method applied to politics. In a sense Burke stands between two worlds: he reflects the old tradition of a transcendental sanction for society, while also influenced by the new romantic idea of emergent will. Having stated this fundamental argument, Burke relaxes into an entertaining comparison between the English Peasant's Revolt of 1381 and the French Revolution. He makes great play with 'the Abbé John Ball, that reverend patriarch of sedition ... Cade, Ket, and Straw at the head of their national guards'. 'The enlightened Dr. Ball', he says 'chose for his text the following couplet: "When Adam delved and Eve span, who was then the gentleman?" This sapient maxim', Burke continues, 'in learning, sense, energy and comprehensiveness is fully equal to all the modern dissertations on the equality of mankind, and it has one advantage over them, that it is in rhyme.' This judgement he reinforces by a footnote quoting Walsingham's account

[1] Op. cit., p. 425.

of the Abbé's Blackheath sermon; 'haec et plura alia deliramenta', Walsingham calls it. 'Think of this old fool's calling all the wise maxims of the French Academy "deliramenta",' comments Burke.[1]

Quoting these 'bulletins of ancient rebellion', which he thinks better written down to popular taste than modern ones, he brings the homely English of 'John Schep' into incongruous contrast with his own. Returning to the main argument, Burke insists that a 'multitude told by the head' is not a people, and has no right to alter the 'seat of power'. He concludes the 'Appeal' by warning of the dangers of entertaining subversive French ideas, by eulogizing the British constitution and the wisdom of the Old Whigs.

'Montesquieu', he says, 'a man gifted by nature with a penetrating aquiline eye, with a judgement prepared by a most extensive erudition . . . chose out of all others the Constitution of England to hold out to the admiration of mankind . . . and shall we Englishmen revoke such a suit?' For his part, he would rather be the least of the men of 1689 than the 'first and greatest of those who have coined to themselves Whig principles from a French die'. So Burke made his political Testament, asserting and summing up his principles of his political career.

It will be apparent that the deepest significance of Burke's thought rests on his repudiation of the current fashion of abstract analysis, of the angular rationalism of the eighteenth century, and his reassertion of a mystical sanction for society. He apprehends, with an artist's intensity of vision, the totality of the social pattern, 'the great contexture of the mysterious whole'. He thus anticipates the outlook of Hegel, with his intuition of the national community extending in space and time. But unlike Hegel, Burke remains within the old tradition, within the framework of Law. In this sense he continues and enriches the habit of thought which descends in an unbroken pedigree from classical times through Aquinas, Hooker, and Locke: 'Arbitrary power is a thing which neither any man can hold nor any man can give'; it is 'against the rights of humanity anywhere in the world'.

The expression of vigorous national life can best be achieved by the proper balance and working of the existing social order; this idea is mediaeval, directly paralleled in the writings of Fortescue; but Burke has a wider vision than any mediaeval writer; his eyes range over the territories of the Empire. He understood the obligations

[1] Op. cit., p. 457.

Empire implied; his influence on the development of the British Commonwealth has been lasting. Rome alone realized a parallel achievement of trusteeship, toleration, and peace; Burke's affinity with the statesmen and writers of Rome needs no emphasis.

Yet Burke belongs to the English eighteenth century. His outlook is neither scientific nor universal. It is profoundly national and to some minds stuffily conservative; it is an aristocratic culture he admires, limited to a privileged *élite*, static, for all its apparent flexibility. He belongs to a silver age, to a relatively provincial culture which was overripe; for all his obvious, if unconscious, debt to Thomism, he lacked the range of the mediaeval tradition. Moreover, the new world of the Industrial Revolution, of scientific discovery, of business enterprise, was alien to him. The fierce tempo of industrial life, the surge of middle-class and proletarian vitality, were as repulsive to his mind as to that of Dr. Johnson.

Yet the modern world has much to learn from Burke; his sense of the organic and hierarchical nature of society, of the value of quality over quantity, of the complexity of political action, of the vast issues which hang upon the statesman's decision, of the world responsibilities of power, these are Burke's legacy. He has left, moreover, a tradition of eloquence and fire, of dignity and brilliance, of the sweep of great affairs, which have continued in English politics and in face of danger have always been reaffirmed.

Thus Rousseau and Burke, living in an age of increasing prosperity and widening political awareness, answer the disturbing influence of rationalism by asserting the importance of the will of the community. Rousseau's State has a democratic basis; Burke's an aristocratic and mystical tradition, confined within the bounds of nationality. But where Burke clung to the values of the past, Rousseau's thought ran with the tide of the future. His 'General Will', originally applicable to the peasant villages of the Swiss cantons, was invoked by his followers to justify the doctrine of democratic national sovereignty. That doctrine dominates most of the world to-day; together with the Industrial Revolution, it formed the politics of the nineteenth century. It was in tune with the forces of an expanding age; with the rise of the new bourgeoisie; with the technical and industrial progress which was to give Europe the political, intellectual, and economic mastery of the world. In tune also with the subversion of the old order, with the jeopardizing of the old values, with the stampedes of mass democracy and with total war.

CHAPTER X

THE INDUSTRIAL REVOLUTION:
RETROSPECT: CONCLUSION

§I

OUR survey of European political thought began with the Neolithic Revolution; with the Industrial Revolution, that other cardinal landmark in material progress, the present volume comes to an end. We have followed, in bare outline, the development of political ideas during the predominantly agricultural phase of Western civilization; with the machine age, both the tempo and the scale of political problems and political speculation break radically with the past. The vast increase in population; the change over from a European to a world economy; the expansion of European settlement overseas; the revolution in transport; the spread of education to the masses, combine to create a civilization far more powerful and dynamic than anything hitherto achieved.

The Industrial Revolution, and the technical revolution which followed it, implied a profound change in social scale and power over nature, together with a vast increase in urban life. For it must be understood that this change was radical: it was an event which, in the material sphere, dwarfed anything which had occurred in human history since the agricultural and urban ways of life were invented in the Middle East. Not only was the scale of living revolutionized, but the pace as well: the new civilization brought the promise of plenty and power; but it brought also the menace of chaos and destruction, of a failure of ideas and institutions to adapt themselves to the tide of political and economic change.

The course of political speculation, as it has hitherto been traced, has been concerned with religious and ethical problems and has largely ignored the economic aspect of society or, at most, relegated it to a very subordinate place. With the Industrial Revolution, the whole traditional order of society was changed and the time was ripe for the development of a new economic science.

The incapacity of intelligent men before the eighteenth century to understand or even to take account of economic processes is best

439

paralleled by the equally striking ignorance displayed of medical science. The seventeenth century produced some of the greatest literature of western Europe; but the doctors regularly killed off many of the leaders in all walks of life before the age now regarded as a normal span. As medicine suffered from the lack of classified data, so it was in the economic field. It was only towards the end of the seventeenth century that the statistical evidence for effective economic knowledge began to be collected.

The outlook of the eighteenth century was, indeed, ill-equipped to deal with economic affairs, but the hard rationality of a Scotsman, Adam Smith, achieved the first brilliant, if over sanguine, analysis and added a new field to human knowledge. Henceforth political theory became increasingly coloured by economic considerations, and it will be well to glance very briefly at this new field of specula-tion before turning to a retrospective survey of the political ideas with which western Europe met the new age, and attempting some assessment of the relevance of this ancient and splendid tradition, the theme of this volume, to the problems of the modern world.

§ 11

The analytic power and mastery of lucid prose which makes Hume's writing so distinguished was shared by his friend Adam Smith,[1] who, in the economic sphere, exercised an influence as penetrating and almost as revolutionary as Hume achieved in philosophy. Smith was the first economist to state comprehensive principles in the light of which the whole economic process might be interpreted; he created the first general hypothesis on which economic science could proceed.

He maintained that natural self-interest drove men to improve their position, each along his own lines. Hence there arises a 'division of labour', each one setting himself to exploit his appropriate skill. The combined result of this process, if left to itself, is the healthy

[1] Adam Smith, born Kirkaldy, 1723. Attended the University of Glasgow, 1737-40. At Oxford, 1740-6. 1751, appointed Professor of Logic at Glasgow, and in the same year to the Chair of Moral Philosophy. 1752, formed a close friendship with Hume. 1759, published the *Theory of Moral Sentiments*. 1764, Tutor to the Duke of Buccleuch, with whom he travelled in France and Switzerland, 1764-6. For this service he was assigned a life pension of £300 a year, and from 1767 to 1776 he devoted himself to writing the famous *Wealth of Nations*, which appeared in the latter year. 1778, Commissioner of Customs at Edinburgh. He died in 1790.

working of society. The labour of all classes increases wealth; all co-operate according to their specialized abilities. In a famous passage,[1] after giving a number of examples of the interdependence of the economic process, Smith concludes: 'If we examine, I say, all these things, and consider what a variety of labour is employed about each of them, we shall be sensible that without the assistance and co-operation of many thousands, the very meanest person in a civilized country could not be provided even according to what we very falsely imagine the easy and simple manner in which he is commonly accommodated.' This co-operation is ensured by self-interest: private and public interests coincide.[2]

Smith admits that specialization is stultifying. 'The man whose whole life is spent in performing a few simple operations . . . has no occasion to exert his understanding . . . He naturally loses, therefore, the habit of such exertion, and generally becomes stupid and ignorant as it is possible for a human creature to become.' He proposes the remedy of compulsory education. He was also far from allowing *carte blanche* for the manufacturer and the merchant, and supports the agricultural interest and the 'lower ranks of the people', who constitute after all, he insists, the greater part of the State. 'No society can surely be flourishing and happy of which the far greater part of its members are poor and miserable.' This humanitarianism, typical of the eighteenth century, was reinforced by an optimistic view of society. Adam Smith in fact imported an optimistic version of Natural Law into the field of economics. The comprehensive and organic view of the economic system, so original and valuable, was reinforced with an assumption that its working will enhance the realization of human values.

Smith takes a low view, natural in an age without an efficient bureaucracy, of the administrative capacity of the State; the eighteenth-century distrust of governmental corruption supplements his Scots admiration of individual enterprise. He allows it indeed a wider function than was admitted by many of his followers. Justice, defence, and the maintenance of certain necessary public institutions, come into its scope, though taxation ought to be within very moderate bounds. Further, there ought to be a measure of state

[1] *Wealth of Nations*, bk. I, chap. i.
[2] The idea of an automatic coincidence of private and public interests had been foreshadowed in a cynical manner by that curious figure, Mandeville, who published, as early as 1714, his interesting *Fable of the Bees, or Private Vices, Public Benefits*, which was suppressed by order of the government.

control of investment, even limitation of interest. None the less, the general trend of his thought was away from the mercantilist doctrines of the eighteenth century; free initiative should be left to private effort. The effect of this justification of individual enterprise was very far-reaching, and Adam Smith's prestige was lent, as Darwin's name was later lent, to countenance doctrines of ruthless competition and anti-social enterprise to which he would have most strongly objected; this individualism was inherited by Bentham and Ricardo.

Thus, though Adam Smith may justly be called the founder of the science of political economy, his influence, and particularly the influence of his followers, on liberal political thought was not always a happy one. The moral principles which inform his outlook were watered down and gradually abandoned by subsequent exponents of *laisser-faire*, who, hypnotized by the easy generalizations of their day, attributed to Providence and nature laws which defied the ethical precepts of the Gospels, the fundamental rights of individuals, and the natural solidarity of human institutions.

The new economists naturally inherited the defects, as well as the lucidity of eighteenth-century thought. They attributed an over-simplified rationality to social laws and conceived of individuals as endowed with a reason and self-control with which no one would have imagined such a worldly society would ever have credited them. This curious innocence of eighteenth-century rationalism assumed throughout society the qualities of clear-headedness and self-control admired by Lord Chesterfield. It was seriously imagined that most men were moved by deliberate calculation and humanitarian prudence; this by a society floating on the top of a mass of ignorance, illiteracy, and misery, aggravated and expanded by the dislocation of uncontrolled economic change. Later, the utilitarian economists, brought up under the influence of this tradition, created that unnatural figure, the 'economic man', a hard little atom in the social cosmos, who makes his priggish choices on the nicest calculations of pleasure and pain and lives in a world psychologically impossible for the majority of men.

Yet the over-optimistic conclusions of these writers should not obscure the great service they rendered to mankind. Just as the Cartesian method in the scientific field brought in its immense returns in practical power, though the materialism which it implied may well have had an adverse effect on the development of Western civilization as a whole, so the contribution of Adam Smith and his followers resulted in a new grasp of economic realities, a new respect for statistical method and notable expansion of knowledge and power.

§III

Meanwhile, as this new range of thought began to open up in response to the demands of the new age, traditional political theory was to be confronted by a new and formidable challenge, the combined result of the industrial and liberal revolutions, following the advent of the middle classes to economic and political power. What, then, was the general sense of the tradition which faced the incalculable future? It will be well here shortly to examine it.

There were four outstanding strains of thought which had come down from the evolution of political ideas described in this volume. They may be defined in terms of rational objectivity; of the rule of universal law; of Christian and humanitarian charity; and of the free individualism of the Renaissance and the seventeenth century.

The first and indispensable inheritance, the tradition of intellectual freedom, of curiosity and initiative, had its origins in Greece. Throughout all the vicissitudes of the ages the tradition of rational objectivity had carried on. First apparent in the writings of the scientists and philosophers of Ionian Greece, it found its superb expression in the political thought of Plato and Aristotle, the one inspired by an idealistic rationality, the other by an empirical and analytical bent closely grounded in reality.

The adequacy of this tradition, carried further by the thinkers of Hellenistic antiquity, for the interpretation of the whole of experience, was challenged by the spiritual expansion of Christianity and by the transformation of values demanded by St. Paul. With Augustine, rationality has become the servant of dogma; quick and complex in argument, the Christian theologians had lost the priceless inheritance of objectivity. With the Dark Ages, the tradition all but perished, but, though conventionalized and distorted, divorced from experiment and bedevilled by ignorance and superstition, the method of rational argument never died.[1] The twelfth century and the high Middle Ages saw the hey-day of 'unbridled rationalism',[2] a sharpening of wits and a widespread habit of exact discussion within the assumptions of the Faith, but it was not until the Renaissance that

[1] *Vide supra*, p. 147.   [2] *Vide* Whitehead, op. cit., p. 13.

the full Hellenic objectivity again came into its own and increasingly established itself on the solid ground of experiment.

As we have seen, with Machiavelli there appears a new business sense, a close attention to the facts of power, along with a falling off in moral vision. With Descartes, the vision widens, comprehending a wide philosophic sweep; his principles, laid down in the *Discours sur la Méthod*, cleared away the jungle of later mediaeval scholasticism and created a new analytical technique. Whatever its philosophical limitations, as an instrument of organizing power unique in the history of mankind, the tradition had come fully into its own. The new cosmography as defined by Galileo, Bruno, and Newton, transformed the outlook of the West, and Cartesian organized common sense was destined to fulfil the discovery of a 'Practical' whereby Europeans were to be made 'Lords and masters of Nature'.[1] Revived Hellenic curiosity and impartiality had been reinforced by a new systematizing skill, a close attention to the facts, a readiness not to despise detail.

The new outlook was reflected in political thought by the justification of State power not as a divine institution, but as a necessity for civilized life. It led to the cynical and over-rigid outlook of Hobbes, and to the more deeply scientific outlook of Locke and Spinoza; both insisting on toleration, and a measure of political freedom; both willing to understand human nature, to believe in it and give it full scope for development. There followed a phase, dominated by French thinkers, of an over-confident rationality, of the brilliant and sanguine generalizations of Montesquieu and Voltaire; but the realism of the Whig tradition, of Halifax and the men of 1688, never allowed itself to be side-tracked into so abstract a world. By the late eighteenth century men's minds were outgrowing the over-confidence of the seventeenth, and although an exclusive faith in the power of reason in human society persisted among influential thinkers — notably, as we have seen, among the economists — Hume had demonstrated the metaphysical limitations of rationalism. The leaders of thought were no longer confident that there exists an ideal pattern of the State, either theological or rational, only to be discovered to be acted on. Hobbes believed it possible to impose a planned and static pattern on society, rationally demonstrable, and universally acknowledged: Burke, and from his contrasting approach, Rousseau, no longer accept this view. Reason, as applied to political

---

[1] *Vide supra*, p. 315.

thought, had, by the eighteenth century, become sufficiently mature to recognize the limitations of its own power as a motive in society, thus attaining a more realistic outlook.

Further, as the expansion of knowledge seemed to lead to a fading of the authority of transcendent Natural Law, embodied in the classical and mediaeval tradition of abstract right reason, and also of the belief in transcendent Revelation, a more sophisticated empirical rationalism began to affirm its own anthropocentric values, immanent and emergent in human experience itself and realized in the process of history. This secularized and modern view increasingly developed the tolerance characteristic of the later seventeenth century; the new imaginative sympathy and sense of emergent values apparent in the writings of Spinoza, and the sense of historical evolution foreshadowed in the works of Vico.

Gradually Scientific Humanism was to assert its own metaphysical justification, affirming that the man-made values of reason, charity, and justice, could be valid without supernatural justification — as the expression of life itself. And such a justification could provide those who could not equate the old transcendental beliefs with the new knowledge with a basis for constructive action. Through the storms and stresses of the nineteenth century this outlook was to persist and expand; the sense of evolution, of scientific objectivity, of emergent values peculiar to the West.

Such was the first and most characteristic aspect of eighteenth-century thought, the promise of a mature, dynamic, and creative rationalism, increasingly feeling its way towards a new basis of value. It was originally and predominantly a Greek inheritance, reinforced by Cartesian method and going beyond the Cartesian conclusions.

The second great element in the European tradition came down from Rome: the inheritance of just law, of the trusteeship of power. The Ciceronic definition of Justice had persisted through the darkest times; the tradition of universal Law had dominated mediaeval thought. It had been reinterpreted by Hooker and his Whig successors: it was fundamental to the tradition of the West. Where Oriental societies developed in slavish submission to the rule of tyrants, themselves closely fettered by chains of custom and tradition, the Greeks had asserted the existence of an impartial and abstract Justice, which gave every man his due. The Romans had defined this principle in imperishable and accurate terms, applicable 'in all times and in all places'; and the Christian Church had inherited the Roman conception of order and impartiality. With the dominance of the Augustinian outlook, which regarded the State as at its best the 'secular arm' of a divinely constituted society and at worst as rooted in iniquity, the concept of just law was incorporated into an hieratic and dualistic vision of the world; but it persisted within that framework, and already defined and elaborated by the great Roman jurists, it received a close and practical definition at the hands of Justinian's lawyers. Though the Roman Law displayed an absolutism uncongenial to the tradition of freedom and responsibility, it retained its impartiality, its comprehensiveness, and its accuracy.

Meanwhile, in the West the idea of justice survived the stresses of the Middle Ages: the tradition that the rule of law could be invoked against a tyrant persisted through the darkest times. Isidore repeats it, parrot-like, out of the depths of the Dark Ages; John of Salisbury, representative of many other writers, in the twelfth century; while the barbarian respect for custom, and the sense that the whole commonwealth is something above the individual king, reinforced this reflection of classical tradition. So the rule of just law was regarded both as the manifestation on earth of a secular aspect of divine authority within the framework of the cosmic order, most clearly defined by Aquinas in the thirteenth century, and as the embodiment of the accumulated wisdom of the past; something to be respected, discovered, and followed, enshrined in the wisdom of the 'oldest men' who 'declared' it. When, therefore, following the disruption of the mediaeval world and the definition of the concept of unbridled sovereign power, the new national rulers claimed an absolute divine right, the rule of law was invoked against them in the most advanced countries of the West. Not only was their authority questioned by religious opponents of the opposite camp, but in England, in particular, the authority of the ancient laws of the kingdom was invoked, the whole accumulated prestige of the tradition of the Common Law. And when again, in the eighteenth century, the English Parliament claimed an unbridled power over the American colonists, they, too, harking back to earlier precedent, to the principles of Locke, invoked the authority of the whole community against an innovating power, and their example was influential in bringing about the Revolution in France.

Further, with the fuller definition of the responsibility of government to the governed, there had grown up a wider sense of public duty, extending outside the privileged classes. Locke directly, and the outlook of Puritan radicalism indirectly, reinforced this tradition. It was widely popularized by Rousseau and Burke and destined in its liberal interpretation to play a growing part in political affairs. By the close of the eighteenth century, then, the tradition of a just, impartial, and declared law, administered by a responsible and independent judiciary; of the responsibility of government to the governed, and of their reciprocal obligations, had become an integral part of the political inheritance of the West, in particular of England, France, and North America.

In the third place, the Christian and Humanitarian tradition remained immensely powerful. The majestic ideal of the unity of Christendom and the responsibility of government continued to be affirmed, within the old theological framework, by the Catholic Church, still the most formidable bastion of Christian influence. Further, although dogmatic Catholicism was fighting a losing battle, the tone of society, with increasing prosperity, was becoming softer. Underneath the theological differences of the warring Churches, the Caritic Christian tradition had been for centuries more and more deeply absorbed. Some of the bitterest enemies of the official Churches were actuated by humanitarian motives which were profoundly Christian. In England it was not the rationalists, the organizers, who were able to avert the social upheaval which threatened as a consequence of the Industrial Revolution; it was the Methodist and Evangelical Movements which calmed the storm. This widespread philanthropy was expressed in the disinterested abolition of slavery initiated by Wilberforce; it inspired innumerable societies and organizations for social betterment, and though confined to a minority, living on the top of a semi-civilized and semi-literate proletariat, it was a notable achievement. The callous indifference with which most aristocracies had usually regarded their inferiors was breaking down: the religious feuds which had made the seventeenth century a nightmare of incessant conflict had subsided. The leaven of Christian teaching and Stoic humanitarianism had permeated the upper ranks of society.

Most fundamental of all, the Christian insistence on the spiritual worth of all individuals, of the 'spiritual priesthood of all believers' had, since the Reformation, been affirmed with greater power. The return to the original gospel, the insistence on the direct relationship between man and his Maker, had created a new sense of personal responsibility and a new sense of spiritual freedom. This assumption, not of equality of talent, but of equality of spiritual status, of Brotherhood in God, had reinforced the second great tradition of impartial law. Here was another strong bulwark against the rule of arbitrary government and the overriding of individual rights and interests by unbridled military power.

Closely bound up with this inheritance was the individualism of Western society. The tradition of individual rights, which owed so much to the Protestant Churches, could, indeed, cut both ways. Together with the atomistic social outlook characteristic of Hobbes, which was to persist in much utilitarian thought, these doctrines sometimes constituted a menace to the healthy working of the social order. But the enterprise, variety, and initiative they implied brought in returns which substantially outweighed their disadvantages. The static hierarchy which was the normal expression of the more advanced societies outside Europe was not reflected in this dynamic part of the world.

The tradition of individual enterprise focused the steady initiative, the determination to subdue environment, the refusal to accept material limitations, which was characteristic of the West, and which, as we have seen, had so long a pedigree, going back to the Neolithic colonists who first undertook the subjugation of the Continent.

This individualism was also expressed in a new form by the Romantic movement, which implied a new confidence, a new enterprise, and a new sense of the past. It was native only to a sophisticated society: in the politically advanced countries of the West it helped to make profound social change possible without the expedient of revolution, since it contributed to undermine the belief of the old order in itself, though in Germany romanticism contributed to pernicious theories of state worship and racial superiority. Many of the new bourgeoisie were anxious to live dangerously, to throw in their lot with the forces of the future, to make an alliance with strange elements outside their usual orbit. The cult of romantic republicanism, of the noble savage, of scenery and travel, of a highly coloured version of the classical and mediaeval past, all these things are original and characteristic of the mentality of the dominant classes at the close of the eighteenth century.

This enterprise, intellectual and practical, was to be reflected in the vast expansions of the nineteenth century, when professionalized knowledge and middle-class drive were to chart new ranges of experience and exploit territories that dwarfed Europe.

By the late eighteenth century, then, these four great traditions — of rationality; of political order and responsibility; of Christian and humanitarian brotherhood; personal initiative and free enterprise — had been stated, in their varying idioms, by the great masters of political thought with uncompromising clarity. They promised to combine to form an ideal of the 'good life' — the first objective, as Aristotle stated of political society. It was an ideal no more splendid than that defined by the Greek philosopher, but one enriched by centuries of experience and achievement, broader, more humane, and more dynamic. And it could still only be an ideal predominantly of a privileged minority, for the masses were materially too poor and too ignorant to participate in it. With the Industrial Revolution an extension of the opportunity to realize such an ideal began to come within the bounds of possibility.

Such, in briefest outline, were the four dominant strains in European thought, which had come down through the centuries and which were destined to survive the upheaval of the Industrial Revolution and the coming of modern mass society; to combine, in our day, it may be, to form an ideal compatible with modern knowledge, capable of inspiring a new phase of popular civilization.

§ I V

We must now glance at the social framework which sustained and determined these ideas — within which the tremendous changes of the nineteenth century were destined to take place, and which these changes were destined to disrupt — and attempt some interim assessment of the relevance of the old tradition to the contemporary situation.

While the development of European political thought since the Renaissance was unbroken and dynamic, the international political situation in which the Industrial Revolution occurred was one of degeneracy in European order. Looking back over the wide field of our survey, it is clear that the intellectual, material, and social progress of European civilization had been immense. Apart from the spiritual, artistic, and intellectual range of experience realized, and the accumulation of knowledge and technical skill, the biological progress of Western society was reflected in a vast increase in population at the end of the century. In spite of setbacks and disasters, the crest of each wave had been higher than the last. Since the Neolithic revolution Western men had come a long and successful road; yet, when the Industrial Revolution overtook this society, the tradition of the unity of European culture was jeopardized by the existence of sovereign nation states, increasingly equipped by administrative efficiency and technical skill to wage war on an unprecedented scale. The power of national sovereignty, cutting across the tradition of intellectual freedom, stabilized law, compassion, and personal freedom, was a tolerable thing in an age of limited material power. When the twin drives of industrialism and democracy were put behind this dangerous anachronism the existence of the fundamentals of European and world order were challenged. The political framework of Europe, during the period of 'warring states' which followed the disruption of mediaeval Christendom and the advent of the nation state, was dangerous and defective. It jeopardized, and continues to jeopardize, the best traditions of European thought and practice.

At the same time, within the nation state, the old aristocratic order was in decline. Middle-class enterprise, based on expanding capitalism, and deeply provincial in its traditions, broke down the old cosmopolitan ideas of order and obligation, while, sanctioned by responsible economists, private enterprise plunged into the exploitation of Europe and the world. Further, in alliance with predominant business interests, the great national states were extending their domination overseas, and the material power of Europe was fated to involve the planet in the promise and the conflicts of the new industrial society.

Meanwhile, behind the power, the enterprise, and the greed of the new capitalism, the demands of the masses began to be heard. Underneath both aristocracy and bourgeoisie, the common people were on the move. The French Revolution, a middle-class movement which, as is the way of revolutions, broke from the control of its initiators and ended in military dictatorship, flooded France, the leading nation in Europe, with ideas subversive not merely of the old order, but of middle-class rule as well. Liberal political ideas increasingly made their appeal to the masses; but within a century and a half, the Totalitarian State was to challenge the tradition of Liberal Democracy.

Enough has been said to show the scale of the opportunities and the dangers which were beginning to confront Europe at the end of the eighteenth century. The Industrial Revolution and the coming of democracy marked the opening of a time of great progress and great peril.

Critical as this situation has now become, it is unthinkable that the inheritance of European political thought, of which we have enumerated four dominant themes, should be inadequate to meet the challenge of the new times. The pattern of ideas, evolved in the predominantly agricultural phase of social development, inherited from Greece, from Rome, and from Israel, enriched and expanded by the contribution of the North, forms a permanent tradition which is likely to survive and to control the convulsions of the modern age.

While taking full account of the complex developments of theory and practice which occurred during the nineteenth century and which it would need a new volume to describe, the wide range of our survey has shown the scope, variety, and strength of the pre-industrial European tradition. The 'materialist' interpretation of history and modern interpretations of thought and conduct in terms of the sub-conscious mind, have deepened and widened the range of specula-tion, but have not rendered the old tradition obsolete; while the tremendous initiatives of America and Russia have altered the perspective, though not the importance, of the political thought of western Europe. But it will be well, in spite of the scale and violence, of nineteenth- and twentieth-century events, both theoretical and practical, to keep them, notwithstanding, in a just perspective.

A mere century and a half, though fraught with fateful and tremendous change, has not diverted the fundamental lines of political thought, though it has developed and extended them. The great European tradition of intellectual liberty and power; of material mastery and theoretical knowledge; of self-government under the Law; of religious experience, of originality and enterprise is unlikely to be swamped in the convulsions of the new Mass Society.

And what a tradition it is, how widespread the sources of its perennial strength! In the course of a chequered, but vigorous and original evolution, the Western races, by the close of the eighteenth century, had built up a cosmopolitan inheritance of political thought, probing the deepest problems of social life, raising, if not answering, all the major questions of theory and practice and transcending the boundaries of national states, though drawing inspiration from national cultures. The spiritual and material success of European society had been due largely to a minority of creative and administrative minds actuated by a common tradition. That legacy, peculiar to the West, is still in the blood of our civilization. It combines at its best, freedom and order, stability and initiative.

How can this tradition, so historic and enduring, be adapted to the pace and scale of the modern world? For there can be no radical break with the past. Plainly the twentieth century must maintain and adapt this inheritance if it is to solve the problems which confront modern mass society, too long swinging without guidance under the influence of unbridled nineteenth-century individualism and *laissez-faire* and imperilled by national and economic strife.

At the beginning of this survey it was remarked that no community can continue healthy — least of all a huge modern society — without some objective, some pattern of belief. We have seen in our opening chapter that periods of cultural achievement have coincided with periods of belief, which bring the drive of the whole society behind its leaders. To-day the tremendous initiative, the sprawling enterprise, of the nineteenth century may well be changing to an age of order, of consolidation. Fascist ideas were a denial of the ancient values of civilization, but they formed a perverted social pattern: the Soviet Socialist order includes the masses behind their rulers in a common drive. The task of the Western world is to create a pattern of freedom, based on the European inheritance of political thought, which will command the allegiance, not only of minorities but of the masses. The aim is the spontaneous generation of initiative in a free society, so planned by the State's authority, that basic stability is assured. This stability is bound to depend on certain fundamental conditions: freedom from fear and want; the provision of popular education; the creation and adaptation of patterns of social behaviour which will satisfy the craving for group loyalty; on the assimilation of the basic common-sense principles of scientific method as applied to politics.

Such a progressive society, reflecting, within its agreed framework of security and order, the initiative of an intellectual and administrative *élite* responsive to public opinion, is imperative for an age of revolutionary change.

Our problem is to combine the old tradition with a society free and flexible, ordered and secure. The attack of the planned Fascist state on Liberal Democracy has brought home with unique force the necessity for an alternative order. The threat to the traditional values of European culture, to free speculation, to justice, to Caritic Christianity, to individual liberty — that challenge may well evoke the response of a new age, destined to harvest the achievements of nineteenth-century initiative and lay the foundations for a better future. If this response can be made, our age of 'tragedy and glory' will open into a new world.

SELECT BIBLIOGRAPHY

THE following books will be found useful for the further study of the major writers on political thought; for critical appreciations of their works; of their relations to one another; and for their historical background. In accordance with the plan of the book no bibliography is given for nineteenth-century writers, but certain general works dealing with contemporary problems raised in the final chapter are included. Primary sources are distinguished from critical and historical works by capitals. Where, owing to war-time difficulties, older editions have been unavoidably used in the text, modern editions are also given below.

A. THE POLITICAL THOUGHT OF ANTIQUITY

Aristotle. THE POLITICS OF ARISTOTLE. Translated by B. Jowett, with introduction by H. W. C. Davis. Oxford, 1923.

Aristotle. THE POLITICS OF ARISTOTLE. Translated with introduction by Sir Ernest Barker. Oxford, 1946.

Augustine, St. DE CIVITATE DEI. B. Dombart. 2 vols. Teubner, Leipzig, 1909-18.

Augustine, St. THE CITY OF GOD. Translated by John Healey, with an introduction by Sir Ernest Barker. London, 1931.

Barker, Sir E. Plato and his Predecessors. London, 1925.

Barker, Sir E. Political Thought of Plato and Aristotle. London, 1906.

Baynes, N. H. Constantine and the Christian Church. Proceedings of the British Association, vol. XV.

Baynes, N. H. The Political Ideas of St. Augustine's City of God. Historical Association, 1936.

Bury, J. B. Cambridge Mediaeval History, vol. II, chap. iii (for Justinian's Codification of Roman Law).

Breasted, J. H. The Dawn of Conscience. New York, 1934.

Breasted, J. H. ANCIENT RECORDS OF EGYPT. Chicago, 1906.

Cicero. DE RE PUBLICA: DE LEGIBUS. Loeb Classical Library.

Cicero. ON THE COMMONWEALTH. Translated with introduction by G. H. Sabine and S. B. Smith. Columbus, Ohio, 1929.

Cochrane, C. N. Christianity and Classical Culture. Oxford, 1940.

Diehl, C. Cambridge Mediaeval History, vol. II, chap. i (for Constantine and the Christian Church).

Figgis, J. N. Political Aspects of St. Augustine's City of God. London, 1921.

Frazer, Sir J. G. The Golden Bough. Abridged edition, London, 1925.

BIBLIOGRAPHY

Gilson, E. Introduction à l'étude de St. Augustin. Second edition, Paris, 1943.

Glotz, G. La Civilisation égéenne. Paris, 1923.

Jaeger, W. W. Aristotle, Fundamentals of the History of his Development. Translated by Robinson. Oxford, 1934.

Jaeger, W. W. Paideia, the Ideals of Greek Culture. Translated by G. Highet. 3 vols. Oxford, 1939-45.

Johns, C. W. H. BABYLONIAN AND ASSYRIAN LAWS. Edinburgh, 1904. (For the Code of Hammurabi.)

Jones, A. H. N. The Greek City. Oxford, 1940.

Keyes, C. W. The Original Elements in Cicero's Ideal Constitution. American Journal of Philology, vol. XLII.

Maine, Sir H. Ancient Law. Edited by F. Pollock. London, 1906.

Malinowski, B. Crime and Custom in Savage Society. New York, 1926.

Mead, M. Co-operation and Competition among Primitive Peoples. London, 1937.

Mommsen, T. The Provinces of the Roman Empire. Translated by W. P. Dickson. 2 vols. London, 1909.

Plato. THE REPUBLIC OF PLATO. Translated with introduction by A. D. Lindsay. Everyman, London, 1937.

Plato. THE REPUBLIC OF PLATO. Translated with introduction by F. M. Cornford. Oxford, 1941.

Plato. THE STATESMAN. Loeb Classical Library.

Plato. THE LAWS. Translated by A. E. Taylor. London, 1934.

Ross, W. D. Aristotle. Third edition, London, 1937.

Rostovtzeff, M. Social and Economic History of the Roman Empire. 2 vols., Oxford, 1926.

Syme, R. The Roman Revolution. Oxford, 1939.

Tarn, W. W. Hellenistic Civilization. London, 1927.

Tarn, W. W. Alexander and the Unity of Mankind. Proceedings of the British Academy, vol. XIX.

Taylor, A. E. Plato, the Man and his Work. London, 1926.

Taylor, A. E. Socrates. London, 1933.

Zimmern, Sir A. The Greek Commonwealth.

B. THE POLITICAL THOUGHT OF THE MIDDLE AGES

Attenborough, F. L. THE LAWS OF THE EARLIEST ENGLISH KINGS. Cambridge, 1922.

Bracton, H. de. DE LEGIBUS ET CONSUETUDINIBUS ANGLIAE. Edited by Sir T. Twiss. Rolls Series. 6 vols. London, 1878.

Carlyle, R. W. and A. J. A History of Mediaeval Political Theory in the West. 6 vols. New York and London, 1903-36.

BIBLIOGRAPHY

Dante. OPERE DI DANTE. Barbi, Firenze, 1921.

Dante. THE LATIN WORKS OF. Translated by P. H. Wicksteed. Temple Classics. London, 1904.

D'Arcy, M. C. Thomas Aquinas. London, 1930.

d'Entrèves, A. P. The Mediaeval Contribution to Political Thought. Oxford, 1939.

Fortescue, Sir J. DE LAUDIBUS ANGLIAE. Edited by G. B. Chrimes. Oxford, 1942.

Fortescue, Sir J. THE GOVERNAUNCE OF ENGLAND. Edited by C. Plummer. Oxford, 1885.

Gierke, O. Political Theories of the Middle Age. Translated by F. W. Maitland. Cambridge, 1900.

Gilson, E. L'Esprit de la Philosophie mediévale. Paris, 1932.

Gilson, E. The Philosophy of St. Thomas Aquinas. Translated by E. Bullough; edited by G. A. Elrington. Cambridge, 1924.

Hull, R. Mediaeval Theories of the Papacy. London, 1934.

Isidore of Seville. ISIDORI HISPALENSIS EPISCOPI ETYMOLOGIARUM, 2 vols. Edited by W. N. Lindsay. Oxford, 1900.

Jacob, E. F. Nicolas of Cusa, in Social and Political Ideas of the Renaissance and Reformation. Edited by F. J. C. Hearnshawe. London, 1925.

Jacob, E. F. The Legacy of the Middle Ages. Edited by C. G. Crump and E. F. Jacob. Chapter on Political Thought. Oxford, 1926.

Jacob, E. F. Cambridge Mediaeval History, vol. VI, chap. i (for Innocent III).

John of Salisbury. POLICRATICUS. Edited by C. C. J. Webb. Oxford, 1909.

John of Salisbury. THE STATESMAN'S BOOK OF. Translated and selection by J. Dickinson. New York, 1927.

John of Salisbury. THE FRIVOLITIES OF COURTIERS AND THE FOOTSTEPS OF PHILOSOPHERS. Translated and selection by J. B. Pike. Minneapolis, 1938.

Ker, W. P. Epic and Romance. London, 1897.

McIlwain, C. H. The Growth of Political Thought in the West. New York, 1932.

McIlwain, C. H. Cambridge Mediaeval History, vol. VII, chap. iii (for Mediaeval Estates).

Marsilio of Padua. THE DEFENSOR PACIS OF. Edited by C. W. Prévité-Orton. Cambridge, 1928.

Olrick, A. Viking Civilization. Translated by A. W. Hartmann and H. A. Larsen. London, 1930.

Pecock, Bishop. REPRESSOR OF OVERMUCH BLAMING OF THE CLERGY. Works, edited by C. Babington. Rolls Series. 2 vols. 1860.

Pirenne, H. Economic and Social History of Mediaeval Europe. Translated by J. E. Clegg. London, 1936.

Pollock, F., and Maitland, F. W. History of English Law before Edward I. 2 vols. Cambridge, 1898.

Poole, R. Lane. Illustrations of the History of Mediaeval Thought and Learning. London, 1930.

Powicke, F. M. Reflections on the Mediaeval State. Transactions of the Royal Historical Society, vol. XIX. 1936.

Powicke, F. M. The Christian Life in the Middle Ages. Oxford, 1935.

Smith, A. L. Church and State in the Middle Ages. Oxford, 1913.

Taylor, H. Osborn. The Mediaeval Mind. 2 vols. London, 1925.

Thomas Aquinas, St. THE SUMMA THEOLOGICA OF. Translated by the Fathers of the Dominican Province. London, 1911.

Thomas Aquinas, St. SELECTIONS. Edited by M. C. D'Arcy. Everyman Library. London, 1939.

Thomas Aquinas, St. SELECTION ET TRADUCTION. Revue des Jeunes. Paris, 1931-5.

Troeltsch, E. The Social Teaching of the Christian Churches. Translated by O. Wyon. London, 1931.

Vigfusson G. and York Powell, F. ORIGINES ISLANDICAE. Oxford, 1905.

Vinogradoff, P. Roman Law in Mediaeval Europe. Edited by F. de Zulueta. Oxford, 1929.

William of Ockham. DE IMPERATORUM ET PONTIFICUM POTESTATE. Edited by C. K. Brampton. Oxford, 1927.

C. THE POLITICAL THOUGHT OF THE RENAISSANCE AND THE AGE OF RATIONALISM

Adams, H. P. Life and Writings of Vico. London, 1935.

Allen, J. W. A History of Political Thought in the Sixteenth Century. London, 1928.

Becker, C. The Heavenly City of the Eighteenth-century Philosophers. New Haven, 1933.

Bodin, J. SIX LIVRES DE LA RÉPUBLIQUE. Paris, 1596.

Bodin, J. THE SIX BOOKS OF A COMMONWEALE. Written by J. Bodin, done into English by Richard Knolles. London, 1606.

Bramhall, Archbishop. THE CATCHING OF THE LEVIATHAN. Works, Library of Anglo-Catholic Theology. 5 vols. Oxford, 1842.

Burckhardt, J. The Civilization of the Renaissance in Italy. London, 1937.

Burke, E. SELECTED WORKS. World's Classics, 1903.

Burke, E. WORKS. 8 vols. Bohn's British Classics. London, 1853.

Burke, E. Works. Revised edition, 12 vols. Boston, Mass., 1865-7.

Bury, J. B. The Idea of Progress. London, 1920.

Butterfield, H. The Statecraft of Machiavelli. London, 1940.

BIBLIOGRAPHY

Calvin, J. INSTITUTES OF THE CHRISTIAN RELIGION. Translated by H. Beveredge. Edinburgh, 1863.

Chauviré, R. Jean Bodin. Paris, 1914.

Clarke Papers. Edited by C. H. Firth. 4 vols. Camden Society. 1891.

Cobban, A. B. Edmund Burke and the Revolt against the Eighteenth Century. London, 1929.

Cobban, A. B. Rousseau and the Modern State. London, 1934.

Doumergue, E. Jean Calvin. 5 vols. Lausanne, 1899-1916.

Febvre, L. Un Destin, Martin Luther. Paris, 1936.

Figgis, J. N. The Divine Right of Kings. Cambridge, 1914.

Figgis, J. N. From Gerson to Grotius. Cambridge, 1923.

Gilbert, A. Machiavelli's Prince and its Forerunners. (Duke Univ. Publications.) Durham, N.C., 1938.

Gooch, G. P. English Democratic Ideas in the Seventeenth Century. Second edition, Cambridge, 1927.

Gooch, G. P. Political Thought in England from Bacon to Halifax. London, 1915.

Gough, J. W. The Social Contract. Oxford, 1936.

Grotius, H. DE JURE BELLI AC PACIS. Text and translations by F. Kelsey. 2 vols. Classics of International Law, edited by J. B. Scott. Washington, 1913; Oxford, 1925.

Grotius, H. THE FREEDOM OF THE SEAS. Translated by Magoffin, edited by J. B. Scott. New York, 1916.

Halifax, Marquis of. THE COMPLETE WORKS OF GEORGE SAVILLE, FIRST MARQUIS OF. Edited with introduction by Walter Raleigh. Oxford, 1912.

Hazard, P. La Crise de la Conscience Européenne (1680-1715). Second edition, Paris, 1946.

Hobbes, T. WORKS. Edited by Sir W. Molesworth. English 11 vols.; Latin 5. London, 1840.

Hobbes, T. LEVIATHAN. Edited by W. G. Pogson Smith. Oxford, 1909.

Hooker, R. OF THE LAWS OF ECCLESIASTICAL POLITY. Works, edited by J. Keble. Oxford, 1836.

Hume, D. ESSAYS, MORAL, POLITICAL AND LITERARY. Edited by T. H. Green. London, 1862.

Hume D. ENQUIRY CONCERNING HUMAN UNDERSTANDING; TREATISE OF HUMAN NATURE. Works, edited by T. H. Green and T. H. Grose. 4 vols. London, 1895-8.

JAMES I, KING OF ENGLAND, POLITICAL WORKS OF. Edited by C. H. McIlwain. Cambridge, Mass., 1918.

Lagarde, G. de. La Naissance de L'Esprit Laïque au Fin du Moyen Age. 4 tom. Paris, 1934.

Lamprecht, S. P. The Moral and Political Philosophy of John Locke. New York, 1918.

Locke, J. Two Treatises on Civil Government. Edited with introduction by J. W. Gough. Oxford, 1946.

Locke, J. Essay on Toleration. Works. 10 vols. London, 1823.

Luther, M. The Three Primary Works of. Translated by Wace and Bucheim. London, 1885.

Luther, M. Correspondence and other Contemporary Letters. Edited by Preserved Smith. Lutheran Publications Society. 2 vols. 1913.

MacCunn, J. The Political Philosophy of Burke. London, 1913.

Machiavelli, N. Il Principe. Edited by L. A. Burd. London, 1891.

Machiavelli, N. The Prince. Translated by W. K. Marriott. Everyman Library. London, 1906.

Machiavelli, N. Discourses on the First Decade of Titus Livius. Translated by N. H. Thomson. London, 1883.

Magnus, Sir P. Edmund Burke. London, 1939.

Maritain, J. Three Reformers, Luther, Descartes, Rousseau. London, 1928.

Martin, Kingsley. French Liberal Thought in the Eighteenth Century. London, 1929.

Mesnard, P. L'Essor de la Philosophie Politique au XVIe Siècle. Paris, 1936.

Milton, John. Prose Works. Edited by Fletcher. London, 1834.

Montesquieu, Charles de Secondat, Baron de. Œuvres Complets. 8 vols. Paris, 1820-3.

Montesquieu, Charles de Secondat, Baron de. The Spirit of the Laws. Translated by T. Nugent, revised by F. V. Pritchard. 2 vols. London, 1878.

More, Sir T. Utopia. Translated by G. C. Richards. Oxford, 1923.

Mornet, D. Les Origines intellectuelles de la Revolution française. Paris, 1933.

Richelieu, Cardinal de. Testament Politique. Mélanges Historiques. Paris, 1873-86. tom. III.

Richelieu, Cardinal de. The Political Will and Testament of. Done out of the French. London, 1695.

Rousseau, J. Du Contrat Social. Edited by M. Halbwachs. Paris, 1943.

Rousseau, J. The Social Contract. With introduction by G. D. H. Cole. Everyman edition. 1913.

Rousseau, J. The Political Writings of. Edited by C. E. Vaughan. 2 vols. Cambridge, 1915.

Sée, H. Les Idées politiques en France au XVIIe Siècle. Paris, 1923.

Sée, H. L'Evolution de la Pensée politique en France au XVIIIe Siècle. Paris, 1925.

Spinoza, Baruch de. Tractatus Theologico — Politicus, and Tractatus Politicus. Translated and edited by R. H. Elwes. London, 1891.

BIBLIOGRAPHY

Stephen, Leslie. Hobbes. English Men of Letters Series. London, 1928.

Strauss, L. The Political Philosophy of Hobbes. Translated by E. M. Sinclair. Oxford, 1936.

Vico, G. B. OPERE. Edited by Nicolini. 8 vols. Bari, 1914-42.

Vico, G. B. OPERE. Edited by Ferrari. 6 vols. Milano, 1836.

Vico, G. B. ŒUVRES CHOISIES. Translated by J. Chaix-Ruy. Paris, 1946.

Vico, G. B. THE AUTOBIOGRAPHY OF. Translated by M. A. Fisch and T. J. Bergier. Ithaca, N.Y., 1944.

Villari, P. Life and Times of Niccolo Machiavelli. Translated by L. Villari. 2 vols. London, 1892.

VINDICIAE CONTRA TYRANNOS. Translated and edited by H. J. Laski. London, 1924.

Weber, M. The Protestant Ethic and the Spirit of Capitalism. Translated by T. Parsons. London, 1930.

Winstanley, G. SELECTION FROM THE WRITINGS OF. Edited by Hamilton. London, 1944.

Wolfe, D. M. LEVELLER MANIFESTOS OF THE PURITAN REVOLUTION. New York, 1944.

Wright, E. H. The Meaning of Rousseau. London, 1929.

D. GENERAL

Acton, Lord. History of Freedom and Other Essays. Edited by J. N. Figgis and R. V. Lawrence. London, 1922.

Collingwood, R. H. The New Leviathan. Oxford, 1942.

Collingwood, R. H. The Idea of History. Oxford, 1946.

Curtis, L. The Commonwealth of God. London, 1934.

Dunning, A. A History of Political Theories. 3 vols. New York, 1905.

Lindsay, A. D. The Essentials of Democracy. Oxford, 1929.

Lindsay, A. D. The Modern Democratic State. Oxford, 1943.

Lippman, W. The Good Society. London, 1938.

Mannheim, K. Ideology and Utopia. London, 1936.

Mannheim, K. Man and Society. London, 1940.

Mannheim, K. Diagnosis of Our Time. London, 1943.

Maritain, J. The Rights of Man and Natural Law. London, 1944.

Maritain, J. Le Crépuscule de la Civilisation. Paris, 1939.

McIlwain, C. H. Constitutionalism. New York, 1940.

Pollock, F. The History of the Law of Nature, in Essays in the Law. London, 1922.

Pollock, F. An Introduction to the History of the Science of Politics. London, 1911.

Popper, K. The Open Society and Its Enemies. 2 vols. London, 1945.

Russell, B. Power. London, 1938.

BIBLIOGRAPHY

Sabine, G. H. A History of Political Theory. London, 1937.

Seignobos, C. The Rise of European Civilization. London, 1939.

Toynbee, A. J. A Study of History. 6 vols. Oxford, 1934.

Whitehead, A. N. Adventures of Ideas. Cambridge, 1933.

Whitehead, A. N. Science and the Modern World. Cambridge, 1926.

INDEX

ADRIAN IV, POPE, John of Salisbury on, 192

Aethelbert, laws of, 165

Aethelred the Redeless, Coronation oath of, 187

Agreement of the People, Leveller manifesto, 339

Alaric, the Goth, 132

Alexander, his idea of Empire, 76-8; Hellenizing policy of, 77-8; quoted by Cicero, 94; Plutarch on, 300

Alexander VI, Pope, death of, 253

Alfred, King of Wessex, 161-4

Amalasnuetha, Queen, 148n

Ambrose, St., as an administrator, 130-1

Anglo-Saxon Chronicle, on the Danes, 173

Anna Komnena, 298

Antiochus Epiphanes, encourages physical fitness, 88n

Aristotle, on the State, 1, 2, 15, 25; scientific outlook of, 60; the *Politics* of, 61; on man as a political animal, 62; on justice, 62; on slaves, 63; on property, 64; on tyranny, 67; on marriage, 69; on music, 71; greatness of, 72; influence on Thomism, 204; Dante on, 234; Marsilio on, 237-40; Spinoza on, 379

Arminian theology, uses of, 293n

Assyrians, militarism of, 39; Isidore on, 153; Vico on, 396 (*see* Toynbee, A. J.)

Athelstan, Laws of, on lordless men, 168

Aubrey, John, his biography of Hobbes quoted, 317n, 345

Augustine, St., on secular state, 100; *De Civitate Dei*, 131ff; early life and conversion of, 131; on original sin, 133-6; on reality of Hell, 137; on Church and State, 138

Augustine of Canterbury, St., corresponds with Gregory the Great, 158

Augustus, conflicting opinions on, 97n; achievement of, 97-9; subsequent prestige of, 190

Aurelius, Marcus, *Meditations* of, 84-5, 100

Averroes, influence of, 210n

Avignon, 151

BACON, FRANCIS, compared with Descartes, 270; condones war, 292, 315n, 345; admired by Diderot, 404; and Hume, 410

Bailey, A., quotes account of Richelieu, 308-9

Balance of Power, mitigates international anarchy, 288-301

Bale, *The Pageant of the Popes* of, on Benedict IX, 198n

Ball, 'Abbé' John, butt of Burke, 436

Barbeyrac, edits Grotius *Of War and Peace*, 295n

Basel, Council of, 241

Bayeaux Tapestry, 183n, 198

Baynes, Prof. N. H., on Constantine, 128n; on St. Augustine, 133n

Bears, uses of, Lactantius on, 126n; favourably compared with philosophers, 415n

Beaumanoir, on feudal custom, 185

Bede, the Venerable, cultural importance of, 159-62; poem by, 160n

Bellarmine, *De Potestate summi Pontificis*, justifies papal power, 284

Belphegor, a scurrilous book, 248n

Benedict IX, excesses of, Gregorovius on, 197n; Sir R. Lane Poole on, 198n; Bale on, 198n

Bentham, 410, 415

INDEX